Notable Poets

MAGILL'S CHOICE

NOTABLE POETS

Volume 1
Anna Akhmatova — George Herbert
1 – 482

from
THE EDITORS OF SALEM PRESS

SALEM PRESS, INC.
Pasadena, California   Englewood Cliffs, New Jersey

Copyright © 1998, by SALEM PRESS, INC.
All rights in this book are reserved. No part of this work may be used or reproduced in any manner whatsoever or transmitted in any form or by any means, electronic or mechanical, including photocopy, recording, or any information storage and retrieval system, without written permission from the copyright owner except in the case of brief quotations embodied in critical articles and reviews. For information address the publisher, Salem Press, Inc., P.O. Box 50062, Pasadena, California 91115.

Essays originally appeared in *Critical Survey of Poetry: English Language Series, Revised Edition*, 1992, and *Critical Survey of Poetry: Foreign Language Series*, 1984, both edited by Frank N. Magill. Material from *Cyclopedia of World Authors, Third Revised Edition*, 1997, edited by Frank N. Magill, and new material have been added.

∞ The paper used in these volumes conforms to the American National Standard for Permanence of Paper for Printed Library Materials, Z39.48-1984.

Library of Congress Cataloging-in-Publication Data
Notable poets
        p.   cm. — (Magill's choice)
"From the editors of Salem Press."
Includes bibliographical references and index.
  ISBN 0-89356-967-4 (set : alk. paper). — ISBN 0-89356-968-2 (v. 1 : alk. paper). — ISBN 0-89356-969-0 (v. 2 : alk. paper). — ISBN 0-89356-974-7 (v. 3 : alk. paper)
  1. Poetry—History and criticism—Dictionaries. 2. Poetry—Bio-bibliography—Dictionaries. 3. Poets—Biography—Dictionaries. I. Series.
PN1021.N68   1998
809.1'003—dc21
[B]   98-26164
                                                    CIP

First Printing

PRINTED IN THE UNITED STATES OF AMERICA

Publisher's Note

Notable Poets comprises biographical sketches and critical studies of 110 of the world's best-known poets from antiquity to the late twentieth century. This set is designed to survey the essential poets whose works comprise the core curriculum of high school and undergraduate poetry studies. The essays, selected from *Critical Survey of Poetry: English Language Series, Revised Edition* (1992) and *Critical Survey of Poetry: Foreign Language Series* (1984), have been updated with new material as well as with pertinent information culled from the *Cyclopedia of World Authors* (1997). More than two-thirds of the essays are illustrated with portraits of the poets.

Of the 110 articles in *Notable Poets*, 75 focus on English-language poets and 35 on foreign-language writers whose works are widely studied in translation. Together, they trace the development of poetry from ancient Greece, Rome, and China, through the great works of the Renaissance and the Romantic era, to the modernist, Beat, and confessional poets of the twentieth century.

The beginnings of poetry are lost in prehistory; poetic devices undoubtedly evolved before written language as ways of facilitating the memorization and oral repetition of historical records, legends, and myths. Included in *Notable Poets* are studies of the masterworks of early poets that have influenced the course of literature through the centuries. From the Greece of c. 800 B.C. come the works of Homer; from the sixth and seventh centuries B.C. come Pindar and Sappho; from Italy in the first century B.C. come Horace, Vergil, and Ovid. From eighth century China come Li Po and Tu Fu. Among the hundreds of poems or collections discussed are such old and new milestones in world literature as Homer's *Odyssey*, Vergil's *Aeneid*, Dante's *Divine Comedy*, Charles Baudelaire's *Flowers of Evil*, Arthur Rimbaud's *A Season in Hell*, Johann Wolfgang von Goethe's *Roman Elegies*, and Federico García Lorca's *Gypsy Ballads*.

Among the often-studied English-language poems included are such standard texts as Geoffrey Chaucer's *Canterbury Tales*, William Shakespeare's sonnets, John Milton's *Paradise Lost*, William Blake's "The Tiger," John Keats's "Ode to a Nightingale," William Wordsworth's "Ode: Intimations of Immortality," Elizabeth Barrett Browning's *Sonnets from the Portuguese*, Robert Browning's "My Last Duchess," Emily Dickinson's "Because I could not stop for Death," and Walt Whitman's "When Lilacs Last in the Dooryard Bloom'd." Twentieth century poets and works include T. S. Eliot's *The Waste Land*, William Butler Yeats's "The Second Coming,"

Robert Frost's "Stopping by Woods on a Snowy Evening," Ezra Pound's *Cantos*, William Carlos Williams's *Paterson*, Marianne Moore's "Poetry," Allen Ginsberg's "Howl," and Sylvia Plath's *Ariel*. Works are discussed in the context of the poet's life, times, and body of work.

Each essay provides essential information at its beginning: the poet's birth and death dates, a list of principal poetic works with publication dates, and an "Achievements" section that encapsulates the poet's central contribution and notes major honors and awards the poet has won. The major sections of the text follow: "Biography" provides a summary of the author's life, and "Analysis" is an in-depth look at the poet's work. This section examines a number of key works in the author's canon, points to the techniques and themes of primary interest to the poet, and describes how the poet's work evolved over time. The text concludes with "Other literary forms," briefly describing other genres in which the writer has worked. A categorized list, "Select works other than poetry," follows. Each essay concludes with a paragraph-style bibliography.

The three-volume set is arranged alphabetically. Four useful reference features are included at the end of volume 3: a glossary of poetical terms, a time line of the poets' birthdates, a geographical index, and a comprehensive index. A list of contributing scholars appears at the beginning of volume 1.

List of Contributors

James Lovic Allen
University of Hawaii

John Alspaugh
Independent Scholar

Andrew J. Angyal
Elon College

Stanley Archer
Texas A & M University

Lowell A. Bangerter
University of Wyoming

James John Baran
Louisiana State University, Shreveport

David Barratt
Independent Scholar

Walton Beacham
Independent Scholar

Kate Begnal
Utah State University

Todd K. Bender
University of Wisconsin, Madison

Eleanor von Auw Berry
Independent Scholar

Franz G. Blaha
University of Nebraska, Lincoln

David Bromige
Sonoma State University

Mary Barnes Bruce
Monmouth College

Mitzi M. Brunsdale
Mayville State College

Allan Chavkin
Southwest Texas State University

Steven E. Colburn
Independent Scholar

John J. Conlon
University of Massachusetts, Boston

Reed Way Dasenbrock
New Mexico State University

William V. Davis
Baylor University

Lloyd N. Dendinger
University of Southern Alabama

Lee Hunt Dowling
University of Houston

Doris Earnshaw
University of California, Davis

Cliff Edwards
Fort Hays State University

Richard A. Eichwald
Independent Scholar

Richard Kenneth Emmerson
Walla Walla College

Bernard F. Engel
Michigan State University

Howard Faulkner
Independent Scholar

William L. Felker
Independent Scholar

Thomas C. Foster
University of Michigan, Flint

Walter B. Freed, Jr.
Independent Scholar

Kenneth E. Gadomski
University of Delaware

Elaine Gardiner
Independent Scholar

Katherine Gyékényesi Gatto
Independent Scholar

Donna Gerstenberger
University of Washington

Richard F. Giles
Wilfried Launier University

Ronald K. Giles
East Tennessee State University

C. Herbert Gilliland
U.S. Naval Academy

Sidney Gottlieb
Sacred Heart University

Stephen I. Gurney
Bemidji State University

Shelley P. Haley
Howard University

Robert Hauptman
Independent Scholar

Michael Hennessy
Southwest Texas State University

Hilary Holladay
Independent Scholar

Kenneth A. Howe
Michigan State University

Irma M. Kashuba
Chestnut Hill College

Arthur Kincaid
Independent Scholar

Frederick Kirchhoff
Independent Scholar

B. G. Knepper
Independent Scholar

Jeanne Larsen
Independent Scholar

Leon Lewis
Appalachian State University

Notable Poets

James Livingston
Northern Michigan University

Perry D. Luckett
U.S. Air Force Academy

John D. Lyons
Dartmouth College

Bruce K. Martin
Drake University

Richard Peter Martin
Princeton University

Richard E. Matlak
Independent Scholar

Laurence W. Mazzeno
Alvernia College

Vasa D. Mihailovich
University of North Carolina

Edmund Miller
Long Island University

Mark Minor
Westmar College

Leslie B. Mittleman
California State University, Long Beach

Ronald Moran
Clemson University

Russell Elliott Murphy
University of Arkansas, Little Rock

Joseph Natoli
Independent Scholar

Evelyn S. Newlyn
Virginia Polytechnic Institute and State University

Chapel Louise Petty
Independent Scholar

Helene M. Kastinger Riley
Washington State University

Samuel J. Rogal
Illinois State University

Victor Anthony Rudowski
Clemson University

Stephanie Sandler
Amherst College

Paul J. Schwartz
Independent Scholar

Anne Shifrer
Utah State University

Katherine Snipes
Manhattan College

Robert Lance Snyder
Georgia Institute of Technology

Janet L. Solberg
Kalamazoo College

Sherry G. Southard
Oklahoma State University

Madison U. Sowell
Brigham Young University

Kenneth A. Stackhouse
Independent Scholar

Karen F. Stein
University of Rhode Island

L. Robert Stevens
North Texas State University

Laura M. Stone
Independent Scholar

Ann Struthers
Coe College

John Clendenin Townsend
University of Minnesota

Thomas A. Van
University of Louisville

Edward E. Waldron
Yankton College

Gary F. Waller
Wilfried Launier University

Marie Michelle Walsh
Independent Scholar

Craig Werner
University of Wisconsin

Barbara Wiedemann
Auburn University at Montgomery

Philip Woodard
National University

Contents – Volume 1

Akhmatova, Anna 1
Apollinaire, Guillaume 9
Arnold, Matthew 20
Auden, W. H. 31

Baudelaire, Charles 44
Berryman, John 55
Bishop, Elizabeth 66
Blake, William 77
Bly, Robert 96
Breton, André 106
Brooks, Gwendolyn 114
Browning, Elizabeth Barrett 125
Browning, Robert 137
Burns, Robert 153
Byron, George Gordon, Lord 165

Celan, Paul 183
Chaucer, Geoffrey 191
Coleridge, Samuel Taylor 208
Crane, Hart 224
Cruz, Sor Juana Inés de la 236
Cummings, E. E. 244

Dante 255
Dickinson, Emily 285
Donne, John 299

Eliot, T. S. 318
Emerson, Ralph Waldo 334

Ferlinghetti, Lawrence 348
Forché, Carolyn 356
Frost, Robert 364

García Lorca, Federico 376
Ginsberg, Allen 386
Goethe, Johann Wolfgang von 399
Graham, Jorie 413
Graves, Robert 421

H. D. 434
Heaney, Seamus 445
Heine, Heinrich 459
Herbert, George 470

Complete List of Contents

Contents — Volume 1

Akhmatova, Anna, 1
Apollinaire, Guillaume, 9
Arnold, Matthew, 20
Auden, W. H., 31
Baudelaire, Charles, 44
Berryman, John, 55
Bishop, Elizabeth, 66
Blake, William, 77
Bly, Robert, 96
Breton, André, 106
Brooks, Gwendolyn, 114
Browning, Elizabeth Barrett, 125
Browning, Robert, 137
Burns, Robert, 153
Byron, George Gordon, Lord, 165
Celan, Paul, 183
Chaucer, Geoffrey, 191
Coleridge, Samuel Taylor, 208
Crane, Hart, 224
Cruz, Sor Juana Inés de la, 236
Cummings, E. E., 244
Dante, 255
Dickinson, Emily, 285
Donne, John, 299
Eliot, T. S., 318
Emerson, Ralph Waldo, 334
Ferlinghetti, Lawrence, 348
Forché, Carolyn, 356
Frost, Robert, 364
García Lorca, Federico, 376
Ginsberg, Allen, 386
Goethe, Johann Wolfgang von, 399
Graham, Jorie, 413
Graves, Robert, 421
H. D., 434
Heaney, Seamus, 445
Heine, Heinrich, 459
Herbert, George, 470

Contents — Volume 2

Hölderlin, Friedrich, 483
Homer, 494
Hopkins, Gerard Manley, 507
Horace, 524
Hughes, Langston, 536
Hughes, Ted, 546
Keats, John, 559
Larkin, Philip, 578
Lawrence, D. H., 591
Levertov, Denise, 604
Li Po, 617
Longfellow, Henry Wadsworth, 627
Lowell, Amy, 639
Lowell, Robert, 650

Mallarmé, Stéphane, 670
Mandelstam, Osip, 679
Marvell, Andrew, 692
Matsuo Bashō, 705
Merrill, James, 713
Millay, Edna St. Vincent, 724
Miłosz, Czesław, 732
Milton, John, 746
Moore, Marianne, 760
Nemerov, Howard, 771
Neruda, Pablo, 780
Nerval, Gérard de, 793

Olds, Sharon, 803
Olson, Charles, 810
Ovid, 821
Paz, Octavio, 832
Petrarch, 841
Pindar, 852
Plath, Sylvia, 861
Poe, Edgar Allan, 874
Pope, Alexander, 886
Pound, Ezra, 903
Raleigh, Sir Walter, 918
Ransom, John Crowe, 929
Rich, Adrienne, 940

Contents — Volume 3

Rilke, Rainer Maria, 953
Rimbaud, Arthur, 964
Robinson, Edwin Arlington, 976
Roethke, Theodore, 988
Rukeyser, Muriel, 1000
Sachs, Nelly, 1009
Sandburg, Carl, 1017
Sappho, 1029
Schiller, Friedrich, 1041
Scott, Sir Walter, 1053
Sexton, Anne, 1063
Shakespeare, William, 1072
Shelley, Percy Bysshe, 1085
Sidney, Sir Philip, 1105
Snyder, Gary, 1119
Spender, Stephen, 1134
Spenser, Edmund, 1146

Stevens, Wallace, 1162
Tennyson, Alfred, Lord, 1174
Thomas, Dylan, 1188
Tu Fu, 1200
Valéry, Paul, 1207
Vallejo, César, 1220
Vergil, 1233
Verlaine, Paul, 1247
Warren, Robert Penn, 1257
Whitman, Walt, 1268
Wilbur, Richard, 1284
Williams, William Carlos, 1296
Wordsworth, William, 1310
Wyatt, Sir Thomas, 1330
Yeats, William Butler, 1342
Yevtushenko, Yevgeny, 1374

Notable Poets

ANNA AKHMATOVA

(Anna Andreyevna Gorenko)

Born: Bol'shoy Fonton, near Odessa, Russia; June 23, 1889
Died: Domodedovo, near Moscow, U.S.S.R.; March 5, 1966

Poetry · *Vecher*, 1912 · *Chetki*, 1914 · *Belaya staya*, 1917 · *Podorozhnik*, 1921 · *Anno Domini MCMXXI*, 1922, 1923 · *Iz shesti knig*, 1940 · *Izbrannye stikhotvoreniia*, 1943 · *Stikhotvoreniia*, 1958, 1961 · *Poema bez geroya*, 1960 (*A Poem Without a Hero*, 1973) · *Rekviem*, 1963 (*Requiem*, 1964) · *Beg vremeni*, 1965 · *Sochineniya*, 1965-1983 (3 vols.) · *Poems of A.*, 1973 · *Selected Poems*, 1976 · *Requiem, and Poem Without a Hero*, 1976 · *You Will Hear Thunder*, 1976 · *Anna Akhmatova: Poems*, 1983

Achievements · Anna Akhmatova enriched Russian literature immeasurably, not only with the quality of her poetry but also with the freshness and originality of her strong talent. Through Acmeism, a literary movement of which she was one of the founders and leading members, she effected a significant change of direction in Russian poetry in the second decade of the twentieth century. The Acmeists' insistence on clarity and precsion of expression—much in the spirit of the Imagists, although the two movements developed independently of each other—represented a reaction against the intricate symbols and otherworldly preoccupations of the Symbolists. Akhmatova's youthful love poems brought her early fame, and her reputation was further enhanced during the long reign of terror in her country, through which

Library of Congress

she was able to preserve her dignity, both as a human being and as a poet. With Boris Pasternak, Osip Mandelstam, and Marina Tsvetayeva, Akhmatova is universally regarded as one of the four great poets of postrevolutionary Russia. Having been generously translated into English, Akhmatova's works are constantly gaining stature in world literature as well.

Biography · Anna Akhmatova—the pen name of Anna Andreyevna Gorenko—was born in a suburb of Odessa in 1889, into the family of a naval officer. Akhmatova began to write poetry when she was eleven, and her first poem was published in 1907. She achieved great popularity with her first books *Vecher* and *Chetki*. After joining the literary movement called Acmeism, she played an important part in it together with Osip Mandelstam and with her husband, Nikolay Gumilyov, from whom she was later divorced. During World War I and the Russian Revolution, Akhmatova stood by her people, even though she did not agree with the ideas and methods of the revolutionaries. Never politically inclined, she saw in the war and the Revolution an evil that might eventually destroy the private world in which she had been able to address herself exclusively to her own problems. When the end of that world came, she refused to accept it, believing that she would be able to continue her sequestered life. She also refused to emigrate, saying that it took greater courage to stay behind and accept what came. The effect of the Revolution on her life and creativity was not immediately evident, for she subsequently published two more collections of poetry. When her former husband and fellow Acmeist Gumilyov was shot, however, Akhmatova realized that the new way of life was inimical to her own. Compelled to silence, she ceased to exist publicly, instead remaining an inner émigré for eighteen years and occupying herself mostly with writing essays and translating. This silence may have saved her life during the purges of the 1930's, although she was not spared agony while trying to ascertain the fate of her only son, a promising scholar of Asian history, who had been sent to a labor camp three times. Only World War II brought a change to Akhmatova's dreary and dangerous life. Like many Soviet writers and intellectuals, she once again sided with her people, suppressing her reservations and complaints. She spent the first several months of the war in besieged Leningrad and then was evacuated to Tashkent, where she stayed almost to the end of the war. In Tashkent, she was brought closer to the other part of her ancestry, for her grandmother, from whom she took her pen name, was a Tartar.

When the war was over and the authorities again resorted to repression, Akhmatova was among the first to be victimized. In a vitriolic speech by Andrei Zhdanov, the cultural dictator at that time, she and the satirist

Mikhail Zoshchenko were singled out as examples of anti-Soviet attitudes among intellectuals and charged with harmful influence on the young. They were expelled from the Writers' Union, and their works ceased to be published. Thus, Akhmatova vanished from public view once again in 1946, this time involuntarily, and did not reappear until ten years later. In 1958, a slender collection of her poems was published as a sign of rehabilitation. A few more of her books were subsequently published, both at home and abroad, thus reinstating the poet as an active member of society. During the last decade of her life, she wrote some of the best poetry of her career. Shortly before her death, she received two richly deserved accolades for her work. Ironically, the recognition came from abroad: She was awarded the prestigious Italian Etna Taormina Prize in 1964, and an honorary doctorate from Oxford University in 1965. Ravaged by long illness, she died in 1966, having preserved her dignity and independence by asking for and receiving a church funeral according to the Russian Orthodox rites. After her death, Akhmatova was almost unanimously eulogized as the finest woman poet in all of Russian literature.

Analysis · Anna Akhmatova's poetry can conveniently be divided into three distinct periods: 1912 to 1923, 1940 to 1946, and 1956 to 1966 (with a few poems published in 1950). The interim periods were those of enforced silence. The first silence, from 1923 to 1940, came as a result of tacit admission on her part that the changed way of life in Russia was not fully acceptable to her. The second, from 1946 to 1956, was a direct result of the authorities' intervention. Needless to say, Akhmatova kept busy by further refining her poetry, by writing essays, and by translating.

Akhmatova's development as a poet can be traced from book to book. Her first books, *Vecher* and *Chetki*, impressed readers with the freshness of a young woman's concern about her feelings of love. In almost all the poems having love as a focal point, Akhmatova presents love from a woman's point of view, in a form resembling a diary. It is difficult to say whether the female voice in these poems belongs to the poet herself; probably it does, but in the last analysis it is immaterial. The beloved is almost always silent, never fully revealed or described, and at times he seems to be almost secondary—only a catalyst for the woman's feelings. She is so entranced by his mere presence that, in her anguish, she draws her "left-hand glove upon [her] right." The poet expresses the whole spectrum of love—from the playfulness of a young woman trying to dismay her partner in order to prove that she, too, can wield some power over him, to moments of flaming passion. To be sure, passion is presented implicitly, in the time-honored tradition of Russian literature, yet it is also vividly indicated in unique ways. As she says, "In human intimacy there is a secret boundary,/ Neither the experience of being in love nor passion can cross it/ Though the lips be joined together in awful silence/ And the heart break asunder with love." Her fervent passion is coupled with fidelity to her partner, but as her loyalty is professed time and again, a note of frustration and a fear of incompatibility and rejection become noticeable. The prospect of unrequited love is confirmed by betrayal and parting. The ensuing feeling of loneliness leads to despair and withdrawal. The woman's reaction shows a mixture of anger, defiance, even resignation: "Be accursed . . ./ But I swear by the garden of angels/ By the holy icon I swear,/ By the passionate frenzy of our nights,/ I will never go back to you!" (These lines, incidentally, prompted Zhdanov, in his merciless attack many years later, to call Akhmatova "a nun and a harlot.") Thus, celebration, parting, and suffering receive equal play in Akhmatova's approach to love, although the ultimate outcome is a markedly unhappy one. Her love poetry is a vivid testimony both to the glories and to the miseries of her sex.

The feminine "I" of the poems seeks refuge, release, and salvation in religion, nature, and poetry. The refuge in religion is especially evident in *Chetki*. The work has a peculiar religious tone, pervaded, like Akhmatova's sentiments of love, with a mood of melancholy and inexplicable sadness. The persona seems to have found consolation for unhappiness in love when she says: "The King of Heaven has healed my/ Soul with the icy calm of love's/ Absence." Her prayers are mostly in the form of confession or intercession. It is easy to see, however, that they are used primarily to compensate for her feeling of loneliness and weariness of life. Thus, privations and misfortunes are closely tied to her religious feelings; sin and atonement are inseparable, and her passions of the flesh are tempered by spiritual fervor. Akhmatova's poems with religious overtones have little in common with customary religious experience. They are also much more complex and psychologically laden than any of her other poetry.

In Akhmatova's third collection, *Belaya staya*, a new theme joins those of love and religion: a presentiment of doom. Nourished by the horrors of war and revolution, this presentiment grows into a wake for a world on the verge of annihilation. As the Revolution dragged on, Akhmatova's mood turned bleaker and more hopeless. She sought rapport with the events by writing poetry with political motifs, but to no avail. The poems in *Anno Domini MCMXXI* clearly reveal Akhmatova's state of mind and emotions at this difficult time, as well as her awareness that an era had come to an end. "All is sold, all is lost, all is plundered,/ Death's wing has flashed black on our sight,/ All's gnawed bare with sore, want, and sick longing," she laments in one poem. She refused to emigrate, however, knowing instinctively, as did Boris Pasternak many years later when he was threatened with expulsion from the Soviet Union, that for a poet to leave his or her native land is tantamount to a death worse than physical death. She did not hesitate to criticize those who had left their country in its worst hour: "Poor exile, you are like a prisoner/ To me, or one upon the bed/ Of sickness. Dark your road, O wanderer,/ Of wormwood smacks your alien bread." These lines have been quoted often by Soviet critics for propaganda purposes, although Akhmatova wrote them sincerely, as a poet who could not tear herself away from her own land.

In the poems in which Akhmatova grappled with the problems of present-day reality, a gradual shift away from intimate love poetry toward more worldly themes can be seen. This shift can be considered as an overture to another kind of Akhmatova's poetry. Tormented by the turbulent years of war and revolution, in which she made many personal sacrifices and witnessed many tragedies (the loss of friends, for example, including her former husband Nikolay Gumilyov), she was forced to face reality and to express her feelings and opinions about it. The silence imposed on her in 1923 only postponed further development in that direction. When she was allowed to reappear shortly before World War II, she wrote little in her old idiom. In many poems written during the war, she extols the beauty of her land and the magnitude of the martyrdom of her people under attack by a ruthless enemy. Leningrad, the city of her life and of her dreams, is especially the object of her affection. Tsarskoe Selo–a settlement near Leningrad that was the residence of the czars, the town of young Alexander Pushkin, and the town of Akhmatova's favorite poetry teacher Innokenty Annensky, as well as of her own youth–remained vividly and forever etched in her memory, even when she saw it almost totally destroyed in the war.

Leningrad and Tsarskoe Selo were not the only places to which Akhmatova paid homage; indeed, all of Russia was her home. Her attitude toward her country is typical of many Russian intellectuals, who, despite a thick veneer of cosmopolitanism, still harbor a childlike, sentimental, and irrational love for their country. From her earliest poems to her last, Akhmatova expressed the same feeling for Russia, a strange mixture of abstract love for her country, on one hand, and down-to-earth concern for its people, on the other. In the poem "Prayer," for example, she prays to the Lord to take even her child and to destroy "the sweet power of song" that she possesses if it would help to change "the storm cloud over Russia . . . into a nimbus ablaze." This willingness to sacrifice what is dearest to her if it would benefit her country is no mere affectation–it is expressed with utmost sincerity and conviction. In a poem written almost thirty years later, "From an Airplane," she again expresses her love for her country in no less sincere terms: "It is all mine—and nothing can divide us,/ It is my soul, it is my body, too." Perhaps the most profound and meaningful testimony to her patriotism can be found in the poem "Native Land," written in the last years of her life. For her, her country was "the mud on our gumboots, the grit in our teeth . . . And we mill, and we mix, and we crumble/ This innocent earth at our feet,/ But we rest in this earth at the roots of the flowers,/ Which is why we so readily say: It is ours!"

Akhmatova did not limit her gaze to European Russia, where she was reared and where she spent most of her life. Through her experiences in Tashkent, the city in which her ancestors had resided, she acquired a great admiration for, and understanding of, the Asian mind and soul. A mystical bond with Asia inspired her to write some of her most beautiful descriptive poems, such as "From the Oriental Notebook."

Nevertheless, Akhmatova could not close her eyes to the Soviet reality, in which she was personally caught in a most tragic way. In a unified cycle of poems, *Requiem*, she expresses her deep sorrow not only about her personal loss but also about the suffering to which the Russian people were being subjected. *Requiem* was her closest approach to public castigation of the regime in her country. The tone for the entire work is set by the motto, which sadly admits that the circumstances are not those of a foreign country but, more personally, those of the poet's own country and people. In a short foreword in prose, Akhmatova tells how during the horrible years of the purges she spent seventeen months waiting in line in front of a prison in order to discover the fate of her son. Another woman recognized her and whispered, "Can you describe this?" "Yes, I can," Akhmatova replied. She kept her promise by writing *Requiem*. Although much of it reflects the universal sorrow and despair of a mother on the verge of losing her son, it is the injustice of her suffering that most pains the poet. Using her personal sorrow to speak for all human beings who suffer unjustly, the poet created in *Requiem* a work of lasting value. Moreover, there is much encouragement to be gained from *Requiem*. The persona does not lose hope and courage. She perseveres, knowing that the victims are unjustly persecuted and that she is not alone in suffering. In the epilogue, she recalls the trying hours and the faces she has seen in those seventeen months; in her final words, she begs that her monument be erected in front of the prison where she has stood for "three hundred hours," so that the thawing snow from the face of her monument will glide like tears. Even if overt references to the political terror are overlooked, *Requiem* is still one of the twentieth century's most eloquent poetic testimonies to human tragedy.

Akhmatova's poetry from the last decade of her life shows the greater maturity and wisdom of old age. Her approach to poetic themes is more epic and historical, with a deeper perspective. This mature poetry is also more philosophical and psychological. The best example is the autobiographical *A Poem Without a Hero*, a panoramic view of the previous century as it pertains to the present. It is a subtle and at times complex poem, difficult to fathom without a proper key. In her last poems, she speaks as if she has realized that her active role is over and that nothing else can hurt her. Her work at this time shows a mixture of sadness, resignation, relief, and even slight bewilderment as to what life really is after more than seven decades of coping with it: "The grim epoch diverted me/ As if I were a river./ I have been given a different life. In a new bed/ The river now flows, past the old one,/ And I cannot find my shores. . . ." She finds solace in her increasing loneliness, contemplating the past, trying to reevaluate it and to find the correct perspective on it. In one of her last poems, written slightly more than a year before her death, she speaks of the "Supreme Mystery." It has been on her mind from the beginning, changing its face from period to period. In her early poetry, it was the mystery of the man-woman relationship. Later, it became the mystery of the man-to-man relationship, with the emphasis on the cruelty of man to man. In her last years, it became the mystery of the relationship of man to eternity, indeed the mystery of the meaning of existence. Through such organic development, Akhmatova reached the pinnacle of her poetic power, the power found in Pasternak's late poetry and in the work of other great poets of the century.

The stylistic aspect of Akhmatova's poetry is just as important as the thematic one, if not more so. She shows several peculiarly Akhmatovian features. Above all, there is the narrative tone that points to a definite affinity with prose. Zhirmunski calls her entire oeuvre "a novel in verse." It is this affinity that enables her to switch easily from emotion to description. Connected with this skill is a dramatic quality, expressed either through inner monologue or dialogue. The second striking feature is the brief lyric form, usually consisting of three to four stanzas, rarely five to seven, and never more than seven. (Later in her career, Akhmatova wrote many poems in free verse.) Parallel to the brevity of form is a pronounced laconism: A few carefully selected details suffice to convey an entire picture. Akhmatova's economy of words, spare almost to the point of frugality, led her to the epigrammatic form and to fragmentation, understatement, and improvisation. As a result, her sentences are sometimes verbless and even without a subject (that being quite possible in Russian). Another peculiarity is the concreteness of her images, especially with reference to space and time. She tells the reader exactly where and when, almost to the minute, the events in her poem take place. The colors are vividly and exactly given. She avoids metaphors, instead using pointed, explanatory epithets. Finally, her intonation, never scrupulously measured or regulated, is that of a syncopated rhythm, approaching the rhythm of some forms of folk poetry. Many of these stylistic features result from her adherence to the tenets of Acmeism, but many others are uniquely her own and are easily recognizable as such.

Of the poets who influenced her, Akhmatova herself admits indebtedness to Gavrila Derzhavin, Pushkin, and Annensky. The latter two can be said to have exerted the greatest influence on her, although traces of other poets' influences—Nikolai Nekrasov, Aleksandr Blok, Mikhail Kuzmin—can be found. Even Fyodor Dostoevski, who never wrote poetry, is sometimes mentioned as a possible source of influence. As for her impact on other poets, Akhmatova's influence—like that of her great contemporaries, Mandelstam, Pasternak, and Marina Tsvetayeva—is pervasive, elusive, impossible to measure. In her old age, she recognized the talent of Joseph Brodsky—then only twenty-two years old—and passed on her mantle, as Nadezhda Mandelstam has said, in a kind of poetic succession. Anna Akhmatova, "Tragic Queen Anna," as Alexander Werth calls her, is a poet without whom modern Russian literature is unthinkable and by whom world literature has been significantly enriched.

Select works other than poetry
NONFICTION: *O Pushkine: Stat'i i zametki*, 1977.

Vasa D. Mihailovich

Bibliography · The best critical biography in English is by Amanda Haight: *Anna Akhmatova: A Poetic Pilgrimage*, 1976. Haight knew Akhmatova well near the end of the poet's life and was given much valuable unpublished material by her. Marc Slonim, in *Soviet Russian Literature: Writers and Problems, 1917-1977*, 1977, and Evelyn Bristol, in *A History of Russian Poetry*, 1991, devote portions of chapters to an evaluation of Akhmatova's achievement. Isaiah Berlin, a distinguished Oxford University philosopher, has a moving chapter in his *Personal Impressions*, 1949, recalling two meetings he had with Akhmatova in 1945, when he worked for the British embassy in Moscow. Anatoly Nayman, *Remembering Anna Akhmatova*, 1991, translated by Wendy Rosslyn, has an introduction by Joseph Brodsky.

GUILLAUME APOLLINAIRE

(Guillaume Albert Wladimir Alexandre
Apollinaire de Kostrowitzky)

Born: Rome, Italy; August 26, 1880
Died: Paris, France; November 9, 1918

Poetry · *Le Bestiaire,* 1911 (*Bestiary,* 1978) · *Alcools,* 1913 (English translation, 1964, 1965) · *Calligrammes,* 1918 (English translation, 1980) · *Il y a,* 1925 · *Le Guetteur mélancolique,* 1952 · *Tendre comme le souvenir,* 1952 · *Poèmes à Lou,* 1955

Achievements · After Guillaume Apollinaire, French poetry was never the same again. Writing at the end of the long Symbolist tradition, a tradition very apparent in his early works, Apollinaire moved into a new perception of the world and of poetry. In the world of his mature verse, spatial and temporal relations are radically altered. Apollinaire's was one of the first voices in French poetry to attempt to articulate the profound discontinuity and disorientation in modern society. At the same time, however, his works reflect hope, frequently ecstatic, in the promise of the future.

Apollinaire's sense of radical discontinuity was reflected in his formal innovations, analyzed in considerable depth by Jean-Claude Chevalier in *Alcools d'Apollinaire.* Immediately before the publication of *Alcools,* Apollinaire went through the volume and removed all punctuation, a device which he continued to use in most of his later works. His most notable poems, such as "Zone,"

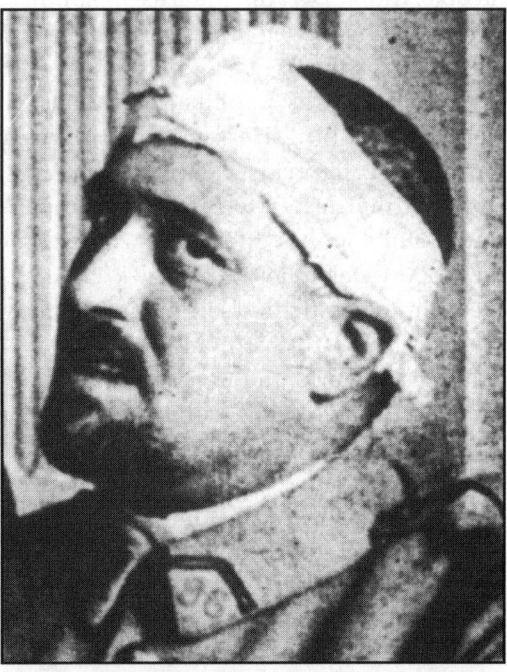

French Embassy Press & Information Division, New York

"Liens" ("Chains"), and "Les Fenêtres" ("Windows"), use free verse with irregular rhyme and rhythm; his most startling works are the picture poems of *Calligrammes*, a form which he falsely claimed to have invented. They consist of verses arranged to give both a visual and an auditory effect in an effort to create "simultaneity."

Like the Cubists and other modern painters who sought to go beyond the traditional boundaries of space and time, Apollinaire desired to create the effect of simultaneity. This ambition is evident in "Zone," with its biographical, geographical, and historical discontinuity. In this single poem, the poet leaps from his pious childhood at the Collège Saint-Charles in Monaco to the wonders of modern aviation and back to the "herds" of buses "mooing" on the streets of Paris. Perhaps his most obvious achievement in simultaneity, though less profound, is in "Lundi rue Christine" ("Monday in Christine Street"), which records overheard bits of conversation in a "sinistre brasserie," a low-class café-restaurant that Apollinaire had frequented as early as 1903.

The friend and collaborator of many important painters during the exciting years in Paris just before World War I, Apollinaire began associating with artists when he met Pablo Picasso in 1904, after which he frequented the famous Bateau-Lavoir on the rue Ravignan with Max Jacob, André Derain, Maurice Vlaminck, Georges Braque, and others. After 1912, he moved into the world of art criticism, not always appreciated by the artists themselves, as Francis Steegmuller has noted. Not unrelated to this interest was Apollinaire's tumultuous liaison with Marie Laurencin from 1907 to 1912. He frequently inspired works and portraits by artists, including Laurencin, Henri Rousseau, and Picasso. Apollinaire's own works further testify to his links with painters: *Bestiary* was illustrated by Raoul Dufy, and "Windows" was the introductory poem to the catalog of the Robert Delaunay exhibit in 1912. His poems often parallel the work of the painters in their spirit of simultaneity; in their subjects, such as the *saltimbanques* of Picasso; and in their moods, such as those of Marc Chagall's dreamworld and inverted figures.

After 1916, Apollinaire became the "chef d'école," the leader of a new generation of poets and painters. Among them were Pierre Reverdy, Philippe Soupault, Jean Cocteau, André Breton, and Tristan Tzara. His own works appeared in the most avant-garde journals: Reverdy's *Nord-Sud*, Picabia's *391*, and Albert Birot's *SIC*. His lecture "The New Spirit and the Poets" called poets to a new prophetic vision, imploring them to create prodigies with their imagination like modern Merlins. Like Paul Claudel, Apollinaire regarded the poet as a creator. The modern poet, he believed, must use everything for his or her creation: new discoveries in science, in the subconscious and the dreamworld, and in the cinema and visual arts.

The Surrealists, in their desire to revolutionize art and literature, saw in Apollinaire their precursor. It was he who coined the word "surréaliste," in the preface to his drama in verse *The Breasts of Tiresias*. In it, he explains that an equivalent is not always an imitation, even as the wheel, though intended to facilitate transportation, is not a reproduction of the leg. Apollinaire conveys his message with a lighthearted tone, employing incongruous rhythms, parody, and sexual imagery. This is essentially the technique he employs in his most avant-garde poetry, and *The Breasts of Tiresias* echoes poems from "Ondes" ("Waves," the first part of *Calligrammes*) such as "Zone," "Le Brasier" ("The Brazier"), "Les Fiançailles" ("The Betrothal"), and "Le Larron" ("The Thief"). Thus, Apollinaire indicated the path to follow in revolutionizing poetry, although much of his work was in some respects traditional. Like Victor Hugo, he served subsequent poets chiefly as a guide rather than as a model, but it was his "esprit nouveau" that gave considerable impetus to a new form of modern poetry.

Biography · Born in Rome on August 26, 1880, Apollinaire was an illegitimate child. His mother was a Polish adventurer of noble ancestry, Angelique Kostrowicka, known in Paris mostly as Olga. His father's identity has never been definitively ascertained. The most plausible supposition points to Francesco Flugi d'Aspermont, a man from a noble Italian family which included many prelates. This theory is based on the careful investigation of biographer Marcel Adéma. Apollinaire's mysterious and involved parentage haunted the poet throughout his life, leaving unmistakable marks on his character and works.

Apollinaire received his only formal education at the Collège of Saint-Charles in Monaco and the Collège Stanislas at Cannes, from 1890 to 1897, where he acquired a solid grounding in religious and secular knowledge. Although his Catholic training was to remain firmly implanted in his memory and is evident in his poetry, he moved away from any outward adherence to religious beliefs after 1897. In 1899, he arrived in Paris, his home for most of the next nineteen years of his life and the center and inspiration of his literary activity. First, however, he made a significant trip to Germany's Rhineland in 1901, as tutor to Gabrielle, the daughter of the Viscountess of Milhau. There, he met and fell in love with Annie Playden, Gabrielle's English governess. This ill-fated romance and the beauty of the Rhineland inspired many of Apollinaire's early poems, which were later published in *Alcools*.

Apollinaire's return to Paris coincided with the beginning of friendships with artists and writers such as André Salmon, Alfred Jarry, Max Jacob, and especially Picasso. In 1903, he began his collaboration on many periodicals, which he continued throughout his lifetime. Most of his prose and poetry were first published in such journals, many of which—such as *Le Festin d'Esope* and *La Revue immoraliste*—were of very short duration. His works appeared under several pseudonyms, of which "Apollinaire" was the most significant. Others included "Louise Lalame," "Lul," "Montade," and "Tyl." In 1907, he met Marie Laurencin, an artist, whose talent Apollinaire tended to exaggerate. Their liaison continued until 1912 and was an inspiration and a torment to both of them. During this period, Apollinaire was deeply marked by the false accusation that he was responsible for the theft of the *Mona Lisa* from the Louvre. A series of six poems in *Alcools*, "À la Santé" ("At the Santé") describes his brief stay in the prison of La Santé in Verlainian imagery.

The year 1912 marked Apollinaire's break with Laurencin and his definite espousal of modern art, of which he became a staunch proponent. During the two years preceding World War I, he gave lectures and wrote articles on modern art and prepared *Alcools* for publication. The beginning of the war, in 1914, was to Apollinaire a call to a mission. Although not a French citizen until the year 1916, he embraced with great enthusiasm his *métier de soldat* as an artilleryman and then as an infantryman, according an almost mystical dimension to his military service. His poetry of these first two years reveals the exaltation of war and the idealization of two women, "Lou" (Louise de Coligny-Châtillon) and Madeleine Pagès, to whom he was briefly engaged.

Wounded in the head in 1916, Apollinaire required surgery and was then discharged from the service. He returned to the world of literature and art with numerous articles, lectures, two plays, and a volume of poetry, *Calligrammes*. In May of 1918, he married Jacqueline Kolb ("Ruby"), the "jolie rousse" (pretty redhead) of the last poem in *Calligrammes*. The marriage was of short duration, however, as Apollinaire died of Spanish influenza on November 9 of the same year.

Analysis · In his poetic style, Guillaume Apollinaire might be characterized as the last of the Symbolists and the first of the moderns. He is considered a revolutionary and a destroyer, yet the bulk of his work shows a deep influence of traditional symbolism, especially biblical, legendary, and mythical. Very knowledgeable in Roman Catholic doctrine from his years with the Marianists at Monaco and Cannes, he uses extensive biblical imagery: Christ, the Virgin Mary, and the Holy Spirit in the form of a dove. Robert Couffignal has analyzed Apollinaire's religious imagery in detail and considers his comprehension of the Bible to be "a cascade of superficial weavings." Scott Bates sees the Last Judgment, with its apocalyptic implications, as central to Apollinaire's works. The concept of Messianism and the advent of a new millennium is evident in both the early works and the war poems, which predict a new universe. In the Symbolist tradition, the poet is the seer of the new kingdom.

Many of Apollinaire's symbols are from the realm of legend and myth. Rosemonde, the idealized woman of the Middle Ages, is present in several poems, though she appears also as a prostitute. In "Merlin et la vielle femme" ("Merlin and the Old Woman"), the medieval seer foreshadows Apollinaire's vision of the future. Ancient mythology is the source for Orpheus, under whose sign *Bestiary* is written. Orpheus is also the symbol of Christ and the poet, as is Hermès Trismégiste. Ancient Egypt appears in frequent references to the Nile, the Israelites in bondage, and Pharaoh, the image of the poet himself. The fantastic abounds in Apollinaire's works: ghosts, diabolic characters, and phantoms, as found, for example, in "La Maison des Morts" ("The House of the Dead") and especially in the short stories.

Much of Apollinaire's early symbolism is directed toward the quest for self-knowledge; his choice of the name "Apollinaire" is a clue to his search. Though it was the name of his maternal grandfather and one of the names given to him at baptism, he seems to have chosen it for its reference to Apollo, the god of the sun. Indeed, solar imagery is central to his poetry, and the introductory poem of *Alcools*, "Zone," ends with the words "Soleil cou coupé" ("Sun cut throat"). Bates argues that the violent love-death relationship between the sun and night, with its corresponding symbolism, is as crucial to the interpretation of Apollinaire as it is to a reading of Gérard de Nerval or Stéphane Mallarmé. Along with love and death is death and resurrection. Apollinaire chooses the phoenix as a sign of rebirth and describes his own psychological and poetic resurrection in "The Brazier" and "The Betrothal," poems that he regarded as among his best. Fire seems to be his basic image, with its multiple meanings of passion, destruction, and purification.

Passion as a flame dominated Apollinaire's life and poetry. Of the many women whom he loved, five in particular incarnated his violent passion and appear in his work: Playden and Laurencin in *Alcools*; Lou, Madeleine, and Jacqueline in *Calligrammes* and in several series of poems published after his death. Apollinaire is capable of expressing tender, idealistic love, as in the "Aubade chantée à Lætare un an passé" ("Aubade Sung to Lætare a Year Ago") section of the "La Chanson du mal-aimé" ("The Song of the Poorly Loved") and in "La Jolie Rousse" ("The Pretty Redhead"), which closes *Calligrammes*. In most cases, Apollinaire is the *mal-aimé*, and as he himself says, he is much less the poorly beloved than the one who loves poorly. His first three loves ended violently; his last was concluded by his death. Thus, the death of love is as important as its first manifestation, which for him resembles the shells bursting in the war.

Autumn is the season of the death of love, wistfully expressed in such nostalgic works as "L'Adieu" ("The Farewell") and "Automne" ("Autumn"). Because the end of love usually involved deep suffering for him, the image of mutilation is not uncommon. The beloved in "The Song of the Poorly Loved" has a scar on her neck, and the mannequins in "L'Émigrant de Landor Road" ("The Emigrant from Landor Road") are decapitated, much like the sun in "Zone." Apollinaire perceives love in its erotic sense, and in many cases he resorts to arcane symbolism, as in the seven swords in "The Song of the Poorly Loved." "Lul de Faltenin" ("Lul of Faltenin") is also typical, with its subtle erotic allusions. Such themes are more overt in Apollinaire's prose; indeed, Bates has compiled a glossary of erotic symbolism in the works of Apollinaire.

Apollinaire was both a lyric poet and a storyteller. In the lyric tradition, he writes of his emotions in images drawn from nature. His work is particularly rich in flora and fauna. *Bestiary* shows his familiarity with and affection for animals and his ability, like the fabulists, to see them as caricatures of people. *Alcools*, as the title indicates, often evokes grapes and wine; it also speaks of fir trees (in "Les Sapins") and falling leaves. "Zone" contains a catalog of birds, real and legendary. The Seine comes alive in Apollinaire's ever-popular "Le Pont Mirabeau" ("Mirabeau Bridge"). In *Calligrammes*, the poet often compares the explosion of shells to bursting buds.

Apollinaire was the author of many short stories, and he maintains a narrative flavor in his poetry. "The House of the Dead" was originally a short story, "L'Obituaire," and it reads like one. Many of the picture poems in *Calligrammes* tell a story; "Paysage" ("Landscape"), for example, portrays by means of typography a house, a tree, and two lovers, one of whom smokes a cigar that the reader can almost smell. Apollinaire's technique often involved improvisation, as in "Le Musicien de Saint-Merry" ("The Musician of Saint-Merry"). Although he claims almost total spontaneity, there are revised versions of many of his poems, and he frequently borrowed from himself, rearranging both lines and poems. In particular, Apollinaire tells stories of the modern city, imitating its new structures as Arthur Rimbaud did in his innovative patterns, and, like Charles Baudelaire, Apollinaire peoples his verse with the forgotten and the poor, the prostitutes and the clowns.

Apollinaire had a remarkable sense of humor, displayed in frequent wordplays, burlesques, and parodies. The briefest example of his use of puns is the one-line poem "Chantre" ("Singer"): "Et l'unique cordeau des trompettes marines" ("And the single string of marine trumpets"). *Cordeau*, when read aloud, might be *cor d'eau* or "horn of water"–another version of a marine trumpet–as well as *corps d'eau* (body of water) or even *coeur d'eau* (heart of water). The burlesque found in his short stories appears in poetry as dissonance, erotic puns, and irreverent parodies, such as in "Les Sept Epées" ("The Seven Swords") as well as in "The Thief," a poem that Bates interprets as parodying Christ. Apollinaire's lighthearted rhythm and obscure symbolism tend to prevent his verse from becoming offensive and convey a sense of freedom, discovery, and surprise.

Bestiary is one of the most charming and accessible of Apollinaire's works. The idea for the poem probably came from Picasso in 1906, who was then doing woodcuts of animals. In 1908, Apollinaire published in a journal eighteen poems under the title "La Marchande des quatre saisons ou le bestiaire moderne" (the costermonger or the modern bestiary). When he prepared the final edition in 1911, with woodcuts by Raoul Dufy, he added twelve poems and replaced the merchant with Orpheus. According to mythology, Orpheus attracted wild beasts by playing on the lyre he had received from Mercury. He is the symbol of Gnosis and Neoplatonic Humanism, and is also identified with Christ and poetry, in a mixture of mystical and sensual imagery.

Apollinaire himself wrote the notes to the volume and uses as its sign a Δ (the Greek letter delta) pierced by a unicorn. He interprets it to mean the delta of the Nile and all the legendary and biblical symbols of ancient Egypt, also suggesting a *D* for Deplanche, the publisher, in addition to the obvious sexual symbolism. He added the motto "J'émerveille" (I marvel), thus giving a fantastic aura to the work. Roger Little sees in the volume a "delicious and malicious" wit, with metamorphoses, syncretism, pride in poetry, carnal love, and mysticism. Like all Apollinaire's early works, it is full of self-analysis. In "La Souris" ("The Mouse"), the poet speaks of his twenty-eight years as "mal-vécus" ("poorly spent").

The animals represent human foibles; the peacock, for example, displays both his best and, unbeknownst to him, his worst. They also speak of love: the serpent, the Sirens, the dove, and Orpheus himself. They point to God and things divine: the dove, the bull, or, again, Orpheus. They speak of poetry: the horse, the tortoise, the elephant, and the caterpillar. For Apollinaire, poetry is a divine gift. He concludes his notes by observing that poets seek nothing but perfection, which is God Himself. Poets, he says, have the right to expect after death the full knowledge of God, which is sublime beauty.

The most analyzed and the best known of Apollinaire's works is *Alcools*, a slender volume published in 1913 with the subtitle *Poèmes, 1898-1913*. A portrait of Apollinaire, an etching by Picasso, serves as the frontispiece. Apollinaire chose fifty-five of the many poems he had written from his eighteenth to his thirty-third year and assembled them in an order that has continued to fascinate and baffle critics. Michel Décaudin says that the order in *Alcools* is based entirely on the aesthetic and sentimental affinities felt by the author, or their discrete dissonances. Very few poems have dates, other than "Rhénanes" (September, 1901, to May, 1902) and "At the Santé" (September, 1911); nevertheless, critics have succeeded in dating many, though not all, of the poems.

The poems have several centers, though not all of those from one group appear together. More than twenty were inspired by Apollinaire's trip to the Rhineland in 1901, including the nine in the cycle "Rhénanes." Several of these poems and some others, such as "The Song of the Poorly Loved," "Annie," and "The Emigrant from Landor Road," refer to his unhappy love affair with Playden. These poems and an interview with her as Mrs. Postings in 1951 by Robert Goffin and LeRoy Breunig are the only sources of information about this significant period in Apollinaire's life. Three poems, "Mirabeau Bridge," "Marie," and "Cors de chasse" ("Hunting Horns"), scattered throughout the volume, refer to Laurencin.

The poems exhibit great variety in form, tone, and subject matter. They range from the one-line "Chantre" to the seven-part "The Song of the Poorly Loved," the longest in the collection. Most of them have regular rhyme and rhythm, but "Zone" and "Vendémiaire," the first and the last, give evidence of technical experimentation. The poems range from witty ("The Synagogue") to nostalgic ("Autumn," "Hunting Horns"), from enigmatic ("The Brazier") to irreverent ("The Thief"). Critics have arranged them in various ways. Bates, for example, sees the volume as a "Dionysian-Apollonian dance of life in three major symbols: fire, shadow, alcools."

Apollinaire chose the beginning and concluding poems of the collection, "Zone" and "Vendémiaire," with great care. "Zone" is overtly autobiographical in a "Romantic-Symbolist" ambience, yet its instant leaps in space and time make it very modern. Also modern is the image of the city, where Apollinaire can see beauty in a poster, a traffic jam, and a group of frightened Jewish immigrants. The city is also the central focus in the concluding poem, "Vendémiaire" (the name given the month of vintage, September 22-October 21, in the Revolutionary calendar), a hymn to the glory of Paris. The poet exuberantly proclaims his immortality and omnipresence: "I am drunk from having swallowed all the universe." Bates sees the end of the poem as a hymn to joy reminiscent of Walt Whitman and Friedrich Nietzsche.

The bizarre juxtapositions, the inner borrowings of lines from one poem to the next, and the absence of punctuation provoked various responses from critics. Cubists hailed Apollinaire as a great poet. Georges Duhamel, writing in the June 15, 1913, issue of *Mercure de France*, called the volume a junk shop. Recent critics such as Adéma, Décaudin, and Marie-Jeanne Durry analyze *Alcools* with depth and scholarship. They discover many platitudes and much mediocrity but find it redeemed by what Steegmuller identifies as a spirit of freedom.

Intended as a sequel to *Alcools*, *Calligrammes* is much more unified than *Alcools*, yet its importance was seen only much later. It consists of six parts. The first part, "Waves," is the most innovative and was written before World War I in the frenzied stimulation of artistic activity in Paris. The other five contain poems inspired by the war and by the poet's love for Lou, Madeleine, and—in the final poem—his future wife, Jacqueline.

Philippe Renaud sees the difference between *Alcools* and "Waves" as one of nature rather than degree. Even the most enigmatic poems of *Alcools* follow a familiar plan, he maintains, whereas in "Waves" the reader is in unfamiliar territory, disoriented in space and time. In "Waves" one feels both the insecurity and the indefiniteness that can only be called "modern art." The introductory poem, "Chains," uses the elements recommended by Apollinaire in "The New Spirit and the Poets" yet remains anchored in the past. It leaps from the Tower of Babel to telegraph wires in disconcerting juxtapositions, speaking of humankind's eternal, frustrating quest for unity. In "The Windows," the window opens like an orange on Paris or in the tropics and flies on a rainbow across space and time.

Beginning with "Waves," and throughout *Calligrammes*, Apollinaire uses what he calls "ideograms," or picture poems. They are the most attractive pieces in the book, though not necessarily the most original. They became excellent vehicles for the war poems, where brevity and wit are essential. The theme of war dominates the majority of poems in *Calligrammes*. The war excited Apollinaire, promising a new universe. He experienced exhilaration as he saw shells exploding, comparing them in the poem "Merveilles de la guerre" ("Wonders of War") to constellations and to women's hair, to dancers and to women in childbirth. He saw himself as the poet-hero, the omnipresent seer, the animator of the universe. In "La Tête étoilée" ("The Starry Head"), his wound was a crown of stars on his head.

Apollinaire was as dependent on love as he was on air, and he suffered greatly in the solitary trenches of France. His brief romance with Lou was intense and violent, as his pun on her name in "C'est Lou qu'on la nommait" ("They Called Her Lou") indicates; instead of "Lou," the word *loup* (which sounds the same in French but means "wolf") is used throughout the poem. In his poems to Madeleine, he devours images like a starving man. The anthology ends serenely as he addresses Jacqueline, "la jolie rousse," the woman destined to be his wife as poetry was destined to be his life. This final poem is also his poetic testament, in which he bequeaths "vast and unknown kingdoms, new fires and the mystery of flowers to anyone willing to pick them."

Other literary forms · Besides poetry, Guillaume Apollinaire wrote a number of prose works. Among the most significant of his short stories and novellas are *L'Enchanteur pourrissant* (1909; the putrescent enchanter), published by Henry Kahnweiler and illustrated with woodcuts by André Derain; *L'Hérésiarque et Cie.* (1910; *The Heresiarch and Co.*, 1965), a contender for the Prix Goncourt; and *Le Poète assassiné* (1916; *The Poet Assassinated*, 1923). They are contained in the Pléiade edition, *Œuvres en prose* (1977), edited by Michel Décaudin.

Apollinaire collaborated on numerous plays and cinema scripts. His best-known individual works in these genres are two proto-Surrealist plays in verse: *Les Mamelles de Tirésias* (*The Breasts of Tiresias*, 1961), first published in the magazine *SIC* in 1918, and *Couleur du temps* (the color of time), which first appeared in the *Nouvelle Revue française* in 1920. They are available in the Pléiade edition of *Oeuvres poétiques*. Apollinaire also published a great deal of art criticism and literary criticism in journals, newspapers, and other periodicals. In 1913, the articles published before that year were collected in *Peintres cubistes: Méditations esthétiques* (*The Cubist Painters: Esthetic Meditations*, 1944). In 1918, *Mercure de France* published his famous manifesto "L'Esprit nouveau et les poètes" ("The New Spirit and the Poets"), which later appeared, along with many other articles, in *Chroniques d'art, 1902-1918* (1960), edited by L. C. Breunig. The same collection has been translated into English as *Apollinaire on Art: Essays and Reviews, 1902-1918* (1972).

Select works other than poetry
LONG FICTION: *L'Enchanteur pourrissant*, 1909; *Le Poète assassiné*, 1916 (*The Poet Assassinated*, 1923).
SHORT FICTION: *L'Hérésiarque et Cie.*, 1910 (*The Heresiarch and Co.*, 1965).
DRAMA: *Les Mamelles de Tirésias*, pr. 1917 (*The Breasts of Tiresias*, 1961); *Couleur du temps*, pr. 1918.
NONFICTION: *Peintres cubistes: Méditations esthétiques*, 1913 (*The Cubist Paint-*

ers: *Esthetic Meditations*, 1944); *Chroniques d'art, 1902-1918*, 1960 (*Apollinaire on Art: Essays and Reviews, 1902-1918*, 1972).

MISCELLANEOUS: *Œuvres complètes*, 1966 (8 volumes); *Œuvres en prose*, 1977 (Michel Décaudin, editor).

Irma M. Kashuba

Bibliography · The best general introduction is Scott Bayes, *Guillaume Apollinaire*, rev. ed., 1989. Apollinaire's influential involvement with cubism is appreciable in Cecily Mackworth's *Guillaume Apollinaire and the Cubist Life*, 1963. In readability and accurate scholarship, Francis Steegmuller's *Apollinaire: Poet Among the Painters*, 1963, has few, if any, peers. A very informative critical study expertly relating Apollinaire to Marius de Zayas, Alberto Savinio, Francis Picabia, and the work of Giorgio de Chirico, is Willard Bohn's *Apollinaire and the Faceless Man: The Creation and Evolution of a Modern Motif*, 1991. Timothy Mathews' *Reading Apollinaire: Theories of Poetic Language*, 1987, is equally informative, but whereas Bohn provides English translations of all French quotations, Mathews translates no French quotations.

MATTHEW ARNOLD

Born: Laleham, England; December 24, 1822
Died: Liverpool, England; April 15, 1888

Poetry · *The Strayed Reveller and Other Poems*, 1849 · *Empedocles on Etna and Other Poems*, 1852 · *Poems*, 1853 · *Poems, Second Series*, 1855 · *New Poems*, 1867 · *Poems, Collected Edition*, 1869 · *Poetical Works of Matthew Arnold*, 1890

Achievements · In 1840, while he was a student at Rugby, Matthew Arnold won the Poetry Prize for "Alaric at Rome," and three years later, then at Oxford, he won the Newdigate Poetry Prize for "Cromwell." From this official recognition of his poetic gift, Arnold began a career which produced what T. S. Eliot calls in *The Use of Poetry and the Use of Criticism* (1933), "academic poetry in the best sense; the best fruit which can issue from the promise shown by the prize-poem." Yet Arnold wrote many poems which rise far above the merely academic, though popular interest in his poetry never approached the following of his more technically and expressively gifted contemporaries, Alfred, Lord Tennyson and Robert Browning. Admittedly, Arnold's poems lack the polished texture that characterizes the great Victorian poetry; critics often complain about Arnold's lack of "ear." The novelist George Eliot, however, early recognized, in the *Westminster Review* (July, 1855), what has been increasingly the opinion: "But when . . . we linger over a poem which contains some deep and fresh thought, we begin to perceive poetic beauties—felicities of expression and description, which are too quiet and subdued to be seized at the first glance." Whatever his prosodic deficiencies, Arnold still composed several lyric and narrative poems which take their place with the best that the age produced.

In a century notable for elegies, "Thyrsis," for Arnold's friend Arthur Hugh Clough, ranks with *Adonais* (1821), "When Lilacs Last in the Dooryard Bloom'd" (1865), and *In Memoriam* (1850) as distinguished additions to the genre. "The Scholar-Gipsy" and "Dover Beach" contain the lyric energy and power which justify both their numerous anthology appearances and a body of criticism that places them among the most frequently explicated poems in the language.

In 1857, Arnold won election as Professor of Poetry at Oxford and, in 1862, was reelected to another five-year term. Receiving permission to abandon the customary Latin, Arnold delivered his lectures in English and

Library of Congress

invigorated the professorship with lectures ranging from the individual (Homer, Dante) to the topical ("The Literary Influence of Academies") to the broadly critical (*On the Study of Celtic Literature*, 1867). Though his critical writings on English culture, literature, and religion made him a controversial figure, Arnold gained respect in his post as Inspector of Schools, serving twice as Assistant Commissioner on official committees dispatched to study European schools and eventually becoming a Senior Inspector in 1870, the same year in which Oxford conferred on him an honorary D.C.L. degree. In 1883, he visited the United States on a lecture tour which, though not triumphal, was at least a measure of his commanding stature as a critic and poet.

Biography · Matthew Arnold, born on Christmas Eve, 1822, in Laleham, England, was the second child and eldest son of five boys and four girls in the family of Dr. Thomas Arnold and his wife, Mary Penrose Arnold. At the time of the poet's birth, Dr. Arnold, a graduate of Oxford, was performing his duties as master at the school in Laleham, preparing himself intellectually and professionally for his appointment in 1828 as Headmaster of Rugby. There Dr. Arnold set about reforming the narrowly classical curriculum to include emphasis on language, history, and mathematics and to reflect his "broad church" liberalism, while insisting that his students maintain his own high standards of discipline and moral conduct. Though his reformist views on both church and school invited attack from traditional quarters, Dr. Arnold exerted over his students, family, and English education a lingering influence after his premature death at the age of forty-seven.

Although there was an undoubtedly tense relationship between headmaster father and poetically inclined son (who, at times, neglected his studies and sported the dress and talk of a dandy), Arnold's elegiac tribute to his father in "Rugby Chapel" confirms his mature appreciation for Dr. Arnold's magisterial qualities of mind and conduct. Likewise, Arnold took a distinct pride in the Cornish ancestry of his mother, whose father was a clergyman named John Penrose and whose mother's maiden name was Trevenen. Arnold's interest in Celtic literature derived from this ancestral connection, received further stimulation from a trip to Brittany in 1859 to visit the Schools, and finally resulted in the lectures *On the Study of Celtic Literature*. Whatever the exact influence of his parents, Matthew Arnold certainly felt the familial strains which, on the one side, tended toward the moral and intellectual honesty and practicality of the headmaster and, on the other, toward the imaginative and expressive charm of the Celtic mother.

Arnold married Frances Lucy Wightman in 1851 after his celebrated infatuation, rendered in the "Switzerland" poems, for the beautiful "Marguerite," a woman now identified by Park Honan in *Matthew Arnold: A Life* (1981) as Mary Claude, "a descendant of French Protestant exiles" who came to live near the Arnold family home at Fox How. Matthew and Frances Lucy had six children, two daughters and four sons, in a happy marriage three times saddened by the early deaths of Basil at two, Thomas at sixteen, and William at eighteen.

Two years after his retirement from the travel-wearying post of school inspector, Arnold entered in his diary, under the date of April 15, 1888, "Weep bitterly over the dead." That day, at Liverpool awaiting the arrival of his daughter and granddaughter from the United States, he collapsed from a heart attack and died.

Analysis · A commonplace beginning for criticism of Matthew Arnold's poetry is one or another of his many well-known critical statements which provide a basis for showing how well or how poorly the critic's precept corresponds with the poet's practice. One must remember, however, that most of Arnold's best work as a poet preceded his finest work as a critic and that his letters reveal dissatisfaction with his poetic "fragments," as he called them. He did believe that his poems would have their "turn," just as Tennyson's and Browning's had, because they followed closely the trend of modern thinking. Indeed, Arnold's modernity—his sense of alienation, moral complexity, and humanistic values—makes his work, both critical and creative, a continuing presence in the literary world.

The sense of alienation which carries so much thematic weight in Arnold's poetry reaches back into his childhood. As a child, he wore a brace for a slightly bent leg. This had an isolating, restricting effect on a boy who enjoyed running and climbing. Also, he early realized the irony of numbers, because, as the second born, he found that his parents' time and attention did not easily spread over nine children, and, at fourteen, he spent what surely seemed like a year in exile at Winchester School. The need for attention influenced his pose as a dandy, and he probably enjoyed his reputation as an idler, especially in his circle of family and friends who upheld and practiced the Victorian principles of work and duty.

Of course, the religious and social atmosphere in which Arnold approached manhood conditioned his perception of the alienating forces at work in England: he entered Oxford during the Tractarian controversy that divided conservative and liberal elements in the Church of England, and he knew about the general economic and social discontent that separated the working class from the wealthy. With such factious elements at work—including the dispute between religion and science on the origin of earth and man—Arnold, facing his own lover's estrangement in "To Marguerite—Continued," could write with justifiable irony that "We mortal millions live alone." With good reason, then, Arnold formed his ideas on the wholesome effect of order and authority, of education and culture recommended in his prose—evident alike in that quest for unity, wholeness, and joy which, in the poems, his lyric and narrative speakers find so elusive.

In the early sonnet "To a Friend," Arnold praises Sophocles, in one of his memorable lines, because he "saw life steadily, and saw it whole." "Wholeness" was the controlling thought behind the poet's vision: "an Idea of the world in order not be prevailed over by the world's multitudinousness," he tells Clough in a letter critical of the "episodes and ornamental work" that distract both poet and reader from a sense of unity. This unity of idea, in perception and execution, is necessary for poetry "to utter the truth," as Arnold says in his essay on William Wordsworth, because "poetry is at bottom a criticism of life . . . the greatness of a poet lies in his powerful and beautiful application of ideas to life,–to the question: How to live." For Arnold, this question is itself "a moral idea."

If Sophocles saw life "whole," he also, according to Arnold, saw it "steadily." For Arnold, Sophoclean steadiness implies two distinct but complementary processes. First, as physical steadiness, *seeing* is the broad sensory reaction to the range of stimuli associated with the poet's "Idea of the world." One may note, for example, the last six lines of "Mycerinus" with their heavy emphasis on auditory imagery–"mirth waxed loudest," "echoes came," "dull sound"–which perfectly conclude the preceding philosophical implications of six long years of reveling by King Mycerinus. These implications appear in a series of "it may be" possibilities, and the imagery underscores the essential uncertainty of the auditors ("wondering people") because the sounds are really once-removed "echoes," partly "Mix'd with the murmur of the moving Nile." There is an attempt to match appropriately the sensations with the subject.

The second point, related to physical steadiness, implies a type of mental fixity on the part of the observer, a disciplined exercise of consciousness operating throughout the temporal context of creative urge and eventual artistic fulfillment. Explaining the difficulty of this exercise for his own poetic practice, Arnold writes to Clough that "I can go thro: the imaginary process of mastering myself and the whole affair as it would then stand, but at the critical point I am too apt to hoist up the mainsail to the wind and let her drive." In short, Arnold recognizes a lack of mental fixity to accompany the poetic inspiration; he can, imaginatively, see the "whole," but, at the critical point of artistic execution, he lets go, becoming, at the expense of the whole, too insistent or expansive in one thematic or descriptive part. The lyric "Despondency" addresses this problem in the typically elegiac tone of Arnold's poetic voice. The lyric speaker says that "The thoughts that rain their steady glow/ Like stars on life's cold sea" have "never shone" for him. He has seen the thoughts which "light, like gleams, my spirit's sky," but they appear "once . . . hurry by/ And never come again." He laments the absence of that conscious persistence which preserves the "steady glow" of thought bearing directly on the moral vastness of "life's cold sea."

In a more general way, seeing life steadily allies itself to the "spontaneity of consciousness" for which Arnold praises Hellenism in *Culture and Anarchy* (1869). This spontaneity suggests a physical and mental alertness which instantly responds to "life as it is," a consciousness prone to thinking but unencumbered by the predisposition to action which describes the force of "conduct and obedience" behind Hebraism, the other major tradition in Western civilization. Sophocles, the model Hellenist, possesses the "even-balanced soul" which holds in steady counterpoise the old dichotomy of thought and feeling, a pre-Christian possibility coming before the "triumph of Hebraism and man's moral impulses." Thus, as a letter to Clough shows, Arnold appreciates the burden of seeing steadily and whole for the modern poet whose subject matter is perforce a criticism of life, a burden compounded because "the poet's matter being the hitherto experience of the world, and his own, increases with every century." This "hitherto experience," both Hellenic and Hebraic, overlaying Arnold's own, accounts for his interest in remote, historical subjects such as "Mycerinus," "Empedocles on Etna," "Tristram and Iseult," "Sohrab and Rustum," and "Balder Dead"–which nevertheless contain critical implications for living morally, even joyfully, in the incipiently modern world of Victorian England.

This "then and now" conception of the human experience has its analogues in the dualities that, as critics often note, Arnold's poems constantly explore: the moral and the amoral, the mind and the body, thought and feeling, the contemplative life and the active life, or, as Professor Douglas Bush labels them in *Matthew Arnold* (1971), the "Apollonian-Dionysian antinomy" of Arnold's ideas. Here again the dynamics for seeing steadily emerge because the poet must look simultaneously in polar directions, resisting all the while the temptation to "hoist up the mainsail to the wind and let her drive."

In his best poems, Arnold seeks the vantage point–call it a poetic situation–from which he can see steadily the dualities that, in the poem's thematic reconciliation, coalesce in the wholeness of the "Idea." Arnold warns, however, in the "Preface to Poems" against the poetic situations "from the representation of which, though accurate, no poetical enjoyment can be derived . . . those in which the suffering finds no vent in action . . . in which there is everything to be endured, nothing to be done." For Arnold, the problem of poetic situation means finding "a vent in action" which does not overwhelm the speculative nature of the idea, and the solution often comes in the form of the "quest," the symbolically active.

"The Scholar-Gipsy" is on a quest, "waiting for the spark from heaven to fall." When the spark falls, he can share with the world the secret art, learned from the "gipsy-crew," of ruling "the workings of men's brains." Until then, he wanders mysteriously from Berkshire Moors to Cumner Hills, pensively cast in an ageless "solitude," exempt from the "repeated shocks" and "strange disease of modern life." The shepherd who lyrically tells the scholar-gipsy's story speaks for the Victorians who also "await" the spark from heaven, but who, with "heads o'ertax'd" and "palsied hearts," cannot acquire the immortalizing agency of a quest with "one aim, one business, one desire." The antithesis is clear: "Arnold's Gipsy," as Honan says, "represents stability in a world of flux and change, creative inwardness in a world of lassitude, stagnation, frustration, and dividedness." The shepherd, a part of the modern world but temporarily secluded in the imaginative distance of "this high field's dark corner," discovers the physical and mental steadiness to tell the story, to see concurrently the past and present, and to indict his society through the quest of the mythic wanderer.

"Thyrsis," a monody for Clough, follows the same stanza form and rhyme scheme of "The Scholar-Gipsy," continuing too the unifying strategy of the quest, this time for the "signal elm-tree" which has itself become a symbol for the perpetual existence of "our friend, the Gipsy-Scholar." In this way, Arnold aligns Clough with the legendary rover; Clough, however, unlike the Gipsy, "could not wait" the passing of the "storms that rage" in their fragmented society. With night descending, Corydon (Arnold's persona) sees, but does not achieve, the object of his quest; but he cries "Hear it, O Thyrsis, still our tree is there!" So lives the Gipsy-Scholar, so remains, in the symbolic activity of the quest, the idea of hope: Corydon will "not despair." As in "The Scholar-Gipsy," Arnold turns the old genre of pastoral elegy to topical account, and the poem achieves a balanced steadiness, as much about Corydon as about Thyrsis, as much about hope as about despair, as much about life as about death.

The idea of the quest—or the hunt or the journey—recurs again and again in Arnold's poetry, providing the "vent in action" required by the expanding idea. The journey may be inward, as in "The Buried Life," where Arnold says that man's impulse to know the "mystery" of his heart sends him delving into "his own breast." Here the poet tries to reconcile the dualities of outward "strife" (in "the world's most crowded streets") and inner "striving" (toward "the unregarded river of our life"). This self-questing journey, however, ironically needs the impetus of "a beloved hand laid in ours," "another's eyes read clear," and then, in the respite of love, one "becomes aware of his life's flow." There is, though faint, an optimistic strain rising through the modern sense of isolation, even permitting the poet, in "Resignation," to make a virtue of necessity by accepting "His sad lucidity of soul."

For Arnold, though, isolation and solitude are not similar; they represent yet another set of opposites: isolation, a state of rejection and loneliness, is to be shunned, while solitude, a state of reflection and inspiration, is to be sought. Away from the "sick hurry" of modern life, the poet in solitude achieves the steadiness of feeling and perception required for the aesthetic fulfillment of his idea. Arnold's lyric speakers enjoy solitude:

the shepherd in "The Scholar-Gipsy" and "Thyrsis," or the lounger in Kensington gardens who finds "peace for ever new" in the "lone, open glade," is analogous, in the "Austerity of Poetry," to the "hidden ground/ Of thought" within the muse herself. Yet there is always the ironic danger: Empedocles, on the verge of suicide, drops his laurel bough because he is "weary of the solitude/ Where he who bears thee must abide." Arnold needs the creative succor of a solitude that carries over, as he says in "Quiet Work," into a life "Of toil unsever'd from tranquillity," a life that, even as Empedocles admits, still "Leaves human effort scope." This "human effort" becomes the dynamic behind Arnold's own quest to focus and balance the idea with the action, to elevate and juxtapose the moral propositions of antagonistic extremes: life and death, love and hate, alliance and alienation.

"Stanzas from the Grande Chartreuse" follows the typically Arnoldian pattern. The first sixty-five lines witness the sensory perception and steadiness of the speaker, his spontaneity of consciousness comprising a mixture of imagery—visual ("spectral vapours white"), auditory ("strangled sound"), tactile ("forms brush by"). There is the anticipatory journey or quest: "The bridge is cross'd, and slow we ride/ Through forest up the mountainside." Then, at line sixty-six, there is the idea, framed in the rhetorical question: "And what am I, that I am here?" The speaker admits that the object of his ultimate quest is really elsewhere, for the "rigorous teachers" of his youth "Show'd me the high, white star of Truth,/ There bade me gaze, and there aspire." That abstract quest, though, must temporarily defer to this cold physical journey to the Grande Chartreuse, a monastery in the French Alps, where the troubled speaker can shed his melancholy tears in the presence of a profound religious faith. No longer young and feeling caught in the forlorn void between the faiths of a past and future time, he is "Wandering between two worlds, one dead,/ The other powerless to be born." The past age of faith, still ascetically practiced in the Carthusian monastery, and a desirable future age "Which without hardness will be sage,/ And gay without frivolity" bracket a divisively inert time in which the sciolists talk, but, with their fathers' history of pain and grief as justification, "The Kings of modern thought are dumb."

Fraser Neiman, in *Matthew Arnold* (1968), summarizes the common emotional ground of the anchorite and Arnold: they both "turn to a quest for inward peace," but Arnold must find his in solitude, in the buried life, in quiet work, in, as Neiman says, "a profound inwardness . . . not incompatible with the world of activity." The poem concludes with images of "action and pleasure"—the "troops," the "hunters," the "gay dames" passing below the monastery—representing a life again rejected by the

Carthusians but, as the reader infers, accepted by the speaker, who has had, at least, the catharsis of his tears. The emphasis, though, is on the idea, an idea which Arnold tries to see steadily and whole through the confrontation of opposites: the ascetic, contemplative life of anchorite, "Obermann," and the past at the top of the Etna-like mountain (where, one gathers, the "suffering finds no vent in action"), versus the secular, restless life of "Laughter and cries" at the bottom of the mountain where "Years hence, perhaps, may dawn an age,/ More fortunate." "Stanzas from the Grande Chartreuse" renders in setting, mood, and idea the predicament of the poet, expressed in Arnold's earlier poem, "Stanza in Memory of the Author of 'Obermann' ":

> Ah ! two desires toss about
> The poet's feverish blood.
> One drives him to the world without,
> And one to solitude.

"Dover Beach" fits into the same structural pattern of imagery, idea, and resolution. The opening of the poem establishes the physical and mental awareness of the speaker, a person attuned to the sensory stimuli of the scene before him. The counterpointed imagery of sight and sound in the first verse paragraph divides as naturally as a Petrarchan sonnet: the visual imagery of the first eight lines suggests peace and serenity ("the moon lies fair," "the tranquil bay"), but the auditory imagery of the next six lines, signaled by the turn of the imperative "Listen!," introduces the "grating roar/ Of pebbles" which, in the climax of the paragraph, "Begin, and cease, and then again begin,/ With tremulous cadence slow, and bring/ The eternal note of sadness in." The Imagistic division, the modulated caesura, and the irregular pattern of end and internal rhymes provide the lyric energy leading up to the emotional dimension of sadness which the second verse paragraph quickly converts to the mental dimension of thought. In a transitional effect, the auditory imagery surrounding the "note of sadness" connects with the image of Sophocles who "long ago/ Heard it on the Aegaean," bringing "Into his mind the turbid ebb and flow/ Of human misery." Critics sometimes object to the shift in imagery from full to ebb tide, but the crucial thematic point lies not so much in the maintenance of parallel imagery as in the formulation of idea: "we/ Find also in the sound a thought/ Hearing it by this distant northern sea." Thus, the perception of dualities—full and ebb tide, present and past time, physical and metaphorical seas—prepares for the "then and now" structure of the third verse paragraph: the "Sea of Faith" was once full, like the tide at Dover, but the lyric speaker can "only hear/ Its melancholy, long, withdrawing roar."

The sociological interpretation, to select just one critical approach, maintains that the disillusioned speaker refers to the debate between religion and science then dominating the intellectual effort of so many Victorians. If the "Sea of Faith" came to full tide with the "triumph of Hebraism and man's moral impulses," the preceding image of Sophocles adds poignance to the speaker's resignation in the face of the constant factor of "human misery." Whereas Sophocles could, in an ancient world, see life steadily and see it whole in its tragic but nevertheless human consequences, the speaker enjoys no such certainty. The retreating "Sea of Faith" takes with it the moral and spiritual basis for "joy" and "love" and "peace." The speaker's own attempt to see modern life steadily and to see it whole, successful or not as the individual critic may determine for himself, leads to the resolution of the lyric cry: "Ah, love, let us be true/ To one another!" The world may no longer offer the comfort of "joy" and "certitude" and "help for pain," but the lovers may create their own interpersonal world where such pleasures presumably exist.

Some critics fault the ending of "Dover Beach," which imaginatively transports the couple to "a darkling plain," leaving behind the sea imagery which guides the speaker's emotional and mental state throughout the poem. The ending, however, maintains the consistency of auditory imagery ("confused alarms," "armies clash") which concludes each of the preceding verse paragraphs, and the "struggle and flight" of the "ignorant armies" echo, in appropriately harsher terms, the "retreating" roar of the "Sea of Faith." Furthermore, the principle of duality, carefully set up in the poem, works at the end: physically, the lovers are still by the quiet, beautiful cliffs of Dover, but, figuratively, at an opposite extreme, they find themselves "as on a darkling plain."

In addition to the ones already mentioned or discussed, the following poems are considered among Arnold's best work: "The Forsaken Merman," "The Strayed Reveller," "Palladium," "The Future," "A Dream," and "A Summer Night." Although Arnold's work has been very influential, even at its best it contains elements which can bother the modern reader, such as the over-reliance on interrogative and exclamatory sentences, giving to his ideas in the former case a weighty, rhetorical cast and, in the latter, an artificial rather than a natural emphasis. There is, however, a consistency in the melancholy, elegiac tone and in the modern concern with man's moral condition in a world where living a meaningful life has become increasingly difficult that makes Arnold's poetry rewarding reading.

Other literary forms · Throughout his life Matthew Arnold wrote critical works on literature, culture, religion, and education which made him the foremost man of letters in Victorian England. This large body of prose is available in a standard edition: *The Complete Prose Works of Matthew Arnold* (1960-1976, R. H. Super, editor), with textual notes and commentary. Essays important to an understanding of Arnold's contribution to the discipline of literary criticism include *Preface to Poems* (1853), "Wordsworth," "The Study of Poetry," and "Literature and Science." "Culture and Anarchy" explains the philosophical positions, and biases, from which Arnold criticized literature and society. Also available are editions containing his letters and notebooks.

Select works other than poetry
DRAMA: *Merope: A Tragedy*, pb. 1858.
NONFICTION: *Preface to Poems*, 1853; *On Translating Homer*, 1861; *Essays in Criticism*, 1865; *On the Study of Celtic Literature*, 1867; *Culture and Anarchy*, 1869; *Friendship's Garland*, 1871; *Literature and Dogma*, 1873; *God and the Bible*, 1875; *Last Essays on Church and Religion*, 1877; *Discourses in America*, 1885; *Civilization in the United States*, 1888; *Essays in Criticism, Second Series*, 1888; *The Complete Prose Works of Matthew Arnold*, 1960-1976 (R. H. Super, editor).
MISCELLANEOUS: *The Works of Matthew Arnold*, 1903-1904 (15 volumes).

Ronald K. Giles

Bibliography · Park Honan's *Matthew Arnold: A Life*, 1981, provides a comprehensive account of Arnold's life. An excellent introduction to Arnold's life and work is Fraser Neiman's *Matthew Arnold*, 1968. Three superb collections of essays are Kenneth Allott, ed., *Matthew Arnold*, 1976; Harold Bloom, ed., *Matthew Arnold*, 1987; and David De Laura, ed., *Matthew Arnold; A Collection of Critical Essays*, 1973. All deal with both the poetry and prose. William E. Buckler's *On the Poetry of Matthew Arnold*, 1982, explores three dominant myths pertaining to Arnold's poetic achievement (that Arnold's poetry is too autobiographically replicative, that it is basically a poetry of statement, and that is extremely derivative). Stefan Collini's *Arnold*, 1988, has chapters on the life of Arnold as a poet and as a literary, social, and religious critic, and on the Arnoldian legacy. It examines briefly the temper of Arnold's mind and his distinctive style.

W. H. AUDEN

Born: York, England; February 21, 1907
Died: Vienna, Austria; September 29, 1973

Poetry · *Poems*, 1930 · *The Orators*, 1932 · *Look, Stranger!*, 1936 (also known as *On This Island*, 1937) · *Letters from Iceland*, 1937 (poetry and prose, with Louis MacNeice) · *Spain*, 1937 · *Journey to a War*, 1939 (poetry and prose, with Christopher Isherwood) · *Another Time*, 1940 · *The Double Man*, 1941 (also known as *New Year Letter*) · *For the Time Being*, 1944 · *The Collected Poetry*, 1945 · *The Age of Anxiety*, 1947 · *Collected Shorter Poems, 1930-1944*, 1950 · *Nones*, 1951 · *The Shield of Achilles*, 1955 · *Homage to Clio*, 1960 · *About the House*, 1965 · *Collected Shorter Poems, 1927-1957*, 1966 · *Collected Longer Poems*, 1968 · *City Without Walls and Other Poems*, 1969 · *Epistle to a Godson and Other Poems*, 1972 · *Thank You, Fog*, 1974 · *Collected Poems*, 1976 (Edward Mendelson, editor) · *The English Auden: Poems, Essays and Dramatic Writings, 1927-1939*, 1977 (Mendelson, editor) · *Selected Poems*, 1979 (Mendelson, editor)

Achievements · At a time when poets no longer enjoyed the wide readership they once did, W. H. Auden achieved a considerable popular success, his books selling well throughout his lifetime. He was also fortunate in having several sympathetic, intelligent critics to analyze and assess his work. It is true that Auden had his share of detractors, beginning, for example, in the 1930's with the negative response to his work in the influential journal *Scrutiny*, and, later, in two essays by Randall Jarrell taking him to task for his various ideological changes. Even today some argue that Auden's work is uneven or that his later poetry represents a serious decline from the brilliance he demonstrated in the 1930's. In a sense, his reputation has been granted grudgingly and, by some, with reservations. Despite all this, however, Auden is generally regarded today as one of the major poets of the twentieth century. Several of his lyrics are well-established as standard anthology pieces—"Lullaby," "As I Walked Out One Evening," "In Memory of W. B. Yeats," "Musèe des Beaux Arts,"—but his larger reputation may well rest not on the strength of individual poems, but on the impressive range of thought and technical virtuosity found in his work as a whole.

Auden's poetry is quintessentially the work of a restless, probing intelligence committed to the idea that poise and clear-headedness are possible,

Jill Krementz

indeed necessary, in a world beset by economic, social, and political chaos. Auden possessed, in the words of Chad Walsh, an "analytic power," an "ability to break a question down into its elements, to find new ways of putting familiar things together." "There is hardly an Auden poem," Walsh concludes, "that does not bespeak, and speak to, the brain at work." Auden's intelligence, however, is rarely ponderous or pedantic, and part of his lasting achievement may be the blending of playfulness and seriousness that he managed to sustain in much of his best work.

While some may doubt the profundity of Auden's thinking, few question his technical virtuosity. No poet in recent times can match the range of traditional forms he used and often revitalized in his work—oratorio, eclogue, sestina, sonnet, villanelle, closet drama, verse epistle, and ode. Auden often boasted, perhaps with justification, that he had written successfully in every known meter. Perhaps even more than for his use of traditional literary forms, however, Auden is admired for his songs, which Monroe Spears sees as "his most distinctive accomplishment and his most popular." Auden borrowed from an array of musical forms, using irony and parody to transcend the limits of the genre in which he was working. His ballads are especially well regarded, as are many of the lyrics he wrote for the stage.

Over the course of his career Auden received numerous literary honors, beginning in 1937 with the King's Gold Medal for poetry. His other awards include Guggenheim fellowships in 1942 and 1945; the Pulitzer Prize in 1948; the Bollingen Prize in 1954; the National Book Award in 1956; and the Austrian State Prize for European literature in 1966. From 1956 to 1960, Auden held the honorary position of Professor of Poetry at Oxford.

Biography · Wystan Hugh Auden was born in York, England, in 1907, the third and youngest son of George and Constance Auden. Before his youngest son was two years old, George Auden gave up a private medical practice in York and moved his family south to Birmingham, where Dr. Auden worked as the city's School Medical Officer. Auden's devout, middle-class family (both his parents were the children of clergymen) gave him a strong sense of traditional religious values and encouraged his early intellectual bent. His mother, Auden frequently said, was the strongest presence in his early years. He was particularly close to her and believed throughout his life that her influence was largely responsible for shaping his adult character. His father, a widely educated man in both the humanities and sciences, acquainted his son at an early age with classical literature and Nordic myths and encouraged his reading in poetry and fiction as well as scientific subjects, including medicine, geology, and mining. This early reading was supported by a close familiarity with nature, and Auden as a child developed a fascination for the landscape of limestone caves and abandoned mines that is recalled in several of his poems. Auden's first inclinations were, in fact, toward the scientific and natural rather than literary, and as a young boy he fancied himself a mining engineer. His interest in science continued throughout his life and is reflected in the frequent use of scientific ideas and images in his poetry, and accounts, perhaps, for the stance of clinical detachment found in his early work.

In 1915, Auden was sent as a boarder to St. Edmund's school in Surrey and, after completing his studies there in 1920, attended Gresham's school, an institution known for its excellence in the sciences. While at Gresham's, Auden gradually came to acknowledge his homosexuality and to question many of his middle-class values and religious beliefs; by the time he left Gresham's, he had abandoned his faith. It was also during this period that Auden, at the suggestion of Robert Medley, began to write his first poems.

In 1925, Auden enrolled at Christ Church, Oxford, where he discovered a congenial social atmosphere far different from the repressive climate at Gresham's. He found in the young don Nevill Coghill a sympathetic, stimulating tutor who was soon informed of Auden's intentions to become a "great poet." After a year of reading in the sciences, Auden turned his interests to English studies and soon developed an enthusiasm for the then unfashionable poetry of the Anglo-Saxon period. This confirmed his preference for the Nordic-Germanic rather than Romance Continental literary tradition, a bias evident in much of his early poetry and, later, in *The Age of Anxiety* (1947), with its close imitation of Old English metric and alliterative patterns.

During the Oxford years and in the decade that followed, Auden was the central figure of a group of writers, including Cecil Day Lewis and Stephen Spender, who shared his liberal political leanings. The 1930's became a sort of golden decade for Auden, a time of intellectual excitement and artistic vitality. With various friends he traveled widely—to Iceland with Louis MacNeice and to China with Christopher Isherwood. Both visits resulted in collaborative books containing poetry by Auden. In 1937 Auden went to Spain, where he worked for the Loyalist cause in the Civil War, which had become a rallying cause for intellectuals of the time. His experience led to the writing of *Spain* (1937), the celebrated political poem which Auden later rejected because of the "wicked doctrine" of its concluding lines; he purged the poem from most subsequent collections of his work. During the 1930's Auden was also active in his home country: He taught school from 1930 to 1935; helped found the Group Theatre in 1932; and published two volumes of poetry that secured for him a reputation as one of the most promising young poets of his generation. In 1935 he married Erika Mann, daughter of the German novelist Thomas Mann, in order to provide her with a British passport.

Auden's writing during the 1930's—both his poetry and the plays written in collaboration with Isherwood—largely constitutes a diagnosis of industrial English society in the midst of economic and moral decay. The diagnosis is made from the perspective of various ideologies that Auden adopted or toyed with during the late 1920's and 1930's—Freudian and post-Freudian psychology, Marxism, and liberal socialism.

In 1939, at the end of a full and brilliant decade, Auden and Isherwood decided to leave England permanently and move to the United States, which they had visited in the preceding year on their return trip from China. Auden's move to New York marked a major turning point in his life and career, for during this period he was gradually shifting away from many of his earlier intellectual convictions and moving toward a reaffirmation of his childhood faith; in October, 1940 he returned to the Anglican communion. Many of his poems in the 1940's record the gradual move toward Christianity, including, most explicitly, his Christmas oratorio, *For the Time Being.* Auden's concern for the ills of modern society did not end, however, with his affirmation of faith, for he pursued this concern in various ways in his poetry, most notably in *The Age of Anxiety,* whose title became a catch phrase for the war-torn decade in which it was written. During the 1940's Auden held teaching posts at several American colleges but continued to write prolifically, working chiefly on his ambitious longer poems.

Auden's life after the 1940's fell into a somewhat more staid routine. In the 1950's he began writing libretti with Chester Kallman, whom he had met shortly after his arrival in America; he and Kallman remained companions and collaborators until the end of Auden's life. From 1948 to 1957 Auden spent each spring and summer on the island of Ischia, prompting some to suggest that he had entered a post-American phase in his career. Then, beginning in 1957, and for the remainder of his life, he stayed half of each year in New York and half in a converted farmhouse that he and Kallman purchased in the village of Kirchstetten, Austria. In a poem written at the time, Auden saw his departure from Ischia as a reaffirmation of his essential northernness. In Kirchstetten he settled into the happy domesticity celebrated in his *About the House* (1965) volume.

In 1972, his health failing, Auden decided to leave New York permanently and spend his winter season each year in a "grace and favour" cottage offered to him by the governing board of his old college, Christ Church, Oxford. As usual, he stayed the following spring and summer in Kirchstetten, and, on his way back to Oxford that fall, died of a heart attack in Vienna. He was buried, as he had wished, in Kirchstetten.

Analysis · Read chronologically, W. H. Auden's poetry moves from alienation to integration; his work is a quest for wholeness, an escape from the isolated self, "where dwell/ Our howling appetites," into a community where the essential goodness of life is acknowledged despite the presence of sin. Over the course of his career, Auden's quest takes many forms, but his goal never varies; from beginning to end, he seeks to discover how love, in all its manifestations, can fulfill man's social and personal needs.

Auden began in the 1930's as a critic of his society, an outsider looking in and finding little to admire in what he saw. His early work is essentially a record of social ills; love is sought, but rarely found. As he matures, however, Auden gradually becomes less of a diagnostician and more of a healer; he arrives eventually at a vision of love informed by human sympathy and, later, by religious belief. Once this vision is affirmed in his poetry, Auden again shifts direction, becoming more fully than before a comic poet, intent on celebrating the redemptive power of love and acknowledging the essential blessedness of life. These shifts in Auden's work are, of course, gradual and subtle rather than abrupt, but the division of his career into three phases provides a way to bring some sense of order to a body of work remarkable, above all else, for its diversity.

The early Auden is very much a poet of the 1930's—a time of economic depression and fascism, war and rumors of war. Faced with such a world, he adopts the pose of a clinical diagnostician anatomizing a troubled society. He sees the social and spiritual malaise of his time as a failure of communication; individuals are trapped inside themselves, unable to escape the forces of psychological and social repression that block the possibility of love.

The poems which record Auden's diagnosis of his society are still considered by some to be his best. Although they are often bewildering to readers, they are admired for their energy and intensity, their brilliant, elusive surfaces. One of the most highly regarded of these early poems is "Consider," which illustrates Auden's early technical skill as well as his characteristic themes. The poem is divided into three verse paragraphs, each addressed to a different auditor by a speaker whose heightened theatrical language gives him an aloofness of tone that matches his arrogant message. Auden's voice in "Consider" typifies the detachment and impersonality of the early poems.

The first verse paragraph addresses the reader directly, asking that he "consider" a symbolic modern landscape "As the hawk sees it or the helmeted airman." From this great height, with the objective eye of the hawk, the speaker observes images of society on the verge of collapse: a cigarette end smoldering at the edge of a garden party; decadent vacationers at a winter resort, surrounded by signs of an impending war; and farmers "Sitting in kitchens in the stormy fens." The vacationers, incapable of emotion, are "Supplied with feelings by an efficient band," while the farmers, separated from them by physical distance and class barriers, yet equally lonely, listen to the same music on the wireless. Though explicitly social and political, the poem is also developed in personal and psychological terms; like the landscape, the individuals in the poem are "diseased," unable to establish genuine personal contacts.

Having drawn this grim picture of "our time," the speaker turns in the second verse paragraph to elucidate the psychological foundation of social ills, addressing, in the process, a "supreme Antagonist," who, according to Edward Mendelson, is the "*inner* enemy" that "personifies the fears and repressions that oppose love." The Antagonist finds an ample number of victims in the decadent society and spreads its evil, "Scattering the people" and seizing them with "immeasurable neurotic dread." In this section, the poem's intense language and deliberate rhetorical excess are beautifully modulated, making the speaker aloof and detached, yet with an edge of hysteria in his voice.

The final verse paragraph is addressed to the banker, the don, and the clergyman (representatives of the social elite), along with all others who seek happiness by following the "convolutions" of the distorted ego. The poem ends by warning the selfish and the elite of the inescapable psychological diseases that the Antagonist holds in store for them, diseases that will further destroy the possibility for love.

Auden's adaptation of various psychological theories in "Consider" is typical of his method in the 1930's, as is the detached clinical posture of the speaker and the explicit social and political concern voiced in the poem. Auden characteristically offers little hope and, given the extent of the ills he describes, his doing so might well have seemed facile. Auden's earliest poetry sometimes offers an idealized, vague notion of Love as a healing force capable of breaking down repression and restoring social and personal relationships to their proper order. Usually, though, this message is faint and clearly secondary to the diagnostic aim of the poems.

In two love poems written somewhat later than "Consider," Auden approaches more explicitly the view of love hinted at in the earliest poems. "Lullaby," his best-known lyric, ends with the speaker's hope that his beloved may be "Watched by every human love." The poem's emphasis, however, rests on the transience of "human love": The arm upon which the sleeping lover rests is "faithless"; love is at best a temporary stay against loneliness. Likewise, in "As I Walked Out One Evening," Auden stresses the limitations of romantic and erotic love. "Time" lurks in the shadows and coughs when the lovers "would kiss," deflating the romantic delusions satirized at the beginning of the poem. Later, though, near the end, the chiming clocks of the city offer an injunction that suggests a new direction: "You shall love your crooked neighbor/ With your crooked heart." Though undercut by a number of ironies, the love described here moves tentatively toward the vision of the 1940's. Even so, the "human love" that Auden evokes in the 1930's seems insufficient to resolve the social and personal ills diagnosed by his poetry.

During the 1930's, Auden gradually left behind the various ideologies he had seriously (and, perhaps, half-seriously) adopted. Humphrey Carpenter, Auden's biographer, suggests that these ideologies—Marxism, post-Freudianism, liberal humanism—all had in common a fundamental belief in the natural goodness of man. Near the end of the decade, Auden began to question his liberal humanism, partly because of its inability to offer, as he put it, "some reason why [Hitler] was utterly wrong." The reason he sought turned out to be in Christianity, particularly the doctrine of man's sinful nature and his need, because of that nature, for forgiveness and redemption. The quest for love that began in the early poetry thus grows in the 1940's into a quest for Christian love. There is, of course, no sudden shift in Auden's poetry as a result of the new direction in his thinking. Rather, at the end of the 1930's, he begins *gradually* to formulate this vision of *agape*; in a sense, he was already doing so in the two love poems previously examined.

The poem "Herman Melville," though written a year before Auden "officially" rejoined the Church in 1940, demonstrates his thinking at this crucial period, a time which coincided with his arrival in the United States. The poem also suggests something of Auden's more relaxed, lucid style, a shift which began in the mid-1930's away from the verbal glitter and rhetorical intensity of poems such as "Consider." "Herman Melville" is thus a good example of Auden's thematic and stylistic direction in the shorter poems published during the 1940's.

In the poem Auden describes Melville's life and literary career as a metaphorical "gale" that had blown the novelist "Past the Cape Horn of sensible success" and "deafened him with thunder." Near the end of his life, after Melville had exorcised his demons, he "sailed into an extraordinary mildness," entering a domestic contentment where he discovered "new knowledge"—that "Evil is unspectacular and always human" (Auden develops a similar idea in "Musèe des Beaux Arts") and "that we are introduced to Goodness every day." What Melville found, in essence, is what Auden himself was in the process of accepting—the universality of man's sinfulness and the possibility that goodness (that is, grace and redemption) can, in an unspectacular fashion, transform the corrupt present, enabling man to transcend his sinfulness.

At the end of the poem Auden describes Melville's exultation and surrender at his discovery of the transforming power of *agape*. The poem, while not autobiographical, certainly seems to be Auden's testing ground, his rehearsal of an idea that had been forming in his mind. Melville's discovery that his love had been "selfish" suggests perhaps that Auden has come full circle from his early poems, now denying completely the efficacy of eros, sexual-romantic love. Auden himself suggests, however, that this is not the case; writing for *Theology* in 1950, he argues that "Agape is the fulfillment of eros, not its contradiction." Perhaps "Herman Melville" contains an early formulation of a position whose full complexity Auden had not yet resolved.

If "Herman Melville" records Auden's initial approach to Christianity, then *The Age of Anxiety* shows his response to a modern society at odds with the directives of *agape*. The poem is the longest of the four extended works Auden wrote in the 1940's. The bulk of his energy during the decade went into these poems, which were ambitious undertakings in an age when the long poem had all but died out. *The Age of Anxiety* is a "baroque eclogue," a pastoral form entirely incongruous with the poem's urban setting (New York) and its subject matter (four modern-day city dwellers during World War II). Auden also achieves irony with his imitation of Old English metric patterns. The contrast between an epic measure and the pettiness of modern life creates a mock-heroic tone.

The poem begins in a Third Avenue bar where four customers—Quant, Malin, Emble, and Rosetta—drink and discuss their lives. The conversation of these four representatives of modern man becomes an effort to find order in an age of chaos and disbelief. At the outset the characters drink in private corners of the bar, each dreaming (as Monroe Spears puts it) "of his own way of escape, but aware . . . of no recourse beyond the human level." Rosetta, for example, has "a favourite day-dream" of "lovely innocent countrysides," while the youthful Emble dreams of success achieved only in a hollow "succession of sexual triumphs." The four dreamers eventually move out of their private corners and begin to discuss the war. As they grow more and more drunk their discussion turns, in the second part of the poem ("The Seven Ages"), to man, "the traveller through time . . . as he bumbles by from birth to death." Their analysis constitutes a psychological study of the maturation process of the individual and leads them to recognize their own failure in coming to terms with life. Their recognition is, however, only momentary, for in the poem's third section ("The Seven Stages") the four figures lapse into a drunken state of unconsciousness and travel over an allegorical dream landscape searching again for a solution of their own, and hence man's, dilemma.

Their journey, however, is doomed to fail, for they seek not spiritual enlightenment, but a way of escaping it. The first six stages of their vision carry them through (and they believe away from) the anxiety and suffering of the world; but they are merely led deeper into themselves. The truth revealed in the dream is that the world and its anxieties—which they can only see in distortion—are unbearable for modern man. The egotism of the dreamer will not allow them salvation.

The first six stages of the dream explore every possible path of escape. In the seventh stage, however, all hope is lost. They are now, as Emble says, "miles" from any "workable world." The quest has taken them into a landscape of "ravenous unreals." As the chaos closes in on them they turn away from it, refusing to attempt the only true quest—the seeking of spiritual knowledge not in their own illusions but in the redemption of the present moment through a religious commitment. At the end of the poem Malin recognizes the failure of their journey. The moment is not redeemed, but the resolution of the poem defines their failure in Christian terms. In his final speech Malin describes modern man's unwillingness "to say Yes" to "That-Always-Opposite" who "Condescended to exist and to suffer death/ And, scorned on a scaffold, ensconced in His life/ The human household."

Thus the poem ends with man's refusal of *agape*, his resignation to loneliness, and his unwillingness to forgo egotism and accept the world as redeemed through the Incarnation. *The Age of Anxiety* takes up two main strands in Auden's work—the diagnosis of social and personal ills and the possibility of *agape* as a release from isolation. The four characters in this poem fail to achieve that release.

The Age of Anxiety brings to an end what some have called Auden's American period. From 1948 to the end of his life he spent half of each year abroad, and many of the poems of this time reflect the change of landscape. There is also a change in perspective, certainly not as radical as some of the earlier changes, but a change nevertheless. Justin Replogle suggests that after 1950 Auden becomes an essentially comic poet whose emphasis shifts away from poetry as a repository for ideas. His work, says Replogle, "begins less to proclaim a belief than to celebrate one." The later poetry, then, is generally lighter in tone and technique than his earlier work, and Replogle's word "celebrate" is especially apt, for there are a variety of celebrations going on in the later work: of the natural world ("Bucolics"); of the five senses ("Precious Five"); of friends ("For Friends Only"); of the ordinary and domestic ("Thanksgiving for a Habitat"); and of earthly happiness ("In Praise of Limestone"). All these celebrations are enacted in *About the House*, a collection which typifies Auden's later style. The book celebrates the rooms of his converted farmhouse in Kirchstetten, Austria, becoming a sort of homage to domesticity.

"Tonight at Seven-Thirty," the dining-room poem, discusses with wit and charm the place where man enacts a ritual of celebration (the dinner party) that is nearly religious or mythical in its implications—the breaking of bread with friends. If many of Auden's poems call on man to love (often with didactic urgency), then the dining-room poem, like all of *About the House*, is informed by a gentle spirit of love. In one sense, the volume is a celebration of friendship; all the poems are dedicated to close friends, and several of them are addressed to people Auden loved. The *agape* proclaimed earlier now unobtrusively informs every poem as each room of the house becomes a celebration of some ordinary human activity—eating, sleeping, conversing, working.

"Tonight at Seven-Thirty" opens with a clever comparison of the eating habits of several species: plants ("one solitary continuous meal"), predators ("none of them play host") and man (who alone can "do the honors of a feast"). This definition is designed, first of all to amuse; it nevertheless makes a serious point in asserting that only man—"Dame Kind's thoroughbred lunatic"—can invite a stranger to the table and serve him first. Auden celebrates man's capacity for kindness, ritual, and even good manners—another recurrent motif in the later poems.

About the House is the work of a poet who, in a sense, has arrived. Auden's quest for love as a cure for man's ills took him in the 1930's to a landscape of desperation, isolation, and decay. Gradually he discovered a basis upon which, in the 1940's, he could build a vision of *agape*, a knowledge that, despite his sinfulness and guilt, man could be forgiven through grace; love was possible. In *About the House*, nearly forty years after his first poems appeared, the "cure" of love is still at the center of Auden's work; in his later work, however, the possibility of love is not so much proclaimed as celebrated.

Other literary forms · Though known primarily as a poet, W. H. Auden worked in a number of other forms, making him one of the most prolific and versatile poets of his generation. During the 1930's he wrote one play on his own—*The Dance of Death* (1933)—and collaborated on three others with his friend Christopher Isherwood. These retain their interest today both as period pieces and, to a lesser degree, as experimental stage dramas. The best of the plays, *The Dog Beneath the Skin: Or, Where Is Francis?* (1935), is an exuberant, wide-ranging work containing some of Auden's finest stage verse and illustrating many of his early intellectual preoccupations, including his interest in post-Freudian psychology. The other plays, *The Ascent of F6* (1936) and *On the Frontier* (1938), are of less interest, especially the latter, which is largely an anti-fascist propaganda piece. After the 1930's, Auden turned his dramatic interests toward the opera, writing his first libretto, *Paul Bunyan*, in 1941 for Benjamin Britten. (The work was not published until 1976, three years after Auden's death.) His better-known librettos, written in collaboration with Chester Kallman, are *The Rake's Progress* (1951), *Elegy for Young Lovers* (1961), *The Bassarids* (1966), and *Love's Labour's Lost* (1972). The assessment of the librettos and their relationship to the poetry has scarcely begun. Auden's prose writing, by contrast, has been quickly and widely recognized for its range, liveliness, and intelligence. His work includes dozens of essays, reviews, introductions, and lectures written over the span of his career. Many of his best pieces are gathered in *The Dyer's Hand and Other Essays* (1962) and *Forewords and Afterwords* (1973);

other prose includes *The Enchafèd Flood* (1950) and *Secondary Worlds* (1969). In addition to his plays, librettos, and prose, Auden wrote for films and radio and worked extensively as an editor and translator. *Plays and Other Dramatic Writings by W. H. Auden, 1928-1938*, edited by Edward Mendelson, was published by Princeton University Press in 1988. It includes Auden's collaborations with Christopher Isherwood and works by Auden alone; it is the first volume of a projected eight-volume series, *The Complete Works of W. H. Auden*.

Select works other than poetry
DRAMA: *Paid on Both Sides: A Charade*, pb. 1930; *The Dance of Death*, pb. 1933; *The Dog Beneath the Skin: Or, Where Is Francis?*, pb. 1935 (with Christopher Isherwood); *The Ascent of F6*, pb. 1936 (with Isherwood); *On the Frontier*, pr., pb. 1938 (with Isherwood); *Paul Bunyan*, pr. 1941 (libretto; music by Benjamin Britten); *The Rake's Progress*, pr., pb. 1951 (libretto, with Chester Kallman; music by Igor Stravinsky); *Delia: Or, A Masque of Night*, pb. 1953 (libretto, with Kallman; not set to music); *For the Time Being*, pr. 1959 (oratorio; musical setting by Martin David Levy); *Elegy for Young Lovers*, pr., pb. 1961 (libretto, with Kallman; music by Hans Werner Henze); *The Bassarids*, pr., pb. 1966 (libretto, with Kallman; music by Henze); *Love's Labour's Lost*, pb. 1972 (libretto, with Kallman; music by Nicolas Nabokov; adaptation of William Shakespeare's play); *The Entertainment of the Senses*, pr. 1974 (libretto, with Kallman; music by John Gardiner); *Plays and Other Dramatic Writings by W. H. Auden, 1928-1938*, pb. 1988.
NONFICTION: *The Enchafèd Flood*, 1950; *The Dyer's Hand and Other Essays*, 1962; *Selected Essays*, 1964; *Secondary Worlds*, 1969; *A Certain World*, 1970; *Forewords and Afterwords*, 1973.
EDITED TEXTS: *The Oxford Book of Light Verse*, 1938; *The Portable Greek Reader*, 1948; *Poets of the English Language*, 1950 (5 volumes; with Norman Holmes Pearson); *The Faber Book of Modern American Verse*, 1956; *Selected Poems of Louis MacNeice*, 1964; *Nineteenth Century British Minor Poets*, 1966; *A Choice of Dryden's Verse*, 1973.
MISCELLANEOUS: *The English Auden: Poems, Essays, and Dramatic Writings, 1927-1939*, 1977 (Edward Mendelson, editor).

Michael Hennessy

Bibliography · Edward Mendelson, *W. H. Auden: Nineteen Hundred Seven to Nineteen Hundred Seventy Three*, 1980, is an indispensable source of material on the poet. Mendelson's personal association with Auden and his consequent access to Auden's letters and other personal material make this biography the most authoritative. Another solid work is Richard Daveport-Hines, *Auden*, 1996; Humphrey Carpenter, *W. H. Auden: A Biography*, 1981, is also thorough. Two critical studies are John R. Boly, *Reading Auden: The Returns of Caliban*, 1991, and Anthony Hecht, *The Hidden Law: The Poetry of W. H. Auden*, 1993. Joseph Warren Beach, *The Making of the Auden Canon*, 1957, sheds light on the meticulousness of Auden's revisions of his work. John G. Blair, *The Poetic Art of W. H. Auden*, 1965, concentrates on the work of Auden's American phase, while Samuel Hynes, *The Auden Generation*, 1972, treats the poet's early development through the 1930's. Monroe Spears, *The Poetry of W. H. Auden: The Disenchanted Island*, 1963, presents a balanced critique of the poet's work by a close analysis of the texts. Despite its age, Richard Hoggart, *Auden: An Introductory Essay*, 1951, is a clear, direct evaluation of Auden's poetry to that time. F. R. Leavis, *New Beginnings in English Poetry*, 1950, presents the view that Auden's poetic quality declined after 1945, while John Bayley, *The Romantic Survival*, 1957, suggests that Auden is the aesthetic heir to Charles Dickens. John Fuller, *A Reader's Guide to W. H. Auden*, 1970, contains a well-researched bibliography.

CHARLES BAUDELAIRE

Born: Paris, France; April 9, 1821
Died: Paris, France; August 31, 1867

Poetry · *Les Fleurs du mal*, 1857, 1861, 1868 (*Flowers of Evil*, 1931) · *Les Épaves*, 1866 · *Petits Poèmes en prose*, 1869 (also known as *Le Spleen de Paris; Poems in Prose*, 1905, also known as *Paris Spleen, 1869*, 1947)

Achievements · Although Charles Baudelaire was close to the major Romantic artists and poets, his work announced something new and difficult to describe. Baudelaire did not introduce a fundamentally new aesthetic principle but made important changes in the proportions of idealism and realism, formal beauty and attention to ideas, social commitment and alienation from society—all categories through which the Romantic poets had expressed their conception of literary art. More than most Romantics, he wrote poetry based on the ugliness of urban life and drew an intense beauty from the prosaic and the unspeakable. Although major Romantics, including Victor Hugo, had broken down many restrictions on subjects that could be treated in poetry, Baudelaire went further, choosing such topics as crime, disease, and prostitution as his points of departure. While many Romantics suggest a transcendent redemptive quality in art, a spiritual enlightenment that gives the readers a kind of religious or social pathway to liberation, Baudelaire tantalizes the reader with religious hope but then pulls it away, suggesting that all hope is in the moment of artistic insight and not in the real future.

The image of the poet as prophet or spiritually superior dreamer, typical of Hugo or Alfred de Vigny, flickers occasionally through Baudelaire's work, but it generally yields to an image of the poet as a sensitive and marginal individual whose only superiority to his contemporaries is his consciousness of his corruption and decadence, something Baudelaire expressed as "conscience [or consciousness] in the midst of evil." Baudelaire thus prepared the way for the decadent poets, and for those poets of the twentieth century who conceived of their work as primarily individual and not social. In this regard, it is significant that Baudelaire introduced Edgar Allan Poe to the French. Poe subsequently came to be a major influence on Stéphane Mallarmé and Paul Valéry and has even played a role in contemporary French psychoanalysis.

In terms of poetic form, Baudelaire's major innovation was undoubtedly in the prose poem, which existed before him but achieved status as a major form principally through *Paris Spleen*. In his verse, Baudelaire often used the highly restrictive "fixed forms" with their set repetition of certain verses, such as the *pantoum*, in which the second and fourth verses of one stanza become the first and third of the following four-verse unit. Such forms were common among the Romantics, but Baudelaire's combination of this formal perfection with surprising and even shocking subjects produces a dissonant and unforgettable music. Baudelaire thus avoids the pitfalls of the school of "art for art's sake," which he denounced for its exclusive attachment to surface beauty.

Although Baudelaire is sometimes grouped with the Symbolists, a movement that constituted itself more than a decade after his death, Baudelaire himself neither belonged to nor founded a school. It is probably fair, however, to designate him as the earliest exponent of modernism. He constantly sought, in both literature and painting, works that expressed

Library of Congress

a beauty specific to the reality of the moment, even if that reality was unpleasant or bizarre.

Biography · Charles-Pierre Baudelaire was born in Paris on April 9, 1821. His father, Joseph-François, was of modest origin but well educated, for he attended seminary and became a priest before the Revolution. Well connected, he became preceptor to the children of the Duke of Choiseul-Praslin and, as a painter, was personally acquainted with Enlightenment figures such as Condorcet and Cabanis. After the Revolution, having left the priesthood, Joseph-François Baudelaire worked on the administrative staff of the French senate. Caroline Archenbaut-Defayis, Baudelaire's mother, was thirty-four years younger than his father. Widowed, she remarried when her son was six years old. Baudelaire's stepfather, Jacques Aupick, was a career military officer who had him placed in a series of boarding schools, first in Lyons, when the child was nine, and then in Paris, at fifteen. The choice of schools permitted Baudelaire to be near his mother as the Aupick household moved in response to the officer's promotions.

As an adolescent, Baudelaire was friendly, religious, and studious. He won prizes in Latin verse composition (one of the poems in *Flowers of Evil* is in Latin). He seems to have had few serious disputes with his stepfather until after obtaining the *baccalauréat* in 1839. After that, however, the now successful general became progressively the object of Baudelaire's dislike and even hatred. Disapproving of the young man's friends and conduct, the general sent him on a long boat trip toward India, but Baudelaire, once embarked, refused to go farther than Mauritius. When Baudelaire reached legal majority in 1842, he broke with the Aupicks and lived prodigally on the money he inherited from his father. The life of ease of the young literary dandy lasted only two years, however, for the Aupicks had Baudelaire placed under conservatorship in 1844 on the grounds that he was incapable of managing his money. This deprivation of his full personal freedom had a devastating effect on Baudelaire, who attempted suicide the following year. Upon his recovery, he apparently resolved to write copiously and seriously, contributing to various reviews, especially *L'Artiste* and *Le Corsaire-Satan*.

Baudelaire was widely acquinted with important Romantic authors, including Charles Sainte-Beuve, Theóphile Gautier, Hugo, Gérard de Nerval, Théodore de Banville, Petrus Borel (the Wolf-man), and Champfleury. He was also close to the active painters of his day and spent much of his time in their studios. His essays on expositions and on individual artists, especially Eugène Delacroix and Constantin Guys, actually occupy twice as many pages in the complete works as his literary criticism. More intermittently, Baudelaire was involved in the political life of his day, manning the barricades in the 1848 Revolution and distributing political tracts. His love of order, or rather his aspiration to order and hatred of disorder, kept him from fitting into the Revolutionary cause, and his hatred of the bourgeoisie prevented him from siding with the conservatives.

By 1845, Baudelaire was already announcing a forthcoming volume of poetry, under the title "Les Lesbiennes." In 1848, he claimed to be working on a volume called "Les Limbes." Finally, in 1855, he settled on the title *Flowers of Evil.* When it appeared in 1857, the collection provoked a scandal that led to the prosecution of the poet and the publisher. Six of the poems were suppressed, and the poet was fined.

The death of General Aupick a few months before the appearance of *Flowers of Evil* led Baudelaire to a reconciliation with his mother. Although he never succeeded in putting his life in what he called "order," living within his means and avoiding debts, his attempt to heal his rift with his respectable middle-class origins may explain the increasingly Christian and even Catholic orientation of his ideas in the last decade of his life. In 1866, while visiting Brussels, Baudelaire was stricken with partial paralysis and became aphasic. He died in Paris after more than a year of suffering.

Analysis · Charles Baudelaire insisted that *Flowers of Evil* should be read as a structured whole and not as a random collection of verse. Whatever one may think about the authority of such claims, the six major divisions of the book, beginning with the longest section, eighty-five poems, entitled "Spleen et idéal" ("Spleen and Ideal"), and ending with the six poems of "La Mort" ("Death"), seem to outline a thematic and perhaps even chronological passage from aspirations toward a transcendence of pain, suffering, and evil (in the earliest section) through the exploration of various kinds of intoxication or escape–glimpsed in the sections "Le Vin" ("Wine"), "Flowers of Evil," and "Révolte" ("Rebellion")–only to end in death, seen itself as a form of escape from the disappointments or boredom of this world.

Throughout *Flowers of Evil,* a major theme is the uncovering of humankind's own contradictions, hypocrisies, desires, and crimes: all the aspects of life and fantasy that the respectable middle-class hides. In the first poem of the book, "Au lecteur" ("To the Reader"), Baudelaire establishes an unusual relationship with his public. The poem begins with a list of vices–stupidity, error, sin, and stinginess–but instead of reproaching humanity and urging the reader to reform, the poet finishes the sentence with an independent clause containing a remarkable simile: "We feed our nice remorse,/ As beggars nourish their lice." Over this humanity presides the

Devil, described two stanzas later as the magician, not Hermes but Satan Trismegistus (three-times great), who turns the rich metal of the will into vapor like an alchemist working backwards. Building toward what will apparently be a crescendo of vice, Baudelaire, in stanza 7, lists sins that man would commit if he had the courage (such as rape, poisoning, stabbing, and arson) and then points to a still greater vice, which he names only three stanzas later in the conclusion: boredom (*ennui*). In the poem's striking concluding lines, Baudelaire claims that the reader knows this "delicate monster," and then calls the reader "Hypocritical reader, my likeness, my brother!"

This strange poem, borrowing so much of its vocabulary and rhetoric from the tradition of religious exhortation, does not choose between good and evil. Instead, it promotes a third term into what is usually a simple dilemma: boredom, as the greatest of vices, is an aesthetic concept that replaces traditional moral concepts of evil as that which must be avoided at all costs, a vice which "could swallow the world in a yawn." In religious verse, the address to the reader as a brother is part of a call, first to recognize a common weakness and, second, to repent. Baudelaire does make an avowal of similarity but calls for an aesthetic rather than an ethical response.

The largest part of *Flowers of Evil* evokes a struggle against boredom through the artistic use of the ugliness of everyday life and ordinary, even abject, passions. The poem "Les Phares" ("Beacons") is an enumeration of eight great painters, including Peter Paul Rubens, Rembrandt, and Michelangelo, not as a celebration of human greatness but as a testimony to human sentiment and sensation, predominantly in the negative. Rubens is described, for example, as a "Pillow of fresh flesh where one cannot love" and Rembrandt as a "sad hospital full of murmuring." The last three stanzas seem at first to point to a religious purpose in this art which depicts a swarming, nightmare-ridden humanity, for Baudelaire uses terms from religion: malediction, blasphemy, *Te Deum*. Humankind's art is called a "divine opium," but this drug is not offered upward as incense to the Deity. It is, rather, an opium for human hearts. The purpose of art is ambiguous in this conclusion, for it is the best testimony to human dignity but is destined to die at the edge of God's eternity. In the historical context of French Romanticism, this vision of art serves at least to set Baudelaire apart from the partisans of "art for art's sake," a movement that Baudelaire himself called the "Plastic school." Clearly, the visual beauty of the paintings alluded to is not their primary characteristic in "Beacons." These works of art are great because of their representative quality and for the tension between their beauty and the suffering on which they are based.

The paradoxical search for an art that draws its beauty from ugliness and suffering appears in a spectacular way in another of the early poems of *Flowers of Evil*, entitled "Une Charogne" ("A Carcass"). Baudelaire's particular delight in the shocking combination of refined form with a crude and repugnant subject is noticeable in the very organization of the stanzas. There are twelve units of four lines each: The first and third lines of each stanza are rhyming Alexandrines (twelve-syllable lines), while the second and fourth lines are rhyming octosyllables. This division imposes a rhythm that heightens the contrast between refined gentleness and sickening sensations. As a whole, the poem is a monologue addressed to a person or character whom the speaker calls "my soul." Although there is a certain ambiguity about the significance of the term (it could represent a division of the self into two parts, a common Baudelairean theme), the poet's "soul" assumes the role of a woman to whom he speaks in words of endearment. He also recalls, however, the discovery, one summer morning, of a carcass lying near a pathway.

The opening stanza illustrates the way in which a tension is created between contrasting tones. The first two lines are addressed to the soul in terms that allow one to expect some pretty image, something that would fit the context of a beautiful, mild summer morning. The end of the second Alexandrine, however, names the object: a "foul carcass." The discovery occurs as the speaker and his soul are coming around a bend in the path (*détour*) which parallels the transition from the first half of the stanza to the somewhat startling second half. The next eight stanzas continue to tell about the discovery of this cadaver in a tone that alternates, sometimes within stanzas and sometimes from one stanza to the next, between a distant aesthetic contemplation and a crude and immediate repulsion. The fourth stanza starts with a presentation of the point of view of the sky witnessing the "blossoming" of the carcass as if it were a flower, while the next two lines ("The stench was so strong that you thought you would faint on the grass") take a distinctly human point of view, even rather sadistically delighting in the soul's weakness. The speaker's reaction is represented as quite different, much closer to that attributed to the sky. In stanza 7, he compares the sounds coming from the carcass, eaten by organisms of decomposition, to flowing water and wind and to the sound of grain being winnowed. Not only does this comparison permit the poet to find beauty in ugliness, but it also permits him to pay homage to the bucolic poetry of the Renaissance (exemplified in such poems as Joachim du Bellay's "D'un vanneur de blé aux vents" ("From a Winnower to the Winds"), showing that classical themes can be presented in a thoroughly modern way.

In the following stanza, the speaker's drift continues from a purely aesthetic contemplation of the object to a comparison of the carcass to an artist's preliminary sketch in the artist's memory. This reverie is broken off in the ninth stanza by the return to the supposed summer morning scene and the recollection that a dog was waiting for the couple to leave so that she could get her meat.

The last three stanzas are quite different, for they depart from the scene, which is in the past, and look forward to the future of the speaker's beloved "soul," foreseeing the time when she will be like that carcass. Yet, even in this section (a form of *envoi*, a traditional closing message to the addressee of a poem), the alteration of tone continues. In the tenth stanza, where the speaker declares "You will be like this filth," he still continues to refer to her as "my angel and my passion." This contrast leads toward the final stanza in which Baudelaire, again recalling the poetry of the French Renaissance, proclaims the immortality of his poetry ("I have kept the form and divine essence/ Of my decomposed loves") in contrast to the fleshly mortality of his "soul," his beloved.

It is impossible to assert that this conclusion is a straightforward poetic doctrine. Perhaps the poet, after having cast the "soul" in the paradoxical role of decomposition, is exercising a final irony toward his own poetry. In any case, it is clear that "A Carcass" represents Baudelaire's reworking of traditional texts from classical and Renaissance tradition. His way of using the tradition sets him apart from those Romantics he called the Pagan school, who preferred to assume the posture of outright return to pre-Christian belief by denying historical evolution. One reason Baudelaire objected to this position was that he himself possessed a deeply tormented Christian character—described by some as Jansenist, that is, as belonging to the most severe, pessimistic, and ascetic form of seventeenth and eighteenth century French Catholicism—penetrated by the sense of sin and guilt. He could not imagine a simple return to classical "innocence." Baudelaire also had an acute sense of the passage of time and of historical change. In calling the work of the neopagans "a disgusting and useless pastiche," he was implicitly drawing attention to his own use of antiquity in a resolutely modernist manner, one that did not copy the ancients but assimilated their ideas into a representation of the reality of modern life.

The poignancy that Baudelaire achieves with such an approach can be seen in his "Le Cygne" ("The Swan"), dedicated, like two other poems in the section "Tableaux parisiens" ("Parisian Pictures"), to Victor Hugo, a deep believer in the historical movement of poetry. "The Swan" is divided into two numbered parts, one of seven and the other of six stanzas. In the first section, the speaker begins by addressing the legendary figure Andromache, the Trojan Hector's widow, captive in the city of Epirus. The Parisian speaker's memory, he says, has been made pregnant by the thought of the "lying Simoïs swelled by your tears." This allusion to the legends of Troy is the key to understanding the rest of the first part of the poem, most of which seems merely to tell of an event in the speaker's own life, an event without apparent connection with Andromache. He was walking across the new Carrousel Square when he recalled a menagerie that once stood on that spot. A swan had escaped from its cage and was bathing its wings in the dust of a gutter.

The allusion to Andromache is now clearer, for the "lying" Simoïs was a replica in Epirus of the small river that once flowed at the foot of the walls of Troy. In an attempt to make the widow happier, her captors had constructed this imitation, described by Baudelaire as "lying" because it is not only false but actively and disappointingly deceitful. It can never replace the Simoïs but can only remind Andromache of the discrepancy between past and present. In the second part of the poem, Baudelaire explains the multiple analogy that had been left implicit in the first part. Returning to the present (the first part had been composed of three chronological layers: the legendary past of Andromache, the moment when the speaker saw the swan, and the approximate present in which he recollects the swan), he exclaims, "Paris changes! but nothing in my melancholy/ Has moved!"

What had seemed in the first part to be a comparison only between the widow and the swan now includes the speaker. Each of the three has an immovable memory on the inside—the speaker compares his to rocks—which cannot match the mutable outside world. This dissonance between mind and world is expressed not only in the image of the swan but also, more subtly and pathetically, in the temporal organization of the poem. Between the time he saw the swan and the time of the creation of the poem, the swan has vanished and the old Carrousel has been changed into the new. The chronological layering of the text has the same function as the simile. Furthermore, the changes in Paris, composed of monumental constructions of carved stone, give the city an ironic and metaphoric significance. Monuments, like the palace of the Louvre near which the menagerie stood, are usually associated with memory. They are meant to last longer than individuals. Here, however, the city represents change. Baudelaire has thus united a commonplace of certain Romantic poets (the indifference of nature to humankind's suffering) with a classical poetry of cities (Troy, Epirus, Rome) to produce a thoroughly modern poetic idiom.

The conclusion of "The Swan" continues the interplay of literary allusion, for it opens still further the analogy involving Andromache, the swan, and the poet to include an African woman exiled in a northern climate, sailors, captives, and the conquered. There is a decidedly epic quality to this expansion of the analogy to include vast numbers of modern exiles. Baudelaire did not, unlike many Romantics, believe in long poems, and he seems here to be condensing the grandeur of the epic into the brevity of the personal lyric. The many components of this epic analogy, stretching from Andromache to the suggestively open-ended last line ("Of captives, of the conquered . . . of still others!), are reminiscent of the multiple symbolic figures (the artists) of "Beacons." With this latter poem "The Swan" also shares the vision of suffering as a defining characteristic of life, for exiles "Suck at the breast of Sorrow as if she were a good wolf." This image is a way of tying in the Roman epic of Romulus and Remus while emphasizing the voluntary or consoling aspect of pain and suffering.

Suffering, inflicted on others or on oneself, is a frequent theme in *Flowers of Evil* and is linked to learning and self-awareness. In the "Heautontimoroumenos" (a Greek term for "The Executioner of Oneself," borrowed from a comedy of Terence), the speaker declares himself a "dissonance in the divine symphony" on account of the irony that eats away at him. In the most remarkable stanza, he declares in part, "I am the wound and the knife!/ I am the blow and the cheek!" In the poem immediately following, "L'Irrémédiable" ("The Irreparable"), after briefly tracing the fall of an ideal being from Heaven into Hell, Baudelaire evokes a "Somber and clear tête-à-tête/ A heart become its own mirror!" This division of the self into two sides, each looking at the other, is then described metaphorically as a "Well of truth, clear and black/ Where a pale star trembles." Although, here, knowledge is stressed more than the pain that is so fiercely displayed in "Heautontimoroumenos," pain must be the outcome of self-examination in this "well of truth" because the inward discovery is the sentiment of a fall from a higher state, an "irreparable" decadence. Yet, there is a tension here between the claim to total clarity and the image of the well, for the latter promises depths which can never be coextensive with the mirroring surface. Working back from this tension, one can see that the whole poem is full of terms for depth, darkness, and entrapment. The lucidity toward which the poem tends will never be complete, for consciousness can only discover the extent, apparently infinite, of its deprivation.

The concluding note of *Flowers of Evil*, the section called "Death," is a reminder of this perpetual quest for new discovery, even at the price of horror. In fact, the last stanza of the concluding poem, "Le Voyage" ("The Trip"), is based on the concept of depth that had already appeared in "The Irreparable": "Plunge into the deeps of the abyss, Hell or Heaven, that difference/ Into the depth of the Unknown to find something *new*!" Here the preoccupation with boredom as supreme evil in "To the Reader" appears coupled with the themes of knowledge and discovery that constitute much of the other sections. "The Trip" is a kind of summary in dialogue of *Flowers of Evil*, beginning with the childlike hope of discovery in the exploration of the real world. When asked later what they discovered, the travelers say that no city they discovered was ever as interesting as the cities they imagined in the shapes of clouds. Then, in passages that seem to recall the "Parisian Pictures," "Wine," and "Rebellion," the world of human sin is sketched out as a monotonous mirror in which humankind sees its own image, "An oasis of horror in a desert of boredom!" The only hope is in death itself, addressed in the last two stanzas as a ship's captain. He alone holds out a balm for our boredom, which itself results from an irresolvable tension between the aspirations of the heart and the outside world, ostensibly a mirror but actually an incomplete reflection because it can capture only actions and not intentions.

Baudelaire's collection of prose poems, *Paris Spleen*, is thematically very similar to *Flowers of Evil*. The prose pieces, however, have greater means to establish a situation for the poetic speaker and to accumulate aspects of life that seem "realistic" but serve ultimately to reveal figurative meanings in the most ordinary surroundings, a process sometimes called "correspondences" after the title of one of Baudelaire's verse poems. Frequently, as in "Le Gâteau" ("The Cake"), Baudelaire dramatically alters the situation of the poetic speaker so that he is not a representative of dissatisfaction with the world but an amazed spectator of the subjectivity of desire. In "The Cake," a traveler finds himself in a country where his plain bread is called "cake," unleashing a fratricidal war for its possession. In "Le Joujou du pauvre" ("The Poor Child's Plaything"), he discovers two children playing on opposite sides of a fence. One child is rich and has a meticulously crafted doll while the other holds his toy in a little cage. It is a living rat. Although these texts include elements of diction, characterization, and setting typical of fiction in the realist or Naturalist vein, Baudelaire always suggests a larger significance that makes the scene or incident figurative. In "The Poor Child's Plaything," the fence between the children is referred to as a symbolic barrier, and the rat is described as a toy drawn from life itself. Baudelaire specifies the metaphoric meaning much less in the prose poems than in his verse. One can, however, easily view the rat as a synecdoche for Baudelaire's aesthetic, based on drawing beauty from those aspects of life that are most repulsive.

Baudelaire's corrosive irony, his suggestive understatement of the metaphoric sense of his images, and his aggressive use of material drawn from the prosaic side of life have had a lasting success and influence. Movements as diverse as Symbolism, Dadaism, and the Italian neorealist cinema have claimed descent from his work.

Other literary forms · Collections of Charles Baudelaire's essays on literature, art, aesthetics, and drugs appeared under the titles *Les Paradis artificiels* (1860), *Curiosities esthétiques* (1868), and *L'Art romantique* (1868). Baudelaire also published translations of several volumes of the prose works of Edgar Allan Poe. The most convenient edition of most of his works is the Pléiade edition, *Œuvres complètes* (1961), edited by Yves Le Dantec and Claude Pichois.

Select works other than poetry
LONG FICTION: *La Fanfarlo*, 1847.

NONFICTION: *Les Paradis artificiels*, 1860 (partial translation as *Artificial Paradises: On Hashish and Wine as a Means of Expanding Individuality*, 1971); *Curiosities esthétiques*, 1868; *L'Art romantique*, 1868; *Mon cœur mis à nu*, 1887 (*My Heart Laid Bare*, 1950); *The Letters of Baudelaire*, 1927; *My Heart Laid Bare and Other Prose Writings*, 1951; *Baudelaire on Poe*, 1952; *The Mirror of Art*, 1955; *Intimate Journals*, 1957; *The Painter of Modern Life and Other Essays*, 1964; *Beaudelaire as Literary Critic: Selected Essays*, 1964; *Art in Paris, 1845-1862: Salons and Other Exhibitions*, 1965.

TRANSLATIONS: *Histoires extraordinaires*, 1856 (of Edgar Allan Poe's short stories); *Nouvelles Histoires extraordinaires*, 1857 (of Poe's short stories); *Aventures d'Arthur Gordon Pym*, 1858 (of Poe's novel); *Eureka*, 1864 (of Poe's poem); *Histoires grotesques et sérieuses*, 1864 (of Poe's tales).

MISCELLANEOUS: *Œuvres complètes*, 1868-1870, 1961.

John D. Lyons

Bibliography · In 1973 Claude Pichois' edition of Baudelaire's correspondence appeared in Paris. A great deal has been written on Baudelaire in English. Two very reliable and well-documented biographies of Baudelaire are Joanna Richardson, *Baudelaire*, 1994, and Claude Pichois, *Baudelaire*, trans. Graham Robb, 1989. The best general introduction in English is Lois Boe Hyslop, *Charles Baudelaire Revisited*, 1992, which also includes an annotated bibliography of important critical studies. A careful stylistic study of *Flowers of Evil* can be found in Graham Chesters, *Baudelaire and the Poetics of Craft*, 1988. The originality of his prose poems has been analyzed in J. A. Hiddleston, *Baudelaire and Le Spleen de Paris*, 1987. A fascinating psychological reading of Baudelaire's poetry and correspondence can be found in Leo Bersani, *Baudelaire and Freud*, 1977.

JOHN BERRYMAN

Born: McAlester, Oklahoma; October 25, 1914
Died: Minneapolis, Minnesota; January 7, 1972

Poetry • *Five Young American Poets*, 1940 (with others) • *Poems*, 1942 • *The Dispossessed*, 1948 • *Homage to Mistress Bradstreet*, 1956 • *His Thought Made Pockets and the Plane Buckt*, 1958 • *77 Dream Songs*, 1964 • *Short Poems*, 1967 • *Berryman's Sonnets*, 1967 • *His Toy, His Dream, His Rest*, 1968 • *The Dream Songs*, 1969 • *Love & Fame*, 1970, 1972 • *Delusions, Etc. of John Berryman*, 1972 • *Henry's Fate and Other Poems*, 1977 • *Collected Poems, 1937-1971*, 1989

Achievements • In *Beyond All This Fiddle* (1968) A. Alvarez remarks that

> John Berryman is one of those poets whom you either love or loathe. Yet even the loathers have grudgingly to admit that the man is extraordinary . . . with a queer, distinct voice of his own.

No doubt, there are "loathers" who would apply "extraordinary" in no laudable sense, and who would use far cruder adjectives than "queer" and "distinct" in describing Berryman's voice. Still, decades after his death, Berryman's place in modern poetry seems as secure as that of any of his contemporaries, living or dead—Robert Lowell, Delmore Schwartz, Richard Wilbur, Adrienne Rich, or W. D. Snodgrass. Though he died a most unsatisfied man, his poetic career certainly brought him his share of recognition and praise: the Levinson and Guarantors Prizes from *Poetry* and the Shelley Memorial Award, 1948; the University of Chicago's Harriet Monroe Poetry Prize, 1957; the Brandies Creative Arts Award,

Daniel A. Lindley

1960; the National Institute of Arts and Letters' Loines Award for Poetry, 1964; the Pulitzer Prize in Poetry for *77 Dream Songs*, 1965; and both the National Book Award and the Bollingen Prize (shared with Karl Shapiro) for *His Toy, His Dream, His Rest*, 1969. In addition, he won grants and fellowships from such organizations as the Guggenheim Foundation (1952, 1966), the Rockefeller Foundation (1944), the National Institute of Arts and Letters (1950), and the Academy of American Poets (1966). He was much in demand for public readings, even though, especially toward the end of his career, his alcoholism and unpredictable personality made some of these appearances traumatic for both poet and audience.

In his poetry, Berryman moved from an ordered, restrained style, imitative of William Butler Yeats and W. H. Auden, to a passionate, energetic, deeply personal mode of expression, held in check—though just barely in places—by skilled attention to rhythm and sound. So decisive was this movement that comparing such early poems as "Winter Landscape" with a random sample from his later work, *The Dream Songs* (1969), is almost like comparing two different poets. It is easy enough to look back at Berryman's early work and find it too poised, too urbane and academic. A number of critics, however, have objected to much of his later work, finding in it too little restraint and much too large a dose of the poet's raw experience. He is placed by some, with Anne Sexton and Lowell, in the "confessional school." The label does not quite apply, for Berryman's work at its best—and, unfortunately, he did frequently allow it to be published at its worst—remained for him a means of using personal experience to get at human experience. He retained too much formal control to be considered a "Beat," and was too inventive in his use of language to be classed with the vernacular mode of William Carlos Williams. Whatever else may be said about him, Berryman is one of the most individual voices in twentieth century American poetry.

In spite of his successes, however, it is difficult not to wonder whether Berryman has been overpraised. His *Homage to Mistress Bradstreet* (1956), for example, was extolled by Robert Fitzgerald (*The American Review*, Autumn, 1960) as "the poem of his generation," while Edmund Wilson, solicited for a back-cover blurb for a 1968 paperback edition of the poem, responded with, "the most distinguished long poem by an American since *The Waste Land*." There must certainly be a middle stance, somewhere between overpraise and Stanton Coblentz's view that "*77 Dream Songs* (1964) has all the imaginative fervor of a cash register." Such a moderate perspective would see Berryman as a major poet of his generation, and view *77 Dream Songs* as one of the major poetic events of the 1960's. His *Collected Poems, 1937-1971*, was published in 1989.

Biography · John Berryman was born John Allyn Smith, in McAlester, Oklahoma, the eldest son of a banker and a schoolteacher. His early childhood, spent in various small Oklahoma towns, was normal enough until his father's work took the family to live in Tampa, Florida; marital problems developed and the boy's father became increasingly troubled and unstable. In June, 1926, he shot himself in the chest at the family's vacation home across Tampa Bay. Young John heard the shot just outside his window—one sharp report that would echo through his consciousness for the rest of his life. When the boy's mother moved to New York and remarried, his name was changed to John Allyn McAlpin Berryman. Berryman wrote many letters to his mother as an adult, which were published as *We Dream of Honour: John Berryman's Letters to His Mother* in 1988.

Berryman attended a Connecticut prep school, South Kent; though he showed great intellectual promise, he was only intermittently moved to apply it. He was graduated in 1933 and went on to Columbia University in New York. There he felt much more at home academically and socially, and there he began a lifelong friendship with Mark Van Doren, who, by Berryman's account, was the first person to inspire and encourage him to be a poet. Not long after this association began, Berryman published his first poem, an elegy on Edwin Arlington Robinson, in the *Nation*. In 1936 he received his Bachelor's degree from Columbia, Phi Beta Kappa, and won the University's Kellett Fellowship, which he used to pursue further studies at Clare College, Cambridge University. Academically, his Cambridge experience was extremely rewarding. In 1937, he served as Oldham Shakespeare Scholar, and received a Bachelor of Arts degree in 1938. His social contacts were rewarding, to say the least, including as they did William Butler Yeats, W. H. Auden, and Dylan Thomas.

Back in New York, Berryman was a friend of another young poet, Delmore Schwartz, and became poetry editor of the *Nation*. His teaching career began in 1939 at Wayne State University in Detroit. After a year there, Berryman took a position at Harvard, where he remained until 1943. During this time, his first published collection of poems appeared in *Five Young American Poets* (1940). His work was well received, as were the poems of another promising young talent, Randall Jarrell. In 1942 Berryman published a self-contained selection, *Poems*. On October 24 of the same year, he married Eileen Patricia Mulligan. From 1943 to 1951, Berryman lectured in creative writing at Princeton, taking time out frequently, with the help of grants and fellowships, to write poetry and criticism, as well as a few short stories. In 1948 he published a new book of poems, *The Dispossessed*, which was received more politely than enthusiastically. His most significant work while at Princeton was his critical study, *Stephen Crane*. His psychoanalytic approach was not popular with most reviewers, but the book, on the whole, attracted a good deal of praise.

In 1951 Berryman accepted a one-year position as Elliston Lecturer in Poetry at the University of Cincinnati, and spent the next academic year in Europe with the help of a Guggenheim Fellowship. While in Europe he completed the poem that, upon its publication in 1956, would bring him his first great critical success as a poet—*Homage to Mistress Bradstreet*. The price of this success, however, was high. Berryman later cited his preoccupation with the poem, coupled with an increasing dependence on alcohol, as the cause of his separation in 1953 from his first wife. Certainly, the marriage had not been helped by an intense, guilt-ridden love affair in which Berryman had indulged during the summer of 1947, an affair portrayed in painful detail in the sequence *Berryman's Sonnets* (1967). In the meantime, however, Berryman's academic and literary careers proceeded without serious hindrance. In the fall of 1954, having spent the preceding spring and summer semesters, respectively, at the University of Iowa and at Harvard, he began his long tenure as a professor of humanities at the University of Minnesota in Minneapolis, where he became a popular, if eccentric academic figure. In 1969 he received the University's most prestigious faculty award, a Regents' Professorship, and he remained on the faculty there until his death.

In 1956, Berryman divorced Eileen and married Ann Levine, who gave birth to a son in 1957. The marriage lasted only until 1959. When he again remarried, in 1961, it was to Kathleen Donahue, twenty-five years his junior. In the same year he lectured at Indiana University, then moved on, in 1962, to a visiting professorship at Boon University. During that year, Kate Berryman gave birth to a daughter, Martha. In 1965, Berryman won the Pulitzer Prize for *77 Dream Songs;* his place as a major contemporary poet seemed secure. He had begun work on these "songs" around 1955, and continued to work in this form for nearly twenty years, publishing in 1968 *His Toy, His Dream, His Rest*, a collection of 308 more poems that won the National Book Award in 1969. The two volumes were combined in *The Dream Songs*.

The 1960's were a time of triumph for Berryman. The decade saw, along with *The Dream Songs*, the long-delayed publication of *Berryman's Sonnets*, and of *Short Poems* (1967), a compilation of the earlier collections, *The Dispossessed* and *His Thought Made Pockets & the Plane Buckt*, with the addition of "Formal Elegy," a poem on the death of John F. Kennedy. Yet, the kind of success that most poets only dream of left Berryman dissatisfied and unfulfilled. His drinking problem became more serious than ever, interfering not only with his family life but with his professional responsibilities as well, disrupting classes and public readings, much to the dismay of students, admirers, and colleagues.

Berryman's next book of poems, *Love & Fame* (1970, 1972), did not fare well with the critics, and the poet took their disapproval hard. He had been, by this time, in and out of alcoholic treatment programs, and, while he had found some consolation in a renewal of his Roman Catholic faith, he could not overcome the addiction to alcohol; drinking had for too long been, in Joel Conarroe's words, "both stabilizer and destroyer, midwife and coroner, focuser and depressant." He spent many weeks of 1971 in the alcohol treatment facility at St. Mary's Hospital in Minneapolis, the hospital that provided the setting for his unfinished novel *Recovery* (1973). He remained, however, busy. He prepared a new book of poems for publication, and his plans for work included a translation of Sophocles and a book or two on Shakespeare. Unfortunately, the prospect of hard work, the comfort of family and friends, his affection for his daughters, Martha and Sarah—these were not enough.

On January 7, 1972, readers of the *St. Paul Dispatch* were greeted with the front page headline: "Poet Berryman Leaps to Death." That afternoon, Berryman had thrown himself some one hundred feet from the railing of a bridge in Minneapolis; his body was recovered from among the rocks on the frozen west bank of the Mississippi. In a circumstance worthy of the most bitterly ironic of his poems, the only identification he carried was a blank check. After a Requiem Mass he was buried in Resurrection Cemetery in St. Paul.

Analysis · In his essay "Tradition and the Individual Talent," T. S. Eliot asserts that

> the more perfect the artist, the more completely separate in him will be the man who suffers and the mind which creates; the more perfectly will the mind digest and transmute the passions which are its material.

Poetry, to Eliot, is "not a turning loose of emotion, but an escape from emotion; it is not the expression of personality, but an escape from personality." Regardless of what Eliot's critical stock is worth these days, there is an essential truth in what he says. Of course, poetry has brought to its readers the sweetest joys and the bitterest sorrows that human flesh is heir to, from "sweet silent thought" to "barbaric yawp." To the extent, however, that a poet presents his passions to the reader undigested, untransmuted, he damages the quality of his work *as poetry*. The more loudly personality speaks in a poem, the more art is forced to falter, to stutter. The poem—and the poet, and the reader—suffers.

To the extent to which "the man who suffers" and "the mind which creates" are not kept separate, to that extent will that poet's art be imperfect. A case in point is John Berryman. There is much in his work that is brilliant; since his death, perhaps, his stature has grown. There is no denying that he suffered much in his life, and risked much, dared much, in his poetry. What he was never really able to do was to find the voice and mode that would allow him not to banish personality from his poems but to keep personality from getting in the way, from obstructing the proper work of the poem.

Berryman's Sonnets, though unpublished until 1967, was mostly written some twenty years earlier. These poems are the poet's first sustained use of what may be called his "mature style," much of his previous work being rather derivative. The 115 sonnets form a sequence that recounts the guilty particulars of an adulterous love affair between a hard-drinking academic named Berryman and a harder-drinking woman named Lise, with the respectively wronged wife and husband in supporting roles. The affair, as the sonnets record it, is a curious mixture of sex, Scotch, and Bach (Lise's favorite, her lover preferring Mozart), punctuated by allusions right out of a graduate seminar, from the Old Testament to E. E. Cummings.

In form, the sonnets are Petrarchan, with here and there an additional fifteenth line. In his adherence, more or less, to the stanzaic and metric demands of the sonnet, Berryman pays a sort of homage to earlier practitioners of the form. At the same time, he is attempting to forge a mode of expression that is anything but Petrarchan, in spite of the fact that, as Hayden Carruth pointed out in a review in *Poetry* (May, 1968), the poems "touch every outworn convention of the sonnet sequence—love, lust, jealousy, separation, time, death, the immortality of art, etc." Carruth points out in the same review that "the stylistic root of *The Dream Songs*" is present in the sonnets, with those attributes that came to be trademarks of Berryman's style—"archaic spelling, fantastically complex diction, tortuous syntax, formalism, a witty and ironic attitude toward prosody generally." A concentrated if somewhat mild example of how Berryman combines any number of these traits within a few lines is the octet of "Sonnet 49":

> One note, a daisy, and a photograph,
> To slake this siege of weeks without you, all.
> Your dawn-eyed envoy, welcome as Seconal,
> To call you faithful . . . now this cenotaph,
> A shabby mummy flower. Note I keep safe,
> Nothing, on a ration slip a social scrawl—

> Not that it didn't forth some pages call
> Of my analysis, one grim paragraph.

There are enjoyable juxtapositions here. Outdated words such as "slake" and "cenotaph," the over-sweetness of "dawn-eyed envoy," ranged about the all-too-contemporary simile, "welcome as Seconal," are no accident. There is an irreverent literary mind at work here, orchestrating intentionally a little out of tune. It is harder to appreciate or justify a phrase such as "not that it didn't forth some pages call/ Of my analysis." Such syntax is a high price to pay for a rhyme, and much more extreme examples could be cited.

On the whole, the sequence is successful, but the seeds of Berryman's eventual undoing are here. The confessional nature of the poems (Berryman did experience just such an affair in 1947, and required a good deal of psychoanalysis afterward) makes it plain enough why their publication was delayed so long, but it also leads the reader to wonder whether they should have been published at all. In his attempts to work within a fairly strict form, he shows a tendency to force rhyme and overburden meter. His literary name-dropping ("O if my syncrisis/ Teases you, briefer than Propertius' in/ This paraphrase by Pound—to whom I owe three letters"), private allusions, and inside jokes present a dangerous intrusion of the idiosyncratic, the personal. With more shaping, more revision, more distance generally, the sequence could have been much more artistically successful than it is. Perhaps part of Berryman's intention was to get the thing on paper "as it was," to share his raw feelings with the reader. The best of the sonnets, by their wit and craft, speak against such a supposition. They contain, as a group, too much undigested Berryman to be placed, as some have placed them, beside the sonnets of William Shakespeare. Lise is all too actual, "barefoot . . . on the bare floor riveted to Bach," no Dark Lady. Further, while Shakespeare's sonnets have much to say about love, loss, youth, age, success, and failure, they tell the reader little if anything about William Shakespeare, while Berryman's sonnets reveal more than one may care to know about Berryman.

Not long after the strenuous summer of the sonnets, Berryman began a poem on the seventeenth century American Puritan poet, Anne Bradstreet. Part of the initial task was to find the right stanza for the job; an eight-line stanza suggested itself, the pattern of feet running 5-5-3-4-5-5-3-6, with a rhyme scheme of *abcbddba*. Neither meter nor rhyme are adhered to inflexibly in the resulting poem, *Homage to Mistress Bradstreet*, but for the most part Berryman succeeded in his choice of a stanza "both flexible and grave, intense and quiet, able to deal with matter both high and low." He achieves beautiful effects in the fifty-seven stanzas of this poem. The birth of Bradstreet's first child after several years of barrenness is portrayed in images wonderfully right: "I press with horrible joy down/ my back cracks like a wrist." The words sweep forward, charged with the urgency of this experience, "and it passes the wretched trap whelming and I am me/ drencht & powerful, I did it with my body!/ One proud tug greens Heaven. . . . " In fact, some of the most touching moments in the poem focus on Bradstreet and her children, whether the occasion be death, as in stanza 41: "Moonrise, and frightening hoots. 'Mother,/ how *long* will I be dead?', " or nothing more than a loose tooth, as in stanza 42: "When by me in the dusk my child sits down/ I am myself. Simon, if it's that loose,/ let me wiggle it out./ You'll get a bigger one there, & bite." Moving outdoors, away from the hearth, there are lovely scenes of natural description: "Outside the New World winters in grand dark/ white air lashing high thro' the virgin stands/ foxes down foxholes sigh. . . . "

Berryman, however, has his problems with the poem. As in the sonnets, he sometimes tangles his syntax unnecessarily: "So were ill/ many as one day we could have no sermons." To write "so were ill many" instead of "so many were ill," without even the excuse of a stubbornly kept rhyme scheme, seems at best eccentric, at worst, sloppy. As in the sonnets, also, there is an unfinished quality about the poem. Tangled phrasing, the inconsistent use of a rather carefully established rhyme scheme—these in spite of the fact that Berryman spent years on the poem, even blamed the demise of his first marriage partly upon the intense effort that the work required. One may wonder, in spite of his long labors, whether he relinquished it to the public a bit unfinished.

The major flaw in *Homage to Mistress Bradstreet*, however, has not so much to do with details of diction or prosody. Anne Bradsteet was, by historical accounts, a happily married, deeply religious woman, devoted to her husband and children, who happened to write poetry. Berryman needed for his poem a passionately suffering artist, plagued by religious doubt, resentful of her husband and family, thwarted in her dream of artistic commitment, so he altered the historical Bradstreet to suit his purposes. This reshaping of history is necessary for the centerpiece of the poem—a seduction scene between a modern poet and a woman three hundred years buried. In an understandably surrealistic dialogue, the poet speaks his love for the poor, tormented Anne in a rather far-fetched variation of the designing rake's "Let-Me-Take-You-Away-From-All-This." Bradstreet (Berryman's, that is) is tempted to religious doubt, to extramarital dalliance (she *does* ask the poet for a kiss), to despair over her misunderstood lot. Her domestic commitments, however, overrule her temptations, and the poem ends with the modern poet standing before Bradstreet's grave and uttering words that are supposed to be touching and solemn, but which somehow fail to convince:

> I must pretend to leave you . . . O all your ages at the mercy of my loves
> together lie at once, forever or
> so long as I happen.
> In the rain of pain & departure, still
> Love has no body and presides the sun . . . Hover, utter, still
> a sourcing whom my lost candle like the firefly loves.

The rhyming of "still" with itself is a nice touch, and "the rain of pain & departure" rings true, but the passage has a disturbing, self-conscious quality that is not at all helped by a reference, in one of the closing stanzas, to contemporary (post-World War II) anxieties—"races murder, foxholes hold men,/reactor piles wage slow upon the wet brain rime."

The above summary oversimplifies and leaves much unsaid. In all fairness, there are a good many brilliant moments in Berryman's poem, but, as a whole, *Homage to Mistress Bradstreet* is somewhat less than brilliant. John Frederick Nims, reviewing the poem in *The Prairie Schooner*, termed it a "gallant failure," finding it "magnificent and absurd, mature and adolescent, grave and hysterical, meticulous and slovenly." In the end, his major complaint is that the poem,

> purportedly concerned with Anne Bradstreet . . . is really about "the poet" himself, his romantic and exacerbated personality, his sense of loneliness, his need for a mistress, confidante, confessor. One might think there would be more satisfactory candidates for the triple role among the living.

Nims's position is persuasively put and strikes at the heart of what is wrong with *Homage to Mistress Bradstreet*. Rather than conveying any true homage to this first American poet, Berryman lets his own personality, his own needs and concerns, dominate the stage, to the extent that the Bradstreet of his poem becomes a just version of himself. Far from "escaping personality," to recall Eliot's term, Berryman forces Bradstreet into the mold of his own personality.

From "Berryman" of the sonnets, to "the poet" of *Homage to Mistress Bradstreet*, Berryman moved on to "Henry," the narrator and protagonist of *The Dream Songs*, the sequence of 385 poems that is considered to be his major work. Berryman apparently began with the notion of writing another long poem, about as long as Hart Crane's *The Bridge* (1930). What resulted, however, was something closer to Ezra Pound's *Cantos* (1925-1972). At the center of the poems is a character known variously as Henry House, Henry Cat, Pussycat, and Mr. Bones. Within flexibly formal songs of three sestets apiece, Berryman reveals Henry's trials and sufferings, which in many cases are the reader's as well. Too often, however, the songs are about Berryman.

There is real feeling in *The Dream Songs*. Too much suffering, however, spread not at all thinly over seven thousand lines and interspersed with proportionately more of the same sort of name-dropping and private allusion encountered in the sonnets, becomes oppressive and even boring. There are wonderful moments, notably in the elegies for dead friends—Jarell, Schwartz, Sylvia Plath. The obsession with suicide that laces many of the poems is lent a special poignance when considered in the light of Berryman's father's, then his own, suicide. Not surprisingly, Henry's father took his life when he was young. Still, readers must be very interested in Berryman as a person to wade through these 385 poems, for Berryman is once again the center of attention, the "star" of his own epic, despite his coy disclaimer that Henry is "not the poet, not me."

In his continuing inability to distance himself sufficiently from his poetry, Berryman places the reader in an awkward position. In *The Personal Heresy: A Controversy* (1939), C. S. Lewis describes the necessity of keeping one's response to a poem separate from one's response to the personality of the poet, a task that Berryman makes unfairly difficult. When readers mix the two, says Lewis, they offend both poet and poem. "Is there, in social life," he asks, "a grosser incivility than that of thinking about the man who addresses us instead of thinking about what he says?" No, says Lewis, "We must go to books for that which books can give us—to be interested, delighted, or amused, to be made merry or to be made wise." As for personalities, living or dead, the response should be some "species of love," be it "veneration, pity," or something in between.

Berryman's personality is hard to love, easier to pity, but what is truly to be pitied is the fact that, had his skills as a poet been a match for his troubled personality, he would without question have been one of the greatest poets of his time.

Other literary forms · In addition to his poetry, John Berryman produced a considerable number of reviews and critical pieces. A posthumous collection, *The Freedom of the Poet* (1976), gathers a representative sample of his criticism, published and unpublished. Berryman did not produce much prose fiction, preferring to use verse as a narrative vehicle. He did, however, write several short stories, and an unfinished novel, *Recovery*

(1973), was published as he left it at his death. Other critical writing includes *Stephen Crane* (1950), a rather psychologized critical biography, and *The Arts of Reading* (1960), a collection of essays coauthored with Ralph Ross and Allen Tate. Berryman also edited a 1960 edition of Thomas Nashe's *The Unfortunate Traveller: Or, the Life of Jack Wilton*. Berryman may be heard reading his poems on several recordings produced by the Library of Congress.

Select works other than poetry
LONG FICTION: *Recovery*, 1973.
NONFICTION: *Stephen Crane*, 1950; *The Arts of Reading*, 1960 (with Ralph Ross and Allen Tate); *The Freedom of the Poet*, 1976; *We Dream of Honour: John Berryman's Letters to His Mother*, 1988.
EDITED TEXT: *The Unfortunate Traveller: Or, the Life of Jack Wilton*, 1960.

Richard A. Eichwald

Bibliography · For a more complete list of sources, readers should investigate Gary Q. Arpin, *John Berryman: A Reference Guide*, 1976, which is an annotated list of secondary sources, or Richard J. Kelly, *John Berryman: A Checklist*, 1972, which is not annotated. John Haffenden, *The Life of John Berryman*, 1982, and Paul Mariani, *Dream Song: The Life of John Berryman*, 1990, provide complete and compelling accounts of Berryman's life. Haffenden also wrote *John Berryman: A Critical Commentary*, 1980, a useful collection of explications of Berryman's major works. An intimate, if more subjective, portrait can be found in *Poets in Their Youth: A Memoir*, 1982, by Eileen Simpson, who was married to Berryman from 1941 to 1953. First-time readers of Berryman will appreciate Joel Conarroe's *John Berryman: An Introduction to the Poetry*, 1977. Harry Thomas, *Berryman's Understanding: Reflections on the Poetry of John Berryman*, 1988, collects interviews with Berryman, memoirs of associates, and criticism of the poetry. Another collection, Richard J. Kelly and Alan K. Lathrop, eds., *Recovering Berryman: Essays on a Poet*, 1993, is notable for its sections focusing on psychological issues and alcoholism in Berryman's work.

ELIZABETH BISHOP

Born: Worcester, Massachusetts; February 8, 1911
Died: Boston, Massachusetts; October 6, 1979

Poetry · *North & South*, 1946 · *Poems: North & South–A Cold Spring*, 1955 · *Questions of Travel*, 1965 · *Selected Poems*, 1967 · *The Ballad of the Burglar of Babylon*, 1968 · *The Complete Poems*, 1969 · *Geography III*, 1976 · *The Complete Poems, 1927-1979*, 1983

Achievements · Elizabeth Bishop was frequently honored for her poetry. Among many awards and prizes, she received the 1956 Pulitzer Prize for Poetry and the 1969 National Book Award for Poetry. Yet, as John Ashbery said, in seconding her presentation as the winner of the *Books Abroad/ Neusadt International Prize for Literature* in 1976, she is a "writer's writer." Despite her continuing presence for over thirty years as a major American poet, Bishop never achieved great popular success. Perhaps the delicacy of much of her writing, her restrained style, and her ambiguous questioning and testing of experience made her more difficult and less approachable than poets with showier technique or more explicit philosophies.

For critics, however, and certainly for other poets–those as different as Marianne Moore and Robert Lowell, or Randall Jarrell and Ashbery–hers is a voice of influence and authority. Writing with great assurance and sophistication from the beginning of her career, she achieved in her earliest poetry the quiet, though often playful, tone, a probing and examining of reality, the exactness of language, and the lucidity of vision that mark all of her best poetry. Her later poetry is slightly more relaxed than her earlier, the formal patterns often less rigorous; but her concern and her careful eye never waver. Because of the severity of her self-criticism, her collected poems, although relatively few in number, are of a remarkably even quality.

Bishop's place in American poetry, in the company of such other twentieth century poets as Moore, Wallace Stevens, and Richard Wilbur, is among the celebrators and commemorators of the things of this world, in her steady conviction that by bringing the light of poetic intelligence, the mind's eye, on those things, she will enrich her readers' understanding of them and of themselves.

Biography · Elizabeth Bishop is a poet of geography, as the titles of her books testify, and her life itself was mapped out by travels and visits as surely as is her poetry. Eight months after Bishop's birth in Massachusetts, her father died. Four years later, her mother suffered a nervous breakdown and was hospitalized, first outside Boston, and later in her native Canada.

Elizabeth was taken to Nova Scotia, where she spent much of her youth with her grandmother; later, she lived for a time with an aunt in Massachusetts. Although her mother did not die until 1934, Bishop did not see her again after a brief visit home from the hospital in 1916–the subject of "In the Village."

Thomas Victor

For the rest of her life, Bishop traveled: in Canada, in Europe, in North and South America. She formed friendships with many writers: Robert Lowell, Octavio Paz, and, most influentially, Marianne Moore, who read drafts of many of her poems and offered suggestions. In 1951, Bishop began a trip around South America, but during a stop in Brazil she suffered an allergic reaction to some food she had eaten and became ill. After recovery, she remained in Brazil for almost twenty years. During the last decade of her life, she continued to travel and to spend time in Latin America, but she settled in the United States, teaching frequently at Harvard, until her death in 1979.

In her early poem "The Map," Bishop writes that "More delicate than the historians' are the map-makers' colors." Her best poetry, although only indirectly autobiographical, is built from those mapmakers' colors. Nova Scotian and New England seascapes and Brazilian and Parisian landscapes become the geography of her poetry. At the same time, her own lack of permanent roots and her sense of herself as an observer suggest the lack of social relationships one feels in Bishop's poetry, for it is a poetry of observation, not of interaction, of people as outcasts, exiles, and onlookers, not as social beings. The relationships that count are with the land and sea, with primal elements, with the geography of Bishop's world.

Analysis · In Elizabeth Bishop's poem "Sandpiper," the title bird runs along the shore, ignoring the sea that roars on his left and the beach that "hisses" on his right, disregarding the interrupting sheets of water that wash across his toes, sucking the sand back to sea. His attention is focused. He is watching the sand between his toes; "a student of Blake," he attempts to see the world in each of those grains. The poet is ironic about the bird's obsessions: he is "finical"; in looking at these details he ignores the great sweeps of sea and land on either side of him. For every time the world is clear, there is another when it is a mist. The poet seems to chide the bird in his darting search for "something, something, something," but then in the last two lines of the poem the irony subsides; as Bishop carefully enumerates the varied and beautiful colors of the grains of sand, she joins the bird in his attentiveness. The reward, the something one can hope to find, lies simply in the rich and multivalent beauty of what one sees. It is not the reward of certainty or conviction, but of discovery that comes through focused attention.

The irony in the poem is self-mocking, for the bird is a metaphor for Bishop, its vision like her own, its situation that of many of her poetic personae. "Sandpiper" may call to mind such Robert Frost poems as "Neither Out Far Nor In Deep" or "For Once, Then, Something," with their perplexity about inward and outward vision and humanity's attempt to fix sight on something, to create surety out of the surroundings. It may also suggest such other Bishop poems as "Cape Breton," where the birds turn their backs to the mainland, sometimes falling off the cliffs onto rocks below. Bishop does share with Frost his absorption with nature and its ambiguities, the ironic tone, and the tight poetic form that masks the "controlled panic" that the sandpiper-poet feels. Frost, however, is in a darker line of American writers: His emphasis is on the transitoriness of the vision, the shallowness of the sea into which one gazes, the ease with which even the most fleeting vision is erased. For Frost's poet-bird, "The Oven Bird," the nature he observes in midsummer is already ninety percent diminished. Bishop rather prefers the triumph of one's seeing at all. In her well-known poem "The Fish," when the persona finally looks into the eyes of the fish she has caught—eyes, the poet notes, larger, but "shallower" than her own—the fish's eyes return the stare. The persona, herself now caught, rapt, stares and stares until "victory fill[s] up" the boat, and all the world becomes "rainbow, rainbow, rainbow." Like the rainbow of colors that the sandpiper discovers, the poet here discovers beauty; the victory is the triumph of vision.

Like the sandpiper, then, Bishop is an obsessive observer. As a poet, her greatest strength is her pictorial accuracy. Whether her subject is as familiar as a fish, a rooster, or a filling station, or as strange as a Brazilian interior or a moose in the headlights of a bus, she enables the reader to see. The world for the sandpiper is sometimes "minute and vast and clear," and because Bishop observes the details so lucidly, her vision becomes truly vast. She is, like Frost, a synecdochist; for her, the particulars entail the whole. Nature is the matter of Bishop's art; to make her readers see, to enable them to read the world around them is her purpose. In "Seascape," what the poet finds in nature, its potential richness, is already like "a cartoon by Raphael for a tapestry for a Pope." All that Bishop must accomplish, then, as she writes in "The Fish," is simply "the tipping/ of an object toward the light."

Although the world for the sandpiper is sometimes clear, it is also sometimes a mist, and Bishop describes a more clouded vision as well. She translated a poem by Paz, "Objects and Apparitions," that might indicate the fuller matter of her own work; the objects are those details, the grains of sand that reveal the world once they are tipped toward the light. The apparitions occur when one sees the world through the mist and when one turns vision inward, as in the world of dreams. Here, too, the goal is bringing clarity to the vision—and the vision to clarity. As Bishop writes in "The Weed," about drops of dew that fall from a weed onto a dreamer's face, "each drop contained a light,/ a small, illuminated scene."

Objects and apparitions, mist and vision, land and sea, history and geography, travel and home, ascent and fall, dawn and night—these oppositions supply the tension in Bishop's poetry. The tensions are never resolved by giving way; in Bishop's world, one is a reflection of the other, and "reflection" becomes a frequent pun: that of a mirror and that of thought. Similarly, inspection, introspection, and insight suggest her doubled vision. In "Paris, 7 A.M., looking down into the courtyard of a Paris house, the poet writes, "It is like introspection/ to stare inside," and there is again the double meaning of looking inside the court and inside oneself.

No verbs are more prevalent or important in Bishop's poetry than those of sight: look, watch, see, stare, she admonishes the reader. From "The Imaginary Iceberg," near the beginning of her first book, which compares an iceberg to the soul, both "self-made from elements least visible," and which insists that icebergs "behoove" the soul "to see them so," to "Objects and Apparitions" near the end of her last book, in which the poet suggests that in Joseph Cornell's art "my words became visible," one must first of all see; and the end of all art, plastic and verbal, is to make that which is invisible—too familiar to be noticed, too small to be important, too strange to be comprehended—visible. In "The Man-Moth," the normal human being of the first stanza cannot even see the moon, but after the man-moth comes above ground and climbs a skyscraper, trying to climb out through the moon, which he thinks is a hole in the sky, he falls back and returns to life below ground, riding the subway backward through his memories and dreams. The poet addresses the readers, cautioning them to examine the man-moth's eye, from which a tear falls. If the "you" is not paying attention, the man-moth will swallow his tear and his most valuable possession will be lost, but "if you watch," he will give it up, cool and pure, and the fruit of his vision will be shared.

To see the world afresh, even as briefly as does the man-moth, to gain that bitter tear of knowledge, one must, according to Bishop, change perspectives. In *Questions of Travel* (1965), people hurry to the southern hemisphere "to see the sun the other way around." In "Love Lies Sleeping" the head of one sleeper has fallen over the edge of the bed, so that to his eyes the world is "inverted and distorted." Then the poet reconsiders: "distorted and revealed," for the hope is that now the sleeper sees, although a last line suggests that such sight is no certainty. When one lies down, Bishop writes in "Sleeping Standing Up," the world turns ninety degrees and the new perspective brings "recumbent" thoughts to mind and vision. The equally ambiguous title, however, implies either that thoughts are already available when one is upright or, less positively, that one may remain unattentive while erect. The world is also inverted in "Insomnia," where the moon stares at itself in a mirror. In Bishop's lovely, playful poem "The Gentleman of Shalott," the title character thinks himself only half, his other symmetrical half a reflection, an imagined mirror down his center. His state is precarious, for if the mirror should slip, the symmetry would be destroyed, and yet he finds the uncertainty "exhilarating" and thrives on the sense of "re-adjustment."

The changing of perspectives that permits sight is the theme of Bishop's "Over 2000 Illustrations and a Complete Concordance." The poet is looking at the illustrations in a gazetteer, comparing the engraved and serious pictures in the book with her remembered travels. In the first section of the poem, the poet lists the illustrations, the familiar, even tired Seven Wonders of the World, moving away from the objects pictured to details of the renderings, until finally the "eye drops" away from the real illustrations which spread out and dissolve into a series of reflections on past travels. These too begin with the familiar: with Canada and the sound of goats, through Rome, to Mexico, to Marrakech. Then, finally, she goes to a holy grave, which, rather than reassuring the viewer, frightens her, as an amused Arab looks on. Abruptly, the poet is back in the world of books, but this time her vision is on the Bible, where everything is "connected by 'and' and 'and.' " She opens the book, feeling the gilt of the edges flake off on her fingertips, and then asks, "Why couldn't we have seen/ this old Nativity while we were at it?" The colloquial last words comprise a casual pun, implying physical presence or accidental benefit. The next four lines describe the nativity scene, but while the details are familiar enough, Bishop's language defamiliarizes them. The poet ends with the statement that had she been there she would have "looked and looked our infant sight away"–another pun rich with possibilities. Is it that she would have looked repeatedly, so that the scene would have yielded meaning and she could have left satisfied? Do the lines mean to look away, as if the fire that breaks in the vision is too strong for human sight? The gazetteer into which the poet first looked, that record of human travels, has given way to scripture; physical pictures have given way to reflected visions and reflections, which, like the imaginary iceberg, behoove the soul to see.

Bishop participates in the traditional New England notion that nature is a gazetteer, a geography, a book to be read. In her poem "The Riverman," the speaker gets up in the night–night and dawn, two times of uncertain light, are favorite times in Bishop's poetic world–called by a river spirit, though at first the dolphin-spirit is only "glimpsed." The speaker follows and wades into the river where a door opens. Smoke rises like mist, and another spirit speaks in a language the narrator does not know but understands "like a dog/although I can't speak it yet." Every night he goes back to the river, to study its language. He needs a "virgin mirror," a fresh way of seeing, but all he finds are spoiled. "Look," he says significantly, "it stands to reason" that everything one needs can be obtained from the river, which draws from the land "the remedy." The image of rivers and seas drawing, sucking the land persists in Bishop's poetry. The unknown that her poems scrutinize draws the known into it. The river sucks the earth "like a child," and the riverman, like the poet, must study the earth and the river to read them and find the remedy of sight.

Not only do the spirits of nature speak, but so too for Bishop does art itself. Her poetry is pictorial not only in the sense of giving vivid descriptions of natural phenomena, but also in its use of artificial objects to reflect on the self-referential aspect of art. Nature is like art, the seascape a "cartoon," but the arts are like one another as well. Bishop is firmly in the *ut pictura poesis* tradition–as is a painting, so a poem–and in the narrower *ekphrastic* tradition: art, like nature, speaks. In "Large Bad Picture," the picture is an uncle's painting, and after five stanzas describing the artist's attempt to be important by drawing everything oversized–miles of cliffs hundreds of feet high, hundreds of birds–the painting, at least in the narrator's mind, becomes audible, and she can hear the birds crying. In the much later "Poem," Bishop looks at another but much smaller painting by the same uncle (a sketch for a larger one? she asks), and this time the painting speaks to her memory. Examining the brushstrokes in a detached and slightly contemptuous manner, she suddenly exclaims, "Heavens, I recognize the place, I know it!" The voice of her mother enters, and then she concludes, "Our visions coincided"; life and memory have merged in this painting as in this poem: "how touching in detail/ –the little that we get for free."

Most explicitly in "The Monument," she addresses someone, asking her auditor to "see the monument." The listener is confused: the assemblage of boxes, turned catty-corner one upon the other, the thin poles hanging out at the top, the wooden background of sea made from board and sky made from other boards: "Why do they make no sound?. . . What is that?" The narrator responds with "It is the monument," but the other is not convinced that it is truly art. The voice of the poet again answers, insisting that the monument be seen as "artifact of wood" which "holds together better than sea or cloud or sand could." Acknowledging the limitations, the crudeness of it, the questions it cannot answer, she continues that it shelters "what is within"–presenting the familiar ambiguity: within the monument or within the viewer? Sculpture or poem, monument or painting, says the poet, all are of wood; that is, all are artifacts made from nature, artifacts that hold together. She concludes, "Watch it closely."

Thus, for Bishop, shifting perspectives to watch the natural landscape (what she quotes Sir Kenneth Clark as calling "tapestried landscape") and the internal landscape of dream and recollection are both the matter and the manner of art, of all arts, which hold the world together while one's attention is focused. The struggle is to see; the victory is in so seeing.

Yet Bishop's poetry is not unequivocally optimistic or affirmative. There are finally more ambiguities than certainties, and–like her double-edged puns–questions, rhetorical and conversational, are at the heart of these poems. Bishop's ambiguity is not that of unresolved layers of meaning in the poetry, but in the unresolvable nature of the world she tests. "Which is which?" she asks about memory and life in "Poem." "What has he done?" the poet asks of a chastised dog in the last poem of *Geography III* (1976). "Can countries pick their colors?" she asks in "The Map." *Questions of Travel* begins with a poem questioning whether this new country, Brazil, will yield "complete comprehension"; it is followed by another poem which asks whether the poet should not have stayed at home: "Must we dream our dreams/ and have them, too?" Bishop poses more questions than she answers. Indeed, at the end of "Faustina," Faustina is poised above the dying woman she has cared for, facing the final questions of the meaning that death gives to life: freedom or nightmare, it begins, but the question becomes "proliferative," and the poet says that "There is no way of telling./ The eyes say only either."

Knowledge, like the sea, like tears, is salty and bitter, and even answering the questions, achieving a measure of knowledge, is no guarantee of permanence. Language, like music, drifts out of hearing. In "View of the Capitol from the Library of Congress," even the music of a brass band "doesn't quite come through." The morning breaks in "Anaphora" with so much music that it seems meant for an "ineffable creature." When he appears, however, he is merely human, a tired victim of his humanity, even at dawn. Yet, even though knowledge for Bishop is bitter, is fleeting, though the world is often inscrutable or inexplicable, hers is finally a poetry of hope. Even "Anaphora" moves from morning to night, though from fatigue to a punning "endless assent."

Bishop's poetry is often controlled by elaborate formal patterns of sight and sound. She makes masterful use of such forms as the sestina and villanelle, avoiding the appearance of mere exercise by the naturalness and wit of the repetitions and the depth of the scene. In "The Burglar of Babylon," she adopts the ballad form to tell the story of a victim of poverty who is destroyed by his society and of those "observers" who watch through binoculars without ever seeing the drama that is unfolding. Her favorite sound devices are alliteration and consonance. In "The Map," for example, the first four lines include "shadowed," "shadows," "shallows," "showing"; "edges" rhymes with "ledges," "water" alliterates with "weeds." The repetition of sounds not only suggests the patterning that the poet finds in the map, but also the slipperiness of sounds in "shadows"/"shallows" indicates the ease with which one vision of reality gives place to another. The fifth line begins with another question: "Does the land lean down to lift the sea," the repeated sound changing to a glide. "Along the fine tan sandy shelf/is the land tugging at the sea from under?" repeats the patterning of questions and the *sh* and *l* alliteration, but the internal rhyme of "tan" and "sandy," so close that it momentarily disrupts the rhythm and the plosive alliteration of "tan" and "tugging," implies more strain.

Being at the same time a pictorialist, Bishop depends heavily on images. Again in "The Map," Norway is a hare that "runs south in agitation." The peninsulas "take the water between thumb and finger/ like women feeling for the smoothness of yard-goods." The reader is brought up short by the aptness of these images, the familiar invigorated. On the map, Labrador is yellow, "where the moony Eskimo/ has oiled it." In the late poem "In the Waiting Room," a young Elizabeth sits in a dentist's waiting room, reading through a *National Geographic*, looking at pictures of the scenes from around the world. The experience causes the young girl to ask who she is, what is her identity and her similarity, not only with those strange people in the magazine but also with the strangers there in the room with her, and with her Aunt Consuela whose scream she hears from the inner room. Bishop's poetry is like the pictures in that magazine; its images offer another geography, so that readers question again their own identity.

This sense of seeing oneself in others, of doubled vision and reflected identities, leads to another of Bishop's favorite devices, the conceit. In "Wading at Wellfleet," the waves of the sea, glittering and knifelike, are like the wheels of Assyrian chariots with their sharp knives affixed, attacking warriors and waders alike. In "The Imaginary Iceberg," the iceberg is first an actor, then a jewel, and finally the soul, the shifting of elaborated conceits duplicating the ambiguous nature of the iceberg. The roads that lead to the city in "From the Country to the City" are stripes on a harlequin's tights, and the poem a conceit with the city the clown's head and heart, its neon lights beckoning the traveler. Dreams are armored tanks in "Sleeping Standing Up," letting one do "many a dangerous thing," protected. In the late prose piece "12 O'Clock News," each item on a desk becomes something else: the gooseneck lamp, a moon; the typewriter eraser, a unicyclist with bristly hair; the ashtray, a graveyard full of twisted bodies of soldiers.

Formal control, a gently ironic but appreciative tone, a keen eye—these are hallmarks of Bishop's poetry. They reveal as well her limitation as a poet: a deficiency of passion. The poetry is so carefully controlled, the patterns so tight, the reality tested so shifting, and the testing so detached, that intensity of feeling is minimized. Bishop, in "Objects and Apparitions," quotes Edgar Degas, " 'One has to commit a painting . . . the way one commits a crime.' " As Richard Wilbur, the writer whom she most resembles, has pointed out, Degas loved grace and energy, strain coupled with beauty. Strain is absent in Bishop's work.

Although there are wonderful character sketches among her poems, the poetry seems curiously underpopulated. "Manuelzinho" is a beautiful portrait of a character whose account books have turned to dream books, an infuriating sort whose numbers, the decimals omitted, run slantwise across the page. "Crusoe in England" describes a man suddenly removed from the place that made him reexamine his existence. These are people, but observers and outsiders, themselves observed. The Unbeliever sleeps alone at the top of a mast, his only companions a cloud and a gull. The Burglar of Babylon flees a society that kills him. Cootchie is dead, as is Arthur in "First Death in Nova Scotia," and Faustina tends the dying.

Crusoe is without his Friday, and in "Sestina," although a grandmother jokes with a child, it is silence that one hears, absence that is present. There is little love in Bishop's poetry. It is true that at the end of "Manuelzinho," the narrator confesses that she loves her maddening tenant "all I can,/ I think. Or do I?" It is true that at the end of "Filling Station," the grubby, but "comfy" design of the family-owned station suggests that "Somebody loves us all," but this love is detached and observed, not felt. Even in "Four Poems," the most acutely personal of Bishop's poems and the only ones about romantic love, the subject is lost love, the conversation internal. "Love should be put into action!" screams a hermit at the end of "Chemin de Fer," but his only answer is an echo.

History, writes Bishop in "Objects and Apparitions," is the opposite of art, for history creates ruins, while the artist, out of ruins, out of "minimal, incoherent fragments," simply creates. Bishop's poetry is a collection of objects and apparitions, of scenes viewed and imagined, made for the moment into a coherent whole. The imaginary iceberg in the poem of that name is a part of a scene "a sailor'd give his eyes for," and Bishop asks that surrender of her readers. Her poetry, like the iceberg, behooves the soul to see. Inner and outer realities are in her poetry made visible, made one.

Other literary forms · In addition to her poetry, Bishop wrote short stories and other prose pieces. She is also known for her translations of Portuguese and Latin American writers. *The Collected Prose*, edited and introduced by Robert Giroux, was published in 1984. It includes "In the Village," an autobiographical revelation of Bishop's youthful vision of, and later adult perspective on, her mother's brief return home from a mental hospital. Like her poetry, Bishop's prose is marked by precise observation and a somewhat withdrawn narrator, although the prose works reveal much more about Bishop's life than the poetry does. Editor Giroux has suggested that this was one reason many of the pieces were unpublished during her lifetime. *The Collected Prose* also includes Bishop's observations of other cultures and provides clues as to why she chose to live in Brazil for so many years.

Select works other than poetry
SHORT FICTION: "In the Village," in *Questions of Travel*, 1965.
NONFICTION: *The Diary of "Helena Morley,"* 1957 (trans. of Alice Brant's *Minha Vida de Menina*); *Brazil*, 1962 (with the editors of *Life*); *One Art: Letters*, 1994.
EDITED TEXT: *An Anthology of Twentieth Century Brazilian Poetry*, 1972 (with Emanuel Brasil).

CHILDREN'S LITERATURE: *The Battle of the Burglar of Babylon*, 1968.
MISCELLANEOUS: *The Collected Prose*, 1984 (fiction and nonfiction).

Howard Faulkner

Bibliography • Brett C. Millier, *Elizabeth Bishop: Life and the Memory of It*, 1993, is a full critical biography, with a generous bibliography of other secondary literature on the writer and her work. See also Joanne Feit Diehl, *Elizabeth Bishop and Marianne Moore: The Psychodynamics of Creativity*, 1993; Harold Bloom, ed., *Elizabeth Bishop: Modern Critical Views*, 1985; C. K. Doreski, *Elizabeth Bishop: The Restraints of Language*, 1993; Marilyn May Lombardi, *Elizabeth Bishop: The Geography of Gender*, 1993; Susan McCabe, *Elizabeth Bishop: Her Poetics of Loss*, 1994; and Gary Fountain and Peter Brazeau, *Remembering Elizabeth Bishop: An Oral Biography*, 1994.

WILLIAM BLAKE

Born: London, England; November 28, 1757
Died: London, England; August 12, 1827

Poetry • *Poetical Sketches*, 1783 • *There Is No Natural Religion*, 1788 • *All Religions Are One*, 1788 • *Songs of Innocence*, 1789 • *The Book of Thel*, 1789 • *The Marriage of Heaven and Hell*, 1790 • *The French Revolution*, wr. 1791 (published posthumously) • *America: A Prophecy*, 1793 • *Visions of the Daughters of Albion*, 1793 • *Songs of Innocence and of Experience*, 1794 • *Europe: A Prophecy*, 1794 • *The [First] Book of Urizen*, 1794 • *The Song of Los*, 1795 • *The Book of Ahania*, 1795 • *The Book of Los*, 1795 • *Vala: Or, The Four Zoas*, wr. 1795-1804 (published posthumously; commonly known as *The Four Zoas*) • *Milton: A Poem*, 1804-1808 • *Jerusalem: The Emanation of the Giant Albion*, 1804-1820 • *The Poems of William Blake*, 1971

Achievements • William Blake's reputation during his lifetime was not a fraction of what it is today. He worked hard at his trade, that of engraving, but his style was not in fashion, and his commissions were few. His poverty and the laborious process of producing his own illuminated books for sale prevented him from producing more than two hundred copies of his own work in his lifetime. Even the *Songs of Innocence and of Experience* (1794), which he sold sporadically throughout his career, remained virtually unnoticed by his contemporaries. What little reputation he had among his contemporaries was as an artist, ingenious but no doubt mad.

In 1863, Alexander Gilchrist's biography of Blake did much to establish Blake's reputation as an artist and a

Library of Congress

poet. The Yeats-Ellis edition of Blake (1893) further enhanced his fame, not as a forgotten painter and poet, but as a purveyor of esoteric lore. Accurate transcription of Blake's texts began only in the twentieth century with the work of Geoffrey Keynes. Modern critical work was pioneered by S. Foster Damon in 1924, but it was not until Northrop Frye's *Fearful Symmetry* in 1947 that Blake's work was treated as a comprehensible, symmetrical whole.

A poet-artist who imaginatively remolds his own age and its traditions and then produces poetry, engravings, and paintings within that re-created world is a poet-artist who will attract a wide variety of readers. Blake's profound understanding of the ways in which humans deal with the warring contraries within their minds has become a fertile source for modern psychology. Carl Jung referred to Blake as a visionary poet who had achieved contact with the potent wellspring of the unconscious. Blake's devotion to a humanistic apocalypse created through the display of exuberant energies and expanded imaginative perceptions has been an inspiration to two generations of twentieth century writers: first D. H. Lawrence, E. M. Forster, William Butler Yeats, and Aldous Huxley, and later, Norman O. Brown, Allen Ginsberg, Theodore Roszak, Colin Wilson, and John Gardner, among others. If a poet can be judged by the quality and quantity of the attention he receives, Blake has certainly risen in the twentieth century from a vague precursor of Romanticism to one of the six major English Romantic poets.

Biography · William Blake was born in Carnaby Market, London, on November 28, 1757. By the age of four, he was having visions: God put his head through the window to look at him, angels walked among the haymakers, and a tree was starred with angels. The visionary child was spared the rigors of formal schooling and learned to read and write at home. He attended a drawing school for four years and in 1772 began a seven-year apprenticeship to James Basire, engraver. He had already begun three years before to write the lyrics which were later printed in *Poetical Sketches* (1783). It was not as a poet, however, that he would make his living but as an engraver who also could do original designs. The Gothic style of engraving which he learned from Basire was unfortunately somewhat passè. In later years, Blake had to sit back and watch other engravers receive commissions to execute his own designs.

At the age of twenty-two, Blake became a student of the Royal Academy, which meant that he could draw from models, living and antique, and attend lectures and exhibitions for six years. The politics of the day, as well as a spreading evangelical fervor, infused his life as an artist-poet.

Blake was part of the 1780 Gordon Riots and was present at the burning of Newgate Prison. He was a vehement supporter of the French Revolution and attended radical gatherings which included William Godwin, Thomas Paine, Mary Wollstonecraft Shelley, and Joseph Priestley. Through John Flaxman, Blake developed an interest in Swedenborgianism. The doctrines of Emanuel Swedenborg seemed both to attract and to repel Blake. *The Marriage of Heaven and Hell* (1790) launched an attack on this movement.

In 1782, Blake married Catherine Boucher, whose life apparently became one with his. He tried his hand at running a printshop, but in 1785 it failed. He continued to make a meager living on commissions for designs and engravings, but these were the work of other men. In 1800, he moved to Felpham near Chichester at the invitation of William Hayley, a minor poet, who attempted for the next three years to guide Blake's life into a financially lucrative mold. Blake returned as impoverished as ever to London in 1803, never to leave it again. In 1804, he was tried for sedition and was acquitted. It is ironic that Blake was not being tried for his pervasive iconoclasm, thoughts expressed in his unpublished work which would have set the eighteenth century on its head, but because a drunk had falsely accused him. In 1809, he had his one and only exhibition of sixteen paintings, an exhibition ignored by everyone except one reviewer, who attacked it viciously.

If the political and religious spirit of this period inspired Blake, it also worked against his prosperity as an engraver. Few in England during the Napoleonic Wars could afford the luxury of commissioning the work of an engraver. In the last ten years of his life, Blake attracted the attention of a group of young painters whose admiration doubtless enriched this period of increasing poverty. On August 12, 1827, Blake died singing of the glories he saw in heaven.

Analysis · William Blake's focus is primarily on inner states; the drama of the later books has been called a *psychomachia*, a drama of the divided psyche. Humanity was once integrated but suffered a Fall when reason sought to dominate the other faculties. The disequilibrium of the psyche, its reduced perception, is the creator of the natural world as it is now known. The notion of "contraries" as defined and developed in *The Marriage of Heaven and Hell* provides a dialectical basis for the regeneration of this psyche. Contraries are to be understood as psychic or mental opposites which exist in a regenerated state, a redeemed paradisiacal state of unlimited energy and unbounded perception. Blake has in his total work depicted the progress to regeneration based on a conflict between contraries. Once contraries are accepted, energy is created, progress is inevitable, and reintegration occurs.

Blake's paradisiacal man differs from fallen man only in that he is aware of his divinity. Paradisiacal man perceives the majesty of the imagination, the passions, the reason, and the senses. The imagination in the redeemed state is called Urthona, and after the Fall, Los. Urthona represents that fourfold, unbounded vision which is the normal attribute of the redeemed person. Such vision is not bound by the particulars it produces through contraction, nor is it bound by the unity it perceives when it expands. Blake, in the imagination's true and saving role as poet, envisions the external world with a fourfold vision. Luvah, the passions or love, is represented after the Fall by Jesus, who puts on the robes of love to preserve some hint of divine love in the fallen world. Urizen, the zoa of reason, is the necessary boundary of energy, the wisdom which supplied form to the energies released by the other contraries. In the fallen world, he is the primary usurper of the dominion of other faculties. Tharmas, the zoa of the senses, has, in his paradisiacal form, unrestrained capacity to expand or contract his senses. In the fallen state, these senses remain but in an enervated condition. Sexuality, the sense of touch shared by two, is a means by which fallen man can regain his paradisiacal stature, but it is unfortunately a suppressed sense. The Blakean Fall, which all the personified contraries suffer, is a Fall from the divine state to the blind state, to the state where none of their powers is free to express itself beyond the severe limitations of excessive reason. Each of the contraries has his allotted place in the Fall; each sins either through commission or omission.

Contraries remain a concern of Blake from *The Marriage of Heaven and Hell* to the later prophecies—*The Four Zoas*, (1795-1804), *Milton: A Poem*, (1804-1808), and *Jerusalem: The Emanation of the Giant Albion*, (1804-1820). SThe metaphysic of contraries, the theoretical doctrine, is never denied. The opposition of energy to reason, however, dramatized in the Orc cycle, is no longer Blake's "main act" in the later books. From Night IX in *The Four Zoas* onward, Los, who embodies something akin to the Romantic concept of the sympathetic imagination, becomes the agent of regeneration. It is he who can project himself into the existence of his polar opposite, can accept the existence of that contrary in the act of self-annihilation and consequently forgive. Thus, the theory of contraries has not altered; any contrary can assume a selfhood in conflict with dialectic progression itself. Los preserves the dialectic while Orc maintains a hierarchy.

Blake's concern with the earthly states of Innocence and Experience, with a fallen body and its contraries, has been associated with religious apocalypse. Blake's apocalypse involves a progression from Innocence to Experience and an acceptance of the contraries in those states. An acceptance of contraries would lead to the destruction of false perception and disequilibrium and eventually to a complete resurrection of the fallen body. Man would again possess divine proportions through a progressive development of his own nature rather than through obedience to the supposed laws of an external deity. Through the faculty of imagination Blake intuits the divinity of man, the falseness of society, and the falseness of laws based upon societal behavior. He perceives the spiritual essence of man, displaying therefore a spiritual rather than a rational brand of humanism. Blake's assumption that man is a fallen god makes his psychology more than a psychology; and it makes his humanism an apocalyptic humanism. His diagnosis of the divided psyche becomes a revelation, and his therapy, an apocalypse. Blake himself dons the mantle of a prophet.

Able to see God and his angels at the age of four, Blake gave precedence in his life to vision over the natural world. He would continue to see through and not with the eye, and what he saw he would draw in bold outline as ineluctable truth. Ultimately, even the heterodoxy of Swedenborgianism was an encroachment upon the supremacy of his own contact with the spiritual world. Early inspired by the revolutionary spirit of the times, he continued throughout his life to advocate a psychic revolution within each person which would lead to regeneration.

Blake's mission throughout his work is always apocalyptic, although he creates a political terrain in the Lambeth books (*The [First] Book of Urizen,* 1794, *The Book of Ahania,* 1795, *The Book of Los,* 1795, and *The Song of Los,* 1795) and a psychological one in his later prophecies (The Four Zoas, Milton, and Jerusalem). His focus moves from a political-societal revolution of apocalyptic proportions to a psychic, perceptual regeneration of each individual person. It is the regenerated person who can perceive both a unity beyond all diversity and a diversity within that unity.

Songs of Innocence and of Experience demonstrates Blake's concern for individual human life, in particular its course from innocence to experience. What are the destructive forces operating early upon man, upon his childhood, which ultimately imprison him and lead to "mind-forged manacles"? In *Songs of Innocence,* a glimpse of energies is uncircumscribed, of what man was and again could be if he rightly freed himself from a limited perception and repressed energies.

The later poems, *The Four Zoas, Milton,* and *Jerusalem,* are large-scale epics whose focus is a particularly Romantic one—epistemological and ontological transformation. Los, hero of the imagination, is not a hero who affirms the values of a culture, nor are his strengths and virtues uniformly admired by that culture. Like traditional epics, Blake's epics begin *in medias res*, but because the natural world is usually seen unclearly, it is worthless to speak of its beginning, middle, or end. Readers who enter the world of Blake's epics enter a psychic world, become "mental travellers," and in purest states reach heights traditionally reserved for deity in the Judeo-Christian tradition and deities in the epics of Homer and Vergil.

Blake's work is not unconnected with the natural world, but he attempts to bracket out all but the irreducible elements of the archetypal, individual human life. Paradoxically, Blake's work is characterized by less structural context than that of any poet of whom one could readily think; yet that work is such a dramatic reaction to the eighteenth century and such a dramatic revelation of the new Romanticism that it is unrivaled as an intense portrait of both sensibilities. In reaction to John Locke's view that the perceiver is separated from the world because of an incapacity to do more than apprehend the secondary qualities of objects, Blake asserted the supremacy of individual perception. Man perceiving is man imagining, an act which encompasses the totality of an individual's energies and personality. What is perceived is dependent upon the imaginative act. The world can only be construed imaginatively. Man, Blake held, can only apprehend the infinity within him through his imagination. The London of Blake's poem of that name is a pitiable place because man's imagination, his poetic genius, is repressed. London is at every moment available for imaginative transformation; so is every object in the natural world. In this view of imagination, Blake foreshadows Samuel Taylor Coleridge and especially Percy Bysshe Shelley and attacks the rationalism of the eighteenth century. The metaphysics of Francis Bacon, Isaac Newton, and Locke were despicable because they elevated rationality and denied imagination, thus standing in the way of regeneration.

Besides disagreeing with the philosophy and psychology of his own day, Blake criticized traditional religious and aesthetic views. Man's fallen perception created the world, not in seven days, but in what became a moment in time. Jesus was a man of revitalized perceptions, a man fully conscious of his unlimited energies. Jesus was thus a supranatural man, one who had achieved the kind of regeneration that Blake felt it was in every person's power to achieve. In art, Blake applauded the firm outline of Michelangelo and Raphael and despised the indeterminacy of Rubens and Titian. The artist who apprehended with strong imagination drew boldly because the truth was clearly perceived. Socially and politically, Blake, unlike Coleridge and William Wordsworth, remained unreconciled to the status quo. Blake's revolutionary zeal, most pronounced in the Lambeth books, remained undiminished, urging him to portray error so that it could be cast out. Only Shelley equals Blake's faith in poetic genius to transform the very nature of man and thus the very nature of the world he perceives.

Songs of Innocence and of Experience shows "the two contrary states of the human soul." The contraries cited in *The Marriage of Heaven and Hell* are "Attraction and Repulsion, Reason and Energy, Love and Hate. . . ." Since, however, these songs are not sung outside either Innocence or Experience but from within those states, the contraries are not fully presented in their ideal forms. The songs are from corrupted states and portray disproportionate contraries. Theoretically, each contrary state acts as a corrective to the other, and contraries in the *Songs of Innocence and of Experience* are suggested either in the text of the poem or in the accompanying design.

The introductory song to the *Songs of Innocence and of Experience* is a good example not only of Blake's view of the role of Innocence and Experience in regeneration but also of the complexity of these seemingly simple songs. This song manages in its twenty lines to present a transition from absolute sensuous Innocence to a recognition of Experience and finally a transition to a higher state. The first stanza presents an almost complete picture of absolute carefree innocence. The adjective "wild" may imply a condemnation of an aspect of absolute Innocence. Because Blake believed that Experience brings an indispensable consciousness of one's actions so that choice becomes possible, the essential flaw in the state of Innocence is that it does not provide the child with alternatives.

The second stanza of this lyric presents the image of the lamb, a symbol of Christ. The lamb, while creating the image of the innocence of Christ, also exhibits the equally true image of Christ crucified. It is this symbol of Experience which brings tears to the child, and on a psychological level, the child is emerging from a "wild" unconscious realm to a realm of consciousness, of Experience.

The third stanza presents two interesting additions: The pipe is replaced by human song and the child weeps with joy. The pipe had first produced laughter and then tears, but it is the human voice which elicits the oxymoronic reaction of joyful weeping. It is only in the human form that the attributes of the two contrary states of Innocence and Experience can exist harmoniously. "Piping down the valley wild" had brought unconstrained laughter, while the figure of the Christ-lamb had brought a more tearful vision of Experience; yet in stanza 3, such contrary reactions exist, unresolved but coexistent, as do the contrary states which foster them.

The fourth stanza alludes to the loss of childhood through the disappearance of the child of the poem and implies that the elemental properties of Innocence remain after the departure of the physical state of childhood. By plucking the hollow reed, Blake, the piper and singer, reveals a move toward creation which is fully realized in the last stanza. From the vision of Experience of stanza 2, and the acceptance of the necessary contrary states of Innocence and Experience through their inherent qualities, laughter and tears, presented in stanza 3, Blake has reached the higher plateau of conscious selflessness described in stanzas 4 and 5. Through the act of creation, the conscious selfless act, which intends to give joy to every child, the conscious selflessness of Blake's paradisiacal reintegrated state is achieved.

In *The Book of Thel* (1789), Thel, a young girl in Innocence, is fearful of advancing to a state of Experience. Lily, cloud, clay, and worm, symbols of innocence and experience, try to allay her fears. Experience may contain key contraries in extreme form; it may be the wrath of the father and the restraint of morality and the curtailment of vision, but it is a state which provides Thel her only opportunity of advancement, of completion and eventual salvation. Experience is a necessary step to the "peace and raptures holy" described by the Cloud. Thel, however, surveys the traditional misfortune of Experience—mortality. She finds no meaningful comfort in the Lily's belief that from Experience, from death, one flourishes "in eternal vales." Thel laments the consciousness that is hers when she takes a trial step into Experience. She finds morality, which represses sexual energy, unbearable. Thus, in spite of the eventual "peace and raptures holy" to which Thel can proceed from a state of Experience, her first look at that state proves too much for her. She flees Experience and consciousness to the vales of Har, the land of superannuated children, described in the poem *Tiriel;* it is a land of unfulfilled innocents who have refused to graduate into the world of Experience. A *Songs of Innocence* poem, "The Lamb," and a *Songs of Experience* poem, "The Tiger," depict the nature of perception in those states and the contraries which abide in each state. The poems may be viewed as "contrary poems."

The questions of the child in "The Lamb" are not reason's questions but imagination's—questions he can answer because he has perceived the identity of himself, the lamb, and God. The equation is formed thus: The lamb is Christ the lamb; the child is Christ as a child; and the lamb and child are therefore joined by their mutual identity with Christ. In Innocence, all life is perceived as one and holy. Since there are two contrary states of the human soul and "The Lamb" is a product of only one, Innocence, it is not possible to conclude that this poem depicts Blake's paradisiacal state. The vines in the design are twisting about the sapling on both sides of the engraving, indicating in traditional symbolism the importance of going beyond childhood into Experience. If the child-speaker can see all life as one, can imaginatively perceive the whole, he cannot perceive the particularity, the diversity, which makes up that unity, which

Experience's reason so meticulously numbers and analyzes. Even as the adult speaker of "The Tiger" can see only a fragmented world which his imagination is too weak to unify, so the child-speaker cannot see the fragments that compose the world.

The spontaneity and carefree abandon of the lamb in Innocence can in Experience no longer be perceived in the form of a lamb. The perceiver in Experience fears the energy of Innocence and therefore shapes it into a form which his reason has deemed frightening—that of a tiger. This form possessed by the tiger of the poem "The Tiger" is symmetrical, its symmetry lying in its perfect relationship with the energy it contains. It is only a "fearful symmetry" to the perceiver in Experience who is riddled with the prejudices of Experience, prejudices regarding what is good and what is evil, what is rational and what is irrational, or wild. The moral hierarchy of Experience—good is good and evil is evil—does not permit the perceiver in Experience to perceive a Keatsian "fineness" in the tiger, a marvelous interrelationship of form and energy.

The reader goes back and forth in this poem from a vision of the energies of the unconscious mind to a perception of the boundaries of those energies. It is the mixture of energy and boundary which the speaker-perceiver finds disturbing. The tiger in the first stanza is seen as a burning figure in the night, perhaps symbolizing the burning vibrant passions repressed in the darkened areas of the mind. The tiger perceived by the speaker can live only in the dark since both reason and moral hierarchy have relegated it to that realm. The tiger is, in its energies, in its fire, too great for the conscious mind to accept; yet, like a recurrent nightmare, the tiger burns brightly and cannot be altogether denied. The tiger cannot be quietly integrated into the personality of the speaker-perceiver without doing severe damage to the structure of self carefully fabricated by reason and moral hierarchy. Rather than transform himself, question himself, the speaker-perceiver questions the tiger's creator. What creator could possibly give form to such uncontrollable energy? How can such energy be satisfactorily bounded? The perceiver in Experience assumes that such energy as the tiger represents can only be denied through repression. It cannot be given necessary form; it must be perceived as having a fearful rather than a fine form. This speaker turns questioner and by his questioning reveals his subservience to analytical reason.

The questioner proceeds under the assumption that no creation can be greater than its creator, that in some way the dangerous, fearful energies of the tiger are amenable to that creator, are somehow part of that creator. Where is such a creator to be found? More specifically, where are those burning energies to be found in the spiritual realm? The questioner is already convinced that the creation of the tiger is a presumptuous act and he therefore concludes that Satan is the great presumer. This tiger is, therefore, in the questioner-perceiver's mind, Satan's work, a hellish creation forged in the fires not of Blake's Hell but of a traditional Hell.

The final questions to be asked are merely rhetorical. The questioner has decided that *his* creator could never have created the tiger. The creator involved here has dared to create the tiger. There exists, therefore, a Manichaean split, a desperate attempt to answer the problem of the existence of evil. Part of man has been made by God and that part is good, while Satan has made the evil part of man, the part symbolized by the tiger. The only symbol of energy that the questioner-perceiver is prepared to face is that of the lamb. Yet, while the lamb suffced in Innocence as representative of certain energies, it is no longer indicative of the growth Sof energy which is a mature person's in Experience. The tiger of Experience expresses the symbolic balance of energy and reason, fire and form; however, only a perceiver whose energies are brought from Innocence and matured in Experience under the guidance of reason in necessary proportions can perceive that balance. This uncorrupted perceiver can see the child lying down with the tiger, as in "A Little Girl Found." That tiger is the perfect symbol of the balance of contraries and is perceived as such; the tiger of "The Tiger" is also a perfect symbol but improperly perceived.

The *raison d'être* of the incorporation of all contraries as they are perceived in the two contrary states, Innocence and Experience, is provided in *The Marriage of Heaven and Hell*. It fulfills more than a mere metaphysical role. It is the foundation of Blake's prophecy, the basis not of extended system but of vision. *The Marriage of Heaven and Hell* preserves the whole body of contraries by a relentless attack upon all divisive factors. Dualism in all areas is negated and the suppressed half of the fallen body, represented by the suppressed division of contraries, is supported and affirmed in opposition to the deadening voices of the "Angels."

The framework of *The Marriage of Heaven and Hell* is traditional Judeo-Christian religion and morality. Blake completely alters and destroys this traditional structure and replaces it with an equal acceptance of the two contrary states of the human soul and their inherent contraries. Energies which are indigenous to childhood must take their place alongside the necessary contraries of Experience—reason, repulsion, and hate. The traditional moral hierarchy of good over evil allows one state and its contraries to have ascendancy over the other. Blake boldly adopts the standard nomenclature and marries good and evil as true opposites, essential contraries. Both the passive and active traits of human nature are assumed. Rather than an exclusive emphasis on good, as in the Judeo-Christian ethic, or evil, as in sadism, Blake seeks the reintegration of the unity of man through the opposition of these strategic contraries. Once Blake's doctrine of contraries as presented in *The Marriage of Heaven and Hell* is understood, it becomes clearer what *Songs of Innocence and of Experience* is describing, what the basis of Orc's battle on behalf of energy in the Lambeth books is, and in what way Los preserves the contraries in the later books.

The Marriage of Heaven and Hell is a theoretical base for Blake's vision; however, the form of the work is by no means expository. It presents a dialectic of contraries in dialectical form. Blake's dialectic is not a system of reason in the Hegelian sense, not a system leading to an external synthesis and to the creation of new contraries. Blake's dialectic is composed of contraries immanent in the human personality, contraries which do not change but which generate increasing energy.

In the "Argument" section, "keeping the perilous path" refers to primal unity, Blakean primal unity, and means maintaining all contraries. The man in the vale maintains the dialectic between conscious and unconscious mind. In Blake's view, once the "path is planted," once the Fall has occurred, man must journey forward through Innocence and Experience to reintegration.

In plate 3, Blake declares the immanence of contraries within the human personality and denies the moral dualism of the Judeo-Christian ethic. These contraries are not illusory; their opposition is real, but one contrary does not subsume or upset another. No hierarchy is imposed. The energies which are traditionally classified as "good" are not superior to the energies traditionally classified as "evil." Neither is the reverse true, since Blake is no disciple of the Marquis de Sade. In Blake's view, the hierarchy of morality is particularly insidious since it prevents people from espousing contraries and achieving the progression resulting from that act.

In plate 4, Blake indicates that the contraries transcend the dualism of body and soul. It is the Devil who proclaims the body as the only portion of the soul and thus Blake's Devil is his hero, his spokesman. This identification of the soul with the observable, physical body, when combined with Blake's notion of progression based on a dialectic of contraries, implies that although the body is a mere portion of the soul, its most debased portion, it is the only medium available to man by which an amplified body, a spiritual body or soul, can be reached. Contraries existing within the body which are perceived in this fallen world are accepted in pursuit of "ideal" or amplified contraries. In Blake's view, the body and its contraries are sacred.

In plates 5 and 6, Blake's Devil says that energies are too often repressed. The person who represses his or her energies in turn suppresses the energies of others. Plate 5 begins the "Proverbs of Hell" section. The proverbs are designed to strengthen the imagination of the reader so that the dynamic of contraries is perceived. Once the reader perceives imaginatively the reality of this dynamic, the dynamic is maintained and energy ensues. Ever-increasing energy leads to ever-expanding perception, and perception, for Blake, ultimately determines ontology. The Proverbs of Hell are pithy "consciousness raisers," each demonstrating the dynamic or dialectic of contraries in both content and form.

Plate 11 continues Blake's assault on the priesthood. In plates 12 and 13, Blake allies himself with the prophets, Isaiah and Ezekiel—voices of "firm persuasion" and "honest indignation." In plates 14 and 15, Blake describes the creative process that produced *The Marriage of Heaven and Hell.* He further defines the psychic terrain in plate 16 by presenting two groups, "Prolific" and "Devourer," that can be seen as personified categories incorporating all dichotomies previously discussed in *The Marriage of Heaven and Hell;* Devil-Evil-Energy-Hell are subsumed by the Prolific, and Angel-Good-Reason-Heaven are subsumed by the Devourer. Plates 17 to 20 contain Blake's "fantastic" satirical drama between an Angel and Blake, as Devil. Limited or bounded perception creates a world and an end for itself that a liberated, diabolical perception can alter in the twinkling of an eye. The Angel perceives such a world of error because he has no sense of the dynamic interplay of contraries, no idea that "Opposition is true Friendship."

Some of the political implications of Blake's doctrines in *The Marriage of Heaven and Hell* are evident in *The French Revolution* (wr. 1791). This poem of twenty pages, posthumously published, has no accompanying designs and was written for the radical publisher Joseph Johnson. It is conjectured that by 1791 it was dangerous for an Englishman to express a revolutionary enthusiasm inspired by the French Revolution. Blake's own political radicalism is not in this poem couched in symbolic terms, and therefore he may have had second thoughts about printing it and risking imprisonment. Blake chronicles, with ample poetic license, the period in France from June 19 to July 15, when the King's troops were dispersed. Louis XVI and his nobles debate their course of action in the light of the growing revolution outside, and they finally decide to remove the troops surrounding Paris. In Blake's telling, this decision represents a renewed perception on the part of the King and his nobles. The Bastille, a symbol of political repression, consequently falls. In actuality, the Bastille fell before the decision was made to remove the King's troops.

There is more of what will become Blake's completed mythology in *America: A Prophecy* (1793) than there is in *The French Revolution.* Besides historical characters such as George Washington, Benjamin Franklin, and Thomas Paine, Blake here introduces Orc and Urizen, personifications of revolutionary energy and reason. In a Preludium or Preface, Vala, the shadowy female who symbolizes North America, is in chains. Her liberation occurs through her sexual relations with the fiery Orc. To Blake, therefore, a successful American revolution is not only political but also sexual. George III is the Angel of Albion (England) who worships Urizen and Urizen's law of the Ten Commandments. These two attempt to saturate America with their own diseases by sending a plague across the Atlantic. The plague is countered, however, by the revolutionary zeal of Orc, who replaces the oppressions of Urizen with genuine political and sexual freedom. All Europe is affected by this revolution, but England, seeking the protection of Urizen, hurries to rebuild the gates of repression, the gates of moral good and evil and a dominant rationality.

Blake's Orc, revolutionary energy, successfully counters Urizen ("your reason") just as the French Revolution countered the *ancien régime*. But the French Revolution lost its revolutionary energy in the tyranny of Napoleonic France. It became obvious to Blake that historical, political solutions—revolutions—could not effect a break in the historical cycle, a break that would be an apocalypse. Thus, in *The Four Zoas*, Orc becomes a destructive force in nature, an opponent of reason totally oblivious to reason's importance on a regenerated scale. Orc becomes as tied to the natural, unregenerated cycle as Vala, the embodiment of the natural process itself.

Although Urizen is easily defeated by Orc in *America*, he remains an important character in Blake's myth. He is at once Nobodaddy, a comical, ridiculous father figure, and the Ancient of Days, depicted with grandeur in the frontispiece to *Europe: A Prophecy* (1794). Urizen represents the urge to structure and systematize, to reduce all to rational terms. In the language of our own day, he recognizes only what can be quantified, and, like a good logical positivist, seeks empirical referents to instill meaning in words.

Europe can be viewed as a continuation of *America* in which revolutionary zeal has been replaced by a repressive conservatism which binds both energies and perceptions. The time is the birth of Jesus, a time of possible regeneration through his example. This possibility is not realized and the world falls into a long sleep, an eighteen-hundred-year sleep of Nature. Los, the poetic genius, naïvely rejoices in a promise of peace while Urizen is attempting to rule outside his own domain; and Los's female counterpart, Enitharmon, is a victim of Urizen's dominion and seeks to bind sexual love with moral law. Urizen solidifies his rule, his brazen book of law which ignores imagination, forgiveness, and the necessity of self-annihilation. Edmund Burke and William Pitt, represented by the characters Palamabron and Rintrah, are also under the dominion of Urizen and Enitharmon. The revolutionary spirit of the youth of England is doomed. Pitt-Rintrah three times attempts to lead England to war, into total devastation. In Blake's view, however, Newton and his system are the real beginning of devastation in England. Newton's blast on the trumpet does not lead to glorious apocalypse but to death-in-life. Enitharmon wakes and calls her perverted children to her—materialism, delusion, hypocrisy, sensualism, and seduction. The poem ends with Orc inspiring the French Revolution, the spirit of which will be challenged by a Urizenic England. Los, the poetic genius, summons his sons to the coming strife, but it is as yet unclear what his precise role will be. That role is defined in *The Four Zoas, Milton,* and *Jerusalem.*

In *The [First] Book of Urizen* and *The Book of Los,* Blake does not present a cryptic intermingling of history and myth but rather a first attempt at describing his cosmogony and theogony. *The Book of Los* tells the story of the Fall from Los's point of view and *The [First] Book of Urizen* from Urizen's point of view. Thus, the texts interconnect and gloss each other. The Fall is a fall into creation, one precipitated by Urizen's desire for painless joy, for laws binding everything, for "One King, one God, one Law." Urizen's usurpation of power is clearly an act of the Selfhood, a condition in which the legitimacy and importance of other energies are not recognized.

Los, as imagination, is the epistemological faculty, by which truth or error is perceived. Urizen's revolt on behalf of reason skews perception and plunges Los into the Fall. The world of time and space, the Natural World, is formed by Los, and both Los and Urizen, fallen, are bound to this Natural World. A fall into sexuality follows the fall into materiality. Sexuality is subject to moral constraints. Science is a woven "woof" which is created to hide the void. Orc is born but his youthful exuberance is bound by the perversions of the Net of Religion, a direct product of the perverted dream of Reason. Urizen explores the dens of the material world and observes the shrunken nature of a humanity which has completely forgotten its eternal life.

The Song of Los can be viewed as the mythological framework for *America* and *Europe.* The first part of Los's song, "Africa," recounts history leading up to George III–Guardian Prince of Albion's war against the Americans, as depicted in *America.* What exists here is also a historical counterpart to the mythology presented in *The [First] Book of Urizen* and *The Book of Los.* Dark delusion was given Moses on Sinai, abstract law to Pythagoras, Socrates, and Plato, a wretched gospel to Jesus, and the reprehensible Philosophy of the Five Senses to Newton and Locke. The second section,

"Asia," is a continuation of *Europe;* it does not speak of events but of the psychological-physiological consequences of Urizen's reign. King, Priest, and Counsellor can only restrain, dismay, and ruin humanity in the service of Urizen. Orc rages over France, but the earth seems too shrunken, humankind too imprisoned to heed. Again, Orc himself, as revolutionary energy, is a questionable savior, since he is described as a serpent. The energy of the French Revolution had become debased, and although Blake hoped for a renewal of its original energies, he was already too skeptical of revolution to present Orc as a hero.

The Book of Ahania takes its name from Urizen's female counterpart or emanation, who comes into existence when Fuzon, an Orc-like figure, battles Urizen. Urizen immediately calls Ahania sin, hides her, and suffers jealousy. Ahania becomes the "mother of Pestilence," the kind of pestilence that is a result of a sexuality restrained by the moral law. Urizen's mind, totally victimized by a repressive rationality and the resulting morality, breeds monsters. From the blood of one of these monsters, Urizen forms a bow and shoots a rock at Fuzon, killing him. Fuzon is pictured as a revolutionary who has assumed the seat of tyranny previously occupied by Urizen. Urizen nails Fuzon to a tree, an act which imitates the death of Christ, Christ as rebel. Fuzon dies because he has not broken the material cycle and is thus vulnerable to the repressive laws of the material world. In the same fashion, the creators of the French Revolution failed to achieve a significant ontological and epistemological revolution and therefore became ensnared once again in nets of mystery which led to the Reign of Terror. Fuzon and the French Revolutionaries achieve no true revolution and fall victim to the "black rock" which is formed by a mind whose energies are repressed in the name of reason and its countless offshoots.

One of the ways to Blakean regeneration is through sexuality, specifically through a reassimilation of the female emanation and the re-creation of the Edenic androgynous body. In *Visions of the Daughters of Albion* (1793), Oothoon is a female emanation; Theotormon is her male counterpart and a victim of a repressive moral code; Bromion is a spokesman of that code. Sexually, Oothoon represents the Prolific; the Devourer equivalent, the opposing sexual nature, must be created in Experience. Jerusalem, in the poem *Jerusalem*, becomes that female emanation cognizant of the nature of the regenerated, androgynous body, and she has gained that knowledge in Experience.

Oothoon is raped by Bromion, and Theotormon treats her like a harlot because she has been raped. Oothoon's imagination gives her a vision of her intrinsic sexual nature. Her vision is of the body, the sexual body no less, a body that is not distinct from the soul. In her newfound identity,

Oothoon tries to bring Theotormon to the same vision, tries to bring him beyond the moral categories; but Theotormon demands a rational proof for all living things. Why, he asks implicitly, should he believe Oothoon is pure when the moral code clearly states that she is not pure? Bromion declares that only what can be perceived by the five senses has merit. Oothoon attacks priests and their restraining moral ethic but finally gives up trying to win Theotormon to her newly liberated vision. Her comprehension of the warped picture of sexuality in Experience as demonstrated by Theotormon and Bromion causes her to conclude that Experience has nothing to offer. Although she is not blinded regarding her own sexual nature, she is unable to reunite with Theotormon, male sexuality, and is denied a vision of sexuality based on energies of both Innocence and Experience. Thus, sexual relations, androgyny, and regeneration are denied both Oothoon and Theotormon.

The Four Zoas is an unengraved poem written in two overlapping stages. The main characters, Luvah, Urizen, Tharmas, and Urthona, are the "zoas" of the human personality, each representing an inherent, indivisible quality of the human personality. But these characters are true characters and not mere allegorical representations. *The Four Zoas* is Blake's account of a split in the Edenic personality of Man, called Albion, of a Fall into the cycle of the natural world, and of the labors of Los, the imagination, to reunite and regenerate the four Zoas. This is both a historical drama inevitably unfolded in time and space and a psychological drama, one in which time and space have no validity. As a historical drama, it is possible to make the kinds of historical connections made in *Europe* or *America*, but this is not a consistent base from which to read the poem, nor will expectations of a conventional narrative structure be at all fruitful.

The poem begins when Luvah and Vala rush from the loins and into the heart and on to the brain, where they replace Urizen's ordering of the body's life with their own cyclical, generative ordering. This sleeping man, Albion, who has within him the whole world—the powers to contract and expand—wakes up in Night VIII of the poem. Albion was asleep because he was in repose in Beulah, a state of threefold perception between Eden (fourfold perception) and Generation (twofold perception). To be in Beulah is to be at rest from the dynamic interplay of contraries of Eden, Blake's paradisiacal state. The aura of Eden pervades Beulah but the threat of the lower state, Generation, is always present. A fall into a reduced perception is always imminent. In *The Four Zoas* that fall occurs. The fall into Generation is a fall into the natural world; it is Blake's version of the biblical Fall.

In the state of Generation, Urizen declares himself God; the "mundane shell," the material world, is built, and Jesus appears and is sacrificed so that regeneration can become possible. Jesus is identified with Luvah, love, with Orc, revolutionary energy battling Urizen in the Lambeth books, and with Albion, Universal Man. Under Jesus' inspiration, Los perceives the errors of the Fall and begins to build Jerusalem, a spiritual freedom in which regeneration is possible. From Night IX in *The Four Zoas* onward into *Milton* and *Jerusalem*, Los, who embodies something akin to the Romantic concept of sympathetic imagination, becomes the agent of regeneration. It is Los who can project himself into the existence of his contrary, can accept the existence of that contrary in the act of "self-annihilation," and can consequently forgive. Thus, in the later books, the theory of contraries is not altered; any contrary can assume a selfhood in conflict with dialectical progression itself. Los preserves the dialectic, while Orc maintains a hierarchy—"saviour" and "villain."

The historical John Milton is revived in Blake's *Milton* so that he can experience a personal self-annihilation which leads to the incorporation of his Spectre, Satan. Blake's Milton is a Milton of energy and imagination, a Milton determined to correct his view (expressed in *Paradise Lost*, 1667) that love "hath his seat in Reason." Through self-annihilation, Blake's Milton acknowledges the validity of Reason, his Spectre. Once Milton is united with his Spectre, he can preach effectively to the public. The repression of the reasoning power is peculiar only to the Blakean "heroes," such as Blake's Milton. Outside this Blakean world, in the world of Innocence and Experience, the reasoning power is not repressed but assumes the role of usurper, a faculty of mind which has overridden the powers of all other faculties. Reason as Blake perceived it in the eighteenth century was in complete control. It is this unrepressed, dominant, reasoning power which Milton calls a "Negation." The reasoning power which Blake's Milton finally accepts is reason as Spectre, not as Negation, reason in its Edenic proportions.

An act of self-annihilation also precipitates the union of female emanation and the fallen male principle. Blake's Milton is reconciled with his emanation, Ololon. What Blake's Milton undergoes here becomes a precedent for what Los and other contraries will undergo. In annihilating his Selfhood, the Los-Blake-Devil Selfhood, Blake's Milton shows that reason is a necessary contrary, that man is not ruled by energies alone. The Spectre as reason has been accepted and Blake's Milton attains an expanded perception. His emanation perceives her power fade. In "delighting in his delight," they are again one in sexuality.

Blake's Milton enables the contraries to be saved, enables a dynamic interplay of contraries once again to take place. In contrast, Orc's obdurate maintenance of his own Selfhood and his denial of Urizen's reality in any proportions does not preserve Edenic contraries and cannot therefore lead to regeneration. Blake's Milton achieves self-annihilation through forgiveness, itself based upon the imagination. It is Los, the imagination, who perceives the dialectic of contraries and recognizes the message of continued forgiveness. It is Los, the imagination, who is employed by each contrary in recognition of its polar opposite.

In *Jerusalem*, Los and the Spectre of Urthona take center stage. Los addresses his Spectre as "my Pride & Self-righteousness," indicating that the Spectre's presence tends to affirm Los's obdurate Selfhood. Throughout *Jerusalem*, the reader witnesses a "compensatory" relationship between the Spectre and Los, although the Spectre seems to be "watching his time with glowing eyes to leap upon his prey." In chapter IV, Los ends this continuing struggle with his Spectre by accepting it. Once Los, identified here with Blake, becomes one with his Spectre, he appears to Albion, fallen humankind, in the form of Jesus and preaches forgiveness based on imaginative identification and self-annihilation. Jesus-Los annihilates himself before Albion and thus points to the necessary destruction of the Selfhood. Overwhelmed by this act, imaginatively caught in Jesus-Los' sacrifice, the albatross drops from Albion's neck, and it is the Selfhood. This is the apocalyptic moment when Albion, like the phoenix, descends to the flames and rises anew. Regeneration is intimately connected with self-annihilation, as it was in *Milton*.

Albion's emanation, Jerusalem, is also spiritual freedom. A reassimilation of Jerusalem generates a climate of freedom in which contraries can interact. Jerusalem as an emanation is beyond morality. She represents the whole of life, but a fallen Albion applies "one law" to her. Because of this application of a rigid "one law," a rigid hierarchical ethic, Jerusalem is separated from Albion. A female emanation repressed becomes a tyrant. Blake gives readers a close view of this "proud Virgin-Harlot," whom he calls Vala. The Vala whom Blake presents is corrupt, since she stands for restraint in all areas, especially moral, as opposed to Jerusalem-as-liberty. The Vala figure, advocate of a repressive morality, both tempts and lures, and also upholds the sense of sin. She thus becomes woman-as-tyrant. She is the femme fatale who incites desire but never acts. Such a morality turns love into prostitution, the free lover into a prostitute.

Again, Los, the imagination, perceives the validity of Jesus' word to Jerusalem regarding forgiveness, annihilation, and regeneration. Los applies what he has learned, unites with his own Spectre, and sends him forth to preach the methods of regeneration—forgiveness and self-annihilation. Albion regains his Jerusalem; spiritual freedom once again exists; and England itself has apocalyptically become Jerusalem, the city of God.

Other literary forms · William Blake's prose includes *An Island in the Moon* (written c. 1784), *To the Public: Prospectus* (1793), *A Descriptive Catalogue* (1809), marginalia, and letters. It is almost a given with Blake scholarship and criticism that the interrelation of poetry and design is vital. David V. Erdman's *The Illuminated Blake* (1975) includes all of Blake's illuminated works, text, and design, with a plate-by-plate commentary.

Select works other than poetry
FICTION: *An Island in the Moon*, wr. c. 1784 (published posthumously); *To the Public: Prospectus*, 1793.
NONFICTION: *A Descriptive Catalogue*, 1809.
ILLUSTRATIONS AND ENGRAVINGS: *The Complaint and the Consolation: Or, Night Thoughts*, by Edward Young, 1797; *Blair's Grave*, 1808; *The Prologue and Characters of Chaucer's Pilgrims*, 1812; *The Pastorals of Virgil*, 1821; *Illustrations of the Book of Job*, 1825; *Illustrations of Dante*, 1827.

Joseph Natoli

Bibliography · On Blake's life, see Peter Ackroyd, *Blake: A Biography*, 1996. G. E. Bentley, Jr.'s *Blake Records*, 1969, and *Blake Records Supplement*, 1988, provide essential information. Bentley's *Blake Books*, 1977, and *Blake Books Supplement*, 1995, are authoritative bibliographies of books by and about Blake. Northrop Frye's *Fearful Symmetry*, 1947, and David Erdman's historicist study, *Prophet Against Empire*, 1954, rev. ed. 1977, have inspired two major approaches. Building on Frye's approach are Leslie Tannenbaum's *Biblical Tradition in Blake's Early Prophecies*, 1982; Nelson Hilton's *Literal Imagination*, 1983; V. A. De Luca's *Words of Eternity*, 1991; and Robert N. Essick's *William Blake and the Language of Adam*, 1991. E. P. Thompson's *Witness Against the Beast*, 1993; Morris Eaves's *The Counter-Arts Conspiracy*, 1992; and Jonathan Mee's, *Dangerous Enthusiasm*, 1992, further examine Blake's relation to history. Robert N. Essick's *William Blake Printmaker*, 1980, and Joseph Viscomi's *Blake and the Idea of the Book*, 1993, are essential for understanding Blake's notions about textuality and his methods of production.

ROBERT BLY

Born: Madison, Minnesota; December 23, 1926

Poetry • *The Lion's Tail and Eyes: Poems Written out of Laziness and Silence*, 1962 (with James Wright and William Duffy) • *Silence in the Snowy Fields*, 1962 • *The Light Around the Body*, 1967 • *The Teeth Mother Naked at Last*, 1970 • *Jumping out of Bed*, 1973 • *Sleepers Joining Hands*, 1973 • *Point Reyes Poems*, 1974 • *Old Man Rubbing His Eyes*, 1974 • *The Morning Glory*, 1975 • *This Body Is Made of Camphor and Gopherwood*, 1977 • *This Tree Will Be Here for a Thousand Years*, 1979 • *The Man in the Black Coat Turns*, 1981 • *Out of the Rolling Ocean and Other Love Poems*, 1984 • *Loving a Woman in Two Worlds*, 1985 • *Selected Poems*, 1986 • *The Apple Found in the Plowing*, 1989 • *The Soul Is Here for Its Own Joy*, 1997

Achievements • Robert Bly is arguably the central poet of his generation. His wide-ranging achievements in poetry, criticism, and translation, as well as his work as editor and itinerant apologist for poetry and various social causes, have made him one of the most conspicuous, ubiquitous, and controversial poets in the United States since the mid-1960's. His significance and influence extend well beyond his own work.

Bly's various accomplishments have been rewarded by a Fulbright Fellowship for translation (1956-1957), the Amy Lowell Traveling Fellowship (1964), two Guggenheim fellowships (1965 and 1972), and a Rockefeller Foundation Grant (1967). In 1968 *The Light Around the Body*, his most controversial collection of poetry, won the National Book Award.

Biography • Born in the small farming community of Madison, Minnesota, Robert Bly grew up, as he said, a "Lutheran Boy-god." He attended a one-room school in his early years. Upon graduation from high school, he enlisted in the navy, where he first become interested in poetry. After the war, Bly enrolled at St. Olaf's College in Northfield, Minnesota, but after only one year there, he transferred to Harvard University. At Harvard he read "the dominant books" of contemporary American poetry, associated with other young writers (among them John Ashbery, Frank O'Hara, Kenneth Koch, Adrienne Rich, and Donald Hall), worked on *The Harvard Advocate* (which he edited in his senior year), delivered the class poem, and graduated magna cum laude in 1950.

Having decided to be a poet, and seeking solitude, Bly moved back to

Minnesota; then, in 1951, still "longing for 'the depths,' " he moved to New York City, where he lived alone for several years, reading widely and writing his early poems. In 1953 he moved to Cambridge, Massachusetts, and in 1954 to Iowa City, where he enrolled in the creative writing program at the University of Iowa. His M.A. thesis consisted of a short collection of poems entitled "Steps Toward Poverty and Death" (1956). Bly was married to Carolyn McLean in 1955, and in 1956 they moved to Oslo, Norway, via a Fulbright grant. In Norway, Bly sought out his family roots, read widely, and translated contemporary Norwegian poetry.

Jerry Bauer

In 1957, back in Minnesota, living now on the family farm, Bly continued his work as a translator. In 1958 he founded a magazine, *The Fifties* (which would become *The Sixties, The Seventies*, and *The Eighties*), in which he published his translations and early literary criticism. His first book of poetry, "Poems for the Ascension of J. P. Morgan," he did not publish, but in 1962 he published two books: *The Lion's Tail and Eyes: Poems Written out of Laziness and Silence* (written with his friends James Wright and William Duffy), and *Silence in the Snowy Fields*, his first independent book of poetry.

By the mid-1960's Bly was actively engaged in the anti-Vietnam War movement. He and David Ray formed a group called American Writers Against the Vietnam War, and they published an anthology entitled *A Poetry Reading Against the Vietnam War* (1966). Bly attended draft card turn-ins, and he demonstrated at the Pentagon in 1967. When his second book of poems, *The Light Around the Body* (1967)—filled with his outspoken poems against the war—won the National Book Award in 1968, Bly donated the prize money to the draft resistance.

During the 1970's, Bly's interests and activities diversified considerably. He studied Sigmund Freud, Carl Jung, Eastern meditation, myths and fairy tales, philosophy, and psychology. He organized conferences on "Great Mother and New Father" culture and consciousness. Bly's poetry, social commentary, and literary criticism during this period reflected his wide-ranging interests. By this point in his career, he said, he believed that he had "gotten about half-way to the great poem."

In 1979 Bly and his wife of more than twenty-five years were divorced. In 1980 he was married to Ruth Ray; they moved to Moose Lake, Minnesota, and lived there for ten years before moving to Minneapolis in 1990.

During the 1980's, Bly continued to work at a rapid pace, writing and publishing widely in several genres, translating, giving readings throughout the United States and overseas, and holding meetings and seminars for groups of women and men. His books during the 1980's document as well as anything the life and activities of this exceedingly visible and yet, finally, extremely private individual.

Analysis · Since Robert Bly has habitually brought his wide-ranging interests in literary history, myth, fairy tales, philosophy, psychology, politics, social concerns, and poetry past and present into his own work, his poetry reflects these interests and is enriched by them. Furthermore, because he has been prolific and unsystematic, even at times seemingly self-contradictory, he is extremely difficult to categorize and analyze. Nevertheless, it is possible—indeed necessary—to consider Bly's poetry in terms of the series of various phases it has gone through. These phases, although they are also reflected in Bly's other writings and involvements, are, finally, most evident in his poetry.

Bly's first published book of poetry, *Silence in the Snowy Fields*, remains the best example to date of his deepest obsession: the notion that a personal, private, almost mystical aura adheres to and inheres with the simplest things in the universe—old boards, for example, or a snowflake fallen into a horse's mane. These things, observed in the silence of contemplation and set down honestly and simply in poems, may, Bly believes, inform human beings anew of some sense of complicity, even communion, they have always had with the world, but have forgotten. Bly's focus has caused his work to be labeled "deep image" poetry. In a 1981 essay, "Recognizing Image as a Form of Intelligence," he explained the term's application to his work: "When a poet creates a true image, he is gaining knowledge; he is bringing up into consciousness a connection that has been largely forgotten." In this sense, these early poems provide the reader with the re-created experience of Bly's own epiphanic moments in the silences of "snowy fields," and they become his means of sharing such silences with his readers.

The epigraph to *Silence in the Snowy Fields*, "We are all asleep in the outward man," from the seventeenth century German mystic Jacob Boehme, points up both the structural and the thematic principles upon which Bly builds his book. The three sections of the book suggest a literal and a mental journey. The second, central section, "Awakening," contains twenty-three of the forty-four poems in the book and serves as a structural and thematic transition from "Eleven Poems of Solitude," the first section, to the final section, "Silence on the Roads," which sends both book and reader, via the central "awakening," outward into the world. The solitude and contemplative silence of this first book, then, prepare both poet and reader for the larger world of Bly's work.

The way the world impinges on private life is immediately evident in Bly's next book, *The Light Around the Body*. This is his most famous (or for some, most infamous) book. Like *Silence in the Snowy Fields*, *The Light Around the Body* shows the strong influence of Boehme (four of the five sections of the book have epigraphs from Boehme), especially in terms of the dichotomy of the inward and the outward person, the "two languages," one might argue, of Bly's first two books. If *Silence in the Snowy Fields* deals primarily with the inward being, clearly the focus of *The Light Around the Body* is on the outward being—here seen specifically in a world at war.

The Light Around the Body was published in the midst of the American obsession with the Vietnam War, and most of the poems in it are concerned with that war, directly or indirectly. The third, central, section of the book (following sections entitled "The Two Worlds" and "The Various Arts of Poverty and Cruelty") is specifically entitled "The Vietnam War." This is the most definitive, the most outspoken and condemnatory group of poems—by Bly or anyone else—on the war in Vietnam. Bly reserves his harshest criticism for American involvement in the war. He does not mince words, and he names names: "Men like [Dean] Rusk are not men:/ They are bombs waiting to be loaded in a darkened hangar" ("Asian Peace Offers Rejected Without Publication").

Perhaps the most famous poem Bly has written is also his most definitive criticism of the Vietnam War. In "Counting Small-Boned Bodies," the speaker of the poem has been charged with keeping the grisly count of war casualties to be reported on the evening news. Shocked by the mounting death tolls, he finds himself trying to imagine ways to minimize these terrifying statistics. The refrain that runs through the poem is, "If we could only make the bodies smaller." The implication is that if the bodies could be made smaller, then people might, through some insane logic, be able to argue the war away. Bly's poems in *The Light Around the Body* ensure that the war will never be forgotten or forgiven.

The last two sections of *The Light Around the Body* ("In Praise of Grief" and "A Body Not Yet Born") move back "inward" from the "outward" world of the war, just as the first two sections of the book had moved "outward" from the "inward" world of *Silence in the Snowy Fields*. Since the war, however, this new inward world can never again ignore or fail to acknowledge the outward world. Therefore, Bly writes "in praise of grief" as a way of getting through, psychologically speaking, both outward and inward conflicts.

The first three poems of the fourth section of the book define a progression back toward a place of rest, calm, peace. In the third poem the body is described as "awakening" again and finding "nourishment" in the death scenes it has witnessed. Such a psychic regeneration, which parallels the inevitable regeneration of nature after a battle, is what is needed to repair the damage the war has done if people are to be restored to full human nature. Thus, in the final section of the book, although the new body is not yet fully born, it is moving toward birth, or rebirth.

Finally, then, although *The Light Around the Body* will no doubt be most often remembered for the overt antiwar poems in it, from the point of view of Bly's developing poetic philosophy it is best seen as a description of the transition from the outer world back into the inner world.

The psychological movement first suggested and then begun in *The Light Around the Body* is followed further inward by Bly's next important book, *Sleepers Joining Hands* (1973). This book contains three distinctly different sections. The first section consists of a series of short lyric poems. Beginning with "Six Winter Privacy Poems," it comes to a climax with a long poem, "The Teeth Mother Naked at Last," Bly's final, psychological response to the war in Vietnam.

The second section of *Sleepers Joining Hands* consists of an essay in which Bly documents many of the philosophical ideas and psychological themes with which he has long been obsessed and which he has addressed both in his poetry and in his criticism. Bly here summarizes his thinking in terms of Jungian psychology, father and mother consciousness, the theory of the three brains, and other ideas that he groups together as "mad generalizations." This essay, although it is far from systematic, remains an important summary of the sources of many of Bly's most important poems and ideas.

Thus, although *Sleepers Joining Hands* does not contain Bly's most important poetry, it does discuss much of the theory behind that poetry, and it is an extremely important book. In the central essay, Bly describes in detail the way in which "mother consciousness" has come to replay "father consciousness" during the last several centuries. Four "force fields" make up the Great Mother (or Magna Mater), which, according to Bly, is now "moving again in the psyche." The Teeth Mother, one of these force fields, attempts to destroy psychic life. She has been most evident in the Vietnam

War and has caused the "inward" harm that that war has brought to the world. "The Teeth Mother Naked at Last," the climactic poem in the first section of *Sleepers Joining Hands*, like the earlier antiwar poems in *The Light Around the Body*, describes the conditions of psychic reality in terms of the presence of the Teeth Mother. It argues that once the Teeth Mother is acknowledged ("naked at last"), she can be dealt with and responded to, and then the outward physical world can be effectively reconnected with the inward psychic or spiritual world.

"Sleepers Joining Hands," the long title poem that constitutes the collection's third section, is an elaborate and challenging poem, a kind of dream journal/journey with overt Jungian trappings. Thematically, it constantly shifts back and forth between dreamed and awakened states. These thematic shifts are evidenced in the structure of the poem. The poem as a whole is a kind of religious quest based in large part on the Prodigal Son story—one of the great paradigms of the journey motif in Western culture. At the end of the poem, bringing to climax so many of his themes, Bly provides "*An Extra Joyful Chorus for Those/ Who Have Read This Far*" in which "all the sleepers in the world join hands."

The next several books in Bly's canon consist of prose poems. Bly believes that when a culture begins to lose sight of specific goals, it moves dangerously close to abstraction, and that such abstraction is reflected in the poetry of the time. Prose poetry, then, often appears as a way of avoiding too much abstraction. Whether this theory holds up historically or not, it certainly can be made to apply in Bly's case, even if only after the fact—the theory having been invented to explain the practice. Certainly, there is ample reason to think that Bly judged that his own work, influenced by the events the world was witnessing, was moving dangerously toward "abstraction," perhaps most conspicuously so in *Sleepers Joining Hands*. For whatever reason, then, Bly turned, in the middle of his career, to the genre of the prose poem. His prose poems of this period are extremely strong work, arguably his strongest poetry.

The two most important collections of prose poems are *The Morning Glory* (1975; which includes as its central section the ten-poem sequence "Point Reyes Poems," published separately the year before, and one of the strongest sequences of poems Bly has written) and *This Body Is Made of Camphor and Gopherwood* (1977). These poems move "deeply into the visible," as the old occult saying Bly quotes as epigraph to *The Morning Glory* demands, and they are poems written "in a low voice to someone he is sure is listening," as Bly suggested they should be in his essay "What the Prose Poem Carries with It" (1977).

The Morning Glory, like *Silence in the Snowy Fields*, contains forty-four poems, suggestive of a new beginning in Bly's career. The poems follow a rather typical pattern. They begin in the most offhand ways, frequently with the speaker alone outdoors, prepared, through his openness to possibilities, for whatever he may find there. These poems are journeys; they move from the known to the unknown. Therefore, what can be learned from them is often difficult to analyze, especially since Bly frequently only suggests what it is or might be. Indeed, often it seems to be something that the body comes to know and only later—if at all—the mind comprehends. In this sense these are poems of preparation, and they frequently imply apocalyptic possibilities.

The Morning Glory ends with several poems that describe transformations. One of the most important of these, "Christmas Eve Service at Midnight at St. Michael's," involves the personal life of the poet, who, six months after his only brother has been killed in an automobile accident, attends a Christmas Eve service with his parents. He and his parents take Communion together and hear the Christian message. Coming so soon after his brother's death, however, this message is "confusing," since the poet knows that "we take our bodies with us when we go." The poem ends in a reverie of transfiguration in which a man (both brother and Christ), with a chest wound, flies out and off over the water like a large bird.

The basic "religious" theme begun in *The Morning Glory* is continued in *This Body Is Made of Camphor and Gopherwood*. Here Bly writes overtly religious "meditations," thus picking up again the aura of the sacred that has been important in his work since the beginning. Indeed, this book immediately reminds the reader of *Silence in the Snowy Fields*, both thematically and in terms of Bly's basic source material.

There are twenty poems in *This Body Is Made of Camphor and Gopherwood;* they are divided into two thematic units. The first ten poems describe, often through dreams, visions, or dream-visions, "what is missing." Not surprisingly, given this theme, Bly frequently uses the metaphor of sleep and awakening. Indeed, the first poem in the book begins, "When I wake." This awakening is both a literal and an imaginative or metaphoric awakening, and it signals at the outset the book's chief concern.

The second section of the book is filled with intensely heightened, almost ecstatic, visionary poems. The crucial transitional poems in *This Body Is Made of Camphor and Gopherwood*—which is itself a crucial transition in Bly's canon—are "Walking to the Next Farm" and "The Origin of the Praise of God." "Walking to the Next Farm" describes the culmination of the transition "this body" has been going through as the poet, his eyes wild, feels "as if a new body were rising" within him. This new body and the energy it contains are further described and defined in the other central poem, "The Origin of the Praise of God." It begins with exactly the same words with which several other poems in this book begin: "My friend, this body." This poem, in the words of Ralph J. Mills, Jr., "a visionary hymn to the body, . . . dramatizes [the] experience of the inner deity" and thus is the paradigm of the entire prose-poem sequence. By the end of the book, this visionary, mystical, yet still fully physical body is finally fully formed and is "ready to sing" both the poems already heard and the poems ahead.

This Tree Will Be Here for a Thousand Years (1979) is a second collection of "snowy fields" poems. Bly has said that it should be understood as a companion volume to *Silence in the Snowy Fields* and has indicated that a third group of "snowy fields poems" would be published in the future. In this sense, then, *This Tree Will Be Here for a Thousand Years* is a specific, overt attempt on Bly's part to return to his beginnings. Just as it is a return, however, it is also a new beginning in the middle of his career. Bly is clearly a poet obsessed with a need for constant renewal, and in many ways each of his books, although taking a different direction, also retraces each earlier journey from a different vantage point.

Yet perhaps it is not surprising that, although *This Tree Will Be Here for a Thousand Years* is a new beginning for Bly, it is also a darker beginning, a darker journey than the journey he took in *Silence in the Snowy Fields*. Here the journey envisions its end. This, then, is the book of a man facing his mortality, his death, and walking confidently toward it. As Bly puts it in one of these poems, "there are eternities near." At the same time, there is the inevitable paradox that poems outlive the poet who has written them—and, thus, even poems that speak of death outlive the death of their speaker.

Two later books may be seen as companions to each other: *The Man in the Black Coat Turns* (1981) and *Loving a Woman in Two Worlds* (1985). Like *This Tree Will Be Here for a Thousand Years*, these books circle back to Bly's beginnings at the same time that they set out on new journeys. Furthermore, these books are among the most personal and private he has published, and thus they are particularly immediate and revealing.

The Man in the Black Coat Turns is divided into three sections, the central section, as in *The Morning Glory* and *This Body Is Made of Camphor and Gopherwood*, being made up of prose poems. The prose poems here, however, are different from their predecessors in being much more clearly related to Bly's personal experiences; as he says in the first of them, "Many times in poems I have escaped—from myself. . . . Now more and more I long for what I cannot escape from" ("Eleven O'Clock at Night").

More than anything else, the poems in *The Man in the Black Coat Turns* are poems about men. The dominant theme of the book is the father-son relationship. This theme and its association with the book's title is immediately, and doubly, announced at the outset of the book, in the first two poems, "Snowbanks North of the House" and "For My Son, Noah, Ten Years Old," as Bly works the lines of relationship through the generations of his own family: from his father to himself as son, then, as father, through himself to his own son, Noah. The third poem, "The Prodigal Son," places the personal family references into a larger context by relating them to fatherhood and sonship in the New Testament parable. In the final poem in this first section of the book, "Mourning Pablo Neruda," Bly extends the father-son relationship again—this time to include one of his own important poetic "father figures," Pablo Neruda, a poet he has often translated.

The final section of *The Man in the Black Coat Turns* draws all these themes together in "The Grief of Men." This poem is clearly the climactic thesis piece for the whole book. There are, however, a number of important poems grouped together in this last section: "Words Rising," "A Meditation on Philosophy," "My Father's Wedding," "Fifty Males Sitting Together," "Crazy Carlson's Meadow," and "Kneeling Down to Look into a Culvert." In the last of these poems, via the account of a symbolic, ritualized sacrificial death, the poet completes his preparations for another new life.

The poems of *Loving a Woman in Two Worlds* are, for the most part, short—almost half of them contain fewer than eight lines, and eleven of them are only four lines long. Technically speaking, however, this book contains poems in most of the forms and with most of the themes Bly has worked in and with throughout his career. In this sense the collection is rather a tour de force. Many of the poems of *Loving a Woman in Two Worlds* are love poems, and some of them are quite explicitly sexual. The book can be read in terms of the stages of a love relationship. These are poems that focus on the female, on the male and female together, and on the way the man and the woman together share "a third body" beyond themselves, a body they have made "a promise to love."

This book thus charts another version of the "body not yet born" journey with which Bly began his poetry. In the final poem in *Loving a Woman in Two Worlds*, Bly, speaking no doubt to one individual, but to all of his readers as well, writes, "I love you with what in me is unfinished.// . . . with what . . . is still/ changing."

In the 1986 *Selected Poems*, in addition to poems from all of Bly's previous major collections (some of the poems have been revised, in some cases extensively), he has included some early, previously uncollected poems. A brief essay introduces each of the sectional groupings of this book. *Selected Poems*, then, is a compact, convenient collection, and it succinctly represents Robert Bly in the many individual phases of his work.

Other literary forms · Bly has been a prolific critic, translator, and anthologist. His work in these areas complements his poetic accomplishments and has been a significant influence on the internationalization of the literary community in the last third of the twentieth century. His most important works include translations of the poems of Georg Trakl, Juan Ramón Jimènez, Pablo Neruda, Tomas Tranströmer, and Antonio Machado. He has also called attention to the work of other poets through anthologies: *News of the Universe: Poems of Twofold Consciousness* (1980) and *The Winged Life: The Poetic Voice of Henry David Thoreau* (1986).

Bly's writings about the practice of poetry have been published as *Leaping Poetry: An Idea with Poems and Translations* (1975) and *American Poetry: Wildness and Domesticity* (1990). His social criticism has ranged from *A Poetry Reading Against the Vietnam War* (1966, with David Ray) to *Iron John: A Book About Men* (1990), the best-seller that became a primer for the men's movement of the 1990's.

William V. Davis

Bibliography · As might be expected of a literary figure whose public renown is based as much on his socio-politics as on his poetic output, much of the secondary material on Bly deals with him in the context of ideas and his impact on popular culture. For example, the relationship between his poetic vision and his wartime politics is the subject of a chapter in James F. Mersmann's *Out of the Vietnam Vortex: A Study of Poets and Poetry Against the War*, 1974. Howard Nelson's *Robert Bly: An Introduction to the Poetry*, 1984, and William Virgil Davis' *Understanding Robert Bly*, 1988, both provide cogent overviews of the poet's place in contemporary thought and literature. A more in-depth study is Victoria Frenkel Harris' *The Incorporative Consciousness of Robert Bly*, 1992, which examines Bly's poetry in terms of his idea of universalizing poetic processes; it also contains an exhaustive bibliography of work by and about Bly.

ANDRÉ BRETON

Born: Tinchebray, France; February 18, 1896
Died: Paris, France; September 28, 1966

Poetry · *Mont de piété*, 1919 · *Clair de terre*, 1923 · *L'Union libre*, 1931 (*Free Union*, 1982) · *Le Revolver à cheveux blancs*, 1932 · *L'Air de l'eau*, 1934 · *Fata Morgana*, 1941 (English translation, 1982) · *Pleine marge*, 1943 · *Young Cherry Trees Secured Against Hares*, 1946 · *Ode à Charles Fourier*, 1947 (*Ode to Charles Fourier*, 1970) · *Poèmes*, 1948 · *Poésie et autre*, 1960 · *Selected Poems*, 1969 · *Poems of André Breton*, 1982 (includes *Free Union* and *Fata Morgana*, among other selected poems)

Achievements · Above all, André Breton will be remembered as the founder and leader of the Surrealist movement. Of all the avant-garde movements which rocked the foundations of the arts at the beginning of the twentieth century, Surrealism has had perhaps the greatest and longest-lived impact. Surrealism, created in Paris in 1924 by André Breton and a small group of friends, was the last inheritor of a long series of "isms," including Dadaism, German Expressionism, French and Spanish Cubism, Italian Futurism, and Anglo-American Imagism and Vorticism, which attempted to transform modern humankind's conception of the world through artistic innovation. Under the leadership of Breton, Surrealism became the most mature expression of this developing sensibility, not only because of its relatively well developed underlying philosophy—which was both far-reaching and systematic in nature—but also because it eventually came to have the greatest international scope of all of these movements and because it stimulated the production of a vast body of work of great diversity in all the major artistic genres—poetry, fiction, drama, philosophy, painting, sculpture, and film.

Biography · André Breton was born on February 18, 1896, in Tinchebray, a small inland town in the old French province of Normandy. The family soon moved, however, to the fishing port of Lorient, in Brittany, on the Atlantic coast of France. This seaside environment was particularly important later in the poet's life. When Breton first began to write in 1914, his highly imaginative lyrical poems expressed the wondrous abundance of nature and were often filled with images of sea life and other details evoking the maritime setting of his youth—which contrasted sharply with his life in Paris.

Breton was an only child, and his parents seemingly had an unusually strong influence on his personality. His father, who was a merchant, seems almost a prototype of the complacent, self-satisfied bourgeois that the Surrealists were later to attack as the epitome of the social conformity they rejected. Breton's mother, whom he described as straitlaced, puritanical, and harsh in her response to any suggestion of impropriety, must have also been responsible, to a large degree, for his later hatred of restraint and his provocative attitude toward anything he considered conventional.

Being the only child of a comfortably situated family, Breton had much attention lavished on him, and, naturally, his parents had great ambitions for him. He attended school in Paris from 1907 until his graduation in 1912, entering the Sorbonne in 1913 to study medicine. This contact with medicine was also important for the later development of the poet and is reflected in Breton's diverse poetic vocabulary. Even more important, however, was the experience which resulted when Breton was sent to work at the neurological center of the hospital at Nantes during World War I instead of into combat. Breton's experiences as a medical assistant during the war—first at Nantes and later at the psychiatric center at Saint-Dizier, to which he was transferred in 1917—introduced the young, impressionable poet to the bizarre aberrations of mental illness.

During this period, Breton was exposed not only to the diverse forms of mental illness from which the soldiers suffered but also to the theories upon which the practical measures used to treat them were based. Among the most important of these theories were those of Jean-Martin Charcot, Sigmund Freud, and Pierre Janet, each of which contributed an important element to the formulation of Breton's view of the operation, structure, and purpose of the human mind. From Charcot's work, Breton learned of the unlocking of the will through the use of hypnosis and saw some of the dramatic cures it was able to effect. From Freud's work, he learned about the existence of the unconscious, its role in determining mental health, and the method of dream interpretation by which one could reveal its secrets to the dreamer. From Janet's work, he learned about the existence of "psychic automatism" and the means by which it might be evoked—which eventually resulted in his own experiments with automatic writing.

These influences were reflected in three important ways in Breton's later work. First, they resulted in the two important prose experiments in automatic writing that he produced: *Les Champs magnétiques*, written with Philippe Soupault, and *Poisson soluble*, which Breton created alone. The second product of his wartime experience was the novel *Nadja* (1928;

English translation, 1960), which describes the encounter of an autobiographical persona with a mysterious woman who suffers a bizarre and debilitating psychosis. The third product of these influences was *L'Immaculée Conception*, a series of writings undertaken with Paul Éluard, with the purpose of simulating, in verbal form, the thought processes of various types of insanity.

Following the war, Breton came under the influence of Dadaism, which by then had moved its base of operation from Zurich to Paris. The heyday of Dada in Paris was brief, however, lasting from January of 1920 until July of 1923. In the meantime, beginning in May of 1921, Breton and some of his friends were forming a new group whose optimistic attitude toward life, experiments with new methods of literary composition, and increasingly systematic philosophical orientation was in marked contrast to Dada's attitude of nihilistic despair. Breton later called this period, which extended from May of 1921 until October of 1924—when the first *Manifesto of Surrealism* was published—the "intuitive phase" of Surrealism. The publication of this first manifesto established, in an explicit way, a new aesthetic and a profoundly optimistic, imaginative conception of the world which its author, André Breton, named "Surrealism." The intense period of Surrealist creative activity, which began at that time and continued unabated until the appearance of the *Second Manifesto of Surrealism* in 1930, Breton was later to call the "reasoning phase" of Surrealism. This period culminated in the appearance of *Les Vases communicants*, a series of lyrical philosophical discourses expressing in mature, fully developed form the central ideas of the Surrealist philosophy and aesthetic.

The period following 1930, the year of the second manifesto, was characterized by two developments. One of these was the Surrealists' increasing involvement with the Communist International movement. The second development was, in a direct sense, an outgrowth of the first, for it was also during this period that Surrealism was disseminated on a worldwide scale and gained adherents outside Western Europe in many places where it was seen as the artistic concomitant of Marxist revolutionary philosophy. This period, which might be called, with some small injustice, the "dogmatic phase" of Surrealism, lasted until the outbreak of World War II. In 1941, Breton left France and lived for five years in New York. When he returned to Paris in 1946, Surrealism was effectively dead, although with those few friends of the original group who still remained, and with the growing support of countless other self-acknowledged "Surrealists" in many other countries where their dream had been carried, André Breton lived on as the universally acknowledged magus of Surrealism until his death on September 28, 1966, in Paris.

Analysis · André Breton's poetry forms a relatively small though important part of his total literary output, being dwarfed in quantity by his lengthy experiments in prose and his numerous polemical writings. His poetry, from the first published collection, *Mont de piété* (mount of piety), to his last major poetic work, *Ode to Charles Fourier*, shows a remarkable consistency of style. As a poet, Breton is best known for his remarkable imagery—which, at its best, expresses the powerful ability of the imagination to reconcile basic human drives and desires with the material conditions of reality and, at its worst, lapses into bizarre forms of irrationality which are incomprehensible to all but the poet himself.

In general terms, Breton's poetic imagery is characterized by comparisons which yoke together extremely disparate objects, by the sudden, sometimes violent shifting of context as the poet moves from one image to the next, and by an extremely indirect method of expressing comparisons between objects. These three qualities, above all, give his poetic imagery the appearance of being spontaneous rather than deliberate. As recent critics have shown, however, much to Breton's credit as a poet, this initial impression is a misleading one.

Breton's imagery is reinforced by other prominent aspects of his style, one of which might be called "devices of syntactic derangement." These devices range from the use of simple paradoxes involving logical and semantic contradictions, to syntactic ambiguity involving multiple or imprecise grammatical modification, to much more unsettling contradictions of reference—where the referent of a speech act is left unidentified, is deliberately misidentified, or is made ambiguous.

One other important element of Breton's style which helps to support the dramatic effect of his poetic images on his readers is his diction, which is characterized by two principal traits. The first of these is the extremely wide range of his vocabulary, which frequently includes the use of words from anatomical, zoological, botanical, and technical contexts that are unfamiliar to most readers of poetry. The second important trait of his diction is the tendency to use words in specialized, atypical ways that emphasize (and often create) their figurative meanings over their denotations. These qualities have two important effects on Breton's work: The first helps make possible his imagery of violent contrasts, and the second is, to a large degree, responsible for the great difficulty his readers and translators encounter searching for paraphrasable or translatable meaning in his work.

Another element of Breton's style which deserves mention is his use of recurring themes and symbolic motifs, such as the revolver as a synecdochic image for rebellion or revolt of any kind. As critics have recently discovered, these recurring thematic and symbolic elements in Breton's work can frequently be used as contextual clues for interpreting his most difficult works.

The poetry of André Breton expresses three key ideas—the liberating power of the imagination, the transformation of the material world into a utopian state, and the exploration of human potentiality through love between the sexes—which recur, with increasing elaboration, throughout the course of his work and constitute the essence of his Surrealist vision.

Breton's faith in the liberating power of the human imagination, although suggested and influenced by his contact with modern psychoanalytic thought, especially that of Freud on the operations of the unconscious, goes far beyond the notion of simply releasing the bound or "repressed" energies which is the therapeutic basis of psychoanalytic practice. For Breton, the unconscious is not an enclosed inner space, or reservoir, of trapped energy; it is, rather, the way out of the everyday world of material reality into the realm of the surreal. According to the Surrealists, this realm—where human reason and imagination no longer struggle against each other but function in harmony—is the ultimate reality, and humanity's goal in life is to seek out continually the signs of this reality, which, when directly experienced, is capable of transforming the life of a person. Although Breton envisioned the realm of the surreal as accessible to all who seek it, it was especially important for the artist, whose goal was to capture the fleeting traces of *le merveilleux* (the marvelous) in his writing.

The Surrealists recommended a number of different methods for attaining this experience. Two, in particular, are frequently used and referred to in Breton's work: the surrendering of the person to the *hasard objectif* (objective chance) of the universe, and the evocation of the "primary processes" of the unconscious through such procedures as automatic writing. The first of these methods is illustrated well in "Au regard des divinités" ("In the Eyes of the Gods"), one of Breton's early poems from *Clair de terre* (the light of Earth):

> 'Shortly before midnight near the landing-stage
> If a dishevelled woman follows you, pay no attention.
> It's the blue. You need fear nothing of the blue.
> There'll be a tall blonde vase in a tree.
> The spire of the village of melted colors
> Will be your landmark. Take it easy,
> Remember. The dark geyser that hurls fern-tips
> Towards the sky greet
> Greets you.'

This poem reads like, and in fact is intended to be, a set of instructions for encountering the marvelous through the technique of objective chance.

Breton's other primary technique for evoking the marvelous—using the unfettered association of ideas in the unconscious to produce automatic writing—is illustrated by "Au beau demi-jour" ("In the Lovely Half-Light"), a poem from *L'Air de l'eau* (air of the water):

> In the lovely half-light of 1934
> The air was a splendid rose the colour of red mullet
> And the forest when I made ready to enter it
> Began with a tree that had cigarette-paper leaves
> For I was waiting for you. . . .

Not only did Breton believe in the power of the creative imagination to transform the lives of individuals, but also he believed in the possibility of transforming society itself into a Socialist utopia, and he came to believe that the Communist International movement was a means to that end. Breton's association with the Communist Party, which began about 1930, was an increasingly divisive force among the French Surrealists. Many who were willing to accept Surrealism's aesthetic and philosophical premises did not believe that this view of life could ever transform the material world of nations and societies. Breton saw this resistance toward political involvement as an indication of insufficient commitment, while those who resisted engagement countered by emphasizing the restrictive nature of the Communist Party, its repressive disciplinary practices, and its hostility to artistic activity that did not directly further the interests of the Party itself. Regardless of the problems it created for him, Breton never gave up this utopian faith, as the choice of subject for his last major poetic work, *Ode to Charles Fourier*, makes clear.

The third key idea that informs Breton's poetry is one which, like his belief in the liberating power of the imagination, was shared by many of the Surrealists: the belief that romantic love was the means by which humankind might establish an enduring link between the mundane world of material reality and the limitless, eternal world of surreality. At times, the mere presence of the beloved is enough to evoke such a response, and some of Breton's most moving poetry deals with this experience. The idea is expressed in two principal forms in Breton's love poetry. The first is the belief in woman as muse: The beloved becomes the source of contact with the realm of surreality, where, Breton's friend Paul Éluard (the greatest of the Surrealist love poets) wrote, "all transformations are possible." This belief is clearly expressed in two of Breton's best poems: the famous "catalog-poem" *Free Union*, which celebrates the magical connection between the poet's beloved and the unspoiled world of nature, and *Fata Morgana*, which celebrates the ecstatic elation of the poet at the advent of a new love. The second form taken by this belief in the magical power of love is the equation of poetic creation itself with sexual love, as in "Sur la Route de San Romano" ("On the Road to San Romano"): "Poetry is made in a bed like love/ Its rumpled sheets are the dawn of things."

These three ideas—together with the support of countless writers, scattered across the world, who identified themselves with the Surrealist ideal—sustained Breton throughout a career that lasted more than fifty years. Although Breton died in 1966, the beliefs that he helped to formulate and that he expressed so brilliantly in his own poetry continue to exist.

Other literary forms · Breton published many experimental works during his career, some of which were written in collaboration with friends. *Les Champs magnétiques* (1921; magnetic fields), the first Surrealist text to employ the technique of "automatic" writing, was done with Philippe Soupault. *L'Immaculée Conception* (1930; immaculate conception), an attempt to simulate the thought processes of various types of insanity, was written with Paul Éluard. Among the basic Surrealist documents were several works by Breton alone, such as *Poisson soluble* (1924; soluble fish) and *Les Vases communicants* (1932; the communicating vessels), which mixed lyrical elements with philosophical speculations cast in the form of prose, as well as the numerous polemical manifestos such as *Manifeste du surréalisme* (1924; *Manifesto of Surrealism*) and *Second Manifeste du surréalisme* (1930; *Second Manifesto of Surrealism*). Breton's numerous essays were also collected in three volumes: *Les Pas perdus* (1924; the lost steps), *Point du jour* (1934), and *Perspective cavalière* (1970). Convenient selections from Breton's prose in English translation have appeared in *Manifestoes of Surrealism* (1969), translated by Richard Seaver and Helen R. Lane, and *What Is Surrealism? Selected Writings* (1978), edited by Franklin Rosemont.

Select works other than poetry
NONFICTION: *Les Champs magnétiques*, 1921 (with Philippe Soupault); *Les Pas perdus*, 1924; *Poisson soluble*, 1924; *Manifeste du surréalisme*, 1924 (*Manifesto of Surrealism*, 1969); *Légitime Défense*, 1926; *Le Surréalisme et la peinture*, 1928, 1945, 1965; *L'Immaculée Conception*, 1930 (with Paul Éluard); *Second Manifeste du surréalisme*, 1930 (*Second Manifesto of Surrealism*, 1969); *Les Vases communicants*, 1932; *Point du jour*, 1934; *Qu'est-ce que le surréalisme?*, 1934 (*What Is Surrealism?*, 1936); *L'Amour fou*, 1937; *Arcane 17*, 1944; *Situation du surréalisme entre les deux guerres*, 1945; *Les Manifestes du surréalisme*, 1955

(*Manifestoes of Surrealism*, 1969); *Perspective cavalière*, 1970; *What Is Surrealism? Selected Writings*, 1978.

LONG FICTION: *Nadja*, 1928 (English translation, 1960).

Steven E. Colburn

Bibliography · For a discussion of Breton's use of Surrealist techniques, especially in his poetry, see J. H. Matthews, *André Breton*, 1967. A more extensive study is Mary Anne Caws's *André Breton*, 1971, which includes a valuable bibliography of secondary sources in both French and English. Also see Herbert Gershman, *The Surrealist Revolution in France*, 1968; Anna Balakian, *André Breton: Magus of Surrealism*, 1971; and Balakian's more recent *André Breton Today*, 1989, which includes a bibliography through 1988. *André Breton and the Basic Concepts of Surrealism*, 1974, by Michel Carrouges, is an analysis of the poet that Breton himself favored. Matthew Josephson's *Life Among the Surrealists*, 1962, is an entertaining account of an American who joined the Surrealists and was "excommunicated" by "Pope" Breton.

Finally, for a general picture of the Surrealist group, see Maurice Nadeau, *History of Surrealism*, 1967, and for chapters on automatic writing, objective chance, passionate love, utopianism, and magic, see Clifford Browder's *André Breton, Arbiter of Surrealism*, 1967.

GWENDOLYN BROOKS

Born: Topeka, Kansas; June 7, 1917

Poetry · *A Street in Bronzeville*, 1945 · *Annie Allen*, 1949 · *The Bean Eaters*, 1960 · *Selected Poems*, 1963 · *In the Mecca*, 1968 · *Riot*, 1969 · *Family Pictures*, 1970 · *Aloneness*, 1971 · *Beckonings*, 1975 · *Primer for Blacks*, 1980 · *To Disembark*, 1981 · *The Near-Johannesburg Boy*, 1986 · *Blacks*, 1987 · *Gottschalk and the Grand Tarantelle*, 1988

Achievements · Working comfortably in relation to diverse poetic traditions, Gwendolyn Brooks has been widely honored. Early in her career, she received numerous mainstream literary awards, including the Pulitzer Prize for Poetry in 1950 for *Annie Allen*. She was named Poet Laureate of Illinois in 1969 and has received more than fifty honorary doctorates. Equally significant, numerous writers associated with the Black Arts Movement recognize her as an inspirational figure linking the older and younger generations of black poets. Brooks's ability to appeal both to poetic establishments and to a sizable popular audience, especially among young blacks, stems from her pluralistic voice which echoes a wide range of precursors while remaining unmistakably black. Her exploration of America in general and Chicago in particular links her with Walt Whitman and Carl Sandburg. Her exploration of the interior landscape of humanity in general and women in particular places her in the tradition of Emily Dickinson and Edna St. Vincent Millay. At once the technical heir of Langston Hughes in her use of the rhythms of black street life and of Robert Frost in her exploration of traditional forms such as the sonnet, Brooks nevertheless maintains her integrity of vision and voice.

This integrity assumes special significance in the context of African-American writing of the 1950's and 1960's. A period of "universalism" in black literature, the 1950's brought prominence to such poets as Brooks, LeRoi Jones, and Robert Hayden, all of whom provided clear evidence that African-American poets matched the technical and intellectual range of their white counterparts. During this period of intellectual and aesthetic integration, Brooks never abandoned her social and racial heritage to strive for the transcendent (and deracinated) universalism associated by some African-American critics with T. S. Eliot. Responding to William Carlos Williams' call in *Paterson* (1946-1951) to "make a start out of particulars and make them general," Brooks demonstrates unambiguously that an African-American writer need not be limited in relevance by concentrating on the black experience.

The 1960's, conversely, encouraged separatism and militancy in African-American writing. Even while accepting the Black Arts Movement's call for a poetry designed to speak directly to the political condition of the black community, Brooks continued to insist on precision of form and language. While Jones changed his name to Amiri Baraka and radically altered his poetic voice, Brooks accommodated her new insights to her previously established style. An exemplar of integrity and flexibility, she both challenges and learns from younger black poets such as Haki R. Madhubuti (Don L. Lee), Sonia Sanchez, Carolyn Rodgers, and Etheridge Knight. Like Hughes, she addresses the black community without condescension or pretense. Like Frost, she writes technically stunning "universal" poetry combining clear surfaces and elusive depths.

Jill Krementz

A recipient of more than fifty honorary doctorates, Brooks was appointed to the Presidential Commission on the National Agenda for the Eighties; she was the first black woman elected to the National Institute of Arts and Letters. She was named Consultant in Poetry to the Library of Congress for 1985-1986.

Biography · Gwendolyn Brooks's poetry bears the strong impress of Chicago, particularly of the predominantly black South Side where she has lived most of her life. Although she was born in Topeka, Kansas, Brooks was taken to Chicago before she was a year old. In many ways she has devoted her career to the physical, spiritual, and, more recently, political exploration of her native city.

Brooks's life and writings are frequently separated into two phases, with her experience at the 1967 Black Writers' Conference at Fisk University in

Nashville serving as a symbolic transition. Prior to the conference, Brooks was known primarily as the first black Pulitzer Prize winner in poetry. Although not politically unaware, she held to a somewhat cautious attitude. The vitality she encountered at the conference crystallized her sense of the insufficiency of universalist attitudes and generated close personal and artistic friendships with younger black poets such as Madhubuti, Walter Bradford, and Knight. Severing her ties with the mainstream publishing firm of Harper and Row, which had published her first five books, Brooks transferred her work and prestige to the black-owned and operated Broadside Press of Detroit, Third World Press of Chicago, and Black Position Press, also of Chicago. Her commitment to black publishing houses remains unwavering despite distribution problems which render her later work largely invisible to the American reading public.

Educated in the Chicago school system and at Wilson Junior College, Brooks learned her craft under Inez Cunningham Stark (Boulton), a white woman who taught poetry at the South Side Community Art Center in the late 1930's and 1940's. Brooks's mother, who had been a teacher in Topeka, had encouraged her literary interests from an early age. Her father, a janitor, provided her with ineffaceable images of the spiritual strength and dignity of "common" people. Brooks married Henry Blakely in 1939 and her family concerns continued to play a central role in shaping her career. The eleven-year hiatus between the publication of *Annie Allen* (1949) and *The Bean Eaters* (1960) resulted at least in part from her concentration on rearing her two children, born in 1940 and 1951. Her numerous poems on family relationships reflect both the rewards and the tensions of her own experiences. Her children grown, Brooks concentrated on teaching, supervising poetry workshops, and speaking publicly. These activities brought her into contact with a wide range of younger black poets, preparing her for her experience at Fisk. As Poet Laureate of Illinois, a position she has held since 1969, she continues to encourage the development of younger poets through personal contact and formal competitions.

The division between the two phases of Brooks's life should not be overstated. She evinced a strong interest in the Civil Rights Movement during the 1950's and early 1960's; her concern with family continued in the 1980's. Above all, Brooks continues to live with and write of and for the Chicagoans whose failures and triumphs she sees as deeply personal, universally resonant, and specifically black.

Analysis · The image of Gwendolyn Brooks as a readily accessible poet is at once accurate and deceptive. Capable of capturing the experiences and rhythms of black street life, she frequently presents translucent surfaces which give way suddenly to reveal ambiguous depths. Equally capable of manipulating traditional poetic forms such as the sonnet, rhyme royal, and heroic couplet, she employs them to mirror the uncertainties of characters or personae who embrace conventional attitudes to defend themselves against internal and external chaos. Whatever form she chooses, Brooks consistently focuses on the struggle of people to find and express love, usually associated with the family, in the midst of a hostile environment. In constructing their defenses and seeking love, these persons typically experience a disfiguring pain. Brooks devotes much of her energy to defining and responding to the elusive forces, variously psychological and social, which inflict this pain. Increasingly in her later poetry, Brooks traces the pain to political sources and expands her concept of the family to encompass all black people. Even while speaking of the social situation of blacks in a voice crafted primarily for blacks, however, Brooks maintains the complex awareness of the multiple perspectives relevant to any given experience. Her ultimate concern is to encourage every individual, black or white, to "Conduct your blooming in the noise and whip of the whirlwind" ("The Second Sermon on the Warpland").

A deep concern with the everyday circumstances of black people living within the whirlwind characterizes many of Brooks's most popular poems. From the early "Of De Witt Williams on His Way to Lincoln Cemetery" and "A Song in the Front Yard," through the later "The Life of Lincoln West" and "Sammy Chester Leaves 'Godspell' and Visits UPWARD BOUND on a Lake Forest Lawn, Bringing West Afrika," she focuses on characters whose experiences merge the idiosyncratic and the typical. She frequently draws on black musical forms to underscore the communal resonance of a character's outwardly undistinguished life. By tying the refrain of "Swing Low Sweet Chariot" to the repeated phrase "Plain black boy," Brooks transforms De Witt Williams into an Everyman figure. Brooks describes his personal search for love in the pool rooms and dance halls, but stresses the representative quality of his experience by starting and ending the poem with the musical allusion.

"We Real Cool," perhaps Brooks's single best-known poem, subjects a similarly representative experience to an intricate technical and thematic scrutiny, at once loving and critical. The poem is only twenty-four words long, including eight repetitions of the word "we." It is suggestive that the subtitle of "We Real Cool" specifies the presence of only seven pool players at the "Golden Shovel." The eighth "we" suggests that poet and reader share, on some level, the desperation of the group-voice that Brooks transmits. The final sentence, "We/ die soon," restates the *carpe diem* motif in the vernacular of Chicago's South Side.

On one level, "We Real Cool" appears simply to catalog the experiences of a group of dropouts content to "sing sin" in all available forms. A surprising ambiguity enters into the poem, however, revolving around the question of how to accent the word "we" which ends every line except the last one, providing the beat for the poem's jazz rhythm. Brooks has said that she intended that the "we" *not* be accented. Read in this way, the poem takes on a slightly distant and ironic tone, emphasizing the artificiality of the group identity which involves the characters in activities offering early death as the only release from pain. Conversely, the poem can be read with a strong accent on each "we," affirming the group identity. Although the experience still ends with early death, the pool players metamorphose into defiant heroes determined to resist the alienating environment. Their confrontation with experience is felt, if not articulated, as existentially pure. Pool players, poet, and reader cannot be *sure* which stress is valid.

Brooks crafts the poem, however, to hint at an underlying coherence in the defiance. The intricate internal rhyme scheme echoes the sound of nearly every word. Not only do the first seven lines end with "we," but the penultimate words of each line in each stanza also rhyme (cool/school, late/straight, sin/gin, June/soon). In addition, the alliterated consonant of the last line of each stanza is repeated in the first line of the next stanza (Left/lurk, Strike/sin, gin/June) and the first words of each line in the middle two stanzas are connected through consonance (Lurk/strike, Sing/thin). The one exception to this suggestive texture of sound is the word "Die" which introduces both a new vowel and a new consonant into the final line, breaking the rhythm and subjecting the performance to ironic revaluation. Ultimately, the power of the poem derives from the tension between the celebratory and the ironic perspectives on the lives of the plain black boys struggling for a sense of connection.

A similar struggle informs many of Brooks's poems in more traditional forms, including "The Mother," a powerful exploration of the impact of an abortion on the woman who has chosen to have it. Brooks states that the mother "decides that *she*, rather than her world, will kill her children." Within the poem itself, however, the motivations remain unclear. Although the poem's position in Brooks's first book, *A Street in Bronzeville* (1945), suggests that the persona is black, the poem neither supports nor denies a racial identification. Along with the standard English syntax and diction, this suggests that "The Mother," like poems such as "The Egg Boiler," "Callie Ford," and "A Light and Diplomatic Bird," was designed to speak directly of an emotional, rather than a social, experience, and to be as accessible to whites as to blacks. Re-creating the anguished perspective of a persona unsure whether she is victim or victimizer, Brooks directs her readers' attention to the complex emotions of her potential Everywoman.

"The Mother" centers on the persona's alternating desire to take and to evade responsibility for the abortion. Resorting to ambiguous grammatical structures, the persona repeatedly qualifies her acceptance with "if" clauses ("If I sinned," "If I stole your births"). She refers to the lives of the children as matters of fate ("Your luck") and backs away from admitting that a death has taken place by claiming that the children "were never made." Her use of the second person pronoun to refer to herself in the first stanza reveals her desire to distance herself from her present pain. This attempt, however, fails. The opening line undercuts the evasion with the reality of memory: "Abortions will not let you forget." At the start of the second stanza, the pressure of memory forces the persona to shift to the more honest first person pronoun. A sequence of spondees referring to the children ("damp small pulps," "dim killed children," "dim dears") interrupts the lightly stressed anapestic-iambic meter which dominates the first stanza. The concrete images of "scurrying off ghosts" and "devouring" children with loving gazes gain power when contrasted with the dimness of the mother's life and perceptions. Similarly, the first stanza's end-stopped couplets, reflecting the persona's simplistic attempt to recapture an irrevocably lost mother-child relationship through an act of imagination, give way to the intricate enjambment and complex rhyme scheme of the second stanza, which highlight the mother's inability to find rest.

The rhyme scheme—and Brooks can rival both Robert Frost and W. B. Yeats in her ability to employ various types of rhyme for thematic impact—underscores her struggle to come to terms with her action. The rhymes in the first stanza insist on her self-doubt, contrasting images of tenderness and physical substance with those of brutality and insubstantiality (forget/get, hair/air, beat/sweet). The internal rhyme of "never," repeated four times, and "remember," "workers," and "singers," further stresses the element of loss. In the second stanza, Brooks provides no rhymes for the end words "children" in line 11 and "deliberate" in line 21. This device draws attention to the persona's failure to answer the crucial questions of whether her children did in fact exist and of whether her own actions were in fact deliberate (and perhaps criminal). The last seven lines of the stanza end with hard "d" sounds as the persona struggles to forge her conflicting thoughts into a unified perspective. If Brooks offers coherence, though, it is emotional rather than intellectual. Fittingly, the "d" rhymes and off-rhymes focus on physical and emotional pain (dead/instead/made/afraid/said/died/cried). Brooks provides no easy answer to the anguished question: "How is the truth to be told?" The persona's concluding cry of "I loved you/ All" rings with desperation. It is futile but it is not a lie. To call "The Mother" an antiabortion poem distorts its impact. Clearly portraying the devastating effects of the persona's action, it by no means condemns her or lacks sympathy. Like many of Brooks's characters, the mother is a person whose desire to love far outstrips her ability to cope with her circumstances and serves primarily to heighten her sensitivity to pain.

Perhaps the most significant change in Brooks's poetry involves her analysis of the origins of this pervasive pain. Rather than attributing the suffering to some unavoidable psychological condition, Brooks's later poetry indicts social institutions for their role in its perpetuation. The poems in her first two volumes frequently portray characters incapable of articulating the origins of their pain. Although the absence of any father in "The Mother" suggests sociological forces leading to the abortion, such analysis amounts to little more than speculation. The only certainty is that the mother, the persona of the sonnet sequence "The Children of the Poor," and the speaker in the brilliant sonnet "My Dreams, My Works Must Wait Till After Hell" share the fear that their pain will render them insensitive to love. The final poem of *Annie Allen*, "Men of Careful Turns," intimates that the defenders of a society which refuses to admit its full humanity bear responsibility for reducing the powerless to "grotesque toys." Despite this implicit accusation, however, Brooks perceives no "magic" capable of remedying the situation. She concludes the volume on a note of irresolution typical of her early period: "We are lost, must/ Wizard a track through our own screaming weed." The track, at this stage, remains spiritual rather than political.

Although the early volumes include occasional poems concerning articulate political participants such as "Negro Hero," her later work frequently centers on specific black political spokespersons such as Malcolm X, Paul Robeson, John Killens, and Don L. Lee. Since the early 1960's, a growing anger informs poems as diverse as the ironic "The Chicago *Defender* Sends a Man to Little Rock," the near-baroque "The Lovers of the Poor," the imagistically intricate "Riders to the Blood-Red Wrath," and the satiric "Riot." This anger originates in Brooks's perception that the social structures of white society value material possessions and abstract ideas of prestige more highly than individual human beings. The anger culminates in Brooks's brilliant narrative poem "In the Mecca," concerning the death of a young girl in a Chicago housing project, and in her three "Sermon on the Warpland" poems.

The "Warpland" poems mark Brooks's departure from the traditions of Euro-American poetry and thought represented by T. S. Eliot's *The Waste*

Land (1922). The sequence typifies her post-1967 poetry, in which she abandons traditional stanzaic forms, applying her technical expertise to a relatively colloquial free verse. This technical shift parallels her rejection of the philosophical premises of Euro-American culture. Brooks refuses to accept the inevitability of cultural decay, arguing that the "waste" of Eliot's vision exists primarily because of our "warped" perceptions. Seeing white society as the embodiment of these distortions, Brooks embraces her blackness as a potential counterbalancing force. The first "Sermon on the Warpland" opens with Ron Karenga's black nationalist credo: "The fact that we are black is our ultimate reality." Clearly, in Brooks's view, blackness is not simply a physical fact; it is primarily a metaphor for the possibility of love. As her poem "Two Dedications" indicates, Brooks sees the Euro-American tradition represented by the Chicago Picasso as inhumanly cold, mingling guilt and innocence, meaningfulness and meaninglessness, almost randomly. This contrasts sharply with her inspirational image of the Wall of Heroes on the South Side. To Brooks, true art assumes meaning from the people who interact with it. The Wall helps to redefine black reality, rendering the "dispossessions beakless." Rather than contemplating the site of destruction, the politically aware black art which Brooks embraces should inspire the black community to face its pain with renewed determination to remove its sources. The final "Sermon on the Warpland" concludes with the image of a black phoenix rising from the ashes of the Chicago riot. No longer content to accept the unresolved suffering of "The Mother," Brooks forges a black nationalist politics and poetics of love.

Although her political vision influences every aspect of her work, Brooks maintains a strong sense of enduring individual pain and is aware that nationalism offers no simple panacea. "The Blackstone Rangers," a poem concerning one of the most powerful Chicago street gangs, rejects as simplistic the argument, occasionally advanced by writers associated with the Black Arts Movement, that no important distinction exists between the personal and the political experience. Specifically, Brooks doubts the corollary that politically desirable activity will inevitably increase the person's ability to love. Dividing "The Blackstone Rangers" into three segments—"As Seen by Disciplines," "The Leaders," and "Gang Girls: A Rangerette"—Brooks stresses the tension between perspectives. After rejecting the sociological-penal perspective of part one, she remains suspended between the uncomprehending affirmation of the Rangers as a kind of government-in-exile in part two, and the recognition of the individual person's continuing pain in part three.

Brooks undercuts the description of the Rangers as "sores in the city/

that do not want to heal" ("As Seen by Disciplines") through the use of off-rhyme and a jazz rhythm reminiscent of "We Real Cool." The disciplines, both academic and corrective, fail to perceive any coherence in the Rangers' experience. Correct in their assumption that the Rangers do not want to "heal" themselves, the disciplines fail to perceive the gang's strong desire to "heal" the sick society. Brooks suggests an essential coherence in the Rangers' experience through the sound texture of part one. Several of the sound patterns echoing through the brief stanza point to a shared response to pain (there/thirty/ready, raw/sore/corner). Similarly, the accent cluster on "Black, raw, ready" draws attention to the pain and potential power of the Rangers. The descriptive voice of the disciplines, however, provides only relatively weak end rhymes (are/corner, ready/city), testifying to the inability of the distanced, presumably white, observers to comprehend the experiences they describe. The shifting, distinctively black, jazz rhythm further emphasizes the distance between the voices of observers and participants. Significantly, the voice of the disciplines finds no rhyme at all for its denial of the Rangers' desire to "heal."

This denial contrasts sharply with the tempered affirmation of the voice in part two which emphasizes the leaders' desire to "cancel, cure and curry." Again, internal rhymes and sound echoes suffuse the section. In the first stanza, the voice generates thematically significant rhymes, connecting Ranger leader "*Bop*" (whose name draws attention to the jazz rhythm which is even more intricate, though less obvious, in this section than in part one) and the militant black leader "*Rap*" Brown, both nationalists whose "country is a Nation on no *map*." "Bop" and "Rap," of course, do not rhyme perfectly, attesting Brooks's awareness of the gang leader's limitations. Her image of the leaders as "Bungled trophies" further reinforces her ambivalence. The only full rhyme in the final two stanzas of the section is the repeated "night." The leaders, canceling the racist association of darkness with evil, "translate" the image of blackness into a "monstrous pearl or grace." The section affirms the Blackstone Rangers' struggle; it does not pretend to comprehend fully the emotional texture of their lives.

Certain that the leaders possess the power to cancel the disfiguring images of the disciplines, Brooks remains unsure of their ability to create an alternate environment where love can blossom. Mary Ann, the "Gang Girl" of part three, shares much of the individual pain of the characters in Brooks's early poetry despite her involvement with the Rangers. "A rose in a whiskey glass," she continues to live with the knowledge that her "laboring lover" risks the same sudden death as the pool players of "We Real Cool." Forced to suppress a part of her awareness—she knows not to ask where her lover got the diamond he gives her—she remains emotionally removed even while making love. In place of a fully realized love, she accepts "the props and niceties of non-loneliness." The final line of the poem emphasizes the ambiguity of both Mary Ann's situation and Brooks's perspective. Recommending acceptance of "the rhymes of Leaning," the line responds to the previous stanza's question concerning whether love will have a "gleaning." The full rhyme paradoxically suggests acceptance of off-rhyme, of love consummated leaning against an alley wall, without expectation of safety or resolution. Given the political tension created by the juxtaposition of the disciplines and the leaders, the "Gang Girl" can hope to find no sanctuary beyond the reach of the whirlwind. Her desperate love, the more moving for its precariousness, provides the only near-adequate response to the pain that Brooks continues to see as the primary fact of life.

Other literary forms · In addition to the poetry on which her literary reputation rests, Gwendolyn Brooks has published a novel, *Maud Martha* (1953); a book of autobiographical prose, *Report from Part One* (1972); and volumes of children's verse. An episodic novel, *Maud Martha* makes some use of autobiographical materials and shares many of the major concerns of Brooks's poetry, particularly concerning the attempts of the person to maintain integrity in the face of crushing environmental pressures. *Report from Part One* recounts the personal, political, and aesthetic influences which culminated in Brooks's movement to a black nationalist stance in the late 1960's. Since that time she has written introductions to, and edited anthologies of, the works of younger black writers. These introductions frequently provide insight into her own work. Several recordings of Brooks reading her own work are available.

Select works other than poetry
LONG FICTION: *Maud Martha*, 1953.
NONFICTION: *The World of Gwendolyn Brooks*, 1971; *Report from Part One*, 1972; *Young Poet's Primer*, 1980.
CHILDREN'S LITERATURE: *Bronzeville Boys and Girls*, 1956; *The Tiger Who Wore White Gloves*, 1974; *Very Young Poets*, 1983.
EDITED TEXT: *Jump Bad: A New Chicago Anthology*, 1971.

Craig Werner

Bibliography · George E. Kent, *A Life of Gwendolyn Brooks*, 1990, provides a thorough biography through 1978, and D. H. Melhem's afterword updates the biography through 1988. An extensive analysis of Brooks's poetry can be found in D. H. Melhem, *Gwendolyn Brooks, Poetry and the Heroic Voice*, 1987. A valuable collection of critical essays is Maria K. Mootry and Gary Smith, eds., *A Life Distilled: Gwendolyn Brooks, Her Poetry and Fiction*, 1987. Henry Taylor, "Gwendolyn Brooks: An Essential Sanity," *Kenyon Review* 13 (1991), is an informative and succinct analysis of most of the poems included in *Blacks*. George Stavros interviews Brooks in *Contemporary Literature* 2 (1970). Other important studies include Arthur P. Davis, "Gwendolyn Brooks: Poet of the Unheroic," *College Language Association Journal* 7 (1963); William H. Hansell, "The Role of Violence in Recent Poems of Gwendolyn Brooks," *Studies in Black Literature* 5 (1974); Patricia H. Lattin and Vernon E. Lattin, "Dual Vision in Gwendolyn Brooks's *Maud Martha*," *Critique: Studies in Modern Fiction* 25 (1984); Cheryl Clarke, "The Loss of Lyric Space and the Critique of Traditions in Gwendolyn Brooks's 'In the Mecca,'" *Kenyon Review* 17 (1995); Ann Folwell Stanford, "Dialectics of Desire: War and the Resistive Voice in Gwendolyn Brooks's 'Negro Hero' and 'Gay Chaps at the Bar,'" *African American Review* 26 (1992); and Ann Folwell Stanford, "An Epic With a Difference: Sexual Politics in Gwendolyn Brooks's 'The Anniad,'" *American Literature* 67 (1995).

ELIZABETH BARRETT BROWNING

Born: Durham, England; March 6, 1806
Died: Florence, Italy; June 29, 1861

Poetry · *The Battle of Marathon,* 1820 · *An Essay on Mind, with Other Poems,* 1826 · *The Seraphim and Other Poems,* 1838 · *Poems, by Elizabeth Barrett Barrett,* 1844 · *Poems,* 1850 (including *Sonnets from the Portuguese*) · *Casa Guidi Windows,* 1851 · *Aurora Leigh,* 1856 · *Poems Before Congress,* 1860 · *Last Poems,* 1862

Achievements · Elizabeth Barrett Browning's principal biographer, Gardner Taplin, wrote that "[i]t is the quality of her life even more than her artistic achievements which will live" (*The Life of Elizabeth Barrett Browning,* 1957). The reasons for this fact, he believes, are to be found "in her fulfillment as [a woman], in her courageous and impassioned protests against injustice to individuals and subject peoples, and in her broad, generous, idealistic, Christian point of view." Literary critics since her time have insisted upon thinking of Browning as a great woman poet, or as the Sappho of the age, or as the first woman to write a sustained sequence of sonnets. Her husband thought of her simply as having written the finest sonnets since William Shakespeare. The headnote to "Seraphim" indicates specifically that she invited comparison with Aeschylus. "A Drama of Exile" is a continuation of the Adamic drama just beyond the events described by John Milton and clearly invites comparison with him. Her sonnets can be compared with those of Petrarch, Shakespeare, Milton, and William Wordsworth. Whether she meets the measure of these models is problematical in some cases, doubtful in others. Still, her aim is consistently high and her achievement is historically substantial. She gave a strong voice to the democratic revolution of the nineteenth century; she was a vigorous antagonist of those she thought were the enemies of children, of the world's dispossessed, and of popular government.

Biography · In 1861, Elizabeth Barrett Browning died in her husband's arms in a rented apartment (unfurnished for the sake of economy). She had been born in one of the twenty marbled bedrooms of her father's estate, Coxhoe Hall. Edward Moulton Barrett, her father, had inherited a substantial fortune and the promise of remunerative properties from his family in

Library of Congress

Jamaica. When Elizabeth was three years old, the family moved to a still larger home, Hope End, in Herefordshire. This was to be her home until the abolition of slavery brought about sharp retrenchments in the Barrett family's affairs in 1832. After three years at Sidmouth, on the channel coasts, the family moved to London. Elizabeth was twenty-nine. Her family's congregational Protestantism and its strong support for the Reform Bill of 1832 had already helped to establish the intellectual landmarks of her poetry—Christian idealism and a sharp social conscience. In London, as her weak lungs became a source of chronic anxiety, the dark and reclusive habits which were to lend a fearful realism to Elizabeth Barrett's ideals became fixed in her mode of life.

Such anxiety found its consolations in a meditative piety which produced an increasingly intense inwardness in the poet. This fact partly explains why her poems are so commonly reflective, and so rarely narrative or dramatic. Eventually, she even gave up attending chapel services. In 1837, her lungs were racked by a persistent cough. In 1838, she left London for Torquay, hoping the sea air would afford her some relief. When her brother Edward ("Bro") had concluded his visit there and planned to return to London, Elizabeth pleaded with him to stay. He did so, but in the summer of 1840, as he was boating with friends, a sudden squall capsized the boat, and Bro was drowned. Elizabeth, who had been using laudanum fairly steadily since arriving in Torquay, almost lost her mind from guilt and distress. Macabre visions came to her and prompted in her a sharply balanced ambivalence between a wish to live and a wish to die.

Elizabeth returned to the family home at 50 Wimpole Street in London, more nervous and withdrawn than ever. She rarely descended the stairs, and in the darkened room came to depend ever more heavily on the morphine, "my amreeta, my elixir," which dulled her physical and spiritual pains. She called her room a "hermitage," a "convent," a "prison." The heavy curtains were always drawn. After her marriage, the images of her poems became less abstract and more concrete as she came to participate afresh in the parade of life's affairs. For readers of her poetry, the Casa Guidi windows of later years seem dramatically open as the colorful banners and the sounds of singing pass by.

In January of 1845, Robert Browning, then an obscure poet, wrote to thank Elizabeth for praising him in a poem she had recently published. She replied to the letter but was not anxious to meet him. She had already declined twice to receive calls from the venerable Wordsworth, whom she had met earlier. She did receive Browning several months later, however, and their famous courtship began. Both parties claimed that they had never been in love before, yet Elizabeth did have a history of strong attachments to men. When she had lived at Hope End, her informal tutor in Greek, H. S. Boyd, had become so confidential with her that quarrels with his wife resulted over the time spent with Elizabeth. At Sidmouth, she had formed a friendship with George Hunter, a minister, whose wife was allegedly mad. Years later, during Browning's courtship, Hunter even followed him once to Elizabeth's room, where an unseemly encounter took place. Browning, on the other hand, characteristically formed strong attachments to women—the Flowers sisters, Fanny Haworth, Julia Wedgwood. Still, for these two idealists, love was something quite particular, not a vague sentiment, and their claim seems authentic enough.

The principal obstacle to their courtship was Elizabeth's father. Strong-willed, pietistic, politically liberal, Edward Moulton Barrett saw Robert Browning as a footloose adventurer with a barely supportable claim to being a sometime-poet. Browning had no reliable means of support, and Barrett was certain that if the two were married Robert would merely live off Elizabeth's ample but not boundless fortune.

On September 12, 1846, while her family was away, Elizabeth, nearly fainting with fear, made her way to Saint Marylebone Parish Church. Robert met her there, and they were married. It was the first time he had seen her away from Wimpole Street. She returned home for one week and then slipped out of the house to begin the long journey to Italy with her husband. She never saw her father again. He wrote her a cruelly condemnatory letter, disinherited her, and sent her books out of the house to be stored (the bills to go to Elizabeth). She was forty years old, a poet widely respected in England and America.

The Brownings' most enduring home in Italy was at Florence in the Casa Guidi, a fifteenth century palace located very near the palace of the Grand Duke of Tuscany. Although Elizabeth's health was a constant concern to them, it is nevertheless clear that in Italy she recovered something of the vitality of her youth. She lived quietly with her husband, but enjoyed occasional walks to the bridges of the Arno and trips to the local churches, which were filled with incomparable treasures of art. She entertained guests more readily than she had in London and was able to accept the praise which great figures of the world brought to her doorstep in recognition of her growing fame.

In 1846, Cardinal Giovanni Masoni-Ferretti was elected Pope Pius IX. He immediately freed thousands of political prisoners, provoking the anger of the Austrian government. Disturbances broke out in Florence. The Grand Duke granted the people of Tuscany a constitution. The ecstatic populace of Florence marched to the Ducal Palace—right beneath the Casa Guidi windows. Later, however, when it appeared that Austria would intervene, the Pope refused to sanction a war between two Catholic countries, and the hopes of Italian nationalists were curtailed. Riots broke out; the liberals saw their near goals slipping away—and, in 1851, Elizabeth published *Casa Guidi Windows*, a reflection on these events.

Elizabeth's health was in fact sufficiently improved that on March 9, 1849, she was able to deliver a child—her only one—without the expected complications. Indeed, she became exhilarated and active just after the birth of her son, seeming much stronger than when she first married.

During the last ten years of her life, Elizabeth traveled extensively between Venice, Paris, and England. She found England, however, a somewhat alien place, more unyielding in manner than the Continent. When she was in London, she wrote seeking a reconciliation with her father, asking him at least to see her child. In reply, she received two packets containing the letters she had written home in the years since her marriage—all unread.

At the close of 1856, back in Italy, Browning published a "novel in verse," *Aurora Leigh.* Critics gave the book a somewhat ungenerous reception, but the public bought out issue after issue. It was a genuine best-seller. She was by now a true celebrity.

One volume of poems remained to her. In many ways it was her most controversial. *Poems Before Congress* is hardly a book, more nearly a pamphlet of poems. In it she praises Louis Napoleon, who had raised the fears of England again—Napoleon *redivivus*. English friends alleged that Elizabeth was politically unsophisticated for supporting the French. Browning replied, however, that this Napoleon would pry Italy loose from Austrian fingers; thus, her refrain is the same—Italian nationalism. The freedom of her adopted land would not be abandoned just because it caused fears at home. In the same spirit with which she had opposed slavery when abolition meant the loss of her family's fortune, she now opposed colonialist friends. Some in her own day said that Browning was politically naïve; but no one has ever denied the magnanimity of her love for humankind.

As the Italian national movement gained strength, Giuseppe Mazzini, Giuseppe Garibaldi, and the Conte di Cavour all unified great territorial patches of the peninsula; but Browning's strength waned. She could no longer keep up with her husband's vitality. She languished under the long struggle with her weak lungs. On a June night in 1861, protesting the fuss made over her, she lay down to sleep. Later she roused and, struggling to cough, relaxed into death.

Analysis · Elizabeth Barrett Browning did not think it a kindness when critics praised her as a "woman poet." She would think it much closer to essentials if she were praised instead as a Christian poet. An evangelical of an old Victorian strain, she prized learning, cultivated Greek as the language of the Christian revelation, studied the work of the church fathers, and brought a fine intellectual vigor to the manifestly Christian ethos which shapes her work.

Like her husband, Elizabeth suffered somewhat at the close of the nineteenth century from the uncritical applause of readers who praised the religious thought in her work merely as religious thought. A century after her death—and again like her husband—Browning began to enjoy the approbation of more vigorous critics who called attention to an element of intellectual toughness in her work which earlier critics had ignored. Now it is widely agreed that her poetry constitutes a coherent working out of evangelical principles into a set of conclusions which bear on the most pressing issues of modern times: the progress of liberal democracy, the role of militant nationalism, the ambivalences of the "woman question," and the task of the poet in a world without decisive voices.

In each case, the resolution she works toward is a further realization of the evangelical principle of the priesthood of persons. In many evangelical thinkers, a contradiction appears at this point: The antinomian doctrine of the depravity of man seems to contravene the doctrine of the high efficacy of individual thought; evangelicalism has, therefore, often encouraged a strong anti-intellectual bias among its followers. Since redemption is a matter of divine grace extended to childlike faith, there is no great need for secular learning. Browning, however, worked out a reconciliation of the dilemma: Fallen men can govern themselves well by a system of checks and balances which allows the many (because it is in their interest to do so) to restrain the venality of the powerful few. This reconciliation of the evangelical paradox allowed Browning not only to affirm the great egalitarian movements of her day, but also to believe that in them history was making "progress" on an enormous, though not continuous, scale. As a result, the poet is able to maintain a rather rigorous evangelicalism which is progressive, yet is not so facile and glibly optimistic as her early readers sometimes supposed. If it is her evangelicalism which endeared her to her own age, it is her wry, even grim sense of the role which personal failures must play in any realistic expectation of progress which has interested more recent critics.

The evolution of the ideas discussed above can be traced from Browning's first serious volume, *The Seraphim and Other Poems*, to her *Last Poems*. The title poem of the first volume is an attempt to transform the story of Jesus' crucifixion into a classical tragedy. She had just finished translating Aeschylus' *Prometheus Bound* and was determined to make of Christ a hero equal in tragic significance to Prometheus. Two angels descend from heaven, attending the death of Christ. The entire perspective given to the reader is through the eyes of these two angels. The poem fails because readers never see its tragic hero; they only hear from afar three among Christ's last sayings. Thus, Jesus never appears in the poem as a dramatic figure. It is possible, of course, that Browning was reluctant to bring Christ on stage and put fictitious words in his mouth. It seems hopeless, then, to expect that the hero will evoke the tragic empathies which Prometheus does; thus, her poem is not a genuinely tragic drama.

In her second major volume, *Poems, by Elizabeth Barrett Barrett*, Browning makes two important advances. The first is that her leading poem, "A Drama of Exile," is no longer a mere account of events. Rather, there is more invention and conflict than in earlier poems: Outside the garden, surrounded by a sinister-seeming nature, Eve meets Lucifer for the first time since her fall. On this occasion she rejects him. Then, in a mystical vision, Adam and Eve see and hear the omnipotent Christ rebuking the taunting spirits of fallen nature and the pride of the triumphant Lucifer. Eve now for- gives Lucifer and Christ forgives Eve. Here, the poet ventures a dramatic representation of her views with a series of invented situations which constitute a small episode in her effort to build a poetically Christian mythology.

The second advance of this volume over her previous one is technical. It is at this point in her career that Browning begins to experiment with the sonnet. The volume contains twenty-eight sonnets on various subjects. All are Italian in form (divided between an octet and a sestet), and in all cases the first eight lines rhyme *abba abba*. In the last six lines, however, Browning uses two different patterns. Some of the poems end with a *cdcdcd* pattern. Others end cdecde. The profit to the poet is that her attempts with the sonnet force on her a verbal economy which is more rigorous than that in her earlier volumes. Petrarch, for example, brought this Italian form to its pitch of perfection, allowing himself the five rhyme values of *abcd* and *e* (two rhyme values fewer than William Shakespeare uses); Mrs. Browning occasionally restricts herself to four rhyme values in a single sonnet—*abcd*. This practice imposes upon her vocabulary even stricter limits than those imposed by either the Petrarchan or the Shakespearean form. Furthermore, the sonnets—some about grief, tears, and work, with two about George Sand—force her to be less diffuse. They force her to find the concrete image which will quickly communicate a complex feeling, rather than simply talking the feeling out as she does earlier: "Experience, like a pale musician, holds a dulcimer of patience in his hand. . . ." Her religious sentiments also are forced into sharper images: "pale-cheeked martyrs smiling to a sword."

It is also in *Poems, by Elizabeth Barrett Barrett* that she includes the romance "Lady Geraldine's Courtship," which was to have significant repercussions for her. It is in this poem that she praises Robert Browning—eliciting his first letter to her—and it is here that she first attempts a theme which will not be fully realized until *Aurora Leigh:* that romance is plausible but handicapped in an unromantic (that is, an industrial, mercantile) age.

The last poem in the volume of 1844, though brief, is an important one in the poet's canon. "The Dead Pan" consists of thirty-nine stanzas, each containing six lines of iambic tetrameters (which do occasionally fall into an unheroic jog-trot), together with a seventh line of four syllables acting as a refrain. The poem produces just the image necessary to give Browning's religious thought the freshness, clarity, and invention necessary if she is to avoid mere clichés of faith in the search for an authenticating power in her poems. The subject of the poem is the ancient claim made by Plutarch (in *De Oraculorum Defectu*) that at the very hour of Christ's crucifixion a supernatural cry went out across the sea, "Great Pan is dead," and that from that moment the pagan oracles lost their vision and power. In the poem, Browning utters a long roll call of the pagan deities, and names them to witness that the prophetic power of an old world, mythopoeic and visionary, personified in the spirits of place—of forest, stream, and grotto—has been subsumed by a Christianity which is the new crown triumphant to a faded, classical past.

The poem is also a challenge to the skepticism and materialism of the poet's own age. The Christian religion has subsumed the ancient gifts of mystery and vision and has sanctified them by a revelation which marks them as being true, and by an ethic which adds to them the imperative to love. For Browning, the oracular voice of the modern world is heard in poetry. Some nineteenth century thinkers believed that, with the death of the mythopoeic consciousness, men had entered an age of rational secularism from which there could be no historical return. Matthew Arnold was such a thinker. For him, the loss of mythopoeic sensibility implied the loss of tragic sensibility. Against this sort of plaintive skepticissm Browning raised her protest. The Christian narrative constitutes the mythos of modern times, and the oracular voice of poetry constantly reinvigorates this mythology. The creativity and the virtuoso invention of Christian poets proves the vitality of the myths from which they draw, to which they add their stories and songs. Pan is dead, but the spirit—now illuminated by science—is as quick as ever.

Browning's next collection appeared six years later, after her famous elopement to Italy. *Poems* is marked by the distinction of containing *Sonnets from the Portuguese*, which prior to this time had been available only in a small private edition. These forty-four sonnets had been completed in 1847. They are technically more sure-handed than the earlier ones. The same Italian octet is here *abba, abba*, but Mrs. Browning has decided unequivocally on a sestet which rhymes *cdcdcd*. The *e* rhyme has disappeared. She limits herself to four rhyme values in each sonnet. The effect is a tight, organically unified sequence of sonnets. This impression of technical unity is enhanced by the single-minded theme of the poems: "this very love which is my boast." The poet has nevertheless avoided sameness in the sonnets by avoiding clichès and by writing from her own varied experience of love. For her, love had been exhilarating and risky during the days of her engagement; it had cruelly forced on her the determination to defy her father; it had sorrowfully juxtaposed her frailty to Robert's vigor; it had pitted her will to live against her expectation of an early death. These experiences provide the images which keep her poems from being merely conventional and confessional. Throughout them all there is a grim sense of herself which tries to avoid melodramatic self-deprecation on the one hand, while expressing an honest sense of her own limits on the other. This ironic view of herself gives the poems an underlying psychological realism which holds their Romanticism in check: "What can I give thee back, O liberal/ and princely giver" (Sonnet VIII); "Accuse me not, beseech thee, that I wear/ Too calm and sad a face" (Sonnet XV); "Unlike are we, unlike, O princely heart" (Sonnet III).

In 1851, Browning published her sustained political poem, *Casa Guidi Windows*. By this time she had found a clear political expression for her evangelical ethic, "Manhood's right divine . . . to elect and legislate." The poem is written in iambic pentameter, which is well suited to protracted discourse. To avoid a too-liberal capitulation to prosaic looseness, however, the poet uses a generalized rhyme scheme: *abababcdcdcdefefef*, through verse paragraphs of various lengths. The interlocking triple rhymes serve as a restraint on the rhetoric of the poem, but it is not a heavy-handed check. The incidents in the poem are few; thus, the burden of success is thrown upon its ideas.

During 1847, the Brownings were living in apartments in the Guidi Palace overlooking the Piazza del Gran Duca, a public square in Florence. From her windows Mrs. Browning was witness to a number of enthusiastic demonstrations of popular support for an Italian nationalism aimed at severing Italy's dependence upon the Austrian hierarchy—a dependence forced upon the country in the post-Napoleonic European settlement engineered by Metternich. This nationalism culminated in a revolt which failed in 1848. From her windows, Browning saw the joyful crowds agitating for national autonomy. Part 1 of her poem celebrates their libertarian hopes, "*O bella libertà.*" The Florence of Dante, Petrarch and Boccaccio is a political prisoner; its poets and artists are suppressed. Still, it is not merely for the sake of its heroic past that Italy deserves to be free. "We do not serve the dead—the past is past. God lives and lifts his glorious mornings up/ Before the eyes of men awake at last. . . ." It is God who has made men free. Piety is on the side of liberty. The first part of the poem is a rhetorical appeal to the Grand Duke of Florence, and especially to Pope Pius IX, to side with the people in this great controversy. The poet's evangelical suspicion of Church authority is laid aside in the hope that "authority" will do justice against Austria.

Part 2 of *Casa Guidi Windows* was written in 1851 after the failure of the revolution. Browning had seen the somber faces of the defeated loitering in the square. The leaders, she believed, had failed the people. The Duke had taken "the patriot's oath," but "Why swear at all," she asks, "thou false Duke Leopold." The Pope has also vacillated: "Priests, priests—there's no such name," she protests. Her evangelical instinct was true; the Pope has failed; "All Christians! Levi's (priestly) tribe is dispossest." Her grim disappointments at the failure of Italian nationalism in part 2 are balanced against the exalted hopes of part 1 and are resolved into a more subdued hopefulness for the future: "We will trust God. The blank interstices/ Men take for ruins, He will build into/ With pillared marbles. . . ." Popular sovereignty will win out.

Browning's longest poem, *Aurora Leigh*, appeared at Christmas, 1856. It is a narrative poem fulfilling her earlier wish to set a romance in an unromantic age. The ironies of such a circumstance are resolved for her when it becomes manifest to the protagonists that love is not only a "romantic" experience, but also a universal ethic. It therefore disarms the meanness of spirit, the poverty of values which the poet associated with the growing skepticism of a scientific and industrial age. The poem consists of nine books of approximately (but by no means uniformly) twelve hundred lines each, all in unrhymed iambic pentameter—blank verse. The poet had by then discovered from her own experience, as so many poets have, the suitability of blank verse for high eloquence upon serious subjects. Although this poem has a more detailed narrative framework than most of Elizabeth Browning's poems, it still is characterized by long reflective passages in which she devotes intense thought to the important ideas that arise from the narrative events. From the beginning, critics have observed that her characters are not persuasive, the incidents seem improbable, and the diction is uniformly stilted. The themes discussed, however, are confronted with a directness and boldness almost unequaled among Victorian poets.

Aurora Leigh is born in Italy of an English father and an Italian mother. Orphaned early, she travels to England to be reared by her father's sister. She becomes a retiring, moderately successful poet. Her cousin Romney, who has inherited the Leigh title and fortune, is a deeply compassionate Christian socialist with a strongly activist disposition. Aurora and Romney are drawn to each other, yet they so little understand each other that there is constant friction between them. This concatenation of events and characters allows Browning to bring together all of the ideas she most cares about and to work them out in a single crowning achievement. The state-of-England question (the poor and the privileged), the Germanic North and the Latin South (England and Italy), the condition of women, the role of the artist in a socially conscious world, the nature of progress, nationalism, and the impact of science are among the issues finally woven into the poem. After years of circling about each other, proposed marriages to third parties, and the exhaustion of Romney's fortune on an ungrateful community of the poor, Aurora and Romney recognize that their ambivalence toward each other is actually a rigorous—that is, a not very sentimental—form of love.

The issues of the poem are resolved in the most comprehensive working out of these problems which Browning ever undertook. Romney acknowledges that his social activism has been too doctrinaire, too manipulative; it has ignored the practical realities of human experiences. Aurora acknowledges that the ferocity of her independence has masked a deep need for intimacy. Each finds that love—as both an ethic and a sentiment—gives complexity and vitality both to the social question (Romney's problem) and to individual identity (Aurora's problem). The poet believes that this kind of love is grounded in an eternal Divine and is therefore the key to resolving the antinomies in an age of conflict—nationalists against empires, poor against rich, men against women, faith against doubt.

According to Lionel Trilling, "Behind the [nineteenth century] struggle of romanticism and rationalism lies . . . the diminution of the power of Christianity" (*Matthew Arnold*, 1939). Browning was keenly interested in this issue, and her poetry, when viewed as an organic whole, is a substantial and single-minded effort to infuse fresh force into Christian thought by a poetic quickening of the Christian mythos, as many of her poetic fictions show. For example, in "A Drama of Exile," Christ appears to Adam and Eve in a vision, "in the midst of the Zodiac"; he rebukes the Earth Spirits who have been taunting the people for their sins. "This regent and sublime Humanity," he tells the spirits "Though fallen, exceeds you . . . by their liberty to fall."

The poet's effort to take the ancient images of Christendom and elaborate them by sheer poetic invention into a revivified myth gives her work its unity; but it also imposes upon her poems certain inherent limitations. She never quite comes to grips with the possibility that if Pan is truly dead, then her own vision lacks oracular authenticity. In "The Seraph and the Poet," however, she presses her case that the modern visionary is the poet:

> Sing, seraph with the glory
> heaven is high;
> Sing, poet with sorrow! earth is low: The universe's inward
>   voice cry "Amen" to either song for joy and woe:
> Sing, seraph—poet,—sing on equally!

By imputing death to Pan, Browning has imputed death to other mythologies than her own. All mythologies, however, share a common epistemology, a common access to the morning-time sense of the world and to the tragic conception of human experience. Browning severs these ties which her mythology shares with the other great visionary images of the universe. This separation imposes upon her conception of faith a somewhat sectarian and doctrinaire limit. It means that her themes tend to be stated as issues (nationalism, poverty) rather than ideas. In her poems, there is no rigorous testing of her own first principles. Still, she is one of the great libertarians of her age, and all the disinherited of the world—children, women, slaves, poets—and all who love freedom will find in her work a brave and unequivocal voice.

Other literary forms · Elizabeth Barrett Browning was an accomplished Greek scholar, and from her translations she learned a great deal of her own prosody. In 1833, she published a weak translation of Aeschylus'

Prometheus Bound (date undetermined). In 1850, she included in her collected poems an entirely new and substantially improved version of the same play. "The Daughters of Pandarus," a selection from the *Odyssey* (c. 800 B.C.), was translated for Anna Jameson's *Memoirs and Essays Illustrative of Art, Literature, and Social Morals* in 1846. She modernized selections from *The Canterbury Tales* (1387-1400) for R. H. Horne's edition of Geoffrey Chaucer in 1841. She submitted occasional translations to periodicals, such as three hymns of Gregory Nazianzen which appeared in the *Athenaeum*, January 8, 1842. Browning also published a modest amount of prose criticism. Four articles on Greek Christian poets appeared anonymously in the *Athenaeum* during 1842. For the same journal, she published five articles (all in 1842) reviewing an anthology of English verse entitled *The Book of the Poets* (1842). Later in the same year, she reviewed a new edition of William Wordsworth. In 1843, she reviewed R. H. Horne's *Orion: An Epic Poem in Three Books* (1843) for the *Athenaeum*, and then she gave up literary criticism in order to devote more time to her poetry.

Select works other than poetry

NONFICTION: *The Letters of Elizabeth Barrett Browning*, 1897; *The Letters of Robert Browning and Elizabeth Barrett Browning*, 1899; *Diary by E. B. B.: The Unpublished Diary of Elizabeth Barrett Browning, 1831-1832*, 1969 (Philip Kelly and Ronald Hudson, editors).

MISCELLANEOUS: *Prometheus Bound, Translated from the Greek of Aeschylus: And Miscellaneous Poems*, 1833.

L. Robert Stevens

Bibliography · A multivolume collection, *The Brownings' Correspondence*, edited by Philip Kelley et al., 1984-, will contain all the Brownings' letters when it is completed. Three other collections of letters are F. G. Kenyon, ed., *Letters of Elizabeth Barrett Browning*, 2 vols., 1897; Elvan Kintner, ed., *Letters of Robert Browning and Elizabeth Barrett Barrett, 1845-1846*, 1969; and Meredith B. Raymond and Mary Rose Sullivan, eds., *The Letters of Elizabeth Barrett Browning to Mary Russell Mitford*, 3 vols., 1983. The definitive biography is Gardner B. Taplin, *The Life of Elizabeth Barrett Browning*, 1957. See also Margaret Forster's *Elizabeth Barrett Browning*, 1988. For the Brownings' life together, see Daniel Karlin, *The Courtship of Robert Browning and Elizabeth Barrett*, 1985, and Julia Markus, *Dared and Done*, 1995. Criticism includes Alethea Hayter, *Mrs. Browning*, 1963; Angela Leighton, *Elizabeth Barrett Browning*, 1986; Helen Cooper, *Elizabeth Barrett Browning*, 1988; and Dorothy Mermin, *Elizabeth Barrett Browning*, 1989.

ROBERT BROWNING

Born: Camberwell, London, England; May 7, 1812
Died: Venice, Italy; December 12, 1889

Poetry · *Pauline*, 1833 · *Paracelsus*, 1835 · *Sordello*, 1840 · *Bells and Pomegranates*, 1841-1846 (published in eight parts and contains *Dramatic Lyrics*, 1842, and *Dramatic Romances and Lyrics*, 1845) · *Christmas Eve and Easter Day*, 1850 · *Men and Women*, 1855 (2 volumes) · *Dramatis Personae*, 1864 · *The Ring and the Book*, 1868-1869 (4 volumes) · *Balaustion's Adventure*, 1871 · *Prince Hohenstiel-Schwangau: Saviour of Society*, 1871 · *Fifine at the Fair*, 1872 · *Red Cotton Nightcap Country: Or, Turf and Towers*, 1873 · *Aristophanes' Apology*, 1875 · *The Inn Album*, 1875 · *Pacchiarotto and How He Worked in Distemper*, 1876 · *The Agamemnon of Aeschylus*, 1877 (drama translation in verse) · *La Saisiaz, and The Two Poets of Croisac*, 1878 · *Dramatic Idyls*, 1879-1880 (in two parts) · *Jocoseria*, 1883 · *Ferishtah's Fancies*, 1884 · *Parleyings with Certain People of Importance in Their Day*, 1887 · *The Poetical Works of Robert Browning*, 1888-1894 (17 volumes) · *Asolando*, 1889 · *Robert Browning: The Poems*, 1981 (2 volumes)

Achievements · Robert Browning is, with Alfred, Lord Tennyson, one of the two leading Victorian poets. Although Browning did not invent the dramatic monologue, he expanded its possibilities for serious psychological and philosophical expression, and he will always be considered a master of the dramatic poem. Browning's best poetry appears in three volumes: *Men and Women, Dramatis Personae*, and *The Ring and the Book*. Browning typically writes as if the poem were an utterance of a dramatic character, either a creation of his own imagination or his re-creation of some historical personage. He speaks through a mask, or dramatic persona, so that his poems must be read as little plays, or as scenes or fragments of larger dramas. The dramatic mask allowed him to create in his audience a conflict between sympathy and judgment: As the reader often judges the dramatic speaker to be evil, he nevertheless sympathizes with his predicament. The dramatic monologue allows the author to explore the thoughts and feelings of deviant psychology to an extent seldom practiced before. On the other hand, when the author always speaks through a character, taking on the limitations and prejudices of a dramatic figure, he conceals his own feelings and ideas from his reader. His critics charge that he evaded the writer's most important duty by failing to pass judgment on his characters, and by

Library of Congress

presenting murders, villains, and whores without a word of moral reprobation. He is accused of valuing passion for its own sake, failing to construct his own framework of values that would allow the reader to evaluate and judge the ethical position of his characters. Nevertheless, Browning deserves to be read as a serious innovator in poetic form; his conception of dramatic character influenced modern fiction as well as poetry.

Biography · Robert Browning was born in a London suburb, Camberwell, on May 7, 1812. His family could be characterized as comfortably middle-class, politically liberal, and dissenting in religion. His father, a prosperous employee of the Bank of England, had collected a large private library.

The family was dominated to some extent by the powerful personality of Browning's mother, the former Sarah Anna Wiedemann from Dundee, who was deeply committed to the Congregational religion. At a time when Oxford and Cambridge were religious institutions, admitting only Anglican students, Browning attended the newly instituted University of London for a short time in 1828, but he did not complete a coherent course of study. Browning was largely self-taught and, like many autodidacts, he had difficulty appreciating how deeply learned he was and judging what his more conventionally educated audience would be likely to know. His poetry bristles with allusions and historical references that require a specialist's explanation.

As a boy, Browning showed remarkable enthusiasm for the work of Percy Bysshe Shelley. Such an admiration is particularly surprising in the light of their divergent beliefs. Shelley was antireligious, especially in his youth, and was in fact expelled from his university for publishing a pamphlet on the necessity of atheism, while Browning's mother was firmly committed to a fundamentalist and emotional Christian belief. In any event, throughout his life, Browning depicted churchmen in an unfavorable light in his poems—a tendency that is perhaps understandable in a follower of Shelley, but one that suggests considerable tension between the mother and her son over religious matters. Shelley glorified the romantic rebel, as in his depiction of Prometheus, for example; Browning's father, on the other hand, was employed by the Bank of England, and the family comfort depended on the stability and success of that existing order. Shelley's extremely liberal ideas about politics and personal relationships must have been difficult to fit harmoniously into the boy's comfortable, religious, suburban home life.

In 1852, when Browning was forty years old, a collection of letters supposed to have been written by Shelley was published, and Browning was engaged to write the "Preface." The letters were discovered later to be spurious and the volume was withdrawn from publication, but Browning's "Preface" remains one of his most important explanations of his artistic theory. In the "Preface," Browning makes his famous distinction between "objective" and "subjective" writers, which can be imagined as the difference between the mirror and the lamp. An objective poet reflects or mirrors the outer world, making it clearer and easier to understand by writing about what takes place outside himself. The subjective poet, however, is like a lamp projecting from his inner flame a light by which the reader sees everything in a new way. Although the words "subjective" and "objective" seem to get hopelessly tangled as the argument proceeds, it appears that Browning views his dramatic characters as lamps, shedding their light on the world, allowing the reader to imagine the inner flame that produces such rays of fancy and imagination, shaping and distorting whatever they fall upon.

At the age of twenty, Browning published *Pauline*, which was to be the first step in a massive work projected to be the utterances of a series of characters distinct from the author himself. The work is in the tradition of Romantic confessional writing. John Stuart Mill wrote an unpublished review of *Pauline*, which eventually came to Browning's attention, in which he accused the poet of having a more intense and morbid self-consciousness than he had ever before seen in a sane man. These cutting words are particularly ironic coming from the author of Mill's *Autobiography* (1873), a totally self-conscious production. Nevertheless, Browning was stung by the criticism and in the future tried to hide his own identity, his personal self, ever more cleverly behind the mask of dramatic speakers. *Pauline* was followed by *Paracelsus* and *Sordello*. These three works all treat the predicament of an artist or seer at odds with his environment and his historical age. The phenomenon of alienation, estrangement from one's own culture and time, is one of Browning's repeated topics, as is the role of the artist and the artist's relationship to society at large. Betty B. Miller in *Robert Browning: A Portrait* (1953) argues that there is a close identification between Browning and the central characters in these three works, so that Paracelsus is Browning, his garden at Wurzburg is identical to Browning's garden at the family home in Camberwell, and so on.

For about ten years, from 1837 to 1847, Browning devoted much of his energy to writing stage plays. These must be considered practical failures, although *Strafford* (1837) ran for five performances on the professional stage with the famous tragedian William Charles Macready in the hero's role. Browning had difficulty in treating external action, which is necessary in a staged performance, and turned instead to internal conflicts which were invisible to his audience. Although the plays simply did not work on stage, they were the workshop for the great dramatic monologues in *Men and Women* and *Dramatis Personae*.

In 1845-1846 Browning courted the semi-invalid poet Elizabeth Barrett. They were married on September 12, 1846, and fled immediately to Italy. The popular imagination has clothed this romance in a gauze of sentimentality, so that Browning appears as a knight in shining armor rescuing his maiden from her ogre of a father. Even a cursory reading of the Browning-Barrett letters suggests that the romance was rather more complicated and contradictory. Miller's *Robert Browning: A Portrait* suggests that Browning had a need to be dominated by a woman. His mother supplied that role until her death in 1840, and then he found her surrogate in Elizabeth

Barrett, who was a considerably more famous writer than he was at the time. Miller points to places where Elizabeth simply took the controlling hand in their relationship and points to the nine-year period of silence between *Men and Women* and *Dramatis Personae* as the consequence of Elizabeth's domination of Browning until her death, June 29, 1861. The truth is probably not so sinister as Miller thinks, nor so blissful as depicted in modern popular plays such as *Robert and Elizabeth*. There appear to have been areas of gross disagreement between Elizabeth and Robert that would have been difficult to reconcile in day-to-day life. For example, Elizabeth, like Browning's mother, believed in the spiritual world, while Browning distrusted those who made supernatural claims.

The publication of *The Ring and the Book*, along with the earlier *Men and Women* and *Dramatis Personae*, established Browning as one of the major writers of the nineteenth century. *The Ring and the Book* tells, from a number of sharply differing points of view, the story of a scandalous murder case. It resembles the plan of Browning's earliest work, *Pauline*, in that it represents the speech of "Brown, Smith, Jones, and Robinson," who are characters quite distinct from the author. It was a project of which Elizabeth had disapproved in her lifetime. Browning's later works became more and more cryptic and complex as he further pushed his ideas of dramatized poetry, but his fame grew rapidly, spurred by the formation of the Browning Society in London in 1881. Following his death in Venice, December 12, 1889, his body was moved to England and interred in Westminster Abbey.

Analysis · "Porphyria's Lover," published along with "Johanes Agricola" under the caption "Madhouse Cells" in *Dramatic Lyrics*, exemplifies Robert Browning's use of the dramatic monologue. Written in sixty lines of iambic quatrameter (rhymed ababb), the poem is spoken entirely by a dramatic character, much like the soliloquies in William Shakespeare's plays. Typically, the monologue can occur only at a moment of inaction, enabling the character to pause from whatever he has been doing and reflect for a moment. What he proceeds to say implies a larger framework of surrounding circumstances: the dramatic situation. Understanding the dramatic situation within a monologue necessitates reader participation in order to discover the circumstances that are only implied in the poem.

By looking closely at the text of "Porphyria's Lover," the reader learns that the speaker is a man who has just strangled his lover, Porphyria. The dead woman's head rests on his shoulder as he speaks, and he looks with approval upon the murder he has committed. The speaker relates the events of the dark, stormy evening: Alone in a cottage, he waited for his beloved Porphyria to enter. Evidently, her absence had been the result of her attendance at a "gay feast," one of the "vainer ties" which Porphyria presumably cultivated. Left alone, the speaker had become obsessed by the need for Porphyria's presence, and, when she finally entered the cottage, her lover could only think, "mine, mine, fair, perfectly pure and good." Strangling her in her own hair, he has propped her dead head on his shoulder, and so he sits as he speaks his monologue. Exultant that he has done the perfect thing, he ends his speech with the words, "And yet God has not said a word."

The dramatic monologue is always spoken by a dramatic character, creating a condition called limited narration. Everything that the reader hears is limited to what the speaker sees, thinks, and chooses to tell. Frequently, limited narration can be "unreliable," so that the reader has reason to believe that the speaker is mistaken or lying. In "Porphyria's Lover" the problem of unreliable narration occurs when the speaker says that the perfect thing to do in his situation was to strangle his beloved.

Some critics point to a poem such as this and assert that Browning's form of writing is vicious, that he evades his duty as a moral teacher by not passing judgment on his characters' actions. In reply, many scholars argue that Browning has indeed provided sufficient guidance for the reader to form a normative judgment, thus overriding the limited and defective judgment of the murderer. The careful reader of this poem will find much evidence to indict the speaker as a madman and criminal. His very mention of God in the closing line reveals an expectation of punishment. Such an expectation could only result from a subconscious admission of guilt. Thus, even the murderer in a deranged way has brought a moral judgment upon himself. Browning has developed a situation that produces a conflict in the reader between sympathy for the character and judgment of him. The beauty rather than the fault of this poem is Browning's mastery at creating such a conflict and involving the reader in its solution.

"My Last Duchess," another poem published in *Dramatic Lyrics*, exhibits many of the features discussed with reference to "Porphyria's Lover," while showing a considerable advance in artistic power and seriousness. Browning's dramatic poems fall into three categories: soliloquies, in which the persona speaks alone or *solus* on stage; monologues, in which a single speaker on stage addresses a defined dramatic audience, who must be imagined present; and epistles, monologues constructed as if they were letters written from one character to another. "My Last Duchess" is a monologue, having a speaking persona and a clearly defined dramatic audience. The dramatic situation of this poem is derived from history. The subtitle of the poem is "Ferrara," and it is likely that the persona is Browning's dramatization of Alfonso II, the fifth Duke of Ferrara. Alfonso II married Lucrezia de' Medici, daughter of Cosimo I de' Medici, Duke of Florence. The Medici family were newly arrived upstarts in comparison with the more ancient house of Ferrara. The Duchess of Alfonso II, Lucrezia de' Medici, died at the age of seventeen in 1561, it being said that she was poisoned. Three years later Alfonso contracted to marry Barbara, niece of the Count of Tyrol.

The dramatic situation of "My Last Duchess" probably involves Duke Alfonso II imagined as addressing an envoy from the Count of Tyrol in order to negotiate the details of his wedding with Barbara. One of the main objectives of the Duke's speech is to "soften up" his adversary in the negotiations so as to extract from him the maximum dowry and to exact the most dutiful compliance with his wishes by his future wife and in-laws. The reader must imagine the Duke walking with his guest in the Duke's art gallery while an entertainment is going on for the other guests in the lower hall of his castle. The Duke pauses before a painting covered by a curtain, asks his guest to sit, and opens the curtain to display a striking portrait of his previous wife, who is dead. While the envoy contemplates the picture of the dead wife, the Duke explains that he was not completely happy with his last mate. She did not appreciate the value of his "nine hundred years old name" and so the Duke "gave commands" and her annoying smiles stopped completely. She stands in the portrait as if alive, and he invites the envoy to gaze on her. Then the Duke suggests that they join the party below, mentioning in passing that he is sure that the Count will give him any dowry that he desires. As they descend the stairs, the Duke points out a statue of the pagan god Neptune taming a sea horse, which recapitulates the struggle of the Duke with the envoy. The envoy has no chance of winning a contest of will with the Duke, just as the sea horse must submit to the god of the sea. The power is all in the Duke's hands.

"The Bishop Orders His Tomb at St. Praxed's Church" appeared in *Dramatic Romances*. Subtitled "Rome, 15–," it appears to refer to a real place, the church of St. Praxed near Rome, but unlike "My Last Duchess" it does not seem to refer to a particular person or historical event. One must construct a general idea of a worldly bishop in Italy in the sixteenth century on his deathbed speaking these lines. The dying man has his "nephews" or illegitimate sons, including his favorite, Anselm, at his bedside to communicate his last wishes to them. From the details of his speech, the reader learns that the sons' mother, the Bishop's mistress, was a beautiful woman, and that the Bishop had a rival for power called old Gandolf, who is buried in St. Praxed's Church. The Bishop orders his sons to build him a tomb in the church that will put Gandolf's to shame by its richness. Such a tomb will be costly to build, but the dying bishop makes a shocking revelation to the boys: There was once a fire in the church from which the Bishop saved an enormous semiprecious stone, a lump of lapis lazuli, which he hid. He now tells the boys where to find the buried treasure, provided they will put it on his funeral statue as a decoration.

The depiction of the Bishop's character is a study in hypocrisy. One expects a churchman to be humble and honest, to deny his physical desires, to abstain from sex and the gratification of worldly lusts. As his mind wanders and he nears death, this bishop appears to be just the opposite. Rather than living celibate, he has fathered these sons who stand around him and he has loved their voluptuous mother. Rather than showing generosity to his enemies, even at the moment of death he is filled with petty jealousy of old Gandolf. He has stolen the church's jewel from the conflagration. He even confuses Christianity and paganism as he describes the frieze he wants on his tomb as a mixture of erotic pagan elements and Christian scenes. Next to the depiction of the virgin martyr St. Praxed, he wants a Bacchic orgy with "one Pan ready to twitch the Nymph's last garment off."

Works such as "The Bishop Orders His Tomb at St. Praxed's Church" were influential on the novel and the short story as well as on modern poetry, for they expanded the notion of character in fiction. Character is sometimes defined as what man habitually chooses to do. A character is said to be a liar if he usually lies. Another is a brave man if he usually refuses to run from danger. Browning writes many poems about churchmen, perhaps because their ethical character is so sharply defined. The minute one sees a character dressed as a bishop, one expects that this man will habitually act in a certain way, that his actions will be loving, self-sacrificing, humble, Christian, and that he will not put his faith in the material world, but concern himself with heavenly goals. Browning puts such a character in a moment of unusual stress in which his expected role crumbles, and one sees through his public face to an inner set of unexpected feelings. At any other time in his life, the Bishop of St. Praxed's, dressed in his robes and healthy and strong, would never have revealed that he was subject to lust, greed, pride, and all the un-Christian characteristics he reveals to his sons on his deathbed. Browning has found a moment when the Bishop's public face cracks and his inner personality is revealed. The poem explores the conflict between the public role and the private personality of a man.

In addition to "The Bishop Orders His Tomb at St. Praxed's Church," Browning wrote a number of other poems about religious hypocrites, including "Bishop Blougram's Apology," published in *Men and Women*. The dramatic situation is a nineteenth century dinner party given by Blougram for a young newspaperman, who is an unbeliever. Blougram talks at length to the younger man and, perhaps a bit intoxicated by his own importance or an unusual amount of wine, confesses some things that he would not normally say in public because they do not fit the expected role of a bishop. The newspaperman Gigadibs despises Blougram because, while the Bishop is intelligent enough to know that miracles and the historically untrue parts of the Bible are mere superstition, he nevertheless publicly professes to believe in them. He must therefore be a hypocrite. Apparently Gigadibs has also accused the Bishop of profiting from his profession of belief and so achieving a comfortable and powerful position in life. Perhaps the poem refers to the Roman Catholic Cardinal Wiseman and Cardinal John Henry Newman, whose *Apologia pro Vita Sua* (1864) may be reflected in the title of Browning's poem.

Blougram's reply to Gigadibs' charges is important for an understanding of Browning's idea of characterization in fiction. At line 375 and following, Blougram suggests that Gigadibs thinks that a few intelligent people will always look at Blougram and "know me whether I believe in the last winking virgin, as I vow, and am a fool, or disbelieve in her and am a knave." Even so, Blougram maintains that these intelligent people will be those most fascinated with him because he maintains an impossibly contradictory balance:

> You see lads walk the street . . . what's to note in that? You see one lad o'erstride a chimney-stack; him you must watch—he's sure to fall, yet stands! Our interest's on the dangerous edge of things. The honest thief, the tender murderer, the superstitious atheist . . . we watch while these in equilibrium keep the giddy line midway: one step aside, they're classed and done with. I, then, keep the line. . . .

Browning's characters are people caught in impossible contradictions, frequently between their expected or usual pattern of behavior and some contrary inner impulse. The situations named by Blougram as fascinating are explored in Browning's poetry: the tender murderer is Porphyria's lover, for example. As in nearly all of Browning's dramatic poems, "Bishop Blougram's Apology" leaves the reader struggling to find a normative judgment. Is Blougram a hypocritical exploiter of religion for his own worldly benefit and therefore subject to scorn, or is he something else? Even though the concluding lines of the poem are spoken as if in the voice of Browning himself, it is still difficult to say whether one should approve of Blougram or despise him. In that impossible "equilibrium" the reader is fascinated.

Browning took the dramatic situation of the poem "Andrea del Sarto" mainly from Giorgio Vasari's *Lives of the Painters* (1550, 1568), which includes a discussion of the painter Andrea del Sarto, called the "faultless painter" because of the technical perfection of his art. Andrea married a widow, Lucrezia del Fede, in 1512 and was subsequently summoned from Florence, Italy, to work at the court of Francis I of France at Fontainebleau. According to Vasari's story, Francis I gave Andrea money to purchase art works in Florence, but he misappropriated the funds and had to live in hiding because he allowed himself to be dominated by the artful and wicked Lucrezia. A self-portrait of Andrea and Lucrezia hung in the Pitti Palace at Florence while the Brownings were residents in Italy. Elizabeth Browning's cousin, John Kenyon, asked Browning to send him a photograph of the painting and, so the story goes, Browning composed and sent him this poem instead.

The poem illustrates the idea of the "magnificent failure," one of Browning's most important concepts. In order to understand the "magnificent failure" the reader must be aware of thinking current in the 1850's concerning the relation of art to society. For example, John Ruskin in *The Stones of Venice* (1851-1853) makes a distinction between slave art and free art. Slave art, such as an Egyptian pyramid, sets up a simple design so that any slave can execute it perfectly. Free art, such as a Gothic cathedral, engages the creative impulses of every worker so that it is never completed and is marked by the luxuriant variety of every worker's creation. A perfect, finished, polished work of art signifies that the artist set his design too low, did not strive to reach beyond the limits of his power. Perfect art is the sign of moral degeneration. Andrea's painting is slave's work because it is perfect.

In the poem, Andrea del Sarto is speaking to his dramatic audience, and his wife Lucrezia, who is impatient with him, wishes to go out in the evening to join her "cousin," or lover, who is whistling for her in the street. In the opening lines, the reader learns that Lucrezia is not kind to the painter and that he must bribe her to stay with him a few minutes. Andrea is unhappy, thinking how his art is not of the highest order despite all its perfection. He never fails to make a perfect drawing because he never sets his design beyond his ability, "but a man's reach should exceed his grasp, or what's a heaven for?" He considers a painting by Raphael and shows how the drawing of an arm in it is poor, but when he corrects the draftmanship, he loses all of the "play, the insight and the stretch" of the imperfect original. He laments his lost productive times when he worked in France and regrets that he must now live in exile. He pathetically asks Lucrezia to be his companion so that he can work more and give her more money. At the conclusion of the poem, Lucrezia's "cousin" whistles for her again while Andrea, who is a faultless painter, envies the glory of less perfect artists.

Andrea paints designs that never challenge his ability and completes perfectly all his undertakings. Ironically, this perfection in art signifies his moral degeneration, for he is a slave to the beautiful but ignorant and unfeeling Lucrezia and to the profit motive, so that he must paint trivial works to earn gold, which Lucrezia simply gives to her "cousin" lover. Artists such as Raphael fail in their work because they set their sights so high that they can never finish or complete their designs perfectly. Although they fail, their works are magnificent. Andrea's perfect works are merely slavish.

In the middle of the nineteenth century, there was a revival of interest in knightly romances and the so-called "matter of Britain," the ancient stories concerning King Arthur's court, evident in Tennyson's *Idylls of the King* (1859) and many other poems of the period. Frequently, the failed quest of the courtly romance was a vehicle for the idea of magnificent failure. Arthur had tried to establish a court of perfect chivalry, but he had failed in the attempt. Nevertheless, his failure was more noble than a practical compromise would have been. Each of his knights must fail in some important way, suffer humiliation and death, even as Christ did, so that the nobility of their endeavor may show forth. Browning's "Childe Roland to the Dark Tower Came" is in this tradition of the courtly failed quest and the magnificent failure.

The subtitle of the poem refers to Shakespeare's *King Lear* (1606), specifically a song by the character Edgar in Act III, Scene 4. Lear on the heath encounters Edgar disguised as a madman. Lear calls him a philosopher and takes him with his company. At the conclusion of the scene, Edgar pronounces some riddling or nonsense lines, including "Child Rowland to the dark tower came." These are apparently garbled snatches of traditional ballads. "Childe" means any untested knight, and Browning's poem constructs a nightmare quest for his untried knight, Childe Roland, who tells of his weird adventure. The poem is best considered a journey into the mind, a psychological rather than a physical quest. Childe Roland tells of his perilous journey across a wasted land in which a cripple advises him to turn into an "ominous tract" where the Dark Tower hides. As soon as he leaves the road, it vanishes. Everything in the enchanted land is sick, wounded, and in torment. Childe Roland thinks of his companions who have failed before him. He crosses a river and stumbles unaware on the "round squat turret." He imagines he sees all his dead companions ranged along the hillside overlooking the arena, yet "dauntless" he sets his horn to his lips and blows the cry, "Childe Roland to the Dark Tower Came."

Like many of Browning's poems, this work seems laden with ambiguity. There are at least three possibilities: the tower is not the true object of a knight's quest and thus Childe Roland is lost when he takes the advice of the cripple to leave the highroad, and he is punished for deviating from his proper goal; or, the tower is the true quest, but Childe Roland's discovery is that it is worthless and ugly when he finds it (therefore, his life is wasted); or, the tower is the quest and is in itself meaningless, but the dedication of Roland creates success out of failure—although the tower is "squat" and ugly, he has played his proper role and even in the face of overwhelming forces, he blows defiance, dauntless to the last.

"Childe Roland to the Dark Tower Came" invites comparison with the surrealist nightmares of Franz Kafka, and Browning's use of a wasteland as a symbol for man's alienation and his evocation of a failed courtly quest foreshadow T. S. Eliot's *The Waste Land* (1922). "Childe Roland to the Dark Tower Came" is one of Browning's most interesting works and it foreshadows developments in the modernist revolution some fifty years after its publication.

The Ring and the Book is Browning's most important poem. Written in blank verse, rhymed iambic pentameter, it appeared in four volumes between November, 1868, and February, 1869. In 1860, Browning came across in Florence a collection of old documents and letters telling the story of the murder trial of Guido Franceschini, who was executed in Rome in 1698. Browning called this volume *The Old Yellow Book;* it has been translated into English by Charles W. Hodell and was published in 1911. From the lawyers' arguments and other documents emerges a particularly sordid case of "divorce Italian style." In 1693, Count Guido Franceschini, an impoverished nobleman forty years old, from the north of Italy, married a thirteen-year-old commoner, Francesca Pompilia, in Rome. She was the daughter of Pietro and Violante Comparini. Pietro had opposed the marriage, knowing that the Count was not as wealthy as he seemed. His wife, however, was attracted by the possibility of a nobleman for a son-in-law and contrived to have the marriage take place. The Comparini family gave all their possessions as dowry to Count Guido, expecting to live in comfort on his estate. The Count, angry to find that the Comparini family was less wealthy than he imagined, harassed them until they were forced to flee from his house. They sued for the return of Pompilia's dowry on grounds that she was not their natural daughter, but a common prostitute's child whom they had adopted. Count Guido increased his cruelty to his child bride, even though she sought help from the local bishop and governor. Pompilia fled from Count Guido's castle with the dashing young priest Caponsacchi in 1697 but Count Guido apprehended the couple near

Rome on April 28, 1697. They were charged with adultery; Caponsacchi was banished, and Pompilia was confined to a nunnery from which she was released on bond to bear her child, a son, at the house of the Comparini on December 18, 1697, almost exactly nine months after her flight from Guido's castle with Caponsacchi. Her son Gaetano stood to inherit the Count's name and estate. Two weeks later, Count Guido broke into the Comparini house and murdered Pietro and Violante, and left Pompilia mortally wounded. Pompilia lived four more days, long enough to accuse Count Guido of the assault. He and his companions were arrested fleeing toward his estate. The bulk of *The Old Yellow Book* presents the legal arguments in this dark case. The murders were admitted, but Count Guido claimed that he was justified as an injured husband to defend his honor. When he was found guilty, he appealed to the Pope, who refused to intervene. Count Guido was beheaded February 22, 1698, in Rome, while his accomplices were hanged. Finally, a convent brought suit to claim the estates forfeited by Pompilia's allegedly adulterous action, but a court ruled that she was innocent and gave all property to her son Gaetano.

Browning converted the material of *The Old Yellow Book* into one of the first relativistic narrative masterpieces. Some authors tell their readers what to think about their characters; others make their readers think for themselves. Browning is one of the latter, presenting his readers with questions rather than giving them answers. In twelve books, Browning tells and retells the story of Pompilia, Count Guido, and the priest Caponsacchi, through their eyes and through the eyes of their lawyers, the eyes of the Pope considering Guido's appeal, and the eyes of three factions of the vulgar population of Rome. Naturally, when Guido explains his action, he not only argues in defense of what he did, but also actually believes that he is right. In his own mind, he is blameless. Likewise, when the reader sees through the limitations and prejudices of Pompilia or of Caponsacchi, the point of view dictates what is right and what is wrong. Many readers coming to Browning's text try to penetrate the tangle of conflicting judgments and opinions presented in these twelve books, and try to say that Browning's sympathy lies with Pompilia or that the Pope speaks for the author. Yet, if there is a single, clear-cut normative judgment, why did Browning feel compelled to write the contradictory monologues that argue against it? More likely, Browning intentionally created a powerful experimental literary form, rather like the limited narration novels of Henry James. Browning's text provides a complicated stimulus, but each reader constructs in his mind his own evaluation of the relative guilt or justification of Count Guido, Pompilia, Caponsacchi, the Pope, and the Comparini family.

Stories are sometimes said to fall into two classes. There are stories such as mediocre mystery tales that cannot bear a second reading. Once the audience has heard the tale to its end, they know "who done it." All questions are solved, so that a second reading would be unnecessary and boring. On the other hand, there is a second kind of story that is so constructed that each reading only deepens the questions in the readers' minds. Every reader is drawn back to the text over and over and the third or fourth reading has as much interest as the first. In *The Ring and the Book* Browning converted a gruesome but mediocre mystery tale into a work of this second type which poses troubling questions about right and wrong, judging and pardoning. Every character evokes some spark of sympathy when allowed to speak for himself or herself. Every character seems subject to guilt when seen through hostile eyes.

The Ring and the Book illustrates Browning's concern with the infinite moment, the instant when a character can act decisively to break out of his characteristic pattern of expected behavior and do the unforeseen. The priest Caponsacchi's flight with the Count's child-bride is an example of the dizzy equilibrium between expected social behavior and contradictory impulse. The reader asks, "How could he do it and still be a priest of God, forsaking his vows of celibacy and all his ordinary rules of conduct?" The reader can imagine what it is to be a priest and what it is to be a lover, but how can there exist such a contradictory character as a lover/priest? The same question can be posed for Pompilia, the childlike innocent yet renegade wife, who is the final winner of them all eventually when her son inherits the estate. The reader has seen many times in literature the childlike, innocent woman, and equally often has encountered the sexual sharpster, but how can these contradictory roles be balanced in a single character?

Boyd Litzinger in *Time's Revenges: Browning's Reputation as a Thinker 1889-1962* (1964) reviews the critical reception of Browning's work during the decade after his death and finds that his immense popularity was based on three chief beliefs among his readers: Browning was a defender of Christianity, although his specific beliefs were subject to considerable doubt; he was admired for an optimistic worldview and his works were thought to urge man to higher and higher efforts to improve his condition; and he was considered to be a serious philosopher and man of ideas. This analysis seems seriously misguided. Browning's religious teachings are contradictory at best. His frequent comic and hostile portraits of churchmen are hard to reconcile with conventional Christian belief. His alleged optimism does not account for the gray sadness of Andrea del Sarto's world, nor the bloody trial of Count Guido, nor even the dauntless but perhaps meaningless call of Childe Roland's horn in the face of the Dark Tower. As a "philosopher," Browning seems to have a taste more for questions than for answers, and although he expands certain ideas such as the conflict of social role versus private personality, or the concept of magnificent failure, he does not develop a coherent system comparable to the philosophic poetry of John Milton.

From the perspective of the present, Browning claims a place of first importance as a protomodernist, a writer who anticipated some of the major developments in art and literature occurring at the beginning of the twentieth century. His use of the dramatic monologue anticipated and to a degree influenced the limited and unreliable narration of such masterpieces of modernism as Joseph Conrad's *Heart of Darkness* (1902) and Ford Madox Ford's *The Good Soldier* (1915). His conception of relativistic and fragmented worlds in which a character is not at home anticipated the vision of T. S. Eliot's *The Waste Land*. His sense of character defined by the conflict between social roles and internal impulses held in a sometimes unstable equilibrium was confirmed by modern psychology. Browning is most interesting when seen not as a Victorian sage but as a forerunner of modernism.

Other literary forms · Robert Browning wrote letters copiously. Published volumes of his correspondence include *Letters of Robert Browning and Elizabeth Barrett Browning, 1845-1846* (1926, Robert B. Browning, editor, 2 volumes), as well as volumes of correspondence between Browning and Alfred Domett, Isa Blagden, and George Barrett. Baylor University holds extensive manuscript and document collections concerning Browning from which *Intimate Glimpses from Browning's Letter File: Selected from Letters in the Baylor University Browning Collection* was published in 1934. An additional collection of about four hundred *New Letters of Robert Browning* has also been published (1950, W. C. DeVane and Kenneth L. Knickerbocker, editors).

For a short time, Browning also attempted to write plays. Unfortunately, the impracticality of performing his particular dramas on stage doomed them to failure. The majority of these works can be found in the *Bells and Pomegranates* series, published between 1841 and 1846.

Select works other than poetry
 DRAMA: *Strafford*, pr., pb. 1837; *Pippa Passes*, pb. 1841; *King Victor and King Charles*, pb. 1842; *The Return of the Druses*, pb. 1843; *A Blot in the 'Scutcheon*, pr., pb. 1843; *Colombe's Birthday*, pb. 1844; *Luria*, pb. 1846; *A Soul's Tragedy*, pb. 1846.

NONFICTION: *Letters of Robert Browning and Elizabeth Barrett Browning, 1845-1846*, 1926 (Robert B. Browning, editor); *Intimate Glimpses from Browning's Letter File: Selected from Letters in the Baylor University Browning Collection*, 1934; *Browning's Essay on Chatterton*, 1948 (Donald A. Smalley, editor); *New Letters of Robert Browning*, 1950 (W. C. DeVane and Kenneth L. Knickerbocker, editors); *The Letters of Robert Browning and Elizabeth Barrett Browning, 1845-1846*, 1969 (Elvan Kintner, editor).

MISCELLANEOUS: *The Works of Robert Browning*, 1912 (10 volumes; F. C. Kenyon, editor); *The Complete Works of Robert Browning*, 1969- .

Todd K. Bender

Bibliography · Biographies include W. H. Griffin and H. C. Minchin, *The Life of Robert Browning*, 1938; Betty Miller, *Robert Browning: A Portrait*, 1952; William Irvine and Park Honan, *The Book, the Ring, and the Poet*, 1974; and Clyde de L. Ryals, *The Life of Robert Browning*, 1993. See also John Maynard, *Browning's Youth*, 1977; Daniel Karlin, *The Courtship of Robert Browning and Elizabeth Barrett*, 1985; and Julia Markus, *Dared and Done*, 1995. Criticism includes G. K. Chesterton, *Robert Browning*, 1903; W. C. DeVane, *A Browning Handbook*, 2d ed., 1955; Roma A. King, *The Bow and the Lyre*, 1957, *The Focusing Artifice*, 1968; Park Honan, *Browning's Characters*, 1961; Thomas J. Collins, *Robert Browning's Moral-Aesthetic Theory, 1833-1855*, 1967; Richard D. Altick and James F. Loucks II, *Browning's Roman Murder Story*, 1968; W. David Shaw, *The Dialectical Temper*, 1968; Philip Drew, *The Poetry of Browning*, 1970; Clyde de L. Ryals, *Browning's Later Poetry*, 1975; and *Becoming Browning*, 1983; Herbert F. Tucker, *Browning's Beginnings*, 1980; and Joseph Bristow, *Robert Browning*, 1991.

ROBERT BURNS

Born: Alloway, Ayrshire, Scotland; January 25, 1759
Died: Dumfries, Scotland; July 21, 1796

Poetry · *Poems, Chiefly in the Scottish Dialect*, 1786 (Kilmarnock edition), 1787 (Edinburgh edition), 1793 (2 volumes)

Achievements · Robert Burns's most significant poetry was written in what may loosely be termed *Scots*–the northern dialect of English spoken regularly by Scottish peasants and informally by Scottish gentry. When the poet attempted to write in standard eighteenth century British English, he came forth as a different person: stiff, conventional, and genteel, seemingly trying too hard to find his place within the poetic tradition of his day. No matter what the dialect, however, literary historians have termed Burns a "pre-Romantic," a poet who anticipated William Wordsworth, gave new life to the English lyric, relied heavily upon literary forms and legends peculiar to the Scottish folk culture, and (certainly the most Wordsworthian quality of them all) wrote in the actual language of the common people. Few realize, however, that the pre-Romantic label is based primarily on Burns's songs, while the bulk of his poetry was written in the forms favored by the majority of eighteenth century poets. He also wrote satire, verse epistles to friends and fellow poets, and even a variation on the mock-epic narrative ("Tam O'Shanter"). An argument could easily be advanced that Burns ranks as a first-rate practitioner of those forms.

Nevertheless, as a writer of satire, epistle, and mock-heroic, Burns does not belong entirely to the neoclassical mainstream which followed John Dryden, Alexander Pope, and Oliver Goldsmith. With his dialect and intricate stanza forms, his poems evinced a heartiness and exuberance, and even a certain "roughness." Burns had little use for Horace, Homer, and the other models for English neoclassicism; instead, he turned to a clearer tradition that had been established during the so-called golden age of Scottish poetry by the major Scottish Chaucerians: Robert Henryson (1430-1506), William Dunbar (1465-1530), and Gavin Douglas (1474-1522). Following the efforts of Allan Ramsay (1686-1758) and Robert Fergusson (1750-1774)–earlier Scottish poets who had collected the ancient poems and had written new ones based on the older models–Burns committed himself to the bards and songs of his native land. He refined the work of his eighteenth century predecessors, but he was also perceptive enough to learn from them and to retain characteristic subjects, forms, stanza patterns, and language.

No matter how academic, the discussion of Burns's poetry seems never to circumvent his songs. Almost to a line, those short pieces have gained wider fame and prompted more discussion than have his longer poems. Burns wrote more than three hundred songs on every subject imaginable within the context of late eighteenth century Scotland. Within the confines of those songs, Burns gave himself almost totally to the emotions of the moment; he reached out, touched the essence of rural Scotland, and brought it lyrically to life. He gave his readers the excitement and the

Library of Congress

genuineness of love, work, friendship, patriotism, and even inebriation (a point that has been greatly overemphasized). He portrayed universal character types, national heroes as well as lowly tavern revelers, and he took delight in sketching the grand parades of humanity as they passed before his vivid and lyrical imagination. Thus, Burns's poetic achievement was really very simple. He assumed the mantle of Scotland's national poet at a time when the country was struggling to preserve its cultural identity. Yet, if Burns spoke for Scotland, he stood also for all English-speaking people, who, as they prepared to undergo the political and technological traumas of the nineteenth century, needed frequent reminders of their national, political, and artistic heritage.

Biography · Robert Burns was born on January 25, 1759, in Alloway, some three miles south of the seaport town of Ayr. He was the first son of William Burnes (the original spelling of the family name that the poet eventually altered) and Agnes Broun. The father belonged to a lowly class of Scots agricultural society: he was a *cotter*, one who occupied a cottage on a farm in exchange for labor. As such, he engaged in a constant struggle to keep himself, his illiterate wife, and their seven children fed and clothed. In 1766, the elder Burnes leased seventy acres near Ayr and committed his family to farming. High rents and poor soil, however, only increased the size of the family debt.

Young Robert studied at a small village school, where, for three years, he read English literature, wrote essays, and learned mathematics. After the practicalities of elementary education had been mastered, further learning came only as time would permit. The local schoolmaster, John Murdock, managed to teach the boy some French, and in 1775, the sixteen-year-old Burns journeyed across the Doon River to Kirkoswald, where he studied the rudiments of surveying. At home, the senior Burnes assumed responsibility for the balance of his son's education: geography, history, devotional and theological literature, and more mathematics. Although chores related to the family farm assumed a high priority, young Burns managed to find time for the Bible, Presbyterian theology, and any books he could beg or borrow from friends and neighbors.

In 1777, William Burnes moved his family some twelve miles to the northwest, to Lochlie Farm, between Tarbolton and Mauchline. There, eighteen-year-old Robert emerged as a sociable, sensitive, and handsome young man. He debated in the Tarbolton Bachelors' Club, a group of serious albeit boisterous young men; he joined the Freemasons; he discovered women. In 1781, he attempted to embark upon a business career in the flax-dressing industry at Irvine, on the coast. The venture proved to be a failure, and for the most part Burns rooted himself to the family farm in central Ayrshire, where he remained until the publication of the Kilmarnock edition of his *Poems* in 1786. William Burnes died in 1784, leaving his family heavily in debt. Robert and his brother Gilbert remained on the farm, however, and the poet's early verse indicates the degree to which he involved himself in the activities, associations, and gossip of the local people.

Burns had begun to write poetry around 1773, when he was fourteen. The poems tended, primarily, to be song lyrics in the Scots vernacular, although (probably as a result of Murdock's influence) he tried his hand at some moral and sentimental pieces in standard English. The manuscripts of those poems reveal considerable roughness. Burns needed models, and not until he came upon the work of two Scots poets, Robert Fergusson and Allan Ramsay, did he learn how to write nonlyric poetry in the Scots vernacular that would appeal to the hearts and minds of his countrymen. Three years prior to the publication of the Kilmarnock edition, he put together a commonplace book (several versions of which have been published), containing both his poems and remarks concerning his poetic development. Thus, the period 1785-1786 marked Burns's most significant literary output. It also proved to be the time when he would have to pay dearly for liaisons with various young women of the area. In May, 1785, his first daughter was born to Elizabeth Paton, a former servant; in all, he fathered nine illegitimate children, four by his future wife, Jean Armour (those were two sets of twins). He accepted responsibility for rearing and supporting all of them. Another affair with a servant girl, Mary Campbell—the "Highland Mary" of the song—ended tragically when the girl died giving birth to another Burns child.

Despite these domestic problems, the Kilmarnock edition of poems was published, bringing Burns success and some money. More important, the volume took him out of Ayrshire and into Edinburgh, where he gained the praise of the critic Henry Mackenzie (1745-1831) and the publisher William Creech (1745-1815), and where he arranged for publication and subscriptions for a new edition of his poems. From November, 1786, to mid-1788, Burns lived in Edinburgh, seeking to establish himself in its social and intellectual atmosphere. Although his congenial personality and intellectual curiosity appealed to the upper levels of Edinburgh society, they were not enough to erase the stigma of low social birth. The upper classes ultimately rejected him. Thus, the young poet drifted to the late-hour social clubs frequented by printers, booksellers, clerks, and schoolmasters. Through it all, he pondered about how to earn a living, since neither poetry nor social contacts enabled him to meet his financial obligations.

Four separate tours throughout Scotland and the editorship of James Johnson's *The Scots Musical Museum* yielded no relief from financial pressures.

In March, 1788, Burns rented a tract of land for farming in Ellisland, Dumfriesshire, after which he finally married Jean Armour. He then began a struggle to support his family, a contest that was not eased even upon his securing an appointment (September, 1789) as tax collector and moving to Dumfries. His literary activities were limited to collecting and writing songs, in addition to the composition of some nonlyric pieces of moderate quality. Although "Tam O'Shanter" belongs to this period, Burns misused his talents by trying to emulate the early eighteenth century poets—composing moral epistles, general verse satires, political ballads, serious elegies, and prologues for theatrical pieces.

Burns died on July 21, 1796, the result of a heart condition that had existed since his youth. The details of his life have been much overstated, particularly the gossip about his drinking and his excessive sexual appetite. For serious students of his poetry, Burns's autobiography can be found within the sound and the sense of his writing.

Analysis · To an extraordinary degree, Robert Burns is *the* poet of Scotland, a Scotland that—despite its union with England—remained for him and his readers a totally independent cultural, intellectual, social, and political entity. Undoubtedly, Burns will always be identified exclusively with Scotland, with its peculiar life and manners communicated to the outside world through its distinctive dialect and fierce national pride. He justly deserves that identification, for he not only wrote about Scottish life and manners, but he also sought his inspiration from Scotland—from his own Ayrshire neighborhood, from its land and its people.

Scotland virtually drips from the lines of Burns's poetry. The scenes of the jocular "Jolly Beggars" have their source in Poosie Nansie's inn at Mauchline, while the poet and Tam O'Shanter meet the witches and the warlocks at midnight on the very real, local, and familiar Alloway Kirk. Indeed, reality obscures even the boldest attempts at erudite romanticism. Burns alludes to actual persons, to friends and acquaintances whom he knew and loved and to whom he dedicated his songs. When he tried his hand at satire, he focused upon local citizens, identifying specific personages or settling for allusions that his eighteenth century Scottish readers would easily recognize. In "The Cotter's Saturday Night"—which features a clear portrait of his own father—the poet reflects his deep attachment to and sincere pride in the village of Alloway and the rural environment of Ayrshire. He viewed the simple scenes in "The Cotter's Saturday Night" as the real essence of Scotland's heritage. Burns began with a sincere love and respect for his neighbors, and he sustained that attitude throughout his life and his work. Without the commitment to Scotland, he never would have conquered the hearts of its native readers nor risen to become the acknowledged national poet of the land north of the Tweed.

Burns's poetry gained almost immediate success among all classes of the Scottish population. He knew of what he wrote, and he grasped almost immediately the living tradition of Scottish poetry, assimilating the qualities of that tradition into his own verse forms and distinct subject matter. For example, the stanzaic forms in such poems as "To a Mouse" (and its companions) had been in existence for more than three hundred years. Burns early had become familiar with the Scottish Chaucerians (John Major, James I of Scotland, Robert Henryson, William Dunbar, Gavin Douglas, Sir David Lindsay) and the folk poets closer to his own day (Allan Ramsay, James Macpherson, Robert Fergusson); he took the best from their forms and content and made them his own. Thus, he probably could not be termed an "original" poet, although he had to work hard to set the tone and style to his readers' tastes. His countrymen embraced his poetry because they found the cadence, the music, and the dialect to be those of their own hearts and minds. The vigor and the deep love may have been peculiar to Burns, but the remaining qualities had existed longer than anyone could determine.

Still, writing in the relatively remote confines of Scotland at the end of the eighteenth century, Burns was not totally alien to the neoclassical norm of British letters. If Alexander Pope or Henry Fielding or Tobias Smollett could focus upon reality and write satires to expose the frailties of humankind, so could Burns be both realistic and satiric. In his most forceful poems—such as "Holy Willie's Prayer," "The Holy Fair," "Address to the Unco Guid"—he set out to expose the religious hypocrites of his day, but at the same time to portray, clearly and truthfully, both the beautiful and the ugly qualities of Scottish life and character. Burns's poetry may not always be even in quality or consistent in force, but it certainly always conveys an air of truthfulness.

If Burns's poetry reverberates with the remoteness of rural Scotland, it is because he found the perfect poetic environment for the universal themes of his works. In 1803, William Wordsworth stood beside his grave and contemplated "How Verse may build a princely throne/ On humble truth." The throne was carved out of Burns's understanding of the most significant theme of his time—the democratic spirit (which helps to explain Wordsworth's tribute). Throughout, the Scottish bard salutes the worth of pure man, the man viewed outside the context of station or wealth.

Certainly, Burns was sensitive to the principles and causes that spawned the revolutions in America and in France; in fact, closer to home, the Jacobite rebellion sparked by the landing of the Young Pretender from France had occurred only nine years before the poet's birth. By nature, he was a political liberal, and his poems take advantage of every opportunity for man or beast to cry for freedom. Again, it was Wordsworth who identified Burns as a poet of the literary revolution—Romanticism—that later rushed through the open gates and into the nineteenth century.

Few will question that, ultimately, Burns's strength as a poet is to be found in the lyrical quality of his songs. That quality simply stood far above his other virtues—his ability to observe and to penetrate until he discovered the essence of a particular subject, his skill in description and satire, and his striving to achieve personal and intellectual independence. In his songs, he developed the ability to record, with the utmost ease, the emotions of the common people of whom he wrote. Burns's reliance on native Scottish tradition was both a limitation and a strength. For example, although he genuinely enjoyed the poetry of James Thomson (1700-1748), the Edinburgh University graduate who ventured to London and successfully challenged the artificiality of English poetry, Burns could not possibly have written a Scottish sequel to *The Seasons* (1726-1730). Instead, he focused upon the simple Scottish farmer, upon the man hard at work and enjoying social relationships, not upon the prevalent eighteenth century themes of solitude and retirement. In Burns, then, the reader sees strong native feeling and spontaneous expression, the source of which was inherited, not learned.

Another quality of Burns's poetry that merits attention is his versatility, the range of human emotions that exists throughout his verse. He could function as a satirist, and he could sound the most ardent notes of patriotism. His humor was neither vulgar nor harsh, but quiet, with considerable control—as in "Address to the Deil," "To a Mouse," and "To a Mountain Daisy." As a lover, as one who obviously loved to love and be loved, he wrote lyrical pieces that could capture the essence of human passion. The lyric forms allowed for the fullest expression of his versatility, most of which came about during the last ten years of his relatively short life.

From 1787 until his death in the summer of 1796, Burns committed himself to steady literary activity. He became associated with James Johnson, an uneducated engraver and enthusiastic collector and publisher of Scottish songs. From 1787 to 1804, Johnson gathered those songs into a five-volume *Scots Musical Museum*, and Burns served as his principal editor. Then the poet became associated with George Thomson, whose *Select Collection of Scottish Airs* reached six volumes between 1793 and 1811.

Burns's temperament seemed suited to such a combination of scholarly activity and poetic productivity, but he never accepted money for his contributions. The writing, rewriting, and transformation of some three hundred old songs and ballads would serve as his most singular gift to his nation. In reworking those antiquated songs and popular ballads, he returned to Scotland, albeit in somewhat modified form, a large portion of its culture that had for so long remained in obscurity. Thus, an old drinking song emerged as "Auld Lang Syne," while a disreputable ballad became "John Anderson My Jo." Finally, the Johnson and Thomson collections became outlets for certain of his more famous original songs: "For A' That and A' That," "Scots, Wha Hae wi' Wallace Bled," as well as such love lyrics as "Highland Mary" and "Thou Lingering Star." Because of his love of and gift for the traditional Scots folk songs and ballads, Burns wrote and sang for Scotland. He became the voice and the symbol of the people and captured the national sentiment.

It would be a mistake, however, to assume that all is happily rustic, nationalistic, or patriotic with Burns. On the contrary, he has a decidedly melancholy or mournful strain. A look at such poems as "A Bard's Epitaph" and the "Epistle to a Young Friend" demonstrates that the intellect and the passion of the poet were far from being comfortably adjusted. A conflict raged within the mind and heart of Burns as the sensibilities of an exceedingly gifted soul vied with the sordid lot that was his by birth and social position (or the lack of it). Despite the appearance and even the actuality of productivity during his last five years, the final stage of Burns's career reflects, in the soberest of terms, the degradation of genius. Nevertheless, his muse remained alive and alert, as his passions seethed within him until they found outlets in rhyme. Burns controlled his passion so that, particularly in his songs, there is abundant evidence of sense and beauty. To his credit, he remained aware of the conflict within him and drew strength from the clash of experiences, of habits, and of emotions which, somehow, he managed to regulate and harmonize. Few will argue that certain of the songs ("Mary Morison," "My Nanie O," and "Of A' the Airts the Wind Can Blow") hang heavy with serious and extremely pathetic and passionate strains. Since such heaviness had its origin in the Scottish tradition, Burns could effectively hide his own melancholy behind the Lugar or the banks of Bonnie Doon.

Such conclusions invariably lead to the question of a religious or moral element in Burns's poetry. Assuredly, the more religious among Burns scholars have difficulty with such poems as "The Holy Fair," "Holy Willie" and the satiric pieces in which the poet ridiculed religious and ecclesiastical ideals and personages. No doubt Burns's own moral conduct was far from perfect, but the careful reader of his poetry realizes immediately that Burns never ridiculed religion; rather, he heaped scorn only upon those religious institutions that appeared ridiculous and lacked the insight to recognize obvious weaknesses. Indeed, the poet often seems to be looking for virtue and morality, seeking to replace the sordid scenes of his own world with the piety of another time and place. He sought a world beyond and above the grotesqueness of his own debauchery, a world dominated by order, love, truth, and joy. That is about the best he could have done for himself. Even had Burns been the epitome of sobriety, morality, and social and religious conformity, religious expression would probably not have been high on his list of poetic priorities. He inherited the poetic legacy of Scotland—a national treasure found outside the limits of the Kirk, a vault not of hymns and psalm paraphrases, but of songs and ballads. Such were the constituent parts of Burns's poetic morality.

Burns's language and poetic methods seem to distract only the impatient among his readers. To begin with, he believed that the vernacular ought never to be seen as low or harsh, or even as prostituted English. Rather, Burns came to know and to understand the Scots dialect and to manipulate it for his own poetic purpose. At the outset, he claimed to have turned his back upon formal bodies of knowledge, upon books, and to have taken full advantage of what he termed "Nature's fire" as the only learning necessary for his art. Nature may have provided the attraction toward the Scots dialect, but Burns himself knew exactly what to do with it. Close attention to his letters and to the details of his life will yield the steps of his self-education. He read Thomas Salmon's *Geographical and Historical Grammar* (1749) and a *New System of Modern Geography, History, and Modern Grammar* (1770), by William Guthrie (1708-1770), both of which provided descriptions and examples of Scotland's traditions and language, although nothing of poetic contexts. Then he turned to Jethro Tull (1680-1740), the Hungerford farmer and inventor, who wrote several volumes on the general subject of "horse-hoeing husbandry" (1731-1739), and to the Reverend Adam Dickson of Edinburgh, who wrote *A Treatise on Agriculture* (1762, 1765, 1769) and the two-volume *The Husbandry of the Ancients* (1788). Thus, Burns was well versed in the specifics of rural Scotland by the time he discovered his most helpful source, the poetry of Robert Fergusson, who had managed successfully to capture the dialect of enlightened Edinburgh. Burns had his models, and he simply shifted the sounds and the scenes from Scotland's capital to rural Ayrshire.

To simplify matters even further, Burns himself had actually stood behind the plow. Little wonder, then, that the Kilmarnock edition of the *Poems* succeeded on the basis of such pieces as "The Twa Dogs," "The Holy

Fair," "Address to the Deil," "Halloween," "The Cotter's Saturday Night," "To a Mouse," and "To a Mountain-Daisy." Burns had effectively described Scottish life as Scots themselves (as well as those south of the Tweed) had come to know it. More important, the poems in that initial collection displayed to the world the poet's full intellectual range of wit and sentiment, although his readers received nothing that had not already been a part of their long tradition. Essentially, the Edinburgh edition of the following year gave the world more of the same, and Burns's readers discovered that the poet's move from Ayrshire to Edinburgh had not changed his sources or his purpose. The new poems—among them "Death and Dr. Hornbook," "The Brigs of Ayr," "Address to the Unco Guid," "John Barleycorn," and "Green Grow the Rushes"—still held to the pictures of Scottish life and to the vernacular, still held to the influence of Robert Fergusson's *Scots Poems* (1773).

By the time Burns had done some substantive work on James Johnson's *The Scots Musical Museum*, however, his art had assumed a new dimension, the writing and revision of the Scots song. The poet became a singer, providing his own accompaniment by the simple means of humming to himself as he wrote, and trying (as he explained) to catch the inspiration and the enthusiasm so strongly characterized in the traditional poetry. He set out to master the tune, then to compose for that particular strain. In other words, he demanded that for the song, musical expression must dictate the poetic theme. Nevertheless, Burns was the first to admit his weakness as a musician, making no claims even to musical taste. For him, as a poet, music was instinctive, supplied by nature to complement his art. Thus, he felt unable to deal with the technical aspects of music as a formal discipline. What he could do, however, was to react quickly to what he termed "many little melodies" and to give new and fresh poetic and musical expression to something like "Scots Wha Hae," one of the oldest of Scottish airs. Through the songs, Burns clearly preserved tradition, while, at the same time, he maintained his originality. This tradition was the genuine expression of the people who, from generation to generation, echoed the essence of their very existence; Burns gave it sufficient clarity and strength to carry it forward into the next century and beyond. The effect of those more than three hundred songs was, simply, to cede Burns the title of Scotland's national poet—a title that he earned because of his poetic rather than his political voice.

Perhaps the one poem that demonstrates Burns's ability as a serious and deliberate craftsman, a true poet, is "Tam O' Shanter" (1790, 1791). More than anything else, that piece of 224 lines transports its creator away from the "Heaven-taught plowman" image, from the label of the boy genius whose poetry is nothing more than one large manifestation of the spontaneous overflow of his native enthusiasm. Burns wrote "Tam O' Shanter" for a volume on Scottish antiquity and based it on a witch story told about Alloway Kirk, an old ruin near the poet's house in Ayr. Yet, he turned that tale into a mockheroic rendering of folk material that comes close, in genre and in poetic quality, to Geoffrey Chaucer's "The Nun's Priest's Tale." Burns specifically set out to construct his most sustained and most artistic production; in his own words, he remained aware of the "spice of roguish waggery" within the poem, but he also took considerable pains to ensure that the force of his poetic genius and "finishing polish" would not go unrecognized. Burns's manipulation of his dipsomaniacal hero and his misadventures constitutes a masterful blending of the serious and the comic. The moralists of his day objected vehemently to the ribald elements of the poem. Early in the next century, William Wordsworth, whose strongest drink was probably water, attacked the attackers of "Tam O' Shanter" (as well as those who objected to all of Burns's poetry on moral grounds) by labeling them impenetrable dunces and narrow-minded puritans. Wordsworth saw the poem as a delightful picture of the rustic adventurer's convivial exaltation; if the poem lacked clear moral purpose, maintained England's laureate, it at least provided the clearest possible moral effect.

The final issue raised by Burns's poetry is his place in literary history—an issue that has always prompted spirited debate. There is no doubt that Burns shares common impulses with Wordsworth and the Romantic movement, particularly in his preoccupation with folklore and the language of the people, yet neither is there any evidence of Burns's fundamental dissatisfaction with the dominant critical criteria and principal literary assumptions of eighteenth century England. The readers of his songs will be hard put to discover lush scenery or majestic mountains, or even the sea—although all were in easy reach of his eye and his mind. If he expressed no poetic interest in such aspects of nature close at hand, however, he turned even less in the direction of the distant and the exotic. Instead, he looked long and hard at the farmer, the mouse, the louse, and he contemplated each; the mountains, the nightingale, the skylark he also saw, but chose to leave them to the next generation of poets. In other words, Burns did not seek new directions for his poetry; instead, he took full advantage of what existed and of what had come before. He grasped literary imitation firmly and gave that form the most significance and prominence it had enjoyed since the late Restoration and the Augustan age. Burns wrote satire and he wrote songs, but he invented neither. Rather, he served as an exploiter of tradition; he gathered inherited motifs, rhetorical conventions, and familiar language and produced art. The reader of the present century should see no less and expect no more from Burns's poetical character.

Other literary forms · As a pure poet, Robert Burns had little time or desire to write in other forms. For *The Scots Musical Museum*, edited by James Johnson between 1787 and 1803, he wrote "Notes on Scottish Song," wherein he tried to collect all of the information he could about the poetic tradition of his native land. He suggested possibilities for authorship, identified the poems' native regions and the occasions of their composition, cited fragments and verses of traditional songs, and set forth critical comments and engaging anecdotes.

Following the publication and success of the 1786 edition of his *Poems*, Burns set off on a series of trips that carried him over much of Scotland. Narratives of two of those journeys, *Journal of a Tour in the Highlands Made in 1787* and *Journal of the Border Tour*, eventually found their way into print in 1834.

Select works other than poetry
NONFICTION: *Journal of a Tour in the Highlands Made in 1787*, 1834 (Allan Cunningham, editor); *Journal of the Border Tour*, 1834 (Cunningham, editor); *The Letters of Robert Burns*, 1931 (2 volumes; John De Lancey Ferguson, editor).

Samuel J. Rogal

Bibliography · James Kinsley, ed., *The Poems and Songs of Robert Burns*, 1968, is the standard edition of Burns's works, and it includes extensive and very informative notes. In his excellent biography, *The Life of Robert Burns*, 1932, reprint, 1968, Franklyn Bliss Snyder describes the land of Burns's Ayrshire and discusses both the man and the poet. David Daiches, *Robert Burns*, 1950, is an accessible introduction to Burns that examines Burns's poetic achievement, considers Burns's place in the Scottish literary tradition, and analyzes individual poems. R. D. S. Jack and Andrew Noble, eds., *The Art of Robert Burns*, 1982, has a collection of critical essays considering Burns's lyrics, satire, musical qualities, narrative verse, letters, relation to the Romantic revolt, and role as the quintessential Scot. Carol McGuirk, *Robert Burns and the Sentimental Era*, 1985, shows how Burns's work achieves the classical standard of universality, shows imaginative power, and delineates a world that is broadly human and familiar; McGuirk believes that Burns's use of dialect neither determines nor excessively restricts his range of poetic vision.

GEORGE GORDON, LORD BYRON

Born: London, England; January 22, 1788
Died: Missolonghi, Greece; April 19, 1824

Poetry · *Fugitive Pieces*, 1806 · *Poems on Various Occasions*, 1807 · *Hours of Idleness*, 1807 · *Poems Original and Translated*, 1808 · *English Bards and Scotch Reviewers*, 1809 · *Hints from Horace*, 1811 · *Childe Harold's Pilgrimage*, Cantos I-IV, 1812-1818, 1819 (the 4 cantos published together) · *The Curse of Minerva*, 1812 · *Waltz: An Apostrophic Hymn*, 1813 · *The Giaour*, 1813 · *The Bride of Abydos*, 1813 · *The Corsair*, 1814 · *Ode to Napoleon Buonaparte*, 1814 · *Lara*, 1814 · *Hebrew Melodies Ancient and Modern*, 1815 · *The Siege of Corinth*, 1816 · *Parisina*, 1816 · *Poems*, 1816 · *The Prisoner of Chillon, and Other Poems*, 1816 · *Monody on the Death of the Right Honourable R. B. Sheridan*, 1816 · *The Lament of Tasso*, 1817 · *Manfred*, 1817 (verse drama) · *Beppo: A Venetian Story*, 1818 · *Mazeppa*, 1819 · *Don Juan*, Cantos I-XVI, 1819-1824, 1826 (the 16 cantos published together) · *Marino Faliero, Doge of Venice*, 1821 (verse drama) · *The Prophecy of Dante*, 1821 · *Sardanapalus*, 1821 (verse drama) · *The Two Foscari*, 1821 (verse drama) · *Cain: A Mystery*, 1821 (verse drama) · *The Vision of Judgment*, 1822 · *Heaven and Earth*, 1822 (verse drama) · *The Age of Bronze*, 1823 · *The Island*, 1823 · *Werner: Or, The Inheritance*, 1823 (verse drama) · *The Deformed Transformed*, 1824 (unfinished verse drama) · *The Complete Poetical Works of Byron*, 1980-1986 (5 volumes)

Achievements · If poets can be judged by the intellectual and cultural myths that they inspire, then George Gordon, Lord Byron must be deemed the most broadly influential of the Romantic writers. Through his creation of a brooding and defiant persona known as the "Byronic Hero"—according to Peter L. Thorslev, Jr., a composite blend of the attributes of Cain, Ahasuerus, Satan, Prometheus, Rousseau's Child of Nature, the Man of Feeling, the Gloomy Egoist, the Gothic Villain, and the Noble Outlaw— Byron exerted a profound impact on the entire nineteenth century and its conception of the archetypal Romantic sensibility. The essential trait that came to be associated with "Byronism" is what Bertrand Russell, in his *History of Western Philosophy* (1945), identifies as "Titanic cosmic self-assertion." Signifying less a specific stance than a generalized attitude, the phrase denotes a proud, often despairing, rebellion against any institutional or moral system that threatens to rob the self of its autonomy, centrality, and independence. Something of the extent to which this outlook captured the imagination of the age can be gauged from a brief list of artists and thinkers whose works reflect Byron's influence: in Germany, Johann Wolfgang von Goethe, Heinrich Heine, Ludwig van Beethoven, and Friedrich Nietzsche; in France, Honorè de Balzac, Stendhal, Hector Berlioz, and Eugène Delacroix; in Russia, Aleksandr Pushkin and Fyodor Dostoevski; and in America, Herman Melville. Even Matthew Arnold, that most Wordsworthian of Victorian critics, admitted in his 1850 poem "Memorial Verses" that the collective English soul "Had *felt* him like the thunder's roll." Thirty-one years later, Arnold's view had not changed: "The power of Byron's personality," he wrote, approvingly quoting A. C. Swinburne, "lies in . . . '*the excellence of sincerity and strength.*' "

What fascinated nineteenth century audiences about Byron was not simply the larger-than-life character of the man transmuted into art, but also the flinty integrity of his mind that penetrated all deception and constantly tested the limits of skepticism. In this respect Byron seems peculiarly modern. Although often considered a Romantic paradox because of various antitheses in his nature (he led the Romantic revolution toward "expression" in poetry, for example, but was thoroughly Augustan in his literary ideals and a lifelong admirer of Alexander Pope), he rarely succumbs to the temptation of believing his own fictions and always examines his experience with obsessive self-honesty. In conversations with his friend and confidante Lady Blessington, Byron thus confessed to being "so changeable . . . such a strange *mèlange* of good and evil, that it would be difficult to describe me," but he goes on to say: "There are but two sentiments to which I am constant—a strong love of liberty, and a detestation of cant." These last qualities undoubtedly explain why the vein of satire was so congenial to him as a poet. In both the barbed heroic couplets of *English Bards and Scotch Reviewers*, the scathing burlesque that launched his career, and the seriocomic use of ottava rima in *Don Juan*, the epic satire which he never lived to complete, Byron sought to expose the smug complacencies and absurd pretensions of his time and, if possible, to restore to it the ability to see itself objectively. The dark *Weltschmerz* of poems such as *Childe Harold's Pilgrimage* may attest his personal despair over whether that goal could ever be accomplished, but in all his varigated moods he writes with energetic conviction born of "sincerity and strength." Byron's seminal achievement, therefore, may be his capacity for embodying the strivings of a deeply restless age, for articulating those longings and doing what all great poets do—namely, to return the imagination to the world.

Library of Congress

Biography · George Gordon, the sixth Lord Byron, was born with a clubbed right foot, a deformity that caused him considerable suffering throughout his life and did much to shape his later character. He was descended from two aristocratic and colorful families: his father, who died when Byron was three years old, was Captain John ("Mad Jack") Byron, a rake and fortune hunter who traced his ancestry back to the time of William the Conqueror; his mother, Catherine Gordon of Gight, was the irascible and outspoken heiress who liked to boast of her lineal connection to James I of Scotland. After her husband squandered the Gordon inheritance, Mrs.

Byron moved to Aberdeen, where she reared her son under straitened financial circumstances and the Calvinistic creed of Scottish Presbyterianism. With the death of his great-uncle in 1798, the ten-year-old Byron became a titled English peer and took up residence at the patrimonial estate of Newstead Abbey in Nottingham. During this period the precocious young lord fell in love with two cousins named Mary Duff and Margaret Parker, was initiated into premature sexual dalliance by a nurse, and began his zealous regimen of swimming, boxing, fencing, and horsemanship to compensate for his physical lameness.

While at Harrow (1801-1805) and subsequently at Cambridge (1805-1807), Byron started to develop some of the strong attachments and habits that remained with him into adulthood. Though he little relished formal schooling, he periodically immersed himself in reading, became infatuated with Mary Chaworth, and cultivated lasting friendships with his half sister Augusta Leigh as well as with John Cam Hobhouse, Scrope Davies, Francis Hodgson, and others. He also incurred sizable debts for his extravagant revelries at Newstead during college vacations, and, simultaneously, he was entering the arena of literary authorship. His first few volumes of juvenilia, *Fugitive Pieces* and *Poems on Various Occasions*, were privately printed and circulated; *Hours of Idleness*, however, his ensuing venture into the public domain, prompted caustic notice by Henry Brougham, which in turn fueled the retaliatory satire of *English Bards and Scotch Reviewers*. Shortly thereafter, tiring of his life of routine dissipation, Byron prepared to leave England.

The next seven years were momentous ones in Byron's life. Before committing himself to what he thought might eventually be a Parliamentary career, he determined to broaden his education by visiting other lands and peoples. Accordingly, in 1809 he embarked with Hobhouse on an exhilarating tour through Portugal, Spain, Malta, Albania, Greece, and Asia Minor. The vivid scenes and experiences of this two-year excursion provided Byron with the materials for Cantos I-II of his autobiographical travelogue *Childe Harold's Pilgrimage* and his several Eastern tales in verse. Eight months after his return to England in 1811, *Childe Harold's Pilgrimage* was published and Byron became an overnight celebrity: "I awoke one morning," wrote the nobleman-poet, "and found myself famous." Because Byron was readily identified with the melancholic, jaded, and quasi-erotic hero of his poem, he was besieged by ladies of fashion and lionized by the beau monde of Regency London. Foremost among those giddily vying for the attentions of the handsome and aristocratic young author was Lady Caroline Lamb, a flamboyant, decidedly eccentric woman who to her delight discovered Byron to be "mad—bad—and dangerous to know." Perhaps as much to escape such frenzied pursuit as for any other reason, Byron in early 1815 married Annabella Milbanke, a demure and somewhat priggish "bluestocking" whom Byron dubbed "my Princess of Parallelograms." The ill-fated marriage dissolved a year later, after the birth of a daughter Augusta Ada, when Lady Byron learned of her husband's incestuous relations with his half sister. Socially ostracized by all but his close friends and beset by creditors, Byron left England on April 25, 1816, never to return.

The legendary final phase of Byron's career, which saw his full maturation as a poet, was crowded with events that ensured his lasting renown. Journeying through France to Switzerland, he spent his first summer in exile near Geneva, where he met two other expatriates, Percy Bysshe Shelley and Mary Shelley, with whom he enjoyed many evenings of intellectual conversation. While there, Byron also completed Canto III of *Childe Harold's Pilgrimage*, began *Manfred*, and tried unsuccessfully to stay uninvolved with Mary Shelley's persistent stepsister Claire Clairmont, who, in January, 1817, bore him a daughter, Allegra. By the spring of that year Byron had established himself in Venice, "the greenest isle" of his imagination, where he diverted himself with numerous affairs while periodically exploring the antiquities of Florence and Rome.

The atmosphere of Italy did much to stimulate his literary creativity in new directions. By the end of 1817 he finished *Childe Harold's Pilgrimage* IV, an elegiac canto signaling Byron's decisive break with the past, and, influenced by John Hookham Frere's *Whistlecraft*, a mock-heroic satirical poem in the flexible form of ottava rima, he completed the experimental *Beppo*, which looks forward to the narrative style of *Don Juan*. The period from 1818 to 1822 brought additional changes. Wearying of his promiscuous debaucheries on the Grand Canal in Venice, Byron met the Countess Teresa Guiccioli of Ravenna, then nineteen years old, and soon became her devoted *cavalier servente*. This attachment, in turn, drew him into the revolutionary Carbonari struggle against Austrian rule in Northern Italy, an interest reflected in his political dramas (*Marino Faliero, The Two Foscari*, and *Sardanapalus*). With the defeat of the Carbonari movement in 1821, Byron followed the Gambas, Teresa's family, to Pisa, where he again joined the Shelley circle, which now included Edward John Trelawny and Thomas Medwin, and composed his devastating satire *The Vision of Judgment*. News of Shelley's drowning in July, 1822, however, stunned and sobered Byron. Shortly thereafter, he left for Genoa with Countess Guiccioli, but found his thoughts increasingly preoccupied with the Greek War of Independence. The final chapter of his life, always dominated by the trait that Lady Blessington called "mobility," forms a fitting memorial to

Byron's restless spirit. Elected a member of the London Greek Committee, a Philhellene organization, the poet felt obligated to translate his political convictions into action. Despite skepticism concerning various Greek leaders' loyalty to the cause and despite a presentiment of his own imminent death, Byron set forth to do what he could. Sailing for Missolonghi in late December, 1823, he devoted his personal fortune and energy to forming a united front against the Turks. Four months later he died of a fever; to this day he is hailed as a national hero by the Greek people.

Analysis · The history of Lord Byron's poetic development intersects at every stage with the saga of his life; yet it is only one of many paradoxes that he valued the writing of poetry primarily for the opportunity it afforded him to escape what he termed "my own wretched identity." More than anything else, poetry for Byron was a means both of sublimation and, ultimately, of self-realization. In his letters he thus suggests the former function when he speaks of poetry as "the lava of the imagination whose eruption prevents an earthquake," the volcanic metaphor signifying the cathartic release that the process of writing afforded him. The precise way in which it fulfilled the second function, however, is less obvious. Through the dynamics of self-projection, of investing much of his own multifaceted character in his personae, Byron strives to transcend the narrow limits of "personality" and achieve a more comprehensive perspective on himself and his experience. The essential goal of this artistic quest, which constitutes a progressive ontology, is delineated in Canto III of *Childe Harold's Pilgrimage*: "'Tis to create, and in creating live/ A being more intense." To trace Byron's growth as a poet, therefore, is to witness him reaching beyond subjectivism and attempting to realize that intensity of being that comes about through the continuous act of self-creation.

Any account of Byron's achievement must begin with the poems collected in *Hours of Idleness* and the early satires. In the Preface to the 1807 miscellany, his highly self-conscious debut as a poet, the nineteen-year-old Byron calls attention to himself by posing as an unlikely author (one "accustomed, in my younger days, to rove a careless mountaineer on the Highlands of Scotland"), by minimizing the merits of his literary endeavor ("to divert the dull moments of indisposition, or the monotony of a vacant hour, urged me 'to his sin' "), and by passing preemptive judgment on his work ("little can be expected from so unpromising a muse"). Such ingenuous posturing is clearly meant to invite, under the guise of dismissing, public recognition and acclaim. Despite the transparency of the subterfuge, the poems comprising *Hours of Idleness* form a revealing self-portrait in which Byron, while paraphrasing past idioms in poetry and exploiting eighteenth century literary conventions, obliquely seeks to discover a mythologized pattern for his emerging sense of himself. The one theme sounded repeatedly is what Robert F. Gleckner designates "the ruins of paradise," or the fall from youthful innocence. As he explores the experience of spiritual loss and shattered illusions, Byron can be seen moving toward this latter belief that "the great object of life is Sensation–to feel that we exist–even though in pain."

Admittedly imitative in style, often to the point of mannerism, *Hours of Idleness* revolves around several episodes of separation and disenchantment that, for the speaker, spell the end of an idealized, prelapsarian past. The short poem "Remembrance," composed in 1806 but not published until 1832, epitomizes both the tone and outlook of the volume as a whole:

> My days of happiness are few:
> Chill'd by misfortune's wintry blast,
> My dawn of life is overcast,
> Love, Hope, and Joy, alike adieu!–
> Would I could add Remembrance too!

Although the lines verge on doggerel, the same mood of melancholic nostalgia informs such other generally more successful poems as "On Leaving Newstead Abbey," "The First Kiss of Love," "On a Distant View of the Village and School of Harrow on the Hill," and "Lachin y Gair." In all of these works Byron cannot disown the power of memory because, though denounced as a curse, it alone provides glimpses of what in "Childish Recollections" he refers to as "the progress of my youthful dream," the foundation for his concept of self. This tension gives rise in other lyrics to a plangent wish to escape the "dark'ning shades" of maturity, regaining the uncompromised or "freeborn soul." Knowing the fatuity of the desire, however, the poet resorts at last to a kind of protective cynicism. In "To Romance," for example, abandoning what he derides as the "motley court" of "Affectation" and "sickly Sensibility," he admits that "'tis hard to quit the dreams,/ Which haunt the unsuspicious soul" but abjures the past as illusory and refuses any longer to be the dupe of his romantic fancy. Embittered by his early discovery, as Byron was later to write in *Childe Harold's Pilgrimage* III, that "life's enchanted cup but sparkles near the brim," the poet in *Hours of Idleness* fluctuates between moments of elegiac regret and tenacious hope, the ambivalent response itself prefiguring the skeptical idealist of the major poems to follow.

The Popean satires, which were composed shortly after the 1807 collection, disclose Byron's reaction to his disillusionment and punctured faith. In *English Bards and Scotch Reviewers*, *Hints from Horace*, and *The Curse of*

Minerva—all written during the next four years—Byron lashes out at various individuals whom he regarded as typifying the literary and moral shortcomings of his age. The motto of "these degenerate days," he announces in *English Bardsb and Scotch Reviewers*, is "Care not for feeling," and so in arraigning nearly all his contemporaries except Samuel Rogers and Thomas Campbell he poses as the hardened realist determined to expose error on every hand: "But now, so callous grown, so changed since youth,/ I've learned to think, and sternly speak the truth." In the diatribe Byron often vents his anger indiscriminately, but the acrimony of his attack stems from a keen sense of embarrassment and outrage at the reception accorded *Hours of Idleness* by such critics as Henry Brougham in the *Edinburgh Review*. Thus, before indicating all those "afflicted," as his Preface charges, "with the present prevalent and distressing *rabies* for rhyming," Byron debunks himself as well:

> I, too, can scrawl, and once upon a time
> I poured along the town a flood of rhyme,
> A school-boy freak, unworthy praise or blame;
> I printed—older children do the same.
> 'Tis pleasant, sure, to see one's name in print;
> A Book's a Book, altho' there's nothing in't.

The same irreverent or inconoclastic spirit pervades *Hints from Horace*, a mocking jab at contemporary literary practice from the vantage point of Horace's *Ars Poetica* (13-8 B.C., *The Art of Poetry*), and *The Curse of Minerva*, a Swiftian condemnation of Lord Elgin for his despoiling Greek sculpture. In these strident satires Byron alters his earlier poetic stance through two mechanisms: by adopting the voice of savage indignation and by spurning the accepted standards of his age. The detachment that he tries to win through both devices is another step toward his large aesthetic goal of self-realization.

A crucial phase in that ongoing process involves the composition, spanning the period from 1809 to 1817, of *Childe Harold's Pilgrimage* and, to a lesser extent, of the exotic Oriental tales that include *The Giaour, The Bride of Abydos, The Corsair*, and *Lara*. These verse narratives are significant because in them two sides of Byron's complexity as an artist are counterbalanced—the usually antithetical modes that Keats, in his letters, conceptualizes as the "egotistical sublime" and "the camelion [sic] Poet." Though Keats associated the first quality with William Wordsworth, the element of the "egotistical sublime" in Byron reveals itself in the highly developed reflexivity of his semiautobiographical poems and in his tendency to concentrate on his own immediate thoughts and emotions. At the same time, however, there emerges an equal but opposite impulse that reflects Byron's essentially centrifugal rather than centripetal habit of mind. This is his characteristic propensity for employing a gamut of masks or personae through which he endeavors to escape the restrictive confines of self-consciousness, especially as molded by memory, and to achieve the intensity of being that comes with self-transcendence. Together, these intertwined modalities—the "egotistical" and the "chameleonic"—make up the unique "strength" of Byron's imagination.

Readers of the time were nevertheless inclined to recognize only the former tendency in his works and so to find him guilty of facile exhibitionism. Certainly when Byronism was rampant no one impersonated Byron better than Byron himself; yet, if one allows for this susceptibility, the earnestness with which the poet responded to his detractors is instructive. Echoing the well-known protest lodged in his 1820 "Reply to Blackwood's *Edinburgh Magazine*," he expostulated a year later to Thomas Moore that "a man's poetry is a distinct faculty, or soul, and has no more to do with the every-day individual than the Inspiration with the Pythoness when removed from her tripod." Similarly, in the privacy of his journal for 1813, while writing the very poems that incurred the charge, he remarks: "To withdraw *myself* from *myself* (oh that cursed selfishness!) has ever been my sole, my entire, my sincere motive in scribbling at all; and publishing is also the continuance of the same object, by the action it affords to the mind, which else recoils upon itself." The vehemence of these statements should not be allowed to obscure Byron's clear point regarding the psychology of composition. The vicarious world of poetry, as he views it, makes possible a release from the concentricity of the mind that otherwise, to borrow two of his favorite images in *Childe Harold's Pilgrimage*, would sting itself to death like the scorpion ringed by fire or consume its scabbard like a rusting sword.

Byron first expands upon this aesthetic in *Childe Harold's Pilgrimage* III-IV, but some attention to the earlier cantos is prerequisite to understanding the later two. When he began the travelogue in 1809 while touring Europe and the Levant, Byron conceived of a work in Spenserian stanza form which would depict, in the eighteenth century tradition of topographical or "locodescriptive" poetry, his vivid impressions of the scenes and peoples he visited, intermixed with meditative reflections. "For the sake of giving some connection to the piece," which otherwise, according to the Preface, "makes no pretension to regularity," Byron introduces the "fictitious character" of Harold, who serves as the nominal hero-protagonist, although this syntactical function is about all that can be claimed for him. Out of "the fulness [sic] of satiety," it is true, Harold "resolve[s]" to leave England behind, having run through "Sin's long labyrinth"; yet in his wandering pilgrimage through Spain, Portugal, Albania, and Greece he remains a curiously static, one-dimensional figure and is little more than a partial projection of Byron's darker moods (for example, misanthropy, remorse, cynicism, and forced stoicism). As such, he adumbrates the explicit theme of Cantos I-II: that is, "Consciousness awaking to her woes." Neither Harold nor Byron, however, has yet learned "what he might be, or he ought," and it is somehow fitting that Canto II should close in a Greece stripped of its ancient grandeur and heroes.

Throughout this half of the poem, Byron's protagonist bears a marked resemblance to the poet himself, but it is well not to overlook the punning assertion made in the 1812 Preface that Harold is "the child of imagination." Shortly before the publication of Cantos I-II, in a letter to Robert Charles Dallas, Byron reinforces the distinction between himself and his central character: "If in parts I may be thought to have drawn from myself, believe me it is but in parts, and I shall not own even to that. . . . I would not be such a fellow as I have made my hero for all the world." The disclaimer has not won wide acceptance, largely because in the holograph copy of the poem Byron initially christened his protagonist "Childe Burun"; yet the first two cantos themselves substantiate the dissociation which Byron's comment to Dallas emphasizes. On the one hand, they dramatize the alienated figure of Harold, who, like the tortured hero of *Lara*, is portrayed as "a stranger in this breathing world,/ An erring spirit from another hurled;/ A thing of dark imaginings"; on the other hand, they are mediated by a separate narrator who, distanced from the foreground objectively recognizes that "the blight of life" that overtakes men like Harold is "the demon Thought," or the canker of self-consciousness. In actuality, both entities are Byron, and through the dichotomy he seeks to plumb his own contradictory nature.

By the time that Byron came to write Canto III, however, life had paradoxically imitated art: Exiled from England by public vilification for his alleged cruelty toward his wife, the poet became that which before he had only imaged. This turn of events contributed to a new coalescence or ironic similarity between the author and his persona. Byron still does not identify himself completely with his titular hero, but he is now able to assimilate Harold as an exponent of himself without capitulating to the kind of Haroldian angst that suffuses Cantos I-II. He seems to register this altered orientation in the following lines: "Yet am I changed; though still enough the same/ In strength to bear what time can not abate,/ And feed on bitter fruits without accusing Fate." Implicit in the passage, with its allusion to John Milton's *Paradise Lost* (1667), is an undertone of confidence that even despair can be transformed into a source of stimulation and proof of his endurance. Byron now is speaking *in propria persona.* No longer rhapsodizing as in Canto I "a youth,/ Who ne in virtue's ways did take delight," he is instead dealing with himself as a social and moral pariah–"the wandering outlaw of his own dark mind." The full assurance that he can avoid entrapment from within remains to be found, but the seeds of spiritual recovery are before him.

The groundwork is laid at the start of Canto III when, after the framing device of an apostrophe to his daughter, Byron declares his artistic manifesto for the work: "'Tis to create, and in creating live/ A being more intense, that we endow/ With form our fancy, gaining as we give/ The life we image, even as I do now." Reflecting Shelley's influence on Byron in 1816, the passage continues and reveals that the poet now views his quotidian identity as "Nothing," as a hollow fiction, while the project of art discloses to him an ideal "other" or truer self which he will appropriate through the act of creating. The poem itself, in short, becomes the vehicle for self-discovery. Thus, although Harold continues to be much the same character as he was in Cantos I-II, what has changed greatly is Byron's positioning of himself as artist *vis-à-vis* the poem. He no longer depends on his protagonist as a surrogate or alter ego; even though the disease of self-consciousness has not been expunged, his faith has been restored in the imagination's ability to locate new horizons of meaning in an otherwise entropic world.

Both the third and fourth cantos of *Childe Harold's Pilgrimage* contain clear evidence of his shift in outlook. The two major scenes visited in Canto III are Waterloo and the Swiss Alps, locales which by their historical associations stand symbolically opposed. In the former, Byron finds only the tragic vanity of life and the futility of worldly ambition; in the latter, he surveys the benign sublimity and undisturbed repose of nature. Initially, it would seem that he is elevating one sphere above the other, idealizing the serenity of "throned Eternity" in contrast to the agitation of "earth-born jars." He is indeed doing this, to some extent, but in a unique manner. Rather than treating these landscapes as discrete alternatives, Byron exploits them as provisional constructs for raising questions and defining some of his own misgivings about the human condition. Thus, if at Waterloo he rejects the "wretched interchange of wrong for wrong" within society, in the Alps he sees nothing "to loathe in nature, save to be/ A link reluctant in a fleshly chain."

In much the same way, he responds ambivalently to the fallen figureheads of each domain–Napoleon Bonaparte and Jean-Jacques Rousseau–whom he envisions as variants of himself. Both the Napoleon who was "conqueror and captive of the earth" and the "inspired" Rousseau whose oracles "set the world in flame" were men of unbounded energy, yet each was responsible for the shambles of the French Revolution and each was subverted by "a fever at the core,/ Fatal to him who bears, to all who ever bore." Byron recognizes their failure as potentially his own as well: "And *there* hath been thy bane," he proclaims. The stanza's rhetoric reverberates with his affinity for these individuals and suggests that Byron, as Jerome J. McGann observes in *Fiery Dust* (1968), is coming to the realization that "to 'know oneself' one must submit to immediate and partial acts of perception." Within *Childe Harold's Pilgrimage* III, therefore, the poet moves further toward the understanding that to be human means to be a pilgrim, but a pilgrim ever in the process of redefining himself and the world that he inherits.

Canto IV continues the archetypal pattern of the journey, in this case one extending from Venice to Rome, but broadens at the end to reveal a significantly matured Byron arriving at the genuine goal or embodiment of his questing spirit. Centered on the elegiac motif or *sic transit gloria mundi*, the last canto weighs the respective claims of both art and nature to permanence as Byron tries to decipher the enigma of man's existence. "The moral of all human tales," he postulates, is the inevitability of ruin and unfulfilled hopes, such that "History, with all her volumes vast,/ Hath but *one* page." This stark lesson occasionally moves the poet to invective, as when he declares that "Our life is a false nature–'tis not in/ The harmony of things." Nevertheless, in the poetry of Torquato Tasso, the sculpture of Venice, and the Colosseum in Rome, he discerns a grandeur and genius which transcend the melancholy attrition of time. That discovery, in turn, rekindles conviction as to the vitality of his own essential self, a realization heightened when Byron finds that he has outgrown the fictive prop of Harold:

> But where is he, the Pilgrim of my song,
> The being who upheld it through the past?
> . . . .
> He is no more–these breathings are his last;
> His wanderings done, his visions ebbing fast,
> And he himself as nothing. . . .

In the poem's concluding apostrophe to the sea near Albano, conceived as a "glorious mirror" and thalassic "image of Eternity," Byron achieves the true goal toward which he has been tending all along. Awesome in its untrammeled energy, the ocean becomes the symbol of the creating self that the poet has reclaimed. "My Pilgrim's shrine is won," writes Byron, for "I am not now/ That which I have been." With that declaration, Byron enters upon the last great phase of his poetic career.

The monumental epic *Don Juan* forms the inspired climax to Byron's evolution as an artist, but to understand how this is so requires brief attention to a disturbing undercurrent in *Childe Harold's Pilgrimage*. Despite the general movement toward self-apprehension in that work, there yet occur moments when the inadequacy of language to articulate "all I seek,/ Bear, know, feel" subverts the poet's faith in his enterprise. Thus, although in Canto III he would willingly believe that "there may be/ Words which are things," he has not found them; nor is he able to disguise from himself the knowledge that language is part of the disintegrated syntax of a fallen world. Along the same lines, after pondering in Canto IV the disappointed ideals of such poets as Dante and Petrarch, he ruefully admits that "what we have of feeling most intense/ Outstrips our faint expression." The intransigence of language, its inherent circularity as an instrument of meditation, was for Byron tied to the kind of Metaphysical despair dramatized in *Manfred* and *Cain*, and by way of overcoming those quandaries he adopts in *Don Juan* a more radically versatile poetics.

The chief difference between *Childe Harold's Pilgrimage* and his later "epic of negation," as Brian Wilke describes *Don Juan* in *Romantic Poets and Epic Tradition* (1965), lies in Byron's refusal any longer to be controlled by "the stubborn heart." After opening with the farce of Juan's sexual initiation, before which he pauses to berate Plato as a charlatan, Byron makes his new outlook resoundingly clear:

> No more—no more—Oh! never more, my heart,
>   Canst thou be my sole world, my universe!
> . . . .
> The illusion's gone for ever, and thou art
>   Insensible, I trust, but none the worse,
> And in thy stead I've got a good deal of judgment,
>   Though heaven knows how it ever found a lodgement.

Cognizant of the fictiveness of all experience, he plans to make his rambling medley of a poem mirror the manifold delusions and deceptions that man allows to impose upon his right of thought. In the face of such knowledge "Imagination droops her pinion," turning "what was once romantic to burlesque"—lines aptly capturing the shift from his stance in *Childe Harold's Pilgrimage*. In composing his "versified Aurora Borealis," however, Byron obviously sensed a creative exhilaration linked to his complete separation of himself from his hero. His letters written during the work's early stages reveal an exuberant confidence in the undertaking which, as he told Thomas Moore, was "meant to be a little quitely facetious upon every thing." Thus, addressing his old friend Douglas Kinnaird in 1819, he expressed a typically high-spirited opinion of his achievement: "As to 'Don Juan'—confess—confess—you dog—and be candid—that it is the sublime of *that there* sort of writing—it may be bawdy . . . but is it not *life*, is it not *the thing*?—Could any man have written it—who has not lived in the world?"

Byron's governing purpose in *Don Juan* is to "show things really as they are,/ Not as they ought to be." Toward that end he does not forbear lampooning all the assorted follies and philistine pretenses of "that microcosm on stilts,/ Yclept the Great World," for he sees its attachment to illusion as the root cause of men's inability to recognize or accept the truth about themselves. Byron's attack is all the more effective because he exempts neither himself as poet nor the function of language from his skeptical scrutiny. Overturning all conventional notions of structure and voice in poetry, he is intent upon making his "nondescript and ever-varying rhyme" demystify itself at every turn. Both serious and cynical, he consequently avers that compared to the epic myths of Vergil and Homer "this story's actually true," then later reminds his audience that his work "is only fiction,/ And that I sing of neither mine nor me." Nearly every stanza of *Don Juan* unmasks itself in similar fashion through the whimsical freedom of Byron's style. Fearless of incongruities in a world permeated by fraud, the poem's narrator defends his fluid cynicism in the name of verisimilitude (his aim is to "show things existent") while simultaneously debunking traditional concepts of authorial integrity: "If people contradict themselves, can I/ Help contradicting them, and everybody,/ Even my veracious self?" True "sincerity" in these terms is equated with inconsistency, paradox, and radical doubt, an outlook anticipated as early as 1813 when Byron, with uncanny self-knowledge and prescience, remarked in his journal that "if I am sincere with myself (but I fear one lies more to one's self than to any one else), every page should confute, refute, and utterly abjure its predecessor." By constantly deflating the artifices on which his own poem is built, Byron seeks to generate a self-critical model for exposing the larger abuses of his society.

Don Juan is, as William Hazlitt was quick to note in *The Spirit of the Age* (1825), a "poem written about itself," but foremost among the vices it satirizes are the contemporary prevalence of cant and the moral blindness or hypocrisy which it fosters. Both traits are first encountered in the character of Donna Inez, Juan's mother, in Canto I. A prodigy of memory whose brain is filled with "serious sayings darken'd to sublimity," she is walking homily—"Morality's prim personification"—who sees to it that her son is taught from only the most carefully expurgated classics. Unable to find anything to censure or amend in her own conduct, Donna Inez nevertheless carries on a clandestine affair with Don Alfonso, the husband of her close friend Julia, and later writes in fulsome praise of Catherine the Great's "maternal" attentions to Juan. Such self-deceiving and myopic piety moves Byron to wish for "a *forty-parson power* to chant/ Thy praise, Hypocrisy," the vice that he regards as endemic to his age and culture at all levels.

On a larger scale, he dramatizes the disastrous consequences of cant and its ability to obscure human realities in the Siege of Ismail episode beginning in Canto VII. Here his target is in part the gazettes and their debased glorification of war, particularly as they promote "the lust of notoriety" within modern civilization. Spurred on by the hope of being immortalized in the newspapers or war dispatches, a polyglot collection of soldiers join with the Russians in devastating the Turkish fortress. Before recounting scene after scene of the mindless butchery, in which thirty thousand are slain on both sides, Byron reflects on whether "a man's name in a *bulletin/* May make up for a *bullet in* his body." The final irony is that the gazettes, preoccupied with trivial gossip of the beau monde at home, generally garble the names of the dead and thoroughly distort the facts of the campaign. Determined to unriddle "Glory's dream," Byron shows that it is founded on nothing more than an abject appetite for fame and conquest. His greatest ire is reserved for someone such as the Russian leader Aleksandr Suwarrow, who, in a dispatch to Catherine after the slaughter, can glibly write, " 'Glory to *God* and to the Empress!' (*Powers/ Eternal! such names mingled!*) 'Ismail's our's.' " The same purblind insensitivity, he charges, makes it possible for Wordsworth to speak of carnage as " 'God's daughter.' " In all these instances, Byron shows how language is a ready instrument for the perversion of thought and action.

His own aesthetic in *Don Juan* thus bases itself on an unswerving respect for truth, "the grand desideratum" in a society glutted with cant and equivocation. Early in the poem he comments that his is "the age of oddities let loose," such that "You'd best begin with truth, and when you've lost your/ Labour, there's sure market for imposture." The lines also echo his mocking Dedication of the work to Robert Southey, who succeeded Henry James Pye as poet laureate in 1813, and his arraignment there of the other so-called Lake Poets. Having disowned the radical politics of their youth, they are depicted as comprising a "nest of tuneful persons" who now warble sycophantic praise for the Tory regime of King George III. Their apostasy in Byron's eyes is all the more reprehensible because they have, in effect, become the hirelings of the "intellectual eunuch Castlereagh," a master of oratorical "trash of phrase/ Ineffably–legitimately vile." To counteract this mounting Tower of Babel in his age, Byron persistently explodes the enchantment of words and their tendency to falsify reality. There is, accordingly, an underlying method to his chameleonic *mobilitè* and digressiveness in the poem, for he demonstrates that only by doubting the language-based constructs, which man imposes upon experience, can he, like the poet himself, avoid the pitfall of "universal egotism." Viewed in this light, the whole of *Don Juan* becomes an open-ended experiment in linguistic improvisation, a poem that demythologizes the very act by which it comes into being.

Because Byron's mock-epic attempts to encompass no less than "life's infinite variety," any synopsis of its innumerable subjects and themes is doomed to failure. From the opening line in which the narrator declaims "I want a hero" and then seems arbitrarily to settle on "our ancient friend Don Juan," it is evident that the ensuing comedy will follow few established conventions or patterns. This impression is reinforced later in Canto XIV, when Byron points out his technique in composing *Don Juan:* "I write what's uppermost, without delay." The stated casualness in approach, however, belies the artistic integrity of the satire. Jerome J. McGann, in *Don Juan in Context* (1976), convincingly shows that the poem is "both a critique and an apotheosis of High Romanticism," primarily because it implicitly denies that any imaginative system can be an end unto itself while also endeavoring to reinsert the poetic imagination back into the context of a fallen world. If there is one crux around which the entire mosaic turns, it is that of the fundamental opposition between nature and civilization. After Juan's idyllic love affair with Haidèe, "Nature's bride," is destroyed by her jealous father in Canto IV, Byron suggests that the Fall is man's permanent condition; he conducts his hero into slavery at Constantinople in Canto V, into the bloodbath of the Siege of Ismail in Cantos VII-VIII, into the lustful tyranny of the Russian Empress in Cantos IX-X, and finally into the fashionable corruptions of English society in Cantos XI-XVII. Not all, however, is moral cannibalism. By the introduction of such unspoiled figures as Haidèe at the start and Aurora Raby at the end, Byron ascribes a certain redemptive value to natural innocence that offsets, even if it does not quite counterbalance, the ruling vices of society. *Don Juan* thus immerses itself in all the unflattering details of "life's infinite variety," but always with the purpose of embodying the human realities with which the artist must deal. Byron distills the complexity of the matter in a few words: "I write the world."

In this century as in his own, Byron has often been criticized as a poet for his many supposed failures—for not projecting a coherent metaphysic, for not developing a consistent attitude to life, for not resisting the Siren call of egotism, for not paying sufficient attention to style, and for not, in short being more like Wordsworth, Samuel Taylor Coleridge, Keats, and Shelley. Because he did not adopt the vatic stance of his contemporaries or espouse their belief in organicism, he has been labeled the leading exemplar of Negative Romanticism. Common to such estimates, however, is a reluctance to recognize or concede Byron's uniqueness as a poet. Although he did not share with others of his time an exalted conception of the imagination as being equivalent, in Keats's metaphor, to "Adam's dream," he was able ultimately to do what the other four poets generally could not—namely, to accept the mixed quality of human experience. Through his ironic detachment and comic vision he permanently enlarged the domain of poetry and made it meaningful in a fresh way. This he accomplished through his skeptical idealism and his acceptance of his own paradoxes as a man and poet. "I am quicksilver," he wrote to a friend in 1810, "and say nothing positively." Therein lies perhaps the essence of his "sincerity" and "strength," traits that continue to make him an enduring cultural force.

Other literary forms · It should be noted that the titles of Byron's principal poetic works include dramatic as well as lyrical and narrative works. Lord Byron wrote eight plays in all, most of which focused on either speculative or historical subjects and were never intended for the stage. He designated them "mental theatre," or closet drama modeled after classical principles, and clearly regarded the plays as among his most important productions. Complementing Byron's extraordinarily prolific and diverse career as a poet is his versatility as a writer of epistolary prose. During his lifetime Byron composed more than 2,900 letters, which have been scrupulously edited by Leslie A. Marchand and published between 1973 and 1982 in twelve volumes under the title *Byron's Letters and Journals.* The sheer immensity of this correspondence is matched only by the unlimited range and immediacy of Byron's voice as he speaks without reserve on a variety of topics. In addition to these private documents, along with John Keats's letters the most revealing correspondence of the British Romantic poets, Byron also published the combative *Letter to [John Murray] on the Rev. W. L. Bowles' Strictures on the Life and Writings of Pope* (1821) and, in the first number of Leigh Hunt's *The Liberal* (1822), "A Letter to the Editor of 'My Grandmother's Review.' " *The Parliamentary Speeches of Lord Byron*, comprising three addresses he made while a member of the House of Lords, was issued in 1824, well after he had grown disillusioned with what he called "Parliamentary mummeries."

Select works other than poetry

NONFICTION: *Letter to [John Murray] on the Rev. W. L. Bowles' Strictures on the Life and Writings of Pope*, 1821; "A Letter to the Editor of 'My Grandmother's Review,'" 1822; *The Blues: A Literary Eclogue*, 1823; *The Parliamentary Speeches of Lord Byron*, 1824; *Byron's Letters and Journals*, 1973-1982 (12 volumes; Leslie A. Marchand, editor).

Robert Lance Snyder

Bibliography · Robert Gleckner's *Byron and the Ruins of Paradise*, 1967, and *Critical Essays on Lord Byron*, 1991, contain valuable readings of Byron and his multifaceted personality, including his nihilistic tendencies. Jerome McGann's *Fiery Dust: Byron's Poetic Development*, 1968, is a fascinating discussion of Byron's desire to find inspiration in the midst of decay. Harold Bloom's collection of essays in his Chelsea House *Byron*, 1986, provides helpful background. Frederick Garber's *Self, Text, and Romantic Irony: The Example of Byron*, 1988, examines Byron's ideas of textuality and the self, and Jerome Christensen's *Lord Byron's Strength: Romantic Writing and Commercial Society*, 1993, examines how Byron was able to commodify himself as perhaps the world's first marketable media star. See also Laura Claridge's *Romantic Potency: The Paradox of Desire*, 1992, and Caroline Franklin's *Byron's Heroines*, 1992. *Byron's Letters*, 1973-1982, is the authoritative text for his correspondence.

PAUL CELAN

(Paul Antschel)

Born: Czernowitz, Romania; November 23, 1920
Died: Paris, France; April, 1970

Poetry · *Der Sand aus den Urnen,* 1948 · *Mohn und Gedächtnis,* 1952 · *Von Schwelle zu Schwelle,* 1955 · *Gedichte: Eine Auswahl,* 1959 · *Sprachgitter,* 1959 (*Speech-Grille,* 1971) · *Die Niemandsrose,* 1963 · *Gedichte,* 1966 · *Atemwende,* 1967 (*Breathturn,* 1995) · *Ausgewählte Gedichte: Zwei Reden,* 1968 · *Fadensonnen,* 1968 · *Lichtzwang,* 1970 · *Schneepart,* 1971 · *Speech-Grille and Selected Poems,* 1971 · *Nineteen Poems,* 1972 · *Selected Poems,* 1972 · *Gedichte: In zwei Bänden,* 2 vols., 1975 · *Zeitgehöft: Späte Gedichte aus dem Nachlass,* 1976 · *Paul Celan: Poems,* 1980 (rev. as *Poems of Paul Celan,* 1988) · *Gesammelte Werke in fünf Bänden,* 5 vols., 1983 · *Gedichte: 1938-1944,* 1985 · *65 Poems,* 1985 · *Last Poems,* 1986 · *Das Frühwerk,* 1989

Achievements · Celan is considered an "inaccessible" poet by many critics and readers. This judgment, prompted by the difficulties Celan's poetry poses for would-be interpreters seeking traditional exegesis, is reinforced by the fact that Celan occupies an isolated position in modern German poetry. Sometimes aligned with Nelly Sachs, Ernst Meister, and the German Surrealists, Celan's work nevertheless stands apart from that of his contemporaries. A Jew whose outlook was shaped by his early experiences in Nazi-occupied Romania, Celan grew up virtually trilingual. The horror of his realization that he was, in spite of his childhood experiences and his later residence in France, a German poet was surely responsible in part for his almost obsessive concern with the possibilities and the limits of his poetic language. Celan's literary ancestors are Friedrich Hölderlin, Arthur Rimbaud, Stéphane Mallarmé, Rainer Maria Rilke, and the German Expressionists, but even in his early poems his position as an outsider is manifest. Celan's poems, called hermetic by some critics because of their resistance to traditional interpretation, can be viewed sometimes as intentense and cryptic accounts of personal experience, sometimes as religious-philosophical discussions of Judaism, its tradition and its relation to Christianity. Many of his poems concern themselves with linguistic and poetic theory to the point where they cease to be poems in the traditional sense, losing all contact with the world of physical phenomena and turning into pure language, existing only for themselves. Such "pure" poems, increasingly frequent in Celan's later works, are largely responsible for the charge of inaccessibility which has been laid against him. Here the reader is faced with having to leave the dimension of conventional language use, where the poet uses language to communicate with his audience about subjects such as death or nature, and is forced to enter the dimension of metalanguage, as Harald Weinrich calls it, where language is used to discuss only language—that is, the *word* "death," and not death itself. Such poems are accessible only to readers who share with the poet the basic premises of an essentially linguistic poetic theory, a demand which is made by many works of modern literature.

In spite of all this, much of Celan's poetry can be made accessible to the reader through focus on the personal elements in some poems, the Judaic themes in others, and by pointing out the biblical and literary references in yet another group.

Biography · Paul Celan was born Paul Ancel, or Antschel, the only child of Jewish parents, in Czernowitz, Romania, in Bukovina, situated in the foothills of the Carpathian Mountains in what is today northern Romania. This region had been under Austrian rule and thus contained a sizable German-speaking minority along with a mix of other nationalities and ethnic groups. In 1918, just two years before Celan's birth, following the collapse of the Austro-Hungarian Empire, Bukovina became part of Romania. Thus, Celan was reared in a region of great cultural and linguistic diversity, the tensions of which energized his poetry.

Little is known of Celan's early childhood, but he appears to have had a very close relationship with his mother and a less satisfying relationship with his father. Positive references to his mother abound in his poems, whereas his father is hardly mentioned. After receiving his high school diploma, the young Celan went to study medicine in France in 1938, but the war forced his return in the following year to Czernowitz, where he turned to the study of Romance languages and literature at the local university. In 1940, his hometown was annexed by the Soviet Union but was soon occupied by the Germans and their allies, who began to persecute and deport the Jewish population. Celan's parents were taken to a concentration camp, where they both died, while the young man remained hidden for some time and finally ended up in a forced-labor camp. These events left a permanent scar on Celan's memory, and it appears that he had strong feelings of guilt for having survived when his parents and so many of his friends and relatives were murdered. After Soviet troops reoccupied his hometown, he returned there for a short time and then moved to Bucharest, where he found work as an editor and a translator. In 1947, his first poems were published in a Romanian journal under the anagrammatic pen name Paul Celan. In the same year, he moved to Vienna, where he remained until 1948, when his first collection of poetry, *Der Sand aus den Urnen*, was published.

After moving to Paris in the same year, Celan began to frequent avant-garde circles and was received particularly well by the poet Yvan Goll and his wife, Claire. Unfortunately, after Goll's death in 1950, Claire Goll, apparently jealous of Celan's growing reputation as a poet, accused him of having plagiarized from her husband. A bitter feud resulted, with many of the leading poets and critics in France and Germany taking sides. During this period, Celan also began his work as a literary translator, which was to be a major source of both income and poetic inspiration for the rest of his life. He translated from the French—notably the writings of Rimbaud, Paul Valéry, and Guillaume Apollinaire—as well as the poetry of William Shakespeare, Emily Dickinson, and Marianne Moore from the English and the works of Aleksandr Blok, Sergei Esenin, and Osip Mandelstam from the Russian.

In the following years, Celan married a French graphic artist, Gisèle Lestrange, and published his second volume of poetry, *Mohn und Gedächtnis* (poppy and memory), containing many poems from his first collection, *Der Sand aus den Urnen*, which he had withdrawn from circulation because of the large number of printing mistakes and editorial inaccuracies it contained. *Mohn und Gedächtnis* established his reputation as a poet, and most of his subsequent collections were awarded prestigious literary prizes.

Celan remained in Paris for the rest of his life, infrequently traveling to Germany. During his later years, he appears to have undergone many crises both in his personal and in his creative life (his feud with Claire Goll is only one such incident), and his friends agree that he became quarrelsome and felt persecuted by neo-Nazis, hostile publishers, and critics. His death in April of 1970, apparently by suicide—he drowned in the Seine—was the consequence of his having arrived, in his own judgment, at a personal and artistic dead end, although many critics have seen in his collections *Lichtzwang*, *Schneepart*, and *Zeitgehöft*, published posthumously, the potential beginning of a new creative period.

Analysis · Paul Celan's poetry can be viewed as an expressive attempt to cope with the past—his personal past as well as that of the Jewish people. Close friends of the poet state that Celan was unable to forget anything and that trivial incidents and cataclysmic events of the past for him had the same order of importance. Many of his poems contain references to the death camps, to his dead parents (particularly his mother), to his changing attitude toward the Jewish religion and toward God. In his early collections, these themes are shaped into traditional poetic form–long, often rhymed lines, genitive metaphors, sensuous images–and the individual poems are accessible to conventional methods of interpretation. In his later collections, Celan employs increasingly sparse poetic means, such as one-word lines, neologisms, and images that resist traditional interpretive sense-making; their significance can often be intuited only by considering Celan's complete poetic opus, a fact which has persuaded many critics and readers that Celan's poems are nonsense, pure games with language rather than codified expressions of thoughts and feelings which can be deciphered by applying the appropriate key.

Mohn und Gedächtnis, Celan's first collection of poetry (discounting the withdrawn *Der Sand aus den Urnen*), was in many ways an attempt to break with the past. The title of the collection is an indication of the dominant theme of these poems, which stress the dichotomy of forgetting–one of the symbolic connotations of the poppy flower–and remembering, by which Celan expresses his wish to forget the past, both his own personal past and that of the Jewish race, and his painful inability to erase these experiences from his memory. Living in Paris, Celan believed that only by forgetting could he begin a new life–in a new country, with a non-Jewish French wife, and by a rejection of his past poetic efforts, as indicated by the withdrawal of his first collection.

Mohn und Gedächtnis is divided into four parts and contains a total of fifty-six poems. In the first part, "Der Sand aus den Urnen" ("Sand from the Urns"), Celan establishes the central theme of the collection: The poet "fills the urns of the past in the moldy-green house of oblivion" and is reminded by the white foliage of an aspen tree that his mother's hair was not allowed to turn white. Mixed with these reflections on personal losses are memories of sorrows and defeats inflicted upon the Jewish people; references to the conquest of Judea by the Romans are meant to remind the reader of more recent atrocities committed by foreign conquerors.

The second part of *Mohn und Gedächtnis* is a single poem, "Todesfuge" ("Death Fugue"), Celan's most widely anthologized poem, responsible in no small part for establishing his reputation as one of the leading contemporary German poets. "Death Fugue" is a monologue by the victims of a concentration camp, evoking in vivid images the various atrocities associated with these camps. From the opening line, "Black milk of daybreak we drink it at sundown . . ."–one of the lines that Claire Goll suggested Celan had plagiarized from her husband–the poem passes on to descriptions of the cruel camp commander who plays with serpent-like whips, makes the inmates shovel their own graves, and sets his pack of dogs on them. From the resignation of the first lines, the poem builds to an emotional climax in the last stanza in which the horror of the cremation chambers is indicated by images such as "he grants us a grave in the air" and "death is a master from Germany." While most critics have praised the poem, some have condemned Celan for what they interpret as an attempt at reconciliation between Germans and Jews in the last two lines of the poem. Others, however, notably Theodor Adorno, have attacked "Death Fugue" on the basis that it is "barbaric" to write beautiful poetry after, and particularly about, Auschwitz. A close reading of this long poem refutes the notion that Celan was inclined toward reconciliation with the Germans—his later work bears this out—and it is hard to imagine that any reader should feel anything but horror and pity for the anonymous speakers of the poem. The beautifully phrased images serve to increase the intensity of this horror rather than attempting to gloss it over. "Death Fugue" is both a great poem and one of the most impressive and lasting documents of the plight of the Jews.

"Auf Reisen" ("Travel"), the first poem of the third part of the collection, again indicates Celan's wish to leave the past behind and to start all over again in his "house in Paris." In other poems he makes reference to his wife, asking to be forgiven for having broken with his heritage and married a Gentile. As the title of the collection suggests, the poppy of oblivion is not strong enough to erase the memory of his dead mother, of his personal past, and of his racial heritage. In poems such as "Der Reisekamerad" ("The Traveling Companion") and "Zähle die Mandeln" ("Count the Almonds"), the optimistic view of "Travel" is retracted; in the former, the dead mother is evoked as the poet's constant travel companion, while in the latter, he acknowledges that he must always be counted among the "almonds." The almonds *(Mandeln)* represent the Jewish people and are an indirect reference also to the Russian Jewish poet Osip Mandelstam, whose work Celan had translated. The irreconcilable tension between the wish to forget and the inability to do so completely is further shown in "Corona," a poem referring to Rainer Maria Rilke's "Herbsttag" ("Autumn Day"). Whereas the speaker of Rilke's poem resigns himself to the approaching hardships of winter, Celan converts Rilke's "Lord: it is time" into the rebellious "it is time that the stone condescended to bloom."

The poems in *Mohn und Gedächtnis* are not, for the most part, innovative in form or imagery, although the long dactylic lines and the flowery images of the first half begin to give way to greater economy of scope and metaphor in the later poems. There is a constant dialogue with a fictional "you" and repeated references to "night," "dream," "sleep," "wine," and "time," in keeping with the central theme of these poems. Celan's next collections show his continued attempts to break with the past, to move his life and his poetry to new levels.

In *Von Schwelle zu Schwelle* (threshold to threshold), Celan abandoned his frequent references to the past; it is as if the poet—as the title, taken from a poem in *Mohn und Gedächtnis*, suggests—intended to cross over a threshold into a new realm. Images referring to his mother, to the persecution of the Jews, to his personal attitude toward God, and to his Jewish heritage are less frequent in this volume. Many German critics, reluctant to concentrate on Celan's treatment of the Holocaust, have remarked with some relief his turning away from this subject toward the problem of creativity, the possibilities of communication, and the limits of language. Indeed, if one follows most German critics, *Von Schwelle zu Schwelle* was the first step in the poet's development toward "metapoetry"—that is, poetry which no longer deals with traditional *materia poetica* but only with poetry itself. This new direction is demonstrated by the preponderance of terms such as "word" and "stone" (a symbol of speechlessness), replacing "dream," "autumn," and "time." For Celan, *Von Schwelle zu Schwelle* constituted a more radical attempt to start anew by no longer writing about—therefore no longer having to think about—experiences and memories which he had been unable to come to grips with in his earlier poems.

Speech-Grille is, as the title suggests, predominantly concerned with language. The thirty-three poems in this volume are among Celan's finest, as the enthusiastic critical reception confirmed. They are characterized by a remarkable discipline of expression, leading in many cases to a reduction of poetry to the bare essentials. Indeed, it is possible to see these poems as leading in the direction of complete silence. "Engführung" ("Stretto"), perhaps the finest poem in the collection and one of Celan's best, exemplifies this tendency even by its title, which is taken from musical theory and refers to the final section of a fugue. A long poem which alludes to "Death Fugue," it is stripped of the descriptive metaphors which characterized that masterpiece, such as the "grave in the air" and "the black milk of daybreak"; instead, experience is reduced to lines such as "Came, came./ Came a word, came/ came through the night,/ wanted to shine, wanted to shine/ Ash./ Ash, ash./ Night."

Celan's attempt to leave the past behind in *Speech-Grille* was not completely successful; on the contrary, several poems in this collection express sorrow at the poet's detachment from his Jewish past and from his religion. It is therefore not surprising that Celan's next collection, *Die Niemandsrose* (the no-one's rose), was dedicated to Osip Mandelstam, a victim of Joseph Stalin's persecutions in the 1930's. One of the first poems in this collection makes mention of the victims of the concentration camps: "There was earth inside them, and/ they dug." Rather than concentrating on the horrors of camp existence, the poem discusses the possibility of believing in an omnipotent, benevolent God in the face of these atrocities; this theme is picked up again in "Zürich, zum Storchen" ("Zurich, the Stork Inn"), in which Celan reports on his meeting with the Jewish poet Nelly Sachs: "the talk was of your God, I spoke/ against him." Other poems contain references to his earlier work; the "house in Paris" is mentioned again, and autumn imagery, suggesting the memory of his mother, is used more frequently. Several other poems express Celan's renewed and final acceptance of his Jewish heritage but indicate his rejection of God, culminating in the blasphemous "Psalm," with its bitter tribute: "Praised be your name, no one."

Celan's poetry after *Die Niemandsrose* became almost inaccessible to the average reader. As the title *Atemwende* (breath turning) indicates, Celan wanted to go in entirely new directions. Most of the poems in Celan's last collections are very short; references to language and writing become more frequent, and striking, often grotesque, portmanteau words and other neologisms mix with images from his earlier poems. There are still references to Judaism, to an absent or cruel God, and—in a cryptic form—to personal experiences. In the posthumously published *Schneepart*, the reader can even detect allusions to the turbulent political events of 1968. The dominant feature of these last poems, however, is the almost obsessive attempt to make the language of poetry perform new, hitherto unimagined feats, to coerce words to yield truth which traditional poetic diction could not previously force through its "speech-grille." It appears that Celan finally despaired of ever being able to reach this new poetic dimension. The tone of his last poems was increasingly pessimistic, and his hopes, expressed in earlier poems, of finding "that ounce of truth deep inside delusion," gave way to silence in the face of the "obstructive tomorrow." It is the evidence of these last poems, more than any police reports, which make it a certainty that his drowning in the Seine in 1970 was not simply the result of an accident.

Celan's poetry can be understood only by grasping his existential dilemma after World War II as a Jewish poet who had to create his poetry in the German language. Desperate to leave behind everything which would remind him of his own and his people's plight, he nevertheless discovered that the very use of the German language inevitably led him back to his past and made a new beginning impossible. Finally, the only escape he saw still open to him was to attempt to abandon completely the conventions of German lyric poetry and its language, to try to make his poetry express his innermost feelings and convictions without having to resort to traditional poetic diction and form. Weinrich suggests that Celan, like Mallarmé before him, was searching for the "absolute poem," a poem which the poet creates only as a rough sketch and which the reader then completes, using private experiences and ideas, possibly remembered pieces of other poems. If this is true, Celan must have ultimately considered his efforts a failure, both in terms of his poetic intentions and in his desire to come to terms with his personal and his Jewish past.

Other literary forms · Paul Celan's literary reputation rests exclusively on his poetry. His only piece of prose fiction, if indeed it can be so described, is "Gespräch im Gebirg" (1959), a very short autobiographical story with a religious theme. Celan also wrote an introductory essay for a book containing works by the painter Edgar Jené; this essay, entitled "Edgar Jené und der Traum vom Traume" (1948), is an important early statement of Celan's aesthetic theory. Another, more oblique, statement of Celan's poetic theory is contained in his famous speech, "Der Meridian" (1960), given on his acceptance of the prestigious Georg Büchner Prize. (An English translation of this speech, "The Meridian," is available in the Winter 1978 issue of *Chicago Review*.)

Select works other than poetry
NONFICTION: *Edgar Jené und der Traum vom Traume*, 1948 (*Edgar Jené and the Dream About the Dream*, 1986); *Collected Prose*, 1986.
TRANSLATIONS: *Der goldene Vorhang*, 1949 (of Jean Cocteau); *Bateau ivre/Das trunkene Schiff*, 1958 (of Arthur Rambaud); *Gedichte*, 1959 (of Osip Mandelstam); *Die junge Parzel/La jeune Parque*, 1964 (of Paul Valéry); *Einundzwanzig Sonette*, 1967 (of William Shakespeare).
MISCELLANEOUS: *Prose Writings and Selected Poems*, 1977.

Franz G. Blaha

Bibliography · John Felstiner, *Paul Celan: Poet, Survivor, Jew*, 1995, is a thoughtful and well-documented critical biography. Israel Chalfen, *Paul Celan: A Biography of His Youth*, trans. Maxmilian Bleyleben, 1991, emphasizing the young Celan's Jewishness, relies heavily on one friend's testimony. Amy D. Colin, *Paul Celan: Holograms of Darkness*, 1991, provides an overview of Celan's cultural background as well as postmodernist textual analysis. James Rolleston, *Narratives of Ecstasy: Romantic Temporality in Modern German Poetry*, 1987, argues that Celan's manipulation of language demonstrates a radical political consciousness. Jerry Glenn, *Paul Celan*, 1973, the first full-length study of Celan in English, focuses narrowly on the bitterness of the Holocaust experience.

GEOFFREY CHAUCER

Born: London(?), England; c. 1343
Died: London, England; October 25(?), 1400

Poetry · *Book of the Duchess*, c. 1370 · *Romaunt of the Rose*, c. 1370 (translation, possibly not by Chaucer) · *Hous of Fame*, 1372-1380 · *The Legend of St. Cecilia*, 1372-1380 (later used as "The Second Nun's Tale") · *Tragedies of Fortune*, 1372-1380 (later used as "The Monk's Tale") · *Anelida and Arcite*, c. 1380 · *Parlement of Foules*, 1380 · *Palamon and Ersyte*, 1380-1386 (later used as "The Knight's Tale") · *The Legend of Good Women*, 1380-1386 · *Troilus and Criseyde*, 1382 · *The Canterbury Tales*, 1387-1400

Achievements · Seldom has a poet been as consistently popular and admired by fellow poets, critics, and the public as has Geoffrey Chaucer. From the comments of his French contemporary, Eustache Deschamps (c. 1340-1410) and the praise by imitation of the fifteenth century Chaucerians to the remarks of notable critics from John Dryden and Alexander Pope to Matthew Arnold and C. S. Lewis, Chaucer has been warmly applauded if not always understood. His poetic talent, "genial nature," wit, charm, and sympathetic yet critical understanding of human diversity are particularly attractive. To D. S. Brewer, Chaucer "is our Goethe, a great artist who put his whole mind into his art."

Yet sometimes this praise has been misinformed, portraying Chaucer rather grandly as "the father of English literature" and the prime shaper of the English language. In fact, English literature had a long and illustrious tradition before Chaucer, and the development of Modern English from the London East Midland dialect of Chaucer has little to do with the poet. Chaucer has also been credited with a series of firsts. G. L. Kittredge identified *Troilus and Criseyde* as "the first novel, in the modern sense, that ever was written in the world." Its characters, to John Speirs, are also poetic firsts: Pandarus "the first rounded comic creation of substantial magnitude in English literature," and Criseyde "the first complete character of a woman in English literature." Others see Chaucer's poetry as "Renaissance" in outlook, a harbinger of the humanism of the modern world. Such views reveal an element of surprise on the critics' part that from the midst of Middle English such a poetic genius should emerge. In fact, typical discussions of Chaucer's career, dividing it into three stages as it develops from French influence (seen in the dream allegories) to Italian tendencies (in *Troilus and Criseyde*, for example) and finally to English realism (in *The Canterbury Tales*), imply an evolutionary view not only of Chaucer's poetry but also of English literary history. These stages supposedly reflect the gradual rejection of medieval conventionalism and the movement toward modern realism.

Whatever Chaucer's varied achievements are, the rejection of conventions, rhetoric, types, symbols, and authorities is not among them. Charles Muscatine has shown, moreover, that Chaucer's "realism" is as French and conventional as are his early allegories. Chaucer's poetry should be judged within the conventions of his time. He did experiment with verse forms, establishing a decasyllabic line which, to become the iambic pentameter of the sonnet, blank verse, and heroic couplet, is English poetry's most enduring line. His talent, however, lies in manipulating the authorities, the rhetoric, and conventional "topics," and in his mastery of the "art poetical." As A. C. Spearing notes, "Once we become aware of Chaucer's 'art poetical,' we gain a deeper insight into his work by seeing how what appears natural in it is in fact achieved not carelessly but by the play of genius upon convention and contrivance."

Such an approach to Chaucer will recognize his achievement as the greatest poet of medieval England, not as a forerunner of modernism. It will note his remaking of French, Latin, and Italian sources and treatment of secular and religious allegory as being, in their own way, as original as his creation of such characters as the Wife of Bath and the Pardoner. Chaucer's achievement is in his ability to juxtapose various medieval outlooks to portray complex ideas in human terms, with wit and humor, to include both "heigh sentence" and "solaas and myrthe," and to merge the naturalistic detail with the symbolic pattern. In this attempt to synthesize the everyday with the supernatural and the homely with the philosophical, and in his insistence on inclusiveness—on presenting both the angels and the gargoyles—Chaucer is the supreme example of the Gothic artist.

Biography · For a medieval poet, much is known about Geoffrey Chaucer's life, his association with the English court, his diplomatic activity on the Continent, and his public appointments. He was born in the early 1340's, the son of John Chaucer, a London wine merchant. He spent time in the military, serving with the English forces in France in 1359 where he was captured; he was ransomed in 1360. Around 1366 he married Philippa Roet and probably fathered two sons. He served the crown most of his life. Originally (c. 1357) he was connected to the household of Princess Elizabeth, who was married to Prince Lionel, the son of King Edward III. He also served another son of the king, John of Gaunt, the Duke of Lancaster, who later married Chaucer's sister-in-law, Katherine Swynford. Chaucer's public service survived the death of Edward III and the tumultuous reign and deposition of Richard II. It included numerous diplomatic missions to the Continent, his appointment as Controller of Customs and Subsidy for the port of London (1374-1386), his service as a justice of the peace and member of parliament for Kent (1386), his demanding duties as Clerk of the King's Works (1389-1391), and, finally, his appointment as deputy forester of North Petherton royal forest in Somerset (after 1391). Chaucer lived in London, Greenwich, and Calais, the French port then controlled by the English. In 1399, he leased a house in the garden of Westminster Abbey. He probably died on October 25, 1400, and was buried in the nearby abbey, the first of a long line of English authors to rest in the Poets' Corner.

These biographical details provide little evidence of Chaucer's position as a poet, although in a general way they do cast light on his poetry. Chaucer's association with courtly circles must have provided both the inspiration for and the occasion of his early poetry. It is certain that he wrote the *Book of the Duchess* to commemorate the death of Blanche, the wife of John of Gaunt. He probably also composed *The Legend of Good Women* for a courtly patron (the queen, according to John Lydgate), and read *Troilus and Criseyde* to a courtly audience, as he is portrayed doing in a manuscript illustration. In more general terms, his early poetry reflects the French literary taste of the English court.

Chaucer's public career, furthermore, reveals that he was far from being the withdrawn versifier of artificial courtly tastes. His duties at the port of London and as chief supervisor of royal building projects suggest that he was a practical man of the world. Certainly these responsibilities brought him into contact with a wide variety of individuals whose manners and outlooks must have contrasted sharply with those of members of the court. In the past, such scholars as J. M. Manly searched historical records to identify specific individuals with whom Chaucer dealt in an attempt to locate models for the portraits of the pilgrims in *The Canterbury Tales*. Like any artist, Chaucer was no doubt influenced by those with whom he worked, but such research gives a false impression of Chaucer's characters. Even his most "realistic" creations are often composites of traditional portraits. Nevertheless, the recent studies of J. A. W. Bennett (*Chaucer at Oxford and at Cambridge*, 1974) show that careful attention to the records of fourteenth century England can enlighten modern understanding of the social, intellectual, and cultural trends of Chaucer's time and thus provide a setting for his life and work.

One aspect of Chaucer's public career must certainly have influenced his poetry. Repeatedly from 1360 to 1387 Chaucer undertook royal missions on the Continent. During these journeys he visited Flanders, Paris, perhaps even Spain. More important, in 1373 and again in 1378 he visited Italy. These trips to what in the fourteenth century was the center of European art brought him into contact with a sophisticated culture. They may have also introduced him to the work of the great Florentine poets, for Chaucer's poetry after these visits to Italy reflects the influence of Dante, Petrarch, and particularly Boccaccio. Finally, the diplomatic missions suggest certain features of Chaucer's personality that lie behind his poetry, although these features seem deliberately masked by his self-portraits in the poetry. Of middle class origin, expert in languages and trusted at court, Chaucer as a diplomat sent on at least seven missions to the Continent must have been not only convivial and personable—the usual view of the poet—but also self-assured, intelligent, and a keen judge of character.

Analysis · When reading Geoffrey Chaucer's works one is struck by a sense of great variety. His poetry reflects numerous sources, Latin, French, and Italian, ranging from ancient authorities to contemporary poets and including folk tales, sermons, rhetorical textbooks, philosophical meditations, and ribald jokes. Equally varied are Chaucer's poetic forms and genres: short conventional lyrics, long romances, exempla, fabliaux, allegorical dream visions, confessions, saints legends, and beast fables. The characters he creates, from personified abstractions, regal birds, and ancient goddesses to the odd collection of the Canterbury pilgrims and the naïve persona who narrates the poems are similarly varied. Finally, the poems present a wide variety of outlooks on an unusual number of topics. Like the Gothic cathedrals, Chaucer's poetry seems all-inclusive. Not surprisingly, also like the Gothic cathedrals, his poems were often left unfinished.

"Experience, though no authority," the Wife of Bath states in the prologue to her tale, "is good enough for me." Unlike her fifth husband, Jankin the clerk, the Wife is not interested in what "olde Romayn gestes" teach, what Saint Jerome, Tertullian, Solomon, and Ovid say about women and marriage. She knows "of the woe that is in marriage" by her own experience. This implied contrast between, on the one hand, authority—the established positions concerning just about any topic set forth in the past by scripture, ancient authors, and the Church fathers and passed on to the present by books—and, on the other hand, the individual's experience of everyday life is central to medieval intellectual thought. It is a major theme of Chaucer's poetry. Often Chaucer appears to establish an authority and then to contrast it with the experience of real life, testing the expected by the actual. This contrast may be tragic or comic; it may cast doubt on the authority or further support it. Often it is expressed by paired characters, Troilus and Pandarus, for example, or by paired tales, the Knight's and the Miller's. The characters' long recital of authorities may be ludicrous and pompous, Chaucer's parody of the pedant; but the pedant may be right. After Chanticleer's concern with what all the past has said about the significance of dreams, readers probably sympathize with Pertelote's comment that he should take a laxative. Nevertheless, once the rooster is in the fox's mouth, the authorities are proven correct. Similarly, the sum total of the Wife of Bath's personal experience is merely the proving, in an exaggerated form, of the antifeminist authorities. As Chaucer states in the prologue to the *Parlement of Foules*, out of old fields comes new corn, and out of old books new knowledge.

Related to the contrast between authority and experience are a series of other contrasts investigated by Chaucer: theological faith versus human reason, the ideal versus the pragmatic, the ritual of courtly love versus the business of making love, the dream world versus everyday life, the expectations of the rule versus the actions of the individual, the Christian teaching of free will versus man's sense of being fated. Again, these contrasts may be treated seriously or comically, may be represented by particular characters and may be brought into temporary balance. Seldom, however, does Chaucer provide solutions. The oppositions are implicit in human nature, in the wish for the absolute and the recognition of the relative. As Arthur Koestler comments on a modern political version of this dilemma (as represented by the extremes of the Yogi and the Commissar), "Apparently the two elements do not mix, and this may be one of the reasons why we have made such a mess of our History." Chaucer's poetic and highly varied treatment of these nonmixers may help to explain why his poetry continues to speak to the present century.

Chaucer's concern with these topics—a fascination not unusual in the dualistic Gothic world—imbues his poetry with a sense of irony. Since the 1930's, readers have certainly emphasized Chaucer's ironic treatment of characters and topics, a critical vogue that may be due as much to the fashions of the New Criticism as to the poetry itself. Yet Chaucer's characteristic means of telling his stories clearly encourages such readings. One can never be sure of his attitude because the poet stands behind a narrator whose often naïve attitudes simply cannot be identified with his creator's. Perhaps the creation of such a middleman between the poet and his audience was necessary for a middle-class poet reading to an aristocratic audience, or perhaps it is the natural practice of a diplomatic mind, which does not speak for itself but for another. Whatever the reasons, Chaucer's narrators are poetically effective. They provide a unifying strand throughout his varied work. Spearing notes that "the idiot-dreamer of *The Book of the Duchess* develops into the idiot-historian of *Troilus and Criseyde* and the idiot-pilgrim of *The Canterbury Tales*." Later, he comments that when Chaucer assigns the doggerel poem, "Sir Thopas," to Chaucer the pilgrim as a joke, he "takes the role of idiot-poet to its culmination."

One result of the use of such narrators is that, in contrast with the contemporary dream vision, William Langland's *The Vision of William, Concerning Piers the Plowman* (c. 1362)—with its acid attacks on English society, the failures of government, and the hypocrisy of the church—Chaucer's poetry seems aware of human foibles yet accepting of human nature. He implies rather than shouts the need for change, recognizing that in this world at least major reform is unlikely. His essentially Christian position, hidden behind the naïve narrator and his concern with surface details, naturalistic dialogue, and sharp description, is implied by the poem's larger structures. They often provide symbolic patterning. The contrast in the *Parlement of Foules* between the steamy atmosphere of the temple of Venus and the clear air of Nature's dominion, or in *Troilus and Criseyde* between the narrator's introductory devotion to the god of love and his concluding epilogue based on Troilus' new heavenly point of view imply Chaucer's position concerning his favorite topic, human love. Similarly, the traditional Christian metaphor identifying life as a pilgrimage and the Parson's identification of Canterbury with the New Jerusalem suggest that the pilgrimage from a pub in Southwark to a shrine in Canterbury is a secular version of an important traditional religious theme. The reader of Chaucer, while paying careful attention to his realism which has been found so attractive should also be aware of the larger implications of his poetry.

Behind the medieval interest in dreams and the genre of dream visions lies a long tradition, both religious and secular, originating in biblical and classical stories and passed on to the Middle Ages in the works of Macrobiuss and Boethius. As a literary type, the dream vision, given impetus by the *Romaunt of the Rose*, was particularly popular in fourteenth century England. The obtuse dreamers led by authoritative guides found in such works as *Piers Plowman* and *The Pearl* (c. 1375-1400) are typical of dream visions and may have suggested to Chaucer the creation of his characteristic naïve narrator. Certainly Chaucer's four dream visions, as different as they are from one another, already develop this narrative voice as well as other typical Chaucerian characteristics.

The earliest of Chaucer's very long poems, *Book of the Duchess* (1,334 lines), is a dream elegy in memory of the duchess of Lancaster. The poem begins with the narrator reading in bed about dreams, specifically the Ovidian story of the tragic love of Ceyx and Alcyone. After her husband's death, Alcyone is visited in a dream by Ceyx, leading to Alcyone's eventual brokenhearted death. This introductory section, which as usual refers to numerous authorities on dreams, combines Chaucer's concern with both dreams and love. These authorities provide background for the narrator's experience in a dream. After praying to Morpheus, the narrator falls asleep to dream of another couple divided by death, a man in black (John of Gaunt) and his lost lover, "faire White" (Blanche). The dreamer's foolish and tactless questions allow the grieving knight to express his love and sense of loss, sometimes by direct statement, on other occasions by such elaborate devices as describing a game of chess in which fortune takes his queen. The traditionally obtuse dreamer is here used in a remarkably original way. The poet is able to place the praise of the dead and the feelings of anguish in the mouth of the bereaved. Thus this highly conventional poem, with its conscious borrowing from Ovid, *Romaunt of the Rose*, Jean Froissart, and Guillaume de Machaut, is an effective elegy in the restrained courtly tradition.

The *Hous of Fame*, Chaucer's second dream vision, breaks off suddenly after 2,158 lines. It creates a series of allegorical structures and figures in an analysis of the relationship between love, fame, rumor, fortune, and poetry. The dreamer is here provided with a guide, Jupiter's eagle, that probably derives from Dante's *Purgatorio IX*. In Book I he relates the romance of Aeneas and Dido, two lovers of some poetic fame whose story is portrayed in panels on a temple of glass dedicated to Venus. This temple is contrasted with the house of Fame which the dreamer sees in Book III when the eagle rather unceremoniously whisks him into the heavens. In this second allegorical structure, the dreamer views the goddess Fame surrounded by the great poets of antiquity on pedestals. They represent the authorities who, like Vergil, record the stories of such lovers as Aeneas and Dido. The dreamer realizes, however, that Fame (and thus presumably the poets of Fame) deals out good and bad at random, suggesting that there is little relationship between actuality and reputation. He next sees the house of Rumor. Full of noise and whispering people, it is perhaps an allegorical representation of the character of everyday life. In any case, this chaotic structure is no more attractive than the house of Fame. Still searching for "tydinges of Loves folk," the dreamer sees "a man of greet auctoritee," but the poem breaks off before the man can speak. The reader, like the dreamer, is left in the air; the poem is left without an ending. As Muscatine comments, "It is hard to conceive of any ending at all that could consistently follow from what we have." In fact, the poem lacks a sense of unity.

Its multiple topics and elaborate descriptions are best studied as set pieces. Of particular interest is the often comic dialogue between the dreamer and the eagle in Book II.

The *Parlement of Foules* (699 lines) is a more satisfactory poem, although it shares much in common with *Hous of Fame*, including a series of allegorical portraits and locales, a guide who tends to shove the dreamer around, and birds as characters. A poem describing the mating of birds on Saint Valentine's day, the *Parlement of Foules* begins, like the *Book of the Duchess*, with the narrator reading a book about a dream. The book is Cicero's *Dream of Scipio*, the standard textbook on dreams, found in the last part of *De republica* (52-51 B.C.). Its guide, Scipio Africanus the elder, becomes the dreamer's guide in the *Parlement of Foules*. He dreams of the typical enclosed garden of romance, guarded by a gate. The gate's contrasting inscriptions alluding to the gates of Dante's *Inferno*, suggest the dual nature of love: bliss, fertility, and "good aventure" on the one hand, and sorrow, barrenness, and danger on the other. Within the garden the dreamer again sees two versions of love, although, as naïve as ever, he seems bewildered and unsure of what he witnesses.

Like the Renaissance masterpiece, Titian's painting of "Sacred and Profane Love," the poem contrasts two traditional ideals of love. One is symbolized by Venus, whose entourage includes Flattery, Desire, and Lust as well as Cupid, Courtesy, and Gentleness. Her religion of love is the subject of the poets and ancient authorities whom the narrator so often reads. Her palace is dark and mannered, painted with the tragic stories of doomed lovers. In contrast, the dreamer next sees in the bright sunlight "this noble goddesse Nature," who presides over the beauty of natural love and mating of the birds. These ceremonies include description of all levels of the hierarchy of the birds, from the pragmatic arrangements of the goose and the love devotion of the turtledove to the courtly wooing of the former by the eagles. The language of the birds, often comic, similarly ranges from the sudden "kek, kek!" and "kukkow" to elaborate Latinate diction. Although lighthearted and sometimes chaotic, the openness and social awareness of Nature's realm is clearly to be preferred to the artificiality and self-absorption of the temple of Venus. The poem ends under Nature's skillful guidance as the birds sing a song of spring, which awakens the dreamer. In the prologue, the narrator states that he wishes to learn of love. This dream has provided much to learn, yet he seems in the end unchanged by his experience and once again returns to his authorities.

Of great interest as a forerunner of *The Canterbury Tales, The Legend of Good Women* is Chaucer's first experiment with decasyllabic couplets and with the idea of a framed collection of stories. Like the much grander later collection, it begins with a prologue and then relates an unfinished series of stories. Although the prologue plans nineteen stories, the poem breaks off near the conclusion of the ninth, after 2,723 lines. Unlike "The General Prologue" to *The Canterbury Tales*, with its detailed portraits of the pilgrims set in the Tabard Inn, the prologue to *The Legend of Good Women* is set as yet another dream. It presents the god of love and his daisy queen in conversation with the Chaucerian narrator. Once again, the narrator is a reader of books anxious to learn from life about love. More interesting, he is here also a writer of books, and is harassed by the god of love for not presenting lovers in a good light in his poetry. Specific reference is made to his translation of the *Romaunt of the Rose* and to *Troilus and Criseyde*. As penance for his grievous sins against the religion of love, the narrator promises to write about the faithful lovers of ancient legend.

Comparisons with *The Canterbury Tales* are perhaps unfair, but the poem, lacking the dynamic characters and varied tales of the later collection, seems grievously repetitious. Its recital of love tragedies is borrowed from Ovid and other authorities. Nevertheless, the legends do encompass a wider range of classical stories than might at first be expected, including the stories of Cleopatra and Medea, who to the modern reader, at least, hardly qualify as "good women." The luscious yet natural scenery of the prologue is superb. Furthermore, the work is fulfillment of Chaucer's poetic development in the courtly tradition. Whatever the poem's weaknesses, it is unlikely that Chaucer would have agreed with Robert Burlin's judgment that the poem was "a colossal blunder."

In his elaborate panegyric, the French poet Émile Deschamps refers to Chaucer as a "Socrates, full of philosophy, Seneca for morality . . . a great Ovid in your poetry. . . ." The poem that most fully deserves such praise is *Troilus and Criseyde*, Chaucer's longest complete poem (8,259 lines) and, to many readers, his most moving work. Here for the first time in a long poem, Chaucer turns from the dream vision form and the participating narrator, but not from his concern with authorities and the nature of love. He now adds, however, a Boethian philosophical touch. Although it is a poem about love, Fortuna rather than Venus is the controlling goddess of Chaucer's "little tragedy." Although the career of Troilus is based on Boccaccio's *Filostrato* (c. 1335-1340), it would seem that *The Consolation of Philosophy* exerted the greatest influence on the poem.

The five books of *Troilus and Criseyde* rather than being, as modern critics like to assert, the first novel or a drama in five acts, represent the various stages of Troilus' tragic love affair. Describing the "double sorrow" of Troilus, the son of King Priam of Troy, the poem begins with his initial love-longing, then traces his increasingly successful courtship of Criseyde culminating in their fulfilled love, the intervention of the Trojan War in the midst of their happiness, their forced separation, Criseyde's eventual acceptance of the Greek Diomede, and finally Troilus' gallant death at the hand of Achilles. While telling this story, Chaucer paints a series of scenes, both comic and serious, sometimes absurd, often movingly romantic, examining various outlooks on human love. Troilus' excessive idealism seems to parody the courtly lovers of French romances, whereas the pragmatic, often cynical attitudes of Pandarus, the uncle of Criseyde and confidant of Troilus, remind one of the waterfowl in the *Parlement of Foules* and the later fabliaux of *The Canterbury Tales*. Criseyde's views of love shift between these two extremes, varying according to her feelings and the exigencies of circumstance.

Calling *Troilus and Criseyde* Chaucer's "great failure," Ian Robinson (*Chaucer and the English Tradition*, 1972) believes that the poem includes "many great parts but they don't cohere into a great whole." Yet the poem does have a unifying structure, based on the rising and falling stages of the Wheel of Fortune. The notion of Fortune turning a wheel which sometimes takes man to the height of success and sometimes drags him down to failure is standard in medieval thought and very popular in both literature and art. The stages of the wheel, along with the poem's narrative units, are set forth in the invocations which introduce the books of *Troilus and Criseyde*. In the first, when Troilus is at the bottom of the wheel, the narrator invokes Tesiphone, "thou cruel fury." As Morton Bloomfield comments ("Distance and Predestination in *Troilus and Criseyde*"), Tesiphone was characterized as the "sorrowful fury" who laments her torments and pities those whom she torments. The choice is thus appropriate for the description in Book I of the hero's initial love torments and for the events of the entire poem. The Chaucerian narrator presents himself as "the sorrowful instrument" of love, required to tell the "sorrowful tale."

The invocation in Book II, to Clio the muse of history, suggests that the second stage represents a rather neutral and objectively historical description of the rise of Troilus on the wheel, whereas the invocation to Venus in Book III is appropriate for the stage when the lovers are at the top of the wheel and consummate their love. As all readers of Boethius know, however, if one chooses to ride to the top of the wheel, one in all fairness cannot be surprised when the wheel continues to turn downward. Thus, Book IV begins with an invocation to Fortune and her wheel, which throws down the hero and sets Diomede in his place. There is also an appropriate reference to Mars, suggesting the growing influence of the war on the romance. Book V follows without an invocation, probably because it is a continuation of the fourth book and implying that the downward movement of the wheel is one continuous stage. Certainly the poem's last book does not introduce any new elements. Its major concerns are Troilus' fatalism and the details of the Trojan War.

This pattern clearly interweaves two problems which dominate the poem: the perplexities of human love and man's sense of being fated. Troilus is the character overwhelmed by both problems. Although many critics are fascinated by the inscrutable Criseyde and attracted by the worldly-wise Pandarus, Troilus is the poem's central figure. Readers may become frustrated by his passive love-longing and swooning and his long-winded and confused discussion of predestination and free will; however, he is treated sympathetically and his situation must be taken seriously. One can argue, using Boethius as support, that the solution to the human predicament is simply never to accept the favors of Fortune–to stay away from her wheel–but what man would not do as Troilus did for the love of Criseyde? Similarly, one can agree with the moralizing narrator at the poem's conclusion that the solution is to avoid worldly vanity and the love associated with Venus and to look instead to heavenly love.

Certainly Troilus recognizes this view as his soul ascends to the seventh sphere. Yet the poem as a whole hardly condemns the love of the two Trojans. On the contrary, it describes their long-awaited rendezvous in bed with great sensitivity and poetic beauty, with warmth and sensuous natural imagery. As Spearing states, "There is probably no finer poetry of fulfilled love in English than this scene." In this great tragic romance, Chaucer seems to juxtapose human and divine love and to intermingle the sense of predestination and the Christian teaching of free will; not until the end does he speak as the moralist and condemn worldly vanity. Perhaps the tragedy of Troilus and of the human situation in general is that the distinctions are not sufficiently clear until it is too late to choose.

Near the end of *Troilus and Criseyde*, Chaucer associates his "little tragedy" with a long line of classical poets and then asks for help to write "some comedie." Donald Howard and others have seen this as a reference to the poet's plans for *The Canterbury Tales*. Whether Chaucer had this collection planned by the time he had completed *Troilus and Criseyde*, *The Canterbury Tales* can certainly be understood as his comedy. If, as the Monk notes at the beginning of his long summary of tragic tales, a tragedy deals with those who once "stood in high degree, and fell so that there was no remedy," in the medieval view comedy deals with less significant characters and with events that move toward happy endings. *The Canterbury Tales* is thus a comedy, not because of its comic characters and humorous stories–several tales are actually tragic in tone and structure–but because its overall structure is comic.

Like Dante's *The Divine Comedy* (c. 1320) which traces the poet's eschatological journey from hell through purgatory to heaven, shifting from a pagan guide to the representatives of divine love and inspiration, and concluding with the beatific vision, Chaucer's comedy symbolically moves from the infernal to the heavenly. From the worldly concerns of the Tabard Inn in Southwark and the guidance of the worldly-wise Host, through a variety of points of view set forth by differing characters on the pilgrimage road, the poem moves to the religious goal of the saint's shrine in Canterbury Cathedral and the Parson's direction of the pilgrims to "Jerusalem celestial."

Although with differing effects, since the Christian perspective of *Troilus and Criseyde* lies beyond the narrative itself, Chaucer's tragedy and comedy thus share a similar moral structure. Like the tragedy, *The Canterbury Tales* moves from an ancient story of pagan heroes to a Christian perspective. In *Troilus and Criseyde* the narrator develops from being the servant of the god of love to being a moralist who condemns pagan "cursed old rites" and advises the young to love Him who "for love upon a cross our souls did buy." The collection of tales similarly moves from the Knight's "old stories" set in ancient Thebes and Athens and relating the fates of pagan lovers to the Parson's sermon beginning "Our swete lord god of hevene." In contrast with the earlier poem, *The Canterbury Tales* is a comedy because its divine perspective is achieved within the overall narrative. Yet as in the earlier poem, this divine perspective at the end does not necessarily cancel out the earlier outlooks proposed. The entire poem with its multiplicity of characters and viewpoints remains.

Such an approach to *The Canterbury Tales* assumes that, although unfinished, the poem is complete as it stands and should be judged as a whole. Like the Corpus Christi cycles of the later Middle Ages, which include numerous individual plays yet can (and should) be read as one large play tracing salvation history from creation to doomsday, *The Canterbury Tales* is more than the sum of its parts. "The General Prologue," that masterpiece of human description with its fascinating portraits of the pilgrims, establishes not only the supposed circumstances for the pilgrimage and the competition to tell the best story, but also the strands that link the tales to the characters and to one another. Although only twenty-four tales were finished, their relationship to one another within fragments and their sense of unity within variety suggest that Chaucer had an overall plan for *The Canterbury Tales*.

The famous opening lines of "The General Prologue," with the beautiful evocation of spring fever, set forth both the religious and the secular motivations of the pilgrims. These motivations are further developed in their description by the pilgrim Chaucer. He again is the naïve narrator whose wide-eyed simplicity seems to accept all, leaving the discriminating reader to see beyond the surface details. Finally, in his faithful retelling of the stories he hears on the way to Canterbury—for once his experience has become an authority to which, he explains, he must not be false—the narrator again unwittingly implies much about these various human types. Several of the prologues and tales that follow then continue to explore the motivations of the individual pilgrims. The confessional prologue of "The Pardoner's Tale" and its sermon filled with moral exempla, for instance, ironically reflects the earlier description of the confidence man, Pardoner, as one "with feigned flattery and tricks, made the parson and the people his apes."

It would be a mistake, however, to interpret the various tales simply as dramatic embodiments of the pilgrims. Certainly Chaucer often fits story to storyteller. The sentimental, self-absorbed, and prissy Prioress tells, for example, a simplistic, anti-Semitic tale of a devout little Christian boy murdered by Jews. The implications of her tale make one question the nature of her spirituality. The tales given the Knight, Miller, and Reeve also reflect their characters. The Knight tells at great length a chivalric romance, a celebration of his worldview, whereas the Miller and Reeve tell bawdy stories concerning tradesmen, clerks, and wayward wives.

Yet these tales also develop the larger concerns of *The Canterbury Tales* implied by Chaucer's arrangement of the tales into thematic groups. "The Knight's Tale," with its ritualized action and idealized characters, draws from Boethian philosophy in its symmetrically patterned examination of courtly love, fate, and cosmic justice. The Miller then interrupts to "quite" or answer the Knight with a bawdy fabliau. Developing naturalistic dialogue and earthy characters, it rejects the artificial and the philosophical for the mundane and the practical. In place of the Knight's code of honor and courtly love, elaborate description of the tournament, and Stoic speech on the Great Chain of Being, the drunken Miller sets the stage for sexual conquest, a complex practical joke, and a "cherles tales" involving bodily functions and fleshly punishment. In "The Miller's Tale," justice is created not by planetary gods but by human action, each character getting what he deserves. The Reeve, offended by both the Miller and his tale, then follows with another fabliau. His motivations are much more personal than those of the Miller: the Reeve feels that the Miller has deliberately insulted him and he insists on returning the favor. Yet even in this tale Chaucer provides another dimension to the issues originally set forth by the Knight.

The clearest example of Chaucer's thematic grouping of tales is the so-called "Marriage Cycle." First noted by G. L. Kittredge and discussed since by various critics, the idea of the cycle is that Chaucer carefully arranged particular tales, told by suitable pilgrims, so that they referred to one another and developed a common theme, as in a scholarly debate. The "Marriage Cycle" examines various viewpoints on love and marriage, particularly tackling the issue of who should have sovereignty in marriage, the husband or the wife. The cycle is introduced by the Wife of Bath's rambling commentary on the woes of marriage and her wishful tale of a young bachelor who rightly puts himself in his wife's "wyse governance." After the Friar and Summoner "quite" each other in their own personal feud, the cycle continues with an extreme example of wifely obedience, "The Clerk's Tale" of patient Griselda. Such an otherworldly portrait of womanly perfection spurs the Merchant, a man who is obviously unhappy in marriage, to propound his cynical view of the unfaithful wife. The saint's legend of the scholarly Clerk is thus followed by the fabliau of the satirical Merchant and the debate is no nearer conclusion. Finally, the Franklin appears to "knit up the whole matter" by suggesting that in marriage the man should be both dominant as husband and subservient as lover. Yet the Franklin's view is hardly followed by the characters of his tale. Interestingly, the two solutions to the issue of sovereignty proposed—those of the Wife of Bath and of the Franklin—are developed in Breton lays, short and highly unrealistic romances relying heavily on magical elements. Is it the case that only magic can solve this typically human problem? Chaucer, at least, does not press for a definitive answer.

The great sense of variety, the comic treatment of serious issues, the concern with oppositions and unsuccessful solutions, and the lively and imaginative verse that so typifies *The Canterbury Tales* are best exemplified by "The Nun's Priest's Tale." A beast fable mocking courtly language and rhetorical overabundance, the tale at once includes Chaucer's fascination with authorities, dreams, fate, and love and marriage, and suggests his ambivalent attitudes toward the major philosophical and social concerns of his day. The elevated speeches of Chanticleer are punctuated by barnyard cries, and the pompous world of the rooster and hen are set within the humble yard of a poor widow.

Here the reader is provided with a comic version of the detached perspective that concludes *Troilus and Criseyde*. After deciding that dreams are to be taken seriously and refusing to take a laxative, Chanticleer disregards his dream and its warning and makes love to his favorite wife in a scene that absurdly portrays chickens as courtly lovers. Interestingly, Chanticleer now cites a standard sentiment of medieval antifeminism: *In principio/ Mulier est hominis confusio* ("In the beginning woman is man's ruin"), which alludes to the apostle John's famous description of the creation (John 1:1). The learned rooster, moreover, immediately mistranslates the Latin as "Womman is mannes ioye and al his blys," perhaps the Priest's subtle comment on the Nun he serves or the rooster's joke on Pertelote. Yet the joke ultimately is on Chanticleer when "a colfox ful of sley iniquitee" sneaks into this romance "garden." Noting that the counsel of woman brought woe to the world "And made Adam from paradys to go," the Nun's Priest then relates the temptation and fall of Chanticleer and the subsequent chasing of the fox and rooster out of the barnyard. The adventure is full of great fun, a hilarious scene, yet strangely reminiscent of the biblical story of the fall of man. It is not clear what one is to make of such a story.

Although Chaucer was not the first author to create a framed collection of stories, *The Canterbury Tales* is assuredly the most imaginative collection. Earlier the poet had experimented with a framed collection in *Legend of Good Women*. His Italian contemporary, Boccaccio, also created a collection of stories in *The Decameron* (1348-1353), although scholars cannot agree whether Chaucer knew this work. Earlier collections of exempla and legends were probably known by the poet, and he certainly knew the great collection of Ovid, *The Metamorphoses* (c. 8 A.D.). Like Ovid's collection, *The Canterbury Tales* is organized by thematic and structural elements which provide a sense of unity within diversity. Chaucer's choice of the pilgrimage as the setting for the tales is particularly effective, since it allows the juxtaposition of characters, literary types, and themes gathered from a wide range of sources and reflecting a wide range of human attitudes.

Here, perhaps, is the key to Chaucer's greatness. Like the medieval view of the macrocosm, in which constant change and movement take place within a relatively unchanging framework, Chaucer's view of the microcosm balances the dynamic and the static, the wide range of individual feeling and belief within unchanging human nature. *The Canterbury Tales* is his greatest achievement in this area, although earlier poems, such as the *Parlement of Foules*, with its portrayal of the hierarchy of birds within Nature's order, already show Chaucer's basic view. Ranging over human nature, selecting from ancient story and supposed personal experience, with a place for both the comic and the tragic, Chaucer's poetry mixes mirth and morality, accomplishing very successfully the two great purposes of literature, what the Host calls "sentence and solas," teaching and entertainment.

Other literary forms · In addition to the early allegorical dream visions, the "tragedy" of *Troilus and Criseyde*, and the "comedy," *The Canterbury Tales*,

Geoffrey Chaucer composed various lyrical poems, wrote a scientific treatise in prose, and translated two immensely influential works from Latin and Old French into Middle English. The shorter works have received little attention from critics. *ABC to the Virgin*, Chaucer's earliest poem adapted from the French of Guillaume Deguilleville, and the various ballades, roundels, and envoys are in the French courtly tradition. They also reflect the influence of the Roman philosopher Boethius and often include moral advice and standard *sententiae*. Somewhat longer are the *Anelida and Arcite* and the complaints to Pity and of Venus and Mars, which develop the conventions of the languishing lover of romance.

The prose works include the interesting astrological study, *A Treatise on the Astrolabe* (1387-1392), written for "little Lewis my son," and the *Boece* (c. 1380) a translation of Boethius' *The Consolation of Philosophy* (523) which particularly influenced Chaucer's *Troilus and Criseyde* and "The Knight's Tale." The prologue to *The Legend of Good Women* notes that Chaucer also translated *Romaunt of the Rose* (c. 1370). Certainly the great Old French dream vision, particularly the first part by Guillaume de Lorris, influenced Chaucer's early dream allegories as well as his portrayal of certain characters and scenes in *The Canterbury Tales*—the Wife of Bath, for example, and the enclosed garden of "The Merchant's Tale." Scholars, however, are uncertain whether the extant Middle English version of *Romaunt of the Rose* included in standard editions of Chaucer is by the poet.

Select works other than poetry

NONFICTION: *Boece*, c. 1380 (translation of Boethius' *The Consolation of Philosophy*); *A Treatise on the Astrolabe*, 1387-1392.

MISCELLANEOUS: *Works*, 1957 (second edition; F. N. Robinson, editor).

Richard Kenneth Emmerson

Bibliography · For editions of Chaucer's work that include extensive notes and insightful introductions, see *The Riverside Chaucer*, 3d ed., edited by Larry Dean Benson, 1988; *The Complete Poetry and Prose of Geoffrey Chaucer*, 2d ed., edited by John H. Fisher, 1989; and *The Works of Geoffrey Chaucer*, 2d ed., edited by F. N. Robinson, 1957. Derek Brewer, *An Introduction to Chaucer*, 1984, provides a useful overview. For biographical studies, see D. Pearsall's *The Life of Geoffrey Chaucer: A Critical Biography*, 1992; Paul Strohm, *Social Chaucer*, 1989; and Jill Mann, *Geoffrey Chaucer*, 1991. Foundational studies include George Lyman Kittredge, *Chaucer and His Poetry*, 1915, and Robert K. Root, *The Poetry of Chaucer*, 1922.

See also D. W. Robertson, *A Preface to Chaucer*, 1962, which examines the role of the Christian tradition in Chaucer; Charles Muscatine, *Chaucer and the French Tradition*, 1957, which considers Continental influences on Chaucer; E. Talbot Donaldson, *Speaking of Chaucer*, 1970, which considers Chaucer from a twentieth century perspective; Henry Ansgar Kelly, *Love and Marriage in the Age of Chaucer*, 1975; and Morton W. Bloomfield, "Chaucer's Sense of History," *Journal of English and Germanic Philology* 51 (1952). More recent studies include Carolyn Dinshaw, *Chaucer's Sexual Poetics*, 1989, and David Aers, *Chaucer*, 1986. Especially helpful to the student are Helen Cooper, *Oxford Guides to Chaucer: "The Canterbury Tales,"* 1989, and B. A. Windeatt, *Oxford Guides to Chaucer: Troilus and Criseyde*, 1992; these compilations provide summaries of criticism and extensive bibliographies.

Other comprehensive critical studies include Piero Boitani and Jill Mann, eds., *The Cambridge Chaucer Companion*, 1986; and Richard J. Schoeck and Jerome Taylor, eds., *The Canterbury Tales*, vol. 1 in *Chaucer Criticism*. For criticism on Troilus and Criseyde, see Stephen A. Barney, ed., *Chaucer's "Troilus": Essays in Criticism*, 1980; J. A. W. Bennett, *Chaucer's "Troilus and Criseyde,"* 1990; Mary Salu, ed., *Essays on "Troilus and Criseyde,"* 1979; A. C. Spearing, *Chaucer: "Troilus and Criseyde,"* 1976; and Robert P. ApRoberts, "Criseyde's Infidelity and the Moral of the *Troilus*," *Speculum* 44 (1969). Chaucer's sources and inspirations are explored in John M. Fyler, *Chaucer and Ovid*, 1979; Alistair Minnis, "Aspects of the Medieval French and English Traditions of the *De Consolatione Philosophiae*," in *Boethius*, edited by Margaret Gibson, 1981; and J. A. W. Bennett, "Chaucer, Dante, and Boccaccio," in Piero Boitani, ed., *Chaucer and the Italian Trecento*, 1983.

SAMUEL TAYLOR COLERIDGE

Born: Ottery St. Mary, England; October 21, 1772
Died: Highgate, London, England; July 25, 1834

Poetry · *Poems on Various Subjects*, 1796, 1797 (with Charles Lamb and Charles Lloyd) · *A Sheet of Sonnets*, 1796 (with W. L. Bowles, Robert Southey, and others) · *Lyrical Ballads*, 1798 (with William Wordsworth) · *The Rime of the Ancient Mariner*, 1798 · *Christabel*, 1816 · *Sibylline Leaves*, 1817 · *The Complete Poetical Works of Samuel Taylor Coleridge*, 1912 (2 volumes; Ernest Hartley Coleridge, editor)

Achievements · It is ironic that Samuel Taylor Coleridge has come to be known to the general reader primarily as a poet, for poetry was not his own primary interest, and the poems with which his name is most strongly linked—*The Rime of the Ancient Mariner*, "Kubla Khan," and *Christabel*—were products of a few months in a long literary career. He did not suffer a decline in poetic creativity; he simply turned his attention to political, metaphysical, and theological issues that were best treated in prose. That Coleridge is counted among the major poets of British Romanticism is, for this reason, all the more remarkable. For most poets, the handful of commonly anthologized poems is a scant representation of their output; for Coleridge, it is, in many instances, the sum of his accomplishment. His minor verse is often conventional and uninspired. His major poems, in contrast, speak with singular emotional and intellectual intensity in a surprising range of forms—from the symbolic fantasy of *The Rime of the Ancient Mariner* (which first appeared in *Lyrical Ballads*) to the autobiographical sincerity of the conversation poems—exerting an influence on subsequent poets far beyond what Coleridge himself anticipated.

Biography · Samuel Taylor Coleridge was born October 21, 1772, in the Devonshire town of Ottery St. Mary, the youngest of ten children. His father, a clergyman and teacher, died in October, 1781, and the next year Coleridge was sent to school at Christ's Hospital, London. His friends at school included Charles Lamb, two years his junior, whose essay "Christ's Hospital Five-and-Thirty Years Ago" (1820) describes the two sides of Coleridge—the "poor friendless boy," far from his home, "alone among six hundred playmates"; the precocious scholar, "Logician, Metaphysician,

Bard!," holding his auditors "entranced with imagination." Both characteristics—a deep sense of isolation and the effort to use learning and eloquence to overcome it—remained with Coleridge throughout his life.

He entered Cambridge in 1791, but never completed work for his university degree. Depressed by debts, he fled the university in December, 1793, and enlisted in the Light Dragoons under the name Silas Tompkyn Comberbache. Rescued by his brothers, he returned to Cambridge in April and resumed his studies. Two months later he met Robert Southey, with whom he soon made plans to establish a utopian community ("Pantisocracy") in America. Southey was engaged to marry Edith Fricker, and so it seemed appropriate for Coleridge to engage himself to her sister Sara. The project failed, but Coleridge, through his own sense of duty and Southey's insistence, married a woman he had never loved and with whom his relationship was soon to become strained.

As a married man, Coleridge had to leave the university and make a living for his wife and, in time, children—Hartley (1796-1849), Berkeley (1798-1799), Derwent (b. 1800), and Sara (1802-1852). Economic survival was, it turned out, possible only with the support of friends such as Thomas Poole and the publisher Joseph Cottle and, in 1798, a life annuity from Josiah and Tom Wedgwood. The early years of Coleridge's married life, in which he lived with his family at Nether Stowey, were the period of his closest relationship with the poet William Wordsworth. Inspired by Wordsorth, whom he in turn inspired, Coleridge wrote most of his major poetry. Together, the two men published *Lyrical Ballads* in 1798, the proceeds of which enabled them, along with Wordsworth's sister Dorothy, to spend the winter in Germany, where Coleridge studied metaphysics at the University of Göttingen.

Returning to England the following year, Coleridge met and fell deeply in love with Sara Hutchinson, a friend of Dorothy who later became Wordsworth's sister-in-law. This passion, which remained strong

Library of Congress

for many years, furthered Coleridge's estrangement from his wife, with whom he moved to Keswick in the Lake District of England, in July, 1800, to be near the Wordsworths at Grasmere. Coleridge's health had always been poor, and he had become addicted to opium, which, according to current medical practice, he had originally taken to relieve pain. Seeking a change of climate, he traveled to Malta and then Italy in 1804 to 1806. On his return, he and his wife "*determined* to part absolutely and finally," leaving Coleridge in custody of his sons Hartley and Derwent (Berkeley had died in 1799).

In 1808, Coleridge gave his first public lectures and in the next two years published the twenty-seven issues of *The Friend*. By now, he was a figure of national standing, but his private life remained in disarray. Sara Hutchinson, who had assisted him in preparing copy for *The Friend*, separated herself from him, and in 1810 he quarreled decisively with Wordsworth. (They were later reconciled, but the period of close friendship was over.) Six years later, after various unsuccessful attempts to cure himself of opium addiction and set his affairs in order, he put himself in the care of James Gillman, a physician living at Highgate, a northern suburb of London. Under Gillman's roof, Coleridge was once again able to work. He wrote the two Lay Sermons, "The Statesman's Manual" and "A Lay Sermon"; completed the *Biographia Literaria*, originally planned as an autobiographical introduction to *Sibylline Leaves* but ultimately two volumes in its own right; and revised the essays he had written for *The Friend*, including among them a version of the "Essay on Method" which he had composed for the first volume of *The Encyclopaedia Metropolitana*. He also resumed his public lectures on philosophy and literature and in time became a London celebrity, enthralling visitors with his conversation and gradually attracting a circle of disciples. Meanwhile, he worked at the *magnum opus* that was to synthesize his metaphysical and theological thought in a single intellectual system. This project, however, remained incomplete when Coleridge died at Highgate, July 25, 1834.

Analysis · Samuel Taylor Coleridge's major poems turn on problems of self-esteem and identity. Exploring states of isolation and ineffectuality, they test strategies to overcome weakness without asserting its antithesis—a powerful self, secure in its own thoughts and utterances, the potency and independence of which Coleridge feared would only exacerbate his loneliness. His reluctance to assert his own abilities is evident in his habitual deprecation of his own poetry and hyperbolic praise of William Wordsworth's. It is evident as well in his best verse, which either is written in an unpretentious "conversational" tone or, when it is not, is carefully dissociated from his own voice and identity. Yet by means of these strategies, he is often able to assert indirectly or vicariously the strong self he otherwise repressed.

Writing to John Thelwall in 1796, Coleridge called the first of the conversation poems, "The Eolian Harp" (written in 1795), the "favorite of *my* poems." He originally published it, in 1796, with the indication "Composed August 20th, 1795, At Clevedon, Somersetshire," which dates at least some version of the text six weeks before his marriage to Sara Fricker. Since Sara plays a role in the poem, the exact date is crucial. "The Eolian Harp" is not, as it has been called, a "honeymoon" poem; rather, it anticipates a future in which Coleridge and Sara will sit together by their "Cot o'ergrown/ With white-flower'd Jasmin." Significantly, Sara remains silent throughout the poem; her only contribution is the "mild reproof" that "darts" from her "more serious eye," quelling the poet's intellectual daring. Yet this reproof is as imaginary as Sara's presence itself. At the climax of the poem, meditative thought gives way to the need for human response; tellingly, the response he imagines and therefore, one must assume, desires, is reproof.

"The Eolian Harp" establishes a structural pattern for the conversation poems as a group. Coleridge is, in effect, alone, "and the world *so* hush'd!/ The stilly murmur of the distant Sea/ Tells us of silence." The eolian harp in the window sounds in the breeze and reminds him of "the one Life within us and abroad,/ Which meets all motion and becomes its soul." This observation leads to the central question of the poem:

> And what if all of animated nature
> Be but organic Harps diversely fram'd,
> That tremble into thought, as o'er them sweeps
> Plastic and vast, one intellectual breeze,
> At once the Soul of each, and God of all?

Sara's glance dispels "These shapings of the unregenerate mind," but, of course, it is too late, since they have already been expressed in the poem. (Indeed, the letter to Thelwall makes it clear that it was this expression of pantheism, not its retraction, that made the poem dear to Coleridge.) For this reason, the conflict between two sides of Coleridge's thought—metaphysical speculation and orthodox Christianity—remains unresolved. If the poem is in any way disquieting, it is not because it exemplifies a failure of nerve, but because of the identifications it suggests between metaphysical speculation and the isolated self, religious orthodoxy and the conventions—down to the vines covering the cottage—of married life. Coleridge, in other words, does not imagine a wife who will love him all the more for his intellectual daring. Instead, he imagines one who will chastise him for the very qualities that make him an original thinker. To "possess/ Peace, and this Cot, and thee, heart-honour'd Maid!," Coleridge must acknowledge himself "A sinful and most miserable man,/ Wilder'd and dark." Happiness, as well as poetic closure, depends upon this acceptance of diminished self-esteem. Even so, by embedding an expression of intellectual strength within the context of domestic conventionality, Coleridge is able to achieve a degree of poetic authority otherwise absent in the final lines of the poem. The ability to renounce a powerful self is itself a gesture of power: the acceptance of loss becomes—as in other Romantic poems—a form of strength.

The structure of "The Eolian Harp" can be summarized as follows: a state of isolation (the more isolated for the presence of an unresponsive companion) gives way to meditation, which leads to the possibility of a self powerful through its association with an all-powerful force. This state of mind gives place to the acknowledgment of a human relationship dependent on the poet's recognition of his own inadequacy, the reward for which is a poetic voice with the authority to close the poem.

This pattern recurs in "This Lime-Tree Bower My Prison" (1797). The poem is addressed to Charles Lamb, but the "gentle-hearted Charles" of the text is really a surrogate for the figure of Wordsworth, whose loss Coleridge is unwilling to face head-on. Incapacitated by a burn—appropriately, his wife's fault—Coleridge is left alone seated in a clump of lime trees while his friends—Lamb and William and Dorothy Wordsworth—set off on a long walk through the countryside. They are, like Sara in "The Eolian Harp," there and yet not there: their presence in the poem intensifies Coleridge's sense of isolation. He follows them in his imagination, and the gesture itself becomes a means of connecting himself with them. Natural images of weakness, enclosure, and solitude give way to those of strength, expansion, and connection, and the tone of the poem shifts from speculation to assertion. In a climactic moment, he imagines his friends "gazing round/ On the wide landscape," until it achieves the transcendence of "such hues/ As veil the Almighty Spirit, when yet he makes/ Spirits perceive his presence."

As in "The Eolian Harp," the perception of an omnipotent force pervading the universe returns Coleridge to his present state, but with a new sense of his own being and his relationship with the friends to whom he addresses the poem. His own isolation is now seen as an end in itself. "Sometimes/ 'Tis well to be bereft of promised good," Coleridge argues, "That we may lift the soul, and contemplate/ With lively joy the joys we cannot share."

"Frost at Midnight," the finest of the conversation poems, replaces silent wife or absent friends with a sleeping child (Hartley—although he is not named in the text). Summer is replaced by winter; isolation is now a function of seasonal change itself. In this zero-world, "The Frost performs its secret ministry,/ Unhelped by any wind." The force that moved the eolian harp into sound is gone. The natural surroundings of the poem drift into nonexistence: "Sea, and hill, and wood,/ With all the numberless goings-on of life,/ Inaudible as dreams!" This is the nadir of self from which the poet reconstructs his being—first by perception of "dim sympathies" with the "low-burnt fire" before him; then by a process of recollection and predication. The "film" on the grate reminds Coleridge of his childhood at Christ's Hospital, where a similar image conveyed hopes of seeing someone from home and therefore a renewal of the conditions of his earlier life in Ottery St. Mary. Yet even in recollection, the bells of his "sweet birth-place" are most expressive not as a voice of the present moment, but as "articulate sounds of things to come!" The spell of the past was, in fact, a spell of the imagined future. The visitor he longed for turns out to be a version of the self of the poet, his "sister more beloved/ My play-mate when we both were clothed alike." The condition of loss that opens the poem cannot be filled by the presence of another human being; it is a fundamental emptiness in the self, which, Coleridge suggests, can never be filled, but only recognized as a necessary condition of adulthood. Yet this recognition of incompleteness is the poet's means of experiencing a sense of identity missing in the opening lines of the poem.

"Frost at Midnight" locates this sense of identity in Coleridge's own life. It is not a matter of metaphysical or religious belief, as it is in "The Eolian Harp" or "This Lime-Tree Bower My Prison," but a function of the self that recognizes its own coherence in time. This recognition enables him to speak to the "Dear Babe" who had been there all along, but had remained a piece of the setting and not a living human being. Like the friends of "This Lime-Tree Bower My Prison," who are projected exploring a landscape, the boy Hartley is imagined wandering "like a breeze/ By lakes and sandy shores." The static existence of the poet in the present moment is contrasted with the movement of a surrogate. This movement, however, is itself subordinated to the voice of the poet who can promise his son a happiness he himself has not known.

In all three poems, Coleridge achieves a voice that entails the recognition of his own loss—in acknowledging Sara's reproof or losing himself in the empathic construction of the experience of friend or son. The act entails a defeat of the self, but also a vicarious participation in powerful forces that reveal themselves in the working of the universe, and through this participation a partial triumph of the self over its own sense of inadequacy. In "Frost at Midnight," the surrogate figure of his son embodies a locomotor power denied the static speaker; but he is also, in his capacity to read the "language" uttered by God in the form of landscape, associated with absolute power itself.

Although written in a very different mode, *The Rime of the Ancient Mariner* centers on a similar experience of participation in supernatural power. At the core of the poem is, of course, the story of the Mariner who shoots the albatross and endures complete and devastating isolation from his fellow man. The poem, however, is not a direct narrative of these events; rather, it is a narrative of the Mariner's narrating them. The result of the extraordinary experience he has undergone is to make him an itinerant storyteller. It has given him a voice, but a voice grounded on his own incompleteness of self. He has returned to land, but remains homeless and without permanent human relationships. In this respect, *The Rime of the Ancient Mariner* is Coleridge's nightmare alternative to the conversation poem. As "conversations," they suggest the possibility of a relationship with his audience that can in part compensate for the inadequate human relationships described in the poem. The Mariner's story is a kind of conversation. He tells it to the Wedding-Guest he has singled out for that purpose, but the relationship between speaker and audience can scarcely be said to compensate for the Mariner's lack of human relationships. The Wedding-Guest is compelled to listen by the hypnotic power of the Mariner's "glittering eye." He "beats his breast" at the thought of the wedding from which he is being detained, and repeatedly expresses his fear of the Mariner. In the end, he registers no compassion for the man whose story he has just heard. He is too "stunned" for that–and the Mariner has left the stage without asking for applause. His audience is changed by the story–"A sadder and a wiser man,/ He rose the morrow morn"–but of this the Mariner can know nothing. Thus, the power of the Mariner's story to captivate and transform its audience simply furthers his alienation from his fellow human beings.

Structurally, the poem follows the three-stage pattern of the conversation poems. A state of isolation and immobility is succeeded by one in which the Mariner becomes the object of (and is thus associated with) powerful supernatural agencies, and this leads to the moralizing voice of the conclusion. Unlike the conversation poems, *The Rime of the Ancient Mariner* prefaces individual isolation with social isolation. The Mariner and his shipmates, in what has become one of the most familiar narratives in English literature, sail from Europe toward Cape Horn, where they are surrounded by a polar ice jam. An albatross appears and accepts food from the sailors; a fair wind springs up and they are able to resume their journey northward into the Pacific; the albatross follows them, "And every day, for food or play,/ Came to the mariner's hollo!"—until the Mariner, seemingly without reason, shoots the bird with his crossbow. Coleridge warned readers against allegorizing the poem, and it is fruitless to search for a specific identification for the albatross. What is important is the bird's gratuitous arrival and the Mariner's equally gratuitous crossbow shot. The polar ice that threatens the ship is nature at its most alien. Seen against that backdrop, the albatross seems relatively human; the mariners, accordingly, "hailed it in God's name"; "As if it had been a Christian soul." Like the "film" in "Frost at Midnight"—a poem in which crucial events are also set against a wintry backdrop—the bird offers them a means of bridging the gap between man and nature, self and nonself, through projecting human characteristics on a creature of the natural world. By shooting the albatross, the Mariner blocks this projection and thus traps both himself and his shipmates in a state of isolation.

The Mariner's act has no explicit motive because it is a function of human nature itself, but it is not merely a sign of original sin or congenital perversity. His narrative has until now been characterized by a remarkable passivity. Events simply happen. Even the ship's progress is characterized not by its own movement but by the changing position of the sun in the sky. The ice that surrounds the ship is only one element of a natural world that dominates the fate of the ship and its crew, and it is against this overwhelming dominance that the Mariner takes his crossbow shot. The gesture is an assertion of the human spirit against an essentially inhuman universe, aimed at the harmless albatross because aimed at the act of self-deceptive projection by which his shipmates attempt to mitigate their sense of isolation.

He is punished for this self-assertion—first, by the crewmen who blame him for the calm that follows and tie the albatross around his neck as a sign of guilt. It is only after this occurs that the Mariner, thirsty and guilt-ridden, perceives events that are explicitly supernatural and the second stage of his punishment begins. Yet the Mariner's isolation, even after his shipmates have died and left him alone on the becalmed ship, remains a consequence of his assertion of self against the natural world; and the turning point of the poem is equally his own doing. In the midst of the calm, the water had seemed abhorrently ugly: "slimy things did crawl with legs/ Upon the slimy sea," while "the water, like a witch's oils,/ Burnt green, and blue and white." Now, "bemocked" by moonlight, the same creatures are beautiful: "Blue, glossy green, and velvet black,/ They coiled and swam; and every track/ Was a flash of golden fire." In this perception of beauty, the Mariner explains, "A spring of love gushed from my heart,/ And I blessed them unaware." At the same moment, he is once again able to pray and the albatross falls from his neck into the sea. Prayer—the ability to voice his mind and feelings and, in so doing, relate them to a higher order of being—is a function of love, and love is a function of the apprehension of beauty. In blessing the water snakes, it should be noted, the Mariner has not returned to the viewpoint of his shipmates when they attributed human characteristics to the albatross. When he conceives of the snakes as "happy living things," he acknowledges a bond between all forms of organic life, but their beauty is not dependent on human projection.

Yet achieving this chastened vision does not end the Mariner's suffering. Not only must he endure an extension of his shipboard isolation, but also when, eventually, he returns to his native land, he is not granted reintegration into its society. The Hermit from whom he asks absolution demands quick answer to his own question, "What manner of man art thou?' " In response, the Mariner experiences a spasm of physical agony that forces him to tell the story of his adventures. The tale told, he is left free of pain—until such time as "That agony returns" and he is compelled to repeat the narrative: "That moment that his face I see,/ I know the man that must hear me:/ To him my tale I teach." The Mariner has become a poet—like Coleridge, a poet gifted with "strange power of speech" and plagued with somatic pain, with power to fix his auditors' attention and transform them into "sadder and wiser" men. Yet the price of this power is enormous. It entails not only the shipboard suffering of the Mariner, but also perpetual alienation from his fellow human beings. Telling his story is the only relationship allowed him, and he does not even fully understand the meaning of his narration. In the concluding lines of the poem, he attempts to draw a moral—

> He prayeth best, who loveth best
> All things both great and small;
> For the dear God who loveth us,
> He made and loveth all.

These words are not without bearing on the poem, but they overlook the extraordinary disproportion between the Mariner's crime and its punishment. Readers of the poem—as well as, one supposes, the Wedding-Guest—are more likely to question the benevolence of the "dear God who loveth us" than to perceive the Mariner's story as an illustration of God's love. Thus, the voice of moral authority that gave the conversation poems a means of closure is itself called into question. The soul that acknowledges its essential isolation in the universe can never hope for reintegration into society. The poet whose song is the tale of his own suffering can "stun" his reader, but can never achieve a lasting human relationship. His experience can be given the aesthetic coherence of narrative, but he can never connect the expressive significance of that narrative with his life as a whole.

It is in part the medium of the poem that allows Coleridge to face these bleak possibilities. Its ballad stanza and archaic diction, along with the marginal glosses added in 1815 to 1816, dissociate the text from its modern poet. Freed from an explicit identification with the Mariner, Coleridge is able both to explore implications of the poet's role that would have been difficult to face directly and to write about experiences for which there was no precedent in conventional meditative verse.

A similar strategy is associated with "Kubla Khan," which can be read as an alternative to *The Rime of the Ancient Mariner*. The poem, which was not published until 1816, nearly two decades after it was written, is Coleridge's most daring account of poetic inspiration and the special nature of the poet. In the poem, the poet's isolation is perceived not as weakness but strength. Even in 1816, the gesture of self-assertion was difficult for Coleridge, and he prefaced the poem with an account designed to diminish its significance. "Kubla Khan" was, he explained, "a psychological curiosity," the fragment of a longer poem he had composed in an opium-induced sleep, "if that indeed can be called composition in which all the images rose up before him as *things*, with a parallel production of the correspondent expressions, without any sensation or consciousness of effort." Waking, he began to write out the verses he had in this manner "composed," but was interrupted by a visitor, after whose departure he found he could no longer remember more than "the general purport of the vision" and a few "scattered lines and images."

The problem with this explanation is that "Kubla Khan" does not strike readers as a fragment. It is, as it stands, an entirely satisfactory whole. Moreover, the facts of Coleridge's Preface have themselves been called into question.

Just what was Coleridge trying to hide? The poem turns on an analogy between the act of an emperor and the act of a poet. Kubla Khan's "pleasuredome" in Xanadu is more than a monarch's self-indulgence; symbolically, it attempts to arrest the process of life itself. His walls encircle "twice five miles of fertile ground," in the midst of which flows "Alph," the sacred river of life, but they control neither the source of the river nor its conclusion in the "lifeless ocean" to which it runs. The source is a "deep romantic chasm" that Coleridge associates with the violence of natural process, with human sexuality, and with the libidinal origins of poetry in the song of a "woman wailing for her demon lover." Kubla's pleasuredome is "a miracle of rare device," but it can exert no lasting influence. The achievement of the most powerful Oriental despot is limited by the conditions of life, and even his attempt to order a limited space evokes "Ancestral voices prophesying war!"

In contrast, the achievement of the poet is not bounded by space and time and partakes of the dangerous potency of natural creativity itself. Yet the nature of inspiration is tricky. The speaker of the poem recollects a visionary "Abyssinian maid" playing a dulcimer, and it is the possibility of reviving "within me/ Her symphony and song" that holds out the hope of a corresponding creativity: "To such a deep delight 'twould win me,/ . . . I would build that dome in air." The poet's act is always secondary, never primary creativity. Even so, to re-create in poetry Kubla's achievement—without its liabilities—is to become a dangerous being. Like the Mariner, the inspired poet has "flashing eyes" that can cast a spell over his audience. His special nature may be the sign of an incomplete self—for inspiration depends on the possibility of recovering a lost recollection; nevertheless, it is a special nature that threatens to re-create the world in its own image.

Nowhere else is Coleridge so confident about his powers as a poet or writer. *Christabel*, written in the same period as *The Rime of the Ancient Mariner* and "Kubla Khan," remains a fascinating fragment. Like "Kubla Khan," it was not published until 1816. By then, the verse romances of Sir Walter Scott and George Gordon, Lord Byron had caught the public's attention, and among Coleridge's motives in publishing his poem was to lay claim to a poetic form he believed he had originated. More important, though, his decision to publish two parts of an incomplete narrative almost two decades after he had begun the poem was also a means of acknowledging that *Christabel* was and would remain unfinished.

To attribute its incompletion to Coleridge's procrastination evades the real question: Why did the poem itself preclude development? Various answers have been offered; the most convincing argue a conflict between the metaphysical or religious significance of Christabel—whose name conflates Christ and Abel—with the exigencies of the narrative structure in which she is placed. As Walter Jackson Bate explains it, the "problem of finding motives and actions for Christabel . . . had imposed an insupportable psychological burden on Coleridge." The problem that Coleridge fails to solve is the problem of depicting credible innocence. Christabel, the virgin who finds the mysterious Lady Geraldine in the forest and brings her home to the castle of her father, Sir Leoline, only to fall victim to Geraldine's sinister spell, is either hopelessly passive and merely a victim, or, if active, something less than entirely innocent. At the same time, Geraldine, who approaches her prey with "a stricken look," is potentially the more interesting character. Christabel is too much like the albatross in *The Rime of the Ancient Mariner;* Geraldine, too much like the Mariner himself, whose guilt changes him from a simple seaman to an archetype of human isolation and suffering. Christabel's name suggests that Coleridge had intended for her to play a sacrificial role; but by promising to reunite Sir Leoline with his childhood friend, Roland de Vaux of Tryermaine, whom she claims as her father, Geraldine, too, has a potentially positive function in the narrative. Whether or not her claim is true, it nevertheless initiates action that may lead to a reconciliation, not only between two long-separated friends, but also between Sir Leoline's death-obsessed maturity and the time in his youth when he was able to experience friendship. There is, therefore, a suggestion that Geraldine is able to effect the link between childhood and maturity, innocence and experience, of particular concern to Coleridge—and to other Romantic poets as well. If Christabel and Geraldine represent the passive and active sides of Coleridge, then his failure to complete the narrative is yet another example of his inability to synthesize his personality—or to allow one side to win out at the expense of the other.

A few other poems from 1797 to 1798 deserve mention. "The Nightingale" (1798), although less interesting than the other titles in the group, conforms to the general structure of the conversation poems and so confirms its importance. "Fears in Solitude" (1798) is at once a conversation poem and something more. Like the others, it begins in a state of isolation and ends with social reintegration; its median state of self-assertion, however, takes the form of a public political statement. The voice of the statement is often strident, but this quality is understandable in a poem written at a time when invasion by France was daily rumored. "Fears in Solitude" attacks British militarism, British materialism, and British patriotism. Yet it is itself deeply patriotic. "There lives nor form nor feeling in my soul," Coleridge acknowledges, "Unborrowed from my country"; and for this reason the poem is not a series of topical criticism, but an expression of the dilemma of a poet divided between moral judgment of and personal identification with his native land.

When Coleridge returned from Germany in the summer of 1799, his period of intense poetic creativity was over. The poems that he wrote in the remaining years of his life were written by a man who no longer thought of himself as a poet and who therefore treated poetry as a mode of expression rather than a calling. "Dejection: An Ode," which Coleridge dated April 4, 1802, offers a rationale for this change and seems to have been written as a formal farewell to the possibility of a career as a poet. The poem's epigraph from the *Ballad of Sir Patrick Spence* and its concern with perception link it with *The Rime of the Ancient Mariner;* its use of the image of the eolian harp links it with the poem by that name and, by extension, with the free-associational style of the conversation poems as a group. Its tone and manner are also close to those of the conversation poems, but its designation as an ode suggests an effort to elevate it to the level of formal statement. At the same time, its recurrent addresses to an unnamed "Lady" (Sara Hutchinson) suggest that the poem was primarily intended for a specific rather than a general audience, for a reader with a special interest in the poet who will not expect the poem to describe a universal human experience. Thus, the poem is at once closely related to Coleridge's earlier verse and significantly different from it.

In keeping with the conversation-poem structure, "Dejection" begins in a mood of solitary contemplation. The poet ponders the moon and "the dull sobbing draft that moans and rakes/ Upon the strings of this Aeolian lute." Together, they portend a storm in the offing, and Coleridge hopes that the violence of the "slant night shower" may startle him from his depression. His state, he explains, is not merely grief; it is "A stifled, drowsy, unimpassioned grief,/ Which finds no natural outlet, no relief,/ In word, or sign, or tear." All modes of emotional expression are blocked: He is able to "see" the beauty of the natural world, but he cannot "feel" it, and thereby use it as a symbol for his own inner state. He has lost the ability to invest the "outward forms" of nature with passion and life because, by his account, his inner source of passion and life has dried up. This ability he calls "Joy"—"the spirit and the power,/ Which wedding Nature to us gives in dower/ A new Earth and new Heaven." The language of apocalypse identifies "Joy" with religious faith; the notion of language suggests a more general identification with the expressive mode of his earlier poetry and its ability to transform an ordinary situation into an especially meaningful event. To have no "outlet. . ./ In word" is to have lost the voice of that poetry; to make the observation within a poetic text is to suggest one more difference between "Dejection" and Coleridge's earlier poetry.

"Dejection" may seem like a restatement of the notion of a possible harmony—now lost—between nature and the human that was expressed in the earlier poetry. In fact, "Dejection" denies the grounds of the harmony advanced in the earlier poems. In "Frost at Midnight," for example, the "shapes and sounds" of the natural world are perceived as an "eternal language, which thy/ God utters." In "The Eolian Harp," man is conceptualized (tentatively) as only one of the media through which the eternal force expresses itself. "Dejection," in contrast, identifies the source of "Joy" in man himself. In feeling the beauty of nature, "we in ourselves rejoice." While the earlier poems toyed with pantheism, this focus on the state of mind of the individual soul is squarely orthodox, but the religious conservatism of "Dejection" does not in itself explain the termination of Coleridge's poetic career.

Coleridge himself attributes this termination to his own self-consciousness. As he explains in "Dejection," he had sought "by abstruse research to seal/ From my own nature all the natural man"; but this scientific analysis of the self got the better of him, and now his conscious mind is compelled to subject the whole of experience to its analytic scrutiny. Nothing now escapes the dominance of reason, and insofar as the power of Coleridge's greatest poetry lay in its capacity to dramatize or at least imagine a universe imbued with supernatural meaning, the power is lost. Theologically, this capacity can be associated with pantheism or the vaguely heterodox natural theology of the conversation poems; psychologically, its potency, derived from primal narcissism, is related to the animism given explicit form in the spirits who supervise the action in *The Rime of the Ancient Mariner*. The power of this poetry, it can be argued, lies in its ability to recapture a primitive human experience of the world.

The psychological awareness that Coleridge gained by his own self-analysis made this primitive naïveté impossible. "Dejection" is thus potentially a poem celebrating the maturity of the intellect–its recognition that its earlier powerful experience of nature, even when attributed to a Christian deity, was a matter of projection and therefore a function of his need to associate himself with an objective expression of his own potency. If the poem is not celebratory, it is because the consequences of this recognition amount to an admission of the importance of his individual self at odds with Coleridge's need for social acceptance. At the same time, it deprives him of that powerful confirmation of self derived from the illusionary sense of harmony with the animistic forces of the natural world. "Dejection" should have been a poem about Coleridge's internalization of these forces and triumphant recognition of his own strength of mind. Instead, he acknowledges the illusion of animism without being able to internalize the psychic energy invested in the animistic vision.

In disavowing belief in a transcendental power inherent in Nature, Coleridge disavows the power of his own earlier poetry. "Dejection" lacks the ease and confidence of the conversation poems, and its structure is noticeably mechanical. The storm that ends "Dejection" replaces the voice of authority that defined their closure; but, despite being anticipated by the opening stanzas, it is a *deus ex machina* without organic connection with the poet and even cause a change in his mood, but for reasons that the poem itself makes clear, it can effect no fundamental transformation of his being. Hence, it is simply unimportant; and to expect it to have greater effect is, in the words of "The Picture" (1802), to be a "Gentle Lunatic."

Having forgone "Gentle Lunacy," the best of Coleridge's later poetry speaks with an intense but entirely naturalistic sincerity. In poems such as "The Blossoming of the Solitary Date-Tree" (1805), "The Pains of Sleep" (1815), and "Work Without Hope" (1826), Coleridge makes no attempt to transform his poetic self into the vehicle for universal truth. He simply presents his feelings and thoughts to the reader. He complains about his condition, but there is no sense that the act of complaint, beyond getting something off his chest for the time being, can effect any significant alteration of the self. Other poems lack even this concern for the limited audience whom he might have expected to be concerned with his personal problems. Poems such as "Limbo" (1817) and "Ne Plus Ultra" (1826?) are notebook exercises in conceiving the inconceivable—in this case, the states of minimal being, in which even the Kantian categories of space and time are reduced to uncertain conceptions, and absolute negation, "The one permitted opposite of God!" With other poems written for a similar private purpose, they are remarkable for the expressive power of their condensed imagery and their capacity to actualize philosophical thought. Coleridge's mastery of language never deserted him.

The greatness of the half dozen or so poems on which his reputation is based derives, however, from more than mastery of language. It derives from a confidence in the power of language that Coleridge, for legitimate reasons, came to doubt. Those half dozen or so poems assume that Coleridge is not a great poet, but that the grounding medium of poetry, like the "eternal language" of nature, is itself great. The very fact of his achievement in 1797 to 1798 presented to him the possibility that it was Coleridge and not poetry in which greatness lay; and, given that possibility, Coleridge could no longer conceive of himself as a poet. He would continue to write, but in media in which it was the thought behind the prose, and not the thinker, that gave meaning to language.

Other literary forms · Samuel Taylor Coleridge's original verse dramas—*The Fall of Robespierre* (1794, with Robert Southey), *Remorse* (1813, originally *Osorio*), and *Zapolya* (1817)—are of particular interest to readers of his poetry, as is *Wallenstein* (1800), his translation of two dramas by Friedrich Schiller. His major prose includes the contents of two periodicals, *The Watchman* (1796) and *The Friend* (1809-1810, 1818), two Lay Sermons, "The Statesman's Manual" (1816) and "A Lay Sermon" (1817), the *Biographia Literaria* (1817), "Essay on Method," originally published in *The Encyclopaedia Metropolitana*, and a series of metaphysical aphorisms, *Aids to Reflection* (1825). His lectures on politics, religion, literature, and philosophy have been collected in various editions, as have other short essays, unpublished manuscripts, letters, records of conversations (*Table Talk*), notebooks, and marginalia. These prose works share common interests with his poetry and suggest the philosophical context in which it should be read. Coleridge's literary criticism is particularly relevant to his poetry.

Select works other than poetry

DRAMA: *The Fall of Robespierre*, pb. 1794 (with Robert Southey); *Remorse*, pr., pb. 1813; *Zapolya*, pb. 1817.

NONFICTION: *The Watchman*, 1796; *The Friend*, 1809-1810, 1818; "The Statesman's Manual," 1816; "A Lay Sermon," 1817; *Biographia Literaria*, 1817; *Aids to Reflection*, 1825; *On the Constitution of the Church and State, According to the Idea of Each: With Aids Toward a Right Judgment on the Late Catholic Bill*, 1830; *Specimens of the Table Talk of the Late Samuel Taylor Coleridge*, 1835; *Letters, Conversations, and Recollections of S. T. Coleridge*, 1836; *Letters of Samuel Taylor Coleridge*, 1855 (2 volumes; E. H. Coleridge, editor); *Coleridge's Shakespearean Criticism*, 1930; *Coleridge's Miscellaneous Criticism*, 1936; *Notebooks*, 1957-1986 (4 volumes).

TRANSLATION: *Wallenstein*, 1800 (of Friedrich Schiller's plays *Die Piccolomini* and *Wallensteins Tod*).

MISCELLANEOUS: *The Collected Works of Samuel Taylor Coleridge*, 1961- (Kathleen Coburn et al., editors).

Frederick Kirchhoff

Bibliography · Jean-Pierre Mileur's *Vision and Revision: Coleridge's Art of Immanence*, 1982, examines Coleridge's attempt to humanize and demythologize Wordsworth's *Prelude*. See also Tilottama Rajan's *The Supplement of Reading*, 1990, and *The Coleridge Connection: Essays for Thomas McFarland*, 1990. Thomas McFarland's *Romanticism and the Forms of Ruin: Wordsworth, Coleridge, and Modalities of Fragmentation*, 1981, is seminal to understanding Coleridge's literary figures; see also William Hazlitt's classic study of Coleridge in his *My First Acquaintance with the Poets*, repr. 1993. Rosemary Ashton, *The Life of Samuel Taylor Coleridge*, 1996, is a solid biography. Three standard biographies are J. D. Campbell, *Samuel Coleridge: A Narrative of Events in His Life*, 1894; E. K. Chambers, *Samuel Taylor Coleridge*, 1938; and Lawrence Hanson, *The Life of Samuel Taylor Coleridge: The Early Years*, 1939. Other sources on the work include Mary Anne Perkins' *Coleridge's Philosophy: The Logos as Unifying Principle*, 1994; Jack Stillinger's *Coleridge and Textual Instability*, 1994; Anya Taylor's *Coleridge's Defense of the Human*, 1986; and Thomas McFarland, *Coleridge and the Pantheist Tradition*, 1969.

HART CRANE

Born: Garrettsville, Ohio; July 21, 1899
Died: Gulf of Mexico; April 27, 1932

Poetry · *White Buildings*, 1926 · *The Bridge*, 1930 · *The Collected Poems of Hart Crane*, 1933 (Waldo Frank, editor)

Achievements · Hart Crane is acknowledged to be a fine lyric poet whose language is daring, opulent, and sometimes magnificent. Although complaints about the difficulty and obscurity of his poetry persist, the poems are not pure glittering surface. When Harriet Monroe, editor of *Poetry*, challenged metaphors of his such as the "calyx of death's bounty" in "At Melville's Tomb," Crane demonstrated the sense within the figure.

Crane is significant, moreover, in being a particularly modern poet. He wrote that poets had to be able to deal with the machine as naturally and casually as earlier poets had treated sheep and trees and cathedrals. His aim was to portray the effects of modern life on people's sensibilities. In his poetry Crane caught the frenzied rhythms and idioms of the jazz age.

Crane's stature also rests on his having created a sustained long poem, *The Bridge*. Early critics looking for a classical epic deplored the poem's seeming lack of narrative structure. Some critics also objected to Crane's joining the party of Walt Whitman at a time when Whitman and optimism were in disfavor. Later critics, however, have seen *The Bridge* as one of the great poems in modern American literature. They find in it a more Romantic structure, the structure of the poet's consciousness or the structure of human consciousness

Biography · Harold Hart Crane's parents were Grace Hart, a Chicago beauty, and C. A. (Clarence Authur) Crane, a self-made businessman who became a successful candy manufacturer. An only child, Crane felt that he was made the battleground of his parents' conflicts. When Crane was fifteen years old, a family trip to his grandmother's Caribbean plantation, the Isle of Pines, erupted in quarreling. Crane subsequently made two suicide attempts.

When he was seventeen, Crane went to New York to become a poet, not to prepare to enter college as his father thought. In the next several years Crane alternated between living in Cleveland and New York, working at lowpaying jobs, primarily in advertising, that drained his energy for writing poetry. Crane received little financial support from his father, who wanted Crane to commit himself to a business career. In 1917, siding with his mother in a family argument, Harold Crane began using the name Hart Crane.

In this period Crane's poems were being published in "little" magazines. To stimulate his creativity, Crane often relied on drink and music, a habit that led him to later problems with alcohol. (His poem "The Wine Menagerie" pays tribute to the connection he found between intoxication and poetic vision.) Crane's homosexual lifestyle, which involved him in brawls and run-ins with the police, also provided him the experience of love.

"For the Marriage of Faustus and Helen" was published in 1923, a breakthrough for Crane, who previously had written only short lyrics. Poor and often unemployed, he applied in 1925 for a grant from Otto Kahn, a financier and patron of the arts. Crane received money to help support him while he worked on *The Bridge*, a poem which was to be a synthesis of the American identity. The next summer Crane wrote a major part of his masterwork at his grandmother's plantation on the Isle of Pines, Cuba. In 1926 a collection of his poetry, *White Buildings*, was published.

Crane's stormy family life continued. In 1928, in California, after helping to nurse his sick grandmother, Crane had a final quarrel with his mother, Grace, and they never saw each other again. Shortly thereafter Crane received a legacy from his grandmother Hart's estate and he traveled to London and Paris. There he met Harry and Caresse Crosby, who offered to publish *The Bridge* in a special edition. In 1930 in Paris and then in New York *The Bridge* was published.

That winter Crane was reconciled with his father. A few months later in 1931 Crane received a fellowship from the Guggenheim Foundation. He spent a year in Mexico preparing to write a poetic drama on the conquest of Mexico. The year was marked by drinking sprees and trouble with the police for brawling and homosexuality. After traveling back briefly to Ohio for his father's funeral, Crane returned to Mexico.

At the end of his stay in Mexico, Crane had a close relationship with Peggy Cowley, who was being divorced from Malcolm Cowley. The two had plans to be married, but Crane had fits of despondency, fears about his difficulty with writing, and anxieties about the quality of his latest poem, "The Broken Tower." After a suicide attempt that Crane feared would attract police attention, he and Peggy Cowley set sail for New York on the *Orizaba*. A stop in Havana, where Crane and Cowley lost track of each other, was followed by a night on board ship during which Crane went on a violent drinking spree and was robbed and beaten. The next day at noon Crane jumped overboard from the deck of the *Orizaba* and was never found.

Analysis · Hart Crane's characteristic mode of poetry is visionary transformation. His language is that of transformation aimed at a reality beyond the surface of consciousness. Crane called the technique that subtly converts one image into another the "logic of metaphor." Like that of the French symbolist poets—Charles Baudelaire, Arthur Rimbaud, Jules Laforgue, and Paul Verlaine—Crane's language is often vivid and obscure, a "jeweled" style that juxtaposes apparently alien entities. It is a poetry of indirection, not naming but suggesting objects or using them for an evocation of mood, for their magic suggestiveness. Sometimes choosing words for their music or texture, Crane employs the technique of synaesthesia, the correspondence between different sense modalities. Symbolists such as Crane, intuiting a correspondence between the material world and spiritual realities, aim to elicit a response beyond the level of ordinary consciousness.

Influenced by T. S. Eliot (but wanting to counteract the pessimism of the early Eliot), Crane used ironic mythological, religious, and literary echoes interspersed with snatches of banal conversation and lines from popular songs and slang. His method of achieving various perspectives almost simultaneously by the juxtaposition of such unlikely elements has been called "cubist." The tension between his cubist and symbolist methods and his Whitmanian sentiments accounts for the unique quality of Crane's style.

Crane's poetry uses visionary transformations in an attempt to encompass the modern experience. In *The Bridge*, historical figures such as Christopher Columbus, legendary characters such as Rip Van Winkle, and mythic figures such as Maquokeeta (the consort of Pocahontas) are made part of the poet's consciousness, associated with personal memories of his childhood and with scenes of modern urban soullessness. The modern scene is transmuted by the elements, which provide a standard of value and a range of alternatives. In "For the Marriage of Faustus and Helen" the classic figure of Helen of Troy is brought together with the Renaissance figure of Dr. Faustus, and the two figures with their complex contexts bring a new perspective to the streetcar, the nightclub, and the aerial battle they visit in Crane's poem. Crane learned from the Symbolists that an image can become symbolic within a private context, calling up a dense network of meanings, emotions, and associations. Such images, unlike traditional symbols, draw on the cumulative force of the poet's personal associations—his personal "language"—rather than on the common cultural heritage. Crane's poetry fuses such personal symbols with traditional symbols from the sweep of Western culture.

"For the Marriage of Faustus and Helen," a poem of almost 140 lines, is Crane's first long poem. It is a marriage song for Faustus, the poet in search of spiritual fulfillment, and Helen, a figure of ideal beauty. The poem begins, however, in the tawdry modern world with the mind fettered by artificial distinctions and smothered with the trivial: stock quotations, baseball scores, and office memos. "Smutty wings" in the first stanza becomes "sparrow wings" in the second as evening brings freedom from the strictures of the office.

The poet enters his experience by getting lost, forgetting his streetcar fare and forgetting to get a transfer. Between green and pink advertisements he sees Helen's eyes across the aisle from him, half laughing. The poet wants to touch her hands as a sign of love. Helen offers him words, inspiring his poetry. The poet's promise of love makes Helen ecstatic, and, like a Romantic poet, the modern poet dedicates his vision to her praise.

The setting of the next section is a rooftop nightclub with dancers cavorting to jazz played by black musicians. The scene of wild revelry is Dionysian. The abandon of the dancers is contrasted with the passivity of relatives, sitting home in rocking chairs. The poet invites the reader to experience a fortunate fall "downstairs" into sensual abandon. ("National Winter Garden" in *The Bridge* presents a much more somber and sordid version of the fall.) Here the scene is a fallen world where people titter at death. The flapper who is the incarnation of Helen in the fallen realm should not be frowned on, however; even though it is "guilty song," sensual love, that she inspires, she is young and still retains some of the innocence of the ideal Helen.

The scene changes again in the third section, with the poet addressing a fighter pilot as an emissary of death (a problem that Crane would explore again in *The Bridge*). Crane treats war and the desecration of the heavens as the ultimate problem for the poet who would love the world and see beauty in it. It is not only eternity and abstract beauty that the poet praises but also the years, and beauty in and out of time, to which the bleeding hands of the poet pray. More advanced than business or religion, the imagination of the poet reaches beyond despair.

The Bridge, a poem of more than twelve hundred lines, is Crane's masterwork, comparable to T. S. Eliot's *The Waste Land* (1922) and William Carlos Williams' *Paterson* (1946-1958). Although it is not a classical epic because it is not a narrative, the poem's seriousness and magnitude are reflected in its theme: the poet tries to find in himself and in America the possibility of the redemption of love and vision. Crane wanted the poem to be not an expression of narrow nationalism but a synthesis of the spiritual reality of America.

The central symbol of the poem is the Brooklyn Bridge, a product of contemporary technology that seemed in its beauty to embody man's aspirations for transcendence. In the poem the bridge is seen as a musical instrument, a harp; as the whitest flower, the anemone; as a ship, a woman, a world. In a letter to Otto Kahn, his patron, Crane said that the bridge symbolizes "consciousness spanning time and space." It is a figure of power in repose, a quality that Crane ascribes in the poem to God. The bridge also symbolizes all that joins and unifies, as the bridge unites the material and the spiritual in its existence.

"To Brooklyn Bridge," the proem, is an invocation to the bridge, in which the central opposition of the poem is sketched out—the life-giving spirituality of the bridge versus the deadening influence of the materialistic, commercial city. The freedom of the soaring seagull in the sky is contrasted with the destructive compulsion of the "bedlamite" who jumps from the bridge, amid the jeering onlookers. The poet asks the bridge to "lend a myth to God," to be the means of belief and transcendence in the city that seems to have no ideals and nothing in which to believe.

In the next section, "Ave Maria," Crane goes back to the beginnings of America and to an age of faith, to Columbus after his discovery. Journeying back to Spain, Columbus meditates that he will tell the Queen and her court that he is bringing back "Cathay." He will announce his discovery of a new reality, something that the poet accomplishes in his journey into history and myth. (In this section the sea acts as a bridge between the two continents.) Columbus' dedication has its counterweight, however, in Fernando, Isabella's husband, who anticipates a "delirium of jewels." Even in the discovery of America the motive for its exploitation was present.

The next section of the poem, "Powhatan's Daughter," includes five sections. The first part, "The Harbor Dawn," is set in the present, with the sounds of fog horns, trucks passing, and stevedores yelling—back by the Brooklyn Bridge but enshrouded in fog. The blurring of sights and sounds by fog and water is in preparation for a blurring of time and space for a visionary journey with the poet. In the sanctuary of his room by the bridge or in his dream, the poet has an experience of love, in which his beloved is portrayed in mythic terms. Her eyes drink the dawn, and there is a forest in her hair. The mythic past lives in the present, or at least in the love of the poet.

The next section, "Van Winkle," shifts abruptly with the mention of macadam roads that leap across the country and seem to take the poet back to his childhood as well as to figures in American history that he learned about in school: Francisco Pizarro, Hernando Cortez, Priscilla Alden, Captain John Smith, and Rip Van Winkle. Van Winkle, who was legendary rather than historical, was a man out of time, displaced, because he refused to grow up. Here Van Winkle forgets the office hours and the pay and so ends up sweeping a tenement. He can get only menial work in a commercial society that demands a dedication to materialistic values. Rip has a different, uncommercial vision. He looks at Broadway and sees a springtime daisy chain. Instead of the lifeless city, he sees a beautiful natural world.

Lines about Van Winkle are interspersed with memories of the poet's own childhood. The memories pick up equivalents for recurring symbols of the poem—the eagle for space and the snake for time. The poet remembers stoning garter snakes that "flashed back" at him. Instead of eagles, his space figures were paper airplanes, launched into the air.

Mythic journeys often involve the search for the father or the mother as a part of the search for identity. Crane introduces a possible need for that search in recounting two memories of disjunction from his parents: a glimpse of his father whipping him with a lilac switch and a more subtle denial by his mother, who once "almost" brought him a smile from church and then withheld it. Together with the smile, the mother seems to be withholding her approval and love. The final image of the section is of Rip, ready for a streetcar ride, warned that it is getting late. It is time for the journey to continue.

"The River" begins with a jumble of sounds, fragments of conversations—perhaps on the streetcar—mention of commercial products such as Tintex and Japalac, and slogans from advertising, with fragments slappeda gainst one another, making no sense. A misplaced faith links "SCIENCE–COMMERCE and the HOLYGHOST." Unlike the sermons in stones that William Shakespeare's world could find, the slogans and jingles are meaningless.

From the streetcar the scene switches to a magnificent train, the Twentieth Century Limited, roaring cross-country. The poem focuses on the hoboes who ride the rails and who, like Van Winkle, refuse to grow up. The men who did grow up, however, killed the last bear in the Dakotas and strung telegraph wires across the mountain streams. Those who want progress and a world of "whistles, wire, and steam" have a different time-sense from that of the wanderers. Although people like the poet's father would call the hoboes useless clods, the wanderers sense some truth and know the body of the land as alive and beautiful. In that knowledge they are like the poet who knows the land "bare"—intimately—and loves it. The eagle of space and the serpent of time appear, adorning the body of the beloved land, but the old gods need to be propitiated because the iron of modern civilization (and especially of the railroad) has split and broken the land and the mythic faith.

The train seems now to follow the river or to become the river. Everyone becomes part of the river, that is timeless because eternal; lost in the river, each one becomes his father's father. The poet and the poem are not only traveling across the country but are journeying back into time as well. Affirming again the possibility of love, the river whose one will is to flow is united with the Gulf in passion.

In "The Dance," the poet returns to the time of Indian greatness, the time of Pocahontas. The poet imagines himself an Indian, initiated into the world view of the brave, at home in nature, speeding over streams in his canoe. He salutes Maquokeeta, the medicine man and priest. He commands Maquokeeta to dance humankind back to the tribal morning, to a time of harmony between people and nature when they had power even over rainbows, sky bridges. Maquokeeta is named the snake that lives before and beyond, the serpent Time itself. The time that he creates in his dance is the time of mythic wholeness. Pocahontas, the earth, is his eternal bride, and in the dance he possesses her; time and space are made one. The poet has become one with Maquokeeta by calling him up and participating imaginatively in the dance.

The next section, "Indiana," a transitional one, is a letdown of poetic energy and drama. The verse is more prosaic and the rhymes seem strained. The explicit function of the piece is to have the national spirit passed from the Indian to the white settlers in a continuation of American history. It also chronicles the parting of a mother from a son, who is now to be independent, (an important struggle in Crane's own life). The mother's pleas and clinging continue to the end of the section and almost beyond, binding the son by his pledge. Unwilling to let go, she begs for remembrance, naming the young man "stranger," "son," and finally "my friend." The relationship of friend, however, seems more request than fact, and nothing is related from the son's point of view.

Once the poet has succeeded in getting away, in the "Cutty Sark" section, his verse returns to the energy and style of "The River" and earlier sections. The narrator is again the poet, introducing a tall, eerie sailor he has met in a South Street bar. Like the hoboes and perhaps like the poet, the sailor is an outcast. (In various ways he resembles Herman Melville's Captain Ahab and Samuel Taylor Coleridge's Ancient Mariner.) Like the hoboes in "The River," this sailor has a different sense of time from that of the commercial city. Instead of being tuned to the cycles of nature, the sailor's time-sense has been disturbed by the expanse of Arctic white, eternity itself. The sailor, who says he cannot live on land any more, is almost run down by a truck as he tries to cross the street, a sign of the break between the inarticulate, prophetic sailor and the cynical city.

The poet starts walking across the Brooklyn Bridge to get home, and his thoughts are still filled with memories of the clipper ships, related to the bridge in shape by being called "parabolas." Just as Ferdinand's greed was part of Columbus' discovery of America, part of the motive for the sailing ships was "sweet opium" and the tea the imperial British sought. The poet's experience and the American experience are still a mixture of the ideal and the sordid.

"Cape Hatteras" is a substantial section of almost 250 lines. It begins with a primitive setting, with a dinosaur sinking into the ground and coastal mountains rising out of the land. In contrast to the impersonal geological processes, the poet, who has been wandering through time and space, tells the reader that he has returned home to eat an apple and to read Walt Whitman. From Marseille and Bombay, he is going home to America, to the body of Pocahontas and the sweetness of the land under the "derricks, chimneys," and "tunnels." He is returning to try to get a perspective on the exotic experiences he has had.

Next, the poet contemplates the infinity of space that is not subjugated by time and the actions of man, even though modern man can know space by "an engine in a cloud." The poet invokes Whitman and asks if infinity was the same when Whitman walked on the beach in communion with the sea. The poet's answer is that Whitman's vision lives even in the stock-market society of the present and in the free paths into the future. Opposed to Whitman's vision, however, is the fallen world of the machine, a demonic world of unleashed power. The din and the violence of slapping belts and frogs' eyes that suddenly appear, vulnerable in the midst of such uncontrolled machinery, make the world a nightmare, an apocalyptic vision. The dance of the machines is a devilish parody of the heavenly, creative dance of the poet as the Indian priest and America as Pocahontas.

The poet presents the scene of the Wright brothers at Kitty Hawk with their silver biplane, praising their daring but deploring the use of the invention for war. A demonic image that is parallel to the later image of the bridge as an anemone is the grenade as a flower with "screaming petals." Such terrible power is rationalized with theories as destructive as hail to the fertile earth. Imaginative vision cannot control the machines that have splintered space, even as the iron railroad split the land. The poet reminds the pilot that at the great speed of the airplane, the pilot has no time to consider what doom he is causing: he is intoxicated with space. The pilot's real mission is to join the edges of infinity, to bring them together in a loving union, to conjugate them. The poet follows his warning with a scene of the fighter pilot's destruction. Hit by a shell, the plane spirals down in a dance of death, and all that bravery becomes "mashed and shapeless debris."

If the fighter pilot represents a false relationship with space and infinity, Whitman is a figure with the right relationship, one whose vision of the earth and its renewal makes possible a new brotherhood. Whitman makes himself a living bridge between the sky and man through song. Whitman is also chief mourner of the men lost in wars, from the Civil War to Crane's time.

The next part of "Cape Hatteras" reads like a Romantic poet's declaration of his awakening to the beauty and inspiration of nature in its rhapsodic description of flowers and of heights that the poet has climbed. The declaration is followed by an apostrophe to Whitman as the awakener of the poet. Whitman is named his poetic master, the bread of angels in a eucharistic sense, and the one who began work on the Bridge, the myth or imaginative construction that the poet is here creating. In Whitman the poet seems to have claimed his poetic father: he says that Whitman's vision has passed into his hands.

In the next section, "Three Songs," the poet tries to work through his relationship with the feminine. In the first song, "Southern Cross," he says that he yearns for a relationship that would be heavenly, ideal, and also real. (He pictures night and the constellation of the Southern Cross.) What he has found, however, is not Woman, nameless and ideal, but Eve and Magdalene, fallen women, and a Venus who is subhuman and apelike. All the women lead to one grave, to death. The poet seems to feel disgust at the physical being of woman. He next pictures woman as a ship. Like the Ancient Mariner in Coleridge's poem, he is revolted by the generative (physical-sexual) nature of the sea. In Crane's poem, however, it is the feminine ship that is pictured as promiscuous, defiled by the masculine sea. The feminine also has qualities of a sea monster that can sting man. The Southern Cross, the poet's idealization of the feminine, drops below the horizon at dawn and what is left is woman's innumerable spawn, evidence of her indiscriminate sexuality.

The next song, "National Winter Garden," may seem to be a continuation of the poet's disgust with women, but it is different in being given an actual, rather than an archetypal, setting. The scene is a striptease in a burlesque show. The stripper's dance is a vulgar parody of sexuality and another parody of the creative, ecstatic dance of the Indian Priest-poet and Pocahontas. The burlesque queen awakens sexual appetite, but she is only pretending to have youth and beauty. Her pearls and snake ring are also fake, and the poet, who is waiting for someone else, runs away from the final "spasm." Here, however, the poet can make a reconciliation with Magdalene, with feminine sexuality, admitting its finality. Both men and women are physical and sexual; their natures are inescapable. If a woman is an agent of death, she is also an agent of birth. If each man dies alone in sexual union with her, he is also somehow born back into life, into his own sexual nature.

A third song for woman is "Virginia." The woman, Mary, is young, childlike, and possibly innocent. The poet seems to be using echoes of a popular song. Mary is working on Saturday at an office tower. She is in chivalric terms; the poet is serenading her, and she is at least temporarily inaccessible. Flowers are blooming and bells are ringing, even if they are "popcorn bells." Like Rapunzel in the fairy tale, Mary is asked to let down her golden hair. All seems light and graceful (even though in the fairy tale the prince pays for his courtship with Rapunzel with a period of wandering in the forest, blinded). At the end of the song the poet calls the girl "Cathedral Mary," sanctifying her, perhaps ironically.

In "Quaker Hill" the tone changes from the light, playful tone of the previous song. The section begins with a diatribe against weekenders descending on the countryside. Self-absorbed, they are out of tune with nature. They also have a distorted relation with time, being eager to buy as an expensive antique a cheap old deal table whose finish is being eaten by woodlice. The poet says that time will make strange neighbors.

Meditating on time as a destroyer, the poet asks where his kinsmen, his spiritual fathers are. To find his heritage, he has to look past the "scalped Yankees" to the mythic world of the Indians and accept his "sundered parentage." The poet says that people must come down from the hawk's to the worm's viewpoint and take on their tongues not the eucharist but the dust of mortality.

This humiliation is associated with the artist's abject position in modern society. Emily Dickinson and Isadora Duncan are introduced as examples of artists scorned in their day, and the only consolation the poet offers is that pain teaches patience. He asserts that patience will keep the artist from despair, implying that time will bring vindication. The section closes with a motif that is parallel to the fall of the fighter pilot to shapeless debris. Like the plane spiraling down, a leaf breaks off from a tree and descends in a whirling motion, but the leaf is part of a natural cycle, and the poet has put his faith in time and nature.

The scene shifts back to the city in the next section, "The Tunnel." The natural world is left behind, and the poet is in the center of the gawdy theater district. References to hell, death, and "tabloid crime-sheets" make the area a wasteland. The subway, the fastest way home, is a descent into hell. The traveler cannot look himself in the eye without being startled and afraid. The sound of the subway is a monotone, but fragments of conversation are lewdly suggestive. The subway riders are the walking dead, living on like hair and fingernails on a corpse, yet "swinging" goes on persistently "somehow anyhow." The sounds of the subway make a phonograph of hell that plays within the poet's brain. This labyrinth of sound even rewinds itself; from this hell there is no exit. Love is a "burnt match." In "For the Marriage of Faustus and Helen," the flapper, the modern embodiment of beauty, was like a skater in the skies. Here the discarded match is skating in the pool of a urinal.

Suddenly the poet sees a disembodied head swinging from a subway strap. The apparition, figure of the artist scorned and destroyed by his society, is Edgar Allan Poe. Poe's eyes are seen below the dandruff and the toothpaste ads. In this banal setting death reaches out through Poe to the poet. At this point the subway comes to a dead stop. A sight of escape is momentary, and then the train descends for the final dive under the river.

As the train lurches forward again, the poet sees a "wop washerwoman." In the midst of the inferno there is a positive figure of a woman. Although she is not a discoverer like Columbus, her work has dignity: she cleans the city at night. A maternal figure, she brings home to her children her eyes and hands, Crane's symbols of vision and love. A victim like Poe and the poet, the cleaning woman is bandaged. Other birth imagery here is demonic: a day being born is immediately slaughtered. The poet's greatest agony is that in this nightmare he failed to preserve a song.

In his great agony the poet feels the train start to ascend. Both the poet and the train are, like Lazarus, resurrected. They are returning to the natural world above ground. His vocation renewed, the poet can affirm the everlasting word. Once above ground again the poet is at the river bank, ready to turn to the bridge.

With the poet resurrected, "Atlantis"—the final section of the poem—is a song of deliverance. It is an ecstatic paean to the bridge, seen as music, light, love, joy, and inspiration. More dynamic than the music of the spheres, the music of the bridge creates a divinity. It is a myth that kills death: It gives death its utter wound, just by its light, its unshadow. By the myth of the bridge the cities are endowed with ripe fields. They have become natural, organic, and fruitful. The bridge is the city's "glittering pledge" forever. It is the Answerer of all questions. In the poet's vision and in the poem it is unutterably beautiful.

"Atlantis" acts as a synthesis, subsuming earlier motifs such as stars, seagulls, cities, the river, the flower, grass, history and myth, circles and spirals. The question "Is it Cathay?" links the end of *The Bridge* with Columbus' discovery of America in the beginning, not in a mood of anxiety but in wonder at an America transfigured. The final two lines bring together time and space—the serpent and the eagle—with the music and radiance and energy of the bridge transcendent.

Other literary forms · Hart Crane's principal literary production was poetry. Other writings include reviews, several essays on literature, and two essays on poetry: "General Aims and Theories" and "Modern Poetry." His letters have been published, including those between Crane and the critic Yvor Winters and Crane's letters to his family and friends.

Select works other than poetry
>NONFICTION: *The Letters of Hart Crane*, 1952 (Brom Weber, editor).
>MISCELLANEOUS: *The Complete Poems and Selected Letters and Prose of Hart Crane*, 1966 (Brom Weber, editor).

Kate Begnal

Bibliography · An excellent biography is John E. Unterecker, *Voyager: A Life of Hart Crane*, 1969. Other book-length studies include Thomas Yingling, *Hart Crane and the Homosexual Text: New Thresholds, New Anatomies*, 1990; Thomas Vogler, *Preludes to Vision in Blake, Wordsworth, Keats, and Hart Crane*, 1971; *Hart Crane: A Collection of Critical Essays*, edited by Alan Trachtenberg, 1982; Sherman Paul, *Hart's Bridge*, 1972; and R. W. B. Lewis, *The Poetry of Hart Crane: A Critical Study*, 1967.

SOR JUANA INÉS DE LA CRUZ

(Juana Inés de Asbaje y Ramírez de Santillana)

Born: San Miguel Nepantla, Mexico; November, 1648
(baptized December 2, 1648)
Died: Mexico City, Mexico; April 17, 1695

Poetry · *Inundación castálida*, 1689 · *Segundo volumen de las obras*, 1692 · *Fama y obras póstumas*, 1700

Achievements · Sor Juana Inés de la Cruz was a Mexican literary virtuoso who was called the "tenth muse" during her lifetime, and who is generally considered the most important writer of colonial Spanish America. Although she wrote more than four hundred poems, twenty-three short plays, two full-length *comedias*, and various prose works, Sor Juana's reputation rests on a handful of poems (about two dozen in all), *El divino Narciso*, and *Respuesta de la poetisa a la muy ilustre Sor Filotea de la Cruz*. Although a reassessment of her works begun in the 1950's promises a more extensive list of her most important writings, it is likely that, with the exception of her extremely complex "Primero sueño" (first dream), the few pieces which earned her the admiration of Marcelino Menendez y Pelayo one hundred years ago will continue to be the ones that will assure her a place of prominence in Spanish letters.

At her best, Sor Juana was able to manipulate the often unwieldy and intricate language of the Spanish Baroque, with its rich heritage from the Golden Age, into expressions of delicate, feminine vision and sensibility. Her aesthetic documentation of the search for knowledge, love, and God is the most complete personal and artistic record of any figure from the colonial period. Sor Juana's love poetry appears to reflect frustrating and painful experiences prior to her entry into the convent at about the age of seventeen. Few of the poems are concerned with fulfillment or the intimate communication of personal feelings; most are, instead, variations on the themes of ambivalence and disillusionment in love. Sor Juana's philosophical poems are linked to her amatory verse by a sense of disenchantment. An exception to her general pessimism is "Primero sueño," in which the poet takes delight in depicting the joys and dangers of her intellectual explorations. More of Sor Juana's writings bear witness to her theological concerns. Although some of her religious lyrics express the same kind of anguish about God's love that she expressed about human love, she clearly attempted in her *villancicos* to use her poetic talent in the service of the Church.

Biography · Juana Inés de Asbaje y Ramírez de Santillana was born in November, 1648, in San Miguel Nepantla, some sixty kilometers southeast of Mexico City. She was the illegitimate child of a Spanish captain and a Creole mother. In the charming *Respuesta de la poetisa a la muy ilustre Sor Filotea de la Cruz*, she tells how she learned to read at the age of three, and tagged along with one of her sisters to La Amiga, an elementary school, where she took her first formal lessons. She says that, at the age of eight, she begged her mother to let her cut her hair and dress like a boy so she could attend the university. That being denied her, she continued her self-education by reading the classics she found in her grandmother's house. Around 1659, she was allowed to go to Mexico City and live with the family of one of her aunts. Although not enrolled in the university, Juana privately continued her studies, which included twenty lessons in Latin. Twenty was apparently sufficient, for subsequently she was able to write Latin poetry as well as anyone in the viceroyalty.

By 1664, Sor Juana was a member of the viceregal court and was the darling of the vicereine. She so impressed the viceroy, the Marques de Mancera, with her knowledge, that he arranged for forty professors from the university to give her tests. Sor Juana passed them all, amazing the local

Ruben Mendoza

elite. Her several years of court life must have been intense, emotional years. She was a beautiful woman and was doubtless wooed by gentlemen of some wealth and position. Nevertheless, by 1669, she had entered the convent and had taken religious vows, as much from aversion to marriage as from attraction to the celibate life. It was her desire to be free to learn, she states in the *Respuesta de la poetisa a la muy ilustre Sor Filotea de la Cruz*, that was the primary motivation for her vocation.

For the next twenty-three years, Sor Juana was the major literary figure in colonial Spanish America, composing everything from love sonnets to a treatise on music, almost all of her writing being done on request from high-ranking officials of the Church or the state. She wrote elaborate pieces for performance at liturgical functions, occasional verse for political events, and scenarios and scripts for afternoons of royal entertainment. Not long after the brilliant defense of her studies in *Respuesta de la poetisa a la muy ilustre Sor Filotea de la Cruz*, and at the height of her career, when her collected works were beginning to be published and acclaimed in Spain, pressures by her religious superiors induced her to give away her library of more than four thousand volumes and all of her scientific and musical instruments, and to abandon her writing altogether. Several years later, on April 17, 1695, she died in an epidemic that swept Mexico City.

Analysis · Although most of the compositions have merit, the lyric poems, in the order of their treatment here, are usually considered to be the best, and they may be used as a point of departure for delineating a canon of Sor Juana Inés de la Cruz's most significant writings.

Sor Juana Inés de la Cruz was a deeply passionate and intelligent woman who dedicated her life to knowledge and spiritual perfection. On the one hand, she seems to have renounced love for intellectual freedom, and from her amatory and philosophical writings, it appears that her renunciation of the world, along with her commitment to learning, paradoxically caused an obsession with intimacy and a profound disillusionment with any reality except that of spiritual intimacy. On the other hand, judging from her other prose and verse, Sor Juana was also a writer engaged with her society, closely involved with its institutions and its native culture. An anthology of Sor Juana's most popular compositions may slight this more social side of her personality, but it is important to remember as one reviews her major poems of love and disillusionment that the poet wrote more concerning religion than about any real or imaginary love, and that she was as adept at elaborate versification about current events and visitors to the viceroyalty as at revealing her most private feelings. It is not difficult to dwell on the more romantic side of the "tenth muse," to use certain of her poems to enhance the image of a jilted, precocious, disenchanted teenage intellectual sequestering herself in a convent and spending her life in extremely elaborate sublimation. Her most famous pieces contribute to such an image, but as the reader is exposed to a wider spectrum of her talents, a more balanced picture emerges; a trajectory of maturation becomes visible in which Catholicism and the Baroque are means to the self-fulfillment and self-expression originally thwarted in her youth by her lack of social position and her fascination with scholarship.

If one reads Sor Juana's writings to observe a progression from human to divine love, it is appropriate to begin with the sonnet "Esta tarde, mi bien" (this afternoon, my love). The poem is one of the few in which she relates a moving encounter with another person, and it contrasts the impotency of words with the efficacy of tears in the communication of love. Here, there is none of the love-hate dialectic which colors most of her amatory poems; instead, one finds the description of a delicately feminine, sensitive, and formidably talented personality in a moment of unguarded abandon. It is only a slight exaggeration to say that after "Esta tarde, mi bien," one sees in Sor Juana's verse the psychological effects of an unhappy affair rather than the experience of love itself. Even the tender *lira* "Amado dueño mio" (my beloved master), while documenting in a poetic sense the dimensions of intimacy, is a conventional lament of the lover separated from the beloved. The lover, like a Renaissance shepherdess, tells her misfortunes to the wind, which carries her complaints, her passion, and her sadness to the distant partner. Alfonso Méndez Plancarte states that the poem contains some of Sor Juana's finest lines, and that it may surpass the eclogues of Garcilaso de la Vega. The comparison with Garcilaso is appropriate, and poetry in his likeness is fitting to express the absence of consummation rather than its presence; significantly, the *lira* keynotes a thematic transformation from completion to emptiness.

The sonnet "Detente, sombra de mi bien esquivo" (stay, shadow of my scornful love) can be considered an introduction to a series of poems which admit both the positive and negative effects of passion as well as the inconclusive status of unconsummated love. In "Detente, sombra de mi bien esquivo," the beloved himself eludes the poet, but his image cannot escape the prison of her fantasy. Important in this and the poems under discussion below is the counterpoint of conceits and emotions about the love "por quien alegre muero" (for whom I would happily die), but also "por quien penosa vivo" (for whom I live in agony), which develops to an extreme in the sonnet "Al que Ingrato me deja, busco amante" (I seek the one who spurns me) and "Que no me quiera Fabio, al verse amado" (that

Fabio does not love me as I love him), and the *redondilla* "Este amoroso tormento" (this torment of love). In the latter piece, as in the other poems of this group, the poet never finds fulfillment, "porque, entre alivio y dolar, hallo culpa en el amor y disculpa en el olvido" (because between relief and pain, I find blame in love and exoneration in forgetfulness).

Beyond frustration and the love-hate duality which the poet attributes to romantic feeling lie disillusionment and bitterness. The sonnets "Silvio, yo te aborezco" (I hate you, Silvio), "Amor empieza por desasosiego" (love begins uneasily), and "Con el dolor de la mortal herida" (with the pain of a mortal wound) are among Sor Juana's strongest denunciations of the men she once might have loved, as well as of herself for having given in to loving them: "no solo a tí, corrida, te aborrezco,/ pero a mí por el tiempo que te quise" (not only do I abhor you/ but myself for the time that I loved you). Here the bittersweet of "Este amoroso tormento" turns to anger. The image of the lover purposely retained in "Detente, sombra de mi bien esquivo" is repeatedly banished, and it is a logical movement from such rejection to the *sátira filosófica*, "Hombres necios" (foolish men), one of Sor Juana's more popular denunciations of men as the source of all women's problems. In these feminist *redondillas*, the poet exposes the ways in which men "acusan lo que causan" (blame us for the things they cause). Why, she asks, do men want women to be good if they tempt them to be bad? Who, she questions, is the greater sinner, "la que peca por la paga o el que paga por pecar" (she who sins for pay or he who pays for sin)?

Since Sor Juana's poems are not usually dated, there is no way of knowing whether the progression from the delicate, loving "Esta tarde, mi bien" to the sarcastic "Hombres necios" reflects the sequential effects of an increasingly unhappy situation. In any case, these poems of erotic experience do fit a pattern which begins with brief reciprocal affection and degenerates into ambivalence, then finally into contempt. There are, at the same time, a great number of poems written to women which do not fit this generalization. Sor Juana apparently had very meaningful relationships with the wives of two of the Mexican viceroys, and her many verses to Lysi show a far more consistent emotional response than that depicted in poems of male-female interaction. Certainly the Lysi poems, perhaps especially the ornate "Lámina sirva el cielo al retrato" (the sky is lamina of your portrait), are a moving contrast to her more widely read poems' heterosexual canon.

Sor Juana's philosophic poems complement her negative attitude toward worldly love. "Verde embeleso de la vida humana" (green charm of human life) rejects illusions and hope as deceptive: "solamente lo que toco veo" (I only see what I can touch). It represents the repression of vain dreams, the acceptance of life without romance or even platonic fantasy. "Diuturna enfermedad de la Esperanza" (lasting infirmity of hope) reiterates this concept, and "Este que ves, engaño colorido" (this painted lie you see), a sonnet on her portrait, is an intense affirmation of the Catholic view that the flesh is "polvo, es sombra, es nada" (is dust, is a shadow, is nothing). Her "Rosa divina" (divine rose) is a variation on the universal theme of the brevity of beauty and life. Perhaps her most powerful renunciation is "Finjamos que soy feliz" (pretend that I am happy), in which she denies the validity of knowledge and maintains that because people can know nothing for certain, ignorance is preferable to imperfect knowing: "aprendamos a ignorar" (let us learn to not know). This poem is a moment of despair within the context of Sor Juana's self-confessed lifelong passion, the pursuit of knowledge. Her monumental "Primero sueño"("First Dream"), the only work which she admitted to writing for her own pleasure and not to please someone else, is far more balanced in presenting her attitude toward learning.

The "Primero sueño," which is among the best philosophic poems in Spanish, is the height of Sor Juana's exploration of the Baroque. The poem begins with a description of nightfall, in which the entire physical world eventually succumbs to sleep. The human spirit, freed from the constraint of the body, soars upward to find a perspective from which it can comprehend the immensity of the universe. Once it glimpses the overpowering dimensions of creation, the soul retreats to the shadows. Finding a mental shore on the sea of knowledge, it decides to approach the challenge of learning by dividing things into categories and mastering each division separately. In spite of doubts that the mind can really know anything, echoes of the dark vision of "Finjamos que soy feliz," the soul continues its search for truth. Dawn arrives, however, and the dream ends inconclusively. Universal knowledge has eluded the soul, but the dreamer has not despaired.

Once considered to be on the fringe of literature because of its purposeful Gongorism, "Primero sueño" is enjoying the positive reconsideration accorded the entire Spanish Baroque, in the course of which Luis de Góngora y Argote himself has been reinstated into the canon of major Spanish poets. Accepting the style of this poem as not only valid but also essential to its meaning, one can better appreciate Sor Juana's most mature and complex statement about the human condition. It is the culmination of a lifetime of study and reflection.

Sor Juana's religious writings include several "sacred ballads," among which "Amante dulce del alma" (sweet love of my soul), "Mientras la Gracia me exita" (while Grace moves me), and "Traigo conmigo un cuidado" (I have a deep concern) are generally held in high regard. All three attempt to express the effects of divine love. "Amante dulce del alma" asks why Christ might have willed to visit the poet in Holy Communion: Has He decided to be present from love or from jealousy? She decides for the former, reflecting that since God knows all things, He can see into her heart and has no reason to be jealous. "Mientras la Gracia me exita" tries to clarify some of the feelings involved in the inner struggle between "la virtud y la costumbre" (virtue and habit). Like "Amante dulce del alma," this is a poem of scruples rather than a meditation of universal religious significance. "Traigo conmigo un cuidado" carries the analysis of spiritual love further and contrasts it with the poet's experience of human love. "La misma muerte que vivo, es la vida con que muero" (the same death that I live is the life in which I die), she writes at the end of the poem, attempting to sum up her contradictory mental state. Even though it is divine love which causes her to feel the way she does, there are parallels between the contrarias penas (contradictory anxieties) of "Este amoroso tormento" and those expressed in "Traigo conmigo un cuidado."

It is more fruitful to look for a developed sense of religious experience in Sor Juana's *villancicos* and her play *El divino Narciso* than in her personal religious lyrics. Although these works have generally been neglected, Méndez Plancarte and others have made convincing defenses of their genres as well as of the verse itself. *El divino Narciso* contains some of Sor Juana's best writing, and, with the *loa* (or one-act play) which precedes it, shows how she introduced Indian themes into her work. The most significant element of the play, however, is the successful depiction of divine love, sufficiently anthropomorphized to give it comprehensible human beauty. Here is also the full evolution of a spiritual maturity which finally quiets the older, worldly concerns.

Sor Juana is easily anthologized, but such selectivity does not provide a proper perspective from which to view her talents or interests. The genius of the "tenth muse" offers almost unlimited fare for those who would dwell on the poems and techniques in themselves; similarly, the literary historian will hardly want to limit his reading to Sor Juana's "best," but will find the richest commentary on colonial Mexico as well as the soul of the poet herself within the diversity of her complete works. There, instead of a facile trajectory from personal rejection to religion, one finds a maze of subtle Rococo revelations.

Other literary forms · Sor Juana Inés de la Cruz's most readable prose work, the *Respuesta de la poetisa a la muy ilustre Sor Filotea de la Cruz* (1700; reply of the poetess to the illustrious Sister Filotea de la Cruz) is an appealing autobiographical defense of her precocious interest in learning, an emotional plea for acceptance as a woman and a scholar, and an obsessive declaration of faith. Sor Juana tries to convince her superiors that, despite her lifelong curiosity about the material world, theological concerns are still the most important to her.

El divino Narciso (c. 1680; *The Divine Narcissus*), a religious one-act play, is a tasteful and imaginative treatment of divine love in which Narcissus, as a figure of Christ, falls in love with human nature as a reflection of himself. With this short play, the fantasy of desire which takes so many forms throughout Sor Juana's work finds its ultimate synthesis of eros and agape.

Select works other than poetry

DRAMA: *Amor es más laberinto*, wr. 1668, pr. 1689 (with Juan de Guevara); *El divino Narciso*, pr. c. 1680 (*The Divine Narcissus*, 1945); *Los empeños de una casa*, pr. c. 1680 (based on Lope de Vega Carpio's play *La discreta enamorada*; *A Household Plagued by Love*, 1942); *El mártir del Sacramento, San Hermenegildo*, pr. c. 1692; *El cetro de José*, pb. 1692.

NONFICTION: *Respuesta de la poetisa a la muy ilustre Sor Filotea de la Cruz*, 1700.

MISCELLANEOUS: *Obras completas de sor Juana Inés de la Cruz*, 1951-1957 (4 volumes: I, *Lírica Personal*, poetry; II, *Villancicos y letras sacras*, poetry; III, *Autos y Loas*, drama; IV, *Comedias sainetes y prosa*, drama and prose; Méndez Plancarte, editor); *A Sor Juana Anthology*, 1988.

William L. Felker

Bibliography · Twentieth century American scholarship on Sor Juana Inés de la Cruz began with Dorothy Schons, "Some Obscure Points in the Life of Sor Juana Inés de la Cruz," and "Some Bibliographical Notes on Sor Juana Inés de la Cruz," *Modern Philology*, vols. 23 and 24, 1926 and 1927. In the 1930's, Ermilo Abreu Gómez published the first modern bibliographical-biographical studies and critical editions of her works in Spanish. Ludwig Pfandl, *Sor Juana Inés de la Cruz: La Décima Musa de México*, 1963, provides a psychoanalytical study. Alan Trueblood, *A Sor Juana Anthology*, 1988, complements Octavio Paz, *Sor Juana: Or, The Traps of Faith*, 1988; both constitute the most authoritative material in translation. Feminist studies on Sor Juana are found in Beth Miller, ed., *Women in Hispanic Literature: Icons and Fallen Idols*, 1983; Jean Franco, *Plotting Women: Gender and Representation in México*, 1989; and Francisco J. Cevallos-Candau et al., eds., *Coded Encounters: Writing, Gender, and Ethnicity in Colonial Latin America*, 1994.

E. E. CUMMINGS

Born: Cambridge, Massachusetts; October 14, 1894
Died: North Conway, New Hampshire; September 3, 1962

Poetry · *Tulips and Chimneys*, 1923 · *&*, 1925 · *XLI Poems*, 1925 · *Is 5*, 1926 · *W: Seventy New Poems*, 1931 · *No Thanks*, 1935 · *1/20 Poems*, 1936 · *Collected Poems*, 1938 · *Fifty Poems*, 1940 · *1 x 1*, 1944 · *Xiape*, 1950 · *Poems, 1923-1954*, 1954 · *Ninety-five Poems*, 1958 · *One Hundred Selected Poems*, 1959 · *Selected Poems*, 1960 · *Seventy-three Poems*, 1963 · *E. E. Cummings: A Selection of Poems*, 1965 · *Complete Poems, 1913-1962*, 1968

Achievements · E. E. Cummings is not usually included in the first rank of modernist poets, which always begins with T. S. Eliot, William Butler Yeats, and Ezra Pound and is, more often than not, rounded out with Wallace Stevens and William Carlos Williams. Two aspects of his career, however, give his achievement a great deal of significance. First, he was on the cutting edge of the modernist, experimental movement in verse. Pound, at the center of that movement, was dedicated to restoring value and integrity to the word by breaking the mold of the past, and in that cause, he evangelically admonished the poets of his generation to "make it new." Although a disciple of no one, Cummings led the assault on conventional verse, pushing experimentation to extremes and beyond with his peculiarly distinctive typography and his unconventional syntax, grammar, and punctuation. Although he paid the price of such experimentation, which brought charges of superficiality and unintelligibility, he served the modernist movement well by helping to educate an audience for the innovations in verse and prose of the second and third decades of the twentieth century.

Second, Cummings was not only a leading experimenter in an age of experimentation but also an intense lyric poet and an effective satirist. As a lyricist, he celebrated those experiences, values, and attitudes which lyric poets of all times have celebrated; and high on his list was love—sexual, romantic, and ideal or transcendental. His love poetry often reminds readers of Renaissance poets because of its subject matter, diction, and imagery. He is often bawdy, often sentimental, sometimes concrete, sometimes abstract, but almost always intense. Many of his lyrics express a childlike joy before nature and the natural state; he also celebrated personal relationships, particularly in his well-known tributes to his father and mother.

Library of Congress

As a satirist, Cummings' principal target is humanity *en masse*. This thrust is the opposite of the celebration of individuality, a principal subject of his lyricism. In poems with a military setting, he satirically attacks not the military but the submergence of the individual into the mass which the military often brings about. He attacks the same submergence in poems that seem to be attacking modern advertising or salesmen. Neither, however, is the real object of his scorn; it is not modern advertising but the mass mind of the mass market which it engenders that he lashes out at in several of his most effective satiric pieces.

Cummings celebrates love, spontaneity, individuality, and a childlike wonder before nature. He attacks conformity, the mass mind, progress, and hypocrisy. His greatest achievement is that in an age of experimentation in verse, and in an age defensive and self-conscious about feeling, he fashioned a personal, highly idiosyncratic style which at its best provided him with effective vehicles for some of the finest lyric and satiric poetry of the modernist period.

Biography · Edward Estlin Cummings, who preferred to be known as e. e. cummings (sans capital letters), was born in Cambridge, Massachusetts, on October 14, 1894, the first of two children born to Edward Cummings and Rebecca Harwell Clarke. His father was a Harvard graduate and lecturer, an ordained Unitarian minister, and pastor of the South Congregational Church from 1909 to 1925. Cummings received his degree *magna cum laude* from Harvard in 1915 and a Harvard M. A. the following year. A landmark in his career came in 1952 when he returned to Harvard to deliver the Charles Eliot Norton Lectures. Subsequently published as *i: six nonlectures*, all of which are highly personal and autobiographical, the first is of particular interest because of its affectionate, idealized portraits of his parents.

Cummings went to France in 1917 to join Norton Harje's Ambulance Corps. A combination of unfortunate and nearly ludicrous events led to his incarceration by the French authorities on suspicion of disloyalty. He and a friend were confined in a concentration camp at La Ferté Macé from late September through December, 1917. That experience is the subject matter of Cummings' first book, *The Enormous Room*, which has come to be regarded as a classic account of personal experience in World War I. Although prose, it launched the poet's career and, because of its style, set the tone and, implicitly, some of the basic themes that were to characterize the responses to his poetry for the next two decades. Before 1922, Cummings had published poems in the *Harvard Monthly*, in *The Dial*, and six poems in *Eight Harvard Poets*, but it was *The Enormous Room* that began his critical reputation. His first book of poems, *Tulips and Chimneys*, was published in 1923.

In 1923, Cummings moved to Patchin Place in New York City and lived there, spending the summers at his family's place in New Hampshire, until his death in 1962. Cummings traveled to Russia in 1931 and converted that experience into the second of his two major prose works, *Eimi*, 1933. In 1932, he married Marion Morehouse, a model, actress, and photographer. It was his third marriage and it survived. She died in 1969. The three decades Cummings spent with Marion and the nearly four decades at Patchin Place deserve emphasis in a biographical sketch because they provide a perspective that brings some balance to the poet's reputation as a bohemian *enfant terrible.* Although he never lost the cutting edge of his capacity to shock, he lived a relatively settled life devoted to painting and writing poetry.

In addition to the Charles Eliot Norton Lectureship, among the honors and awards he received were the Dial Award in 1925 for "distinguished service to American letters"; two Guggenheim Fellowships, in 1933 and 1951; and a special citation by National Book Awards in 1955 for *Poems, 1923-1954.* In 1957, he received the Bollingen Prize in Poetry and the Boston Arts Festival Award.

Analysis · Since E. E. Cummings rarely used titles, all those poems without titles will be identified by reference to the Index of First Lines in *Complete Poems, 1913-1962.* An analysis of Cummings' poetry turns, for the most part, upon judgments about his innovative, highly idiosyncratic versification. Some of Cummings' critics have thought his techniques to be not only cheap and shallow tricks but also ultimately nonpoetic. There was, from the early stages of his career, general agreement about his potential as a lyric and satiric poet. As that career developed through his middle and late periods, negative criticism of his verse diminished as affirmation grew. Although there always will be dissenting voices, the consensus for some time has been that his innovative verse techniques and his lyric and satiric talents were successfully blended in the best of his work.

Cummings wrote both free verse and conventional verse, particularly in the form of quatrains and sonnets. He also imposed on conventional verse the combination of typographical eccentricities and grammatical and syntactical permutations which constitute his distinctive hallmark. There is a considerable range between his most extreme free-verse poems, where the hallmark is superimposed, and his most conventional sonnets, where the hallmark is barely discernible. An example of the extreme is his "grasshopper" poem, "r-p-o-p-h-e-s-s-a-g-r," which is at the same time a masterpiece and a failure. The poem is a masterful blending of form and content, an achievement that might be described as pure technique becoming pure form. It fails as a poem, however, to move the reader or to matter very much except as a witty display of pyrotechnics. Its achievement, nevertheless, is a considerable one, and it serves as a useful model of one kind of poem for which Cummings is best known.

"r-p-o-p-h-e-s-s-a-g-r" is structurally a free-verse poem in which Cummings employs many of his distinctive typographical devices. The word "grasshopper" occurs four times in the poem, its letters jumbled beyond recognition the first three times. The grasshopper's leap, capturing the essence of grasshoppers, brings its name into proper arrangement. Cummings also uses parentheses to break up words and to signal recombinations of letters and syllables resulting in conventional spelling, syntax, and meaning. At the literal and figurative center of the poem is the word "leaps," which links the first two versions of the word "grasshopper" to the final two, culminating in the resolution of the proper arrangement of letters. Cummings' diagonal typography for the word "leaps" is intended to render spatially, in the visual terms of a painter, the conceptual meaning of the word.

A poem of even less substance than "r-p-o-p-h-e-s-s-a-g-r," and therefore illustratively useful in the same way, is the "leaf-falling" poem "1(a." The four words of the poem, "a," "leaf," "falls," and "loneliness," are arranged along a vertical line with two or three letters or characters on each horizontal line, except for the final five of "iness." Thus, the poem begins with "1(a," with the rest of the poem directly below, two or three letters at a time, spaced out to suggest two triplets, set off by an opening, an intervening, and a closing single line. The use of the two parentheses, setting off "a leaf falls," actually helps in the reading of the poem. To the extent that the slender column of letters on the relatively vast whiteness of the page visually complements the theme of the poem, human loneliness engendered by the cyclical dying of the natural world in the fall of the year, Cummings has again succeeded in an effective union of form and content.

Other examples of this kind of verse are poems depicting a black, ragtime piano player ("ta"), a sunset ("stinging"), and a thunderstorm ("n(o)w/the"). The arrangement on the page of the portrait of the piano player is very much like that of "loneliness," as is the second half of the poem depicting a sunset by the sea. Cummings attempts in the thunderstorm poem to create visual effects to complement the conceptual meaning of the words "lightning" and "thunder." In one line, he states that the world "iS Slapped:with;liGhtninG"; thunder in the poems appears as "THuNdeR." These five poems represent some of Cummings' more effective uses of several of his most representative devices, particularly eccentric typography and spatial arrangement intended to create special visual effects. Often successful, these same devices at times fail completely, merely producing involved semantic puzzles hardly worth the effort necessary to solve them. More important, however, is the fact that the same features of versification exemplified by these poems of relatively little substance are to be found in his very best lyric and satiric poetry, the best of which stands between the highly eccentric versification of "r-p-o-p-h-e-s-s-a-g-r" and his relatively conventional uses of the sonnet form.

Cummings wrote many sonnets. A convenient sampling of his uses of the form is to be found in *Is 5*, which begins with five sonnets and closes with five. The first five are portraits or sketches of prostitutes and are among the few Cummings poems with titles—in this example, the respective names of each of the women. The subject matter of the final five sonnets of the collection, in sharp contrast to the portraits, is romantic love, and this set is more conventional than the portraits of the prostitutes. Cummings' best lyric poetry tends to be his more conventional verse: a comparative reading of the second and the tenth sonnets of *Is 5* will illustrate Cummings' mastery of conventional lyric forms.

Three observations can be made about the second sonnet of *Is 5*, the portrait of Mame ("Mame") and the tenth ("if I have made, my lady, intricate"). First, the former is a portrait of a prostitute, while the latter is addressed to "my lady." Second, Mame speaks in a Brooklyn dialect, such as "duh woild," "some noive," and "dat baby." What little quoted speech there is in "if I have made, my lady, intricate" is not dialect and would not be obtrusive in a Renaissance sonnet. Third, Mame's sonnet is relatively loose structurally, while my lady's is one of Cummings' most conventional. The loose structure of the former results largely from the dramatic presentation, particularly as it calls for the use of fragmented speech in dialect. Both sonnets are conventional syntactically, grammatically, and typographically. Formally and thematically, "if I have made, my lady, intricate" stands in dramatic contrast to "r-p-o-p-h-e-s-s-a-g-r." The sonnet is one of Cummings' better lyric poems, the best of which make use of the formal eccentricities of "r-p-o-p-h-e-s-s-a-g-r" in the poet's successful blending of traditional subject matter with his personally distinctive, modern verse forms.

Cummings' principal lyric subject matter is his celebration of romantic, sexual, and transcendental love and of the beauty, physical and spiritual, of lovers. A good example of a successful blend of his distinctive versification with a traditional lyric subject is "(ponder,darling,these busted statues." Formally, the poem might be thought of as standing near the middle of the range defined by the extremes of "r-p-o-p-h-e-s-s-a-g-r" and "if I have made, my lady, intricate." As such, it represents well the characteristics of Cummings' poetry. The blend of versification with a traditional subject is effective because of the appropriateness of the fragmented verse to the imagery of broken statuary and architectural ruins and of both to the poem's *carpe diem* theme.

The most obvious aspect of Cummings' distinctive verse is typographical, his sparse and erratic use of capitals and of parentheses. These particular details function in this poem of lyric substance to further understanding. Two sets of parentheses clearly delineate the three sections of the poem, the first and last being enclosed by them. The capitalization gives emphasis to the "Greediest Paws" of time and to the all-important "Horizontal" business. In addition to the typography, two examples of Cummings' manipulation of syntax also contribute to understanding his style: verse paragraphs three and six. As with the typography, the unconventional syntax contributes to the unmistakable distinctiveness of Cummings' verse without in any way impeding the reader's comprehension and hence appreciation of the poem.

The poem "(ponder,darling,these busted statues" is the modern poet's address to the perennially coy mistress. As in Andrew Marvell's poem "To His Coy Mistress" (1650), the woman is asked to consider the mutability of all things and urged, since time passes irrevocably, to get on with meaningful "horizontal" business. Marvell's plea turns on his images of the grave and the desert of eternity. Cummings, the quintessential modern, stands with the woman among the architectural ruins of a past that must be not so much denied as ignored, or, at least, turned away from. Although it is a lesser poem than T. S. Eliot's *The Waste Land* (1922), it shares with that landmark of the modernist period the fragmented artifacts of the past. More important, Cummings, like Eliot, is addressing the fundamental question of their time: What does one do in the midst of such ruins? Cummings' answer, "make love," is direct, obvious, and highly ironic; it is not simply flippant and clever. The poet's urgent request to get on with the important horizontal business is one of the most traditional lyric responses to the overt awareness of mortality, one of man's principal talismans down through the centuries against the certainty of death.

The poems "somewhere i have never travelled,gladly beyond" and "you shall above all things be glad and young" provide good examples of Cummings' celebration of transcendental love. It should be noted that the categories, physical or sexual love and transcendental love, are not mutually exclusive. That is, nothing in "(ponder,darling,these busted statues" precludes the possibility that the lovers see something in each other deeper and more enduring than sex. Yet, it would be foolish to deny the sexual suggestiveness of the imagery of "somewhere i have never travelled,gladly beyond."

The poem "since feeling is first" is an explicit celebration of feeling, the wellspring of all lyricism. Examples of his affirmation of spontaneity, of nature, and of the natural and the childlike selves can be found in "when god lets my body be," "i thank You God for most this amazing," "in Just-," and "O sweet spontaneous." Cummings' intense tribute to his father, "my father moved through dooms of love," and his slight but moving poem for his mother, "if there are any heavens my mother will(all by herself)have," extend the range of lyric subject matter to include filial affection. The poem "anyone lived in a pretty how town" is Cummings' allegorical "everyman" which has a poignancy similar to that of Thornton Wilder's *Our Town* (1938).

These poems provide examples of Cummings' principal lyric subject matter. They also constitute a group useful for studying the formal variety found in some of his best poetry. Two of them, the poem on his father and "anyone lived in a pretty how town," are fairly conventional quatrains given a twist by Cummings' characteristic grammatical distortion: the parts of speech exchange roles. For example, the father moves "through griefs of joy" and sings "desire into begin." Everyman of "anyone lived in a pretty how town" "sang his didn't" and "danced his did." In general, the key to this special vocabulary, here and in other poems, is that the present, immediate, concrete, and spontaneous are being affirmed, while their opposites are being rejected. "Is" is superior to "was." The "dooms of feel" are to be celebrated; the "pomp of must and shall" scorned. In addition to these examples of Cummings' quatrains, this group also contains another of his fairly conventional sonnets, "i thank You God for most this amazing," and several free verse poems, including "in Just-," and "O sweet spontaneous." As a group, they illustrate and support the generalization stated earlier that Cummings makes the most effective use of his distinctive devices in his more substantive lyric poetry.

Because satirists use lyricism to intensify their satirical thrusts, there is often no hard line between satiric and lyric poetry. The distinction for Cummings in particular is more a matter of emphasis than a clear-cut distinction. Because so much of his poetry is primarily satirical, however, it is profitable to consider several appropriate examples. It is also instructive to note that, as with his best lyric poetry, his best satiric pieces are those characterized by an effective blending of his distinctive devices with the resources of traditional verse. An excellent example of such blending and of the use of lyric intensity for satiric purposes is "i sing of Olaf glad and big."

The poem looks and even sounds like free verse. It is, however, an intricately constructed set of interlocking quatrains and couplets in four-stress lines. The loosening of what sounds like very regular verse is effected by the spacing on the page and by the counterpoint of sentence or sense structure against the verse structure. That tension between verse and sense is intensified by the characteristic use of parentheses and syntactical inversions. As in "(ponder,darling,these busted statues," the parentheses are used conventionally for humorous asides, as when readers are told that colonel left the scene "hurriedly to shave," and for emphasis, as in the passages on Olaf's knees and Christ's mercy. The syntactical inversions effectively provide emphasis and hardly impede understanding. The hyphenating of the word "object-or" catches the genius of Cummings' style at its best. The poem is about a conscientious objector who becomes an "object" in the hands of his fellow soldiers.

The satire is directed not at the military or against war, but at the lockstep, group mentality which, although fostered particularly by the military, may be found in the highly organized structures of all institutions: corporate, religious, academic. For Cummings, affirmation of the bravery of the individual places heavy emphasis on "individual," and it is the group, crowd, or gang that is being indicated. The irony of the closing lines strongly suggests that the military is but the protective arm of the nation or culture locked into value systems symbolized by abstractions such as the nation's "blueeyed pride." Olaf, blond and blue-eyed, fits the abstraction and hence his culpability is compounded. He was "blonder," however (that is, nearer the ideal of bravery and of manhood), than most and willing to pay lip service to the ideal, while others lose themselves in the false security of the crowd.

Two other satires set in the context of war but directed at more fundamental targets are "my sweet old etcetera" and "plato told." The first satirizes, in a light vein, attitudes very close to those of the soldiers of "i sing of Olaf glad and big." Aunts, sister, mother, and father all think war is glorious, while the soldier, who describes them, lies in the muddy trenches, thereby refuting the grandiose notions of those safe and comfortable at home. The satire "plato told" comes closest to being an indictment of war, but its focus is really on the obtuseness of "him," on his failure to understand what everyone has been telling him, which is that war is hell. All three of these "war" poems satirize a failure to see reality.

"POEM, OR BEAUTY HURTS MR. VINAL," one of Cummings' few titled poems, is a harsh but clever indictment of modern advertising and, implicitly, of the culture from which it derives. Cummings piles up actual lines from advertisements for garters, gum, shirt collars, drawers, Kodaks, and laxatives juxtaposed with fragments of lines from "America the Beautiful" and fragmented allusions to Robert Browning in the sixth verse paragraph. The poem makes fun of the glibness and excessive claims of advertising but then takes a turn toward the end to focus on Cummings' primary satiric target: men and women, "gelded" or "spaded," who have allowed themselves to be manipulated into anonymous units of the "market." Cummings makes the same point in one of his harshest sonnets, "a salesman is an it that stinks Excuse." Almost savage in tone, the poem once again links various seemingly incongruous activities in terms of the marketplace: the selling of "hate condoms education . . . democracy." The focus of Cummings' attack shifts from its ostensible targets—the military, advertising, and a salesman—to processes which rob people of their individuality and freedom of choice.

Cummings' innovative genius as a versifier, excessive in many of the lesser poems, is modified and restrained in his poems of substance, effecting in many of them happy unions of form and content. He is, as a result, a modernist poet of consequence.

Other literary forms · In addition to poetry, E. E. Cummings also published two long prose narratives, *The Enormous Room* (1922) and *Eimi* (1933); a translation from the French of *The Red Front*, by Louis Aragon (1933); a long play, *Him* (1927); two short plays, *Anthropos: The Future of Art* (1944) and *Santa Claus: A Morality* (1946); a ballet, *Tom* (1935); a collection of his own drawings in charcoal, ink, oil, pastels, and watercolor, *CIOPW* (1931); his autobiographical Harvard lectures, *i: six nonlectures* (1953); and a collection of his wife's photographs with captions by Cummings, *Adventures in Value* (1962).

Of these, *The Enormous Room* and *Eimi* are of particular interest because of their contributions to Cummings' critical reputation and to his development as an artist. The former is the poet's account of his three-month confinement in a French concentration camp in 1917. It was hailed upon its appearance as a significant firsthand account of the war and has become one of the classic records of World War I. It is also significant in that it is Cummings' first book, and, although prose, it reflects the same kinds of linguistic experimentation and innovation apparent in his poetry. Also reflecting his stylistic innovations is *Eimi*, Cummings' account of a trip to Russia, which has a topical vitality similar to the war experiences. The major themes of the critical response to Cummings' poetry, which developed in the 1920's, were implicit in the responses to *The Enormous Room*. Those themes, explicit by 1933, also helped to shape the criticism of *Eimi*.

Similar to the two prose narratives, *Him*, a long, expressionistic drama, is also representative of Cummings' development and of his critical reputation. Experimental and distinctive, the drama was produced in 1928 by the Provincetown Players. In the program notes, Cummings cautioned the audience against trying to understand the play. Instead, he advised the audience to "let it try to understand you." As with the poetry and the prose, there were outraged cries claiming that the play was unintelligible, although there was also an affirmation of the lyrical originality and intensity of the play. The recognition of Cummings' lyrical talents was gradually to replace the often angry rejections of his work because of its eccentricity.

Stylistically distinctive and therefore important in any full assessment of his achievement is the collection of Cummings' presentations as the annual Charles Eliot Norton Lecturer in Poetry at Harvard, *i: six nonlectures*. Of immediate interest, however, is the autobiographical content of the lectures. Lecture One is entitled "my parents" and contains poetic and affectionate sketches of his mother and father; Lecture Two is entitled "their son." The final four, less pointedly autobiographical in the usual sense of the word, are an exploration of the relationship between the poet's values and his sense of personal identity, between what he believes and what he is.

Select works other than poetry

DRAMA: *Him*, pb. 1927; *Tom: A Ballet*, pb. 1935; *Anthropos: The Future of Art*, pb. 1944; *Santa Claus: A Morality*, pb. 1946.

NONFICTION: *The Enormous Room*, 1922; *CIOPW*, 1931 (drawings); *Eimi*, 1933; *i: six nonlectures*, 1953; *Adventures in Value*, 1962 (photographs by Marion Morehouse).

Lloyd N. Dendinger

Bibliography · The Twayne series on United States authors includes a fine Cummings introduction: Joseph M. Flora, *E. E. Cummings Revisited*, 1994. One of the most fascinating approaches to Cummings is a critical book that contains many pages of his color prints and picture-like poems, Milton A. Cohen, *Poet and Painter: The Aesthetics of E. E. Cummings' Early Work*, 1987. A thorough collection of criticism is *Critical Essays on E. E. Cummings*, 1984, edited by Guy Rotella. Other writings on Cummings: Robert E. Wegner, *The Poetry and Prose of E. E. Cummings*, 1965; R. P. Blackmur, *The Double Agent*, 1935; Allen Tate, *Reactionary Essays in Poetry and Ideas*, 1936; Barbara Deutsch, *Poetry in Our Time*, 1956; and Norman Friedman, *E. E. Cummings*, 1960.

DANTE

(Dante Alighieri)

Born: Florence, Italy; May or June, 1265
Died: Ravenna, Italy; September 13 or 14, 1321

Poetry · *La vita nuova*, c. 1292 (*Vita Nuova*, 1861; better known as *The New Life*) · *La divina commedia*, c. 1320 (*The Divine Comedy*, 1802; 3 volumes)

Achievements · Dante is among the greatest and most influential figures in the long history of Western literature, and no brief summary can do justice to the scope of his achievements. Perhaps his most enduring legacy has been the astonishing supply of signs and symbols for describing and evaluating inner experience which succeeding generations of readers have found in *The Divine Comedy*. Dante was ultimately a mystic in his approach to God, but he wrote with systematic clarity about every spiritual event, stopping only at the point where language and reason had to be abandoned. Probably the most learned, articulate voice in the Christian West since Saint Augustine, Dante created a powerful mindscape able to reflect every movement of the soul. He did this without subjectivism and narcissism. Dante's vision is both a mirror of the self and a window onto the outside world, the cosmos, and the divine. His inward journey is recounted with great intensity and variety, but with no surprises, for that inner world is no more ambiguous or mysterious than the outer world, and Dante did not confront either world in a metaphysical void. His vision is not a hallucinatory refuge, but a site where the interconnectedness of all things can be rationally presented and the consequent need for spiritual discipline and social duty can be argued.

  Dante responded to two primary imaginative impulses. One drove him to put all of his experiences into an ordered relationship: eros, history, politics, faith. Behind these ideal forms and schematizations lies a genuine love of the created world in all its density. Dante insists that experience be known as actual *and* metaphorical, and that virtue be attained through historical processes. The other impulse moved him continually beyond each part of his creation, always ascending, so that each epiphany becomes a curtain to be drawn back to reveal a higher one. One reads Dante with an awareness of the elaborations of each part and the upward movement of the whole.

Dante was the most important voice in the vernacular love lyric before William Shakespeare. Dante's mastery of lyric form and meter was unparalleled, and he used the intellectually demanding conventions of *dolce stil nuovo* (sweet new style) with simplicity and ease. Had he taken Holy Orders, he could have given the world a pastoral voice worthy of John Donne or George Herbert. Dante's vocational decision was singular and uncompromising. He decided to be a citizen and a philosophical poet. The pains of citizenship fired the creator in him, so that he ultimately became the grandsire of Italian literature and indeed of much of Western literature written since his time. Dante excelled in the poetry of direct statement, in making thought melodic. He found ways to energize moral knowledge, so that it could both persuade and delight. He never wrote to be obscure or ambiguous, but it is important to remember that he was addressing keen, well-educated medieval minds. His mastery of narrative technique and symbolic detail encourages some readers to evaluate his art for its own sake, but Dante always wrote to make the reader look beyond his words to the vision that they served.

Biography · Dante Alighieri was a citizen, and his city was Florence. Medieval Italian cities were for the most part independent states, free of feudal allegiances, with power based not on land, but on harbors, commerce, and industry. The nobility within these cities had gradually yielded power to the new bourgeois interests, but the traditional lines of that struggle were still evident, the nobles seeking support from the Emperor and the bourgeois and popular elements tending to oppose the Empire and join with the Pope.

Those in the imperial faction were called Ghibellines, and the Papal, or at least the anti-imperial faction, were known as Guelphs. The faction one chose to support often had more to do with current and particular needs and where one's friends and enemies were, than with hereditary considerations. Dante's Florence was Guelph, which was enough to make rival cities support the Ghibelline cause—not that the Florentine Guelphs were able to live peaceably for long among themselves. A feud between two branches of a family in Pistoia, who called themselves "Whites" and "Blacks," spread to the Florentine upper classes. The Whites attracted the older families and Papal supporters, while the Blacks tended to attract the newly rich commercial classes.

Little is known of Dante's youth in Florence. It is clear that he read widely among Provençal and contemporary Italian poets as well as classical Latin writers; his writing also reveals a practical knowledge of music and painting. He may have attended the University of Bologna. He fought in the Florentine army and seems to have enjoyed many friendships throughout his city. The most important event in his life occurred at a May Day festival when he was nine years old. There he first saw Beatrice Portinari, who was eight at the time. They did not see each other again until nine years later, but Dante's devout fascination with her image and its significance lasted throughout his life. When she died in 1290, Dante diverted his grief by plunging into the difficult politics of the city and the study of philosophy. Between 1296 and 1301, the government of Florence entrusted him with high responsibilities in politics, finances, and diplomacy. His election as one of the city's six priors in the summer of 1300 exemplifies the public trust he enjoyed, a trust he justified when he validated the banishment of his close friend, the poet Guido Cavalcanti.

The year 1300 brought a convergence of several crises, political, spiritual, and economic, in the poet's life. So far as Dante's personal misfortunes are concerned, there are few details in the historical records. The larger event involved Charles de Valois, whom Pope Boniface had invited into Italy to help with the reconquest of Sicily. Charles was permitted to enter Florence with all of his troops, after assurances that he would not take part in the struggle between the Whites and the Blacks. Almost immediately, Charles allowed the Blacks to have the upper hand, at which point they began severe reprisals against the Whites. Dante was in Rome at the time as part of a delegation sent to secure guarantees from the Pope that the French forces would not interfere in Florentine politics. Dante was accused in absentia of barratry, extortion, impiety, and disloyalty, accusations which ultimately carried with them the death sentence. Dante never returned to Florence. As an exile, he drew closer to the exiled Whites and Ghibellines, but neither negotiations nor armed conspiracy succeeded in restoring them to power in Florence. Dante became disenchanted and impatient with his fellow exiles, who resented him, and may even have blamed him for the military reversals they were suffering.

A restless Dante may have spent time in at least a half dozen Italian cities and perhaps Paris at one point. He was unable to right things between himself and Florence, so that he might return. When Henry VII was elected Emperor, Dante envisioned an Italy unified under the Empire, with an end to the destructive rivalry between Church and State, but several key cities, aided by Florentine money, resisted Henry. When Dante angrily urged the Emperor to conquer Florence, he probably eliminated his last chance of entering the city alive. Florence excluded him from the general amnesty offered to the Whites, and then withstood the Emperor's assault; Henry died shortly thereafter. In 1315, probably because it needed talented citizens to help against a rival army, Florence declared itself willing to have Dante return, but he proudly rejected the terms. He was in Verona shortly after that, at work on *The Divine Comedy* under the patronage of Can Grande della Scala and his family. He spent his last days in Ravenna at the court of Guido da Polenta. In 1321, da Polenta sent him on a diplomatic mission to Venice. On his return, Dante fell desperately ill and did not recover. He was buried in Verona wearing Franciscan dress.

Analysis · Dante wrote *The New Life* to give an essential history of his own spirit, which was first aroused, then illuminated by his love for a woman. Here together are the narcissism and ecstasy of youth with the intricate design and perceptions of an older, uncompromising intelligence. The work consists of forty-two passages of prose commentary in which thirty-one poems are set at varying intervals. There are twenty-five sonnets, five canzones, and one ballad. The reader is not meant to abide the prose patiently until he reaches the next poem. Medieval poets believed that it should be possible to state in prose the core idea of any poem they created. Furthermore, no poem existed for its own sake—that is, solely for an aesthetic purpose. The prose keeps the reader in touch with the invisible realities and spiritual implications which were far more important to Dante than personal expression or artistic technique. The poems of *The New Life* describe and deal with romantic and sexual passion. Within the close boundaries and strict internal laws of poetic form, they either exemplify the point Dante is making in prose, or give way to a prose examination of the meanings beneath their surfaces. The poetic voice contains the original turmoil; the prose voice carries the more complete understanding of later personal reflection. The reader is thus able to share in the warmth of the original feelings and the sequence of epiphanies about them.

The topic of *The New Life* is love-suffering, which the poet will complain about but never abandon, for love-suffering is a way of life—indeed, part of the credentials of a noble person. The nobles whom Dante addressed constituted an elite, intelligent group who shared a sensitivity about love and who communicated easily with one another about its subtle doctrines. Traditionally, the medieval love poet did not concentrate on the real presence of the lady so much as on his own feelings about her. The poet would cry out against the upheavals his passions were causing and voice his fear and resentment of her coldness and elevated distance. Despite it all, he would vow to continue his martyrdom. These conventions of refined love were distorted and exaggerated, but they proved fit equipment for capturing the values of romantic experience. They take the reader past appearances into mental and spiritual realities which a camera eye can never see. The new ideas about love, which began emerging less than a century before Dante was born, caused a revolution in the sensibilities of Western European culture. Dante mastered them, then added a revolution of his own. He transcended the devouring egotism of his predecessors by identifying his own erotic drive and the mental processes it stimulated with the Divine Love which beckons to every soul. The lady thus becomes not merely the outer boundary of the lover's consciousness but a mediating presence between self and Deity. No longer a mirror of the poet's feelings, she stands as a window onto the infinite beauty of the Divine Presence and the way of salvation. *The New Life* records Dante's discovery of what he owed to several "God-bearing" ladies whom he encountered on his journey, Beatrice foremost among them.

The work begins with the intelligent and chastened voice of experience: Dante has learned to read the book of Nature, and he knows that the mystical significance of numbers can validate his spiritual discoveries. He has found a *vita nuova*, a new and miraculous life epitomized by the number nine, which the word *nuova* also signifies. Nine is the square of three, a number which, to the medieval imagination, represented perfection and the spiritual life. Dante explains how he first saw Beatrice when she was in her ninth year of life, and not again until nine years later, at the ninth hour of the day. Numbers are the clues to what Heaven has planned for him, so that when Dante writes this book of personal memory, made according to the laws of sequence and cause and effect, the reader is also aware of the perennial present of an unchanging ideal realm. For example, in section 3 of *The New Life*, Dante has a dream which is not only an erotic fantasy but also a prophecy. After he has seen Beatrice for the second time, the God of Love appears in a fiery cloud carrying Beatrice, who is asleep and flimsily clothed. Love wakens her and skillfully makes her eat of Dante's burning heart. Then the God begins to weep, folds his arms around her, and the two ascend heavenward. Dante notes that he had this dream at the first of the last nine hours of the night. Thus, the historical event of the lady's death, through the significance of numbers, reflects eternity.

The structure of Dante's book of memory suggests infinite harmony and reconciliation, particularly through the numbers three and nine. The thirty-one poems of *The New Life* fall into three groups, each group attached to one of the three canzones, or longer poems. At the center of the second or middle group is a canzone with four poems on either side of it. The first and third groups each have ten poems and one canzone; in the first group the poems precede the canzone, and in the second they follow it. Besides the obvious symmetry of the entire structure, there are nine poems in the middle group. If Dante had intended the first poem to be an introduction and the thirty-first to be an epilogue, the numbers nine and one would dominate the plan, although this is only a reasonable conjecture. Of more significance is the merger of numerical sign and literary idea in the middle group: The canzone which is at the exact center of the work refers to Beatrice's possible death with imagery traditionally associated with the Crucifixion of Christ. Thus, the center of the poet's book of memory and the center of Christian history are connected, through the analogy drawn between Beatrice and Christ.

The cast of *The New Life* is small, and the narrative is almost without setting and background. There are really only two actors: the poet, and the feminine presence who provides all the imaginative milestones in his life. Some women are useful distractions to prying eyes, so that he can conceal his true love's identity. The death of one of them tunes his grief for the eventual death of Beatrice, as does the death of Folco Portinari, Beatrice's father. If one takes this little history of a pilgrim's soul as an analogy for God's created time, where events can be understood either to anticipate or to look back toward Christ's Passion, death, and Resurrection, one immediately appreciates the suggestiveness of the format. When Dante contemplates the possibility of Beatrice's death, it seems to him that the sun grows dark and violent earthquakes occur. The next dream presents Beatrice following her beautiful friend, Giovanna, just as Christ followed John the Baptist. Her death will be comparably momentous and fruitful for his own life and later ages. Not that these insights enabled the poet to bear the actual death of Beatrice; the sonnets and canzones which follow that event are almost all to which a lyric poet can aspire, fusing intellect and pathos so perfectly that readers are reminded how imperfectly united their own souls are; at the same time, they are uplifted by the unity Dante has found. For long moments, the reader can believe that the alleged incompatibility between poetry and philosophy is but a jealous rumor.

As Dante decorates his own love story with signs of what he would come to understand about it in retrospect, he also means to show the progress of his own mind as events teach and shape him. He remembers himself as a self-preoccupied courtly lover, more educated and intellectually demanding than the troubadour poets from whom he learned, but, like them, emaciated by love-suffering, anxious, easily embarrassed, inclined to enjoy nursing his wounds in private, and completely under the rule of his master, Love. When, out of concern for her good name, Beatrice refuses to recognize him, he takes to his bed like a punished child. Then he begins to realize the limitations of this infantile mode. That night in a dream, the god appears and tells Dante that not he, but Love, is at the center of things, equidistant from all points on the circumference. Until he can accept the possibilities of this subtler and more comprehensive definition, the paradoxically painful and pleasurable qualities of his subjective experience will continue to vex him. Then, some town women, gently ridiculing his emaciated condition, suggest logically what Love had put more mysteriously: Happiness can come from the words he uses to praise Beatrice, not the words which concentrate on his own condition. With this nobler theme, his new life begins.

The famous canzone from section 19 which begins "Donne ch'avete intelletto d'amore," or "Ladies who can reason out Love's ways," describes the source of the lady's nobleness and perfection, which make all in Heaven want her with them, so that Heaven itself can be more perfect. On Earth, her glance can banish an evil intention or transform it to a noble one, and the worthy will feel salvation from having looked at her, for God has granted that whoever has talked with her will not come to a bad end. Having shifted his attention to a site outside himself, and having identified Beatrice as an emissary of Divine Love (able like It to create something where nothing has existed), Dante now has a talismanic axiom that will help him meet all future experience—even Beatrice's death, for everything coming to him from her will lead heavenward.

After Beatrice's death, a disconsolate Dante is temporarily distracted by the earthly beauty and compassion of a lady who looks at him sympathetically, but a vision of Beatrice resolves his inner struggle between reason and sensuality, and from then on the image of Beatrice is all he contemplates. The last sonnet of *The New Life* tells how his sigh passed the world's outermost sphere, moved by a new intelligence to the radiance of Beatrice in Heaven. When the sigh tries to report what it saw, its words are too subtle for Dante's comprehension; he is certain only that he hears Beatrice's name again and again. The highest and most serene image of the poet's renewed life is, paradoxically, beyond words. In the final section, Dante tells of a miraculous vision which included sights so profound that he made the resolution to say no more about Beatrice until he could find a suitably elevated vehicle. He closes with the wish that the Lord will grant him a few more years, so that he can compose a work about her which will contain things never said about any woman.

A diary unlike any written before it, *The New Life* was the work of a poet ready for sublime tasks who chose to review the development of his spiritual vision and poetic powers as the first step in the direction of carrying out those tasks. A finished masterpiece in its own right, it also served as a prelude to the greatest sustained poetic achievement in the West since Homer.

There probably never has been a piece of literary imagination as great in scope, as intricate in relationships among its parts, as fastidiously shaped to the smallest detail as Dante's *The Divine Comedy*. Besides the exacting challenge of maintaining poetic intensity for some fourteen thousand lines, there were the perils of dealing with interpretations of religious doctrine and Holy Writ in a fictional context. Even more perilous was the interpretation of Divine Justice, as it applied to specific historical incidents and individuals. Dante's genius and pious imagination flourished among these boundaries and obstacles. He used the appearances of the created world to describe the human heart in a theocentric universe. The three-part narrative pictures the soul deprived of God, in hope of God, and with God. Dante needed a design to mirror the unchanging realities beyond time and space, and he needed an action which would be an imitation of the soul's movements toward these realities. The symmetrical design of the entire work reflects divine perfection, as does its threefold narrative division and three-line stanzas. Each part, *Inferno, Purgatorio (Purgatory)*, and *Paradiso (Paradise)*, is divided into thirty-three cantos. With the introductory canto, these total one hundred, a number which also traditionally suggested divine unity and perfection.

The world of Dante's *The Divine Comedy* is vertical. The reader always moves downward or upward with the poet: the spiral descent into Hell, the climb up the purgatorial mountain, then up through the various planetary spheres, until the notions of movement up and down are no longer pertinent. The medieval model of the universe was similarly vertical, with Heaven above, Earth at the middle, and Hell below. Everything in God's creation was located at some point or other on a chain or ladder of being, which descended from His divine presence to the lowest form of inert matter. Each being was put at a particular step or degree on this scale, so that it could realize whatever purpose the Creator intended for it, but each thing or being was also understood in terms of what was above it and what was below it. The three realms of Dante's *The Divine Comedy* are vertically related, and each realm has its own vertical plan. The reader is continually urged to compare each spectacle with the one viewed previously and to ponder in retrospect its connection to the spectacle which follows it.

Writing a comedy was also imitating the world, at least as Dante used the term "comedy." In the medieval conception, comedy presented the happy resolution of a difficult situation. Thus, time and history could be seen as parts of a comic action, because Providence, working behind the superficial chaos of Fortune's wheel, would ultimately turn every earthly change to good. Human time and all of its pains began with the Fall of Adam, but that Fall looked forward to Christ's redemptive sacrifice. The sacrifice of Christ, who is often referred to as the "Second Adam," made it possible for the pattern of each life to be comic—that is, for man to conquer sin and win salvation. Dante's *The Divine Comedy* takes place at the end of Holy Week, during the most spiritually intense hours of the Christian year. For a time, darkness appears to triumph, as the God-Man is slain and buried, but out of seeming defeat comes a victorious descent into Hell and a resurrection which is the archetype of every spiritual rebirth which will come after it. When Dante descends into Hell on Good Friday and reaches Purgatory on Easter morning of the year 1300, the reader contemplates that holier comedy thirteen hundred years before.

The Divine Comedy offers more than structural symmetry and Christian values. It is also an imitation of the swarming variousness of the world of time and space: dreams, boasts, accusations, haunting beauties and catastrophes, wisdom, and reconciliation. The opening words hurry the reader into the narrator's dilemma and impasse, until, ninety-nine cantos later, the vision moves beyond human language and sensation. In his treatment of things invisible, Dante makes the reader touch with understanding almost every texture of earthly existence. To the medieval mind, the world was a book to be read, but a book could imitate the world by being an exhaustive compendium of information about geography, history, the nature of flight, even the spots on the moon. Dante's imagination is alert and curious, not satisfied with building a warehouse of facts. Dante further wishes the reader to visualize and experience the logistics of every step of the journey, feeling the heat, smelling the foulness, seeing different kinds of light and darkness, confronting the monstrosities, and struggling along the broken causeways.

The Divine Comedy is Dante's report of a journey he took into the anagogical realm of existence—that is, the afterlife—to witness the rewards and punishments which God's justice apportions to humankind on the basis of choices freely made in life. Dante himself said this much about his masterpiece. The reader learns while watching him learn, and because of that, even in the *Inferno*, moving toward the center of the Earth, the place farthest from God, there is a sense of the intelligence and soul expanding. The journey around which the narrative is constructed is also about the movement of every individual life. *The Divine Comedy* was intended to provide equipment for living in a City of God on Earth until the grander city of Jerusalem can be attained.

Although the meticulous physical detail encourages the reader to imagine himself on a journey in time and space, he is moving in a mindscape, a spectacle of the sinful human heart. Nowhere in Hell is he shown an attitude or act of which every living soul is not capable. Dante's descent involves a lowering of self through the admission of fault and capacity for fault, and the realization that the difference between man's sin and Satan's sin is one of degree rather than kind. Self-accusation and contrition make cleansing and regeneration possible, so that the climb to salvation can begin. Dante makes himself fall so that he may rise a stronger man, but his is a controlled fall. The vision of Hell could lead to despair and insane fascination, but with a guide who has been there before, Dante can have this terrible knowledge and survive. Having a second individual on the journey is also a useful narrative strategy, because the guide can interact dramatically with Dante the pilgrim and provide a normative presence, so that Dante the poet need not stultify the narrative with endless digressions about what the pilgrim cannot see.

That Dante should choose Vergil, the greatest of all Latin poets, to accompany him is not surprising. In one way or another, Vergil's writings had nourished every medieval poet. In his epic, the *Aeneid* (29-19 B.C.), Vergil had described a hero's visit to the underworld, and in that sense had been there once himself. His medieval admirers believed him to be a saint, a moralist, a prophet, even a magician. He was also a pagan and, as Dante strictly reasoned, had not been saved, but he was thought to embody natural wisdom unaided by revelation, which would make him a fit companion for a trip into the region of the damned. Vergil was also a poet of the Empire. He used the story of the fall of Troy to celebrate the founding of Rome and all the achievements of the divinely favored nation which followed it. Vergil predicted an era of world order and prosperity under Roman imperial rule. Many Christians believed that he foresaw in one of his pastorals the coming of the Redeemer and the Christian era. In his essay *On World Government*, Dante had argued that the Empire and the Church were two discrete but complementary modes by which divine purposes could be realized in human history, one emphasizing reason, the other revelation. Vergil epitomizes both the grandeur and the limitations of that gift of natural reason. He travels with Dante as far as he—that is, reason—can, and then is replaced by Beatrice, who personifies the light of divine revelation denied to pagans.

The world of *The Divine Comedy* is so wide and various that a comprehensive introduction to it is not possible in a brief essay, but canto 1 of the *Inferno* is a useful place to begin observing how Dante's composition works. It is Maundy Thursday night, the day before Good Friday in the year 1300. The poet's first words are about personal time, the midpoint of life at which he awakened to discover himself in a dark wood, with no idea where the right road was. Because the very first line refers to a stage of life, the reader is not likely to imagine a search through a literal wood for an actual road. A few lines later, as Dante painfully recalls the harshness and recalcitrance of the forest, it becomes clear that he is talking about his own former willfulness. As horrid as this time of error was, says Dante, good came of it. This mixture of fear and optimism sets the tone perfectly for the *Inferno* and for the rest of *The Divine Comedy*. The opening lines involve the reader in the experiences of another being as though they were his or her own (which, in a sense, they are). Eschewing biographical or historical detail, Dante presents only the essential, the elementary: At a crosspoint in life, another human realized that he had lost touch with an important part of himself.

The poet does not know exactly how he lost his way in that wood, but the torpor from which he suffered at the time was obviously spiritual. Struggling out of the wood, he is aware of a steep mountain, and as he looks up at the sun which lights the ways of men, he feels some comfort. Somehow, his awareness of his own poor spiritual state and the grace of a loving God have helped him through a dangerous maze, a place, he notes, from which no one has escaped, once entrapped there. Clearly, the forest is a form of spiritual death, or sin, but all the pilgrim has done so far is avoid the worst. To climb the mountain and achieve the spiritual perfection it implies, he will need to gain control of the complicated forces within himself.

A quick-stepping leopard first impedes his progress, but a look at the morning sun, as beautiful as it was during the first moments of Creation, restores Dante's hopes, which are again shattered when a lion, head held high, approaches menacingly. Most intimidating is a gaunt, ravenous wolf, which Dante says has conquered many men. The wolf begins to edge Dante back down the path into the dark forest. Dante does not say what each of these beasts symbolizes, but probably they represent types of sinful living. This notion exists because, to the medieval mind, beasts usually stood for the lower or unreasonable parts of the personal hierarchy. The leopard seems to have the flair and energy of youth, the lion the more powerful intellectual pride which can dominate later years, and the wolf the avarice for possessions which comfort advanced years. Any one of these sins could weigh down a traveler throughout life. Dante makes the point that inability to deal with the three brings despair and spiritual disaster. The light of the sun offers encouragement; grace is available, but it has to be used. As he stumbles downward, Dante sees a shadow. Although it seems unaccustomed to speaking, the shadow answers when Dante calls to it for help, just as the way out of the woods appeared when Dante admitted to himself that he was lost. The shadow is Vergil, who stands for the natural good sense that Dante had allowed to lie dormant.

Vergil does not want Dante to take on the she-wolf directly, for she has been the ruin of many. There is another way out of the wood, Vergil says.

The person who confronts his own demons without a guide or a strategy is inviting failure. Dante first needs to use his reason to understand the nature of unforgiven sin and its punishment. Then he can visit the purgatorial realm, where the vestiges of forgiven sins are removed, and finally a worthier guide will show him the vision of ultimate reward. Vergil also cautions Dante against becoming preoccupied with the sins of his fellow countrymen. In time, says Vergil, a greyhound will come to chase the avaricious wolf from Italy. Whether this greyhound represents a great earthly prince or some divine apocalypse is not clear. The central point of this first canto is that, beginning with his own conscience, then using the legible signs in the book of the natural world and the revival of his own rational faculty, Dante is ready to journey toward whatever perfection he can hope to attain.

The above remarks are not an ambitious reading of obscure material. Dante saw clearly and wrote to be understood. He did, however, believe that it was natural and beneficial to require an audience to be alert to more than the literal in what he said. An extremely sophisticated tradition of biblical interpretation had prepared his audience to do that and to take pleasure in understanding more than surface meanings in a piece of writing. If the created world was a fair field of symbols, and if the revealed word could be read on several metaphorical levels, why not a story of the mind's journey to God? Thus, Dante wrote allegorical fiction, in which what is said is frequently intended to mean something else. The "literal" aspect of allegorical narrative is usually the least important, for it is the sense of the figurative and the symbolic which the author wants to exercise. The reader needs a fine set of interchangeable lenses in order to see the multiple levels.

Dante's Hell is in the center of the Earth, which was thought to be the center of the created world, but in a theocentric universe, the Earth was really on the outside looking in. The lowest point in Dante's Hell is therefore the farthest possible point from God; it is frozen, signifying the total absence of human or divine love. This Hell is fashioned from religious tradition and popular belief. Spectacular as some of the punishments are, the chief source of pain is indescribable: the eternal loss of the sight of God.

Although many modern readers reject the idea of eternal punishment, medieval Christian thinkers had concluded that an all-perfect Being had to embody justice as well as mercy. When an individual died, the reign of mercy ended and that of justice began. In this view, the damned have willfully rejected the power of grace, the teachings of the Church, and the Sacraments. If after this, God relented, He would be unjust. Justice also determines the nature of the punishments and the consequent degree of suffering. The punishment Dante imagines for each sin is a symbolic definition of the sin itself, which the sinner has to repeat for eternity. Only the living can learn from this infernal repetition. For all the uproar and movement in Hell, nothing changes. A medieval definition of change would be the movement of things toward the ideal form which God intended for them; not a single gesture in Hell does that.

Dante's Hell is an inverted hierarchy, with each level revealing a more serious sin below. Hell has nine circles, in addition to an outer vestibule. The upper five circles contain punishments for sins committed through misdirected or uncontrolled emotions; they reflect the perils of natural vitality and appetites, as the image of the leopard suggested. Next, behind the walls of the city of Dis, are crimes which require a stronger determination of the will to disrupt the plan of existence. The violence which appears here (circles six and seven) may be connected with the lion which threatened Dante earlier. The eighth circle is a long sheer drop below this and contains the violators of the various kinds of promise-keeping which make social life possible. The more complicated frauds of treason and betrayal in the ninth and lowest circle may be related to the ravenous wolf. Far more ingenious than the schematic layout of Hell is Dante's ability to keep a sense of spontaneity and discovery in what could have been merely a dutiful walk through a catalog of sin. Dante's skill at variation, which every medieval poet would have coveted, is perhaps the chief source of the poem's excellence. Even in *Purgatory*, where the treatment of each sin runs to a pattern, Dante somehow handles every section uniquely.

One of the sources of variety and sense of forward movement in the *Inferno* is the interaction between Dante and Vergil. Vergil chides, encourages, and revives his pupil as they travel through Hell. The pilgrim Dante becomes stronger and more sure of himself, less frightened by the nightmarish circus about him and more able to despise intelligently the evil he sees. At first, Dante does not believe himself to be fit for such a journey, but when Vergil tells him that Beatrice wills it, he immediately agrees to follow. Two cantos later, in Limbo, the greatest pagan poets are welcoming him to their company. Whenever he has need of Reason, Vergil is always there—even literally at one point—to lift and carry him out of danger. The danger and inhospitableness increase as the two proceed deeper. Everything they see is an inversion or distortion of Charity, the love of God and neighbor in which every Christian act is rooted. At the start, Charon, the underworld boatman, refuses to ferry Dante and Vergil across the river Acheron; in the ninth and lowest circle, Count Ugolino devours the head of the bishop whose betrayal caused the Count and his sons to be starved to death. The reader becomes increasingly aware of Dante's obsession with the two Florences: the City of God on Earth that he wanted it to become and the ungrateful zone of corruption it had been to him. In his darkest hour, Dante was nearer to Beatrice and all that she stood for than Florence would ever be to Jerusalem. Almost until the final instants of *Paradise*, Dante rails against the city that nourished and exiled him.

Somewhat like a Gothic cathedral, *The Divine Comedy* is a huge structural support covered with crafted sections of varying size and content, each section somehow finding a place in the totality. A very limited sampling of sections might begin with Upper Hell, where the sins of the incontinent are punished. It may be surprising to find that lust is the first sin viewed here, which makes it the least serious offense in Hell. Medieval moralists tended to treat sexual love as a natural behavior in need of a supernatural perspective. This is quite different from treating sexuality as a taboo, as later ages would. Even so, the reader should consider the mixture of feelings within Dante—who began as a lyric poet in the tradition of erotic courtship—as he watches the souls of the lustful tossed on a roaring black wind, an image of the uncontrollable passion to which they surrendered their reasoning power. They are like flocks of starlings and cranes borne up and down forever, shrieking as they go. The scene conveys the restlessness of human passion and the crowded commonness of the sin itself. The world's most famous lovers are in those flocks: Dido, Helen, Paris, Tristram. Seeing them, Dante grows dizzy with sympathy.

Two of the lovers are still together, dovelike as they waft along hand in hand. They are Paolo and Francesca, who suffered and died for love at the hands of Francesca's husband. Francesca delivers a courtly lyric celebrating the power of love which brought her and Paolo together, a lyric which ends with the assurance that damnation awaits the one who murdered them. Deeply moved by the lovers' tragedy, Dante asks to know more. What he hears is not the spell of romance but a rather ordinary process of young lechery: leisure time, suggestive reading, and the knowing glances which precede coupling. Dante has to be true to the old conventions of love here, the ones he transformed in *The New Life*; he also has to maintain the clear-eyed antiromanticism of Christian morality. It is all too much for the pilgrim, who falls into a dead swoon, until he awakes to find himself in the third circle, with the gluttonous.

Like the lustful, the gluttonous have allowed themselves to be controlled and distorted by a natural urge. The image Dante uses to describe the punishment here is startling in the manner of a metaphysical conceit. First, he describes a cold, heavy rain soaking a putrid earth. Cerberus, the three-headed watchdog of the Underworld, is there, each head gorging on the souls of the gluttonous as they wallow in the mud. To distract the monstrous beast, Vergil throws filthy mud down its throats. Cold rain seems to have no connection with excessive eating, until one considers the motivation which is often behind that excess: self-centered loneliness with indiscriminate sieges of oral gratification. One Ciacco ("Fats"), a fellow Florentine, addresses Dante from the slime. He vents his own alienation and misery, then gives an acid survey of the rottenness which will continue to seep from their native city.

The metaphoric effect is equally powerful in canto 12, when Dante and Vergil enter the pathless wood of the suicides, where the souls have been turned to dead trees which bleed at the touch and are fed on by Harpies, who represent the guilt of self-destruction. Through this same wood run the souls of persons who in life madly spent all they owned. They are being chased and torn to pieces by hunting dogs. Dante's decision to put suicides here among souls who have been violent against themselves seems reasonable. That he should sense a comparable wish for death among those who are impatient to destroy their wealth shows a marvelous awareness of the darker corners of the human situation. Like the cold rain upon the gluttonous, it is a superb reach of intelligence and intuition.

The last four cantos describe the ninth and lowest circle of Hell, which contains the perpetrators of the subtlest, most complicated frauds imaginable. First described are the giants of classical legend who tried to scale Heaven and challenge Jove, and the biblical Nimrod, who directed the attempt to build the Tower of Babel. At the bottom of Hell's pit is the frozen lake Cocytus. There, the traitors, who through intellect and will achieved the most drastic perversion of love, are frozen in unrepentant attitudes of hatred. These are the souls of those who betrayed kin, fatherland, guests, and, lowest of all, those who betrayed their lords. Fed ultimately by all the rivers of Hell, the ice itself may be blood-colored. Tears, a symbol of compassion, freeze instantly there. The famous agony of Count Ugolino of Pisa, who, with his children, starved to death in prison, mirrors perfectly these pitiless surroundings. Ugolino and the others are at Hell's bottom because they violated the promise-keeping which is the root of every social and spiritual relationship, for man becomes ethical on the basis of his fidelity to promises of loyalty, hospitality, and the like. The cannibalism which the traitor Ugolino enacts as he devours the skull of the person who betrayed him suggests the ultimate negation of social behavior, where humanity and bestiality are no longer distinguishable.

Satan, the angel once nearest to God, now occupies the lowest extremity of Hell, held in ice up to his chest. This is the summary image of the first third of *The Divine Comedy*. At the center of the heart of darkness is this living death, presided over by the first of God's creatures to defy Him.

Satan has three faces here, red, yellow, and black, which probably refer to the races of humanity through which his first evil is continued. A parody of the Triune God, his face is the inversion of the spiritual number three. Two batlike wings flap under each face, making a freezing wind which keeps the lake frozen. There is no other movement observable here, unless one includes the tears from those three pairs of eyes, which drip in a bloody mixture from Satan's chins. The draft from his wings evidently freezes all tears but his own. If these tears and blood, which are appalling reminders of the sacramental water and blood which flowed from the side of the Redeemer on the first Good Friday, represent the misery which sin causes, they reveal no contrition whatsoever, for the wings are operated by a will which is still rebellious and an icy egotism which will never cease to oppose God. Even the blindly passionate wind which heaved Paolo and Francesca about would be a welcome alternative to those hopeless gusts.

Each of Satan's mouths chews on a famous traitor. Situated highest, the mouth of the red face tortures the most notorious traitor of all: Judas Iscariot. In the lower mouths are the two others who make up this Satanic Eucharist, Brutus and Cassius, who subverted God's plan for world empire under Rome by assassinating Julius Caesar. In Dante's conception, sacred and imperial history, although they are separate, are both founded on God's will, and therefore must stand responsible before His justice. In this sense, the things of God and the things of Caesar must ultimately converge. In the midst of these ironies is the supreme irony of Satan's powerlessness, which makes him, for all of his gigantic size, ridiculous. He and the giants are mastodons in a museum. Dante and Vergil climb down this hulk out of Hell and see the stars for the first time since early Friday morning.

When Vergil and Dante have climbed down past Satan's navel, they have reached the point farthest from God. What was below is now above them, and Satan appears upside down, a fitting final aspect of the Arch-Rebel. The pair are now in the Earth's southern hemisphere, facing an island with a mountain called Purgatory, formed of the land which retreated to avoid Satan when he fell. The Earthly Paradise is on the top of that mountain. It was closed at the expulsion of Adam and Eve, but since Christ's death it has been open to souls purified in Purgatory. Actually, Scripture gives few specific details about Hell, and none at all about Purgatory.

In Purgatory, medieval Christians believed, the residual effects of sins admitted, confessed, and forgiven were removed before the soul entered Paradise. The soul permitted to enter Purgatory was saved and would surely see God someday. Furthermore, these souls could be helped by the prayers of people still on Earth and could enjoy communication with the suffering souls around them. This is quite different from the isolation and hopeless sense of loss in Hell.

If the topic of the *Inferno* is the just punishment of sin, the topic of *Purgatory* is the discipline of perfection. It is a more serenely organized piece of writing, with a pace which is generally more constant. After the terraces of the ante-Purgatory, the mountain has seven cornices, each devoted to purging the stain of one of the deadly sins. Every cornice contains a penance, a meditation, a prayer, a guardian angel, and a benediction. The ascent from one area to another is often accompanied by a brief essay on some topic in natural or moral philosophy. The idea of an ante-Purgatory was probably Dante's own. In its two terraces are the souls of those who delayed repenting until the moment of their death. Having waited too long in life to do what was necessary to be saved, they must wait for some time before they can begin the ascent. In the first terrace, are the souls who, although excommunicated by the Church, delayed repentance until the last moments of life. In terrace two, are those who delayed similarly, although they always lived within the Church; included here are the souls of the indolent, the unshriven, and the preoccupied.

Saint Peter's Gate is the entrance to Purgatory proper. Three steps of Penance lead up to it: confession, contrition, and satisfaction. At the gate, an angelic custodian inscribes seven *P*'s, signifying the Seven Deadly Sins (*peccatum* is the Latin for sin), on the forehead of each soul. The letters will be erased one at a time as the soul passes from cornice to cornice. The Seven Deadly Sins were the most widely used description of human evil in the Middle Ages. Somehow or other, every transgression was thought to have come from one of those seven: Lust, Gluttony, Avarice, Sloth, Wrath, Envy, and Pride. Each cornice has a penance appropriate to the stain left by one of those sins. The soul may be made to perform a penitential exercise which symbolically describes the effects of the sin committed, or as counterbalance it may have to perform actions which suggest the virtue directly opposed to the sin. Sometimes souls are assigned to do both.

The meditation in each cornice consists of a whip, or example of the opposing virtue, and a bridle, which is made up of horrid instances of the sin in question. These are followed by a prayer taken from the Psalms or hymns of the Church, then by a benediction (one of the Beatitudes), which is spoken by the angel of the cornice, who then erases a *P* from the soul's forehead. The soul then moves up the Pass of Pardon to the next cornice.

The boundary line for a Hell or Purgatory can be difficult for even a severely legalistic planner to draw. Those souls closest to the entrance of Hell had lost all hope of salvation, though by a narrow margin. In *Purga-*

tory, those closest to the boundary have avoided that loss by a similarly narrow margin. Dante's Hell begins with the neutrals, those who chose not to choose. They are a faceless mob condemned to chase a whirling standard forever. Next is the Limbo of the unbaptized and virtuous pagans. Dante could not imagine salvation for them, even though their poetry and ideas had nurtured him, but neither could he condemn them for light denied. Thus, the virtuous pagans appear in a dim but pastoral setting, and the poets among them admit Dante to their number. The first terrace of Purgatory also involves fine distinctions, but ones in which the poet is less personally involved. To be excommunicated was not a sin in itself, but a person who was separated from the Church by a sin which called for excommunication, and who put off repentance until the last minutes of life, was grasping salvation by its coattails. Appropriately, these excommunicates and the other late repentants in the second terrace are the only souls in Purgatory who have to undergo a punishment–that is, a wait. All of the others are cheerfully engaged in a healing process which will continue until they are ready for Paradise.

Ascending through the cornices of Purgatory is in one way like backing up the spiral road out of Hell. The lowest part of Hell, where the proudest act ever committed is being punished, corresponds to the first cornice, where the stains of pride are being removed. The cornice of Lust, the least of the Seven Deadly Sins, is nearest the top of the mountain, as Lust was farthest from the frozen lake at the bottom of Hell. The descent became increasingly difficult for Dante and Vergil as each circle delivered something more bleak or dangerous. The trek upward in Purgatory is a happy jettisoning of old heaviness, done in the midst of general enthusiasm and encouragement. Instead of Charon, who grudgingly ferried the two across Acheron, an angel of the Lord lightly takes a hundred singing souls across to the island where Mount Purgatory stands. Indeed, the change of mood exhilarates Dante so thoroughly that he all but loses his sense of mission as he listens to the singing of Casella, an old friend and musician.

There are subtle changes in Vergil's presence at this point. He is temporarily eclipsed in the early cantos by the appearance of the astringent Cato, who represents the discipline that will be needed for the lively chores ahead. Moreover, Vergil has not been here before, so although he is still a fount of good sense, he is seeing everything for the first time. He can only partly answer certain questions Dante asks, such as the one about the efficacy of human prayer. Dante will have to wait for Beatrice to explain such matters fully, and interpreters will come forth intermittently to talk about what Vergil cannot be expected to recognize.

Dante and Vergil emerge from Hell on Easter morning at dawn and reach the island shortly after that. They are in the second terrace of ante-Purgatory when the sun begins to set. Night-climbing is not permitted, so the two are led to a beautiful valley, where the souls of preoccupied rulers dwell. The cycle of day and night and the natural beauty of the valley indicate their presence still on Earth, in the middle state. The significance of not attempting a penitential climb in the dark is fairly clear, but as night falls, two angels descend to keep watch over the valley. They immediately chase off a serpent who has marauded there. Dante is brilliantly suggestive here. The sentry angels are dressed in green, which is a sign of both hope and penance, but that they should be there at all is puzzling. The point seems to be that, at least in ante-Purgatory, temptation is still a possibility. The fiery swords that the angels bear and the presence of the enemy serpent recall the Fall in Eden, and indeed the theme at the core of this journey is the return to that garden and man's state before he sinned.

The morning dream which Dante has in that valley is also charged with details which add significance to all that will happen. Having his own share of Old Adam's nature, he says, he nods off, and in the first light, the time of holy and prophetic dreams, he sees a golden eagle in midair, about to swoop toward its prey. He thinks of Zeus snatching the boy Ganymede up to Heaven, but then he conjectures that this eagle must always hunt here, so it need not have anything to do with him. Then the eagle comes for him like lightning, and takes him up to the circle of fire which surrounds the Earth, where they burn together with a heat which wakens him and ends the dream. He finds that Saint Lucy has carried him to Saint Peter's Gate—the beginning of Purgatory proper.

This dream illuminates the rest of the story until the final line, although it is possible to interpret its simpler elements at once. Lucy is one of the three ladies (the other two are Beatrice and the Blessed Virgin) who decided to help Dante out of the dark wood earlier. Lucy personifies the beckoning power of Divine Light by literally transporting Dante to the start of this second phase of his journey. The golden eagle, a bird sacred to Jove and also an emblem of the empire, is doing a comparable thing. Here are two faces of the Godhead, one maternally encouraging, the other ravenously assertive, together making up a richly complicated insight which comes not from a Vergilian lecture or the remark of a dead soul, but from a dream, where the discourse is intuitive and mystical. The progress up the mountain will for the most part involve intellectual and ethical knowledge, but as it is happening the totality of Dante's being will be moving toward a Divine Love which is beyond language and rational understanding, and for which a burning heaven is the most appropriate metaphor. The movement up the cornices will be clear and steady, so uniform as to be tedious at times. It will require the light of day, but the total movement of the self with the Deity is perhaps best reflected in dreamlight, because Dante is giving his readers not only an encyclopedia of morality but also an imitation of a psychological process.

The removal of the vestiges of sin will render the soul fitter and more able to see the Beatific Vision in its full glory. In Purgatory, all souls are headed homeward, and each step is easier and more satisfying. Innocence, humanity's state before sin, is the first destination, and from there a more glorious vision will begin, one which the most artful words can only partially describe.

Signs that Eden is near begin in the sixth cornice, with the gluttonous. By this time, Publius Papinius Statius, a pagan Latin poet who became a Christian, has joined the party; Dante believes that Vergil's reason and literary art need the supplement of revelation so that everything that is about to happen can be fully appreciated. Vergil had pagan glimmerings of Eden and the prelapsarian state when he wrote of a virtuous Golden Age once enjoyed by humankind, but glimmerings are not enough. Before them in the path, they see a tall tree, watered from above by a cascade. The tree bears ambrosial fruit, but a voice forbids anyone to eat it. Examples of Temperance are then described, which are the goad or whip to counter the vice. The souls of the gluttonous, all emaciated, suffer from being denied the sweet-smelling fruit, but, as one of them tells Dante, they come to the tree with the same desire that Christ brought to the Cross, for both sufferings bring redemption. They see another tree which also keeps its fruit from a gathering of gluttonous souls. A voice tells them to ignore the tree, which is the sort that fed Eve's greed. The connection between the sin of gluttony and the eating of the forbidden fruit was a point commonly made from medieval pulpits. Particularly noteworthy here is the easy flow of allusions to the Fall of Man and to the suffering on the Cross which compensated for it. The classical story of Tantalus' punishment in the Underworld may have inspired Dante's description of the gluttonous, but the tree of Eden and the tree of the Cross are clearly the central points of reference here.

When the three travelers finally reach the Earthly Paradise, they see not a garden but a forest, a sacred wood wherein dwells the primal innocence which seemed so far away in the dark wood of the *Inferno*, in canto 1. The sacred wood has a single inhabitant, Matilda, who is there to explain these environs and make straight the way of Beatrice, who appears in a spectacular allegorical event called the Procession of the Sacrament. Only eyes which have regained the first innocence are ready for such a vision.

Looking eastward, which is by tradition the holiest direction, Dante sees a brilliant light spread through the forest, and a procession led by seven candlesticks to a chanting of "Hosanna." Next come twenty-four elders, heads crowned with lilies, and after them four beasts surrounding the triumphal cart drawn by a griffin, whose birdlike features are gold, and elsewhere red and white. Three ladies, colored respectively, red, green, and white, dance in a circle by the right wheel; four in purple dance by the left wheel, led by one who has a third eye. Two old men come next, one dressed as a physician, the other carrying a sword. They are followed by four humbly dressed processants, and then by a very old man, going in a visionary trance. These last seven all wear red flowers.

Medieval religious processions were usually staged to affirm a crucial matter of doctrine or devotion. The key notion in this masquelike procession is the unity of sacred revelation since the Fall of Man. The twenty-four elders refer to the books of the Old Testament, their lily crowns suggesting pure righteousness. The Benedictus they sing is a reminder that the Old Testament symbolically anticipates events in the New Testament. The four beasts are the beasts of the Apocalypse and the signs of the four Evangelists. The griffin, which is part eagle and part lion, traditionally refers to the two natures of Christ, its gold suggesting divinity, its red and white, humanity. White and red are also the colors respectively of the Old and New Testaments, and of the bread and wine in the Eucharist. The ladies by the right wheel are Faith (white), Hope (green), and Charity (red); by the left wheel are the four cardinal virtues: Prudence (with the third eye), Temperance, Fortitude, and Justice. Behind the cart are Luke, Paul, and the Epistles of Peter, James, John, and Jude. The old man is the Revelation of Saint John. The red flowers they all wear signify the New Testament.

Then Beatrice appears on the cart in a red dress and green cloak, her head crowned with olive leaves. At this moment, Dante realizes that Vergil, the man of natural wisdom, is no longer with him. Beatrice, who might as well be called Revelation here, tells Dante to look at the entire procession. All of it is she, Beatrice says. Beatrice's words are the fullest manifestation so far of the significance of one passionate event which occurred when the poet was nine years old. What the God-Man brought into history, she is. The Incarnation which the Old Testament faintly surmised, and which the New Testament celebrates, she is, with every holy virtue in attendance. The same can be said of the transsubstantiated Host on the altar.

After a rebuke from Beatrice for the wandering ways of his own life, which is perhaps his own rightful dose of the purgatorial suffering he has been content to watch, Dante faints with shame. When he revives, Matilda is drawing him across the stream of forgetfulness. With the memory of evil now gone, he can watch with original innocence as the procession heads toward the Tree of Knowledge, where human sin began. Many medieval writings connected the Tree of Knowledge with the tree on which Christ was crucified. Lore had it that the seeds of the fruit from the first tree were buried on the tongue of Adam and then grew to become the tree of the Cross. Christ was often referred to as the Second Adam, come to reverse the catastrophe caused by the first. Here, the Griffin (Christ) moves the cart with Beatrice (the Word and its Incarnation) past the site on which the temptation and Fall occurred and joins the shaft of the cart to a barren tree, which immediately blossoms. The Griffin then ascends, leaving Beatrice at the roots of the tree. She now represents the Church which Christ at his ascension left behind to care for the humankind He had redeemed.

The role of the Empire in God's plan is stressed here, too. An eagle slashes at the tree, just as Roman persecution maimed the Church. Then a gaunt fox appears, probably to represent the heresies of the Church's early history. After the fox has prowled about the cart, the eagle descends again, this time to feather the cart from its own breast. This no doubt represents the symbiotic relationship between Church and State in the Holy Roman Empire. That liaison is followed by a dragon which damages the cart, causing it to change into the many-headed beast of the Apocalypse, on top of which is enthroned a whore consorting with giants. The imagery suggests the later corruption of the Church caused by its consorting with earthly powers. Thus, Dante sketches a symbolic history of the decay of the Church which Christ and Peter founded. The point is one he makes directly in many places: that in Christian history, Church and Empire need to maintain separate identities as they pursue God's plan. The atmosphere of these last cantos has been gradually shifting toward Apocalypse, which Beatrice continues by prophesying revenge for what has been allowed to happen to Christendom, but the final canto returns to the theme of a purgatorial journey. Dante now drinks from Eunoe, the water of Good Remembrance, which renders him finally free from the tarnish of an earthly life and ready for a direct vision of the Godhead.

Readers who think of Dante as the poet of Hell often have read only the first third of his masterpiece. The joy which quickens every step of the *Purgatory* makes it an exhilarating sequel to the *Inferno*, but that joy is only a hint of what awaits Dante in the vision of Paradise. The *Inferno* and *Purgatory* are preparatory visions, the first stressing the reality of evil and its effects, the second showing that it is possible to remove every one of those effects. *Purgatory* and *Paradise* form the main part of the comedic structure, which leaves the unhappiness of the *Inferno* far behind.

Dante's *Paradise* is a description of Godhead, as much of it as his eyes could register, and as much as his memory could retain. Medieval literary audiences loved well-executed descriptions, and the *Inferno* and *Purgatory* contain some extraordinarily effective ones. Once the poet has left the substantive world, images on which to base descriptions are no longer obvious. Hell and Purgatory are constructed and described according to sinful human actions, which had been traditionally identified and discussed in concrete images. Social history abounds with vivid examples of depravity, but there has never been a great store of fictions or metaphors to describe the state of the soul enjoying Heavenly rewards. Moreover, the step-by-step journey into Hell and up the purgatorial mountain involves a sense of time and space which is inappropriate to the simultaneity of eternity. Thus, the metaphor of the journey does not quite fit a vision of Heaven, although to accommodate human communication and understanding, the vision had to be subdivided and presented in some sequence. Dante reminds his audience, however, that this is only a strategy to help them see.

Until one reaches the presence of God, the Being than Whom none is higher, one has to understand every phenomenon, even heavenly bliss, hierarchically. Every soul in Heaven is completely happy, but even heavenly bliss has its degrees. To describe Paradise, Dante looks outward from Earth to the concentric spheres of the planets and beyond them to the Empyrean, where the Divine Presence begins. Because, moving outward, each successive planet is closer to God, each one can be a gathering point for increasingly elevated forms of blessedness. With the rather technical exception of the souls on the Moon, the imagery Dante uses to describe the souls he meets is nonrepresentational, even approaching abstraction with voices, lights, and patterns. Dante was familiar with the tradition of the cosmic voyage, a literary form which went back to the Stoic philosophers, in which a guide takes a troubled individual to the outer spheres, to provide consolation by demonstrating the littleness of troubled Earth when compared to the grand harmony of all Creation. A powerful counterpoint develops in *Paradise* between accounts of the sordidness of contemporary Italian society and the charity and communion above. Part of the image of Paradise is thus accomplished through negative description, using earthly examples to emphasize what Heaven is not.

The *Inferno* does not start with a poetic invocation. Dante rushes directly into the troubled middle of things. *Purgatory* has an invocation to Calliope, the Muse of epic poetry. It is crucial but perfunctory, and it suits the hopeful premises of that work. The invocation to *Paradise* is a fitting start to a sublime task. It tells what a poet requires to describe his Creator. He starts with the notion that what he has seen is not possible to relate, because when the mind nears that which it has always wanted, memory weakens. Even so, he will sing about that part of it which has remained with him. He calls upon Apollo, a god traditionally associated with light, wisdom, and prophecy, to breathe into him and use him like a bellows to utter song worthy of what memory of Paradise he still has left. Dante's audience would have been comfortable with an invocation to a pagan deity, because they believed that many pagan myths were glimpses of Christian light which could be used to make poetry more articulate. As an inspiration to soul and art, Apollo resembles the Holy Spirit, but he also carries all the rich associations of the classical literary tradition.

If Apollo will be generous, Dante continues, he will approach the laurel tree to take those famous leaves, now so neglected by an unheroic and unpoetic age, to create poetry which will ignite better imaginations than his own. From that tree, then, may come light for all future ages. The highly prophetic *Paradise* deserves to be under the keeping of Apollo. The poet approaches the laurel tree sacred to Apollo as he gathers strength to take his pilgrim self from Eden and the last visible traces of earthly things. The tree of tantalizing punishment for the gluttonous and the tree of the first sin are replaced here by a tree reflecting the highest moral calling of art. As the images of Eden and sin recede, the laurel tree and the tree of Redemption converge. Dante looks at Beatrice looking at the sun, which is both Apollo's planet and a traditional symbol for God. It is the same sun he saw that morning in the dark wood, but then he was looking through sinful eyes. The eagle, Dante's symbol for the Empire, was thought to be able to look directly into the sun; the suggestion here is that Beatrice, who stands for all revelation, and the eagle are one. It might seem curious that an image of imperial order should be presented at a moment of intimacy between self and Godhead, but Dante will make a similar point throughout *Paradise*: that religious mysticism and social history are different but not antithetical routes to God. The eagle which seized Dante in a dream and took him on high to burn was as much the call of empire as it was a private religious impulse.

Dante is not able to look directly at the sun for long. As he looks at Beatrice looking at eternity, he begins to hear the music coming from the harmonious motion of the heavenly spheres, a sound no mortal has heard since Adam sinned. Instantly, Dante realizes that he has left Earth with Beatrice. The vision which follows, the organization of which is only a metaphor for the ineffable, involves ten Heavens, each of the first seven associated with a planet–Moon, Mercury, Venus, Sun, Mars, Jupiter, Saturn–the eighth Heaven with the zodiac and fixed stars, the ninth the Crystalline Heaven of the *Primum Mobile*, or First Mover, through which motion was imparted to all the other spheres, and beyond that the Empyrean, or realm of God. In the first seven Heavens, the souls are located in the planet with which their earthly activities could be associated, although in actuality each of them is in the Empyrean with God. According to Dante, the first three Heavens are touched by the shadow of Earth. On the Moon, the planet nearest Earth, are those souls who through no fault of their own proved inconstant in vows they had made to God. They were not sinners, only less perfect in salvation. Next is the Heaven of Mercury, filled with souls who lived virtuous lives serving the social order, but who were motivated at least in part by worldly ambition. The sphere of Venus is for those who followed Eros in life but now are delighted to wheel with celestial movement.

In the Heaven of the Sun are spirits whose wisdom furthered the understanding of God on Earth. Mars houses those who gave their lives for the Christian faith, while Jupiter houses the souls of the Just. The second three Heavens (Sun, Mars, and Jupiter) celebrate the virtuous achievements of the active life, but the contemplatives abide above them, in the circle of Saturn. The theme of the eighth Heaven is the Church triumphant, with Christ and the saints in full radiance. The ninth and tenth Heavens, respectively the *Primum Mobile* and the Empyrean, are given to the various direct manifestations of God. They take up the last six cantos, which trail off as even Dante's imagination begins to fade before its task.

The mood of *Paradise* is perfect joy which has no end and which leaves not even a trace of unfulfilled desire. The spirits describe that joy by what they do and say. There is a hierarchy of blessedness here, but it exists without anyone feeling envy or deprivation. Just as the courtesy and charity of Purgatory take one above the hatred and cupidity of Hell, so the perfect happiness here lifts one even higher, particularly through the praises for its perfect Source. The points of Christian doctrine and philosophy which are explained to Dante as he moves from Heaven to Heaven with Beatrice are rarefied, some barely fixable in mind or language. To follow these thoughts, the reader must move with Dante past the recognizable specifics of time and place. This commentary can only sample that exquisite brightness. One might begin with the notion that the rewards of Heaven justify everything that man can know about God's plan. *Paradise* is a celebration and vindication of the Church and all of its traditions, and of the plan for justice on earth through empire. It is also an opportunity for a citizen poet and visionary to justify himself to the audience of the world.

The Heaven of the Sun provides a satisfying example of Dante's love for the true Faith and the ideal Church. When he and Beatrice ascend to this Heaven, twelve lights carol around them, and one, Saint Thomas

Aquinas, speaks. Aquinas belongs with the wisdom and illumination of the Sun. Mastering Aristotelian thought, he put its processes at the service of Christian theology. Among medieval Scholastic philosophers, he was supreme, and as a member of the Dominican Order (whose standard is a blazing sun), he studied and wrote to combat the heresies of unbelievers. Aquinas speaks not to praise a great university scholastic, however, but to praise Saint Francis of Assisi. Saint Francis was a street preacher, a disciple of the poor, whose spontaneous, instinctive love of God did not move through learned syllogisms. Aquinas tells a lively allegory about Saint Francis and the woman in his life, Lady Poverty. Poverty had been a neglected widow since her first spouse died on the Cross twelve centuries before. Indeed Poverty and Christ were so inseparable that during the Crucifixion she leapt on the Cross, like a wanton lover. Aquinas compares Francis' taking the vow of poverty to a wedding, an orgiastic celebration at which the guests (Saint Francis' followers) all hasten to follow this couple; as an Order, they will spread preaching and conversion throughout the world. This earthy description of Saint Francis' love for an ideal is no blasphemy: It is a charming reminder of how far the saint actually was from sensuality.

Then a Franciscan, Saint Bonaventura, praises the life work of Saint Dominic, founder of the order to which Aquinas belonged. Dominic, says Bonaventura, was the skillful gardener, sent to cull, trim, and order the plot of Faith and bring it new vitality. It is, like Aquinas' remarks about Francis, a graceful compliment, from lights which glow more brightly as they praise others. The ecstatic preacher and the systematizer of doctrine both work God's will and complement each other. At the same time, the reader cannot forget the diatribes of Aquinas and Bonaventura against the state of those orders.

Dante continually arranges his descriptions of Heaven to portray the idea of perfect happiness, although he relentlessly turns to bitter reminders of what human choice has rendered impossible on Earth. He never puts down the lash of satire for long. If *Paradise* is the happy conclusion of a comedy, it is also filled with astringent reminders that human history is a process of social and moral decay, much like the image of the Old Man of Crete in *Inferno* 14, which starts with a golden head and ends with rotting feet. At points Dante is apocalyptic about this decay, and he foretells destruction for his sinful age. He also implies that one day a strong figure will punish those selfish wrongdoers and usher in an age of justice.

Despite his outcries as an embittered satirist and doomsayer, Dante knows that both sacred and secular history are processes of God's justice, even when they seem to be operating at cross-purposes. In the Heaven of

Mercury, Dante interviews Justinian, the Roman Emperor and codifier of law, who outlines the historic progress of the Empire. For Justinian, history is the flight of God's sacred eagle. He describes the earliest tribes in Italy, the Punic Wars, and the emperors. Justinian's most startling point is that the highest privilege of Roman justice was the punishment of Christ. The Crucifixion was a legal act, conducted by duly constituted Roman authority, with Pontius Pilate as the agent. It made the Redemption possible. At the same time, as Beatrice will later explain, the legality of the act under Roman law did not remove the need to avenge what had been done to Christ's person, so, somewhat paradoxically, the destruction of Jerusalem was also justified. The path of Divine Justice moved from ancient Rome to the Holy Roman Empire, thanks to Charlemagne, but that magnificent progress has fallen to puny, contemptible heirs, as the Guelphs and Ghibellines of Dante's time continually ruin that justice with their feuding.

Dante's view of the workings of Divine Justice comes with surprises, as when he puts in the Heaven of Jove one Rhipeus, whom Vergil in the *Aeneid* called the most just among the Trojans. Presumably, Rhipeus was a pagan. That he should be in Heaven and the author who wrote about him in Hell is an irony, but Dante means to emphasize the presence of an appetite for justice in the Trojan line even before it settled in Italy.

If the ways of Justice can seem mysterious, Dante had no doubt that they would someday set in balance all the wrongs he had suffered. In Hell, Dante's anger at old enemies sometimes made him spiteful and almost pruriently interested in their pain. He paid particular attention to the part of Hell where barratry, the crime of making personal profit out of public trust, is punished by immersion in a pit of boiling tar. The episode is personal, for Dante was convicted and sentenced to exile on charges of barratry. For all the thrashing about among devils and damned souls in the pit of barrators, not so much as a drop of tar touches the poet. That is his answer to the capricious charges against him.

By placing his fictional journey in 1300, several years before the beginning of the political turmoil in Florence which resulted in his exile, Dante was able to present himself as a pilgrim ignorant of what is to come. This allows the heavenly hosts to refer to his coming suffering as an unjust but transient ordeal. It is a powerful response to his oppressors, because it allows him to assert the righteousness of his own cause and the maliciousness of his enemies through voices which are not to be contradicted, because their foreknowledge comes from the Divine Presence. The highest and most justified reaction to his future sufferings will come when Dante sees how little they amount to in the eye of eternity.

Dante's self-justification in *Paradise* shows a legitimate holy pride in ancestry and a certainty about his own destiny, despite the disgrace which is brewing for him. In the Heaven of Mars, the souls of those who died for the Faith form a cross. One of them, Dante's great-great-grandfather Cacciaguida, reminds him of the simple and virtuous old stock from which he is descended, in a line extending back to ancient Roman times. Cacciaguida hails Dante as a solitary continuation of this earlier nobility, then names clearly what had been hinted about in Hell and Purgatory: exile, poverty, a life at tables and under roofs not his own. Cacciaguida instructs Dante not to temper so much as a word, but to be a gadfly to degenerate Florence as Justice works its way.

Paradise is always ascending toward the vision of God, at which paradoxically it will evaporate, because it is only a human artifact. Actually, Dante is given three manifestations of God's presence. In the *Primum Mobile*, he sees God symbolically as a point of light surrounded by nine rings, each ring representing an order of angels. These nine rings of angels are in pointed contrast to the geocentric world, where the most slowly moving sphere, that of the Moon, is closest to the corruptible center. Here, as Beatrice explains, the fastest and brightest angelic circle, that of the Seraphim, is closest to the point of light. The definition of God as an indivisible point of light may seem unusual, given the traditions of a transcendent, all-encompassing Divinity. Dante was familiar with a definition of God as a sphere whose center is everywhere and whose circumference is nowhere, a concept which neatly implies the traditional idea of God's absolute and indivisible simplicity and His absolute interminability and simultaneity. The image of the point of light and the concentric circles of angels is perhaps as close as the human intelligence can come through symbols to understanding God's essence.

The image of God which Dante is given when he enters the Empyrean is a product of faith and revelation; it is the closest Dante can come directly to God, and this is the image with which *The Divine Comedy* must end. The Empyrean contains the souls of the Blessed on ascending tiers of thrones arranged to form petals of a white rose, as they will appear on Judgment Day. With the rose, a symbol of Divine Love, Dante moves finally beyond time and space in a blinding brightness as a river of Divine Grace pours from an incalculable height. In the center of the rose is a circle of light, the glory of God. It is time now for the final vision, but Dante discovers that Beatrice has left him to take her place among the Blessed. She has sent the great mystic and contemplative Saint Bernard to be his final guide. Doctrine and revelation, which Beatrice represented, have advanced as far as they can. Only ecstasy can go beyond that.

Under Bernard's direction, Dante's journey ends where it was first conceived, for there are the Virgin, and Lucia, whom the Virgin had sent to Beatrice, who in turn summoned Vergil to aid Dante in the descent to Hell. Now Saint Bernard prays for Mary's intercession, so that they can look at God without the instruments of metaphor or symbol. It is, as Dante says, the end of all yearning, satisfying and rendering obsolete the last vestiges of desire in the soul. In one mystical moment, Dante sees all creation held together by love. Then he sees three circles, each one a different color, occupying one space. It is the Trinity. The first two circles (the Father and the Son) reflect on each other, and the third (the Holy Ghost) seems a flame coming equally from the first two. It is a vision beyond logic and intellect. In trying to encompass it, Dante falls, like Icarus, back to his everyday human self. Dante ends with the remark that, whatever the limitations of his own understanding, Love was at the heart of what he saw, that same Love which moves the sun and the stars.

Other literary forms · Dante's prose works are not usually taken as major literary achievements in themselves, although they provide many useful sidelights and clarifications to a reader of *The Divine Comedy*. Dante entitled the work *Commedia*. It was Boccaccio, forty years after Dante's death, who called the work *La divina commedia*, the name by which it is commonly known. *Il convivio* (c. 1307; *The Banquet*, 1903) was probably written between 1304 and 1307. An unfinished work of some seventy thousand words in Italian prose, it is a commentary on three canzones or odes in which the poet proposes a theory of allegory for moral readings of his poetic compositions, so that it will be clear that virtue, not passion, is the topic. A digressive apologia, *The Banquet* is a mine of information about medieval literary culture. *De vulgari eloquentia* (c. 1306; English translation, 1890), a Latin prose work of nearly twelve thousand words, was probably composed in the period from 1304 to 1306. It is believed to be the first study ever written about vernacular language and poetic style and contains fascinating conjectures about the origin of language, Romance linguistics, verse forms, metrics, and poetic sounds. *De monarchia* (c. 1313; *On World Government*) is a Latin prose work of nearly eighteen thousand words, probably written in 1312 and 1313; it is a series of arguments for world rule unified under the Holy Roman Empire. Dante's explanations of his ideas about the separate but complementary functions of Church and State are particularly valuable. Only a few of Dante's letters survive, but several of them contain seminal passages of Dantean thought.

Many of Dante's lyrics are probably lost forever, but if the eighty or so miscellaneous ones attributed to him are a fair sampling of his efforts, he put his finest in *The New Life*. Many of these smaller poems show only average craftsmanship and are interesting because they reveal a poet who actively participated in his society. Some of the sonnets are exchanges of opinions with friends; six are part of an invective, a contest both socially and intellectually (which was common then), between Dante and Forese Donati. There are love poems to various ladies, some of them real individuals, others clearly allegorical. The lyrics show a very human poet, playful and experimental, heated by anger and love, embittered by exile.

Select works other than poetry

NONFICTION: *Epistolae*, c. 1300-1321 (English translation, 1902); *De vulgari eloquentia*, c. 1306 (English translation, 1890); *Il convivio*, c. 1307 (*The Banquet*, 1903); *De monarchia*, c. 1313 (English translation, 1890; also known as *Monarchy*, 1954; better known as *On World Government*, 1957); "Epistola X," c. 1316 (English translation, 1902); *Eclogae*, 1319 (*Eclogues*, 1902); *Quaestio de aqua et terra*, 1320 (English translation, 1902); *Translation of the Latin Works of Dante Alighieri*, 1904; *Literary Criticism of Dante Alighieri*, 1973.

Thomas A. Van

Bibliography · Charles E. Singleton's edition of *The Divine Comedy*, 1970-1975, is the best available to English readers. It includes Dante's original and Singleton's translation and commentary. The standard biography is Michele Barbi, *Life of Dante*, 1960. Also helpful are Dorothy L. Sayers, *Introductory Papers on Dante*, 1954, and *Further Papers on Dante*, 1957. More recent studies useful for background are Rachel Jacoff, ed., *The Cambridge Companion to Dante*, 1993, and Peter Dronke, *Dante and Medieval Latin Traditions*, 1986. Studies of Dante's works might begin with T. S. Eliot's seminal essay, *Dante*, 1929, and work through Charles Williams, *The Figure of Beatice*, 1943, and Eric Auerbach, *Dante: Poet of the Secular World*, 1961. Singleton's Dante Studies series, *Comedia: Elements of Structure*, 1954, *Journey to Beatrice*, 1957, and *An Essay on the Vita Nuova*, 1957, are important older studies. More recent valuable studies include John Freccero, *Dante: The Poetics of Conversion*, 1986; Teodolinda Barolini, *Dante's Poets: Textuality and Truth in the Comedy*, 1984; and Anthony K. Cassell, *Dante's Fearful Art of Justice*, 1984. On works other than the *Commedia*, see J. F. Took, *Dante: Lyric Poet and Philosopher*, 1990. A good collection of a variety of critical perspectives is Harold Bloom, ed., *Dante: Modern Critical Views*, 1986.

EMILY DICKINSON

Born: Amherst, Massachusetts; December 10, 1830
Died: Amherst, Massachusetts; May 15, 1886

Poetry · *Poems,* 1890 · *Poems: Second Series,* 1891 · *Poems: Third Series,* 1896 · *The Single Hound,* 1914 · *Further Poems,* 1929 · *Unpublished Poems,* 1936 · Bolts of Melody, 1945 · The Poems of Emily Dickinson, 1955 (3 volumes; Thomas H. Johnson, editor) · *The Complete Poems of Emily Dickinson,* 1960 (Thomas H. Johnson, editor)

Achievements · As surely as William Faulkner and Ernest Hemingway, different as they were, brought American fiction into the twentieth century, so Walt Whitman and Emily Dickinson brought about a revolution in American poetry. By the mid-nineteenth century, American lyric poetry had matured to an evenly polished state. Edgar Allan Poe, Ralph Waldo Emerson, and Herman Melville were creating poetry of both power and precision, but poetry in this country was still hampered by certain limiting assumptions about the nature of literary language, about the value of regular rhythm, meter, and rhyme, and about imagery as ornamental rather than organic. Were the medium not to become sterile and conventionalized, poets had to expand the possibilities of the form.

Library of Congress

Into this situation came Dickinson and Whitman, poets who—except in their commitment to writing a personalized poetry unlike anything the nineteenth century had thus far read—differ as widely as do Faulkner and Hemingway. Whitman rid himself of the limitations of regular meter entirely. Identifying with the common man, Whitman attempted to make him a hero who could encompass the universe. He was a poet of the open road; Whitman journeyed along, accumulating experience and attempting to unite himself with the world around him. For him, life was dynamic and progressive. Dickinson, however, was the poet of exclusion, of the shut door. She accepted the limitations of rhyme and meter, and worked endless variations on one basic pattern, exploring the nuances that the framework would allow. No democrat, she constructed for herself a set of aristocratic images. No traveler, she stayed at home to examine small fragments of the world she knew. For Dickinson life was kinesthetic; she recorded the impressions of experience on her nerves and on her soul. Rather than being linear and progressive, it was circular: "My business is circumference," she wrote, and she often described the arcs and circles of experience. As carefully as Whitman defined himself by inclusion, Dickinson defined herself and her experience by exclusion, by what she was not. Whitman was a poet of explanation; Dickinson, having rejected expansion, exploited suggestion.

Different as they were, however, they are America's greatest lyric poets. Although Dickinson was barely understood or appreciated in her own lifetime, she now seems a central figure—at once firmly in a tradition and, at the same time, a breaker of tradition, a revolutionary who freed American poetry for modern thought and technique.

Biography · "Renunciation is a piercing virtue," wrote Emily Dickinson, and her life can be seen as a series of renunciations. Born in 1830 of a prominent Amherst family, she rarely left the town, except for time spent in Boston and trips to Washington and Philadelphia. She attended the Amherst Academy and Mount Holyoke Female Seminary. Although she was witty and popular, she set herself apart from the other girls by her refusal to be converted to the conventional Christianity of the town. Her life was marked by a circle of close friends and of family: a stern and humorless father; a mother who suffered a long period of illness and who was cared for my Emily; her sister Lavinia, who likewise never married and remained in the family home; and her brother Austin, who married Sue Gilbert Dickinson and whose forceful personality, like that of his wife, affected the family while Emily Dickinson lived, and whose affair with Mrs. Todd, the editor of the poems, precipitated family squabbles that affected their publication.

Additionally, there was a series of men—for it almost seems that Dickinson took what she called her "preceptors" one at a time—who formed a sort of emotional resource for her. The first of these was Samuel Bowles, the editor of the neighboring Springfield, Massachusetts, *Republican*, which published some of her poetry. Charles Wadsworth was the minister of a Philadelphia church; a preacher famous for his eloquence, he preached one Sunday when Dickinson was in Philadelphia, and afterward they corresponded for several years. In 1862, however, he and his family moved from Philadelphia to the West Coast. Dickinson immediately sent four of her poems to Thomas Wentworth Higginson, at the *Atlantic Monthly*, for his advice, and they began a long friendship; although Higginson was never convinced that Dickinson was a finished poet, he was a continuing mentor. Finally, late in life, Dickinson met Judge Otis Lord, and for a time it seemed as if they were to be married; this was her one explicitly romantic friendship, but the marriage never took place. There were also less intense friendships with women, particularly Mabel Todd, who, despite her important role in Dickinson's life, never actually met her, but, like the writer Helen Hunt Jackson, was one of the few to accept Dickinson's poetry as it was written.

The nature of the relationships with the "preceptors" and their effect on the poetry is a matter of much controversy. It is complicated by three famous and emotional "Master" letters which Dickinson wrote between 1858 and 1862 (the dates are partly conjectural). Who the master was, is uncertain. For Johnson, Dickinson's editor, her great influence was Wadsworth, and although their relationship was always geographically distant. His who was the great love. His moving to California was the emotional crisis that occasioned the great flood-years of poetry—366 poems in 1862 alone—according to Johnson. For Richard B. Sewall, author of the standard biography, Bowles was the master.

Whatever the case, it is true that after 1862, Dickinson rarely left her house, except for a necessary visit to Boston where she was treated for eye trouble. She wore white dresses and with more and more frequency refused to see visitors, usually remaining upstairs, listening to the conversations and entering, if at all, by calling down the stairs or by sending in poems or other tokens of her participation. She became known as the "Myth of Amherst," and from this image is drawn the popular notion of the eccentric old maid that persists in the imagination of many of her readers today. Yet it is clear that whatever the limits of her actual experience, Dickinson lived life on the emotional level with great intensity. Her poetry is dense with vividly rendered emotions and observations, and she transformed the paucity of her outward life into the richness of her inner life.

Richard Wilbur has suggested that Dickinson suffered three great deprivations in her life: of a lover, of publication and fame, and of a God in whom she could believe. Although she often questioned a world in which such deprivations were necessary, she more frequently compensated, as Wilbur believes, by calling her "privation good, rendering it positive by renunciation." That she lived in a world of distances, solitude, and renunciation her biography makes clear; that she turned that absence into beauty is the testimony of her poetry.

Analysis · During her lifetime, only seven of Emily Dickinson's poems were published, most of them edited to make them more conventional. After Dickinson's death, her sister Lavinia discovered about nine hundred poems, over half of the 1,775 poems that now compose the Dickinson canon. She took these to a family friend, Mrs. Mabel Loomis Todd, who, with Dickinson's friend Thomas Wentworth Higginson, published 115 of the poems in 1890. Together they published a second group of 166 in 1891, and Mrs. Todd alone edited a third series in 1896. Unfortunately, Mrs. Todd and Col. Higginson continued the practice of revision that had begun with the first seven published poems, smoothing the rhymes and meter, revising the diction, and generally regularizing the poetry.

In 1914, Dickinson's niece, Martha Dickinson Bianchi, published the first of several volumes of the poetry she was to edit. Although she was more scrupulous about preserving Dickinson's language and intent, several editorial problems persisted, and the body of Dickinson's poetry remained fragmented and often altered. In 1950, the Dickinson literary estate was given to Harvard University, and Thomas H. Johnson began his work of editing, arranging, and presenting the text. In 1955, he produced the variorum edition, 1,775 poems arranged in an attempt at chronological order, given such evidence as handwriting changes and incorporation of the poems in letters, and including all variations of the poems. In 1960, he chose one form of each poem as the final version and published the resulting collection as *The Complete Poems of Emily Dickinson.* Johnson's text and numbering system are accepted as the standard. His job was thorough, diligent, and imaginative. This is not to say, however, that his decisions about dates or choices among variants must be taken as final. Many scholars have other opinions, and since Dickinson herself apparently did not make final choices, there is no reason to accept every decision Johnson made.

One of Emily Dickinson's poems (#1129) begins, "Tell all the Truth but tell it slant," and the oblique and often enigmatic rendering of Truth is the theme of Dickinson's poetry. Its motifs often recur: love, death, poetry, beauty, nature, immortality, the self; but such abstractions do not indicate the broad and rich changes that Dickinson obliquely rings on the truths she tells.

Dickinson's truth is, in the broadest sense, a religious truth. Formally, her poetry plays endless variations on the Protestant hymn meters that she knew from her youthful experiences in church. Her reading in contemporary poetry was limited, and the form she knew best was the iambic of hymns: common meter (with its alternating tetrameter and trimeter lines), long meter (four lines of tetrameter), and short meter (four of trimeter) became the framework of her poetry. That static form, however, could not contain the energy of her work, and the rhythms and rhymes are varied, upset, and broken to accommodate the feeling of her lines. The predictable patterns of hymns were not for Dickinson, who delighted in off-rhyme, consonance, and, less frequently, eye-rhyme.

Dickinson is a religious poet more than formally, but her thematic sense of religion lies not in her assurance, but in her continual questioning of God, in her attempt to define his nature and that of his world. Although she is always a poet of definition, straightforward definition was too direct for her: "The Riddle we can guess/ We speedily despise," she wrote. Her works often begin, "It was not" or "It was like," with the poem being an oblique attempt to define the "it." "I like to see it lap the Miles" (#585) is a typical Dickinson riddle poem. Like many, it begins with "it," a pronoun without an antecedent, so that the reader must join in the process of discovery and definition. The riddle is based on an extended metaphor; the answer to the riddle, a train, is compared to a horse; but in the poem both tenor (train) and vehicle (horse) are unstated. Meanwhile, what begins with an almost cloying tone, the train as an animal lapping and licking, moves through subtle gradations of attitude until the train stops at the end "docile and omnipotent." This juxtaposition of incongruous adjectives, like the coupling of unlikely adjective and noun, is another of Dickinson's favorite devices; just as the movement of the poem has been from the animal's (and train's) tame friendliness to its assertive power, so these adjectives crystallize the paradox.

"It sifts from Leaden Sieves" (#311), another riddle poem, also begins with an undefined "it," and again the movement of the poem and its description of the powerfully effacing strength of the snow, which is the subject of the poem and the answer to the riddle, is from apparently innocent beauty through detailed strength to a quietly understated dread. The emotional movement in the famous riddle poem "A Route of Evanescence" (#1463) is less striking, since the poet maintains the same awed appreciation of the hummingbird from beginning to end; but the source of that awe likewise moves from the bird's ephemeral beauty to its power.

Riddling becomes less straightforward, but no less central, in such a representative Dickinson poem as "It was not Death, for I stood up" (#510), in which many of her themes and techniques appear. The first third of the poem, two stanzas of the six, suggest what the "it" is not: death, night, frost, or fire. Each is presented in a couplet, but even in those pairs of lines, Dickinson manages to disconcert her reader. It is not death, for the persona is standing upright, the difference between life and death reduced to one of posture. Nor is it night, for the bells are chiming noon—but Dickinson's image for that fact is also unnatural. The bells are mouths, their clappers tongues, which are "Put out"; personification here does not have the effect of making the bells more human, but of making them grotesque, breaking down as it does the barriers between such normally discrete worlds as the mechanical and the human, a distinction that Dickinson often dissolves. Moreover, the notion of the bells sticking out their tongues suggests their contemptuous attitude toward people. In stanza two, it is not frost because hot winds are crawling on the persona's flesh. The hackneyed phrase is reversed, so it is not coolness, but heat that makes flesh crawl, and not the flesh itself that crawls, but the winds upon it; nor is it fire, for the persona's marble feet "Could keep a Chancel, cool." Again, the persona is dehumanized, now grotesquely marble. While accomplishing this, Dickinson has also begun her inclusion of sense-data, pervasive in the first part of the poem, so that the confrontation is not only intellectual and emotional but physical as well.

The second third of the poem changes the proportions. Although the experience is not actually any of the four things she has mentioned above, it is like them all; but now death, the first, is given seven lines, night three, frost only two, and fire is squeezed out altogether. It is like death because she has, after all, seen figures arranged like her own; now her life is "shaven,/ And fitted to a frame." It is like night when everything that "ticked"—again mechanical imagery for a natural phenomenon—has stopped, and like frosts, which in early autumn morns "Repeal the Beating Ground." Her vocabulary startles once more: the ground beats with life, but the frost can void it; "repeal" suggests the law, but nature's laws are here completely nullified.

Finally, in the last stanza, the metaphor shifts completely, and the experience is compared to something new: drowning at sea. It is "stopless" but "cool"; the agony that so often marks Dickinson's poetry may be appropriate to the persona, but nothing around her, neither people nor nature, seems to note it. Most important, there is neither chance nor means of rescue; there is no report of land. Any of these conditions would justify despair, but for the poet, this climatic experience is so chaotic that even despair is not justified, for there is no word of land to despair of reaching.

Thus, one sees many of Dickinson's typical devices at work: the tightly patterned form, based on an undefined subject, the riddle-like puzzle of defining that subject, the shifting of mood from apparent observation to horror, the grotesque images couched in emotionally distant language. All this delineates that experience, that confrontation—with God, with nature, with the self, with one's own mind—which is the center of Dickinson's best poetry. Whether her work looks inward or outward, the subject matter is a confrontation leading to awareness, and part of the terror is that for Dickinson there is never any mediating middle ground; she confronts herself in relation to an abyss beyond. There is no society, no community to make that experience palatable in any but the most grotesque sense of the word, the awful tasting of uncontrollable fear.

Dickinson often questions the nature of the universe; she senses that God is present only in one's awareness of his absence. She shares Robert Frost's notion that God has tricked humankind, but while for Frost, God's trick is in the nature of creation, for Dickinson it is equally in God's refusal to answer our riddles about that creation. She writes of the "eclipse" of God, and for Dickinson, it is God himself who has caused the obscurity. The customary movement in her explicitly religious poetry is from apparent affirmation to resounding doubt. Poem #338 begins with the line "I know that He exists." While Dickinson rarely uses periods even at the end of her poems, here the first line ends with one: a short and complete affirmation of God's existence, but an affirmation that remains unqualified for only that one line. God is not omnipresent, but exists "Somewhere—in Silence"; Dickinson then offers a justification for God's absence: his life is so fine that he has hidden it from humans who are unworthy. The second stanza offers two more justifications: he is playing with people, and one will be that much happier at the blissful surprise one has earned. Yet the play, in typical Dickinson fashion, is a "fond Ambush," and both the juxtaposition of incongruous words and the reader's understanding that only villains engage in ambush indicate how quickly and how brutally the tone of the poem is changing.

The last half begins with "But," and indeed 256 of Dickinson's poems, nearly fifteen percent, have a coordinate conjunction as the first word of the middle line—a hinge that links the deceptive movement of the first half with the oblique realization that takes place in the second. The lines of poem #338 then become heavily alliterative, slowing the reader with closely linked, plosive *p*'s before she begins the final question: "Should the glee—glaze—/ In Death's—stiff—stare." The quasi subjunctive, another consistent poetic stance in Dickinson, cannot mask the fact that there is no open possibility here, for death must come, the glee will glaze. Then the fun—it is God's fun of which she writes—will look too expensive, the jest will "Have crawled too far!" Although the last sentence is in the form of a question, the poem closes with an end mark stronger than the opening period, an exclamation point which leaves no doubt as to the tone the poem takes.

This same movement appears in Dickinson's other overtly religious poems. Poem #501 ("This World is not Conclusion.") likewise begins with a clear statement followed by a period and then moves rapidly toward doubt. Here God is a "Species" who "stands beyond." People are shown as baffled by the riddle of the universe, grasping at any "twig of Evidence." Man asks "a Vane, the way," indicating the inconstancy of that on which people rely and punning on "in vain." Whatever answer is received is only a narcotic, which "cannot still the Tooth/ That nibbles at the soul." Again, in "It's easy to invent a Life" (#724), God seems to be playing with people, and although the poem begins with humankind's birth as God's invention, it ends with death as God's simply "leaving out a Man." In poem #1601, "Of God we ask one favor," the favor requested is that he forgive humanity, but it is clear that humans do not know for what they ask forgiveness and, as in Frost's "Forgive, O Lord," it is clear that the greater crime is not humankind's but God's. In "I never lost as much but twice" (#49), an early but accomplished work, God is "Burglar! Banker—Father!" robbing the poet, making her poor.

One large group of Dickinson's poems, of which these are only a sample, suggests her sense of religious deprivation. Her transformation of the meter and rhythm of hymns into her own songs combines with the overt questioning of the ultimate meaning of her existence to make her work religious. As much, however, as Dickinson pretends to justify the ways of her "eclipsed" God, that justification never lasts. If God is Father, he is also Burglar. If God in his omnipotence finds it easy to invent a life, in his caprice he finds it just as easy to leave one out.

Dickinson just as persistently questions nature, which was for her an equivocal manifestation of God's power and whims. Although there are occasional poems in which her experience of nature is exuberant ("I taste a liquor never brewed," #214, for example), in most of her work the experience is one of terror. A synecdochist rather than a symbolist, she describes and confronts a part of nature, that scene representing the whole. For her nineteenth century opposite, Whitman, the world was one of possibilities, of romantic venturing forth to project oneself onto the world and form an organic relationship with it. For Dickinson, the human and the natural give way to the inorganic; nature is, if like a clock, not so in its perfect design and workings, but in its likeliness to wind down and stop.

"I started Early–Took my Dog" (#520) is characteristic in its treatment of nature, although uncharacteristic in the romantic venturing forth of the persona. For the first third of the poem, she seems to be in control: she starts early, takes her pet, and visits the sea. The sea is treated with conventional and rather pretty metaphor; it is a house with a basement full of mermaids. Even here, however, is a suggestion that something is amiss. The frigates extend "Hempen Hands"; the ropes that moor the ships are characteristically personified, but the substitution of "hempen" for the similar sounding and expected "helpin'" (the missing *g* itself a delusive familiarity) suggests that the hands will entwine, not aid, the poet. As so often in Dickinson, the natural world seems to be staring at her, as if she is the chief actor in an unfolding drama, and suddenly, with the coordinate conjunction "but," the action begins. The sea is personified as a man who would attack her. She flees. He pursues, reaching higher and higher on her clothes, until finally she achieves the solid ground, and the sea, like a docile and omnipotent train, unconcerned but "Mighty," bows and withdraws, his power there for another day.

Whenever Dickinson looks at nature, the moment becomes a confrontation. Although she is superficially within the Puritan tradition of observing nature and reading its message, Dickinson differs not only in the chilling message that she reads, but also because nature refuses to remain passive; it is not simply an open book to be read–for books remain themselves–but active and aggressive; personification suggests its assertive malevolence. In #348 ("I dreaded that first Robin, so"), the initial part of the poem describes the poet's fear: Spring is horrible; it shouts, mangles, and pierces. What Dickinson finally manages is merely a peace with spring; she makes herself "Queen of Calvary," and in deference to that, nature salutes her and leaves her alone.

The same accommodation with nature occurs in #986, "A narrow Fellow in the Grass," where the subject, a snake that she encounters, is first made to seem familiar and harmless. Then the poet suggests that she has made her peace with "Several of Nature's People," and she feels for them "a transport/ Of cordiality," although one expects a more ecstatic noun than cordiality after a sense of transport. Dickinson concludes with a potent description of her true feelings about the snake, "Zero at the Bone," a phrase which well reflects her emotion during most confrontations, internal or external.

One of Dickinson's finest poems, #1624 ("Apparently with no surprise"), a poem from late in her life, unites her attitudes toward nature and God. Even as Frost does in "Design," Dickinson examines one destructive scene in nature and uses it to represent a larger pattern; like Frost, she sees two possibilities for both microcosm and macrocosm: accident or dark design. The first two lines of her short poem describe the "happy Flower." The personified flower is unsurprised by its sudden death: "The Frost beheads it at its play–/ In accidental power–/ The blonde Assassin passes on–." In common with many American writers, she reverses the conventional association of white with purity; here the killer, the frost, is blonde. While she suggests that the power may be accidental, in itself not a consoling thought, the two lines framing that assertion severely modify it, for beheading is rarely accidental; nor do assassins attain their power by chance.

Whichever the case, accident or design, there is finally little significant difference, for nothing in the world pays attention to what has happened. "The Sun proceeds unmoved," an unusual pun, since unmoved has the triple meaning of unconcerned, stationary, and without a prime mover; it measures off the time for a God who does approve.

Thus, when Dickinson turns her vision outward, she looks at essential reality translated, often appallingly, into human terms. The alternative vision for Dickinson is inward, at her own self, and despite the claims of her imperial language, what she sees there is just as chaotic and chilling as what she sees without. "The Soul selects her own Society," she writes (#303), and she makes that society a "divine Majority." "I'm Nobody," another Dickinson poem begins (#288); but in her poetry the explicit movement is from no one to someone, from the self as beggar to the self as monarch: empress or queen. Out of the deprivation of her small society, out of the renunciation of present pleasures, she makes a majority that fills her world with aristocratic presence. Yet, for all that affirmation, the poems that look directly inward suggest something more; her assurance is ambiguously modified, her boasting bravado is dissipated.

Occasionally, Dickinson's poetry justifies her internal confusion in conventional terms. Poem #435, "Much Madness is divinest Sense," makes the familiar assertion that, although the common majority have enough power to label nonconformists as insane and dangerous, often what appears as madness is sense, "divinest Sense–/ To a discerning Eye." Usually, however, her poetry of the mind is more unsettling, her understanding more personal. "I Felt a Funeral, in my Brain" (#280) and "'Twas like a Maelstrom, with a notch" (#414), employing the drowning imagery of "It was not Death," are the most piercing of Dickinson's poems about the death of reason, the chaotic confrontation with the instability within. They also indicate the central ambiguity that these poems present, for the metaphor that Dickinson favors for the death of reason is literal, physical death: the tenor, insanity; the vehicle, death. Yet one is never quite sure whether it might not be the other way around: the central subject death; the metaphoric vehicle, the death of reason. Through this uncertainty, these poems achieve a double-edged vitality, a shifting of idea and vehicle, foreground and background.

The awareness of one's tenuous grasp on one's own reason seems clearest in "I felt a Funeral, in my Brain," for there the funeral is explicitly "in," although not necessarily "of," the speaker's brain. The metaphor is developed through a series of comparisons with the funeral rites, each introduced by "and," each arriving with increasing haste. At first the monotony of the mourners' tread almost causes sense to break through, but instead the mind reacts by going numb. Eventually the funeral metaphor gives way to that of a shipwreck—on the surface, an illogical shift, but given the movement of the poem, a continuation of the sense of confusion and abandonment. The last stanza returns to the dominant metaphor, presenting a rapid series of events, the first of which is "a Plank in Reason" breaking, plunging the persona—and the reader—back into the funeral imagery of a coffin dropping into a grave. The poem concludes with "And Finished knowing—then," an ambiguous finish suggesting both the end of her life and of her reasoning, thus fusing the two halves of the metaphor. These two readings of the last line do not exhaust its possibilities, for there is another way to read it: the speaker finished with "knowing" not as a gerund object, but as the participial modifier, so that even at the moment of her death, she dies knowing. Since for Dickinson awareness is the most chilling of experiences, it is an appropriately horrible alternative: not the end of knowing, but the end while knowing.

Death is not merely metaphorical for Dickinson; it is the greatest subject of her work. Perhaps her finest lyrics are on this topic, which she surveyed with a style at once laconic and acute, a tone of quiet terror conveyed through understatement and indirection. Her power arises from the tension between her formal and tonal control and the emotional intensity of what she writes. She approaches death from two perspectives, adopts two stances: the persona as the grieving onlooker, attempting to continue with life—her own faith tested by the experience of watching another die—and the persona as the dying person.

In such poems as "How many times these low feet staggered" (#187), where the dead person has "soldered mouth," and "There's been a Death, in the Opposite House" (#389), where the windows of the house open like "a Pod," the description of death is mechanical, as if a machine has simply stopped. The reaction of the onlookers is first bewilderment, then the undertaking of necessary duties, and finally an awful silence in which they are alone with their realization of what has occurred. Poem #1100 ("The last Night that She lived") best illustrates all of these attitudes. It oscillates between the quietly dying person—whose death is gentle, on a common night, who "mentioned—and forgot," who "struggled scarce—/ Consented"—and those, equally quiet but less capable of giving consent, who watch the death occur. First there is the conventional idea that they who watch see life differently: death becomes a great light that italicizes events. Yet as the poem continues with the onlookers' random comings and goings and their feelings of guilt over continuing to live, there is little sense that their awareness is complete. After the death, Dickinson provides one stanza, neatly summarizing the final understanding: "And We—We placed the Hair," the repeated pronoun, the little gasp for breath and hint of self-dramatization, fills part of the time with what must be done. Then there is nothing left to do or to be said: "And then an awful leisure was/ Belief to regulate." The strange linking of "awful" with "leisure," the disruption of syntax at the line break, and the notion that the best belief can do is regulate leisure, all suggest in two lines the confusion and disruption for those who remain alive.

By consensus the greatest of all Dickinson's poems, "Because I could not stop for Death" (#712) explores death from the second perspective, as do such poems as "I Heard a Fly buzz—when I died" (#465) and "I died for Beauty (#449), in which one who has died for beauty and one who has died for truth agree, with John Keats, that truth and beauty are the same—the poet adding the ironic commentary that their equality lies in the fact that the names of both are being covered up by moss.

"Because I could not stop for Death" unites love and death, for death comes to the persona in the form of a gentleman caller. Her reaction is neither haste to meet him, nor displeasure at his arrival. She has time to put away her "labor and . . . leisure"; he is civil. The only hint in the first two stanzas of what is really occurring is the presence of Immortality, and yet that presence, although not unnoticed, is as yet unfelt by the persona. The third stanza brings the customary metaphor of life as a journey and the convention of one's life passing before his eyes as he dies: from youth, through maturity, to sunset. Here, however, two of the images work against the surface calm: the children out for recess do not play, but strive; the grain is said to be gazing. "Grazing" might be the expected word, although even that would be somewhat out of place, but "gazing" both creates unfulfilled aural expectations and gives the sense of the persona as only one actor in a drama that many are watching.

Again, as is common in Dickinson, the poem is hinged by a coordinate conjunction in the exact middle. This time the conjunction is "Or," as the speaker realizes not that she is passing the sun, but that "He passed us."

The metaphoric journey through life continues; it is now night, but the emotions have changed from the calm of control to fright. The speaker's "Zero at the Bone" is literal, for her clothing, frilly and light, while appropriate for a wedding, is not so for the funeral that is occurring. The final stop—for, like the first two stanzas, the last two are motionless—is before the grave, "a House that seemed/ A Swelling of the Ground." The swelling ground also suggests pregnancy, but this earth bears death, not life. The last stanza comments that even though the persona has been dead for centuries, all that time seems shorter than the one moment of realization of where her journey must ultimately end. Death, Dickinson's essential metaphor and subject, is seen in terms of a moment of confrontation. Absence thus becomes the major presence, confusion the major ordering principle.

Dickinson's poetry is at times sentimental, the extended metaphors occasionally too cute, the riddling tone sometimes too coy. Like any poet, that is, she has limitations, and because her poetry is so consistent throughout her life, those limitations may be more obvious than in a poet who changes more noticeably. They do not, however, diminish her stature. If she found her place in American literature only decades after her death, it is a place she will not forfeit. Her importance is, of course, partly historical: with Whitman she changed the shape and direction of American poetry, creating and fulfilling poetic potentials that make her a poet beyond her century. Her importance, however, is much greater than that. The intensity with which she converted emotional loss and intellectual questioning into art, the wit and energy of her work, mark the body of her poetry as among the finest America has yet produced.

Other literary forms · In addition to her poetry, Emily Dickinson left behind voluminous correspondence. Because she was so rarely out of Amherst—and in her later life so rarely left her house—much of her contact with others took place through letters, many of which include poems. Like her poetry, the letters are witty, epigrammatic, and often enigmatic. They are available in *The Letters of Emily Dickinson* (1958, Thomas H. Johnson and Theodora Ward, editors, 3 volumes).

Select works other than poetry
   NONFICTION: *Letters*, 1894 (2 volumes); *The Letters of Emily Dickinson*, 1958 (3 volumes; Thomas H. Johnson and Theodora Ward, editors).

Howard Faulkner

Bibliography · Among the many important critical and biographical works is Paul Ferlazzo's 1976 introductory-level critical biography *Emily Dickinson*. Another is Cynthia Griffin Wolff's critical biography *Emily Dickinson*, 1988. Another biography is Helen McNeil, *Emily Dickinson*, 1986. Older biographical works include Richard Chase, *Emily Dickinson*, 1951, and T. H. Johnson, *Emily Dickinson: An Interpretive Biography*, 1955. Two books by Millicent Todd Bingham are also useful as source material: *Ancestor's Brocades*, 1945, an account of the early publishing of poems and letters, and *Emily Dickinson's Home: Letters of Edward Dickinson and His Family*, 1955. *Feminist Critics Read Emily Dickinson*, 1983, edited by Suzanne Juhasz, is a collection of essays by some of the most respected feminist scholars in Dickinson studies. Joseph Duchac's *The Poems of Emily Dickinson: An Annotated Guide to Commentary in English, 1978-1989*, 1989 is a helpful source for finding information on individual poems. Other critical works include Judith Farr, ed., *Emily Dickinson: A Collection of Critical Essays*, 1996; David Higgins, *Portrait of Emily Dickinson: The Poet and Her Prose*, 1967; Ruth Miller, *The Poetry of Emily Dickinson*, 1968; Richard B. Sewall, ed., *Emily Dickinson: A Collection of Critical Essays*, 1963; and Albert J. Gelpi, *Emily Dickinson: The Mind of the Poet*, 1965.

JOHN DONNE

Born: London, England; between January 24 and June 19, 1572
Died: London, England; March 31, 1631

Poetry · *An Anatomy of the World: The First Anniversary*, 1611 · *Of the Progress of the Soule: The Second Anniversary*, 1612 · *Poems, by J. D.: With Elegies on the Authors Death*, 1633, 1635, 1639, 1649, 1650, 1654, 1669

Achievements · John Donne was a remarkably influential poet in his day. Despite the fact that it was only after his death that a substantial body of his poetry was published, the elegies and satires (and to a lesser extent the divine poems and the songs and sonnets) had already created a new poetic mode during Donne's lifetime as a result of circulating in manuscript. Thomas Carew, in a memorial elegy published in the first edition of Donne's poems, described him as ruling the "universal monarchy of wit." The poetry of the School of Donne was usually characterized in its own day by its "strong lines." This characterization seems to have meant that Donne and his followers were to be distinguished from the Sons of Ben, the poets influenced by Ben Jonson, chiefly by their experiments with rough meter and conversational syntax; Jonson, however, was also—somewhat confusingly—praised for strong lines. Donne's own characteristic metrics involve lines densely packed with syllables. He makes great use not only of syncope (dropping of an unstressed vowel within a word) and elision (dropping of an unstressed vowel at the juncture between words) but also of a device almost unique to Donne among English poets—synaloepha (speeding up

Library of Congress

of adjacent vowels at the juncture between words with no actual dropping). By hindsight Donne, Edward Lord Herbert of Cherbury, Henry King, George Herbert, John Cleveland, Richard Crashaw, Abraham Cowley, Henry Vaughan, Andrew Marvell, and others of the School of Donne share not only strong lines but also a common fund of imagery. Eschewing for the most part classical allusions, these poets turned to the imagery of everyday life and of the new learning in science and philosophy.

In the middle of the seventeenth century there occurred what T. S. Eliot has memorably described as a "dissociation of sensibility," after which it became increasingly difficult to see Donne's secular and religious values as part of a consistent whole. The beginnings of this attitude were already apparent in Donne's own day; in a letter, for example, he describes *Biathanatos* as the work not of Dr. Donne but of the youthful Jack Donne. Toward the end of the century, the change of perspective is complete when John Dryden describes Donne unsympathetically as one who "perplexes the Minds of the Fair Sex with nice Speculations of philosophy." The Restoration and the eighteenth century had lost Donne's sense of religious commitment and thus scrutinized a style in isolation from the content it intended to express. Donne's poetry was condemned as artificial, and his reputation disappeared almost overnight.

This was the situation when Samuel Johnson wrote the famous strictures on Donne in his "Life of Cowley." That these remarks occur in the *Life of Cowley* is perhaps a commentary on the fallen stature of the earlier poets: Donne did not himself merit individual treatment in *Lives of the Poets* (1779-1781). Conceding that to write like Donne "it was at least necessary to read and think," Johnson describes the wit of the School of Donne–accurately enough–as the "discovery of occult resemblances in things apparently unlike." While many readers of the earlier seventeenth century and of the twentieth century would consider the description high praise, for Johnson it was a condemnation. For him, the "most heterogeneous ideas are yoked by violence together." He popularized the term "Metaphysical poetry" for this yoking; the term had, however, been used earlier, even in Donne's own day.

Donne's stature and influence today are equal to his great stature and wide influence in the seventeenth century, but the attitude represented by Johnson remained the norm for the centuries between. Donne's current prestige is based on values different from those that accounted for his prestige in his own day. The seventeenth century took its religion seriously but understood religion as part of the whole fabric of life. Donne's stature as a preacher was for this reason part of his prestige as a poet. In addition, the fact that he wrote love poetry and sometimes used graphic erotic imagery did not in his own day seem incongruous with his calling as a preacher.

The current century has not, of course, recovered the intense religiosity of the early seventeenth century, but what T. S. Eliot, Ezra Pound, and other poets of their circle had discovered in the 1920's was an aestheticism as intense as this religiosity. Their values naturally led them to praise lyric poetry in preference to epic and to prize intensity of emotion in literary work of all kinds. They disparaged the poetry of John Milton because it was an expression of ideas rather than of feeling and offered Donne as a model and a more appropriate great author for the period. The restoration of Donne's prestige was remarkably complete; but, paradoxically, precisely because the triumph of Donne was so complete, the denigration of Milton never quite occurred. The values that Eliot and others praised in Donne were looked for—and discovered—in Milton as well.

Although Donne was perhaps a more exciting figure during his mid-twentieth century "rediscovery" than he is today, because to appreciate him meant to throw over the eighteenth and nineteenth century allegiance to Milton as the great poet of the language, Donne's stature as a major figure is now assured. Contemporary scholarly opinion has, however, been moving inevitably toward seeing the divine poems as the capstone of his career. Scholarly opinion has, in fact, moved beyond Eliot's position and come to value literary works simply because they have religious content, since intensity of feeling will surely be found in a poetry of religious commitment. This is not a way of appreciating Donne and the Metaphysicals that would have been understood in the seventeenth century.

Biography · Born in St. Nicholas Olave Parish, London, sometime between January 24 and June 19, 1572, John Donne came from a Welsh paternal line (originally Dwn) with some claim to gentility. His father, however, was an ironmonger, although important enough to serve as warden of his professional guild. On his mother's side, Donne's connections were distinguished both for their intellectual attainments and their recusancy—that is, allegiance to the Church of Rome in the face of the Elizabethan Church Settlement. Donne's maternal grandfather was the epigrammatist and playwright John Heywood. A greatgrandfather, John Rastell, was a minor playwright. Two of Donne's uncles were Jesuits who died in exile for their faith, as did his great-uncle Judge William Rastell; and another great-uncle, the monk Thomas Heywood, was executed, having been caught saying mass. Finally, a great-grandmother was the sister of Sir Thomas More, whose skull Donne inherited and very characteristically kept as a *memento mori*. Donne's brother, Henry, died in prison, where he had been sent for harboring a seminary priest; and Donne justifiably said in *Pseudo-Martyr* that no family had suffered more for the Roman Church.

His father died while Donne was still in infancy. His mother married twice more. The step-father of Donne's youth was a prominent physician. At first educated at home by Roman Catholic tutors, in 1584, Donne and his younger brother, Henry, were admitted to Hart Hall, Oxford. While they were a precocious twelve and eleven at the time, they were entered in the register as even younger in order to circumvent the requirement that students of sixteen and over subscribe to the Oath of Supremacy. Donne spent probably three years at Oxford altogether.

Although records are lacking for the next period of Donne's life, one hypothesis is that he spent some of this time in travel abroad. With his brother, Donne eventually took up residence at the Inns of Court to prepare for a legal career. Unsettled in these career plans by the arrest and death of Henry, Donne began serious study of the relative claims of the Anglican and Roman Churches and finally abandoned the study of law entirely.

In 1596, he participated in the Earl of Essex's military expedition to Cadiz. Donne's affability and his growing reputation as a poet—sustained by the private circulation of some of his elegies and lyrics—recommended him to a son of Sir Thomas Egerton who had also participated in the sack of Cadiz; and Egerton, who was Lord Keeper, was persuaded to appoint Donne as his secretary. In this position and also in Parliament, where he served briefly in 1601, he had many opportunities to meet people of note, and he improved his reputation as a poet by composing satires and occasional poems as well as additional lyrics.

In 1601, Donne was already in his late twenties, and, during Christmastide, he contracted a secret marriage with Anne More, the sixteen-year-old niece of Lady Egerton. Since the marriage was contrary to her father's wishes, Donne was imprisoned for his offense; he also permanently lost his position as Egerton's secretary, and the couple were forced to live for several years on the charity of friends and relations. A comment made at the time, sometimes attributed to Donne himself, was, "John Donne, Anne Donne, Undone."

Although his career hopes had been dashed by the impetuous marriage, his winning personality and poetic skill won for him new friends in high places. He traveled abroad with Sir Walter Chute in 1605; he became a member of the salon of Lucy, Countess of Bedford; and he even attracted the attention of King James, who saw what a useful ornament Donne would be to the Church and urged him to take orders. Not completely resolved in his conscience to do so, Donne, for a considerable time, temporized. Yet, his activity during this period led him inevitably toward this step. A substantial body of Donne's religious verse was written during this period and sent to Magdalen Herbert, mother of George Herbert and Lord Herbert of Cherbury. Finally, he committed himself to seeking advancement within the Anglican Church with the publication of *Pseudo-Martyr*, a work of religious controversy on a problem strongly vexing the King—the refusal of Roman Catholics to subscribe to the Oath of Allegiance. Thereafter, the King refused to consider Donne for any post outside the Church. In 1610, Oxford University awarded an honorary master's degree to Donne, who had been prevented by his former religion from taking an undergraduate degree.

Having composed the *Anniversaries* under the patronage of Sir Robert Drury of Hawsted, he accompanied Sir Robert to Paris and then to Frankfort. After the return of the party to England in 1612, Donne and his family resided with Sir Robert. Although he continued to write occasional verse, Donne had definitely decided to take orders. Having prepared himself through further study, he was ordained early in 1615, and numerous avenues for advancement immediately became available to him. The King made him a royal chaplain. Cambridge awarded him the degree of Doctor of Divinity by royal command. Lincoln's Inn appointed him Reader in Divinity to the Society. In addition, he was able to turn down offers of fourteen country livings in his first year as a priest, while accepting two. The one blight on his early years as a priest was the death of his wife in 1617. In 1619, Donne took time out from his regular duties to serve as chaplain accompanying Lord Doncaster on an embassy to Germany.

Donne's fame as a preacher had been immediate, and it continued to grow each year. As Walton reports, even his friends were surprised by the continuous growth of his pulpit eloquence after such a striking beginning. Such genius received its proper setting in 1621 when Donne was appointed Dean of St. Paul's Cathedral. The position was also a lucrative one, and the Dean's residence was as large as an episcopal palace.

The winter of 1623-1624 was a particularly eventful time in Donne's life. Having contracted relapsing fever, he was on the verge of death, but with characteristic dedication—and also characteristic self-consciousness—he kept a meticulous record of his illness as an aid to devotion. The resulting work, *Devotions upon Emergent Occasions*, was published almost immediately. During the same period, Donne's daughter, Constance, married the aging Elizabethan actor Edward Alleyn, founder of Dulwich College. From circumstances surrounding the wedding, the publishing history of *Devotions upon Emergent Occasions* has been reconstructed. It now seems clear that Donne composed this highly structured work in just a few weeks while still physically incapacitated.

In 1624, he took on additional duties as Vicar of St. Dunstan's-in-the-West. After the death of King James in the following year, Donne was chosen to preach the first sermon before the new king. This and other sermons were printed at the request of King Charles. Also printed was his memorial sermon for Lady Danvers, as Magdalen Herbert had become.

Even when Donne again became gravely ill in 1629, he would not stop preaching. Ever conscious of his mortality during these last months, he sat for a portrait wearing his shroud. When he delivered his last sermon on Ash Wednesday in 1631, it was the famous *Death's Duell*. Walton gives a vivid account of the writing and preaching of this sermon during Donne's last illness, and some of the sermon's special urgency is perhaps explained by the fact that the king's household called it Donne's own funeral sermon. Indeed, a few weeks later, on March 31, 1631, he died, having been preceded only a few months before by his aged mother.

Analysis · The traditional dichotomy between Jack Donne and Dr. Donne, despite John Donne's own authority for it, is essentially false. In the seventeenth century context, the work of Donne constitutes a fundamental unity. Conventional wisdom may expect devotional poetry from a divine and feel a certain uneasiness when faced with love poetry, but such a view misses the point in two different ways. On the one hand, Donne's love poetry is philosophical in its nature and characterized by a texture of religious imagery; and, on the other hand, his devotional poetry makes unexpected, bold use of erotic imagery. What Donne presents is two sides of a consistent vision of the world and of the mortality of man.

In the nineteenth century, when Donne's poetry did occasionally attract some attention from the discerning, it was not for the lyrics but for the satires. The satirical mode seemed the most congenial use that Donne had found for his paradoxical style. This had also been the attitude of the eighteenth century, which, however, valued metrical euphony too highly to accept even the satires. In fact, Alexander Pope tried to rescue Donne for the eighteenth century by the curious expedient of "translating" his satires into verse, that is, by regularizing them. In addition to replacing Donne's strong lines and surprising caesurae with regular meter, Pope, as Addison C. Bross has shown, puts ideas into climactic sequence, makes particulars follow generalizations, groups similar images together, and untangles syntax. In other words, he homogenizes the works.

While today Donne's lyrics are preferred to his satires, the satires are regarded as artistically effective in their original form, although this artistry is of a different order from that of the lyrics. Sherry Zivley has shown that the imagery of the satires works in a somewhat different way from that of the imagery of the lyrics, where diverse images simply succeed one another. With images accumulated from a similarly wide range of sources, the satires build a thematic center. N. J. C. Andreasen has gone even further, discerning in the body of the satires a thematic unity. Andreasen sees Donne as having created a single persona for the satires, one who consistently deplores the encroaching materialism of the seventeenth century.

Satire III on religion ("Kind pity chokes my spleen") is undoubtedly the most famous of the satires. Using related images to picture men as engaging in a kind of courtship of the truth, the poem provides a defense of moderation and of a common ground between the competing churches of the post-Reformation world. Although written in the period of Donne's transition from the Roman Catholic Church to the Anglican, the poem rejects both of these, along with the Lutheran and the Calvinist Churches, and calls on men to put their trust in God and not in those who unjustly claim authority from God for churches of their own devising.

In addition to the fully developed satires, Donne wrote a small number of very brief epigrams. These mere witticisms are often on classical subjects and therefore without the occasional focus that turns Ben Jonson's epigrams into genuine poetry. This is the only place where Donne makes any substantial use of classical allusion.

In his own day, Donne's most popular poems were probably his elegies. While in modern usage the term *elegy* is applied only to a memorial poem, Donne's elegies derive their form from a classical tradition that uses the term, as well, for poetry of love complaint written in couplets. Generally longer than the more famous songs and sonnets, the elegies are written on the model of Ovid's *Amores (Loves).* Twenty or more such poems have been attributed to Donne, but several of these are demonstrably not his. On the basis of manuscript evidence, Dame Helen Gardner has suggested that Donne intended fourteen poems to stand as a thematically unified Book of Elegies and that "The Autumnal" (Elegy IX), which has a different manuscript history, and "The Dream" (Elegy X), which is not in couplets, although authentic poems by Donne, do not form a part of it.

Elegy IX, "The Autumnal," is a praise of older women as more seasonable to the appetite because the uncontrollable fires of their youth have passed. There is a long tradition that this poem was specially written for Magdalen Herbert. If so, it is particularly daring since, although not a seduction poem, it is frankly erotic in its praise; inasmuch as Magdalen Herbert did take as her second husband a much younger man, however, it may be supposed that she would have appreciated the general recognition that sexual attractiveness and interest can endure and even ripen. On the other hand, the poem's praises are not without qualification. The persona admires autumnal beauty, but he can see nothing attractive in the truly aged, whom he rejects as death's heads from which the teeth have been scattered to various places—to the vexation of their souls since the teeth will have to be gathered together again for the resurrection of the body at the Last Judgment. Thus the poem shows Donne's typical combination of eroticism and contemplation of mortality in a mode of grotesque humor.

In Elegy XIX, "To His Mistress Going to Bed," the persona enthusiastically directs his mistress in her undressing. Aroused, he uses his hands to full advantage to explore her body. In a famous passage, he compares his amazement to that of someone discovering a new land. He next directs her to bare her body to him as fully as she would to the midwife. This graphic request is followed by the poem's closing couplet, in which the persona points out that he is naked already to show his mistress the way and thus poignantly reveals that he is only hoping for such lasciviousness from her and not already having his wanton way. Even this poem uses religious imagery—most clearly and most daringly when it advocates a woman's baring of her body to her lover by analogy with the baring of the soul before God. In an influential explication, Clay Hunt suggests that Donne is, in fact, ridiculing the Neoplatonic school of love that could seriously advance such an analogy. If so, Donne is clearly having it both ways and making the analogy available for its own sake as well.

The songs and sonnets, as the other love poems are usually called, although no sonnets in the conventional sense are included, show an imaginative variety of verse forms. They are particularly famous for their dramatic, conversational opening lines. In addition, these poems are a great storehouse of the kind of verbal ambiguity that William Empson has shown the modern world how to admire.

In "The Canonization," the persona justifies his love affair in explicitly sacred terms by explaining that his relationship with his beloved makes the two of them saints of love. John A. Clair has shown how the structure of "The Canonization" follows the five stages of the process of canonization in the Roman Catholic Church during the Renaissance: proof of sanctity, recognition of heroic virtue, demonstration of miracles, examination of relics and writings, and declaration of worthiness of veneration. The poem is thus addressed to a devil's advocate who refuses to see the holiness of erotic love. It is this devil's advocate in love who is asked to hold his tongue, in the famous first line. "The Canonization" illustrates Donne's typical use of ambiguity as well as paradox, not as merely decorative wit, but to reveal deepest meanings. William H. Machett suggests that, for example, when the lovers in this poem become a "piece of chronicle," the word *piece* is a triple pun meaning masterpiece, fragment, and fortress. There is also a much more obvious meaning–piece of artillery–a meaning that interacts with the title to give a richer texture to the whole poem: The poem is not only about the making of saints of love but also about the warfare between this idea and conventional notions of sex and religion. Consequently, yet another meaning of *piece* comes into play, the sexual.

"The Flea" is a seduction poem. Like many of the songs and sonnets, it takes the form of a logical argument making full use of the casuistries and indeed sophistries of the dialectic of Peter Ramus. In the first of the poem's three stanzas the persona asks the lady to contemplate a flea he has discerned upon her person. Since his blood and hers are mingled in the flea that has in succession bitten each of them, the mingling of the bloods that takes place during intercourse (as was then believed) has already occurred. In the second stanza the persona cautions the lady not to kill the flea. By joining their bloods the flea has become the place of their joining in marriage, so for her to kill the flea would be to murder him and also to commit both suicide and sacrilege. In the last stanza, the persona discovers that the lady has ignored his argument and killed the flea, but he is ready with another argument. When the lady triumphantly points out that they have survived this death of the flea, surely she is also showing how false her fears of sex are, since sex involves no greater loss of blood and no greater death. Implicit in these last lines is the traditional pun on "death," which was the popular term for sexual climax. The pun and the poem as a whole illustrate Donne's characteristic mingling of the sacred and the profane. It should be noted that a love poem on the subject of the lady's fleas was not an original idea with Donne, but the usual treatment of the subject was as an erotic fantasy. Donne's originality is precisely in his use of the subject for dialectic and in the restraint he shows in ending the poem before the lady capitulates, in fact without indicating whether she does.

"The Ecstasy," the longest of the songs and sonnets, has, for a lyric, attracted a remarkable range of divergent interpretations. The poem is about spiritual love and intermingling as the culmination of physical love, but some critics have seen the Neoplatonism, or spiritualizing of love, as quite serious, while others have insisted that it is merely a patently sophistical ploy of the persona to convince his mistress that, since they are one soul, the physical consummation of their love is harmless, appropriate, inevitable. If the critics who see "The Ecstasy" as a seduction poem are right, the conclusion is even more salacious than they have supposed, since it calls on the addressee to examine the lovers closely for the evidence of true love when they have given themselves over to their bodies—in other words, to watch them make love. In fact, the poem, like so many of Donne's, is quite content to be theological and erotic by turns—beginning with its very title, a term used of both religious experience and sexual experience. That the perfect soul brought into being by the union of the lovers should combine the flesh and spirit eternally is an understandable religious hope and also a good sexual fantasy. In this way, the poem illustrates Donne's philosophy of love. Although not all his poems use this theme, Donne has, in fact, a unique ability for his day to perceive love as experienced by equals.

Another famous poem of love between equals is "A Valediction: Forbidding Mourning." The poem rushes through a dazzling spectrum of imagery in just the way deplored by Samuel Johnson. In addition, in the *Life of Cowley* Johnson singles out the poem for his ultimate condemnation, saying that in the extended metaphor of the last three stanzas "it may be doubted whether absurdity or ingenuity has the better claim." During the present century, ingenuity has once again become respectable in poetry, and modern readers come with more sympathy than Johnson did to this famous extended metaphor, or conceit, comparing lovers who have to suffer a temporary separation to a pair of pencil compasses. Even the improbability of the image—which Johnson castigated as absurdity—has been given a context by modern scholarship. W. A. Murray, for example, has shown that the circle with a dot in the center, which is inscribed by the compasses reflecting the lovers who are separated yet joined, is, in fact, the alchemical symbol for gold, mentioned elsewhere in the poem and a traditional symbol of perfection. More ingeniously, John Freccero has seen Donne's compasses as inscribing not simply a circle but, as they close, a spiral. The spiral has some history of use in describing the motion of the planets. Since the spiral is also a conventional symbol of humanity, this spiral reading helps readers see in "A Valediction: Forbidding Mourning" Donne's characteristic balance of the celestial and the personal.

In fact, Donne's inclusiveness is even wider than it is usually assumed to be. He collapses not only physical and spiritual but also male and female. Donne has the unusual perspicacity to make the persona of "Break of Day" explicitly female, and although no critic has made the point before, there is nothing to prevent seeing a similar female persona in "A Valediction: Forbidding Mourning." Such a reading has the advantage of introducing some erotic puns in the compass conceit as the man (the fixed center in this reading) harkens after his beloved as she roams and then grows erect when she returns to him. More important, such a reading makes further sense out of the image of a circle inscribed by compasses.

The circle is a traditional symbol of woman, and woman's life is traditionally completed—or, as the poem puts it, made just—with a man at the center. Since the circle is a natural sexual image for woman, in this reading, the poem illustrates the practical sex as well as the theoretical sociology behind its imagery as the lover's firmness makes the woman's circle taut. An objection that might be made to this reading is that the poem's various references to parting show that it is the speaker who is going away. While a woman of the seventeenth century would be unlikely to do extensive traveling apart from her lover (or even in his company), a woman may have to part as well as a man, and lovers might well think of themselves as roaming the world when kept apart only by the daily round of pedestrian business. There is no more reason in the poem for believing that the absent one will literally roam than for believing that this absent one will literally run.

While Walton assigns this poem to the occasion of Donne's trip to France with Sir Robert Drury in 1611, the apocryphal nature of Walton's story is sufficiently indicated by the fact that it does not appear until the 1675 version of his *Life of Donne*. This dating would, at the least, make "A Valediction: Forbidding Mourning" extremely late for the songs and sonnets. Nevertheless, were the poem occasioned by Donne's preparation to travel to France in 1611, reading it as spoken by a woman would still be appropriate, since Donne prepared for this trip by sending his wife and children to stay with relatives on the Isle of Wight several months before he was himself able to embark. In addition, a general knowledge of how poets work suggests that a lyric inspired by a specific occasion is seldom in every particular a document congruent with the poet's actual experience. Perhaps the poem finally says that a woman can make a virtue of necessary separation as well as a man can.

Among the songs and sonnets are a few poems that seem to have been written for patrons. Since Twickenham is the seat of the Earls of Bedford, "Twickenham Garden" is assumed to have been written for Lucy, Countess of Bedford. According to the poem, the garden is a refuge like Eden, but the persona admits that with him the serpent has been let in. He wishes he were instead an aphrodisiac plant or fountain more properly at home in the place. In the last stanza, he seems to become such a fountain, but he is disappointed to discover that all the lovers who visit the garden are false. The poem ends—perhaps rather curiously for a patronage poem—with the obscure paradox that the only true woman is the one whose truth is killing.

A similar depersonalization characterizes the riddling poem "A Nocturnal upon St. Lucy's Day, Being the Shortest Day." While the ironies of darkness and light and of the changing movement of time (*Lucy* means light, but her day provides less of it than any other) would have recommended the subject to Donne anyway, it must have been an additional stimulus that this astronomically significant day was the saint's day of one of his patronesses. Clarence H. Miller, seeing the poem as unique among the songs and sonnets in describing the union with the lady as exclusively sacred without any admixture of the profane, relates the poem to the liturgy for St. Lucy's Day. In the body of the poem, however, the persona sees himself as the epitaph for light, as every dead thing. Finally, he becomes St. Lucy's Day itself—for the purpose of providing lovers with a longer nighttime for lust. Despite a certain bitterness or at least coarseness of tone, the poem is usually seen as a lament for the Countess' death (1627); the death of Donne's wife, however, has also been suggested, although Anne More has no special association with St. Lucy and his love for her could not have been exclusively spiritual. Richard E. Hughes has considered the occasion of the poem from a different point of view and usefully suggested that, though commemorating the Countess of Bedford, the poem is not an improbably late lyric for the songs and sonnets but a lament from an earlier period for the loss of the Countess' friendship. If the tone is considered in the least charitable light, the poem might even be read as an accusation of patronage withdrawn.

The familiar letter came into its own as a genre during the seventeenth century, and collections even began to be published. About two hundred of Donne's letters survive. This is a larger number than for any other figure of the English Renaissance except Sir Francis Bacon, and Bacon's correspondence includes many letters written in his official capacity. Since the familiar letter had only begun to surface as a genre, much of the impersonality and formality of earlier letter writing persist in Donne's correspondence. Donne's son was a rather casual editor, and in light of the sometimes general nature of Donne's letters, the date and intended recipient of many remain unknown. One curiosity of this period of epistolary transition is the verse letter. Almost forty of Donne's letters are written in verse. Some of these are true occasional poems datable from internal evidence, but many are of a more general, philosophical nature.

The most famous of the verse letters are "The Storm" and "The Calm," the first certainly and the second probably addressed to Christopher Brooke. Traditionally, shipwrecks and other dangers of the sea are used to illustrate the unpredictability of fortune in men's lives, but, as B. F. Nellist has shown, Donne does not follow this convention; instead, he teaches that frustration and despair are to be accepted as part of man's lot.

While many of the verse letters seem to have been exchanged with friends as *jeux d'esprit*, some are attempts to influence patrons. A group of poems clearly written with an eye to patronage are the epithalamia. Among the weddings that Donne celebrated was that of Princess Elizabeth to Frederick V, Elector of the Palatinate and later briefly King of Bohemia. Donne also celebrated the wedding of the royal favorite Robert Carr, Earl of Somerset, to Frances Howard, Countess of Essex. Since the Countess was shortly afterward convicted of murdering the essayist Sir Thomas Overbury for having stood in the way of her marriage, this epithalamion must later have been something of an embarrassment to Donne. An occasional poem for which no occasion is ascribed is the "Epithalamion Made at Lincoln's Inn." This is the most interesting of the epithalamia to contemporary taste. Its satiric tone, verbal crudities, and scoffing are a pleasant surprise in a genre usually characterized by reverence, even obsequiousness. The problem of what wedding could have been appropriately celebrated with such a poem has been resolved by David Novarr's suggestion that the "Epithalamion Made at Lincoln's Inn" was written for a mock wedding held as part of the law students' midsummer revels.

Other poems written for patrons are those usually called the epicedes and obsequies. These are eulogies for the dead—elegies in a more modern sense of the term. Donne was one among the many poets who expressed regret at the death of Prince Henry, the hope of the dynasty.

Also in the general category of memorial verse are the two so-called *Anniversaries* (*An Anatomy of the World: The First Anniversary* and *Of the Progress of the Soule: The Second Anniversary*) but these two poems are so unlike traditional eulogies as to defy inclusion in the genre. In their search for moments of intense feeling, the Metaphysical poets, with their love of paradox, did not often try to write long poems. Most of the attempts they did make are unsatisfactory or at least puzzling in some fundamental way. The *Anniversaries* are, indeed, primary texts in the study of the difficulties of the long poem in the Metaphysical mode.

Ostensibly written as memorial poems to commemorate Elizabeth Drury, who died as a child of fourteen and whom Donne had never seen, these poems range over a broad canvas of history. "Shee," as the subject of the two poems is called, is eulogized in an extravagant fashion beyond anything in the obsequies. While O. B. Hardison has shown that these poems were not regarded as bizarre or fulsome when originally published, they were the first of Donne's works to lose favor with the passing of time. Indeed, of *An Anatomy of the World* Ben Jonson objected to Donne himself that "if it had been writ of the Virgin Marie it had been something." Donne's answer is reported to have been that he was describing not Elizabeth Drury specifically but the idea of woman; but this explanation has not been found wholly satisfactory. Many candidates have been suggested for Shee of the *Anniversaries*—from Saint Lucy and Astraea (Goddess of Justice) to the Catholic Church and Christ as Divine *Logos*. Two critics have suggested Queen Elizabeth, but one finds her eulogized and the other sees her as satirized, indicting in a particularly striking way the problematic nature of these difficult, knotty poems.

Hardison, and, more recently Barbara Kiefer Lewalski, have made the case for the poems as part of a tradition of epideictic poetry—poetry of praise. In this tradition, extravagant compliments are the norm rather than the exception, and all of Donne's individual extravagances have precedents. What such a reading leaves out of account is, on the one hand, the extraordinary density of the extravagant praise in Donne's *Anniversaries* and, on the other hand, the presence of satire, not only the possible satire of the heroine but also explicit satire in the exploration of the decay of nature that forms the subject of the poems. Marjorie Hope Nicholson sees the *Anniversaries* as companion poems, the first a lament for the body, the second a meditation on mortality. Louis L. Martz suggests, further, that the *Anniversaries* are structured meditations. Martz sees *An Anatomy of the World* as a mechanical application of Ignatian meditation and *Of the Progress of the Soule* as a more successful organic application. Meditation theory, however, fails to resolve all the interpretive difficulties. Northrop Frye's theory that the poems are Menippian satire, and Frank Manley's that they are wisdom literature, also leave unresolved difficulties.

Perhaps these interpretive difficulties are fundamentally beyond resolution. Rosalie L. Colie has usefully pointed out that, in the *Anniversaries*, Donne seems not to be trying to bring his disparate materials to a conventional resolution. The poems accept contradictions as part of the flux of life and should be seen within the Renaissance tradition of paradox. Donne is demonstrably a student of paradox in many of his other works. More specifically, Daniel B. Rowland has placed *An Anatomy of the World* in the Mannerist tradition because in it Donne succeeded in creating an unresolved tension. His purpose may be just to raise questions about the relative weight of praise and satire and about the identity of the heroine Shee. Mario Praz goes further—perhaps too far—when he sees all the work of Donne as Mannerist, as illustrative not of wit but of the dialectics of passion; Mannerism does, however, provide a useful description for what modern taste finds a strange combination of materials in the *Anniversaries*.

An even more difficult long poem is an unfinished one called "Infiniati Sacrum." This strange parable of original sin adapts Paracelsus' theory of the transmigration of souls to follow through the course of subsequent history the spirit of the apple plucked by Eve. W. A. Murray has seen in this poem the beginnings of a *Paradise Lost* (1667). While few other readers will want to go so far, most will agree with Murray and with George Williamson that "Infinitati Sacrum" is a preliminary use of the materials and themes treated in the *Anniversaries*.

Donne has been called a poet of religious doubt in contrast to Herbert, a poet of religious assurance; but Herbert has real doubts in the context of his assurance, and the bold demand for salvation in audacious, even shocking language characteristic of the holy sonnets suggests, on the contrary, that Donne writes from a deep-seated conviction of election.

Louis Martz, Helen Gardner, and others have shown the influence of Ignatian meditation in the holy sonnets. Dame Helen, in fact, by restoring the manuscript order, has been able to see in these poems a sequential meditative exercise. The sensuous language, however, suggests not so much the meditative technique of Saint Ignatius Loyola as the technique of Saint Francis de Sales. In addition, Don M. Ricks has argued cogently that the order of the poems in the Westmorland Manuscript may suggest an Elizabethan sonnet sequence and not a meditative exercise at all.

Holy Sonnet XIV (10 in Dame Helen's numbering), "Batter my heart, three-personed God," has been seen by Arthur L. Clements and others as hieroglyphically illustrating the Trinity in its three-part structure. This poem opens with the striking dramatic immediacy typical of Donne's best lyrics. Using both military and sexual imagery, Donne describes the frightening, ambivalent feelings called up by the thought of giving oneself over to God's power and overwhelming grace. The soul is a town ruled by a usurper whom God's viceroy, Reason, is inadequate to overthrow. The soul is also the beloved of God though betrothed to his enemy and longing for divorce. The resolution of this sonnet turns on a paradoxical sexual image as the persona says that his soul will never be chaste unless God ravishes him. A similar complex of imagery is used, though in a less startling fashion, in Holy Sonnet II (1), "As due by many titles I resign."

Holy Sonnet IX (5), "If poisonous minerals," begins audaciously by accusing God of unfairness in the consequences He has decreed for original sin. In the sestet the persona abruptly realizes that he is unworthy to dispute with God in this way and begs that his tears of guilt might form a river of forgetfulness inducing God to overlook his sins rather than actually forgiving them. While this poem does not turn on a sexual image, it does contrast the lot of fallen man unfavorably with that of lecherous goats, who have no decree of damnation hanging over them.

Holy Sonnet XVIII (2 in Dame Helen's separately numbered group from the Westmorland Manuscript), "Show me, dear Christ, Thy spouse so bright and clear," has some of the most shocking sexual imagery in all of religious literature. While the tradition of using erotic imagery to describe the soul's relationship with God has a long history, particularly in exegesis of the Song of Songs, that is helpful in understanding the other holy sonnets, the imagery here is of a different order. Like Satire III, the poem is a discussion of the competing claims of the various Christian churches, but it goes well beyond the courtship imagery of the satire when it praises the Anglican Church because, like a promiscuous woman, it makes itself available to all men.

A distinctly separate series of holy sonnets is "La Corona." Using paradoxes such as the fact that the Virgin is her Maker's maker, and including extensive allusions to the divine office, this sequence of seven poems on the life of Christ has been called by Martz a rosary of sonnets, not so much because of the devotional content as because of the interlaced structure: The last line of each poem is repeated as the first line of the next. While the ingenious patterning renders the sequence less personal than Donne's best religious poetry, within its exquisite compass it does make a beautiful statement of the mysteries of faith.

In "A Hymn to Christ, at the Author's Last Going into Germany," Donne exaggerates the dangers of a Channel crossing to confront his mortality. Then even in the face of death, the persona pictures Christ as a jealous lover to be castigated if He withdraws His love just because it is not reciprocated; yet the persona does call for a bill of divorcement from all his lesser loves. The poem ends with the thought that, just as dark churches (being free of distractions) are best for praying, death is the best refuge from stormy seas.

"Good Friday, 1613: Riding Westward" is a witty paradox built on Ramist dialectic. Forced to make a trip to the West on Good Friday, the persona feels his soul drawn to the East. Although the heavens are ordered for westward motion, he feels a contradiction even as he duplicates their motion because all of Christian iconology urges him to return to the East where life began—both human life in Eden and spiritual life with the Crucifixion. He reasons that through sin he has turned his back on the Cross—but only to receive the correction that his sins merit. He hopes such flagellation will so change his appearance that he will again become recognizable to God as made in His Own image. Then he will at last be able to turn and face God.

Another divine poem of witty paradox is "A Hymn to God the Father." Punning on *Son/sun* and on his own name, Donne demands that God swear to save him. Having done so, God will at last have Donne. Because of its frankness and its very personal use of puns, this poem is not really a hymn despite its title—although it has been included in hymnals.

The chapter headings of *Devotions upon Emergent Occasions* as laid out in the table of contents should also be included among the divine poems. Joan Webber has made the illuminating discovery that this table of contents is a Latin poem in dactylic hexameters. This is a particularly surprising element of artistry in a work composed in such a short time and under such difficult conditions. Thus even more self-conscious than had been supposed, *Devotions upon Emergent Occasions* can finally be seen as an explication of the Latin poem.

Other literary forms · Although John Donne is known today chiefly as a lyric poet, the posthumous volume *Poems, by J.D.*, which includes the lyrics, represents only a small part of his literary output. Donne was famous in his own age mainly as a preacher; in fact, he was probably the most popular preacher of an age when preaching held the same fascination for the general public that the cinema has today. Various sermons of Donne's were published during his lifetime, and several collections were published in the following decades. Without a commitment to Donne's religious values, few today would want to read through many of his sermons–grand as their style is. Donne must, however, be credited with the careful articulation of the parts of his sermons, which create a resounding unity of theme; and his control of prose rhythm and his ingenious imagery retain their power, even if modern readers are no longer disposed to see the majesty of God mirrored in such writing.

Excerpts from Donne's sermons thus have a continuing vitality for general readers in a way that excerpts from the sermons of, for example, Lancelot Andrewes cannot. In the early seventeenth century, Andrewes had been the most popular preacher before Donne, and, as Bishop of Winchester, he held a more important position. He also had a greater reputation as a stylist, but for modern readers, Andrewes carries to an extreme the baroque fashion of "crumbling a text" (analyzing in minute detail). The sermons of Andrewes are now unreadable without special training in theology and classical languages. On the other hand, though also writing for an educated audience with a serious interest in divinity, Donne wears his scholarship more easily and can still be read by the general student without special preparation. His sermon to the Virginia Company is the first sermon in English to make a missionary appeal.

The single most famous of Donne's sermons was his last. *Death's Duell* (1632), preached before King Charles on February 25, 1631, is a profound meditation on mortality. Mortality is always a major theme with Donne, but here he reaches a new eloquence. Full of startling imagery, the sermon takes as its theme the paradox that life is death and death is life–although Christ's death delivers humankind from death. When this last sermon of

Donne's was published, Henry King, Bishop of Chichester, remarked that "as he exceeded others at first so at last he exceeded himself."

A work of similar theme but published by Donne in his own lifetime is the *Devotions upon Emergent Occasions* (1624). Composed, as R. C. Bald has shown, with extreme rapidity during a serious illness and convalescence in 1623, this work is based on the structured meditational technique of Saint Francis de Sales, involving the sensuous evocation of scenes, although, as Thomas F. Van Laan has suggested, the work is perhaps also influenced by the *Spiritual Exercises* (1548) of Saint Ignatius Loyola. It is divided into twenty-three sections, each consisting of a meditation, an expostulation, and a prayer. The work is an artfully constructed whole of sustained emotional power, but the meditations have achieved a special fame with their vivid evocations of the theme that sickness brings people closer to God by putting them in touch with their frailty and mortality. Various meditations from the *Devotions upon Emergent Occasions* present famous pictures of the tolling of the death knell, of the body as a microcosm, and of the curious medical practices of the day, for example, the application of live pigeons to Donne's feet to try to draw the vapors of fever from his head. By this last practice, Donne discovers that he is his own executioner since the vapors are believed to be the consequence of his melancholy, and this is no more than the studiousness required of him by his calling as a preacher. While in past centuries most readers found the work's self-consciousness and introspection alienating, the contemporary sensibility finds these characteristics especially congenial. The three meditations on the tolling of the bells have, in particular, provided titles and catchphrases for popular writers.

A posthumously published early study of mortality by Donne is *Essayes in Divinity* (1651). The *Essayes in Divinity*, written in a knotty, baroque style, is a collection of curiously impersonal considerations of the Creation and of the deliverance of the Israelites from bondage in Egypt. The work shows none of the fire of the sermons and of the *Devotions upon Emergent Occasions*. A very different sort of contemplation of mortality is provided in *Biathanatos* (1646). The casuistical reasoning perhaps shows evidence of Donne's Jesuit background. The same approach to logic and a similar iconoclasm are apparent in *Juvenilia: Or, Certaine Paradoxes and Problems* (1633; the first complete version was, however, not published until 1923).

The earliest of Donne's publications were two works of religious controversy of a more serious nature. These works also show Donne's Jesuit background, but in them, he is reacting against his upbringing and presenting a case for Anglican moderation in the face of Roman Catholic—and especially Jesuit—pretensions. *Pseudo-Martyr* (1610) was written at the explicit request of King James, according to Donne's first biographer, Izaak Walton. Here and throughout his subsequent career, Donne is a strongly committed Erastian, seeing the Church as properly subordinate in this world to secular authority.

The other of these early works of controversy, *Ignatius His Conclave* (1611), which appeared in Latin as well as English, is still amusing to modern readers who are unlikely to come to it with quite the strong partisan feeling of its original audience.

Select works other than poetry
NONFICTION: *Pseudo-Martyr*, 1610; *Ignatius His Conclave*, 1611; *Devotions upon Emergent Occasions*, 1624; *Death's Duell*, 1632; *Juvenilia: Or, Certaine Paradoxes and Problemes*, 1633, 1923; *Six Sermons on Several Occasions*, 1634; *LXXX Sermons*, 1640; *Biathanatos*, 1646; *Fifty Sermons*, 1649; *Essayes in Divinity*, 1651; *Letters to Severall Persons of Honour*, 1651; *XXVI Sermons*, 1660; *A Collection of Letters*, 1660.

Edmund Miller

Bibliography · An authoritative biography is R. C. Bald, *John Donne: A Life*, 1970. Izaak Walton's *The Life and Death of Dr. Donne*, originally prefixed to *LXXX Sermons*, 1640, and separately published in an enlarged edition in 1658, though not always accurate, shows the viewpoint of a contemporary admirer and friend. For a comprehensive survey of Donne criticism through 1987, see Deborah Aldrich Larsen, *John Donne and Twentieth Century Criticism*, 1989. For prose criticism see Evelyn M. Simpson, *A Study of the Prose Works of John Donne*, 1924, and Joan Webber, *Contrary Music: The Prose Style of John Donne*, 1986. For bibliography, see John Roberts, *John Donne: An Annotated Bibliography of Modern Criticism, 1912-1967*, 1973, and his *John Donne: An Annotated Bibliography of Modern Criticism, 1968-1978*, 1982.

Criticism of the poetry is extensive. For a sampling, see Theodore Spencer, ed., *A Garland for John Donne*, 1931; Helen Gardner, ed., *John Donne: A Collection of Critical Essays*, 1962; Raymond-Jean Frontain and Frances Malpazzi, eds., *John Donne's Religious Imagination: Essays in Honor of John T. Shawcross*, 1994. Book-length treatments include: George Williamson, *The Donne Tradition*, 1930; J. B. Leishman, *The Monarch of Wit*, 1951; David Novarr, *The Disinterred Muse: Donne's Texts and Contexts*, 1980; John Carey, *John Donne, Life, Mind, and Art*, 1981; M Thomas Hester, *Kinde Pitty and Brave Scorn: John Donne's Satyres*, 1982; Arthur Marotti, *John Donne, Coterie Poet*, 1986; Thomas Docherty, *John Donne Undone*, 1986.

T. S. ELIOT

Born: St. Louis, Missouri; September 26, 1888
Died: London, England; January 4, 1965

Poetry · *Prufrock and Other Observations*, 1917 · *Poems*, 1919 · *Ara Vos Prec*, 1920 · *The Waste Land*, 1922 · *Poems, 1909-1925*, 1925 · *Ash Wednesday*, 1930 · *Triumphal March*, 1931 · *Sweeney Agonistes*, 1932 · *Words for Music*, 1934 · *Collected Poems, 1909-1935*, 1936 · *Old Possum's Book of Practical Cats*, 1939 · *Four Quartets*, 1943 · *The Cultivation of Christmas Trees*, 1954 · *Collected Poems, 1909-1962*, 1963 · *Poems Written in Early Youth*, 1967 · *The Complete Poems and Plays*, 1969

Achievements · T. S. Eliot's achievements are such that he became the premier poet of his own generation and enlivened literary criticism by contributing such phrases as "objective correlative," "dissociation of sensibility," and "impersonal" poetry. He greatly helped to foster a resurgence of interest in Dante, in the Metaphysical poets of the seventeenth century, and in Elizabethan and Jacobean drama at a time when such a resurgence was needed. He also provided a strong critical and poetic voice that chided the Victorian and Edwardian poets while furnishing a new poetry that served as a practical criticism of theirs.

The one title he preferred, and the one by which he is best and justly remembered, is "poet." His poetry is not, on first acquaintance, easy; and it may not be so on second or third acquaintance. He is, as

The Nobel Foundation

he said of his own favorite writer, Dante, "a poet to whom one grows up over a lifetime." His poetic originality, called into question in his early days by those who charged him with plagiarism, lies in the careful crafting and arrangement of lines and phrases, the introduction of literary, historical, and cultural allusions, and the elaboration of image and symbol in highly charged and often dramatic language that both describes and presents a personal emotion or experience and generalizes it. Eliot's careful husbanding of words, phrases, images, and symbols results in a recurrence of those elements and a continuity of subject matter from his juvenilia through his first and second masterpieces ("The Love Song of J. Alfred Prufrock" and *The Waste Land*) to his last (*Four Quartets*). The themes of his greater poems, as of his lesser ones, involve indentity, sexuality, the nature of love, religious belief (or its absence), and the telling of a tale/writing of a poem in language adequate to the emotion or state that the telling/writing seeks to express.

It is a short step from the dramatic situations of Eliot's early and middle poetry, situations that owe something to the poetry of Robert Browning, more to John Donne and the Elizabethan and Jacobean dramatists, and most to the symbolist poetry of Jules Laforgue. One of Eliot's chief aspirations and limited achievements countered the thrust of modern drama since Henrik Ibsen (the Nō drama of William Butler Yeats excepted): Eliot was dedicated to the revivification of verse drama in the twentieth century. He succeeded in doing this, to some extent, in *The Rock*, more so in *Murder in the Cathedral*, and less so in *The Family Reunion* and subsequent plays. Although his account of the martyrdom of Thomas à Becket clearly inspired Jean Anouilh's *Becket* (1959), Eliot's attempt to revive the poetic drama amounted to a false start, perhaps attributable in part to the highly poetic but *un*dramatic and static nature of his plays.

Eliot's achievements have led at least one critic to state that in the area of humane letters the larger part of the twentieth century may be called the Age of Eliot. Eliotatry aside, there is some merit in the remark. No stranger to prizes and awards, Eliot may have valued, and needed, the *Dial Award* of 1922 for *The Waste Land*. In the course of his long career he received doctoral degrees (*honoris causa*) from a score of British, European, and American universities; was Clark Lecturer at Trinity College, Cambridge (1926), and Charles Eliot Norton Professor of Poetry at Harvard University (1932-1933); and won the Hanseatic Goethe Prize (1954), the Dante Gold Medal (Florence, 1959), the Emerson-Thoreau Medal (American Academy of Arts and Sciences, 1959), and the U.S. Medal of Freedom (1964). In 1948 he achieved a dual distinction: not only was he awarded the British Order of Merit, but he also won the Nobel Prize in Literature for, he surmised, "the entire corpus."

In another sense, Eliot's continuing achievement may be measured by the extent to which innumerable students, teachers, and researchers have surrendered to him. Each year several books or portions of books, as well as numerous essays, swell the number of works about him, his thought, and his writing; they stand as monuments to his still-unfolding mind and meaning. A legend in his own time, he remains one today.

Biography · To see Thomas Stearns Eliot's end in his beginning is to recall that Andrew Eliot (1627-1704) emigrated from East Coker, Somerset, to Beverly, Massachusetts, in a century that his twentieth century scion would explore and reexplore in poetry and criticism for most of his life. Eliot's grandfather, the Reverend William Greenleaf Eliot, forsook his native New England and went with missionary zeal to the outpost of St. Louis, Missouri, in 1834. There he founded the (first) Unitarian church of the Messiah and later founded Washington University (originally, Eliot Seminary) where he became Chancellor (1870-1887). In the year after William Eliot's death, on September 25, 1888, Thomas Stearns Eliot, the seventh child of a second son, was born to Henry and Charlotte (Stearns) Eliot. As the Eliots did, the American Stearns family hailed from seventeenth century Massachusetts: Members of both families had done what they considered the right thing in the Salem witch trials, Andrew Eliot as a juror, a Stearns as a judge. Eliot's schooling at Smith Academy was punctuated by summers in New England, chiefly at Gloucester and Rockport, Massachusetts (on Cape Ann), not far from the Dry Salvages. After a year at Milton Academy, Eliot matriculated at Harvard College, where he received a B.A. degree (1909) and pursued graduate studies (1910-1914), completing but not defending a doctoral dissertation on the philosophy of F. H. Bradley (published, 1964).

During the years 1910 to 1917, Eliot visited Paris and Germany (1910-1911) and studied at the Sorbonne; back in Cambridge (1911-1914), he studied philosophy (with Bertrand Russell), Sanskrit, Pali, along with other subjects, and received a fellowship stipend to study at Marburg, Germany, in 1914—an award which he promptly transferred to Merton College, Oxford, at the onset of World War I. On September 22, 1914, Eliot met Ezra Pound; it was an event that marked the forging of a spiritual bond that endured for the rest of Eliot's life. Since much has been made of Pound's influence on Eliot's poetry, especially *The Waste Land*, it may be useful to recall Pound's statement that Eliot had "trained himself *and* modernized himself *on his own.*" It was largely through Pound's influence, however, that the poems of *Prufrock and Other Observations* were first published in American and English periodicals.

Eliot's marriage to Vivien Haigh-Wood, on June 26, 1915, was followed by brief periods of teaching (High Wycombe Grammar School, Highgate School) and lecturing (Oxford University Extension Lectures, 1915-1917). In March, 1917, Eliot secured a post in the Colonial and Foreign Department of Lloyd's Bank, London, where he worked continuously, except for three months' leave for reasons of health in the autumn of 1921, until he joined the publishing firm of Faber and Gwynn (later, Faber and Faber) in 1925. His marriage lasted until Vivien's death in 1947, although she and Eliot were officially separated (by letter) in 1933, and thereafter, according to written accounts, they met again only once, and briefly (at one of Eliot's lectures). Several critics have seen the extremely unhappy marriage as fundamental to some of his poems.

Eliot's literary activity between 1916 and 1922 was prodigious: It was the time of his numerous essays and reviews for *The Egoist, The Dial,* the *Athanaeum,* the *Times Literary Supplement,* and many other journals, of *Prufrock and Other Observations, Ara Vos Prec, Poems,* and his masterpiece, *The Waste Land.* That work would catapult him to a prominence attained by no other poet of the twentieth century. In 1922 he assumed the editorship of *The Criterion.* In 1927 Eliot experienced a sea-change: First, he became a communicant in the Church of England (June 29); then he became a British subject (November). In 1928 a statement in *For Lancelot Andrewes* characterized his newly adopted perspectives: "The general point of view may be described as classicist in literature, royalist in politics, and Anglo-Catholic in religion." The formulation is one that should be approached with caution. Although accurate in some respects and misleading in others, it does help to explain the many turnings in the road from "The Hollow Men" (1925) through the Ariel poems to *Ash Wednesday.*

Before returning from his post as Norton Professor of Poetry at Harvard (1932-1933), Eliot obtained a legal separation from his wife (to whom he had dedicated *Ash Wednesday*) and lectured at the University of Virginia on Christian apologetics, a subject of increasing interest for him. His poetry of the 1930's centered on verse drama and on such disparate efforts as "Five Finger Exercises," "Triumphal March," and *Old Possum's Book of Practical Cats;* but the poetic highlights of the decade are *Ash Wednesday, Murder in the Cathedral,* and his best poem of those years, "Burnt Norton."

The first of the poems later to comprise *Four Quartets,* "Burnt Norton" was followed by "East Coker" (1940), "The Dry Salvages" (1941), and his own *Paradiso,* "Little Gidding" (1942). In the years following the publication of *Four Quartets,* Eliot wrote little poetry; but he kept on writing verse drama and began to enjoy generous recognition of his work; notably, he received the Nobel Prize in Literature in 1948, a year after the death of Vivien. His marriage to Valerie Fletcher (January 10, 1957) marked another of the many turning points of his life—this time a turn for the better in a happy marriage. Eliot truly became, in the 1940's, 1950's, and 1960's, the Elder Statesman of letters. His position in the history of modern poetry became unassailable.

Eliot died on January 4, 1965, survived by his wife, Valerie. His ashes were interred in the parish church at East Coker, Somerset, the church of his English ancestors, and a memorial was placed in the Poets' Corner, Westminister Abbey.

Analysis · One useful approach to T. S. Eliot's poetry is to examine voices and fragments as they announce and illustrate themes. In the concluding section of *The Waste Land*, one of Eliot's speakers provides a key to that poem, to Eliot's poetry generally, and to the theory and practice of poetic composition that marked his career as a writer: "These fragments I have shored against my ruins." These fragments consist mainly of highly allusive phrases and quotations, of intricately wrought verbal symbols, of lines of direct simplicity and complex opacity, of passages of sheer beauty and crabbed commonality fixed in formulated phrases, arranged and rearranged until, in the best of the poetry, one finds the complete consort dancing together. Upon first coming to Eliot's poetry, especially to "The Love Song of J. Alfred Prufrock" or *The Waste Land*, the reader's usual (and perfectly acceptable) reaction is one of bewilderment, excitement, and, at best, an appreciation of the poetic statements that does not necessarily involve an understanding of precisely what is said, the conditions under which it is said, the full nature of the speaker, or his or her aims, intentions, or situation.

The fragments owe much to Eliot's youthful experience in St. Louis, summers on the New England coast, his Harvard education, his visits to Paris and Munich, and the Oxford and London years. Furthermore, they stem from his lifelong immersion in Dante and the Bible and from his omnivorous reading. He was particulary drawn to French symbolist poetry (especially Laforgue), the Elizabethan and Jacobean playwrights, especially John Webster, Cyril Tourneur, Christopher Marlowe, William Shakespeare, and Donne and the other Metaphysical poets. To come to Eliot's poetry with such a literary background is to see the phrases of other writers whom Eliot admired take on new and sometimes surprising meanings. To read Eliot's work without such a background may mean that the reader will miss both the larger and the particular allusions; but still the reader may grasp possible meanings of individual poems. The unwary reader may of course be carried along on the surface of the poem or find himself in sympathy with an expressed emotion without clearly knowing what is at issue. All readers should have recourse to those works to which Eliot seems to allude so that they may proceed the more intelligently with the poem at hand. The fragments that Eliot quotes or alludes to are the necessary baggage of the intelligent reader, *impedimenta* that include much of the Western European tradition and elements from Middle and Far Eastern culture.

In many respects, Eliot the poet became not unlike Joseph Conrad's Mr. Kurtz or, indeed, Marlow: He became "A Voice," an "invisible poet" (Hugh Kenner's phrase) who speaks. The voice or voices in the poems are usually those that repeat formulas embedded in literary, cultural, and religious traditions—uncertain voices that often betray their speakers' lack of self-knowledge or clear identity; they may be voices (especially in the Ariel poems) whose certitudes are affirmed only as they speak them (word becomes act) and which may be truly chimerical. The voices speaking the fragments, even the unified voice of *Four Quartets*, are the voices of humanity (though often a special order of humanity) seeking, as they turn over the fragments and seek the sense of sounds, to understand, explain, and identify themselves in terms of the past, present, and future. The voices, desiderative, expectant, seek in the expression of a word or words to communicate themselves to other communicants (the reader) and to educate those communicants in the mystery of a common life, the implications of action or inaction, the generalizable elements of a particular experience or emotion.

Long before his Paris year (1910-1911), Eliot had read Arthur Symons' *The Symbolist Movement in Literature* (1899) and had come under the sway of French Symbolist poetry. He had published some undergraduate poetry (phrases of which he used in later poems) and had begun two major poems, "Portrait of a Lady" and "The Love Song of J. Alfred Prufrock." He completed the latter at Munich (1911) but it remained in manuscript until Ezra Pound persuaded Harriet Monroe to publish it in *Poetry* (1915); it then formed the nucleus for Eliot's first volume of poetry, *Prufrock and Other Observations*, in which he may justly be said to have inaugurated modern poetry in English. It is with "The Love Song of J. Alfred Prufrock," the first masterpiece of an apprentice, that a just appreciation of Eliot's oeuvre should begin.

Like "Portrait of a Lady" and most of his poetry prior to *Four Quartets*, "The Love Song of J. Alfred Prufrock" is a dramatic, if static, monologue. It is heavily influenced by Jules Laforgue's poetic technique in that it presents an interior landscape of atomized consciousness. The male narrator (the voice) worries about the possibility of an erotic encounter as he worries and puzzles over his own identity, his too conscious sense of self, his meaning and place in a surreal and menacing universe of his own devising, and his observations (objective and subjective genitive, as James Joyce phrased it) while he confides to a reader (who is called upon to become part of Prufrock's divided self) the fragmented perceptions of himself and his situation. Prufrock does not, however, arrive at any conclusions about the encounter or about his own identity and meaning.

The epigraph (Dante, *Inferno*, XXVII) provides a key to the incongruous "love song" of an impossible lover and sets the reader squarely in Hell listening to a reluctant speaker (who cannot say what he means) who will confide in the auditor/reader as Guido did in the character Dante, "without fear or infamy," without fear that the secret will be revealed on earth (will become the subject of "observations"), particularly in the hearing of the perplexing women who "come and go" in the troublesome room or of the desirable but distant and somewhat fearsome recumbent woman. It is possible to exclude the "reader" as the addressee of this poem and to read it as an interior dialogue between "self" and "soul": Such a reading would heighten to a clinical level the disorder of identity that is sensed in Prufrock's divided self.

The voice that addresses the reader in scraps of experience remembered and fearfully anticipated and in fragments of historical- and self-consciousness does so in response to a question, presumably posed by the reader in a Dantesque role. As Hugh Kenner aptly points out, the reader enters a "zone of consciousness" in the poem, not a verifiable or constant "realistic" setting. Prufrock is not a "real" character who tells a logical or temporally sequential story. Indeed, the reader participates in the unfolding narrative by hearing and deciding what is part of the world of recognizable experience and what is intrinsic to a fragmented, disjointed, disordered, diseased consciousness that speaks familiarly ("you and I") of a shared boredom of social rounds and obligations, of the terror of rejection, and (the greater Prufrockian terror) of acceptance and surrender in sexual contact—all of which contribute to a sense of cognitive and emotional paralysis (accidia) for which Prufrock finds a disordered "objective correlative" in the "sky/Like a patient etherised upon a table."

The literary fragments in the poem include the central situational analogue in the *Inferno*, the Polonian self-caricature, and grotesque visions of Saint John the Baptist and Lazarus returned from the dead. None of the characters in the fragments belongs to the realm of the living and all represent an inability "to say just what I mean."

"Gerontion" (1919) carries on the pattern of monologue that Eliot established in "The Love Song of J. Alfred Prufrock" and "Portrait of a Lady." Here Eliot presents another voice speaking, besides words of his own devising, words from the Bible, William Shakespeare, Cyril Torneur, Thomas Middleton, Ben Jonson, and George Chapman. He intended "Gerontion" to be a prolegomenon to *The Waste Land*, and as such it is more than adequate. It deals with concerns and embodies themes common to the longer poem: themes such as aridity, the inadequacies of the common experience of sexuality and love, history's "contrived corridors," the function of memory, the Christian economy of salvation, and the attempts of consciousness to order disparate experiences and make them comprehensible. Structurally, both works are collages that use allusive language to make human history manageable; technically, they both employ a stream of consciousness tentatively centered on the centrifugal thoughts of a "dry brain in a dry season."

Gerontion and the foreign figures who flit through the Inferno and Purgatorio of his memory are figures of desolation who have reaped the whirlwind of their own personal histories and of history generally. The characters, from Mr. Silvero to Mrs. Cammel, represent some of the dry thoughts that Gerontion houses. They typify one major difficulty that the poem presents: the tension between the past, the past remembered in the present, and the present—the past dominating the present and vitiating it as memory mixes with desire in a futile nostalgia that prevents the narrator from acting (reaching conclusion). This temporal tension is at the poem's core and is resolved only in the poem's emphasis on the act of remembering. Once again, as in "The Love Song of J. Alfred Prufrock" and *The Waste Land*, the self-conscious voices utter personal and historical fragments that illuminate consciousness speaking. The point of remembering these fragments is to identify a fundamental problem of meaning that attaches to peripheral love (of art, for example) and to *love* (possibly of the poem's addressee), its meaning in personal and general historical context, and the relationship of those meanings to the meaning of the death for which Gerontion waits and the possibility of another kind of life hereafter.

The transition from "Gerontion" to *The Waste Land*, in which Gerontion is transformed into Tiresias, is a movement from considerable opacity to relative clarity, though the later poem is indeed perplexing. In 1953, Eliot wrote that he did not look forward with pleasure either to literary oblivion or to a time when his works would be read only by a few graduate students in "Middle Anglo-American, 42B." Together with "The Love Song of J. Alfred Prufrock" and *Four Quarters, The Waste Land* ensures that neither of those ends is probable. Eliot stunned all, and outraged some, of the literary world in 1922 with the publication (in *The Criterion* and *The Dial*) of *The Waste Land,* a work that has engendered more commentaries, interpretations, and discussions than any other poem of the twentieth century. Structurally, the work is a series of five poems that constitute one poem; parts of it were written and rewritten over the course of at least seven years, with editorial help for the final version from Ezra Pound. When he published it in book form, Eliot added more than fifty notes to the poem, some of which are not helpful and some of which emphasize the importance of vegetation ceremonies and direct the reader to Sir James Frazer's *The Golden Bough* (1890-1915) and to Jessie L. Weston's work on the Grail legend, *From Ritual to Romance* (1920).

The wealth of literary fragments, clues, and allusions to other works, the inclusion of foreign words and phrases and of arcane material, may produce some bafflement and has inspired numerous exegetical tracts. It is of primary importance not to treat the poem as a highly sophisticated double-crostic; instead, one should, before beginning a search for sources and analogues, surrender to it as an emotional, intellectual, puzzling, and disquieting poem. It is only in allowing for the experience of communicable and precisely incommunicable emotion that the poem can work as a poem rather than as an occasion for the exercise of literary archaeology.

Eliot wrote (note to 1.218), "Tiresias, although a mere spectator and not indeed a 'character,' is yet the most important personage in the poem, uniting all the rest. . . . What Tiresias *sees,* in fact, is the substance of the poem." One may, on Eliot's authority, read the poem as an account of Tiresias' observations as he guides the reader through his own memory to various locations in *The Waste Land* as seen or remembered on a journey that is both in and out of time. Thus, many elements fall into place as Tiresias subsumes all the characters or speakers in a multilayered, cyclical ritual of death and rebirth. Alternatively, one may read the poem as a series of fragmented monologues, in the manner of "The Love Song of J. Alfred Prufrock," so that Tiresias' becomes only one among many voices. So to read it, of course, is to find Eliot's note somewhat misleading.

Assuming that this is a symbolist poem, perhaps *the* symbolist poem of the twentieth century, the historical and cultural dimensions that many critics have so ably attributed to it (as being a poem about the disillusionment of a particular generation, about the 1920's, about London, and so on) recede. So, too, do the ubiquitous anthropological considerations of barren land, infertility, initiation rites, and the death of gods. Both sets of data may, then, be treated as "objective correlatives" for emotions that the poet seeks to express. What remain as underlying themes are sexual disorder (basic to the Grail and to vegetation myths), the lack of and need for religious belief (accented negatively by the presence of Madam Sosostris and positively in "The Fire Sermon" and "What the Thunder Said"), and the process of poetic composition (fragments "shored against my ruins"). These may be seen as elaborations in *The Waste Land* of themes present in "Portrait of a Lady," "The Love Song of J. Alfred Prufrock," "The Hippopotamus" (1917), and "Gerontion"; they are themes that also relate directly to Eliot's lessons from Dante's *La vita nuova* (c. 1292; *The New Life*) and *La divina commedia* (c. 1320; *The Divine Comedy*).

The diverse interpretations of what the poem is about have obvious implications for how one values the fragments of which it is composed and, to return to the question of voice, how one identifies the speaker and the burden of his speech. If, for example, one assumes that the blind, androgynous Tiresias speaks in many voices and does so with foreknowledge of all, one may conclude that the work stands as a monument to the disillusionment not of one generation but of many. One may also find that the slight progress of the Fisher King from the dull canal behind the gashouse (III) to the shore (V) has slight significance and that the question about setting his lands in order is, like shoring fragments against ruins, all that can be done before capitulating to the inevitable continuation of a condition in which the land will remain waste. Tiresias has, after all, foreseen this, too. If one assumes a multiplicity of voices, however, beginning with Marie, the Hyacinth Girl (or, in the epigraph, with the Sibyl's complaint and the voice speaking of it), and ending with the Fisher King, the Thunder, and a new voice (or many voices) speaking in the poem's last lines, one has a quite different experience of the poem. In the second reading one treats the work as a series of soliloquies or monologues all mixing memory with quite different desires, all commenting on various meanings (or lack of meaning) or love, and all concerned with hope or its opposite, hope negated in self-irony, hope centered on the release from individual prisons, hope tempered by trepidations attendant upon the "awful daring of a moment's surrender," and, possibly, hope that the Fisher King has finally thrown off accidia by asking himself the one needful question.

In either reading, how one treats the speaker and the meaning of the fragments raises other questions that drive one back into the poem; and each new reading raises new questions. There is no doubt that sexual disorder is a dominant theme, that the disorder concerns the dissociation of appetitive action from the intellectual and emotional aspects that would make the action human and not merely a reflex action, and that the symptoms of disorder are common to such characters as the typist, Mr. Eugenides, Mrs. Porter, Elizabeth I, Tiresias, Philomel, and the Fisher King. Add to this the abiding sense of death and its meaning, and the spiritual teachings of Buddhism and the mystery religions (Christianity among them), and new complexities emerge, as do new questions that only the Thunder can answer.

The poem's last verse paragraph displays little overt coherence once the Fisher King asks his question, but it does nevertheless offer a direct key to understanding the poem. That the Fisher King has traversed the arid plains, has put them behind him and now may have some power to set his kingdom in order, provides a sense of closure. In the next line (1. 427), London Bridge, crossed by so many who had been undone by death in the unreal City (Part I), is falling down. This action will end the procession of dead commuters; in the nursery rhyme there is no adequate means to rebuild the bridge permanently. The next line is from Dante, who is a source for many of the attitudes, emotions, and possibly the situational contexts of many of the poem's speakers: here Arnaut Daniel, suffering in Purgatory for sins of lust, leaps back into the refining fire of his own accord; this may be seen as a gloss on the "Fire Sermon" and as a cure for the various forms of lust in the entire poem. There follow lines from "Pervigilium Veneris," a reference to Philomela (echoes of Parts II and III) and from Gérard de Nerval's "El Desdichado." This last may have metapoetical implications for the authorial Eliot and may also recall another quest for rightful inheritance—in Sir Walter Scott's novel *Ivanhoe* (1819). In "These fragments I have shored against my ruins" (1. 430), "these fragments" are the preceding 429 lines, the immediately preceding seven lines, the fragmented speeches, the fragments of poetic and religious traditions, and the fragments of verses composed over many years to form the poem itself. The reference to Thomas Kyd's *The Spanish Tragedy* (c. 1585, 1. 431), in which Hieronymo proposes to "fit" a play using fragments of poetry in several languages (tongues) could, as Bernard Bergonzi indicates, comment directly on *The Waste Land* itself. The penultimate line repeats the Thunder's statements, giving them more point; and the final line is translated by Eliot as equivalent to "The Peace which passeth understanding."

What do these keys unlock? Surely they suggest what a reader should know of European and Eastern literary, cultural, and religious traditions in order to grasp some of the poem's meanings. They may also serve to help the reader see, to paraphrase Eliot, the end in the beginning and the beginning in the end. Having come to the end of the poem, one must be prepared to read it anew from the beginning. Bernard Bergonzi, following C. K. Stead's analysis of the pattern and meaning of *Four Quartets*, provides an invaluable guide to the significance of each of the poem's five sections. "The Burial of the Dead" concerns movement in time (seasons, change, reluctant birth); "A Game of Chess" reveals patent dissatisfaction with worldly experience; "The Fire Sermon" leads through purgation in the world and a divesting of the soul of love for created things; "Death by Water" is a brief lyric containing a warning and an invocation; "What the Thunder Said" deals with the issues of spiritual health and artistic wholeness. To read the work as a poem about the artist's concern for artistic wholeness allied to spiritual health offers extraordinary and suggestive possibilities for revaluing it and the poetry that preceded it.

"The Hollow Men" has often been read as a poem written at the nadir of the poet's emotional life, a depressing and depressed poem. This may be a correct reading; it may also be, however much it is favored by scores of writers who seek autobiographical confessions in Eliot's poetry, wide of the mark. The poem seems, indeed, to have been composed from fragments discarded from earlier drafts of *The Waste Land*. Again, voice and fragment should guide the wary reader. The epigraph, from Joseph Conrad's *Heart of Darkness* (1902), should put the reader on guard. The speech is that of an African worker reporting the death of Mr. Kurtz to Conrad's narrator-once-removed, Marlow, whose account is passed on to the reader by one who heard him tell the tale. The reader is, like the hollow men, at several removes from anything like experience at first hand; and several emotional layers separate Conrad's reader from Kurtz: Eliot adds another emotional layer of separation but strikes a responsive note of limited sympathy in his readers who have read Conrad. This is only one small reflection of the ways in which *Heart of Darkness* stands in relation to this poem and, by extension, to *The Waste Land* and its "preface," "Gerontion."

This poem, like earlier poems and the later *Ash Wednesday*, is obsessed with death. One of Dante's dead, a "hollow man" (*Inferno*, III) who lived, without blame and without praise, a life of accidia, addresses the reader in self-explanation and communal confession. Two other major sources inform the poem and quicken the sense of death: the history of the Gunpowder Plot and the Elizabethan dramatic account of assassination found in Shakespeare's *Julius Caesar* (c. 1599-1600, in which the phrase "hollow men" occurs). The reader is clearly in the presence of the dead, just as Dante's Pilgrim listened to the hollow men, who were neither for Jehovah nor against him, in the hell of their own making. Like the addressee of *Heart of Darkness* the reader hears, perhaps seated in a club chair, a story of Marlow telling a tale prompted by his observation that his present location (seated on a yawl on the Thames) was once one of the dark places of the earth (and may still be so). In each case, the reader/addressee is told a story of darkness, a story of the Shadow, a story of failure and, ultimately, of inconsequence, a story told to pass the time.

In *Ash Wednesday,* so named for the first day of Lent, a day for the turnings of Christian metanoia, Dante's mysticism and its correlative tension between flesh and spirit are elaborated. The situation of which the voice speaks, a conversion that is not without difficulty and contention, is told not in logical, sequential narrative but in a disciplined symbolist dream. Here, for example, the Lady subsumes many ladies (the rejected one of blesséd face, Beatrice, Theologia, Ecclesia) and Eliot's earlier expressions of dehumanization (such as the classic "ragged claws" of "The Love Song of J. Alfred Prufrock") now become expressions of Christian humility. Unquestionably influenced by Eliot's own turning to the Anglican church in 1928, this poem, together with the Ariel poems, represents poetic pilgrimages of hope that do not necessarily find resolution of the tensions between flesh and spirit but which indicate possibilities for subliminal resolution in transcendence.

The assured masterpiece of his poetic maturity, *Four Quartets* is more immediately accessible than Eliot's early and middle work. The poems which comprise it, like his earlier poetry, grew incrementally from "Burnt Norton," which sprang from lines discarded from *Murder in the Cathedral,* to "Little Gidding," with "East Coker" and "The Dry Salvages" intervening. Unlike his earlier poetry, the poems of *Four Quartets* lack a dramatic character who speaks; instead, they are in the lyric tradition of direct poetic speech in which the speaker has a constant voice that may well be the poet's own. Unfortunately, the speaker sometimes assumes the hortatory voice of the preacher. This shift in poetic style, away from masks and personae, is a new element in Eliot's verse.

Each of the poems adopts a musical and frequently iterative pattern, as if the reader is meant to hear the instrumental conversations endemic to musical quartets. In reading these poems, one is frequently reminded of Walter Pater's dictum that "all art continually aspires to the condition of music." The poems are set pieces in the eighteenth century tradition of verse inspired by a visit to a specific place. Taken together, they constitute some of Eliot's most beautiful (and, in places, most banal) poetry, as the lyricist adopts a consistent poetic voice that muses on the process of cognition and composition.

The essential structure of these poems, filled as they are with local references dear to Eliot, follows the five-part structure of *The Waste Land.* C. K. Stead admirably analyzes the fivefold structure of each of the sections of *Four Quartets* as follows: (1) the movement of time, in which brief moments of eternity are caught; (2) worldly experience, leading only to dissatisfaction; (3) purgation in the world, divesting the soul of love of created things; (4) a lyric prayer for, or affirmation of the need of, Intercession; and (5) the problems of attaining artistic wholeness which become analogues for, and merge into, the problems of achieving spiritual health.

The poems of *Four Quartets* in some way negate, by their affirmations, the fragmented, disparate, and "unreal" elements in Eliot's earliest poems; but, on the whole, they present a synthesis of Eliot's poetic concerns and his varied statements about the problems and business of being a poet. They stand not at the end of his artistic career but at the summit of his career as a poet whose later work, in both bulk and intensity, is minimal. *Four Quartets* constitutes a compendium of the themes that Eliot pursued from his earliest days as a poet, but with the decided difference that sex has become part of love, belief has been ratified, and the world has become flesh again. The fire and the rose are one.

Other literary forms · When he startled the poetic world with the publication of *Prufrock and Other Observations* in 1917, T. S. Eliot was already on his way to becoming a prolific, formidable, and renowned literary critic of extraordinary originality and depth. Between 1916 and 1920, for example, he contributed almost a hundred essays and reviews to several journals, some of which he helped to edit. While his most enduring and famous criticism (except for his superb work on Dante Alighieri) is contained in such essays as "Hamlet and His Problems" and "Tradition and the Individual Talent" (*The Sacred Wood*, 1920), he published thirty books and pamphlets and scores of essays, many of which remain uncollected. Chief among his other volumes of prose are *Homage to John Dryden* (1924), *Shakespeare and the Stoicism of Seneca* (1927), *For Lancelot Andrewes* (1928), the celebrated *Dante* (1929), *Selected Essays* (1932, 1950), *The Use of Poetry and the Use of Criticism* (1933), *After Strange Gods* (1934), *Essays Ancient and Modern* (1936), *Poetry and Drama* (1951), and *On Poetry and Poets* (1957). From its inception in 1922 until its last issue in 1939, Eliot was editor of *The Criterion* and an important contributor to that and other journals concerned with literary, cultural, political, and religious matters.

Eliot came to drama later than to poetry and criticism, though the seeds of drama are clearly in his early poetry, and the drama occupied much of his criticism. His dramatic writing ranges from religious pageant-plays in verse, *The Rock: A Pageant Play* (1934) and *Murder in the Cathedral* (1935), to quite diverse efforts such as *The Family Reunion* (1939), *The Cocktail Party* (1949), *The Confidential Clerk* (1953), and *The Elder Statesman* (1958). All of his dramatic work has as one of its objects the restoration of poetic drama to the popular theater.

The record of Eliot's achievement is by no means complete. Many of his essays are available only in the journals in which they were published, and his notebooks have not been fully mined. *The Letters of T. S. Eliot: Volume I, 1898-1922*, edited by Valerie Eliot, his second wife, was published in 1988. The letters exemplify Eliot's characteristic civility, and they give glimpses of his occasional insecurities as a young American determined to succeed in England on England's terms. Eliot's thousand or so letters to Emily Hale have not been published; they are in the Princeton University Library and may be made public after January 1, 2020. Mrs. Valerie Eliot has edited and published *The Waste Land: A Facsimile and Transcript of the Original Drafts Including the Annotations of Ezra Pound* (1971) and Eliot's *Poems Written in Early Youth*. Several of Eliot's manuscripts are in the Berg Collection of the New York Public Library and in the Hayward Collection at King's College, Cambridge.

Select works other than poetry
DRAMA: *Sweeney Agonistes*, pb. 1932 (fragment); *The Rock*, pb., pr. 1934; *Murder in the Cathedral*, pb., pr. 1935; *The Family Reunion*, pb., pr. 1939; *The Cocktail Party*, pr. 1949; *The Confidential Clerk*, pr. 1953; *The Elder Statesman*, pr. 1958; *Collected Plays*, pb. 1962.

NONFICTION: *Ezra Pound: His Metric and Poetry*, 1917; *The Sacred Wood*, 1920; *Homage to John Dryden*, 1924; *Shakespeare and the Stoicism of Seneca*, 1927; *For Lancelot Andrewes*, 1928; *Dante*, 1929; *Thoughts After Lambeth*, 1931; *Charles Whibley: A Memoir*, 1931; *John Dryden: The Poet, the Dramatist, the Critic*, 1932; *Selected Essays*, 1932, 1950; *The Use of Poetry and the Use of Criticism*, 1933; *After Strange Gods*, 1934; *Elizabethan Essays*, 1934; *Essays Ancient and Modern*, 1936; *The Idea of a Christian Society*, 1939; *The Music of Poetry*, 1942; *The Classics and the Man of Letters*, 1942; *Notes Toward the Definition of Culture*, 1948; *Poetry and Drama*, 1951; *The Three Voices of Poetry*, 1953; *Religious Drama: Medieval and Modern*, 1954; *The Literature of Politics*, 1955; *The Frontiers of Criticism*, 1956; *On Poetry and Poets*, 1957; *Knowledge and Experience in the Philosophy of F. H. Bradley*, 1964; *To Criticize the Critic*, 1965; *The Letters of T. S. Eliot: Volume I, 1898-1922*, 1988.

John J. Conlon

Bibliography · For overviews of Eliot's life and work, see Russell Kirk, *Eliot and His Age: T. S. Eliot's Moral Imagination in the Twentieth Century*, 1971; Robert Sencourt, *T. S. Eliot: A Memoir*, 1971; Bernard Bergonzi, *T. S. Eliot*, 1972; T. S. Matthews, *Great Tom: Notes Towards the Definition of T. S. Eliot*, 1973; Caroline Behr, *T. S. Eliot: A Chronology of His Life and Works*, 1983; and Peter Ackroyd, *T. S. Eliot: A Life*, 1984. For excellent critical biography, see two books by Lyndall Gordon, *Eliot's Early Years*, 1977, and *Eliot's*

New Life, 1988. See also Kenneth George Asher, *T. S. Eliot and Ideology*, 1995, and, as a general guide to Eliot's work, A. David Moody, ed., *The Cambridge Companion to T. S. Eliot* (1994). Bibliographies and collections of essays about Eliot include *T. S. Eliot: The Critical Heritage*, 1982, edited by Michael Grant; *T. S. Eliot: Modern Critical Views*, 1985, edited by Harold Bloom; Donald Gallup, *T. S. Eliot: A Bibliography*, 1969; Mildred Martin, *A Half-Century of Eliot Criticism: An Annotated Bibliography of Books and Articles in English, 1916-1965*, 1972; and Beatrice Ricks, *T. S. Eliot: A Bibliography of Secondary Works*, 1980.

RALPH WALDO EMERSON

Born: Boston, Massachusetts; May 25, 1803
Died: Concord, Massachusetts; April 27, 1882

Poetry · *Poems*, 1847 · *May-Day and Other Pieces*, 1867 · *Selected Poems*, 1876

Achievements · Although Ralph Waldo Emerson's poetry was but a small part of his overall literary output, he thought of himself as very much a poet—even in his essays and lectures. He began writing poetry early in childhood and at the age of nine composed some verses on the Sabbath. At Harvard he was elected class poet and was asked to write the annual Phi Beta Kappa poem in 1834. This interest in poetry continued throughout his long career.

During his lifetime he published two small volumes of poetry, *Poems* (1847) and *May-Day and Other Pieces* (1867), which were later collected in one volume for the Centenary Edition of his works. Altogether, the Centenary volume contains some 170 poems, of which perhaps only several dozen are noteworthy.

Although Emerson produced a comparatively small amount of poetry and an even smaller number of first-rate poems, he stands as a major influence on the subsequent course of American poetry. As scholar, critic, and poet, Emerson was the first to define the distinctive qualities of American verse. His broad and exalted concept of the poet—as prophet, oracle, visionary, and seer—was shaped by his Romantic idealism. "I am more of a poet than anything else," he once wrote, although as much of his poetry is found in his journals and essays as in the poems themselves. In "The American Scholar" he called for a distinctive American poetry, and in his essay "The Poet" he provided the theoretical framework for American poetics. Scornful of imitation, he demanded freshness and originality from his verse, even though he did not always achieve in practice what he sought in theory. Rejecting the derivative verse of the "Hartford Wits" and the sentimental versifiers of his day, he sought an original style and flavor for an American poetry close to the native grain. The form of his poetry was, as F. I. Carpenter argues (*Emerson Handbook*, 1953), the logical result of his insistence upon self-reliance, while its content was shaped by his Romantic idealism. Thus his cumulative influence on American poetry is greater than his verse alone might imply.

Expression mattered more than form in poetry, according to Emerson.

Library of Congress

If he was not the completely inspirational poet called for in his essays, that may have been more a matter of temperament than of any flaw in his sense of the kind of poetry that a democratic culture would produce. In fact, his comments often closely parallel those of Alexis de Tocqueville on the nature of poetry in America. Both men agreed that the poetry of a democratic culture would embrace the facts of ordinary experience rather than celebrate epic themes. It would be a poetry of enumeration rather than elevation, of fact rather than eloquence; indeed, the democratic poet would have to struggle for eloquence, for poetry of the commonplace can easily become flat or prosaic. Even Emerson's own best verse often seems uneven, with memorable lines interspersed with mediocre ones.

Part of the problem with Emerson's poetry arose from his methods of composition. Writing poetry was not for him a smooth, continuous act of composition. Nor did he have a set formula for composition, as Edgar Allan Poe advocated in "The Philosophy of Composition"; instead, he trusted inspiration to allow the form of the poem to be determined by its subject matter. This "organic" theory of composition shapes many of Emerson's best poems, including "The Snow-Storm," "Hamatreya," "Days," and "Ode." These poems avoid a fixed metrical or stanzaic structure and allow the sense of the line to dictate its poetic form. Emerson clearly composed by the line rather than by the stanza or paragraph, in both his poetry and prose, and this self-contained quality often gives his work a gnomic or orphic tone.

Although some of his poems appear to be fragmentary, they are not unfinished. They lack smoothness or polish because Emerson was not a lyrical but a visionary, oracular poet. He valued poetry as a philosophy or attitude toward life rather than simply as a formal linguistic structure or an artistic form. "The poet is the sayer, the namer, and represents beauty," he observed in "The Poet." With Percy Bysshe Shelley he believed that the poet was the visionary who would make people whole and teach them to see anew. "Poets are thus liberating gods," Emerson concluded, because "they are free, and they make free." Poetry is simply the most concentrated expression of the poetic vision, which all people are capable of sharing.

Thus Emerson's poems seek to accomplish what the essays announce. His poems attempt to reestablish the primal relationship between humans and nature that he sought as a substitute for revelation. Emerson prized the poet as an innovator, a namer, and a language-maker who could interpret the oracles of nature. In its derivation from nature, all language, he felt, was fossil poetry. "Always the seer is a sayer," he announced in his Harvard Divinity School address, and through the vision of the poet "we come to look at the world with new eyes."

Of the defects in Emerson's poetry, the chief is perhaps that Emerson's muse sees rather than sings. Because his lines are orphic and self-contained, they sometimes seem flat and discontinuous. Individual lines stand out in otherwise undistinguished poems. Nor do his lines always scan or flow smoothly, since Emerson was virtually tone-deaf. In "The Poet" he rejects fixed poetic form in favor of a freer, more open verse. For Emerson, democratic poetry would be composed with variable line and meter, with form subordinated to expression. The poet in a democracy is thus a "representative man," chanting the poetry of the common, the ordinary, and the low. Although Emerson pointed the way, it took Walt Whitman to master this new style of American poetry with his first edition of *Leaves of*

Grass (1855), which Emerson promptly recognized and praised for its originality. Whitman thus became the poet whom Emerson had called for in "The American Scholar"; American poetry had come of age.

Biography · Born in Boston on May 25, 1803, Ralph Waldo Emerson was the second of five sons in the family of William and Ruth Emerson. His father was a noted Unitarian minister of old New England stock whose sudden death in 1811 left the family to struggle in genteel poverty. Although left without means, Emerson's mother and his aunt, Mary Moody Emerson, were energetic and resourceful women who managed to survive by taking in boarders, accepting the charity of relatives, and teaching their boys the New England values of thrift, hard work, and mutual assistance within the family. Frail as a child, Emerson attended Boston Latin School and Harvard, where he was graduated without distinction in 1821. Since their mother was determined that her children would receive a decent education, each of her sons taught after graduation to help the others through school. Thus Emerson taught for several years at his brother's private school for women before he decided to enter divinity school. His family's high thinking and plain living taught young Emerson self-reliance and a deep respect for books and learning.

With his father and step-grandfather, the Reverend Ezra Ripley of Concord, as models, Emerson returned to Harvard to prepare for the ministry. After two years of intermittent study at the Divinity School, Emerson was licensed to preach in the Unitarian Church. He was forced to postpone further studies, however, and travel south during the winter of 1826 because of poor health. The next two years saw him preaching occasionally and serving as a substitute pastor. One such call brought him to Concord, New Hampshire, where he met his future wife, Ellen Louisa Tucker. After his ordination in March, 1829, Emerson married Ellen Tucker and accepted a call as minister of the Second Church, Boston, where his father had also served. The position and salary were good, and Emerson was prepared to settle into a respectable career as a Boston Unitarian clergyman. Unfortunately his wife was frail, and within a year and a half she died of tuberculosis. Grief-stricken, Emerson found it difficult to continue with his duties as pastor and resigned from the pulpit six months after his wife's death. Private doubts had assailed him and he found he could no longer administer the Lord's Supper in good conscience. His congregation would not allow him to dispense with the rite, so his resignation was reluctantly accepted.

With a small settlement from his wife's legacy he sailed for Europe in December, 1832, to regain his health and try to find a new vocation.

During his winter in Italy he admired the art treasures in Florence and Rome. There he met the American sculptor Horatio Greenough and the English writer Walter Savage Landor. The following spring, Emerson continued his tour through Switzerland and into France. Paris charmed him with its splendid museums and gardens and he admired the natural history exhibits at the Jardin des Plantes. Crossing to England by August, he met Samuel Taylor Coleridge in London, then traveled north to visit Thomas Carlyle in Craigenputtock and William Wordsworth at Rydal Mount. His meeting with Carlyle resulted in a life-long friendship.

After returning to Boston in 1833, Emerson gradually settled into a new routine of study, lecturing, and writing, filling an occasional pulpit on Sundays, and assembling ideas in his journals for his essay on "Nature." Lydia Jackson, a young woman from Plymouth, New Hampshire, heard Emerson preach in Boston and became infatuated with him. The young widower returned her admiration, although he frankly confessed that he felt none of the deep affection he had cherished for his first wife. During their engagement he renamed her "Lidian" in their correspondence because he disliked the name Lydia. She accepted the change without demur. Within a year they were married and settled in a house on the Boston Post Road near the Old Manse of Grandfather Ripley. Emerson was now thirty-two and about to begin his life's work.

The next decade marked Emerson's intellectual maturity. "Nature" was completed and published as a small volume in 1836. In its elaborate series of correspondences between humanity and nature, Emerson established the foundations of his idealistic philosophy. "Why should not we also enjoy an original relation to the universe?" he asked. Humans could seek revelations firsthand from nature, rather than having them handed down through tradition. A year later Emerson gave his "The American Scholar" address before the Harvard Phi Beta Kappa Society, an event that Oliver Wendell Holmes later called "our intellectual Declaration of Independence." In his address, Emerson called for a distinctively American style of letters, free from European influences. Invited in 1838 to speak before the graduating class of Harvard Divinity School, Emerson affirmed in his address that the true measure of religion resided within the individual, not in institutional or historical Christianity. If everyone had equal access to the Divine Spirit, then inner experience was all that was needed to validate religious truth. For this daring pronouncement he was attacked by Harvard president Andrews Norton and others for espousing "the latest form of infidelity." In a sense each of these important essays was an extension of Emerson's basic doctrine of self-reliance, applied to philosophy, culture, and religion.

His self-reliance served him equally well in personal life, even as family losses haunted him, almost as if to test his hard-won equanimity and sense of purpose. Besides losing his first wife, Ellen Tucker, Emerson saw two of his brothers die and a third become so feeble-minded that he had to be institutionalized. Worst of all, his first-born and beloved son Waldo died in 1841 of scarlet fever at the age of six. Emerson's melioristic philosophy saw him through these losses, although in his journals he later chided himself for not feeling his son's death more deeply. Despite the hurt he felt, his New England reserve would not allow him to yield easily to grief or despair. Nor would he dwell in darkness while there was still light to be found.

During these years, Emerson found Concord a congenial home. He established a warm and stimulating circle of friends there and enjoyed the intellectual company of Nathaniel Hawthorne, Henry David Thoreau, and Bronson Alcott. As his fame as a lecturer and writer grew, he attracted a wider set of admirers, including Margaret Fuller, who often visited to share enthusiasms and transcendental conversations. Emerson even edited *The Dial* for a short time in 1842; but for the most part he remained aloof from, although sympathetic to, the transcendentalist movement that he had so largely inspired. His manner at times was even offhand. When asked for a definition of transcendentalism, he simply replied, "Idealism in 1842." When George Ripley invited him to join the Brook Farm Community in 1840, Emerson politely declined. Reform, he believed, had to begin with the individual. Thoreau later rebuked him for not taking a firmer stand on the Fugitive Slave issue, but Emerson was by nature apolitical and skeptical of partisan causes. His serenity was too hard-won to be sacrificed, no matter how worthy the cause.

So instead he continued to lecture and write, and his essays touched an entire generation of American writers. Thoreau, Whitman, and Emily Dickinson responded enthusiastically to the appeal of Emerson's thought, while even Hawthorne and Herman Melville, although rejecting it, still felt compelled to acknowledge his intellectual presence. Lecture tours took him repeatedly to the Midwest and to England and Scotland for a second time in 1847-1848. Harvard finally awarded him an honorary degree in 1866 and elected him overseer the following year. His alma mater also invited him to deliver a series of lectures on his philosophy in 1869-1870. When Emerson's home in Concord burned in 1877, friends sent him on a third visit to Europe and Egypt, accompanied by his daughter Ellen, while the house and study were rebuilt with funds from admirers. He spent his last few years in Concord quietly and died in the spring of 1882. Of his life it can be said that perhaps more than any of his contemporaries he embodied the qualities of the American spirit—its frankness, idealism, optimism, and self-confidence. For the American writer of his age, all things were possible. If, finally, he was as much prophet as poet, that may be due to the power of his vision as well as to its lyrical intensity: a power that suffused his prose and was concentrated in his poems.

Analysis · Ralph Waldo Emerson's poetic achievement is greater than the range of his individual poems might suggest. While perhaps only a handful of his poems attain undisputed greatness, others are rich in implication despite their occasional lapses, saved by a memorable line or phrase. As a cultural critic and poetic innovator, moreover, Emerson has had an immense influence through his essays and poetry in suggesting an appropriate style and method for subsequent American poets. He tried to become the poet he called for in "The American Scholar," and to a degree his poems reflect those democratic precepts. Determined to find distinctively American art forms, he began with expression—not form—and evolved the forms of his poems through their expression. Inspired by the "organic aesthetic" of the American sculptor Horatio Greenough, whose studio in Rome he visited in 1833, Emerson abandoned traditional poetic structure for a loose iambic meter and a variable (though often octosyllabic) line. Instead of following a rigid external form, the poem would take its form from its particular content and expression. This was the freedom Emerson sought for a "democratic" poetry.

Emerson's best poetry is thus marked by two qualities: organic form and a vernacular style; his less successful pieces, such as "The Sphinx," are too often cryptic and diffuse. These strengths and weaknesses both derive from his attempt to unite philosophical ideas and lyricism within a symbolic form in which the image would evoke its deeper meaning. "I am born a poet," he wrote to his fiancée, Lydia Jackson, "of a low class without doubt, yet a poet. That is my vocation. My singing, to be sure, is very 'husky,' and is for the most part in prose. Still I am a poet in the sense of a perceiver and dear lover of the harmonies that are in the soul and in matter, and specially of the correspondence between these and those." Correspondence, then, is what Emerson sought in his poetry, based on his theory of language as intermediary between humanity and nature.

In his essay "The Poet," Emerson announced that "it is not metres, but metre-making argument that makes a poem." His representative American poet would be a namer and enumerator, not a rhymer or versifier. The poet would take his inspiration from the coarse vigor of American vernacular speech and in turn reinvigorate poetic language by tracing root metaphors back to their origins in ordinary experience. He would avoid stilted or artificial poetic diction in favor of ordinary speech. This meant sacrificing sound to sense, however, since Emerson's "metre-making arguments" were more often gnomic than lyrical. As a result, his poems are as spare as their native landscape. They are muted and understated rather than rhapsodic, and—with the exception of his Orientalism—tempered and homey in their subject matter, since Emerson was more of an innovator in style than in substance. Emerson's "Merlin" provides perhaps the best definition of what he sought in his poetry:

> Thy trivial harp will never please
> Or fill my craving ear;
> Its chords should ring as blows the breeze,
> Free, peremptory, clear.

Emerson's poems fall into several distinct categories, the most obvious being his nature poems; his philosophical or meditative poems, which often echo the essays; his autobiographical verse; and his occasional pieces. Sometimes these categories may overlap, but the "organic" aesthetic and colloquial tone mark them as distinctly Emersonian. Two of his most frequently anthologized pieces, "Days" and "The Snow-Storm," will serve to illustrate his poetic style.

"Days" has been called the most perfect of Emerson's poems, and while there is a satisfying completeness about the poem, it resolves less than might appear at first reading. The poem deals with what was for Emerson the continuing problem of vocation or calling. How could he justify his apparent idleness in a work-oriented culture? "Days" thus contains something of a self-rebuke, cast in terms of an Oriental procession of Days, personified as daughters of Time, who pass through the poet's garden bringing various gifts, the riches of life, which the poet too hastily rejects in favor of a "few herbs and apples," emblematic of the contemplative life. The Day scorns his choice, presumably because he has squandered his time in contemplation rather than having measured his ambition against worthier goals. The Oriental imagery employed here transforms a commonplace theme into a memorable poem, although the poet never responds to the implied criticism of his life; nor does he identify the "morning wishes" that have been abandoned for the more sedate and domestic "herbs and apples," although these images do suggest meanings beyond themselves.

A thematically related poem is "The Problem," in which Emerson tries to justify his reasons for leaving the ministry, which he respects and admires but cannot serve. Perhaps because he was more poet than priest, Emerson preferred the direct inspiration of the artist to the inherited truths of religion. Or it may have been that, as a romantic, he found more inspiration in nature than in scripture. The third stanza of "The Problem" contains one of the clearest articulations of Emerson's "organic" aesthetic, of form emerging from expression, in the image of the artist who "builded better than he knew." The temples of nature "art might obey, but not surpass."

This organic theory of art reached its fullest expression in "The Snow-Storm," which still offers the best example in Emerson's poetry of form following function, and human artistry imitating that of nature. Here the poem merges with what it describes. The first stanza announces the arrival of the storm and the second stanza evokes the "frolic architecture" of the snow and the human architectural forms that it anticipates. Nature freely creates and humanity imitates through art. Wind and snow form myriad natural forms that humans can only "mimic in slow structures" of stone. As the windsculpted snowdrifts create beauty from the materials at hand, the poem rounds upon itself in the poet's implicit admiration of nature's work.

One of the most intriguing of Emerson's poems is "Hamatraya," which contains an attack on Yankee land-greed and acquisitiveness, cast as a Hindu meditation on the impermanence of all corporeal things. In "Hamatraya" the crass materialism of his countrymen evokes Emerson's serenely idealistic response. No one finally owns the land, he asserts, and to pretend so is to be deceived. The land will outlive successive masters, all of whom boast of owning it. In the enduring cycle of things, they are all finally returned to the earth they claimed to possess. Emerson uses dramatic form and the lyrical "Earth-Song" as an effective counterpoint to the blunt materialism of the first two stanzas. His theme of all things returning unto themselves finds its appropriate metaphor in the organic (and Hindu) cycle of life. Hindu cosmology and natural ecology complement each other in Emerson's critique of the pretensions of private land-ownership.

Another of Emerson's Oriental poems, his popular "Brahma," is notable for its blend of Eastern and Western thought. Here Emerson assumes the perspective of God or Brahma in presenting his theme of the divine relativity and continuity of life. Just as Krishna, "the Red Slayer," and his victim are merged in the unity of Brahma, so all other opposites are reconciled in the ultimate unity of the universe. This paradoxical logic appealed to Emerson as a way of presenting his monistic philosophy in poetic terms. The poem owes much to Emerson's study of the *Bhagavad Gītā* and other Oriental scriptures, the first stanza of "Brahma" being in fact a close parallel to the Hindu text. The smooth regularity of Emerson's ballad stanzas also helps to offset the exotic quality of the Hindu allusions and the novelty of the poem's theme.

Religious myth is also present in the poem "Uriel," which Robert Frost called "the greatest Western poem yet." Even if Frost's praise is overstated, this is still one of Emerson's most profound and complex poems. Again it deals with the reconciliation of opposites, this time in the proposed relativity of good and evil. Borrowing the theme of the primal revolt against God by the rebellious archangels, Emerson uses the figure of the angel Uriel as the prototype of the advanced thinker misunderstood or rejected by others. Uriel represents the artist as the rebel or prophet bearing unwelcome words, roles that Emerson no doubt identified with himself and the hostile reception given his "Divinity School Address" in 1838 by the Harvard theological faculty. Uriel's words,

> "Line in nature is not found;
> Unit and universe are round;
> In vain produced, all rays return;
> Evil will bless, and ice will burn,"

speak with particular force to our age, in which recent discoveries in theoretical physics and astronomy seem to have confirmed Emerson's intuitions about the relativity of matter and energy and the nature of the physical universe.

Emerson's monistic philosophy also appears in "Each and All," in which the poem suggests that beauty cannot be divorced from its context or setting without losing part of its original appeal. The peasant, sparrow, seashell, and maid must each be appreciated in the proper aesthetic context, as part of a greater unity. Beauty cannot be possessed, Emerson argues, without destroying it. The theme of "Each and All" perhaps echoes section III on Beauty of his essay "Nature," in which Emerson observes that "the standard of beauty is the entire circuit of natural forms–the totality of nature. . . . Nothing is quite beautiful alone; nothing but is beautiful in the whole. A single object is only so far beautiful as it suggests this universal grace." The poem "Each and All" gives a more concentrated and lyrical expression to this apprehension of aesthetic unity. The poetic images lend grace and specificity to the philosophical concept of the beauty inherent in unity.

Emerson's fondness for paradoxical logic and the union of apparent opposites appears in yet another poem, "Give All to Love," which initially appears to falter upon the contradiction between yielding to love and retaining one's individuality. The first three stanzas counsel a wholehearted surrender to the impulse of love, while the fourth stanza cautions the lover to remain "free as an Arab." The final two stanzas resolve this dilemma by affirming that the lovers may cherish joys apart without compromising their love for each other, since the purest love is that which is free from jealousy or possessiveness. Emerson reconciles the demands of love and those of self-reliance by idealizing the love relationship. Some commentators have even suggested that Emerson envisions a Neoplatonic ladder or hierarchy of love, from the Physical, to the Romantic, to the Ideal or Platonic—a relationship which in fact Emerson described in another poem entitled "Initial, Daemonic, and Celestial Love"—but the theme of "Give All to Love" seems to be simply to love fully without surrendering one's ego or identity. The last two lines of the poem, "When half-gods go,/ The Gods arrive," are often quoted out of context because of their aphoristic quality.

A poem that has led some readers to charge Emerson with coldheartedness or lack of feeling is "Threnody," his lament for the loss of his beloved son Waldo, who died of scarlet fever at the age of six. Waldo, the first-born child of his second marriage, died suddenly in January, 1842. Emerson was devastated by grief, yet he seems in the poem to berate himself for his inability to sustain his grief. In his journals Emerson freely expressed his bitterness and grief and he gradually transcribed these feelings into the moving pastoral elegy for his son. "Threnody," literally a death-song or lamentation, contains a mixture of commonplace and idealized pastoral images that demonstrate Emerson's ability to work within classical conventions and to ameliorate his grief through his doctrine of compensation. Some of the most moving lines in the poem describe the speaker's recollection of the child's "daily haunts" and unused toys, although these realistic details are later muted by the pathetic fallacy of external nature joining the poet in mourning the loss of his son.

Emerson's muse most often turned to nature for inspiration, so it is no accident that his nature poems contain some of his best work. "The Rhodora" is an early poem in which Emerson's attention to sharp and precise details of his New England landscape stands out against his otherwise generalized and formal poetic style. The first eight lines of the poem, in which Emerson describes finding the rhodora, a Northern azalea-like flower, blooming in the woods early in May of the New England spring, before other plants have put out their foliage, seem incomparably the best. Unfortunately the second half of the poem shifts from specific nature imagery to a generalized homily on the beauty of the rhodora, cast in formal poetic diction. Here Emerson's impulse to draw moralistic lessons from nature reminds one of another famous early nineteenth century American poem, William Cullen Bryant's "To a Waterfowl." This division within "The Rhodora" illustrates some of Emerson's difficulties in breaking away from the outmoded style and conventions of eighteenth century

English landscape poetry to find an appropriate vernacular style for American nature poetry. Here the subject matter is distinctly American, but the style—the poem's manner of seeing and feeling—is still partially derivative.

"The Humble Bee" is a more interesting poem in some respects, in that Emerson uses a form adequate to his expression—a tight octosyllabic line and rhymed couplets—to evoke through both sound and sense the meandering flight of the bumble bee. As the poem unfolds, the bee gradually becomes a figure for the poet intoxicated by nature. Some of the poem's conceits may seem quaint to modern taste, but "The Humble Bee" is innovative in its use of terse expression and symbolic form. Its style anticipates the elliptical language and abbreviated form of Emily Dickinson's poetry.

"Woodnotes" is a long and somewhat prosy two-part narrative poem that appears to be extracted from Emerson's journals. Part I introduces the transcendental nature lover ("A Forest Seer") in terms perhaps reminiscent of Thoreau, and part II describes the reciprocal harmony between humanity and nature, in which each is fully realized through the other. The vagueness of part II perhaps illustrates Emerson's difficulty in capturing transcendental rapture in specific poetic language.

"Ode" ("Inscribed to W. H. Channing") and "Concord Hymn" are both occasional poems that otherwise differ markedly in style and technique. "Concord Hymn" is a traditional patriotic poem in four ballad stanzas that Emerson composed to be sung at the placing of a stone obelisk on July 4, 1837, to commemorate the Battle of Concord, fought on April 19, 1775, on land later belonging to Reverend Ezra Ripley. The lines of the first stanza, now so well known that they are part of American national folklore, demonstrate that Emerson could easily master traditional verse forms when he chose to do so. The images of the "bridge" and the "flood" in the first stanza ripen imperceptibly into metaphor in the poem's implied theme that the Battle of Concord provided the impetus for the American Revolutionary War.

Emerson's "Ode" is a much more unconventional piece, written in terse, variable lines, usually of two or three stresses, and touching upon the dominant social and political issues of the day—the Mexican War, the Fugitive Slave Law of 1850, the threat of secession in the South, and radical Abolitionism in the North. This open form was perhaps best suited to Emerson's oracular style that aimed to leave a few memorable lines with the reader. His angry muse berates Daniel Webster for having compromised his principles by voting for the Fugitive Slave Law, and it denounces those materialistic interests, in both the North and the South, that would profit from wage or bond slavery. Emerson's lines "Things are in the saddle,/ And ride mankind" aptly express his misgivings about the drift of American affairs that seemed to be leading toward a civil war. His taut lines seem to chant their warning like a Greek chorus, foreseeing the inevitable but being helpless to intervene. By the 1850's Emerson had become an increasingly outspoken opponent of the Fugitive Slave Law, and on occasion risked his personal safety in speaking before hostile crowds.

Despite his commitment to a new American poetry based upon common diction and ordinary speech, Emerson's poetry never quite fulfilled the promise of his call, in "The American Scholar" and "The Poet," for a new poetics. Emerson wanted to do for American poetry what William Wordsworth had accomplished for English lyrical poetry, to free it from the constraints of an artificial and dead tradition of sensibility and feeling. Yet, he was not as consistent or as thoroughgoing a poetic innovator as the Wordsworth of the "Preface" to the Second Edition of *Lyrical Ballads* (1800), who both announced and carried out his proposed revision of the existing neoclassical poetic diction; nor did he apply his theory to his poetic composition as skillfully as Wordsworth did. Emerson could envision a new poetics but he could not sustain in his poetry a genuine American vernacular tradition. That had to wait for Whitman and Dickinson. Perhaps Emerson was too much the philosopher ever to realize fully the poetic innovations that he sought; but even with their flaws his poems retain a freshness and vitality lacking in contemporaries such as Henry Wadsworth Longfellow and James Russell Lowell, who were probably more accomplished versifiers. Emerson's greatness resides in the originality of his vision of a future American poetry, free and distinct from European models. It can be found in the grace of his essays and the insights of his journals, and it appears in those select poems in which he was able to match vision and purpose, innovation and accomplishment. His "Saadi" was no less a poet for the restraint of his harp.

Other literary forms · Ralph Waldo Emerson's *Journals*, written over a period of fifty-five years (1820-1875), were ultimately the source of everything else he wrote. These have been edited in ten volumes by Edward W. Emerson and Waldo Emerson Forbes (1909-1914). From the *Journals* a fine one-volume collection has been edited by Bliss Perry, *The Heart of Emerson's Journals* (1926). Ralph L. Rusk has also edited *The Letters of Ralph Waldo Emerson* in six volumes (1939). Emerson was a noted lecturer in his day, although many of his addresses and speeches were not collected until after his death. These appear in three posthumous volumes—*Lectures and Biographical Sketches, Miscellanies,* and *Natural History of Intellect*—which were published as part of the Centenary Edition (1903-1904). A volume of Emerson's *The Uncollected Writings: Essays, Addresses, Poems, Reviews, and Letters* was published in 1912. A sixteen-volume edition of journals and miscellaneous papers was published between 1960 and 1982.

Select works other than poetry

NONFICTION: *Nature*, 1836; *An Oration Delivered Before the Phi Beta Kappa Society, Cambridge*, 1837 (better known as *The American Scholar*); *An Address Delivered Before the Senior Class in Divinity College, Cambridge* . . . , 1838 (better known as *Divinity School Address*); *Essays: First Series*, 1841; *Orations, Lectures and Addresses*, 1844; *Essays: Second Series*, 1844; *Addresses and Lectures*, 1849; *Representative Men: Seven Lectures*, 1850; *English Traits*, 1856; *The Conduct of Life*, 1860; *Representative of Life*, 1860; *Society and Solitude*, 1870; *Works and Days*, 1870; *Letters and Social Aims*, 1876; *Lectures and Biographical Sketches*, 1884; *Miscellanies*, 1884; *Natural History of Intellect*, 1893; *The Journals of Ralph Waldo Emerson*, 1909-1914 (10 volumes; E. W. Emerson and W. E. Forbes, editors); *The Letters of Ralph Waldo Emerson*, 1939 (6 volumes; Ralph L. Rusk, editor); *The Journals and Miscellaneous Notebooks*, 1960-1982 (16 volumes).

EDITED WORK: *Parnassus*, 1874.

MISCELLANEOUS: *Uncollected Writings: Essays, Addresses, Poems, Reviews, and Letters*, 1912.

Andrew J. Angyal

Bibliography · Many good secondary works on Ralph Waldo Emerson exist. Gay Wilson Allen, *Waldo Emerson: A Biography*, 1981, is an extremely readable study of Emerson's life and works. For a study of Emerson's early life, see Evelyn Barish, *Emerson: The Roots of Prophecy*, 1989. Len Gougeon, *Virtue's Hero: Emerson, Antislavery, and Reform*, 1990, presents a picture of Emerson as a fighter for social justice, an aspect of his life that earlier biographies slight. Good starting places for information about Emerson's ideas are Stephen E. Whicher, *Freedom and Fate: An Inner Life of Ralph Waldo Emerson*, 1953, and Jonathan Bishop, *Emerson on the Soul*, 1964. R. A. Yoder, *Emerson and the Orphic Poet in America*, 1978, is a readable book-length study of the poems. Studies of the darker side of Emerson's works include B. L. Packer, *Emerson's Fall: A New Interpretation of the Major Essays*, 1982, and John Michael, *Emerson and Skepticism: The Cipher of the World*, 1988. See also Carlos Baker, *Emerson Among the Eccentrics: A Group Portrait*, 1996, and a standard biography by Ralph L. Rusk, *The Life of Ralph Waldo Emerson*, 1949.

LAWRENCE FERLINGHETTI

Born: Yonkers, New York; March 24, 1919

Poetry · *Pictures of the Gone World*, 1955, rev. 1995 (with 18 new poems) · *Selections from "Paroles" by Jacques Prévert*, 1958 (translation) · *A Coney Island of the Mind*, 1958 · *Starting from San Francisco*, 1961 · *An Eye on the World: Selected Poems*, 1967 · *The Secret Meaning of Things*, 1969 · *Tyrannus Nix?*, 1969 · *Back Roads to Far Places*, 1971 · *Open Eye, Open Heart*, 1973 · *Who Are We Now?*, 1976 · *Landscapes of Living and Dying*, 1979 · *A Trip to Italy and France*, 1981 · *Endless Life: Selected Poems*, 1981 · *Over All the Obscene Boundaries: European Poems and Transitions*, 1984 · *Roman Poems*, 1988 (trans.) · *These Are My Rivers: New and Selected Poems, 1955-1993*, 1993 · *A Far Rockaway of the Heart*, 1997

Achievements · In 1957, Lawrence Ferlinghetti first received national attention as a result of the "Howl" obscenity trial. At that time, Ferlinghetti was recognized not as a poet but as the publisher and distributor of Allen Ginsberg's *Howl and Other Poems* (1955). After winning the controversial trial, Ferlinghetti received enough attention to boost his own collection of poems, *A Coney Island of the Mind*, into a best-seller position. His name became strongly associated with the new, or "beat," poetry being developed on the West Coast. Since then, Ferlinghetti has been recognized as a poet of movements and protests. Being often antigovernment in his responses, Ferlinghetti has gone so far as never to accept government grants for either his own writing or the City Lights publishing house. Ferlinghetti is noted for the many public readings he has given in support of free speech, nuclear disarmament, antiwhaling, and so on. In 1977, the city of San Francisco paid tribute to Ferlinghetti by honoring him at the Civic Art Festival–the first time a poet was so recognized. Often overlooked by critics, Ferlinghetti has remained an active voice speaking for the American people against many institutions and practices–government, corporate, and social alike–that limit individual freedom; he stands out as a poet and a true individual.

Biography · Lawrence Ferlinghetti–born in Yonkers, New York, in 1919–was the youngest of five sons of Charles and Clemence Ferlinghetti. Several months before Lawrence's birth, Charles Ferlinghetti died unexpectedly of a heart attack, and Lawrence's mother, Clemence, suffered a breakdown as a result. She was unable to care for Lawrence and was eventually institutionalized at the state hospital in Poughkeepsie, New York.

After these humble and tragic beginnings, it is ironic that Lawrence was taken and cared for by his mother's well-to-do uncle, Ludwig Mendes-Monsanto, and his wife, Emily, in their Manhattan home. It is also ironic that American-born Lawrence Ferlinghetti learned French as his first language. In fact, throughout his childhood he actually believed himself to be French, having been taken in by his great-aunt Emily, who left her husband and returned to France, her homeland. Lawrence spent the first five years of his life in Strasbourg with Emily, whom he refers to as his "French mother." Emily was eventually persuaded to return to New York to rejoin Ludwig, but the reunion lasted only for a short time. Lawrence—who knew himself only as Lawrence Ferling Monsanto—was placed in an orphanage for seven months. Eventually Emily reclaimed him and took him away, after leaving Ludwig again. This time they remained in New York.

Emily took on work as a French tutor for the daughter of the very wealthy Presley and Anna Lawrence Bisland. Emily and Lawrence lived in a small room in the third floor servants' area until one day Emily mysteriously disappeared, whereupon Lawrence was adopted by the Bislands.

The Bislands had had a son who died in early childhood. His name—and Mrs. Bisland's maiden name—was Lawrence, her father having founded Sarah Lawrence College near Bronxville. Mr. Bisland was also a man of letters, with a profound interest in contemporary literature, although his experiences included being one of the last men to ride the Chisholm trail on the last of the great cattle drives. The Bislands were aristocratic, adventuresome, cosmopolitan, but also creative in spirit. In fact, Ferlinghetti maintains that Presley Bisland's writings gave him the idea that being an author was a dignified calling.

At the age of ten, Ferlinghetti was told about his natural mother, Clemence Ferlinghetti, whom he met one traumatic Sunday afternoon. He was given the choice to go with her, whom he considered a stranger, or to stay with the Bislands. He chose to stay. Unknown to Ferlinghetti, the Bislands had arranged to send him away to school. A few weeks later he found himself boarding with a family named Wilson in one of New York City's rougher neighborhoods. Their son Bill, being older, became a hero to young Ferlinghetti. Lawrence joined the Boy Scouts and went to baseball and football games and was far less lonely than he had been at the Bisland mansion.

At the age of sixteen, Lawrence began to write poetry. His stepsister, Sally Bisland, gave him a book of Charles Baudelaire in translation. Ferlinghetti remembers it as the first collection of poems he read from cover to cover. He was then sent to a private high school, Mount Hernon, near Greenfield, Massachusetts. In his senior year, Mrs. Bisland took him for the first of a series of visits to see his natural mother and brothers at their home in Ossining.

Ferlinghetti attended college at the University of North Carolina at Chapel Hill and was graduated in 1941, after which he joined the Navy and served in World War II. It was while he was in the Navy that he received a telegram from Central Islip State Hospital saying that Emily Monsanto, Lawrence's "French mother," had died, having listed Ferlinghetti as her only living relative. This was the first he had heard of her since she had left him with the Bislands when he was ten.

In World War II, Ferlinghetti was on one of the primary Naval sub-chasers coming in for the Normandy invasion. Later, in 1945, on the first day of United States occupation of Japan, his ship landed there. Eventually he was able to visit Nagasaki where he witnessed the aftermath of the atomic bombing of that city. The devastation he witnessed left an indelible impression.

After his discharge from the Navy, Ferlinghetti returned to New York City and lived in Greenwich Village, taking on work as a mail clerk for *Time* magazine. His interest in poetry revived, and he returned to Columbia University under the G.I. Bill, receiving his M.A. degree in 1947. That summer Presley Bisland died. Soon afterward, Ferlinghetti left for Paris, where he met many literary figures. He completed work on a thesis, and was awarded a degree from the Sorbonne. He also wrote a novel, which was rejected by Doubleday. In 1949, Ferlinghetti returned to America for a two-week visit with Mrs. Bisland. In 1951, both she and Ferlinghetti's natural mother died. In the same year, after several trips back and forth between Europe and the United States, Ferlinghetti married Selden Kirby-Smith, who was known as Kirby. They moved to San Francisco, where Ferlinghetti wrote articles for *Art Digest* and book reviews for the *San Francisco Chronicle.*

Influenced greatly by Kenneth Rexroth and Kenneth Patchen, who both lived in San Francisco, Ferlinghetti soon came to be considered a political poet. He was published in Peter Martin's magazine *City Lights* and eventually the two men collaborated to open the City Lights Bookstore in 1953. In 1955, the same year that Ferlinghetti's first book of poetry, *Pictures of the Gone World*, was published under the City Lights imprint, Peter Martin sold Ferlinghetti his interest in the store. At about that time, Ferlinghetti became acquainted with James Laughlin, president of New Directions. It was through Laughlin that Ferlinghetti's second book of poems, *A Coney Island of the Mind*, became a best-seller.

Allen Ginsberg came into Ferlinghetti's life from the East, bringing a poem entitled "Howl" with him. Ferlinghetti was impressed with Ginsberg and published *Howl and Other Poems*. It was this book that caused Ferlinghetti to be arrested, the charge against him being that he printed and sold obscene writings. He was eventually cleared, and, partly because of the publicity, City Lights flourished.

Although Ferlinghetti and his wife Kirby were divorced in the early 1970's, their marriage had been relatively stable; in 1962 a daughter, Julie, was born, and in 1963 a son, Lorenzo. During the 1960's Ferlinghetti traveled to South and Central America, to Europe, and to the Soviet Union, giving poetry readings whenever possible. In 1974 he met Paula Lillevand; they moved in together in 1978, but they parted two years later.

Ferlinghetti first took LSD in 1967, the poem "Mock Confessional" resulting from that experience. Throughout the 1970's and 1980's Ferlinghetti remained actively interested in political and environmental matters, his poetry inevitably reflecting his political and social concerns. During these years he traveled extensively in Europe and sometimes in Latin America, giving readings of his poems. In 1977 Ferlinghetti took up drawing, an interest he had left behind some twenty years earlier, and soon he was painting as well. His expressionist-style works were displayed in a formal exhibition in the mid-1980's in the Bay Area, and another show was organized in Berlin in 1990. In 1997 Ferlingetti published *A Far Rockaway of the Heart*, a companion volume to *A Coney Island of the Mind*, published nearly thirty years before.

Analysis · Lawrence Ferlinghetti's poetry may be looked on as a kind of travelog in which he has subjectively recorded choice experiences or montages from experience—often jazzlike or free-associative. For Ferlinghetti, "reality" itself becomes metaphorical, something he endows with mythical import, although he is not a poet given to hidden meanings. While his poetry is largely autobiographical, an adequate analysis of his poetry is possible without thorough biographical knowledge; Ferlinghetti's poetry is not excessively self-contained.

Whereas Ferlinghetti's poems are for the most part historical, or autobiographical, Ferlinghetti the man is a myth, appearing as a cult hero, one of the original "beats." Sometimes a martyr to a cause, Ferlinghetti will occasionally insert his political ideologies into a poem for no apparent reason other than that they seem to fit his role. Halfway through the sometimes absurd, sometimes delightful poem "Underwear," Ferlinghetti overextends his metaphor by becoming politically involved:

> You have seen the three-color pictures
> with crotches encircled
> to show the areas of extra strength
> and three-way stretch
> promising full freedom of action
> Don't be deceived
> It's all based on the two-party system
> which doesn't allow much freedom of choice

The reader is often seduced, but behind Ferlinghetti's seemingly spoken voice, full of American colloquialisms, is an intellect schooled in the classics, highly knowledgeable of literature, past and present—a voice full of allusions. Rather surprisingly, Ferlinghetti makes many direct references to greater works of literature by borrowing lines to suit his own purposes. Even the title of Ferlinghetti's best-selling book *A Coney Island of the Mind* is taken from Henry Miller's *Into the Night Life* (1947). One repeatedly discovers lines and phrases such as T. S. Eliot's "Let us go then you and I" and "Hurry up please it's time" ironically enlisted for use in such poems as "Junkman's Obbligato." Ferlinghetti frequently employs fragments from literature without alerting his audience to his borrowing. In the poem "Autobiography" he states, "I read the Want Ads daily/ looking for a stone a leaf/ an unfound door"—an oblique reference to Thomas Wolfe's opening in *Look Homeward, Angel* (1929). He makes even more esoteric references to W. B. Yeats's "horsemen" in poems such as "Reading Yeats I Do Not Think" and again in "Autobiography." In "Assassination Raga" one finds a variation on Dylan Thomas' "The force that through the green fuse drives the flower." In its stead, Ferlinghetti writes of "The force that through the red fuze/ drives the bullet"—the poem being in honor of Robert Kennedy and read in Nourse Auditorium, San Francisco, June 8, 1968, the day Kennedy was buried. In his role as a subjective historian and political rebel, Ferlinghetti never orates with so much pomp as to raise himself above his audience. In his meager "Charlie Chaplin" manner—Chaplin being a persona to whom he continuously compares himself in poems such as "Constantly Risking Absurdity," "In a Time of Revolution for Instance," and "Director of Alienation"—Ferlinghetti is just as capable of making fun of himself as he is of harassing various institutions and aspects of society.

Whereas some poets seek to find metaphorical reflections of themselves in nature, Ferlinghetti rarely looks there for inspiration. Furthermore, being more fond of philosophy than of drama, Ferlinghetti projects a sense of conflict mainly through his own personal quest—for his true self. His feelings of alienation and the quest for environmental constants that do not restrict one's freedom are depicted in the poem "Dog," which begins: "The dog trots freely in the street/ and sees reality/ and the things he sees/ are bigger than himself." As the poem progresses the reader comes to understand that this is an ordinary stray dog—and also Ferlinghetti in a stray-dog suit. "And the things he sees/ are his reality/ Drunks in doorways/ Moons on trees." The dog keeps on going with a curiosity that demands diversity from experience. Ferlinghetti goes deeper, allowing the reader also to don a dog suit, to see "Ants in holes/ Chickens in Chinatown windows/ their heads a block away." Thus the reader learns that he is roaming the streets of San Francisco. The dog trots past the carcasses that are hung up whole in Chinatown. At this point the reader learns that he "would rather eat a tender cow/ than a tough policeman/ though either might do." The reader has already been told that the dog does not hate cops; he merely has no use for them. Here the reader begins to wonder whether being stray is conditional on having no preferences. Is the dog a Democrat or a Republican? The reader later learns that this dog is at least "democratic." Ferlinghetti does deal with unusual specifics as the dog trots past the San Francisco Meat Market, and keeps going: "past the Romeo Ravioli Factory/ and past Coit's Tower/ and past Congressman Doyle of the Unamerican Committee." Here Ferlinghetti manages to make a political statement that is alien to a dog's perspective. This "Unamerican Committee" is obviously something that Ferlinghetti the Beat poet has recognized— not the Ferlinghetti in the dog suit. The Ferlinghetti in the dog suit says that ultimately "Congressman Doyle is just another/ fire hydrant/ to him." Thus the reader knows how the Ferlinghetti in a dog suit might treat Congressman Doyle—symbolically or not. A few lines earlier, Ferlinghetti alludes to Dylan Thomas by labeling the dog "a sad young dog" (see Thomas' *Portrait of the Artist as a Young Dog,* 1940): The dog appears to be metaphorical of all poets and artists, especially Ferlinghetti himself.

Ferlinghetti proceeds to declare that a dog's knowledge is only of the senses. His curiosity already quite obvious, the day becomes:

> a real live
> > barking
> > > democratic dog
> > engaged in real
> > > free enterprise
> > with something to say

>   about ontology
>   something to say
>   about reality.

In this segment, a major change can be noted: Ferlinghetti has abandoned flush left margins. Beginning with the line "barking," Ferlinghetti demonstrates a newfound freedom through his staggered, free-form typography. The poem continues, and the dog himself trots more freely, cocking his head sideways at streetcorners "as if he is just about to have/ his picture taken/ for Victor Records." His ear is raised, and it is suggested that he embodies a question mark as he looks askew into the "great gramophone of puzzling existence," waiting and looking, just like Ferlinghetti, for an answer to everything—and it all sounds like poetry.

Other literary forms · Early in his career, Lawrence Ferlinghetti was very much interested in the French Symbolist poets, and in 1958 City Lights published his first and only translation of French poetry: *Paroles*, by Jacques Prévert. His translations of pieces by an Italian poet, Pier Paolo Pasolini, appeared in 1986 as *Roman Poems*. Ferlinghetti has rarely published anything except poetry in book form, although he has written many critical and review articles that have appeared in both magazines and newspapers. Even his prose works—*Her* (1960) and *The Mexican Night* (1970)—sound so much like his poetry that it is questionable whether one should actually call them prose. He published another novel, *Love in the Days of Rage*, in 1988.

Ferlinghetti's two books of plays, *Unfair Arguments with Existence* and *Routines*, were published by New Directions in 1963 and 1964, respectively. His interest in the theater and oral poetry led to various filmings and recordings of his readings. The two best-known of Ferlinghetti's performances, "Tyrannus Nix?" and "Assassination Raga," are preserved on both film and record. *Leaves of Life: Drawing from the Model* (1983), published under the pseudonym Mendes Monsanto, is a collection of his drawings.

Select works other than poetry

LONG FICTION: *Her*, 1960; *Love in the Days of Rage*, 1988.

DRAMA: *Unfair Arguments with Existence*, pb. 1963; *Routines*, pb. 1964.

NONFICTION: *The Mexican Night*, 1970; *Literary San Francisco: A Pictorial History from Its Beginnings to the Present Day*, 1980 (with Nancy J. Peters); *Leaves of Life: Drawing from the Model*, 1983.

John Alspaugh

Bibliography · Biographies include Barry Silesky, *Ferlinghetti: The Artist in His Time*, 1990, and Neeli Cherkovski, *Ferlinghetti: A Biography*, 1979. A general review of Ferlinghetti's writings may be found in Larry R. Smith, *Lawrence Ferlinghetti: Poet-at-Large*, 1983, and in Michael Skau, *Constantly Risking Absurdity*, 1989. David Kherdian, *Six Poets of the San Francisco Renaissance: Portraits and Checklist*, 1967, includes a chapter entitled "Lawrence Ferlinghetti" that describes a day in the life of the poet and publisher. David Meltzer, ed., *Golden Gate: Interviews with Five San Francisco Poets*, 1976, presents an extended interview with Ferlinghetti. Gregory Stephenson, *The Daybreak Boys: Essays on the Literature of the Beat Generation*, 1990, contains the chapter "The 'Spiritual Optics' of Lawrence Ferlinghetti," which offers a general view of Ferlinghetti's writings. See also Thomas Francis Parkinson, "Phenomenon or Generation," in his *A Casebook on the Beat*, 1961; Crale D. Hopkins, "The Poetry of Lawrence Ferlinghetti: A Reconsideration," *Italian Americana* 1, no. 1 (1974); and L. A. Ianni, "Lawrence Ferlinghetti's Fourth Person Singular and the Theory of Relativity," *Wisconsin Studies in Contemporary Literature* 8 (1967). Two good interviews are *The Cool Eye: Lawrence Ferlinghetti Talks to Alexis Lykiard*, 1993, and "Lawrence Ferlinghetti," *Paris Magazine* (Summer, 1989), where he is interviewed by John Foy and Kyle Jarvard.

CAROLYN FORCHÉ

Born: Detroit, Michigan; April 28, 1950

Poetry · *Gathering the Tribes*, 1976 · *The Country Between Us*, 1981 · *The Angel of History*, 1994

Achievements · Carolyn Forché's poems focus on people—her ancestors, her childhood friends, Native Americans, and El Salvadorans, to name a few—and emphasize place—often Detroit, the Southwest, or Central America. Her commitment to speaking for those who have been silenced, whether for economic, ethnic, racist, or political reasons, has won for her many readers and much critical acclaim. Her first book, *Gathering the Tribes*, concerning a girl's initiation into adulthood, received the Yale Series of Younger Poets Award. Her second, *The Country Between Us*, concerning a young woman's development of a social conscience, was the Lamont Selection of the Academy of Poets (1981) and the *Los Angeles Times* Book Award nominee in 1982. The commitment to politics that surfaced clearly in the second volume is also evident in *El Salvador: The Work of Thirty Photographers*, in many of her essays, and in her work-in-progress.

She has received numerous awards for her poetry and various fellowships, including a National Endowment for the Arts Fellowship (in 1977) and a John Simon Guggenheim Memorial Fellowship (in 1978). Forché is a member of a number of literary organizations, including the International Association of Poets, Playwrights, Editors, Essayists, and Novelists (PEN) and the Academy of American Poets, and of political and government groups such as Amnesty International, the Institute for Global Education, and the Commission on United States-Central American Relations.

Biography · Born in 1950 to Michael Joseph Forché, a tool and die maker, and Louise Nada Sidlosky Forché, a homemaker, Carolyn Louise Forché, the oldest of seven children, spent her first five years in Detroit, Michigan, before moving to the suburbs with her family. With the encouragement of her mother, Forché began writing poems at nine, often as an escape, much like daydreaming. At eighteen, she published her first poem, "Artisan Well," in the October, 1968, issue of *Ingenue*.

At Justin Morrill College, an experimental college of Michigan State University, she attracted the attention of several professors, who became mentors and encouraged her writing. In 1970 and again in 1971 she won first prize in Michigan State University's poetry competition. At college she majored in creative writing and minored in English literature and French but also took courses in international relations, philosophy, and history. In addition to French she studied Russian, Spanish, Serbo-Croatian, and Tewa (Pueblo Indian)—perhaps following an interest generated by her Slavic-speaking relatives. After receiving her B.A. in 1972, she entered the M.F.A. program at Bowling Green State University in Ohio; she received her master's degree in 1975. Her M.A. thesis, "Secret Histories," suggests the direction that her poetry would take: the chronicling of the lives of those who have been forgotten.

As a student she worked on the poems that formed her first collection, *Gathering the Tribes*, and she completed it at age twenty-four. The collection was well received, entering its third printing only a year after its publication. She then turned her attention to the period involving Vietnam. In high school she and her working-class friends had been supportive of the war, but in college she had joined the antiwar movement. She struggled to understand Vietnam partly because her first husband, whom she married when she was nineteen, was psychologically scarred by the war and partly because her political conscience had been stimulated by Terrence Des Pres's *Survivors: An Anatomy of Life in the Death Camps* (1976), which she had read while convalescing from viral meningitis in 1976. She made Des Pres's acquaintance, and the two writers entered into a correspondence that lasted until his death in 1987. His last work, *Praises and Dispatches* (1988), explores the relationship between poetry and politics, a subject that is of importance in understanding Forché's poems.

During the 1970's, Forché developed an interest in Central America. Working on the translation of the poems of Claribel Alegría, she traveled to Spain in 1977 to consult the exiled poet. There she met a number of Latin American writers and began to learn about the region's human rights problems. Returning to California, she taught English at San Diego State University but also worked for Amnesty International. When she received a Guggenheim Fellowship, Leonel Gomez, Alegría's nephew, suggested that she use it to travel in El Salvador; other friends, however, suggested Paris. Gomez argued, "Do you want to write poetry about yourself the rest of your life?" Answering in the negative, she chose El Salvador. From 1978 to 1980, as a journalist and human rights activist reporting to Amnesty International, she traveled in El Salvador, witnessing the poverty of the peasants, the ill health of the children, the rural hospitals where operations were often performed without anesthesia, and also the luxurious homes of the military. During this period the notorious death squads were becoming active, and she learned about the missing people and the torture of political dissidents. Once back in the United States, she lectured and wrote articles concerning her experiences, following the Salvadorans' plea: "Document it. . . . go back and tell them what you've seen." Her poems on El Salvador are included in *The Country Between Us*, which gained for Forché a reputation as a political poet. Perhaps that designation is not, or should not be, unusual, for as Forché points out, "History and politics affect everyone's life, everywhere, always."

As she had after her first collection, she again took a hiatus from poetry, explaining that reflection and solitude were necessary for writing poetry and the political situation allowed her neither. Instead she turned to writing a series of essays on places she had visited. The first, on El Salvador, appeared in *American Poetry Review* in 1981, and she planned additional essays on Lebanon and on Northern Ireland. While in Lebanon, she presented a series of news documentaries on Beirut (parts of which reminded her of Detroit) for National Public Radio's program *All Things Considered*.

Forché was married on December 27, 1984, to Henry E. Mattison, a photographic correspondent with *Time* magazine whose assignments included Nicaragua, El Salvador, Lebanon, and South Africa. They were together in South Africa but left in 1986 for the birth of their son, Sean Christophe, for they did not want their child to be born under the apartheid system.

Since 1974 Forché has taught English and writing or has been a writer-in-residence at various universities, including Michigan State University, San Diego State University, the University of Virginia, New York University, Vassar College, and Columbia University. She has continued to give frequent poetry readings.

Analysis · In her first collection, *Gathering the Tribes*, Carolyn Forché recounts the experiences of her youth and maturation, focusing on places and people of importance to her development. She writes of her grandmother and Michigan but also of Teles Goodmorning (a Pueblo Indian) and the Southwest, claiming a spiritual kinship. Her second volume, *The Country Between Us*, is marked by a similar emphasis on places and people, but this time the place is often El Salvador or Czechoslovakia and the people are victims of oppression.

The first volume charts the growth of a child entering adulthood, and the second completes the process, chronicling the development of a social conscience with an emphasis on commitment and responsibility. Criticized for being an activist poet, Forché counters, "There is no such thing as a nonpolitical poetry." Her belief that "we are, as a species, now careening toward our complete destruction with ever-greater velocity" explains her political involvement and her commitment to speak out.

In *Gathering the Tribes*, Forché links the process of her maturation to the influence of specific people and places. These poems display a strong sense of place, whether it be the Michigan of her childhood, the Wakhan region of northern Afghanistan, or the Pueblo villages of New Mexico. Yet there is also a strong sense of dislocation: Her Slavic ancestors left their homeland; the narrator can never be part of the Southwest. Thus strong bonds between people are essential; the tribes must be gathered together. The people whom she cherishes might be her Slavic ancestors, her childhood friends, or those she considers spiritual ancestors—the Indians of the Southwest. It is often women who provide guidance—her peasant grandmother; the Indians Rosita and Alfansa; the narrator's lover, Jacynthe. Reinforcing the prominent position of women in the collection are many domestic images, such as bread making and pea shelling, and images drawn from nature and the natural cycles. This emphasis on women has led to questions about Forché's position on the women's movement; she responds, "I think any intelligent woman would have to consider herself a feminist."

Gathering the Tribes is divided into three parts. The first, "Burning the Tomato Worms," focuses primarily on the narrator's Slavic ancestors and their history, including their probably forced migration from northern Afghanistan, across Turkey, to the region where Russia borders Czechoslovakia. The poems suggest a connection between the past of the ancestors and the present of the narrator's girlhood. In other words, her life is a continuation of their lives, especially that of the peasant grandmother, Anna. The poems are imbued with Anna's wisdom and knowledge of the Old World's folkways and folklore, knowledge that the narrator needs: "Grandma, come back, I forgot/ How much lard for these rolls" ("The Morning Baking"). Throughout the poems, there is a transference of the past to the present. Eventually the narrator becomes, in a sense, her grandmother: "But I'm glad I'll look when I'm old/ Like a gypsy dusha hauling milk."

The strong bond between the speaker and her grandmother is evident in the central poem "Burning the Tomato Worms." The poem is set in the Midwest, with its "ploughed land" and "horse-breath weather," reminding the narrator of her deceased grandmother Anna. The narrator is directly linked to her grandmother's ancestors:

> Before I was born, my body as snowfat
> Crept over Wakhan
> As grandfathers spat into fires and thawed
> Their tarpaulin
> Sending crackled paths of blood
> Down into my birth.

She inherits these memories and those of her grandmother's youth in eastern Europe, when political oppression forced her family to leave home:

> When time come
> We go quick
> I think
> What to take.

Carrying nothing but the bare essentials, the grandmother eventually settled in Michigan.

It is Anna who, "shelling snow peas" with Uzbek hands that once were "known for weaving fine rugs," teaches the narrator and guides her, relying on Old World maxims such as "Eat bread and salt and speak the truth." Anna wants the speaker to confront "something/ That was sacred and eternal." The meaning of this "something" is left ambiguous until the final section of the poem, when the reader understands that the grandmother is leading the speaker to an acceptance of the natural cycles of life. Her grandmother shapes the speaker's life, yet the narrator is not frozen to the past but is part of the present and future. Her life is a counterbalance to her grandmother's death. Thus the poem tells of the younger woman's sexual awakening and ends with a transferring of life from the grandmother to the speaker.

Just as the first part of *Gathering the Tribes* examines the influence of Forché's biological ancestors, the second, "Song Coming Toward Us," shows the influence of her spiritual forebears, primarily the Indians of the Southwest. The bonds are again clear: "What has been/ and what is becoming/ are all of the same age" ("Calling Down the Moose"). The Indians, such as Alfansa (in "Alfansa") and Rosita ("Mientras Dure Vida, Sobra el Tiempo"), are her teachers, just as her grandmother was. This section ends with "Plain Song," which expresses her acceptance of her eventual death, since death, like sex, is part of the natural cycle:

> When it happens, let the birds come.
> Let my hands fall without being folded.
> . . . .
> Close my eyes with coins, cover
> my head with agave baskets
> that have carried water.

The final section, "The Place That Is Feared I Inhabit," draws predominantly on Forché's personal experiences rather than on her ancestors. The poems chronicle the development of the narrator's sexuality, from her infatuation with Joey, a childhood boyfriend, in "Taproot" and "This Is Their Fault" to a more adult understanding of sexuality as a young mother in "Year at Mudstraw," followed by a sense of disillusionment in "Taking Off My Clothes"; here the speaker voices the suspicion that her lover cannot appreciate her, just as he could not appreciate a Ming bowl. One of the final poems, "Kalaloch," presents a lesbian relationship against the backdrop of nature. The first few stanzas of the erotic poem focus on Jacynthe and the speaker's stay at the coast, where they gather mussels, pick berries, and watch the fog and the tide at day and the moon and the campfire at night. Their love is as natural as the setting in which it is expressed.

If *Gathering the Tribes* can be said to chronicle an initiation into adulthood, Forché's second volume, *The Country Between Us*, explores the responsibilities and commitments of that adulthood. The catalyst for this collection was Forché's stay in El Salvador. Eight of the poems in the volume have to do with that experience, and the first section of the volume is dedicated to Oscar Romero, the archbishop who, in 1980, was murdered as he said Mass in San Salvador. Yet Vietnam and Czechoslovakia are also highlighted in this collection. As in the first collection, people are central. Included are a steelworker troubled by Vietnam; a woman with whom the speaker shared childhood dreams and who now lives in a trailer with her husband and children, wondering what happened to her life; Terrence Des Pres, Forché's confidant and mentor; a dissident from Eastern Europe; and a political prisoner in El Salvador.

The prose poem "The Colonel," the most frequently quoted piece in *The Country Between Us*, is autobiographical, like much of Forché's work, and is based on an encounter with a Salvadoran military officer. At first, the evening described seems unexceptional, even ordinary. The speaker and her friend have dinner (lamb, wine, and fruit) with the colonel and his wife. Typical household items such as newspapers, a pet dog, and a television set make the setting comfortable and tranquil—yet the broken glass embedded in the wall surrounding the compound suggests otherwise. The family's activities—one child files her nails, the other goes out for the evening, the wife serves coffee—are also familiar. Nevertheless, the horror of the situation is soon apparent. The colonel dumps a sackful of human ears on the dining table, emphasizing his intolerance for human rights activists: "He spilled many ears on the table. They were like dried peach halves. There is no other way to say this. He took one of them in his hands, shook it in our faces, dropped it into a water glass. It came alive there. I am tired of fooling around he said." While the colonel might have power now, the poem suggests that the situation will not last: "Some of the ears on the floor caught this scrap of his voice. Some of the ears on the floor were pressed to the ground." The ears assume a life of their own and a memory, and they will be avenged.

While the volume's first part, "In Salvador, 1978-80," focuses on that country, the second, "Reunion," examines oppression found elsewhere: Turkey ("Expatriot"), Czechoslovakia ("Letter from Prague, 1968-78"), and the United States with its economic oppression. In "As Children Together," Victoria and the speaker grow up together and speak of their girlish dreams; Victoria envisions herself in Montreal, living a romantic life filled with flowers, "a satin bed, a table/ cluttered with bottles of scent." She wants desperately to escape her parents' house with "its round tins of surplus flour,/ chipped beef and white beans, relief checks," where her father whittles aimlessly on soap cakes. Victoria becomes promiscuous and eventually marries a serviceman, who returns from Vietnam "broken/ cursing holy blood at the table/ where nightly a pile of white shavings/ is paid from the edge of his knife." Her life, a legacy of Vietnam and poverty, is circumscribed by the trailer in which she lives. Still, the poem ends on a note of hope. One of the girls, the speaker, has broken the cycle: "If you read this poem, write to me./ I have been to Paris since we parted."

In "Joseph," the character of that name, the narrator's childhood companion and first boyfriend, has also lost his dreams. His life now consists of working in the steel mill, meeting women in bars ("You take her panties to your face/ and it is all you have and all/ your father had and all your brothers"), and fishing. The narrator recognizes the emptiness of his working-class life: "It is not enough, the fish,/ the white heads of beer, your winnings." His youth held a promise that was not fulfilled because of the oppression of poverty. Now the gap between the two former friends prevents communication.

The final part of the collection, "Ourselves or Nothing," contains one long poem of the same title, dedicated to Terrence Des Pres. The poem suggests the importance of remembering, of not letting "Belsen, Dachau, Saigon, Phnom Penh/ and the one meaning Bridge of Ravens,/ Sao Paulo, Armagh, Calcutta, Salvador" be forgotten, and the importance of not remaining behind the "cyclone fence," of not hovering "in a calm protected world like/ netted fish, exactly like netted fish." It is crucial to become involved, for, as the poem concludes, "It is either the beginning or the end/ of the world, and the choice is ourselves/ or nothing."

Forché has been praised by some critics for her ability to blend the political with a personal poetic mode. Yet others disagree, claiming that Forché is too much a part of her poems and that her poetic diction is unsuited to her subject. Forché counters that all subjects should be appropriate for poetry and that she has a responsibility to speak as a witness: "In my own life, the memory of certain of those who have died remains in very few hands. I can't let go of that work if I am of that number." Forché includes the political in her work, but, most important, she never forgets that she is writing poetry, poetry that is lyrical, honest, sensual, tender, courageous, and intelligent.

Other literary forms · Carolyn Forché has provided translations of the poems of Central American writers Claribel Alegría (*Flowers from the Volcano*, 1982) and, working with William Kulik, Robert Desnos (*Selected Poems of Robert Desnos*, 1991). In addition, she wrote the text for a series of photographs of El Salvador, covering the period from 1979 to 1982, in *El Salvador: The Work of Thirty Photographers* (1983). Her essays, reviews, and poems have appeared in major publications, including *The New York Times Book Review, The Atlantic Monthly, Ms., American Poetry Review, The New Yorker, Antaeus,* and *Virginia Quarterly Review.*

Select works other than poetry
NONFICTION: *El Salvador: The Work of Thirty Photographers*, 1983 (text for photographs).
TRANSLATIONS: *Flowers from the Volcano*, 1982 (by Claribel Alegría); *The Selected Poems of Robert Desnos*, 1991 (with William Kulik).
EDITED TEXT: *Against Forgetting: Twentieth-Century Poetry of Witness*, 1993.

Barbara Wiedemann

Bibliography · Stanley Plumly analyzed the strengths and weaknesses of *Gathering the Tribes* in *American Poetry Review* 5 (November/December, 1976); he faults the poet's efforts at creating the effects of Native American speech. Katha Pollitt discussed *The Country Between Us* in an essay that considers the question of "public" poetry in *The Nation* (May 8, 1982). Forché discusses her work in an interview with David Montenegro in *The American Poetry Review* 17, no. 6 (November/December, 1988), and in "Twentieth-Century Poetry of Witness," *The American Poetry Review* 22, no. 2 (March/April 1993), she defines her understanding of poetry as testimony. See also Lenora Smith, "Carolyn Forché: Poet of Witness," in Sheila Roberts and Yvonne Pacheco Tevis, eds., *Still the Frame Holds: Essays on Women Poets and Writers*, 1993, and "Jill Taft-Kaufman Talks with Carolyn Forché," *Text and Performance Quarterly* 10, no. 1 (January, 1990). Brief biographical information can be found in Frank N. Magill, ed., *Contemporary Authors*, vol. 117.

ROBERT FROST

Born: San Francisco, California; March 26, 1874
Died: Boston, Massachusetts; January 29, 1963

Poetry · *A Boy's Will*, 1913 · *North of Boston*, 1914 · *Selected Poems*, 1923 · *New Hampshire: A Poem with Notes and Grace Notes*, 1923 · *West-Running Brook*, 1928 · *Collected Poems*, 1930 · *A Further Range*, 1936 · *Collected Poems*, 1939 · *A Witness Tree*, 1942 · *A Masque of Reason*, 1945 · *Steeple Bush*, 1947 · *A Masque of Mercy*, 1947 · *Complete Poems*, 1949 · *How Not to Be King*, 1951 · *In the Clearing*, 1962 · *The Poetry of Robert Frost*, 1969

Achievements · Perhaps the most successful of American poets, Robert Frost reached a large and diversified readership almost immediately after the publication of *North of Boston*. He sustained both popular and critical acclaim throughout his entire career, which spanned fifty years and ended with his death in 1963, shortly after the publication of his last collection, *In the Clearing*. He is the only writer to have won the Pulitzer Prize in poetry four times (in 1924 for *New Hampshire*, in 1931 for the first *Collected Poems*, in 1937 for *A Further Range*, and in 1943 for *A Witness Tree*). He was nominated for the Nobel Prize in 1950 upon publication of the *Complete Poems*, but did not receive it, perhaps because the two preceding Nobel Prizes had been awarded to Americans: T. S. Eliot in 1948 and William Faulkner in 1949.

Few American poets have laid claim to both an enormous critical and popular reputation. Much of Frost's contribution to American literature has come from his ability to speak in poetic but plain language to both common people and scholars and to observe ordinary occurrences with irony and wit. If modern American poetry began with Walt Whitman and Emily Dickinson and evolved through Edgar Lee Masters, Robinson Jeffers, and Edward Arlington Robinson, Frost's poetry is the culmination, combining all elements of poetic craft and modern themes. Frost liberated American poets by proving the potential success of traditional forms, even during a period when form was giving way to free verse under the influence of T. S. Eliot and Ezra Pound.

Frost's most important contribution may be as the model for a clearly identifiable twentieth century *American* poet. Unlike the expatriate Americans, Frost never lost touch with American persistence, folk humor, plain speech, and attachment to the land. His pragmatic, clever intelligence

Library of Congress

never became pedantic, never abstract, condescending, or introverted, but remained full of mischief and horseplay. In both his poetry and his public image, although his private life was different, Frost embodied the American ideals of rugged gentleness, quiet reflection, and an unconquerable spirit. His poetry is compassionate without falling into sentimentality, and positive without being naïve.

Biography · A native of New Hampshire and a graduate of Harvard University, Robert Lee Frost's father, William Prescott Frost, moved to San Francisco in 1873 to escape post-Civil War bitterness against the South. Shortly before his untimely death at thirty-five, William Prescott requested that he be buried in New England. Fulfilling this request, Robert, his sister

Jeanie Florence, and their mother accompanied the casket across the country to Massachusetts. Because they could not afford the return trip, the Frosts settled in Salem, New Hampshire, when Robert was eleven years old. In 1892 Robert Frost was graduated as co-valedictorian from Lawrence High School and entered Dartmouth College to study law. He dropped out, however, before completing his first semester, spending the following two years working at odd jobs and writing poetry. In 1894 he published his first poem, "My Butterfly," and became engaged to Elinor White, with whom he had shared the valedictorian honor. After his marriage in 1895, Frost helped his mother run a small private school, studied for two years at Harvard, then moved to Derry, New Hampshire, for a life of farming. Between 1900 and 1905 Frost raised poultry and wrote most of the poems that would constitute his first two volumes; after 1905 he taught school in Plymouth, New Hampshire, and in 1912 he sailed for England with Elinor and his two children, where he collected and published *A Boy's Will* and *North of Boston*. By the time the Frosts returned to New York in 1915, *North of Boston* had become an enormous critical and popular success, and Frost spent the next year, and indeed most of his life, in the limelight giving readings and lectures.

Because Frost is so strongly identified as a New England poet whose poems are inextricably rooted in the land of New Hampshire and Vermont, readers expect a high correlation between the events of his life and the resultant poetry. While Frost certainly invested most of his life in New England, there is a surprising dichotomy between his biography and his poetic themes. His family life was tragic because premature death beset many of its members. His father died of tuberculosis, his mother of cancer. He lost his sister; two of his children died in infancy; his married daughter died in childbirth; and his son committed suicide. While being operated on for cancer, his wife died of a heart attack. In spite of his long wait for recognition and the private disasters which befell him, however, Frost's poetry is free from bitterness and from any direct personal references. Instead of writing about his own experiences, as so many modern American poets have done, Frost wrote about the process of discovery and the relationship between people and their surroundings.

Frost's particular world was New England, but his landscapes are metaphorical, not specific; his speech universal, not regional; and his themes archetypal, not autobiographical. His official biographer, Lawrence Thompson, unveiled many shocking characteristics of Frost's personality—including jealousy and vindictiveness—but, much to Frost's credit, his art rises above these frailties and speaks not of pettiness but of deep matters of the heart.

Analysis · The most distinctive characteristic of Robert Frost's work is elusiveness. Frost operates on so many levels that to interpret his poems confidently on a single level frequently causes the reader to misunderstand them completely. This elusiveness makes Frost one of the most interesting and continually intriguing American poets. He teaches the joys of discovering what lies beneath the veil, and readers grow to appreciate how he has cleverly masked what seems so intuitively obvious.

The veils themselves are constructed of technical devices such as symbol, rhyme, stanzation, imagery, and dramatic situation, and they are rooted in language play, which Frost uses to effect sleight-of-hand tricks. He is a magician whose devices are so artful that readers usually cannot see how he transforms one theme into another; they may be delighted with the effect, yet they cannot help wondering how they have been tricked so completely.

Because Frost's poems operate on so many levels, it is possible for almost everyone to find his or her own beliefs about life reflected in his poetry. Optimists can argue that Frost understands the complexities of life while still affirming humanity's ability to make creative choices which determine the future. Realists can argue that Frost is not an optimist, although, having acknowledged that doubt is more prevalent than faith, he still derives pleasure from the process of living life in the present. Skeptics can point out Frost's irony, noting that he affirms nothing but the dualities and contradictions of life and human nature. Each type of reader has interpreted Frost correctly; one must consider all levels of Frost's poems before being certain of any particular meaning. Because Frost writes about familiar experiences in what appears to be conversational language, the overwhelming impulse is to accept what he says at face value.

The fact that most readers seem to see their own beliefs reflected in Frost's poetry certainly accounts for his popular success, but this point also raises some serious questions about his poetic achievement. If his poems advance no universal truths, Frost may well be accused of having no philosophy—of being too vague and complex for any clear interpretation to be derived from his works. "Stopping by Woods on a Snowy Evening" is only one of many examples of a poem which has been read with many contradictory interpretations. Readers have variously explained its meaning, ranging from the serenity of a snowy night, to the virtues of duty, to the lure of death, to self-mockery. One who reads Frost moralistically, believing that "Stopping by Woods on a Snowy Evening" is a lesson about keeping promises, has fallen into Frost's trap. Readers must be exceedingly careful not to impose their own ideas on the poems or to blindly accept any interpretations.

The place to begin an explication of Frost's poetry is with the narrative persona and dramatic situation, for it is here that Frost draws the reader into the poems and begins his illusions. Only a few of his poems have no dramatic context—most of his celebrated ones do, such as "Mending Wall," "Two Tramps in Mud Time," "Death of the Hired Man," "West-Running Brook," "Tree at My Window," "Two Look at Two"—and except for such very short lyrical poems as "Nothing Gold Can Stay," the dramatic context offers the surest chance of discovering Frost's themes.

In "After Apple-Picking," for example, a great deal can be established about the dramatic situation, the dramatic moment, and the narrative persona. The reader knows that the narrator has been harvesting apples, perhaps in great numbers, and that he is now "done" with apple-picking. He has collected his apples in barrels, one of which remains unfilled, and the narrator speculates that there may be a few applies left unpicked, although he does not know for certain. His ladder, long and two-pointed, is in the tree where he has left it, and it points "toward heaven still."

In these first six lines, Frost has already begun his sleight of hand by introducing some facts within the dramatic situation which seem extraneous to the poem's development. For example, why does he describe a "twopointed" ladder when it does not make any difference what kind of ladder it is as long as the narrator can reach the apples with it? Why does he say that it is "sticking" toward heaven? These details of course help to bring the poem alive, but as part of the dramatic situation they add implications far beyond their descriptive use. Heaven is not simply a direction; if it were, Frost could have said "skyward," or not said anything at all since it is obvious that a ladder which sticks through a tree must be pointing up. The empty barrel is similarly suggestive: Readers want to know whether it is empty because somebody miscalculated the number of barrels needed, whether the narrator simply quit before the job was "done," or whether there is a more sinister suggestion that something which should have been filled is empty. Both the ladder and the barrel are facts within the dramatic situation, but they are more than simple details because they raise questions which fall outside the realm of the poem. The reader should be careful to recognize that these questions arise only if one wishes to read the ladder and barrel as suggestive. Clearly, however, Frost did not place them in the poem by accident and therefore they are important. The same kind of suggestiveness can be found in phrases throughout the poem: "winter sleep," "pane of glass," "my dreaming," "cellar bin," "rumbling sound," "cider-apple heap," "woodchuck," and "human sleep."

Complicating the dramatic moment, the narrator tells some things about himself which help to explain why he has left the barrel empty.

Readers know that the time is late fall because it is the end of apple-picking season and the beginning of winter sleep. Readers also know that the narrator is tired as he remembers visions which he saw "this morning through a pane of glass" and as he recognizes what form his dreaming is about to take. The morning world of "hoary grass" was strange to him, and as the ice pane melted, the narrator intentionally let it fall and break. Now, at the end of the day, he is embarking upon a nightmare of apples; his ladder sways precariously as the boughs bend. He is no longer safe in the apple tree where he had once been certain of his purpose; now, it is the source of his fears. Too many apples "rumble" into the cellar, a place beneath the earth, in the opposite to that direction in which the ladder is pointing. What worries the narrator most is that some of the good apples "not bruised or spiked" will end up in the "cider-apple heap," a place which offends the narrator's sense of justice. Just as readers want to know why the barrel was left unfilled, the narrator asks why good apples which he let fall by accident are sent to the heap. If readers can understand why he is so troubled by this, they will know a great deal more about the poem's meaning.

With his typical magic, however, Frost sets readers up to accept the easy explanation as he tempts them to explain the narrator's anxieties merely as a fear of failure to do his job properly. Frost has planted a host of potentially misleading elements which encourage conventional interpretations. The ladder, with its image of outstretched arms, implores heaven, perhaps even suggesting Jacob's ladder. Because apples have such a strong traditional association with the story of the garden of Eden, one might also conclude that apples represent the narrator's fall into mortal existence—his banishment from the grace of God. He has not, himself, sinned but carries the burden of original sin, and even though he has done the best he can with his life—he has dutifully picked apples until the very end—he is still plagued by nightmares. He knows that he has let slip from his grasp some apples which went undeservedly to the cider-apple heap; it is he who has condemned them to unworthy destruction by the apple grinder, and it occurs to him that his destiny might be similar to one of the good apples that is banished to destruction by chance. The narrator, then, is plagued by two doubts: The first is his own failure to fulfill all his earthly obligations, knowing that time is running out for him ("essence of winter sleep is on the air"); the second is a fear that there is no ultimate mercy—fallen apples like fallen men are disposed of indiscriminately. The hoary world he saw through the pane of glass (with its biblical allusion: "For now we see through a glass, darkly; but then face to face") was the image of life and death, and of his own mortality.

Frost has gone to a great deal of trouble to establish this as the proper reading: The narrator is frightened by the thought of death because he is uncertain whether he has satisfied his earthly duties. A simple moralistic conclusion might be that people should work harder before finding themselves, like the narrator, on the verge of death without salvation. Frost first offered the reader those suggestive objects, then presented a narrator filled with visions, dreams, and sleep, and finally, he produced a dozen highly recognizable and traditional biblical symbols. Why should not "After Apple-Picking" (and "Stopping by Woods on a Snowy Evening," for that matter) be interpreted as a poem about the virtues of steadfastness and singleness of purpose? Yet, one cannot read the poem only at that level; Frost has effected a sleight of hand. Any good magician must continually remind the audience that this is not reality; it is, indeed, a magic show where they have come to be fooled. If Frost wants readers to catch on, he has to provide some means for them to spot the trickery. With Frost's poetry, the price of admission to the magic show is high, and there are no easy explanations as to how the trick is performed, but Frost usually plays fair and gives the reader important clues.

One of the clues in "After Apple-Picking" is the use of personal pronouns. In line 16, and throughout the poem, the narrator continually refers to himself as "I," but in line 37 he shifts to say "one" ("one can see what will trouble this sleep of mine"). He could have said "*I* can see," but there is that deliberate shift to "one," who can be no one else but the reader, and Frost might as well have said "you" can see. All along, the reader has been thinking that the narrator is troubled about his sleep because he is unprepared for death, but now he begins to suspect that this interpretation is incorrect. "This sleep of *mine*" is not the sleep the reader originally understood, and the narrator corrects the misconception by adding, "whatever sleep it is." The reader believed it was death, and for good reason: again tricked into it, and having allowed himself to be tricked, the reader has fallen into the poem's message.

The "one" who can see the narrator's sleep is not the reader but the woodchuck who could "say" whether "it's like his long sleep or just some human sleep." In reality, the woodchuck could not *say* anything, nor could the woodchuck fear death because of any failure to fulfill religious obligations. The narrator can speak of and fear death, unsure of salvation, but not the woodchuck. Even more trickily, the narrator projects or imagines what the woodchuck's long sleep is ("as I describe its coming on"); so readers have the woodchuck, who cannot possess human vision, telling the narrator only what the narrator imagines and ascribes to the animal. It is through *imagination* that humans conceive death, just as readers have used their imaginations to create the symbols in the poem. So moments of life may be misinterpreted to create concepts of death. For Frost, human imagination is the trickster, not death, and men often use it to torment themselves about a mortality which they have fabricated.

This theme of "After Apple-Picking" reflects Frost's larger worldview and helps to account for the frequent misreading of his poems. Even though "After Apple-Picking" seems to be concerned with death, Christian fate, redemption, and the virtuous life—abstract ideas about the afterlife—Frost is much more concerned with earthly existence. He seldom speaks of anywhere else, and when he does, it is always in terms of how one is on earth. Frost neither believes nor disbelieves in religious or philosophical abstractions; yet, time and again, readers insist that he is promoting one view or the other. Frost's code, both in his art and in his public life, is an appreciation of wit and irony; Frost the magician is also the most appreciative audience of life's magic show, and it is important to remember that when there is a strong presence of a narrative persona, the poem is most likely to turn ironic. Frost is most ironic toward himself, and he becomes most poignant when he sees that he has become his own victim in the magic show. In "Birches," for example, the narrator is searching for connections which he does not fully understand, while in "At Woodward's Gardens," a remarkably similar poem, the narrator is more amused by a much too clever comparison between people and monkeys. By comparing these two poems, readers have an illustration of how, when the narrator is aloof and haughty, and when he is able to be more of an observer than a participant, the irony is weakened. When the narrator is as much the audience as the magician, however, the poems reverse themselves as the narrator, himself, comes to appreciate life's sleight of hand.

Many of Frost's most popular and critically acclaimed poems employ what might be called "sleight of tongue." Notice how, when the narrator in "After Apple-Picking" says "this sleep of *mine*," he is also saying "this sleep of *mind*"; in "Tree at My Window," when the narrator says "not all their *light tongues* could be profound," he is not only referring to an image of leaves blowing on the tree but also to the process of photosynthesis which nourishes the plant. In his celebrated sonnet "Design," Frost mixes a set of provocative objects (spider web, delicate white flower, moth) within a dramatic situation, and for twelve lines asks a traditional poetic question which in traditional sonnet fashion will be answered in the couplet. Instead of giving an answer, however, Frost proffers another question which is keyed to the various uses of the parts of speech and the equivocal meanings of the words "design" and "appall." Similarly, in "Stopping by Woods on a Snowy Evening," Frost establishes a dramatic situation with an involved narrator, offers a solution to the dramatic question in line 15 ("And miles to go before I sleep"), then reverses the entire tone of the poem by repeating the line to give it a different meaning.

In the longer poems, dramatic situation and narrative persona are the important elements of irony, while in the shorter poems rhyme and stanzation provide the clues. The poems written in couplets are more playful and bemused than they are ironic because, in this cynical century, it is difficult for poets to sustain through couplets the solemnity which irony demands. A single couplet or triplet judiciously placed can create exactly the right ironic effect, but an entire poem in couplets tends toward ridicule rather than the reverse. Knowing this, Frost works to overcome the effect, but his couplet poems tend to reflect longing or sadness and are, in fact, more sincere than ironic. Curiously, some of the most ironic poems are those which use triple and quadruple rhyme schemes, such as "Stopping by Woods on a Snowy Evening" and "After Apple-Picking." The least ironic are those with an abcb structure; these poems present such personal and impossible questions that no answer is acceptable, and thus there is no irony. The impossibility of his question allows the narrator to be distanced from the dramatic tension, and the absence of personal involvement reduces the narrator's commitment to discovery. Comparing "Stopping by Woods on a Snowy Evening" to "Come In," two very similar poems, the reader can see that the rhyme scheme of "Come In" does not permit as strong a potential for a shift in tone as does the aaba of "Stopping by Woods on a Snowy Evening." The locked third line in the aaba form allows the narrator much less chance of escaping, and because the fourth line returns the poem to the first two, the narrator must turn internally to the poem for a resolution.

More adaptable to irony than the abcb stanzation are the alternating quatrains, octaves, and sonnets, but these are more openly philosophical and convey a sense of pleasant discovery rather than deep involvement. The narrator feels good about his discovery, as in "Two Tramps in Mud Time" and "Design," and these poems tend to contain elements of irony without making any final ironic statement. The forms in which Frost is most consistently ironic are stanzas with framed segments (such as abba, abca, abbba, aaba). In the longer, rhymed poems, such as "The Grindstone" and "After Apple-Picking," and in the four-line strophic poems, such as "Stopping by Woods on a Snowy Evening" and "Choose Something Like a Star," the ironic tone is strong, especially when Frost begins shortening lines, as in "Fire and Ice," and altering the number of syllables per line. Without ever reading the poem, one could speculate that "After Apple-Picking" is ironic because of the framed segments (such as the opening six lines), enjambment, shortened lines (line 2 following the long first line, and lines 14 and 16), and the double and triple rhymes (lines 5-6 and lines 14-16, for example). With this combination of techniques, there is little doubt that one cannot accept the poem at face value.

More important than the technical devices for discovering Frost's irony and major themes is the presence of "opposites," which set up patterns of reversal. Frost frequently presents "pairs" of contrasting personae, ideas, images, or symbols, such as in "Tree at My Window," where man faces nature with only a curtain between; in "Two Look at Two," where identical pairs confront each other; in "West-Running Brook," "Home Burial," and "Death of the Hired Man," where husband and wife take opposite views; in "Two Tramps in Mud Time," where the narrator faces the lumberjacks in a confrontation of vocation and avocation; and perhaps most famously in "Mending Wall," where narrator and neighbor, pine and apple trees, civilized man and savage, father and son, light and dark, ego and alter ego square off against each other with yet another barrier—the wall—between them.

Most of the "opposite" poems use some kind of physical barrier to identify territory, and the wall in "Mending Wall" has been consciously constructed in violation of nature which "doesn't love the wall." To the narrator, the wall serves no useful purpose and is only an annoying reminder of his neighbor's foolish platitudes and the inability of the neighbors to communicate except once a year at spring mending time. Before the narrator built a wall, he would want to know what he "was walling in or walling out," but there is a more important question implied: If there were no wall, would he and his neighbor still be opposites? Because the narrator knows that the answer is "yes," and because he is deliberately antagonistic ("Spring is the mischief in me, and I wonder if I could put a notion in his head"), the presence of the wall is a purely academic argument for the narrator. The wall is unnatural—nature wants it down and topples it every winter—just as the wife in "West-Running Brook" thinks it is unnatural that the brook runs west instead of east like all the other country brooks. Fred, her husband, however, knows that there is a more important issue: not one of "opposites" or dualities but one of "contraries." He says that "our life runs down in sending up the clock" and extends this comparison to the sun, which runs down in sending up the brook. The ultimate question is, What sends up the sun? What happens when the water flings backward on itself in a movement toward the source? There is *something* sending up the sun; *something* that does not love a wall. The persistence of "unnatural" barriers, like the wall, the brook, the apples, and the curtain in "Tree at My Window," reminds the narrator that he cannot explain the existence of contraries any more than his neighbor can explain why good fences make good neighbors, but he does know that in contraries lie the secrets of living; that through the self-conscious process of witnessing contraries one is most likely to discover one's own life's forces rather than any profound secrets of life.

Unlike the English Romantic poets and "nature poets" with whom he is frequently compared, Frost does not look to nature for an affirmation of life, for solace, or for a road to self-discovery. For Frost, humankind is alone in the world, unable to answer questions about God and death but having some control over earthly destiny. For Frost, who is not a fatalist or a determinist, who believes things happen neither for good nor evil but simply occur, who does not fear death nor embrace promises of heaven, the only way is "to go by contraries," making creative choices, accepting paradoxes, questioning walls and brooks.

Through wit and irony people can remind themselves that much of their fallibility is self-induced; that they trick themselves and then despair when they think their manufactured illusions have become reality. They have not. Good fences do not necessarily make good neighbors; brooks do not wave at human beings in any annunciation; death does not come as a thrush, or a snowy night, or a spider.

In "Fire and Ice," the entire doctrine of "Opposites" and irony is at work, and this poem, perhaps most directly of all his work, illustrates Frost's themes and techniques. Arranged as a single stanza of nine lines (in framed segments), the poem establishes the opposites of fire and ice, hot and cold, love and hate, and centers on the middle (fifth) line of the poem. Fire is presented in the first four lines, ice in the last four. The center line asks, "But *if* it had to perish twice," and that becomes the ironic key. Whether the world will be destroyed a second time makes no difference to Frost's narrator; it is a moot question reserved for the gullible reader who interprets "After Apple-Picking" as a Christian manifesto. Frost is much more concerned with the power of hate, an opposite of love, which he says "will suffice," but one must not be tricked by that simple explanation either, to conclude that humnity is beset by hate any more than it is pursued by death. It "would suffice," if readers wanted it to, just as the woodchuck "would say" if he were asked, but the world does not have to "perish twice" except as one fears destruction, and readers do not have to ask the woodchuck, and one does not have to stoop to hate. "Some say the world will end in fire," but not Frost.

During an age when the thrust of literature has been to question illusion and reality, and to lament the lonely plight and desperation of the isolated person in an overwhelming universe, Frost presents a more positive vision, rooted in the American search for the good life. Human beings may struggle to discover their tormented spirit, but they are also capable of creative choices and of accepting contraries and uncertainties. Frost delights in the mysteries of life without being burdened by debilitating responsibilities for them, and while human beings might not become the conquerors of the universe, neither are they suppressed by it, and in that Frost rejoices.

Other literary forms · Although the majority of Robert Frost's published work is poetry, it is worth noting that he published a one-act play entitled *A Way Out* in 1929. By this point in his career, Frost had established himself as a fine narrative poet capable of both monologue and dialogue within the poetic narrative mode and with a strong visual mind capable of creating powerful dramatic situations. While Frost never made a serious effort to adapt these dramatic strengths to the stage, much of his poetic success lies with his sense of stage and dramatic persona. His only other literary publications include letters, particularly to his friend Louis Untermeyer, and lectures in which he discusses in detail his own work and poetic theory. He recorded many of his poems on records and film.

Select works other than poetry
DRAMA: *A Way Out*, pb. 1929 (one act).
NONFICTION: *The Letters of Robert Frost to Louis Untermeyer*, 1963 (with commentary by Untermeyer); *The Record of a Friendship*, 1963 (Margaret Bartlett, editor); *Selected Letters of Robert Frost*, 1964 (Lawrance Thompson, editor); *Selected Prose*, 1966 (Hyde Cox and Edward C. Lathem, editors).

Walton Beacham

Bibliography · An excellent introduction to the life and work of Frost for the general reader is Philip L. Gerber's *Robert Frost*, 1982, which contains a chronology and selected bibliography. A solid full-length biography is Jeffrey Meyers, *Robert Frost*, 1996. Mordecai Marcus, *The Poems of Robert Frost: An Explication*, 1991, contains short explications of all of Frost's poems together with information about the poet's use of history, geography, literary allusions, and obscure words. Three superb collections of essays on Frost's poetry are James M. Cox, ed., *Robert Frost: A Collection of Critical Essays*, 1962; Philip L. Gerber, ed., *Critical Essays on Robert Frost*, 1982; and Harold Bloom, ed., *Robert Frost*, 1986.

FEDERICO GARCÍA LORCA

Born: Fuentevaqueros, Spain; June 5, 1898
Died: Víznar, Spain; August 19, 1936

Poetry · *Libro de poemas*, 1921 · *Canciones, 1921-1924*, 1927 (*Songs*, 1976) · *Romancero gitano, 1924-1927*, 1928 (*The Gypsy Ballads of García Lorca*, 1951, 1953) · *Poema del cante jondo*, 1931 (*Poem of the Gypsy Seguidilla*, 1967) · *Llanto por Ignacio Sánchez Mejías*, 1935 (*Lament for the Death of a Bullfighter*, 1937, 1939) · *Primeras canciones*, 1936 · *Poeta en Nueva York*, 1940 (*Poet in New York*, 1940, 1955) · *Diván del Tamarit*, 1940 (*The Divan at the Tamarit*, 1944)

Achievements · The typically Spanish character of his plays and poetry, enhanced by rich and daring lyrical expression, have made García Lorca one of the most universally recognized poets of the twentieth century. His tragic death in 1936 at the hands of the Falange, the Spanish Fascist party, in the flower of his manhood and literary creativity, merely served to further his fame. The first milestone of García Lorca's short but intense career was the publication of *Gypsy Ballads*, which solidly established his reputation as a fine poet in the popular vein. His dark, brooding, foreboding ballads of gypsy passion and death captured the imagination and hearts of Spaniards and foreigners, Andalusians and Galicians, illiterate farmers and college professors. Critics saw in García Lorca's poems the culmination of centuries of a rich and diverse Spanish lyric tradition. For example, Edwin Honig has noted that García Lorca's poetry took its inspiration from such diverse sources as the medieval Arabic-Andalusian art of amorous poetry; the early popular ballad; the Renaissance synthesis in Spain of classical traditions, as exemplified by the "conceptist" poetry of Luis de Góngora y Argote; and the *cante jondo*, or "deep song," of the Andalusian gypsy.

Living in an era of vigorous cultural and literary activity, called by many Spain's second Golden Age, García Lorca clearly maintained his individuality. His innate charm and wit, his strong and passionate presence, his *duende*, or "soul," as a performer of Andalusian songs and ballads, and his captivating readings of his own poetry and plays drew the applause and friendship of equally talented writers and artists, such as Rafael Alberti, Pedro Salinas, Jorge Guillén, Vicente Aleixandre, Salvador Dalí, and Luis Buñuel.

The poet reached the peak of his popular success in the late 1920's. Both his *Songs* and his *Gypsy Ballads* were published to great critical acclaim. In the same period, he delivered two memorable lectures, the first at the *cante jondo* festival organized jointly with composer Manuel de Falla in Granada, and the second at the festival in honor of Góngora's tercentenary. His play *Mariana Pineda* (performed 1927, published 1928; English translation, 1950) was produced in Barcelona, and the following year he founded and published the literary journal *Gallo*. Despite these achievements, however, García Lorca suffered a grave spiritual crisis, to which he alludes in his correspondence but never really clarifies. This crisis led him to reevaluate his artistic output and turn to new experiences and modes of expression.

The result of García Lorca's soul-searching can be seen in his later works, especially *Poet in New York* and *Lament for Ignacio Sánchez Mejías* (also known as *Lament for the Death of a Bullfighter*). In the former, García Lorca fully unleashes his imagination in arabesques of metaphor which on first reading appear incomprehensible. *Poet in New York* is a difficult and frequently obscure work that has been viewed as a direct contrast to his earlier poetry. Yet, as Predmore has so painstakingly demonstrated, these poems extend rather than depart from García Lorca's established preference for ambiguous and antithetical symbolism.

The two threads that run throughout García Lorca's work are the themes of love and death: They lend a poetic logic and stability to what may otherwise appear chaotic and indecipherable. A study of these themes in García Lorca's poetry and plays reveals a gradual evolution from tragic premonition and foreboding, through vital passion repressed and frustrated by outside forces, to bitter resignation and death. Throughout his life, García Lorca's constant companion and friend was death. The poet Antonio Machado described this intimacy with death in his lament for García Lorca: "He was seen walking with Her, alone,/ unafraid of her scythe.// Today as yesterday, gypsy, my Death,/ how good to be with you, alone/ in these winds of Granada, of my Granada."

García Lorca's gift of imagination, his genius for metaphor and volatile imagery, and his innate sense of the tragic human condition make him one of the outstanding poets of the twentieth century. With García Lorca's execution in Víznar in 1936 at the outbreak of the Spanish Civil War, the frustrated personas of his poetry and plays, who so often ended their lives in senseless tragedy, materialized in his own person. In García Lorca, life became art and art became life. Combining the experience of two cultures, he addressed in both, the Andalusian and the American man's primal needs and fears within his own interior world.

Biography · Federico García Lorca was born on June 5, 1898, in Fuentevaqueros, in the province of Granada. His father, Don Federico García

Rodríguez, was a well-to-do landowner, a solid rural citizen of good reputation. After his first wife died, Don Federico married Doña Vicenta Lorca Romero, an admired schoolteacher and a musician. García Lorca was very fond of his mother and believed that he inherited his intelligence and artistic bent from her and his passionate nature from his father. It was in the countryside of Granada that García Lorca's poetic sensibility took root, nourished by the meadows, the fields, the wild animals, the livestock, and the people of that land. His formative years were centered in the village, where he attended Mass with his mother and absorbed and committed to memory the colorful talk, the folktales, and the folk songs of the *vega* (fertile lowland) which would later find a rebirth in the metaphorical language of his poetry and plays.

In 1909, his family moved to Granada, and García Lorca enrolled in the College of the Sacred Heart to prepare for the university. This was the second crucial stage in his artistic development: Granada's historical and literary associations further enriched his cultural inheritance from the *vega* and modified it by adding an intellectual element. García Lorca wanted to be a musician and composer, but his father wanted him to study law. In 1915, he matriculated at the University of Granada, but he never was able to adapt completely to the regimentation of university studies, failing three courses, one of them in literature. During the same period, he continued his serious study of piano and composition with Don Antonio Segura. García Lorca frequented the cafés of Granada and became popular for his wit. In 1916 and 1917, García Lorca traveled throughout Castile, Léon, and Galicia with one of his professors from the university, who also encouraged him to write his first book, *Impresiones y paisajes*. He also came into contact with important people in the arts, among them Manuel de Falla, who shared García Lorca's interest in traditional folk themes, and Fernando de los Ríos, an important leader in educational and social reforms, who persuaded García Lorca's father to send his son to the University of Madrid.

In 1919, García Lorca arrived in Madrid, where he was to spend the next ten years at the famous Residencia de Estudiantes, in the company of Rafael Alberti, Jorge Guillén, Pedro Salinas, Gerardo Diego, Dámaso Alonso, Luis Cernuda, and Vicente Aleixandre. There García Lorca published his first collection of poems, *Libro de poemas*, and became involved with the philosophical and literary currents then in vogue. In 1922, García Lorca returned to Granada to conduct with Manuel de Falla a "Festival of Cante Jondo."

The years from 1924 to 1928 were successful but troubled ones for García Lorca, marked by moments of elation followed by depression. During these years, García Lorca developed a close friendship with Salvador Dalí and spent several summers with the Dalí family at Cadaqués. He published his second book of poems, *Songs*, in 1927 and in that same year saw the premiere of *Mariana Pineda* in Barcelona and Madrid. In December of 1927, García Lorca participated in the famous Góngora tricentennial anniversary celebrations in Seville, where he delivered one of his most famous lectures, "The Poetic Image in Don Luis de Góngora." Gradually, García Lorca's fame spread, and his *Gypsy Ballads* became the most widely read book of poems to appear in Spain since the publication of Gustavo Adolfo Bécquer's *Rimas* in 1871. During the period from May to December of 1928, García Lorca suffered an emotional crisis which prompted him to leave Spain to accompany Fernando de los Ríos to New York. After spending nine months in the United States, a stay that included a visit to Vermont, García Lorca returned to Spain by way of Cuba with renewed interest and energy for his work. The clearest product of this visit was *Poet in New York*, one of his greatest books of poems, published four years after his death.

Upon his return to Madrid in 1930, García Lorca turned his focus increasingly to the dramatic. In 1932, under the auspices of the Republic's Ministry of Education, García Lorca founded La Barraca, a university theater whose aim was to bring the best classical plays to the provinces. In the same period, he saw the successful staging of *Blood Wedding* and *El amor de don Perlimplín con Belisa en su jardín* (performed 1933, published 1938; *The Love of Don Perlimplín for Belisa in His Garden*, 1941). His achievements in Spain were capped by another trip to the New World, this time to Argentina, where *Blood Wedding, Mariana Pineda*, and *La zapatera prodigiosa* (performed 1930, published 1938; *The Shoemaker's Prodigious Wife*, 1941) were staged and received with great enthusiasm. The years 1934 and 1935 saw the writing of the *Lament for Ignacio Sánchez Mejías* and the premieres of at least four new plays. By 1936, García Lorca had decided to return to Granada for the celebration of his name day and also to bide his time until the political turmoil in Madrid abated. During his stay, the Civil War broke out, and amid the fighting between the Nationalist and the Popular forces in Granada, García Lorca was detained and executed on August 19, 1936, in the outskirts of Víznar. His body was thrown into an unmarked grave.

Analysis · In imagery that suggests an "equestrian leap" between two opposing worlds, García Lorca embodies a dialectical vision of life, on one hand filled with an all-consuming love for humankind and nature and, on the other, cognizant of the "black torso of the Pharaoh," the blackness symbolizing an omnipresent death unredeemed by the possibility of immortality. The tension between these two irreconcilable forces lends a tautness as well as a mystery to much of his poetry.

A recurring theme throughout García Lorca's work which is expressive of this animating tension is that of thwarted love, repressed by society or simply by human destiny and ending inevitably in death. This obsession with unfulfilled dreams and with death is evident in the poet's first collection. In a moving elegy to the Castilian princess Juana la Loca entitled "Elegía a doña Juana la Loca," García Lorca details in fifteen stanzas the lamentable fate of a woman driven to madness by her unrequited love for her husband, Felipe el Hermoso. Throughout the poem, García Lorca addresses her as a red carnation in a deep and desolate valley, to whom Death extended a bouquet of withered roses instead of flowers, verses, and pearl necklaces. Like other great tragic heroines of Spanish literature, such as Isabel de Segura and Melibea, and those of García Lorca's own creative imagination, she is a victim of fate. The themes of violent passion and death, later more fully expressed in the *Gypsy Ballads*, are latent in the description of Juana as a princess of the red sunset, the color of blood and fire, whose passion is like the dagger, whose distaff is of iron, whose flax is of steel. Here, metallic substances are symbols of death; Juana lies in her coffin of lead, and within her skeleton, a heart broken into a thousand pieces speaks of her shattered dreams and frustrated life.

In contrast to the bleak symbolism of these works, children and their world interested and delighted García Lorca, and he futilely sought in their charm and innocence a respite from the anguish of existence. In another poem from his first collection, "Balada de la placeta" ("Ballad of the Little Square"), the poet is listening to children singing. In a playful dialogue, the children ask the poet what he feels in his red, thirsty mouth; he answers, "the taste of the bones of my big skull." The poet's consciousness of death's presence mars his contemplation of youthful fun. Although he might wish to lose himself in the child's world, he clearly recognizes in a later poem, "Gacela de la huida" ("Gacela of the Flight"), that the seeds of death are already sown behind that childish exterior: "No one who touching a newborn child can forget the motionless horse skulls." Still, he tries to reject the physical destruction, the putrefaction of death which he so vividly describes in "Gacela de la muerte oscura" ("Gacela of the Dark Death") and in the *Lament for Ignacio Sánchez Mejías*.

García Lorca was a master of the dramatic ballad, full of mystery, passion, and dark, sudden violence. His tools were simple words and objects culled from everyday living, that contrasted with and intensified the complex emotions underlying the verse. García Lorca's mastery of the ballad form is exemplified in "Canción de jinete" ("The Song of the Horseman"), from *Songs*. The horseman's destination is the distant city of Córdoba. Although he knows the roads well and his saddlebags are packed with olives, he fatalistically declares that he will never reach Córdoba. García Lorca never tells a story outright; he makes his audience do the work. Thus, Death is looking at the horseman from the towers of Córdoba, as he cries "Ay! How long the road! Ay! My valiant pony! Ay! That death should wait me before I reach Córdoba." How? Why? Who? Where? These questions are left to the imagination.

It is through the figure of the Andalusian gypsy that García Lorca best conveys his personal vision of life. With his characteristic techniques of metaphorical suggestion and dramatic tension, enriched by an artist's palette of colors, García Lorca in the *Gypsy Ballads* treats his usual subject matter of love and death, passion and destruction, with great lyrical fantasy. The refrain "Green, how much I want you green" establishes the enchanted atmosphere of the famous "Romance sonambulo" ("Somnambule Ballad"), where everything possesses the greenish cast of an interior world: "Green wind, green flesh, green hair." The best known of García Lorca's ballads, it only implies the story behind the death of a pair of lovers: his the result of a wound that runs from his chest to his throat, hers from drowning in the sorrow of having waited for him so long in vain. The themes of passion and violence are underscored by the theme of liberty, denied to the lovers by fate and a false social order. The gypsy girl's death is already intimated in the first stanza, where she is described as having a shadow on her waist, with green flesh, hair of green, and eyes of cold silver that cannot see. On a first reading, the two lines "The ship upon the sea/ and the horse in the mountain," which precede the description, seem to be a discordant and senseless addition to the narrative. To understand their function, the reader must see them in relation to the theme of liberty. Man is imprisoned by his passions, by destiny, death, a sense of honor, and social institutions. In contrast, the images of the ship upon the sea and the horse in the mountain suggest total freedom. The horse, which in García Lorca's work often represents male virility, prefigures the gypsy's attainment of the freedom that is his by nature. The image of the ship, on the other hand, has a long tradition of symbolizing liberty, especially in the Romantic period; its interpretation here, as such, is logical and expected. The description of the stars as white frost and the mountain as a filching cat foreshadows the violence of the characters' deaths.

Thus, "Somnambule Ballad" offers a profusion of surrealistic and seemingly disconnected images governed by a vigorous inner logic. In this, it is representative of García Lorca's finest works. The repetition of key images–of green, cold silver, the moon, water, and the night–unifies the poem. The gypsy girl and the gypsy are together in death and cannot hear the pounding of the drunken Civil Guard on the door. Death has granted them freedom, and all is as it should be: "The ship upon the sea, and the horse on the mountain." Using the local color and ambience of gypsy life, García Lorca gives voice to his own frustrations and those of humanity in general. Fettered by passion, destiny, and social norms, humankind's only escape is through death.

The strange poems of *Poet in New York* are the work of a mature poet. In New York, García Lorca, who had loved life in all its spontaneity, who had grieved over the death of gypsies, their instinctive and elemental passions suffocated, was confronted with the heartless, mechanized world of the urban metropolis. In *Poet in New York*, the gypsy is replaced by the black man, whose instinctive impulses and strengths are perverted by the white man's civilization and whose repression and anguish is embodied in the figure of the great King of Harlem in a janitor's suit. The blood of three hundred crimson roses that stained the gypsy's shirt in "Somnambule Ballad" now flows from four million butchered ducks, five million hogs, two thousand doves, one million cows, one million lambs, and two million roosters. The disrepect for life in this landscape of vomiting and urinating multitudes is portrayed in the death of a cat, within whose little paw, crushed by the automobile, García Lorca sees a world of broken rivers and unattainable distances. Alone, alienated, and frustrated in his endeavors, man cannot appeal to anyone for help, not even the Church, which in its hypocrisy and heathen materialism betrays the true spirit of Christianity. The poet sees death and destruction everywhere. His own loneliness and alienation, described in "Asesinato" ("Murder"), recall the haunting words and melody of the *cante jondo:* "A pinprick to dive till it touches the roots of a cry."

Considered by many to be García Lorca's supreme poetic achievement, the *Lament for Ignacio Sánchez Mejías* is the quintessence of the Spanish "tragic sense of life." In this lament, García Lorca incorporated aspects of a long poetic tradition and revitalized them through his own creativity. Based on a true incident, as were most of García Lorca's poems, the elegy was written upon the death of his good friend Ignacio, an intellectual and a bullfighter, who was gored by a bull and died in August of 1934. The bullfight is elevated by García Lorca to a universal level, representing humanity's heroic struggle against death. Death, as always in García Lorca's poetry, emerges triumphant, yet the struggle is seen as courageous, graceful, meaningful.

The elegy is divided into four parts: "La cogida y la muerte" ("The Goring and the Death"), "La sangre derrameda" ("The Spilling of the Blood"), "Cuerpo presente" ("The Body Present"), and "Alma ansente" ("Absent Soul"). In general, the poem moves from the concrete to the abstract, from report to essay, from the specific to the general. Part 1 describes the events, the chaos, the confusion, the whole process of death in a series of images appealing to all the five senses. Phones jangle, the crowd is mad with grief, the bulls bellow, the wounds burn. What dominates is the incessant and doleful bell, reminding the poet, with each repetition of "at five o'clock in the afternoon," of the finality of death, worming its way into Ignacio's being, hammering its way into the public mind and into the poet's consciousness. The macabre sights and smells of death are detailed in all their colorful goriness: the white sheet, a pail of lime, snowy sweat, yellow iodine, green gangrene. Time ceases for Ignacio as all the clocks show five o'clock in the shadow of the afternoon. Refusing to look at Ignacio's blood in the sand, García Lorca vents his anger and frustration at seeing all that beauty, confidence, princeliness, strength of body and character, wit, and intelligence slowly seeping out as the moss and the grass open with sure fingers the flowers of Ignacio's skull.

The poet's initial reaction of shock and denial slowly softens into gradual acceptance. Utilizing the slower Alexandrine meter in "The Body Present," García Lorca contemplates the form of Ignacio laid out on a sterile, gray, cold stone. The finality of death is seen in the sulphur yellow of Ignacio's face and in the rain entering his mouth in the stench-filled silence. García Lorca cannot offer immortality. He can only affirm that man must live bravely, and that death, too, will one day cease to exist. Hence, he tells Ignacio to sleep, fly, rest: Even the sea dies. Death, victorious, challenged only by the value of Ignacio's human experience, is dealt with in the last part. By autumn, the people will have forgotten Ignacio, robbed by death and time of the memory of his presence. Only those like the poet, who can look beyond, will immortalize him in song.

The *Lament for Ignacio Sánchez Mejías* expresses the fundamental attitude of the Spaniard toward death: One must gamble on life with great courage and heroism. Welcoming the dark angels of death, the "toques de bordón" or the black tones of the guitar, the poet is paradoxically affirming life. This is man's only consolation.

García Lorca's evolution as a poet was characterized throughout by this movement toward an all-encompassing death. Synthesizing a variety of themes and poetic styles and forms, García Lorca embodied, both in his life and in his verse, modern humankind's struggle to find meaning in life despite the over-whelming reality of physical and spiritual death.

Other literary forms · Aguilar of Madrid has issued a one-volume edition of Federico García Lorca's works, compiled and annotated by Arturo del Hoyo, with a prologue by Jorge Guillén and an epilogue by Vicente

Aleixandre. In addition to the poetry, it includes García Lorca's plays, of which the tragic rural trilogy *Bodas de sangre* (performed 1933, published 1935; *Blood Wedding*, 1939), *Yerma* (performed 1934, published 1937; English translation, 1941), and *La casa de Bernarda Alba* (written 1936, published 1945; *The House of Bernarda Alba*, 1947) are world famous and represent García Lorca's best achievement as a poet become director-playwright. In order to portray all the facets of García Lorca's artistic personality, the Aguilar edition also includes his first play, *El maleficio de la mariposa* (performed 1920, published 1957; *The Butterfly's Evil Spell*, 1963); an example of his puppet plays, *La tragicomedia de don Cristóbal y la señá Rosita* (performed 1937, published 1949; *The Tragicomedy of Don Cristóbal and Doña Rosita*, 1955); selections from *Impresiones y paisajes* (1918; impressions and landscapes), García Lorca's first published prose works, in which his genius is already evident in the melancholic, impressionistic style used to describe his feelings and reactions to the Spanish landscape and Spanish life; several short prose pieces and dialogues; a number of lectures and speeches, including "Imaginación, inspiración y evasión en la poesía" (1929; imagination, inspiration, and evasion in poetry), "La imagen poética en Don Luis de Góngora" (given in 1927, published 1932; "The Poetic Image in Don Luis de Góngora," 1950), and "Teoría y juego del duende" (given in 1930, published 1938; "Theory and Function of the Duende," 1963). Finally, there is a variety of representative letters to friends, texts of newspaper interviews, poems from the poet's book of suites, fifteen of his songs, and twenty-five of his drawings. Although the Aguilar edition reflects a consummate artist, still missing from its pages are a number of works which are known to have existed and either have not been published or have been lost in the years since García Lorca's death. Either lost or unpublished are the complete manuscript of a five-act play, *El público* (written 1930; the public), and the first part of a dramatic biblical trilogy entitled "La destrucción de Sódoma" (written 1936; the destruction of Sodom), on which García Lorca was working at the time of his death. Also lost are "Los sueños de mi prima Aurelia" (the dreams of my cousin Aurelia) and "La niña que riega la albahaca y el príncipe pregunton" (the girl who waters the sweet basil flower and the inquisitive prince), a puppet play presented in Granada on January 5, 1923. "El sacrificio de Ifigenia" (Iphigenia's sacrifice) and "La hermosa" (the beauty) are titles of two plays whose existence cannot be substantiated. Reportedly, García Lorca also collected a group of poems entitled "Sonetos del amor oscuro" (sonnets of dark love), the title suggesting to certain critics the poet's preference for intimate masculine relationships. Until the 1960's, most of the works evaluating García Lorca centered on the events of his life and death and were only interspersed with snatches of literary criticism. In the last fifteen years, thematic and stylistic studies by such noted scholars as Rafael Martínez Nadal, Gustavo Correa, Arturo Barea, Rupert C. Allen, and Richard L. Predmore have served to illuminate García Lorca's symbolic and metaphorical world.

Select works other than poetry

DRAMA: *El maleficio de la mariposa*, pr. 1920 (*The Butterfly's Evil Spell*, 1963); *Mariana Pineda*, pr. 1927 (English translation, 1950); *Los títeres de Cachiporra: La tragicomedia de don Cristóbal y la señá Rosita*, wr. 1928, pr. 1937 (*The Tragicomedy of Don Cristóbal and Doña Rosita*, 1955); *El paseo de Buster Keaton*, pb. 1928 (*Buster Keaton's Promenade*, 1957); *La doncella, el marinero y el estudiante*, pb. 1928 (*The Virgin, the Sailor, and the Student*, 1957); *Quimera*, wr. 1928, pb. 1938 (*Chimera*, 1944); *El público*, wr. 1930, pb. 1976 (fragment; *The Audience*, 1958); *La zapatera prodigiosa*, pr. 1930 (*The Shoemaker's Prodigious Wife*, 1941); *Así que pasen cinco años*, wr. 1931, pb. 1937 (*When Five Years Pass*, 1941); *El amor de don Perlimplín con Belisa en su jardín*, pr. 1933 (*The Love of Don Perlimplín for Belisa in His Garden*, 1941); *Bodas de sangre*, pr. 1933 (*Blood Wedding*, 1939); *Yerma*, pr. 1934 (English translation, 1941); *Doña Rosita la soltera: O, El lenguaje de las flores*, pr. 1935 (*Doña Rosita the Spinster: Or, The Language of the Flowers*, 1941); *El retablillo de don Cristóbal*, pr. 1935 (*In the Frame of Don Cristóbal*, 1944); *La casa de Bernarda Alba*, wr. 1936, pr., pb. 1945 (*The House of Bernarda Alba*, 1947).

NONFICTION: *Impresiones y paisajes*, 1918.

MISCELLANEOUS: *Obras completas*, 1938-1946 (8 volumes); *Obras completas*, 1954, 1960; *Obras completas*, 1973.

Katherine Gyékényesi Gatto

Bibliography · Robert Lima's *The Theatre of García Lorca*, 1963, analyzes Garciá Lorca's major works, highlighting their social and political contexts. Jane Miller, "Silent Exchange of Smiles." *Ohio Review* 49 (1993), focuses on nature and aesthetics in García Lorca's work. Catherine Arturi Parilla, *A Theory for Reading Dramatic Texts: Selected Plays by Pirandello and García Lorca*, 1955, discusses reader response criticism in her comparative study. Candelas Newton, *Understanding García Lorca*, 1995, analyzes García Lorca's major dramatic and poetic works. Beth Wellington, *Reflections on Lorca's Private Mythology: Once Five Years Pass and the Rural Plays*, 1993, offers an interesting view of García Lorca's use of symbolism. Robert Havard, *Lorca, Poet and Playwright*, 1992, discusses García Lorca's major dramas in their political and cultural contexts.

ALLEN GINSBERG

Born: Newark, New Jersey; June 3, 1926
Died: New York, New York; April 5, 1997

Poetry · *Howl and Other Poems*, 1956, 1996 · *Empty Mirror: Early Poems*, 1961 · *Kaddish and Other Poems, 1958-1960*, 1961 · *The Change*, 1963 · *Reality Sandwiches*, 1963 · *Kral Majales*, 1965 · *Wichita Vortex Sutra*, 1966 · *T.V. Baby Poems*, 1967 · *Airplane Dreams: Compositions from Journals*, 1968 · *Ankor Wat*, 1968 · *Planet News, 1961-1967*, 1968 · *The Moments Return*, 1970 · *Ginsberg's Improvised Poetics*, 1971 · *Bixby Canyon Ocean Path Word Breeze*, 1972 · *Iron Horse*, 1972 · *Open Head*, 1972 · *The Fall of America: Poems of These States, 1965-1971*, 1972 · *The Gates of Wrath: Rhymed Poems, 1948-1952*, 1972 · *First Blues: Rags, Ballads, and Harmonium Songs, 1971-1974*, 1975 · *Sad Dust Glories: Poems During Work Summer in Woods*, 1975 · *Mostly Sitting Haiku*, 1978 · *Poems All over the Place: Mostly Seventies*, 1978 · *Plutonian Ode: Poems, 1977-1980*, 1982 · *Mind Breaths: Poems, 1972-1977*, 1977 · *Collected Poems, 1947-1980*, 1984 · *White Shroud: Poems, 1980-1985*, 1986 · *Hydrogen Jukebox*, 1990 (music by Philip Glass) · *Collected Poems*, 1992 · *Cosmopolitan Greetings*, 1994 · *Making It Up: Poetry Composed at St. Marks Church on May 9, 1979*, 1994

Achievements · The publication of "Howl" in 1956 drew such enthusiastic comments from Allen Ginsberg's supporters and such vituperative condemnation from conservative cultural commentators that a rift of immense proportions developed which has made a balanced critical assessment very difficult. Nevertheless, partisan response has gradually given way to an acknowledgment by most critics that Ginsberg's work is significant, if not always entirely successful by familiar standards of literary excellence. The "voice" that Ginsberg employed in "Howl" not only has directed the style of several generations but also combines the rhythms and language of common speech with some of the deepest, most enduring traditions in American literature. In both his life and his work, Ginsberg set an example of moral seriousness, artistic commitment, and humane decency that made him one of the most popular figures in American culture. The best of his visionary and innovative creations earned for him recognition as one of the major figures of the twentieth century.

Biography · The second son of Naomi Ginsberg, a political activist, and Louis Ginsberg, a traditional lyric poet and schoolteacher, Allen Ginsberg attended primary school in the middle-class town of Paterson, New Jersey. Except for his mother's hospitalization for mental stress, he grew up in a conventional and uneventful fashion. He entered Columbia University in 1943, intending to pursue a career in labor law, but the influence of such well-known literary scholars as Lionel Trilling and Mark Van Doren, combined with the excitement of the Columbia community, which included fellow student Jack Kerouac and such singular people as William Burroughs and Neal Cassady, led him toward literature as a vocation. He was temporarily suspended from Columbia in 1945 and worked as a welder and apprentice seaman before finishing his degree in 1948. Living a "subterranean" life (to use Kerouac's term), Ginsberg was counseled to commit himself to Columbia Presbyterian Psychiatric Institute to avoid criminal charges; there, in 1949, he met Carl W. Solomon, to whom "Howl" is dedicated. During the early 1950's, he began a correspondence with William Carlos Williams, who guided and encouraged his early writing, and traveled in Mexico and Europe. He was living in San Francisco when he wrote "Howl," and he read the poem for the first time at a landmark Six Gallery performance that included Gary Snyder, Philip Whalen, and Michael McClure. His mother died in 1956, the year *Howl and Other Poems* was published, and he spent the next few years traveling, defending *Howl* against charges of obscenity, working on "Kaddish"—his celebration of his mother's life—and reading on college campuses and in Beat venues on both coasts.

George Holmes

The growing notoriety of the Beat generation drew Ginsberg into the media spotlight in the early 1960's, and he was active in the promotion of work by his friends. He continued to travel extensively, visiting Europe, India, and Japan, and he published widely in many of the prominent literary journals of the counterculture. His involvement with various hallucinatory substances led to the formation of LeMar (Organization to Legalize Marijuana) in 1964 with the poet, songwriter, and publisher Ed Sanders, and his continuing disaffection with governmental policies took him toward active political protest. In 1965 he was invited to Cuba and Czechoslovakia by Communist officials, who mistakenly assumed that his criticism of American society would make him sympathetic to their regimes, but Ginsberg's outspoken criticism of all forms of tyranny and suppression led to his expulsion from both countries.

His political activity reached a peak in 1968, when he was arrested in Chicago at the Democratic National Convention with many other demonstrators, and in 1969, when he testified at the Chicago trials. In the early 1970's, he spent some time on a farm in rural New York, formally accepted the teachings of Buddhism from Chögyam Trungpa, who initiated him with the name "Lion of Dharma," and founded, with Anne Waldman, a school of literary inquiry at the Naropa Institute in Colorado. He was inducted into the American Institute of Arts and Letters in 1974, an indication of recognition as an artist in the mainstream of American culture, and he further confirmed this status by traveling with Bob Dylan's Rolling Thunder Review as a "poet-percussionist" in 1975. Continuing to combine artistic endeavor with a commitment to social justice, Ginsberg took part in protests at the Rocky Flats Nuclear Facility in 1978 and wrote the "Plutonium Ode," which expressed his concern about the destructive forces humans had unleashed.

During the 1980's, Ginsberg continued to travel, teach, write, and perform his work. The publication of his *Collected Poems, 1947-1980* in 1984 was received with wide attention and respect, and he was appointed distinguished professor at Brooklyn College in 1986, the year he published *White Shroud*, which includes an epilogue to "Kaddish" along with other poems from the 1980's. His ability as a teacher was clearly demonstrated in his appearance on the Public Broadcasting System series *Voices and Visions* in 1987. As the decade drew to a close, he was involved in a collaboration with Philip Glass on a chamber opera called *Hydrogen Jukebox* (a phrase from "Howl"), which was performed in 1990. Continuing to write with energy while teaching a graduate-level course on the Beats at the City University of New York Graduate Center, Ginsberg described his goals in the 1990's, in a poem called "Personals Ad," as similar to the ones he had always pursued: "help inspire mankind conquer world anger & guilt." It was an appropriate task for a "poet professor in his autumn years." Ginsberg died on April 5, 1997, in New York City.

Analysis · "Howl," the poem that carried Allen Ginsberg into public consciousness as a symbol of the avant-garde artist and as the designer of a verse style for a postwar generation seeking its own voice, was initially regarded as primarily a social document. As Ginsberg's notes make clear, however, it was also the latest specimen in a continuing experiment in form and structure. Several factors in Ginsberg's life were particularly important in this breakthrough poem, written as the poet was approaching thirty and still drifting through a series of jobs, countries, and social occasions. Ginsberg had been more heavily influenced by his father than was immediately apparent. Louis Ginsberg's very traditional, metrical verse was of little use to his son, but his father's interest in literary history was part of Ginsberg's solid grounding in prosody. Then, a succession of other mentors—including William Carlos Williams, whose use of the American vernacular and local material had inspired him, and great scholars such as the art historian Meyer Shapiro at Columbia, who had introduced him to the tenets of modernism from an analytic perspective—had enabled the young poet to form a substantial intellectual foundation.

In addition, Ginsberg was dramatically affected by his friendships with Jack Kerouac, Neal Cassady, Herbert Hunke, William Burroughs, and other noteworthy members of an underground community of dropouts, revolutionaries, drug addicts, jazz musicians, and serious but unconventional artists of all sorts. Ginsberg felt an immediate kinship with these "angelheaded hipsters," who accepted and celebrated eccentricity and who regarded Ginsberg's homosexuality as an attribute, not a blemish. While Ginsberg enthusiastically entered into the drug culture that was a flourishing part of this subterranean community, he was not nearly as routed toward self-destruction as Burroughs or Hunke; he was more interested in the possibilities of visionary experience. His oft-noted "illuminative audition of William Blake's voice simultaneous with Eternity-vision" in 1948 was his first ecstatic experience of transcendence, and he continued to pursue spiritual insight through serious studies of various religions—including Judaism and Buddhism—as well as through chemical experimentation.

His experiments with mind-altering agents and his casual friendship with some quasi-criminals led to his eight-month stay in a psychiatric institute. He had already had an unsettling series of encounters with mental instability in his mother, who had been hospitalized for the first time when he was three. Her struggles with the torments of psychic uncertainty were seriously disruptive events in Ginsberg's otherwise unremarkable boyhood, but Ginsberg felt deep sympathy for his mother's agony and also was touched by her warmth, love, and social conscience. While not exactly a "red diaper baby," Ginsberg had adopted a radical political conscience early enough to decide to pursue labor law as a college student, and he never wavered from his initial convictions concerning the excesses of capitalism. His passionate call for tolerance and fairness had roots as much in his mother's ideas as in his contacts with the "lamblike youths" who were "slaughtered" by the demon Moloch—his symbol for the greed and materialism of the United States in the 1950's. In conjunction with his displeasure with what he saw as the failure of the government to correct these abuses, he carried an idealized conception of "the lost America of love" based on his readings in nineteenth century American literature, Walt Whitman and Henry David Thoreau in particular, and reinforced by the political and social idealism of contemporaries such as Kerouac, Gary Snyder, and Michael McClure.

Ginsberg brought all these concerns together when he began to compose "Howl." Yet while the social and political elements of the poem were immediately apparent, the careful structural arrangements were not. Ginsberg found it necessary to explain his intentions in a series of notes and letters, emphasizing his desire to use Whitman's long line "to *build up* large organic structures" and his realization that he did not have to satisfy anyone's concept of what a poem should be, but could follow his "romantic inspiration" and simply write as he wished, "without fear." Using what he called his "Hebraic-Melvillian bardic breath"—a rhythmic pattern similar to the cadences of the Old Testament as employed by Herman Melville—Ginsberg wrote a three-part prophetic elegy, which he described as a "huge sad comedy of wild phrasing."

The first part of "Howl" is a long catalog of the activities of the "angelheaded hipsters" who were his contemporaries. Calling the bohemian underground of outcasts, outlaws, rebels, mystics, sexual deviants, junkies, and other misfits "the best minds of my generation"—a judgment that still rankles reactionary social critics—Ginsberg produced image after image of the antics of "remarkable lamblike youths" in pursuit of cosmic enlightenment, "the ancient heavenly connection to the starry dynamo in the machinery of night." Because the larger American society had offered them little support, Ginsberg summarizes their efforts by declaring that these people had been "destroyed by madness." The long lines, each beginning with the word "who" (which was used "as a base to keep measure, return to and take off from again"), create a composite portrait that pulses with energy and excitement. Ginsberg is not only lamenting the destruction of his friends but also celebrating their wild flights of imagination, their ecstatic illuminations, and their rapturous adventures. His typical line, or breath unit, communicates the awesome power of the experiences he describes along with their potential for danger. Ginsberg believed that by the end of the first section he had expressed what he believed "true to eternity" and had reconstituted "the data of celestial experience."

Part 2 of the poem "names the monster of mental consciousness that preys" on the people he admires. The fear and tension of the Cold War, stirred by materialistic greed and what Ginsberg later called "lacklove," are symbolized by a demon he calls Moloch, after the Canaanite god that required human sacrifice. With the name Moloch as a kind of "base repetition" and destructive attributes described in a string of lines beginning with "whose," the second part of the poem reaches a kind of crescendo of chaos in which an anarchic vision of frenzy and disruption engulfs the world.

In part 3, "a litany of affirmation," Ginsberg addresses himself to Carl W. Solomon, a poet he knew from the Psychiatric Institute; he holds up Solomon as a kind of emblem of the victim-heroes he has been describing. The pattern here is based on the statement-counterstatement form of Christopher Smart's "Jubilate Agno" ("Rejoice in the Lamb"), and Ginsberg envisioned it as pyramidal, "with a graduated longer response to the fixed base." Affirming his allegiance to Solomon (and everyone like him), Ginsberg begins each breath unit with the phrase "I'm with you in Rockland" followed by "where . . ." and an exposition of strange or unorthodox behavior that has been labeled "madness" but that is actually a form of creative sanity. The poem concludes with a vision of Ginsberg and Solomon together on a journey to an America that transcends Moloch and madness and offers utopian possibilities of love and "true mental regularity."

During the year that "Howl" was written, Ginsberg wondered whether he might use the same long line in a "short quiet lyrical poem." The result was a poignant tribute to his "old courage teacher," Walt Whitman, which he called "A Supermarket in California," and a meditation on the bounty of nature, "A Strange New Cottage in Berkeley." He continued to work with his long-breath line in larger compositions as well, most notably the poem "America" (1956), which has been accurately described by Charles Molesworth as "a gem of polyvocal satire and miscreant complaint." This poem gave Ginsberg the opportunity to exercise his exuberant sense of humor and good-natured view of himself in a mock-ironic address to his country. The claim "It occurs to me that I am America" is meant to be taken as a whimsical wish made in self-deprecating modesty, but Ginsberg's growing popularity through the last decades of the century cast it as prophetic as well.

Naomi Ginsberg died in 1956 after several harrowing episodes at home and in mental institutions, and she was not accorded a traditional orthodox funeral because a *minyan* (a complement of ten men to serve as witnesses) could not be found. Ginsberg was troubled by thoughts of his mother's suffering and tormented by uncertainty concerning his own role as sometime caregiver for her. Brooding over his tangled feelings, he spent a night listening to jazz, ingesting marijuana and methamphetamine, and reading passages from an old bar mitzvah book. Then, at dawn, he walked the streets of the Lower East Side in Manhattan, where many Jewish immigrant families had settled. A tangle of images and emotions rushed through his mind, organized now by the rhythms of ancient Hebrew prayers and chants. The poem that took shape in his mind was his own version of the Kaddish, the traditional Jewish service for the dead that had been denied to his mother. As it was formed in an initial burst of energy, he saw its goal as a celebration of her memory and a prayer for her soul's serenity, an attempt to confront his own fears about death, and ultimately, an attempt to come to terms with his relationship to his mother.

The poem begins in an elegiac mood, "Strange now to think of you gone," and proceeds as both an elegy and a kind of dual biography. Details from Ginsberg's childhood begin to take on a sinister aspect when viewed from the perspective of an adult with a tragic sense of existence. The course of his life's journey from early youth and full parental love to the threshold of middle age is paralleled by Naomi's life as it advances from late youth toward a decline into paranoia and madness. Ginsberg recalls his mother "teaching school, laughing with idiots, the backward classes—her Russian speciality," then sees her in agony "one night, sudden attack . . . left retching on the tile floor." The juxtaposition of images ranging over many years reminds him of his own mortality, compelling him to probe his subconscious mind in order to face some of the fears that he has suppressed about his mother's madness. The first part of the poem concludes as the poet realizes that he will never find any peace until he is able to "cut through—to talk to you" and finally to write her true history.

The central incident of the second section is a bus trip the twelve-year-old Ginsberg took with his mother to a clinic. The confusion and unpredictability of his mother's behavior forced him to assume an adult's role, but without any previous preparation. For the first time, he realizes that this moment marked the real end of childhood and introduced him to a universe of chaos and absurdity. As the narrative develops, the emergence of a nascent artistic consciousness, poetic perception, and political idealism is presented against a panorama of life in the United States in the late 1930's. Realizing that his growth into the poet who is revealing this psychic history is closely intertwined with his mother's decline, Ginsberg faces his fear that he was drawing his newfound strength from her as she failed. As the section concludes, he squarely confronts his mother's illness, rendering her madness in disjointed scraps of conversation while using blunt physical detail as a means of showing the body's collapse—an effective analogue for her simultaneous mental disorder. There is a daunting authenticity to these details, as Ginsberg speaks with utter candor about the most intimate and unpleasant subjects (a method he also employs in later poems about sexual contacts), confirming his determination to bury nothing in memory.

This frankness fuses Ginsberg's recollections into a mood of great sympathy; he is moved to prayer, asking divine intervention to ease his mother's suffering. Here he introduces the actual Hebrew words of the Kaddish, the formal service that had been denied his mother because of a technicality. The poet's contribution is not only to create an appropriate setting for the ancient ritual but also to offer a testament to his mother's most admirable qualities. As the second section ends, Ginsberg sets the power of poetic language to celebrate beauty against the pain of his mother's last days. Returning to the elegiac mode (after Percy Bysshe Shelley's "Adonais"), Ginsberg has a last vision of his mother days before her final stroke, associated with sunlight and giving her son advice that concludes, "Love,/ your mother," which he acknowledges with his own tribute, "which is Naomi."

The last part of the poem, "Hymmnn," is divided into four sections. The first is a prayer for God's blessing for his mother (and for all people); the second is a recitation of some of the circumstances of her life; the third is a catalog of characteristics that seem surreal and random but coalesce toward the portrait he is producing by composite images; and the last part is "another variation of the litany form," ending the poem in a flow of "pure emotive sound" in which the words "Lord lord lord," as if beseeching, alternate with the words "caw caw caw," as if exclaiming in ecstasy.

By resisting almost all the conventional approaches to the loaded subject of motherhood, Ginsberg has avoided sentimentality and reached a depth of feeling that is overwhelming, even if the reader's experience is nothing like the poet's. The universality of the relationship is established by its particulars, the sublimity of the relationship by the revelation of the poet's enduring love and empathy.

The publication of "Kaddish" ended the initial phase of Ginsberg's writing life. "Howl" is a declaration of poetic intention, while "Kaddish" is a confession of personal necessity. With these two long, powerful works, Ginsberg completed the educational process of his youth and was ready to use his craft as a confident, mature artist. His range in the early 1960's included the hilarious "I Am a Victim of Telephone" (1964), which debunked his increasing celebrity, the gleeful jeremiad "Television Was a Baby Crawling Toward That Deathchamber" (1961), the generously compassionate "Who Be Kind To" (1965), the effusive lyric "Why Is God Love, Jack?" (1963), and his tribute to his mentor William Carlos Williams, "Death News" (1963), which describes his thoughts upon learning of Williams' death.

In 1965, after he had been invited to Cuba and Czechoslovakia, Ginsberg was expelled from both countries for his bold condemnation of their policies. In Prague, he had been selected by students (including the young Vaclav Havel) as Kral Majales (King of May), an ancient European honor that has lasted through centuries of upheaval; in the poem "Kral Majales" (1965), he juxtaposed Communist and capitalist societies at their most dreary and destructive to the life-enhancing properties of the symbolic May King—a figure of life, love, art, and enlightenment. The first part of the poem is marked by discouragement, anger, and sorrow mixed with comic resignation to show the dead end reached by governments run by a small clique of rulers. Yet the heart of the poem, a list of all the attributes that he brings to the position of Kral Majales, is an exuberant explosion of joy, mirth, and confidence in the rising generation of the mid-1960's. Written before the full weight of the debacle in Vietnam had been felt, and before the string of assassinations that rocked the country had taken place, Ginsberg reveled in the growth of what he thought was a revolutionary movement toward a utopian society. His chant of praise for the foundations of a counterculture celebrates "the power of sexual youth," productive, fulfilling work ("industry in eloquence"), honest acceptance of the body ("long hair of Adam"), the vitality of art ("old Human poesy"), and the ecumenical spirit of religious pluralism that he incarnates—"I am of Slavic parentage and Buddhist Jew/ who worships the Sacred Heart of Christ the blue body of Krishna the straight back of Ram the beads of Chango." In a demonstration of rhythmic power, the poem builds and builds until it tells of the poet's literal descent to earth from the airplane he took to London after his expulsion. Arriving at "Albion's airfield" with the exultation of creative energy still vibrating through his mind and body, he proudly presents (to the reader or listener) the poem he has just written "on a jet seat in mid Heaven." The immediacy of the ending keeps the occasion fresh in the poet's memory and alive forever in the rhythms and images of his art.

The "Prague Spring" that was to flourish temporarily in events such as the 1965 May Festival was crushed by Soviet tanks in 1968. By then, the United States had become fully involved in the war in Southeast Asia, and

Ginsberg had replaced some of his optimism about change with an anger that recalled the mood of the Moloch section of "Howl." In 1966 he was in Kansas to read poetry, and this trip to the heartland of America became the occasion for a poem that is close to an epic of American life as the country was being torn apart. "Witchita Vortex Sutra," one of Ginsberg's longest poems, combines elements of American mythological history, personal psychic exploration, multicultural interaction, and prophetic incantation. The poem is sustained by a twin vision of America: the submerged but still vital American spirit that inspired Whitman and the contemporary American realities by which "many another has suffered death and madness/ in the Vortex." A sense of a betrayal informs the narrative, and the poet is involved in a search for the cause and the cure, ultimately (and typically) discovering that only art can rescue the blighted land.

The first part of the poem depicts Kansas as the seat of American innocence, where the spirit of transcendental idealism is still relatively untouched by American actions in Vietnam. Whitman's dream of an open country and worthy citizens seems to remain alive, but events from the outside have begun to reach even this sheltered place. The land of Abraham Lincoln, Vachel Lindsay, William Jennings Bryan, and other American idealists is being ruined by the actions of a rogue "government" out of touch with the spirit of the nation. The poet finds himself trying to understand why this is happening and what consequences it has for him, for any artist. After this entrance into the poem's geopolitical and psychic space, the second part presents, in a collage form akin to Ezra Pound's *Cantos*, figures, numbers, names, and snatches of propaganda about the conflict in Vietnam. Following Pound's proposal that a bad government corrupts a people by its misuse of language, Ginsberg begins an examination of the nature of language itself to try to determine how the lies and deceptions in "black language/ writ by machine" can be overcome by a "lonesome man in Kansas" who is "not afraid" and who can speak "with ecstatic language"–that is, the true language of human need, essential human reality. Calling on "all Powers of imagination," Ginsberg acts as an artist in service to moral being, using all the poetic power, or versions of speech, that he has worked to master.

Ginsberg's "ecstatic language" includes, in particular, the language of the Far Eastern religions he has learned in his travels. To assist in exorcising the demons of the West, he implores the gods of the East (fitting, since the war is in the East) to merge their forces with those of the new deities of the West, whose incarnation he finds in such American mavericks as Bob Dylan. He summons them as allies against the Puritan death wish he locates in the fanaticism of unbending, self-righteous zealots such as Kansas' Carry Nation, whose "angry smashing ax" began "a vortex of hatred" that eventually "defoliated the Mekong Delta." Through the poem, Ginsberg has cast the language artist as the rescuer, the visionary who can restore the heartland to its primal state as a land of promise and justice. In an extraordinary testament to his faith in his craft, Ginsberg declares, "The war is over now"—which, in a poem that examines language in "its deceits, its degeneration" (as Charles Molesworth says), "is especially poignant being only language."

Other poems, such as "Bayonne Entering NYC" (1966), further contributed to the mood of a collection entitled *The Fall of America: Poems of These States, 1965-1971*, but Ginsberg was also turning again toward the personal. In poems such as "Wales Visitation" (1967), a nature ode written in the spirit of the English Romantics, and "Bixby Canyon" (1968), which is an American West Coast parallel, Ginsberg explores the possibilities of a personal pantheism, attempting to achieve a degree of cosmic transcendence to compensate for the disagreeable situation on Earth. His loving remembrance for Neal Cassady, "On Neal's Ashes" (1968), is another expression of this elegiac inclination, which reaches a culmination in "Mind Breaths" (1973), a meditation that gathers the long lines of what Ginsberg has called "a chain of strong-breath'd poems" into a series of modulations on the theme of the poet's breath as an aspect of the wind-spirit of life. As he has often pointed out, Ginsberg believes that one of his most basic principles of organization is his ability to control the rhythms of a long line ("My breath is long"). In "Mind Breaths," he develops the idea that the voice of the poet is a part of the "voice" of the cosmos—a variant on the ancient belief that the gods spoke directly through the poet. Ranging over the entire planet, Ginsberg gradually includes details from many of the world's cultures, uniting nations in motive and design to achieve an encompassing ethos of universality. Beneath the fragmentation and strife of the world's governments the poet sees "a calm breath, a silent breath, a slow breath," part of the fundamentally human universe that the artist wishes to inhabit.

The tranquillity of such reveries did not replace Ginsberg's anger at the social system but operated more as a condition of recovery or place of restoration, so that the poet could venture back into the political arena and chant, "Birdbrain is the ultimate product of Capitalism/ Birdbrain chief bureaucrat of Russia" (from "Birdbrain," written in 1980). Castigating the idiocy of organizations everywhere, Ginsberg's humor balances his anger, but there is an implication that neither humor nor anger will be sufficient against the forces of "Birdbrain [who] is Pope, Premier, President, Commissar, Chairman, Senator!" Yet in spite of his decades of experience as a political activist, Ginsberg has never let his discouragement overcome his sense of civic responsibility. In "Plutonian Ode" (1978), he offers another persuasive poetic argument to strengthen the "Mind-guard spirit" against the death wish that leads some to embrace "Radioactive Nemesis." Recalling, once again, "Howl," in which Moloch stands for the death-driven impulses of humankind gone mad with greed, Ginsberg surveys the history of nuclear experimentation. The poem is designed as a guide for "spiritual friends and teachers," and the "mountain of Plutonian" is presented as the dark shadow-image of the life force that has energized the universe since "the beginning." Addressing himself, as well, to the "heavy heavy Element awakened," Ginsberg describes a force of "vaunted Mystery" against which he brings, as always, the "verse prophetic" to "wake space" itself. The poem is written to restore the power of mind (which is founded on spiritual enlightenment) to a civilization addicted to "horrific arm'd, Satanic industries"—an echo of William Blake's injunctions at the dawn of an era in which machinery has threatened human well-being.

The publication of Ginsberg's *Collected Poems, 1947-1980* in 1984 secured his reputation as one of the leading writers of late twentieth century American literature, but it did not diminish his production. The poems in *White Shroud* (1986) continue his political orations, identifying the demons of contemporary American life as he sees them: "yes I glimpse CIA's spooky dope deal vanity." His introspective side is expressed in the lyric sadness of his "Personals Ad" (1990), in which he communicates his quest for a "companion protector friend/ young love w/ empty compassionate soul" to help him live "in New York alone with the Alone." There is a discernible sense of time's passage in this poem, as well as in "White Shroud" (1984), which is a kind of postscript to "Kaddish." Once again, Ginsberg recollects the pain of his family relationships—his difficulties in dealing with aging, irascible relatives merging with his responsibility to care for those who have loved him, his feeling for modern America fusing with his memories of the Old Left past of his immigrant family. The poem tells how Ginsberg, in search of an apartment, finds himself in the Bronx neighborhood where his family once lived. There he meets the shade of his mother, still berating him for having abandoned her, but now offering him a home as well. There is a form of comfort for the poet in his dream of returning to an older New York to live with his family, a return to the "lost America" his poetry has leaned toward from the beginning. In that search for the mythic America that has inspired millions of American dreams, Ginsberg's poetry has been central to the social and aesthetic history of his time.

Other literary forms · Allen Ginsberg recognized early in his career that he would have to explain his intentions, because most critics and reviewers did not have the interest or experience to understand what he was trying to accomplish. Consequently, he published books that include interviews, lectures, and letters to friends as means of conveying his theories about composition and poetics. Among the most interesting and informative are his epistolary exchange with William Burroughs, *The Yage Letters* (1963), his *Improvised Poetics* (1971), *Gay Sunshine Interview* (1974), *Allen Verbatim: Lectures on Poetry, Politics, Consciousness* (1974), *As Ever: The Collected Correspondence of Allen Ginsberg and Neal Cassady* (1977), *Journals: Early Fifties Early Sixties* (1977), and *Composed on the Tongue*, 1980.

Select works other than poetry

NONFICTION: *The Yage Letters*, 1963 (with William Burroughs); *Indian Journals*, 1963; *Indian Journals: March 1962-May 1963—Notebooks, Diary, Blank Pages, Writings*, 1970; *Gay Sunshine Interview*, 1974; *Allen Verbatim: Lectures on Poetry, Politics, Consciousness*, 1974; *Visions of the Great Rememberer*, 1974; *To Eberhart from Ginsberg*, 1976; *As Ever: The Collected Correspondence of Allen Ginsberg and Neal Cassady*, 1977; *Journals: Early Fifties, Early Sixties*, 1977, 1992; *Composed on the Tongue: Literary Conversations, 1967-1977*, 1980; *Allen Ginsberg Photographs*, 1990; *Snapshot Poetics: A Photographic Memoir of the Beat Era*, 1993; *Journals Mid-Fifties, 1954-1958*, 1995.

MISCELLANEOUS: *Beat Legacy, Connections, Influences: Poems and Letters by Allen Ginsberg*, 1994.

Leon Lewis

Bibliography · A good critical discussion of Ginsberg's life and poetry is Paul Portugés, *The Visionary Poetics of Allen Ginsberg*, 1978. Another excellent discussion of Ginsberg's life and its influence on his work is Thomas F. Merrill's *Allen Ginsberg*, 1969, rev. ed. 1988. For an interesting firsthand account of Ginsberg's life among the Beat poets, see Carolyn Cassady, *Off the Road: My Years with Cassady, Kerouac, and Ginsberg*, 1990. Comprehensive biographies include Barry Miles, *Ginsberg, A Biography*, 1989, and Michael Schumacher, *Dharma Lion: A Critical Biography of Allen Ginsberg*, 1992. See also Bill Morgan, *The Works of Allen Ginsberg, 1941-1944: A Descriptive Bibliography*, 1995.

JOHANN WOLFGANG VON GOETHE

Born: Frankfurt am Main, Germany; August 28, 1749
Died: Weimar, Germany; March 22, 1832

Poetry · *Neue Lieder*, 1770 (*New Poems*, 1853) · *Sesenheimer Liederbuch*, 1775-1789, 1854 (*Sesenheim Songs*, 1853) · *Römische Elegien*, 1793 (*Roman Elegies*, 1876) · *Reinecke Fuchs*, 1794 (*Reynard the Fox*, 1855) · *Epigramme: Venedig 1790*, 1796 (*Venetian Epigrams*, 1853) · *Xenien*, 1796 (with Friedrich Schiller; *Epigrams*, 1853) · *Hermann und Dorothea*, 1797 (*Herman and Dorothea*, 1801) · *Balladen*, 1798 (with Schiller; *Ballads*, 1853) · *Neueste Gedichte*, 1800 (*Newest Poems*, 1853) · *Gedichte*, 1812, 1815 (2 volumes; *The Poems of Goethe*, 1853) ·*Sonette*, 1819 (*Sonnets*, 1853) · *Westöstlicher Divan*, 1819 (*West-Eastern Divan*, 1877)

Achievements · Goethe's overwhelming success as a lyricist was primarily the result of an extraordinary ability to interpret and transform direct, intimate experience and perception into vibrant imagery and symbols with universal import. In the process of overcoming the artificiality of Rococo literary tendencies, he created for the first time in modern German literature lyrics that were at once deeply personal, dynamically vital, and universally valid in what they communicated to the reader. Beginning with the poems written to Friederike Brion, and continuing through the infinitely passionate affirmations of life composed in his old age, Goethe consistently employed his art in a manner that brushed away the superficial trappings and façades of existence to lay bare the essential spirit of humankind.

In his own time, Goethe became a world figure, although his immediate acclaim derived more from his early prose and dramatic works than from his lyrical writings. Even after the turn of the nineteenth century, he was still recognized most commonly as the author of *The Sorrows of Young Werther*, the novel that had made him instantly famous throughout Europe. Nevertheless, the simple power, clear, appealing language, and compelling melodiousness of his verse moved it inexorably into the canon of the German literary heritage. Much of his poetry was set to music by the great composers of his own and subsequent generations, and the continuing popularity of such creations as "Mailied" ("Maysong") and "Heidenröslein" ("Little Rose of the Heath") is attributable at least in part to the musical interpretations of Franz Schubert and others.

The real importance of Goethe's lyric legacy is perhaps best measured in terms of what it taught other writers. Goethe established new patterns and perspectives, opened new avenues of expression, set uncommon standards of artistic and aesthetic achievement, assimilated impulses from other traditions, and mastered diverse meters, techniques, and styles as had no other German poet before him. His influence was made productive by figures as different as Heinrich Heine and Eduard Mörike, Friedrich Hölderlin and Hugo von Hofmannsthal, Stefan George and Rainer Maria Rilke. As a mediator and motivator of the literary and intellectual currents of his time, as a creator of timeless poetic archetypes, as an interpreter of humanity within its living context, Goethe has earned an undisputed place among the greatest poets of world literature.

Biography · Three aspects of Johann Wolfgang von Goethe's childhood contributed substantially to his development as a literary artist. A sheltered existence, in which he spent long hours completely alone, fostered the growth of an active imagination. A complicated attachment to his sister Cornelia colored his perceptions of male-female relationships in ways that had profound impact on the kinds of experience from which his works were generated. Finally, contrasts between his parents in temperament and cultural attitudes gave him an early awareness of the stark polarities of life upon which the central tensions of his major literary creations are based.

Library of Congress

While studying law in Leipzig between 1765 and 1768, Goethe began to write poems and simple plays in the prevailing Anacreontic style. Although some of these productions relate to his infatuation with Kätchen Schönkopf, an innkeeper's daughter, they are more the product of his desire to become a part of the contemporary intellectual establishment than a direct outpouring of his own inner concerns. Among the important figures who influenced his education and thinking during this period were Christoph Martin Wieland, Christian Fürchtegott Gellert, and Adam Friedrich Oeser.

The experiences that resulted in Goethe's breakthrough to a distinctly individual and characteristic literary approach began when he entered the University of Strasbourg in 1770. Encounters with two very different people during the winter of 1770-1771 sharply changed his life. Johann Gottfried Herder introduced him to the concepts and ideals of the *Sturm und Drang* movement, providing him with new models in Homer and Shakespeare and moving him in the direction of less artificial modes of expression. Of equal consequence for the immediate evolution of his lyrics was an idyllic love affair with Friederike Brion that ended in a parting, the emotional implications of which marked his writings long afterward.

Upon his return to Frankfurt in 1771, Goethe was admitted to the bar. During the next five years, he fell in love with at least three different women. A painful involvement with Charlotte Buff, the fiancé of his friend Johann Christian Kestner, was followed by a brief attraction to Maximiliane Laroche. In April, 1775, he became engaged to Lili Schönemann, the daughter of a wealthy Frankfurt banker. Of the three relationships, only the interlude with Maximiliane Laroche failed to have a significant impact on his art. *The Sorrows of Young Werther* derived much of its substance from Goethe's experiences with Charlotte Buff, while the powerful internal conflicts generated by his feelings for Lili gave rise to a small group of very interesting poems.

When the engagement to Lili became intolerable because of its demands and restrictions, Goethe went to Weimar, where he settled permanently in 1776. For the next ten years, he served as adviser to Carl August, Duke of Weimar, whom he had met in Frankfurt in 1774. A broad variety of political and administrative responsibilities, ranging from supervision of road construction to irrigation, from military administration to direction of the court theater, left Goethe little time for serious literary endeavor. The resulting lack of personal fulfillment coupled with the prolonged frustrations of an unhappy platonic love affair with Charlotte von Stein caused him to flee to Italy in search of artistic and spiritual rejuvenation. While there, he perfected some of his most significant dramatic works.

The combination of exposure to Roman antiquity, classical Italian literature, and a uniquely satisfying love alliance with the simple, uneducated Christiane Vulpius formed the basis for renewed poetic productivity when Goethe returned to Weimar. In *Roman Elegies*, he glorified his intimate involvement with Christiane in imagery of the Eternal City. A second, more disappointing trip to Italy in 1790 provided the stimulus for the less well-known *Venetian Epigrams*.

In 1794, Goethe accepted Friedrich Schiller's invitation to collaborate in the publication of a new journal. There followed the most fruitful creative friendship in the history of German letters. Among the famous lyrical compositions that emerged from their relationship were the terse, pointed forms of the so-called "Epigram War" that they waged against their critics in 1796, and the masterful ballads that were written in friendly competition in 1797. Goethe regarded Schiller's death, in 1805, as one of the major personal tragedies of his own life.

The two specific experiences of later years which provided the direction for Goethe's last great productive period were exposure to the works of the fourteenth century Persian poet Hāfez and a journey to the places of his own childhood. While in Frankfurt in 1814, Goethe fell in love with Marianne von Willemer, the wife of a friend. The Hāfez-like dialogue of their intense spiritual communion is the focus of *West-Eastern Divan*, in which Goethe reached the culmination of his career as a lyricist. After it was published, only the final work on his immortal masterpiece *Faust* remained as a substantial task to be completed before his death.

Analysis · In his famous letter to Johann Wolfgang von Goethe of August 23, 1794, Schiller identified the addressee as a writer who sought to derive the essence of an individual manifestation from the totality of natural phenomena. More particularly, he saw Goethe's goal as the literary definition of humankind in terms of the organization of the living cosmos to which it belongs. Only to the extent that Goethe viewed himself as representative of humanity in general does Schiller's assessment offer a valid approach to the understanding of his friend's lyric poetry. The focus of Goethe's verse is less humankind in the abstract than it is Goethe himself as a distinct, feeling, suffering, loving, sorrowing, longing being. From the very beginning, his works assumed the character of subjective poetic interpretations of his specific place in society, the implications of direct encounters with nature and culture, and the significance of concrete interpersonal relationships. He later described his creative writings as elements of a grand confession, pinpointing the fact that a major key to them lay in the penetration of his own existence.

Goethe's development as a lyric poet is clearly a continuum in which internal and external events and circumstances contribute to sometimes subtle, sometimes obvious modifications in approach, technique, and style. It is nevertheless possible to recognize a number of well-defined stages in his career that correspond to important changes in his outward situation and his connections with specific individuals. The predominant tendency of his growth was in the direction of a poetry that reaches outward to encompass an ever-broader spectrum of universal experience.

The Anacreontic creations of Goethe's student years in Leipzig are, for the most part, timebound, occasional verse in which realistic emotion, feeling, and perception are subordinated to the artificial conventions and devices of the time. Typical motifs and themes of the collection *New Poems* are wine, Rococo eroticism, the game of love with its hidden dangers, stylized pastoral representations of nature, and a peculiarly playful association of love and death. Individual poems often move on the border between sensuality and morality, mirroring the prevailing social patterns. Especially characteristic is the employment of language that magnifies the separation of the world of the poem from experienced reality. In their affirmation of the elegant façades, the deliberate aloofness, the uncommitted playfulness of Rococo culture, these lyrics document Goethe's early artistic attitudes, even though they reveal little of his unique poetic gift.

Under the influence of Herder in Strasbourg, Goethe began to move away from the decadent artificiality of his Leipzig songs. A new appreciation for the value of originality, immediacy of feeling, unmediated involvement in nature, and directness of approach is apparent in creations that are notable for their vivid imagery, plastic presentation of substance, force of expression, and power of language and rhythm.

Two types of utterance dominate the verse of this period. Highly personal outpourings of the soul, in which the representation of love is more passionate, serious, and captivating than in the Leipzig productions, are couched in formal stanzas that arose from Goethe's fondness for Friederike Brion. Free-verse poems that focus on *Sturm und Drang* ideals of individuality, genius, and creativity reflect the lyrical influence of Pindar and the dramatic legacy of Shakespeare in their form and tone. In what they reveal of Goethe's worldview, the love poetry and the philosophical reflections are deeply intertwined. Without love, Goethe's perception of life is empty; without the depth of awareness of individual responsibility in creation, love loses its strength and vitality. Love forms the basis for the experience of nature, while the external surroundings with their beauties, tensions, conflicts, and potential for joy give full meaning to love.

The most important new feature of the Strasbourg poetry is the visible emphasis on existential polarities in the description of the poet's relationship to people and things. Love and suffering, defiance and submission, danger and ecstasy are juxtaposed in the portrayal of a world of change, growth, and struggle. In endless variation, Goethe offers the intimate revelation of loneliness, longing, and lack of final fulfillment that are the fundamental ingredients of life viewed as a pattern of restless wanderings. The very acts of searching, striving, creating, and loving are communicated with an energy and a spiritual intensity that carries the reader along in a rush of emotional participation in universal experience.

Among Goethe's most interesting early works are the sometimes tender, often intensely painful lyric documents of his courtship of Lili Schönemann. Few in number, these writings illustrate the poet's cathartic use of his talent in a process of self-analysis and clarification of his position with respect to external events. At the same time, they underscore a growing tendency to come to grips with and master life through his art. Consisting of occasional pieces that are connected by recurring themes related to the tension between the attractions of love and the devastating torments of an accompanying loss of freedom, the Lili poems combine visions of joy with ironically biting yet dismal portraits of despair. A gem of the period is the famous "Auf dem See" ("On the Lake"), a vivid projection of both physical and spiritual flight from oppressive love, written in Switzerland, where Goethe had taken temporary refuge from the demands of life with Lili.

During Goethe's first years in Weimar, the frustrations of an unsatisfying association with Charlotte von Stein, the all-consuming responsibilities of the court, and his own inability to overcome completely the break with Lili contributed to his lyrics a new preoccupation with themes of melancholy, resignation, and self-denial. The heavy moods that characterize his works of this period inform short meditative poems as well as longer philosophical reflections, mournful love songs, and a few haunting ballads. Especially profound are two eight-line stanzas, each entitled "Wanderers Nachtlied" ("Wanderer's Night Song"), in which the poet longs for and admonishes himself to courage, comfort, hope, belief, and patience. "Warum gabst du uns die tiefen Blicke?" ("Why Did You Give Us the Deep Glances?"), the most powerful of his poems to Charlotte von Stein, presents love as a mystical mystery. The two dramatic ballads, "Erlkönig" ("Elf King") and "Der Fischer" ("The Fisherman"), emphasize man's psychological subjection to the demoniac power of his own impressions of nature.

The experience of Italy completely changed Goethe's poetry. Among the most important developments which the journey inspired were the abandonment of suggestion and tone in favor of pure image, the transition from lyrical song to epic description, and the replacement of extended elaboration of worldview with terse epigrams and short didactic verse. During Goethe's classical period, his ballads achieved perfected form, while his depictions of nature attained their final goal in brightness and joyful plasticity. Where earlier poems feature colors that flow softly together, or points of color that invoke mood and an impression of the whole, the works created after 1790 are dominated by structure and the placement of objects in space. Ideas are presented in classical meters, especially hexameter, and as a result confessional poetry loses much of its melody.

Three groups of poems are particularly representative of the new directions in Goethe's lyrics: *Roman Elegies*, the epigrams, and the classical ballads. In their rich mural presentation of the poet's life in Rome, the *Roman Elegies* document the author's increasing tendency to circumscribe his own existence in verse, while their form, style, and combination of classical dignity with inner lightheartedness reflect the direct influence of Ovid, Catullus, and Propertius. The poems of *Venetian Epigrams* were similarly motivated by direct exposure to elements of classical Italian culture. They are especially notable for their rich imagery and their realism in depicting the emotional intensity of the poet's longing for Germany. In structure and style, they were models for the more famous epigrams written by Goethe and Schiller in 1796. Unlike the elegies and epigrams, Goethe's powerful ballads of 1797 arose out of materials that he had carried within him for a long time. The lyrical and melodic aspects that are absent from the other forms remain strong in rhythmic creations that emphasize passion and excitement while developing themes related to the classical ideal of pure humanity. Goethe viewed the ballad as an archetypal lyric form. His "Die Braut von Korinth" ("The Bride of Corinth") and "Der Gott und die Bajadere" ("The God and the Bayadere") are among the greatest German ballads ever written.

The erotic poetry of Goethe's old age had its beginnings in a group of sonnets that he wrote to Minchen Herzlieb in 1807. During the seven years that followed their creation, he wrote verse only occasionally. At last, however, the combination of stimuli from the deeply meaningful love affair with Marianne von Willemer and exposure to the works of Hāfez moved him to compose his greatest poetic accomplishment, *West-Eastern Divan*. In the framework of a fantasy journey of rejuvenation, Goethe entered a friendly competition with Hāfez while simultaneously declaring his own newly regained inner freedom. The central themes of the collection include longing for renewal of life, recognition of the need for spiritual transformation, coming to grips with Hāfez as a poet, love, wine, worldly experience, paradise, looking upward to God, and looking downward to the human condition. In some of the poems, Goethe returned to a kind of Anacreontic love poetry. In the heart of the cycle, he made of Hatem and Suleika timeless archetypal models for man and woman bound in the love relationship.

After *West-Eastern Divan*, Goethe wrote only a few poems of consequence. Among them, "Uworte, Orphisch" ("Primeval Words, Orphic"), in which he attempted to develop the core problems of human existence in five eight-line stanzas, and "Trilogie der Leidenschaft" ("Trilogy of Passion"), a tragic document of unfulfillment that was inspired by his final love experience, attained the power and stature of earlier lyrics. In these two creations, Goethe pin-pointed once more the essence of his own spiritual struggle between the light and the night of human existence.

While living in Strasbourg and courting Friederike Brion, Goethe created for the first time sensitive love poetry and descriptions of nature that exude the vitality of immediate experience. Perhaps the most characteristic of these works is the famous "Willkommen und Abschied" ("Welcome and Farewell"). The substance of the poem is a night ride through the countryside to Sesenheim and a joyful reunion with Friederike, followed by a painful scene of parting when morning comes. Significant elements include a new and plastic rendering of nature, fresh and captivating imagery, and melodic language that is alive with rhythm and motion. A special power of observation is demonstrated in the poet's representation of that which cannot or can hardly be seen, yet the scenery is not portrayed merely for its own sake; rather, it is symbolic, for the uncanny aspects of the ride through the darkness are overcome by a courageous heart that is driven by love. Landscape and love thus become the two poles of the poem generating an inner tension that culminates in a peculiar equation of the beloved with the world as a whole. The portrayal of Friederike is especially notable for its psychological depth, while the expression of Goethe's own feelings of passion and eventual guilt lends the entire picture qualities of a universal experience of the heart.

Deeply personal yet broadly valid content is also typical of the so-called "genius" poems of Goethe's *Sturm und Drang* period. The intensity of emotional extremes is particularly vivid in the sharply contrasting hymns "Prometheus" and "Ganymed," which reflect the poles of Goethe's own spirit even more strongly than do his dramas. In depicting the two mythological titans, the poet concentrated on the creation of dynamic archetypes. "Prometheus" is a hard, even harsh portrait of modern man. The speaker of the lines is loveless and alone. Emphasis is placed on "I"; the focus is inward and limiting. In his defiant rejection of Father Zeus and the attendant process of self-deification, Prometheus champions the value of individuality and independence. Important themes of his declaration of emancipation from gods who are less powerful than humankind include faith in self, belief in the power of action, knowledge of the difficulty and questionability of life, and the divinity of humanity's creative nature. The tone of "Ganymed" is completely different. In the soft language of a prayer, the title figure proclaims his total submission to the will of the Father and his desire to return to the divine presence. A new side of Goethe's religiosity is revealed in the transformation of his sensitivity to nature into a longing for God's love. The central concern is no longer "I" but "you"; the direction is outward toward the removal of all boundaries in a coming together of deity and humankind. In the manner in which they play off the real world against the ideal realm, "Prometheus" and "Ganymed" are especially representative of the existential polarity lyrics that Goethe wrote during the pre-Weimar years.

Roman Elegies, the major lyrical product of Goethe's first Italian journey, comprises twenty confessional hexameter poems knit tightly together in a cycle that documents the poet's love for a fictitious young widow (Christiane Vulpius in Roman disguise). Two primary thematic configurations dominate creations that are among Goethe's most beautiful, most sensuously erotic works. The story of the tender love affair with Faustine, integrated into the Italian framework, is played off against the problems associated with renewal and adaptation of antiquity by the modern poet. Within this context, love becomes the key that makes entry into the Roman world possible.

Lively, direct reflection of the writer's enthusiasm for Rome sets the tone for the cycle. At the center of the introductory elegy, which forms an overture to the love adventure, there is a longing for the beloved who gives the city its true character. This yearning is followed in the next segment by a cynical glance backward at the boredom of Weimar society, which is in turn contrasted with the first report of the developing amorous relationship. An attempt to idealize the new situation, focusing specifically on the rapidity with which Faustine gives herself, leads to the elaboration of the described experiences in the light of ancient mythological gods. Through the creation of a new goddess, "Opportunity," as a symbol for the woman he loves, Goethe effectively connects the motifs of the sequence with classical themes. The fifth elegy provides the first high point in the poetic chain with its projection of the spirit of the author's existence in Rome as a blend of antiquity, art, and the erotic which mutually illuminate, intensify, and legitimize each other to yield a true "life of the gods." Other important sections of the cycle touch on questions of jealousy, gossip about the lovers, a Homeric idyll of the hearth, and a variety of encounters with Rome and its traditions, history, and secrets. Elegy thirteen is especially interesting for the tension that it establishes between the demands of lyric art and those of love for Faustine. A dialogue between Amor and the poet develops the idea that the former provides plenty of material for poetry but does not allow enough time for creative activity. Colorful pictures of the joys of love culminate in imagery of the couple's morning awakening together in bed. There is grand irony in the fact that the lament about not having enough time to write becomes a magnificent poem in itself.

Throughout the collection, love is the focus of polar conflicts on several levels. The intense need for unity with Faustine in the physical alliance is juxtaposed to the act of self-denial that provides the quiet enjoyment of pure observation and contemplation in the creative process. Within the social frame, the fulfilled love that is sought and attained cannot be brought into harmony with reality. Fear of discovery necessitates disguise of the beloved, deception of relatives, secret meetings, and isolation from the surrounding world. In the final elegy, however, Goethe is forced to conclude that the beautiful secret of his love cannot remain hidden for long because he himself is incapable of remaining quiet about it. The result is a many-faceted revelation of love as a timeless human situation.

Careful examination of Goethe's most representative ballads reveals a clear progression from verse stories in which humankind is at the mercy of a potentially destructive, magically powerful natural world to lyric accounts that proclaim the supremacy of the human spirit over the restrictions of mortal experience. Influenced by the popular pattern established in Gottfried August Bürger's "Lenore," Goethe's early ballads such as "Elf King" and "The Fisherman" describe the fatal resolution of inner conflicts in terms of individual surrender to seductive impressions of external reality. Later, philosophically more complex works ("The Bride of Corinth" and "The God and the Bayadere") portray death as a process of transcendence that purifies the individual while preparing the soul for joyful fulfillment on a higher plane of existence.

"Elf King" is somewhat similar to "Welcome and Farewell" in its representation of a night landscape's malevolent lure as it impresses its terror on the minds of those who encounter it. The substance of the narrative is the homeward night ride of a father and son; the darkness gives uncanny form and life to things that would appear harmless by day. The boy, who is ill with fever, believes that he hears the elf king enticing him, describes what he sees and feels to his father, and dies of fright when the older man's reassurances fail to convince him of the falseness of his delirious vision. Rhythmic language that conveys the beat of the horse's hooves through the countryside, immediacy created by dialogues involving the child, the phantom elf king, and the father, and moods evoked by contrasts between light and shadow, intimate fear and pale comfortings, all contribute to the psychological intensity of a presentation in which the poet attempted to find accurate formulation for the fantastic, indefinite problem of human destiny.

In "The God and the Bayadere," a confrontation with death is handled much differently. The legend of the prostitute who spends a night providing the pleasures of love to the god Siva in human form, only to awaken and find him dead on the bed, is a forceful lyrical statement about the redeeming properties of love. Denied her widow's rights because of her way of life, the bayadere makes good her claim by springing into the flames that arise from the funeral pyre. In response to this act of purification, Siva accepts the woman as his bride. Strong Christian overtones exist in the first stanza's emphasis on the god's humaneness and in the obvious parallels to the relationship between Christ and Mary Magdalene. The poem's thrust is that the divine spark is present even in a degraded individual and that even the lowest human being can be transformed and exalted through the cleansing influence of pure love.

A major key to the literary productions of Goethe's old age is found in the notion of personal fulfillment through direct sensual and spiritual enjoyment of life. The implications of that approach to experience are most thoroughly and splendidly elaborated in *West-Eastern Divan*, a carefully constructed collection of verse that attempts to blend and join the artistic legacies of East and West in a book about love in all its manifestations. Both the pinnacle of Goethe's lyric oeuvre and one of the most difficult of his creative works, *West-Eastern Divan* is a conscious declaration of the validity of humanity's unending search for joy in the world.

As revealed in the opening poem, the focal metaphor of the volume is the Hegira, which Goethe uses as an image for his flight from oppressive circumstances into the ideal realm of foreign art. Two central relationships dominate the twelve sections of his dream journey to the Orient. On one level, the individual poems are portions of a playful fantasy dialogue between Goethe and his Eastern counterpart Hāfez. The object of their interchange is a friendly competition in which the Western poet seeks to match the achievements of a revered predecessor. Conversations between two lovers, Hatem and Suleika, develop the second complex of themes, derived from elements of the love experience shared by Goethe and Marianne von Willemer.

"Buch des Sängers" ("Book of the Singer"), the most important of the first six cycles, sets the tone for the entire work. In the famous poem "Selige Sehnsucht" ("Blessed Longing"), Goethe explored the mystery of how one gains strength through the transformation that occurs as a result of sacrifice. Borrowing from a ghazel by Hāfez the motif of the soul that is consumed in the fire of love like a moth in a candle flame, he created a profound comment on the necessity of metamorphosis to eternal progress. The uniting of two people in love to generate the greatest possible joy is made to stand for the longing of the soul to be freed from the bonds of individuality through union with the infinite. The antithesis of "Blessed Longing" is presented in "Wiederfinden" ("Reunion"), a creation of extremely vivid imagery from "Buch Suleika" ("Book of Suleika"), the eighth and most beautiful section of *West-Eastern Divan*. Based on Goethe's separation from Marianne and their coming together again, the poem develops the idea that parting and rediscovery are the essence of universal existence. In a uniquely powerful projection of creation as division of light from darkness and their recombination in color, Goethe produced new and exciting symbols for love's power, rendered in lines that form a high point in German lyric poetry.

Other literary forms · The unique significance of Johann Wolfgang von Goethe's contribution to German letters lies in the fact that his best creations provided models which influenced, stimulated, and gave direction to the subsequent evolution of literary endeavor in virtually every genre. Among more than twenty plays that he wrote throughout his career, several have special meaning for the history of German theater. *Götz von Berlichingen mit der eisernen Hand* (1773; *Götz von Berlichingen with the Iron Hand*, 1799) was a key production of the *Sturm und Drang* movement, mediating especially the influence of William Shakespeare upon later German dramatic form and substance. With *Iphigenie auf Tauris* (1787; *Iphigenia in Tauris*), Goethe illustrated profoundly the ideals of perfected form and style, beauty of language, and humanistic education that characterized German literature of the classical period. His famous masterpiece *Faust* (published in three distinct versions, 1790, 1808, 1833; *The Tragedy of Faust*), with its carefully programmed depiction of the spiritual polarities that torment the individual, rapidly became the ultimate paradigm for the portrayal of modern humankind's fragmented nature.

Goethe's major narratives, including *Die Leiden des jungen Werthers* (1774; *The Sorrows of Young Werther*), *Wilhelm Meisters Lehrjahre* (1795-1796; *Wilhelm Meister's Apprenticeship*), *Die Wahlverwandtschaften* (1809; *Elective Affinities*), and *Wilhelm Meisters Wanderjahre: Oder, Die Entsagenden* (1821-1829; *Wilhelm Meister's Travels*), are powerful illuminations of fundamental human problems. The monumental saga of Wilhelm Meister established the pattern for the German *Bildungsroman* of the nineteenth century, and it also had a substantial impact on Romantic novel theory.

A large portion of Goethe's oeuvre is nonfiction. He completed more than fourteen volumes of scientific and technical writings, the most important of which are *Versuch die Metamorphose der Pflanzen zu erklären* (1790; *Essays on the Metamorphosis of Plants*) and *Zur Farbenlehre* (1810; *Theory of*

Colors). His historical accounts, specifically *Campagne in Frankreich, 1792* (1822; *Campaign in France in the Year 1792*) and *Die Belagerung von Mainz, 1793* (1822; *The Siege of Mainz in the Year 1793*), are vividly readable reports of firsthand experience. Writings that reveal a great deal about Goethe himself and his perception of his artistic calling are his autobiography, *Aus meinem Leben: Dichtung und Wahrheit* (1811-1814; *Poetry and Truth from My Own Life*), and the many published volumes of his correspondence.

Select works other than poetry

DRAMA: *Die Laune des Verliebten*, wr. 1767, pr. 1779 (*The Wayward Lover*, 1879); *Die Mitschuldigen*, first version wr. 1768, pr. 1780, second version wr. 1769, pr. 1777 (*The Fellow-Culprits*, 1879); *Götz von Berlichingen mit der eisernen Hand*, pb. 1773 (*Götz von Berlichingen with the Iron Hand*, 1799); *Götter, Helden und Wieland*, pb. 1774; *Clavigo*, pr., pb. 1774 (English translation, 1798, 1897); *Erwin und Elmire*, pr., pb. 1775 (libretto; music by Duchess Anna Amalia of Saxe-Weimar); *Stella*, first version pr., pb. 1776, second version pr. 1806 (English translation, 1798); *Claudine von Villa Bella*, first version pb. 1776, pr. 1779, second version pb. 1788 (libretto); *Die Geschwister*, pr. 1776; *Iphigenie auf Tauris*, first version pr. 1779, second version pb. 1787 (*Iphigenia in Tauris*, 1793); *Jery und Bätely*, pr. 1780 (libretto); *Die Fischerin*, pr., pb. 1782 (libretto; music by Corona Schröter; *The Fisherwoman*, 1899); *Scherz, List und Rache*, pr. 1784 (libretto); *Der Triumph der Empfindsamkeit*, pb. 1787; *Egmont*, pb. 1788 (English translation, 1837); *Torquato Tasso*, pb. 1790 (English translation, 1827); *Faust: Ein Fragment*, pb. 1790 (*Faust: A Fragment*, 1980); *Der Gross-Cophta*, pr., pb. 1792; *Der Bürgergeneral*, pr., pb. 1793; *Was wir bringen*, pr., pb. 1802; *Die natürliche Tochter*, pr. 1803 (*The Natural Daughter*, 1885); *Faust: Eine Tragödie*, pb. 1808 (*The Tragedy of Faust*, 1823); *Pandora*, pb. 1808; *Die Wette*, wr. 1812, pb. 1837; *Des Epimenides Erwachen*, pb. 1814; *Faust: Eine Tragödie, zweiter Teil*, pb. 1833 (*The Tragedy of Faust, Part Two*, 1838).

LONG FICTION: *Die Leiden des jungen Werthers*, 1774 (*The Sorrows of Young Werther*, 1779); *Wilhelm Meisters Lehrjahre*, 1795-1796 (4 volumes; *Wilhelm Meister's Apprenticeship*, 1825); *Die Wahlverwandtschaften*, 1809 (*Elective Affinities*, 1849); *Wilhelm Meisters Wanderjahre: Oder, Die Entsagenden*, 1821, 1829 (2 volumes; *Wilhelm Meister's Travels*, 1827).

SHORT FICTION: *Unterhaltungen deutscher Ausgewanderten*, 1795 (*Conversations of German Emigrants*, 1854); *Novelle*, 1826 (*Novel*, 1837).

NONFICTION: *Von deutscher Baukunst*, 1773 (*On German Architecture*, 1921); *Versuch die Metamorphose der Pflanzen zu erklären*, 1790 (*Essays on the Metamorphosis of Plants*, 1863); *Beyträge zur Optik*, 1791, 1792 (2 volumes); *Winckelmann und sein Jahrhundert*, 1805; *Zur Farbenlehre*, 1810 (*Theory of Colors*,

1840); *Aus meinem Leben: Dichtung und Wahrheit,* 1811-1814 (6 volumes; *The Autobiography of Goethe,* 1824; better known as *Poetry and Truth from My Own Life*); *Italienische Reise,* 1816, 1817 (2 volumes; *Travels in Italy,* 1883); *Zur Naturwissenschaft überhaupt, besonders zur Morphologie,* 1817, 1824 (2 volumes); *Campagne in Frankreich, 1792,* 1822 (*Campaign in France in the Year 1792,* 1849); *Die Belagerung von Mainz, 1793,* 1822 (*The Siege of Mainz in the Year 1793,* 1849); *Essays on Art,* 1845; *Goethe's Literary Essays,* 1921; *Goethe on Art,* 1980.

MISCELLANEOUS: *Works,* 1848-1890 (14 volumes); *Goethes Werke,* 1887-1919 (133 volumes).

Lowell A. Bangerter

Bibliography · General introductions to the study of Goethe include Nicholas Boyle, *Goethe: The Poet and the Age,* 1991; Ronald Gray, *Goethe: A Critical Introduction,* 1967, which is especially useful as an introduction to Goethe's lesser writings; Richard Friedenthal, *Goethe: His Life and Times,* 1965; and Victor Lange, ed., *Goethe: A Collection of Critical Essays,* 1968. Cyrus Hamlin, ed., *The Norton Critical Edition of "Faust,"* trans. Walter Arndt, 1976, is a useful source for that work, containing introductory essays by the translator and editor, as well as substantial interpretive notes and other critical essays. Additional excellent analyses of *Faust* from preeminent Goethe scholars include Alexander Gillies, *Goethe's Faust: An Interpretation,* 1957, an important and careful scene-by-scene study (with, however, original-language excerpts); Stuart Atkins, *Goethe's Faust: A Literary Analysis,* 1958; and Jane K. Brown, ed., *Interpreting Goethe's Faust Today,* 1994. For studies of other works, see Marc Redfield, "The Dissection of the State: *Wilhelm Meisters Wanderjahre* and the Politics of Aesthetics, *German Quarterly* 69, no. 1 (Winter, 1996); Fritz Gutbrodt, "The Worth of Werther: Goethe's Literary Marketing," *Modern Language Notes* 110, no. 3 (April, 1995); and Martin Swales, " 'Die neue Sitte' and Metaphors of Secular Existence: Reflections on Goethe's *Iphigenie,*" *Modern Language Review* 89, no. 4 (October, 1994). See also Maura C. Flannery, "Goethe and Arber: Unity in Diversity," *American Biology Teacher* 57, no. 8 (November/December, 1995); Claudia Brodsky Lacour, "Grounds of Comparison," *World Literature Today* 69, no. 2 (Spring, 1995); Wilhelm Hennis and Fiona Elliot, "Goethe, Goya, and the Threat to Modernity, *Times Literary Supplement* (November 11, 1994); and Wendell E. Wilson, "Johann Wolfgang von Goethe (1749-1832)," *Mineralogical Record* 25, no. 6 (November/December, 1994).

JORIE GRAHAM

Born: New York, New York; May 9, 1951

Poetry · *Hybrids of Plants and Ghosts*, 1980 · *Erosion*, 1983 · *The End of Beauty*, 1987 · *Region of Unlikeness*, 1991 · *Materialism*, 1993 · *The Dream of the Unified Field: Selected Poems, 1974-1994*, 1995 · *The Errancy*, 1997

Achievements · In an era of lyric poetry in minor modes and moods, Jorie Graham's work is strikingly grand in scope. Her imagination is both galactic and intensely particular, at times more reminiscent of Dante than of her contemporaries. She is also an extremely self-demanding poet, one who attempts to think where thought cannot seem to go and to feel what seems too painful to feel. The poem, Graham has said, should be an act in the *present* tense, which holds genuine risks (instead of risks invented for the sake of the poem) and thus holds the possibility of personal transformation.

After an apprentice volume in lyric moods and miniatures (poems, for example, about her mother's sewing box and her own pencil sketches of wildflowers) and after the superb volume *Erosion*, Graham began to write what she calls "books"— breathless, ferociously intelligent cascades of language— rather than individual poems. The sections of these volumes do have titles but are recursively structured so that they avoid self-containment. *The End of Beauty* and *Region of Unlikeness* flow like vigorous and troubled rivers of incalculable force. Their architecture as

Jeannette Montgomery Barron

volumes, their substance, and their streaming prosody make these two volumes innovations of a high order.

Graham's creativity has secured for her a MacArthur Fellowship, recognition from the Academy of American Poets, and Pushcart prizes for "I Was Taught Three," "My Garden, My Daylight," and "Remembering Titian's Martyrdom of Saint Lawrence."

Biography · Though born of American parents, Jorie Graham grew up in Italy. Many of her poems reflect this background, especially those about Italian Renaissance paintings and European mystics, such as Saint Francis of Assisi, Saint Clare of Assisi, and Saint Teresa of Avila. She was educated at the Sorbonne, where she studied philosophy, and received a B.A. at New York University, where she studied cinema and began writing poetry. She received an M.F.A. at the University of Iowa in 1978 and later became a member of the permanent faculty in the Writers Workshop. She lives in Iowa City with her husband and daughter.

Analysis · Jorie Graham's first volume of poetry, published in the Princeton Series of Contemporary Poets, is in many respects unlike her later work. The poems are self-contained lyrics, densely figured and elaborately wrought. They have little of the impetuosity of style and subject and the rapidity and evasion of closure that characterize Graham's later work.

The poems, though more slight, are often lovely in themselves and occasionally press upon the enigmas that evolve into the great intellectual labyrinths that Graham explores in her major works. "The Geese," for example, anticipates the theme of what Graham would eventualy call, in her own distinctive metaphysical code, "hurry" and "delay"—which can be translated, but roughly, into the paradoxes of temporality and timelessness. Alternatively one might translate these terms as "flux" and "form," the changing temporal body and the permanent body of beauty, or as designations of the longing human beings have for change against their longing for fixity and stability.

In "The Geese" Graham incarnates the paradoxical terms with which people think their reality into simple, earthly activities and forms. While she is hanging out clothes, she sees geese flying overhead. Their flight becomes an "urgent" and "elegant" code for "hurry," for the flowing onwardness of time. Spiders that spin filaments between the clotheslines become an emblem for those forces in the world that hold things together—that bind, as the poem says, "pins to the lines, the lines to the eaves." More largely, the spiders on their clothesline loom signify the desire to keep human meanings intact and to mend the rifts and wounds of time. Between these two contending forces is an "astonishing delay": "And somewhere in between/ these geese forever entering and/ these spiders turning back,// this astonishing delay, the everyday, takes place."

Graham has been called a gnostic poet, and it is true that she presses thought against the secret places and conundrum points of the universe. She asks not only, "Why this strange process called time?" but also, "How do consciousness and flesh coincide?" The title of her first volume signals Graham's interest in these ontological questions. Friedrich Nietzsche's contention that even the wisest man "is only a discord and hybrid of plant and of ghost" provides a conjunction of incommensurables that stirs Graham's imagination.

In later volumes, *The End of Beauty* and *Region of Unlikeness*, Graham would extend these ontological concerns by undertaking to explore woman or the anima and its relationship to the animus through rewritings of the stories of Eve and Adam, Penelope and Ulysses, Eurydice and Orpheus, Daphne and Apollo. In recasting these cultural mythologies, Graham portrays woman as the will toward change and transformation that chooses against the stasis of paradise and perfection, and the overlords who would paralyze woman within the form of the beautiful. Eve's coming out of Adam's body is, for Graham, the tragedy that makes time and history, an ongoing tragedy that she embraces and loves, though with suffering. Similarly, Eurydice and Daphne are used to signify the will to change. Eurydice goes back to Hell because Orpheus tries to fix her form with his backward gaze. Daphne transforms herself when Apollo tries to snare her within the trammels of beauty. In Graham's rewritings of all these stories, woman becomes that principle of escape from fixities that makes time and history. "Gnosis," for Graham, will entail not only an exploration of the unthinkable interface of body and soul but also an exploration of an archetypal Eve-life within and outside the body of Adam.

The quest for knowledge of self and selfhood begins in *Hybrids of Plants and of Ghosts*. The self-portraits of this volume initiate an analysis that will become an analysis of "Selfhood," of the mystery of being. Three poems are notable in this respect: "Self Portrait," "My Face in the Mirror Tells a Story of Delicate Ambitions," and "On Why I Would Betray You." Graham's self-renderings in all of these are wonderfully ethereal. Their ghostliness comes from the fact that she depicts a generic, nongendered selfhood. Rather than painting herself as individual presence, Graham paints "the self" people share. Her self-portraits in this first volume and in later volumes are ontological rather than projections of a particularized identity.

In "Self Portrait," she draws herself as a field of snow she "makes tracks on" by merely looking out her window. At the end of the poem, she describes herself as a record whose delineations are made by the needle moving around and across the record surface. This record is, however, like the records Graham imagined as a child, an unmarked darkness that the needle must cut anew each time it is played. Such is her lovely, precise, haunting image of the self, with its simultaneous presentness and lack of presence.

Despite their alluring concretions, however, the ontological questings of these poems have caused some critics to describe Graham as an "intellectual poet," as if this were a fault. Were she to moderate her intellect, one wonders whether she would be adjudged a "merely personal poetess." Fortunately, the philosophical dimensions of Graham's poetry show no signs of shrinking to ladylike size and have actually grown with each new volume. In *The End of Beauty* and *Region of Unlikeness* Graham begins to paint herself at once in more intensely personal terms and more abstractly and philosophically: as "hurry" and "delay" in "Self-Portrait as Hurry and Delay" or the gesture between Adam and Eve. Growing more expansive, Graham's self-portraits begin to render not only the bare ontological bones of being but also the self as an individual and an archetypal gesture toward more being.

Hybrids of Plants and of Ghosts also prefigures what would become for Graham a major theater for thought—the world of painters and painting. In this first volume Graham writes poems for Paul Cézanne and Mark Rothko which pay tribute to these painters by distantly emulating their paintings in her images. In her next book, *Erosion*, painting figures much more largely. While one poem describes a Goya painting and another two paintings by Gustav Klimt, most address paintings from the Italian Renaissance. She often seems to want to argue with the paintings, to change them. Indeed, in an interview, Graham remarked that by being so fixed and immovable, paintings stimulate her rage to change. The repose of these aesthetic forms has the paradoxical effect of making her want to transform the image and its meanings.

In "San Sepolcro," the first poem of the volume, Graham invites the reader to look at *Madonna del Parto* by Piero della Francesca. Graham's description of the painting is like a film fast-forward. "And the dress keeps opening/ from eternity// to privacy, quickening. . . . each breath/ is a button// coming undone, something terribly/ nimble-fingered/ finding all of the stops." In the painting itself, Mary is notably tranquil, her hand reposing rather than unbuttoning. Clearly Graham has added to the painting the metaphysical force of "hurry." As if finding the "on switch" to this fixed aesthetic form, Graham injects temporality into the painting, making it come alive in her own era.

Similarly, Graham urges the figures of Adam and Eve in Massacio's *The Expulsion* to come alive. She tells the sorrowing couple to take their hands from their faces, to accept the lives, the process of change they have chosen by eating from the tree of knowledge. Although the repose of paintings holds great allure for Graham, their stillness is also a provocation to change and to a conception of art that emphasizes acts rather than objects.

Not surprisingly, Graham's next volume, *The End of Beauty*, adds the canvases of Jackson Pollock to her gallery of paintings. "The end of beauty" is, among other things, the end of poems as finished forms and the beginning of poems as tumultuous futural projections and acts of personal change. These aesthetic commitments of Graham are importantly linked to her ethical commitments, which become clearly enunciated in *Region of Unlikeness*. Here, in a series of poems about Eve, Graham endorses the step out of Eden, the moment when Eve seeks knowledge and in doing so initiates change, movement away from perfection. Graham's sense of the poetic enterprise might be compared to Wallace Stevens' idea of the Supreme Fiction, the aesthetic project that seeks not final form but to change as people change.

Although Graham embraces change–the Eve-acts that make history– she also values what her metaphysical lexicon terms "delay." "Delay" is the self when it looks in the mirror and sees a story of delicate ambitions. "Delay" is a mind-absorbing painting by Rothko or a Renaissance master. "Delay," as becomes clear in *The End of Beauty* and *Region of Unlikeness*, is the attempt to stay married. It is the attachment to one's particular backyard and its red birds. It is what people know of love.

"Delay" is also present in the depth of the world. Though Graham's advocacy of change links her to the open-ended aesthetic projects of postmodern art, the link is only partial. She obviously appreciates the writings of experimental postmodernists such as the "language poets," but her own aesthetic is far from the aesthetics of surface that many postmoderns embrace. Her images, for example, are nothing like Andy Warhol's soup labels, and her poetry makes everywhere evident a commitment to depth in both image and event.

Two poems in *Erosion*, "At Luca Signorelli's *Resurrection of the Body*" and "Two Paintings by Gustav Klimt," demonstrate with particular force Graham's commitment to depth. In the latter poem she writes of one of Klimt's last works, *The Bride*. An unfinished painting, it suggests that the glittering mosaic surfaces for which Klimt is famous may conceal mutilation scenes. As Graham describes it, after Klimt's death an incomplete painting was found in his studio. It pictured "a woman's body/ open at its point of/ entry," with "something like/ a scream" rising between her legs. The painter had begun to cover "this mouth/ of her body" with a garment rendered in soft, delicate brushstrokes. *The Bride* makes Graham wonder whether even Klimt's landscape paintings, like his painting of beech trees called *Buchenwald*, conceal death scenes. The beech grove may be Buchenwald concentration camp, whose myriad dead may be lingering in the leaves of Klimt's forest floor, longing to come back.

"At Luca Signorelli's *Resurrection of the Body*" describes a resurrection painting of the Renaissance master in which skeletons crawl out of their graves and climb into physical bodies that await them on the earth's surface. Graham talks to the painting and asks its figures why they are in such a hurry to get bodies back. Then the poem flicks to a description of the painter cutting into the body of his son after his son dies. The way in which Graham enacts this scene is much too marvelous to be told. She describes the cutting as an act of love, a healing process for the father. He needs to see that his son's soul cannot be found in the body. Having awaited "the best/ possible light," the father begins cutting "with beauty and care." It is a slow, painstaking process that takes days. At the end of this "deep/ caress," the father's mind "could climb into/ the open flesh and/ mend itself." Although the father must, in terrible pursuit of gnosis, lovingly explore his son's body, he cannot cut deep enough to reach the spirit. It will always recede before him. Like the vanishing point used in painting with perspective, "the flesh/ open endlessly,/ its vanishing point so deep/ and receding// we have yet to find it."

The poem also embodies the thematics of discord and dissolve between the material and immaterial, the hybridization of plant and ghost that shapes Graham's first volume. This poem discovers, though, that the body is a depth that leads to a vanishing point for thought. The images in Graham's poetry seem similarly fathomless. The point at which mind and matter meet, meaning and image merge, cannot be finally thought: Thought can only disappear into the mystery.

The other depth that grows larger and larger in Graham's poetry is the depth of the tragic. Graham is, as critics so often note, "relentlessly cerebral." As her corpus grows, it also becomes clear that she is relentlessly committed to feeling, and to feeling beyond the point at which one blacks out for the pain. It is this combination of intense intellect and growing depth and range of feeling that would cause one to compare Graham to Dante.

Like Dante's *Divine Comedy*, Graham's poems in *The End of Beauty* and *Region of Unlikeness* attempt to link disparate realms, the sublime and the hellish, the agonies of the personal life with cultural tumult at large. A montage strategy, which was at times disconcerting in her early work, is in these volumes fully mature and profoundly disturbing. The poems are often in two parts, the second seeming to be of a totally different substance; these two parts, though, by the end of the poem become a sort of liquid montage that blends the disparate and discordant experiences and implies without stating an endlessly reticulating realm of subterranean connections.

"Imperialism," the last poem of *End of Beauty*, juxtaposes an acrimonious argument between a couple, one in which the form of marriage cannot seem to hold their feeling, to a childhood experience of being made to enter the Ganges River. The river is teeming with people washing their bodies and their personal effects; it is also thick with ashes and remains from funeral pyres that burn along the Ganges night and day. The child cannot contain her terror. In the hotel afterward, neither Demerol nor her mother's arms can console her. At first the two parts of the poem seem arbitrarily conjoined; as one thinks the poem and feels it, however, connections begin to appear. As the marriage form cannot hold the feelings of its partners, the mother-daughter relationship cannot absorb the terror of the child. Like many of Graham's poems, "Imperialism" deals with the fact that people's forms for experience—parenting, marriage, the idealistic phantasms of imperialists—are finally unable to absorb and hold their teeming reality. The poem leaves the reader with an awed and awful feeling that one is ultimately on one's own in a river of life turbulent with human suffering.

Region of Unlikeness begins with a poem called "Fission" that also forces disparate experiences into the montagelike structure described earlier. The poem's speaker is watching the Stanley Kubrick film *Lolita* (1962) when a man bursts into the theater announcing the Dallas shooting of John F. Kennedy. *Lolita*, as presented in the poem, makes the female body into a too-large and physical surface of desire, so that desire itself becomes obscenely grandiose and public. As the light of the theater, the projector light, the house lights, and light from a skylight beam into the room, the speaker begins to feel that the lights converge on her, the leprous gray of blended film light and daylight. The spotlight seems to be on her own body and its sexual potential. She feels stripped, torn from herself, and it is at just this moment that she must absorb Kennedy's death, with her father beside her crying. This collision of disparate realms of experience causes fission, an explosion of troubled energy that one's psyche can hardly contain.

This process of fission moves through much of the volume. In "From the New World," for example, Graham painfully brings together "the story about the girl who didn't die/ in the gas chamber, who came back out asking/ for her mother" with her own family experience of placing a grandmother in a nursing home. The grandmother is "in her diaper sitting with her purse in her hand all day every/ day, asking can I go now." In these poems Graham seems to be dealing with the bad conscience of a whole people—how human beings have survived only by compartmentalizing the painful, glossing the tragic.

As *Region of Unlikeness* grows poem by poem, the sense of human temporality as a fragile surface to an immense tragedy also grows. Graham is, as she says, now writing books, not poems, and these books push and push toward a gnosis that is at once too painful and absolutely necessary.

Select works other than poetry
 EDITED TEXT: *The Best American Poetry, 1990*, 1990 (with David Lehman).

Anne Shifrer

Bibliography · Charles Berger, "Laurels," *Poetry* 115, no. 1 (April, 1982), praises Graham's first book of poetry with some reservations about her style. Jessica Greenbaum, "Evolution," *The Nation* (September 5, 1987), praises the style and thought of Graham's *The End of Beauty*. Helen Vendler, *The Given and the Made*, 1995, is a full discussion of Graham's poetry. Vendler's *The Breaking of Style*, 1995, is an excellent discussion of the changes in Graham's style from book to book.

ROBERT GRAVES

Born: Wimbledon, England; July 24, 1895
Died: Deyá, Majorca, Spain; December 7, 1985

Poetry · *Over the Brazier*, 1916 · *Goliath and David*, 1916 · *Fairies and Fusiliers*, 1917 · *Treasure Box*, 1919 · *Country Sentiment*, 1920 · *The Pier-Glass*, 1921 · *The Feather Bed*, 1923 · *Whipperginny*, 1923 · *Mock Beggar Hall*, 1924 · *The Marmosite's Miscellany*, 1925 (as John Doyle) · *Welchman's Hose*, 1925 · *Poems: 1914-1926*, 1927 · *Poems: 1914-1927*, 1927 · *Poems: 1929*, 1929 · *Ten Poems More*, 1930 · *Poems: 1926-1930*, 1931 · *To Whom Else?*, 1931 · *Poems: 1930-1933*, 1933 · *Collected Poems*, 1938 · *No More Ghosts: Selected Poems*, 1940 · *Work in Hand*, 1942 (with others) · *Poems: 1938-1945*, 1946 · *Collected Poems: 1914-1947*, 1948 · *Poems and Satires: 1951*, 1951 · *Poems: 1953*, 1953 · *Collected Poems: 1955*, 1955 · *Poems Selected by Himself*, 1957 · *The Poems of Robert Graves Chosen by Himself*, 1958 · *Collected Poems: 1959*, 1959 · *The Penny Fiddle: Poems for Children*, 1960 · *Collected Poems*, 1961 · *More Poems: 1961*, 1961 · *The More Deserving Cases: Eighteen Old Poems for Reconsideration*, 1962 · *New Poems: 1962*, 1962 · *Ann at Highwood Hall: Poems for Children*, 1964 · *Man Does, Woman Is*, 1964 · *Love Respelt*, 1965 · *Collected Poems: 1965*, 1965 · *Seventeen Poems Missing from "Love Respelt,"* 1966 · *Colophon to "Love Respelt,"* 1967 · *Poems: 1965-1968*, 1968 · *The Crane Bag*, 1969 · *Love Respelt Again*, 1969 · *Beyond Giving: Poems*, 1969 · *Poems About Love*, 1969 · *Advice from a Mother*, 1970 · *Queen-Mother to New Queen*, 1970 · *Poems: 1969-1970*, 1970 · *The Green-Sailed Vessel*, 1971 · *Poems: Abridged for Dolls and Princes*, 1971 · *Poems: 1968-1970*, 1971 · *Poems: 1970-1972*, 1972 · *Poems: Selected by Himself*, 1972 · *Deyá*, 1972 (with Paul Hogarth) · *Timeless Meetings: Poems*, 1973 · *At the Gate*, 1974 · *Collected Poems: 1975*, 1975 (2 volumes) · *New Collected Poems*, 1977

Achievements · *The White Goddess: A Historical Grammar of Poetic Myth* (1948), and Robert Graves's other studies in mythology, *The Greek Myths* (1955, 2 volumes), *Hebrew Myths: The Book of Genesis* (1964, with Raphael Patai) and *The Nazarine Gospel Restored* (1953, with Joshua Podro), together with his novels and poetry based on myth, have undoubtedly had a subtle and pervasive influence on modern literature. Their impact cannot, of course, be distinguished precisely from that of other writers, such as James Frazer, T. S. Eliot, Joseph Campbell, and others, who have contributed to the renewed interest in mythology and ancient patterns of belief. With the

Washington Post/D.C. Public Library

passing of the enthusiasm for social realism, the old patterns of myth have reasserted themselves with a surprising vigor—perhaps in direct proportion to discomfort with the demythologized, purely practical bent of technological society. Graves contributed significantly to this rediscovery of the past.

For the novel *I, Claudius*, Graves received the Hawthornden Prize, the oldest of the famous British literary prizes, and the James Tait Black Memorial Prize, administered through the University of Edinburgh for the year's best novel. Collections of his poetry gained the Loines Award for Poetry (1958), the William Foyle Poetry Prize (1960), the Arts Council Poetry Award (1962), and the Queen's Gold Medal for Poetry (1968).

Graves held only one full-time salaried position in his life—in 1926, when he taught for one year at the Egyptian University of Cairo. He was Clark Lecturer at Trinity College, Cambridge, in 1954, however, and Arthur Dehon Little Memorial Lecturer at the Massachusetts Institute of Technology in 1963. He also lectured in California, Hungary, Israel, and Spain. In 1970, he became an Honorary Member of the American Academy of Arts and Sciences.

Biography · Robert Graves was born July 24, 1895, in Wimbledon, near London, to Alfred Percival Graves and Amalie von Ranke Graves. His father was an inspector of schools, a Gaelic scholar, and a writer of poetry of a conventional sort. His German mother was related to the historian Leopold von Ranke. Robert was one of ten children, five of them from his father's first marriage. The Graves household was conventionally religious, a tradition which Graves dispensed with in his maturity, but which left him, according to his autobiography, *Goodbye to All That* (1929), with "a great capacity for fear . . . a superstitious conscience and a sexual embarrassment." To the age of twelve, Robert and the other Graves children sometimes visited their German relatives, including their aunt, Baronin von Aufsess, who lived in a medieval castle in the Bavarian Alps. These romantic environs undoubtedly colored his early poetry.

When Graves attended Charterhouse, where he was listed as R. von R. Graves, his German connections were an embarrassment because of the anti-German sentiment developing in England. Graves did not find his school-mates particularly congenial until he won their respect by becoming a competent boxer. He did find one prominent friend in George Mallory, a famous mountaineer who later died climbing Mount Everest. Mallory introduced Edward Marsh, then secretary to Winston Churchill, to Graves's poetry. Marsh, a patron of the contemporary Georgian school of poetry, encouraged Graves in his writing; but, he said, Graves should modernize his diction, which was "forty years behind the time."

Graves joined the Royal Welsh Fusiliers when World War I began and went to France as a nineteen-year-old officer. He became a close friend of the well-known war poet Siegfried Sassoon. Graves's autobiography, *Goodbye to All That*, written when he was thirty-five, includes one of the best accounts of trench warfare to come out of the war. Both Graves and Sassoon survived the war, though they suffered physical and mental wounds in the process. Graves received multiple wounds from an exploding shell and was, in fact, listed among the casualties, but eventually someone noted that the "corpse" in the hospital tent had moved and Graves lived to fight again. One lung was seriously damaged, however, and he was soon brought back to England to serve in a training role.

The more lasting damage that Graves suffered from trench warfare, however, was psychological and helped to determine the nature of his poetry for nearly ten years. He suffered from war neurasthenia; he was prone to nightmares, obsessed with military strategy even in peaceful surroundings, and had waking hallucinations about comrades who had died in the war. He became acquainted with Dr. W. H. R. Rivers, a Freudian psychologist who was an expert in war neurasthenia and was also interested in the role of the subconscious in poetic creativity. Under his influence, Graves became fascinated with dreams and developed a theory about poetry as a way of expressing and resolving mental conflicts. His poetry of this period was haunted by images of guilt, despair, and entrapment. Though he seldom wrote specifically about war experiences, he translated the emotions aroused there into more gothic visions. Only years later, after he had achieved some distance from combat, could he treat it in both poetry and prose with a certain gritty objectivity.

In 1918, Graves married Nancy Nicholson, a painter, socialist, and ardent feminist who kept her maiden name. The couple had four children. Although it had seemed positive, the marriage failed in a shattering domestic crisis in which the American poet Laura Riding, who had been staying with the Graves family, made a dramatic exit from a fourth-story window. She survived with a broken back and gradually recovered over a period of months. Graves and Riding were companions for the next thirteen years. They established the Seizin Press and later moved to Majorca, where Graves lived until his death in 1985 except when lecturing at universities or when political conditions forced the evacuation of British nationals. On one such occasion while Graves and Riding were living temporarily in the United States, Riding fell in love with and married the American poet Schuyler Jackson. Graves went back to England and eventually married Beryl Hodge, with whom he lived in Majorca until his death. He had four children from this marriage.

Laura Riding had a considerable influence on Graves's writing. She was more obsessed with "truth" than with emotional expression in poetry, and was fascinated with word-meanings. She encouraged Graves to forgo the Gothic effects he was using when he looked upon poetry as emotional therapy. She insisted on more rigorous thinking and verbal precision. Perhaps she merely supported a development which was already under way in Graves's writing; in any case, his poetry became more philosophic and ironic. After Riding severed her association with Graves, he developed his fascination with the mythological White Goddess, which provided a pattern of images for almost all his subsequent poetry.

Some critics suggest that the White Goddess mythology universalized Riding's personality, though Graves claimed that he simply discovered, and did not invent, the great Triple Goddess of moon, earth, and underworld who dominated preclassical religion. He became interested in the concept while doing research for a novel about Jason and the Golden Fleece, and studied such anthropologists as James Frazer, J. J. Bachofen, Jane Harrison, and Margaret Murray as well as recent archaeological studies. He finally worked out his theory while examining thirteenth century Welsh minstrel poems. These investigations culminated in *The White Goddess,* a unique combination of esoteric lore and inspired speculation. He was convinced (or claimed to be, at least) not only that the goddess cult once dominated the Western world, but also that most of the social evils of civilization stemmed from her overthrow and the subsequent domination by the male. The mythology of the goddess inspired much of Graves's subsequent writing.

Analysis · Robert Graves was perhaps the most significant inheritor of the Romantic tradition in twentieth century poetry. After articulating his devotion to the White Goddess, he specialized in love poetry. He wrote significant poetry, however, at every stage of development, sometimes dealing with psychological or philosophical ideas as well as with mythological themes.

According to Graves, the art of poetry requires long experience with and attention to the meanings of words, a carefully developed craftsmanship, and an intuitive openness to what he called the poetic trance. He explained this process lucidly in one of his Oxford lectures, "The Poet in a Valley of Dry Bones" (published in *Mammon and the Black Goddess,* 1965):

> A poet lives with his own language, continually instructing himself in the origin, histories, pronunciation, and peculiar usages of words, together with their latent powers, and the exact shades of distinction between what Roget's *Thesaurus* calls 'synonyms.'

The use of the English language depends largely upon precedent. One needs to know the precedents and when to deviate from them. Graves says that "The exact rightness of words can be explained only in the context of a whole poem: each one being related rhythmically, emotionally, and semantically to every other."

This meticulous sense for shades of meaning is demonstrated in an ironic poem called "The Naked and the Nude." "Nude" is associated with sly seduction, showmanship, and mock-religious poses, while the state of nakedness is appropriate in contexts of love, medicine, and "true" religious devotion: "naked shines the Goddess when/ She mounts her lion among men." The poet warns that though the brazen nude may defeat the naked in life, in the world of the dead they shall be pursued by Gorgons with whips. There, in a final play on meaning, "How naked go the sometime nude!" Here, of course, "naked" means exposed in its actuality. Thus, in the poet's personal lexicography, "nude" implies exploitation and prostitution, while the term "naked" fuses connotations of love, beauty, and truth.

Graves has other poems which explore in a more serious tone the function of language. One of the most perceptive is "The Cool Web," where language serves as a buffer between the speaker and the intensity of raw experience. It is one of the best poems written on the theme of language as a cocoon that protects but also embalms:

> There is a cool web of language winds us in,
> Retreat from too much joy or too much fear:
> We grow sea green at last and coldly die
> In brininess and volubility.

This state of insulation from the stark reality of experience contrasts with the clearer perception that he attributes to children: "Children are dumb to say how hot the day is . . . How dreadful the black wastes of evening sky." The poet suggests that one must either smother in a sea of words or throw off language and die of madness, "Facing the wide glare of the children's day." Besides being a unique expression of the function of language in controlling emotional reaction to experience, the poem also suggests a view of alternative fates somewhat analogous to Achilles' dilemma in Homer's *Iliad* (c. 800 B.C.). Achilles was supposed to have two possible destinies: a short life of violent action in obedience to his passions which would bring him everlasting fame, or a long, uneventful life if he chose to return home. Of course, the romantic traditionally prefers the short, intense life to the long, dull, conventional existence. Graves, however, gives a new turn to the screw: the ferocious quality of reality is not a romantic illusion, but its true color. It is the dull, conventional life which is an error—an illusion of order conceived and perpetuated by language.

Although Graves had the romantic's distrust of cold reason uninformed by the heart, the poem called "The Philosopher" seems to entertain at least the possibility of some benefit derivable from logic—given a suitable environment. The ideal housing for the logical mind is, unfortunately, a barren prison cell where the mind might be "free" of all the usual distractions of living. There one might weave a more perfect web of thought,

"Threading a logic between wall and wall,/ Ceiling and floor more accurate by far/ Than the cob-spider's." In this paradoxically ideal situation, one might attain "Truth captured without increment of flies." The poet imagines the cell becoming a

> spacious other head
> In which the emancipated reason might
> Learn in due time to walk at greater length
> And more unanswerably.

The poem achieves an ironic fusion of contradictory attitudes—only persons quite dead to the world are in a position to form a logically consistent philosophy. This may suggest an outright parody of philosophers, but one fancies that the poet would really like to reconcile the worlds of experience and thought if he could. Perhaps Graves was struggling with Laura Riding's rather obscure requirement that poetry express "Truth."

Graves meticulously avoided schools and movements in poetry. Having emerged from the Georgian school popular in his early youth, he deliberately disregarded T. S. Eliot and Ezra Pound, who were dictating poetic taste somewhat later. Graves maintained that one does not write good poetry by imitating popular fashions or even recognized geniuses in the genre. The style should always be one's own and the idea or experience itself should determine form, diction, and rhythm. He despised what he saw as the tendency in modern poetry to cultivate obscurity for its own sake or to throw out rhyme or rhythm simply to rebel against nineteenth century Romanticism. He did, however, modernize his diction, as Edward Marsh once told him to do, weaning himself away from all decorative elaboration that served no function in the poem. When the cult of Eliot and Pound was on the wane, Graves became a model to many younger poets for his craftsmanship and his ability to match rhythm and diction with content.

Graves repeatedly displayed this versatility of language. During the time when he was haunted by his war experiences, he became adept at the Gothic mode. The collection called *The Pier-Glass* contains some of his best poems of that period. The title poem uses the ambience of a haunted house to convey the acute emotional trauma of its female persona, who returns obsessively to a deserted bedroom, "Drawn by a thread of time-sunk memory." She gazes at her pale reflection in a cracked pier-glass and at the curtained bed which is likened to a "puppet theatre where malignant fancy/ Peoples the wings with fear."

In spite of the Gothic touches of such poems as "The Pier-Glass," Graves was soon writing other poems in an altogether different mode, as cool and ironic as anyone could wish. "The Legs," for example, is entirely original in subject matter, though surrealism may have inspired the wry humor and absurdity of the scene:

> There was this road,
> And it led down-hill,
> And round and in and out.
> And the traffic was legs,
> Legs from the knee down,
> Coming and going,
> Never pausing.

The persona is apparently feeling rather smug because he is standing firmly in the grass by the roadside, clearly self-possessed in the midst of this mindless activity of legs. Suddenly, his feeling of superiority becomes slightly clouded with doubt:

> My head dizzied then:
> I wondered suddenly,
> Might I too be a walker
> From the knees down?
> Gently I touched my shins.
> The doubt unchained them.
> They had run in twenty puddles
> Before I regained them.

The simplicity of diction, the clarity of the symbolic action, and the delicately modulated tempo make this poem delightful.

Graves became increasingly objective in his poetry as the urgencies of war and domestic upheavals receded, abandoning his notion of poetry as therapy, and writing more and more in a philosophic or ironic vein. With the disappearance from his life of Laura Riding and his subsequent fascination with ancient myth, he found a reservoir of symbols and metaphors that contributed to a burst of creative activity during which he wrote some of the best love lyrics of his age. As he affirmed in "To Juan at the Winter Solstice," one of the best-known of the poems inspired by the White Goddess mythology, "There is one story and one story only/ That will prove worth your telling." That is the love story between the Great Goddess of moon, earth, and the underworld (or a woman who embodies her) and her champion, who represents in ancient myth the Sacred King (the god of the waxing and waning year)–or, by extension, the poet inspired by his muse. As he explains his discovery in *The White Goddess*:

The Theme, briefly, is the antique story, which falls into thirteen chapters and epilogue, of the birth, life, death and resurrection of the God of the Waxing Year; the central chapters concern the God's losing battle with the God of the Waning Year for love of the capricious and all-powerful Threefold Goddess, their mother, bride and layer-out. The poet identifies himself with the God of the Waxing Year and his Muse with the Goddess; the rival is his blood-brother, his other self, his weird.

The God of the Waxing Year is, of course, a variation of the primitive vegetation god. He suffers death in the fall but revives in the spring, like the Egyptian Osiris, murdered by his brother Set, god of desert and drought, only to be restored to life by his wife Isis. The poet sees himself in both creative and sacrificial roles, alternately inspired by the love of the Goddess Muse and suffering ritual death when her love grows cold.

The historical and religious origins of the goddess, nevertheless, have some purely literary precedents in the numerous fatal women of Romantic poetry—John Keats's supernatural "La Belle Dame sans Merci," and Samuel Taylor Coleridge's weird women who dice with Death for the life of the Ancient Mariner. This is exactly the guise in which Graves often meets her, stressing her more frightening implications over her occasional gentleness. In "Darien," the poet tells his son about the Muse. "Often at moonrise I had watched her go./ And a cold shudder shook me/ To see the curved blaze of her Cretan axe." The Cretan axe is an emblem of the ancient Moon Goddess, having both convex and concave surfaces, suggesting different stages of the moon. The axe forebodes the price of being her chosen lover, for it is an instrument of sacrifice.

In the poem entitled "The White Goddess," the persona also hints at the price of seeking the favor of the goddess. Spring, the poet suggests, always celebrates the Mountain Mother:

> But we are gifted, even in November
> Rawest of seasons, with so huge a sense
> Of her nakedly worn magnificence
> We forget cruelty and past betrayal,
> Heedless of where the next bright bolt may fall.

In ancient times, certain animals were associated with the Goddess, particularly the cat, bitch, cow, sow, owl, dove, and crane. (Her consort had other animal forms, such as the snake, bull, or the white roebuck.) In Graves's poem "Cat-Goddesses" the triad expands to nine (like the powerful ninefold-mountain mother of Parnassus whom Apollo reduced to nine little nymphs, the Muses). The poem speaks of the "perverse habit of cat-goddesses" who, "With coral tongues and beryl eyes like lamps/ Long-legged, pacing three by three in nines," offer themselves indiscriminately to "tatter-eared and slinking alley-toms." They do this simply to provoke jealousy. They promptly desert the "gross-headed, rabbit-coloured litters" that result from such casual unions. None of these careless offspring is the sacred child whom the Goddess bears to her chosen Sacred King, symbolizing the rejuvenation of spring and the fertility of the land.

In "Return of the Goddess," the Queen appears as a crane, reclaiming errant frogs who had unwisely crowned a king of their own devising. "The log they crowned as king/ Grew sodden, lurched and sank"; the frogs, "loud with repentance," await the Goddess' judgment day. At dawn, the Goddess returns as a "gaunt red-legged crane" to claim them, "Lunging your beak down like a spear/ To fetch them home again." This clever fable perhaps suggests that men, too, erred in transferring their allegiance to a male deity. Sooner or later, the impostor will sink, and the immortal Goddess will return.

Sometimes the Goddess is invoked only indirectly in a more realistic context. The excellent short poem "The Sweet Shop Around the Corner" tells of a little boy who, losing track of his mother in a crowd, grabs a strange woman's hand and drags her boisterously into a sweet shop, demanding candy. Only gradually does he realize with dread that something is wrong:

> Were Mother's legs so lean, or her shoes so long,
> Or her skirt so patched, or her hair tousled and grey?
> Why did she twitter in such a ghostly way?
> *O, Mother, are you dead?*
> What else could a child say?

It is, of course, unnecessary for the appreciation of this poem to realize the mythic quality of Mother turned Crone. The poem is a model of clarity and brevity, yet achieves a striking revelation. The child, so confident in himself and his world of indulgent Mother and animal joys, looks suddenly upon the face of old age and death.

Although Graves's long love affair with the White Goddess inspired many good poems, such exclusive attention to this mythic framework ultimately limited his further development. It was hard for even so expert a craftsman to go on telling the "one story only" in fresh and exciting ways. The change or deepening of perspective that one might expect from age never appeared. Moreover, sometimes the reader may yearn for a real woman with a distinctive personality to emerge from the repeated avowals of love. Nevertheless, Graves wrote some very good poetry at almost every stage of his long and devoted career. Through his investigations in mythology and his celebration of it in poetry, he reactivated a past which makes the present richer.

Other literary forms · Robert Graves published fifteen novels, including one (*No Decency Left*, 1932) written in collaboration with Laura Riding. His novels are usually based on historical events or mythology. *I, Claudius* (1934) and *Claudius the God and His Wife Messalina* (1934) borrow heavily from Suetonius' *Lives of the Caesars* (c. A.D. 120). *Count Belisarius* (1938) concerns the brilliant general of the Byzantine emperor Justinian. *Sergeant Lamb of the Ninth* (1940) and *Proceed, Sergeant Lamb* (1941) fictionalize the life of an actual English soldier in the American Revolution. *The Story of Marie Powell, Wife to Mr. Milton* (1943) elaborates imaginatively on John Milton's marital problems. *The Islands of Unwisdom* (1949) is based on the abortive attempt by the Spanish in the sixteenth century to colonize the Solomon Islands. *They Hanged My Saintly Billy* (1957) is a minor work about the notorious career and execution of Dr. William Palmer for poisoning his friend, John Parsons Cook.

Biblical topics inspired two novels: *My Head! My Head!* (1925), about Elisha and Moses, and *King Jesus* (1946), his most significant attempt to fuse his ideas about the Triple Goddess with Christian and Hebrew myth. Greek mythology inspired *The Golden Fleece* (1944, published as *Hercules, My Shipmate* in America) and *Homer's Daughter* (1955), while *Seven Days in New Crete* (1949, *Watch the North Wind Rise* in America) is an entertaining fantasy about a mythological future when the worship of the Goddess is reestablished in Crete, the ancient stronghold of the Goddess cult.

Graves published more than fifty works in the nonfiction category, including literary criticism, books about writing and language, an autobiography, a biography of T. E. Lawrence, social commentaries, and studies in Greek and Hebrew myths. In addition, he translated such writers as Suetonius, Homer, Hesiod, Lucius Apuleius, Lucan Pharsalia, and Manuel de Jesus Galvan. He was one of the most versatile writers of the twentieth century, a persistent maverick often embroiled in intellectual arguments with other scholars because of his sometimes eccentric views.

Select works other than poetry
LONG FICTION: *My Head! My Head!*, 1925; *No Decency Left*, 1932 (as Barbara Rich, with Laura Riding); *I, Claudius*, 1934; *Claudius the God and His Wife Messalina*, 1934; "*Antigua, Penny, Puce*," 1936 (also known as *The Antigua Stamp*, 1937); *Count Belisarius*, 1938; *Sergeant Lamb of the Ninth*, 1940 (also

known as *Sergeant Lamb's America*); *Proceed, Sergeant Lamb*, 1941; *The Story of Marie Powell, Wife to Mr. Milton*, 1943 (also known as *Wife to Mr. Milton, the Story of Marie Powell*); *The Golden Fleece*, 1944 (also known as *Hercules, My Shipmate*, 1945); *King Jesus*, 1946; *Watch the North Wind Rise*, 1949 (also known as *Seven Days in New Crete*); *The Islands of Unwisdom*, 1949 (also known as *The Isles of Unwisdom*); *Homer's Daughter*, 1955; *They Hanged My Saintly Billy*, 1957.

SHORT FICTION: *The Shout*, 1929; *¡Catacrok! Mostly Stories, Mostly Funny*, 1956; *Collected Short Stories*, 1964.

NONFICTION: *On English Poetry*, 1922; *The Meaning of Dreams*, 1924; *Poetic Unreason and Other Studies*, 1925; *Contemporary Techniques of Poetry: A Political Analogy*, 1925; *Another Future of Poetry*, 1926; *Impenetrability: Or, The Proper Habit of English*, 1926; *The English Ballad: A Short Critical Survey*, 1927; *Lars Porsena: Or, The Future of Swearing and Improper Language*, 1927; *A Survey of Modernist Poetry*, 1927 (with Laura Riding); *Lawrence and the Arabs*, 1927 (also known as *Lawrence and the Arabian Adventure*, 1928); *A Pamphlet Against Anthologies*, 1928 (with Riding, also known as *Against Anthologies*); *Mrs. Fisher: Or, The Future of Humour*, 1928; *Goodbye to All That: An Autobiography*, 1929; *T. E. Lawrence to His Biographer Robert Graves*, 1938; *The Long Week-End: A Social History of Great Britain, 1918-1938*, 1940 (with Alan Hodge); *The Reader over Your Shoulders: A Handbook for Writers of English Prose*, 1943 (with Hodge); *The White Goddess: A Historical Grammar of Poetic Myth*, 1948; *The Common Asphodel: Collected Essays on Poetry, 1922-1949*, 1949; *Occupation: Writer*, 1950; *The Nazarene Gospel Restored*, 1953 (with Joshua Podro); *The Crowning Privilege: The Clark Lectures, 1954-1955*, 1955; *Adam's Rib and Other Anomalous Elements in the Hebrew Creation Myth: A New View*, 1955; *The Greek Myths*, 1955 (2 volumes); *Jesus in Rome: A Historical Conjecture*, 1957 (with Podro); *Five Pens in Hand*, 1958; *Greek Gods and Heroes*, 1960; *Oxford Addresses on Poetry*, 1962; *Nine Hundred Iron Chariots: The Twelfth Arthur Dehon Little Memorial Lecture*, 1963; *Hebrew Myths: The Book of Genesis*, 1964 (with Raphael Patai); *Majorca Observed*, 1965 (with Paul Hogarty); *Mammon and the Black Goddess*, 1965; *Poetic Craft and Principle*, 1967; *The Crane Bag and Other Disputed Subjects*, 1969; *On Poetry: Collected Talks and Essays*, 1969; *Difficult Questions, Easy Answers*, 1972.

CHILDREN'S LITERATURE: *The Big Green Book*, 1962; *The Siege and Fall of Troy*, 1962; *Two Wise Children*, 1966; *The Poor Boy Who Followed His Star*, 1968.

TRANSLATIONS: *Almost Forgotten Germany*, 1936 (Georg Schwarz; trans. with Laura Riding); *The Transformation of Lucius, Otherwise Known as "The Golden Ass,"* 1950 (Lucius Apuleius); *The Cross and the Sword*, 1954 (Manuel de Jesús Galván); *Pharsalia: Dramatic Episodes of the Civil Wars*, 1956 (Lucan); *Winter in Majorca*, 1956 (George Sand); *The Twelve Caesars*, 1957

(Suetonius); *The Anger of Achilles: Homer's "Iliad,"* 1959; *The Rubáiyát of Omar Khayyám,* 1967 (with Omar Ali-Shah).

EDITED TEXTS: *Oxford Poetry: 1921,* 1921 (with Alan Porter and Richard Hughes); *John Skelton: Laureate,* 1927; *The Less Familiar Nursery Rhymes,* 1927; *The Comedies of Terence,* 1962; *English and Scottish Ballads,* 1975.

MISCELLANEOUS: *Steps: Stories, Talks, Essays, Poems, Studies in History,* 1958; *Food for Centaurs: Stories, Talks, Critical Studies, Poems,* 1960; *Selected Poetry and Prose,* 1961.

Katherine Snipes

Bibliography · For a thorough biography, see Miranda Seymour, *Robert Graves: Life on the Edge,* 1995. Richard Perceval Graves, Robert Graves's cousin, has written a detailed account of Graves's early life in *Robert Graves: The Assault Heroic, 1895-1926,* 1986, which covers the same period as *Goodbye to All That.* For an account of events leading to the break with Laura Riding, see T. S. Matthews, *Jacks or Better,* 1971. For a discussion of the impact of World War I on writers, including Graves, see Paul Fussell, *The Great War and Modern Memory,* 1975. Studies of Graves's work include D. N. Carter, *Robert Graves: The Lasting Poetic Achievement,* 1989; Daniel Hoffman, *Barbarous Knowledge: Myth in the Poetry of Yeats, Graves, and Muir,* 1967; John B. Vickery, *Robert Graves and the White Goddess,* 1972; Sydney Musgrove, *The Ancestry of the White Goddess,* 1962. Katherine Snipes in *Robert Graves,* 1979, traces the Goddess mythology not only in the poetry but also in the historical novels. See also Douglas Day, *Swifter than Reason: The Poetry and Criticism of Robert Graves,* 1963; Michael Kirkham, *The Poetry of Robert Graves,* 1969; D. J. Enright, *Robert Graves and the Decline of Modernism,* 1960; Martin Seymour-Smith, *Robert Graves: His Life and Work,* 1983; and George Stade, *Robert Graves,* 1967.

H. D.

Hilda Doolittle

Born: Bethlehem, Pennsylvania; September 10, 1886
Died: Zurich, Switzerland; September 27, 1961

Poetry · *Sea Garden*, 1916 · *Hymen*, 1921 · *Heliodora and Other Poems*, 1924 · *Collected Poems of H. D.*, 1925 · *Red Roses for Bronze*, 1931 · *The Walls Do Not Fall*, 1944 · *Tribute to the Angels*, 1945 · *The Flowering of the Rod*, 1946 · *By Avon River*, 1949 · *Selected Poems of H. D.*, 1957 · *Helen in Egypt*, 1961 · *Hermetic Definition*, 1972 · *Collected Poems, 1912-1944*, 1983 · *Selected Poems*, 1988

Achievements · Hilda Doolittle, or H. D. as she signed her work, was at the center of the pre-World War I literary movement known as Imagism. It had a profound influence on twentieth century poetry, insisting on direct treatment through concrete imagery, freshness of language, economy of expression, and flexible versification. H. D. was a protégée of Ezra Pound, and the images in her poems best demonstrated Pound's definition of the image as "that which presents an intellectual and emotional complex in an instant of time." "Priapus" and "Hermes of the Ways," H. D.'s first Imagist poems, published in 1913, were hailed as innovative breakthroughs; with the publication of *Collected Poems of H. D.* in 1925, she came to be regarded as the finest of the Imagists. A number of these early poems, such as "Orchard," "Oread," "Heat," and "Sea Gods," have been repeatedly anthologized. (Unless otherwise noted, all poems cited are from *Collected Poems of H. D.*).

H. D.'s productive literary career spanned some fifty years. Her later poetry, somewhat neglected, includes *Red Roses for Bronze*; the World War II trilogy, *The Walls Do Not Fall, Tribute to the Angels*, and *The Flowering of the Rod*; her long "epic" poem, *Helen in Egypt*; and *Hermetic Definition*.

H. D. has received less critical attention than others of her generation. Although her early Imagist poetry was highly acclaimed, critical response to her later work has been mixed. Some critics have argued that this later work is marred by patches of triteness and sentimentality and a too-narrow focus; others have praised its spiritual richness and the undeniable beauty of many of its passages, and more recent critics have called attention to its feminist aspects. Although she was awarded *Poetry*'s Levinson Prize in 1938, she was near the end of her life before there were signs of renewed interest in her work: she received the Harriet Monroe Memorial Prize in 1958; the Brandeis Award in 1959; and the prestigious poetry award of the American Academy of Arts and Letters in 1960—a prize given only once every five years. Several books appraising H. D. appeared in the 1960's, and since the mid-1970's numerous articles and the first full-length biography have been published. Her *Collected Poems, 1912-1944* was published in 1983.

Biography · Hilda Doolittle was born in Bethlehem, Pennsylvania, the first Moravian community in America, on September 10, 1886. Her mother, Helen Wolle Doolittle, was artistic and musical; her father, Charles Leander Doolittle, was professor of mathematics and astronomy at Lehigh, later director of the Flower Observatory at the University of Pennsylvania. Hilda had a rich childhood in a setting of mystical Moravianism that exerted a lasting influence on her poetry.

At the age of fifteen she met Ezra Pound, the first of several extraordinary figures who profoundly influenced her life. Pound, then a precocious graduate student at the University of Pennsylvania, encouraged her to become broadly read, and together they studied Latin, Greek, the classics, yogic texts, and a great diversity of authors. Pound, according to their fellow student William Carlos Williams, "was wonderfully in love with her," but their relationship was somewhat stormy. In 1908, he proposed that they elope to Europe, but her family ties and her suspicions of his other romantic liaisons deterred her. This estrangement was equivocal, however, and in 1911 Hilda joined Pound and his literary circle in London, never again to live in America. Her first Imagist poems were published in *Poetry* (January, 1913), under the signature that Pound suggested,

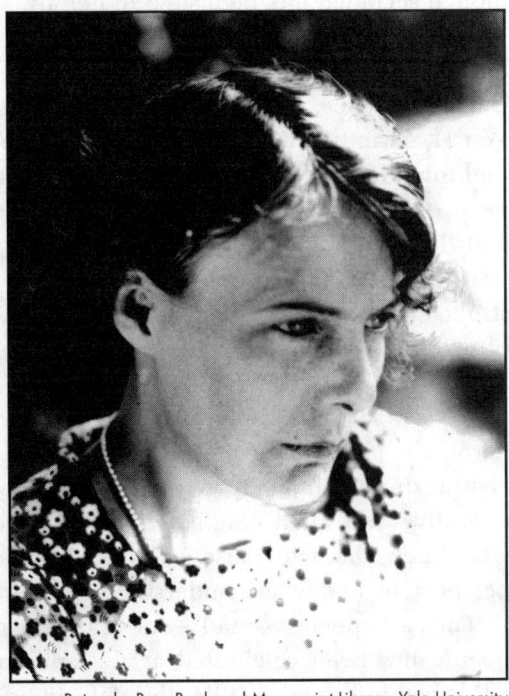

Beinecke Rare Book and Manuscript Library, Yale University and New Directions Publishing Corp.

"H. D., Imagiste." Active in the Imagist movement, she published her first collection, *Sea Garden*, in 1916.

The intense experiences of the World War I years forever after dominated H. D.'s life and art. Although still attached to Pound, in 1913 she married her fellow Imagist, Richard Aldington. Their marriage, initially happy, was troubled by infidelity and the turmoil of war. In 1914, H. D. met D. H. Lawrence. Their strong mutual attraction persisted through the war years, and their relationship was ever afterward present in H. D.'s life and work. In 1915 her first child was stillborn; in 1916 Aldington enlisted, and at the same time began an extramarital affair. In 1917 H. D.'s favorite brother was killed in France, and in 1919 her father died. In 1919, gravely ill with pneumonia, she gave birth to her daughter, Perdita; H. D. never revealed who the father was, and she and Aldington separated. Distressed by these events to the point of collapse, she was aided by a young woman from a wealthy English family, Winifred Ellerman, known by her pen name Bryher. For a time they lived together, and traveled to Greece, America, and Egypt. In 1922, H. D. settled near Zurich, with Bryher nearby, to rear her daughter and write. Her literary reputation established by the 1925 publication of *Collected Poems of H. D.*, she lived an active though secluded life, dedicated to her art.

In 1933, dissatisfied with her imperfect understanding of the events of her life and how they related to her art, she entered analysis under Freud. This experience, together with her experiences in London during World War II, permitted her to crystallize her own "legend," to expand upon the multiple meanings in her writing. She wrote much during the last fifteen years of her life, including her most ambitious long poem, *Helen in Egypt*, and the autobiographical novel, *Bid Me to Live* (1960). Following a brief visit to America to accept an award for her poetry, she was disabled by a stroke and died on September 27, 1961, at a clinic near Zurich, at the age of seventy-five.

Analysis · H. D. was a lyric poet with one overarching dramatic theme: a heroine's quest for love and spiritual peace. Her poetry about this one central drama, although written in concise and crystalline images, is an evocative and often enigmatic reworking of scenes, a retelling of tales, where new characters fuse with old, where meanings subtly shift with the perspective, and where understanding interchanges with mystery.

The early poem "Oread"—one of the most often anthologized of H. D.'s poems—has been celebrated as the epitome of the Imagist poem. First published in February, 1914, this deft six-line poem not only illustrates the essence and freshness of the Imagist approach but also foreshadows and reflects many of the themes to which H. D. would turn and return in her art. The six lines of the poem rest upon a single image:

> Whirl up, sea—
> whirl your pointed pines,
> splash your great pines
> on our rocks,
> hurl your green over us,
> cover us with your pools of fir.

The image in this poem is a "presentation," not a representation; it is a tangible, immediate manifesting of a physical thing, not a description of a scene or an abstract feeling. On the immediate level, the poem is an image of a stormy sea whose wavecrests are like forest pines as they crash against the shore and recede, leaving rocky pools in their wake. The image evokes a complex picture suggesting color, the beating of waves on a coast, sounds crashing and hushed, and even fragrance.

"Oread" has, as the Imagists insisted free verse should have, a rhythmic and linguistic development that is musical rather than metrical, corresponding to the sense of the poem. The first three lines describe an active, thrashing sea advancing on a rocky coast, and the last three suggest a lessening forcefulness, still powerful but withdrawing. The rising and falling movement is created in part by emphatic, initial-stress spondees and trochees in the beginning lines of the poem, which then give way to the more yielding dactyls, anapest, and iambic of the last two lines. These prosodic modifications are paralleled by the vowel and consonantal sounds: rough plosives and fricatives dominate the first half; the last half employs liquid continuants to suggest waning flow and submarine calm. This shift in tone is also underscored by the appearance of back vowel sounds in the last three lines only, giving the lines a more sonorous and less frenzied sound.

Various devices give unity to the poem. It is set as one sentence, in lower case. The imperative mood of the verbs that begin all but the fourth line emphasizes the thrusting force of the waves. Internal rhymes subtly reinforce the central metaphor, fusing sea and forest. The aspirated h and the liquid r and l of "whirl" are repeated in "hurl," and the last word, "fir," is a partial assonantal echo of the first word, "whirl," while "green" similarly echoes "sea." Consonants are repeated with like effect. For example, the h, l, p, and s of "whirl up, sea" are forcibly compressed in "splash," and quietly recapitulated in "pools of fir." Line 4 ("on our rocks"), which introduces character and location, is distinguished from the preceding lines by its lack of a verb, its use of back vowel sounds, and its triseme (or anapest); yet it is yoked to line 3 by enjambment, again subtly sustaining the fusion metaphor.

"Oread" has an elusiveness that is typical of H. D.'s poetry: the identity of the speaker is obscure, the location of the seacoast is unspecified. Who is "us"? Why are the rocks "our rocks"? The answers lie hidden in the title, which contains much that is enigmatic and unspoken. An oread is a nymph of Greek myth—in particular, a mountain nymph. Like naiads, nereids, dryads, sylphs—the nymphs of rivers, the sea, woods, air—oreads were usually personified as beautiful young girls, amorous, musical, gentle, and shy virgins, although occasionally identified with the wilder aspects of nature and akin to satyrs. The oread is one of the multiple forms that H. D. used to develop the central feminine consciousness in her writings. The oread inhabits the lonelier reaches of nature, rocky places of retreat; as H. D. put it in her children's novel, *The Hedgehog* (1936), "The Oreads are the real mountain girls that live furtherest up the hill."

Mountain nymphs were especially identified in myth as companions of the goddess Artemis, the virgin huntress associated with the moon; Artemis guarded the chastity of her nymphs as jealously as her own. It is one of the finer aspects of H. D.'s poetry that she can evoke the presence of things that are not mentioned yet shimmer ghostlike somewhere just out of poetic range: The goddess Artemis is an offstage presence in this poem, as in others. Her figure, white, distant, cold, virginal, yet passionate, is another of the complex manifestations of consciousness that appear in odd guises throughout H. D.'s poetry. In *Helen in Egypt*, for example, the moon goddess is symbolized by the white island in the sea where Helen encounters her lover Achilles. Artemis is embodied in the form of another island in "The Shrine" (subtitled "She Watches over the Sea," and dedicated to Artemis when initially published); it is an island whose difficult approaches can wreck mariners but can also reward those who reach "the splendor of your ragged coast": "Honey is not more sweet/ than the salt stretch of your beach." There is a sexuality, even a bisexuality, about this Artemis apparent in such lines as these, or in the opening lines of "Huntress": "Come, blunt your spear with us,/ our pace is hot."

The title "Oread" is an allusion to both the moon goddess Artemis, the virgin huntress, and her nymph-companions, wild and free in the mountains. This allusion is but one of many in H. D.'s poems to the Greek world, which was, along with Egyptian, Roman, and other civilizations of antiquity, a frame of reference and an abiding source of inspiration for her. A reader with only a slight familiarity with H. D.'s writings will thus recognize in a title such as "Oread" resonances of the classical world. Virtually all of her poems and prose writings allude to it, either directly or by implication. Many of her early poems are explicitly set in the ancient world; others, such as "Sea Iris" and "Sea Lily," are located there only by reference to "temple steps" or "murex-fishermen," or, like "Oread" and "Lethe," have their settings implied solely by their titles.

In the classical world, H. D. found a metaphor for her own loneliness; as she once wrote to William Carlos Williams, "I am, as you perhaps realize, more in sympathy with the odd and the lonely—with those people that feel themselves apart from the whole." It was a far country of the imagination where she could find retreat both from the pain of love and the strain of war and modern life. Ancient Greece or Egypt is envisioned as a stark and beautiful world, a world of cold purity in harmony with nature, where an austere peace could be found in the harsher aspects of the natural landscape. Cities are squalid (as in "The Tribute"), crowded, hideous, and menacing (as in "Cities"); H. D. finds the starker elements of sea, rocky coasts and mountains, trees and wild flowers, storms and wind, the moon and stars, rain, snow and frost, to be sympathetic as well as remote. "I go," she says in the epigraph to *The Flowering of the Rod*, "where I love and where I am loved: Into the snow." The wild seacoast of "Oread" is a manifestation of this nameless land. Linked to the classical world, it appears and reappears throughout H. D.'s work, a dense metaphor for the mental landscape of the particular feminine consciousness present in her writings.

This piling up of associations to be evoked by allusion, as in "Oread," is a stylistic device that H. D. used in both poetry and prose. Her object was to create a many-layered work, dense with meaning, rich with metaphor, and evocative of mystery and legend. She labeled this style *palimpsest* (also the title of her 1926 novel), a palimpsest being a parchment on which earlier writing has been erased but is still faintly discernible under new writing. H. D. thought of her writing as a superimposition of recurring, almost archetypal feelings and behaviors, like photographic negatives placed on top of one another, yielding a new yet old picture or pattern.

"Oread" illustrates this style. Against the background of rich allusion that is implied in the title, "Oread" is seen to have many layers of superimposed meaning. One step beyond the level of the surface imagery, the poem becomes an incantation, a prayer almost, spoken by the remote-dwelling oread on behalf of herself and her cloistered sisters. They seek, through communion with the elemental natural forces that sustain them in their retreat from the world of men, to be cleansed and strengthened, purified and rededicated to the harmonies of the natural world they have chosen for their refuge. There is also, in the call to the sea to "cover us with your pools," an implied wish to be suspended oblivious in the healing waters, to be reunited with the sea-matrix. This hint is echoed in many poems, such as the similar plea found in "Lethe" for release from the pain of loveless existence: "The roll of the full tide to cover you/ Without question,/ Without kiss." The subject of women hurt and deserted by men whom they loved recurs throughout H. D.'s poems about goddesses, demigoddesses, and other women of antiquity (of whom there are many in her verse—Demeter, Simaethea, Circe, Leda, Phaedra, Helen, Thetis, Cassandra, Calypso, Eurydice, and more). These poems present passionate women ill-treated by men.

Many of H. D.'s poems are about the foundering of a passionate impulse through indecision or rejection and the compensating retreat to colder climes that are clean and pure and white, yet haunted by memories of what was and what might have been. These poems are not only about retreat from the pitch and toss of emotion, but they are also poems about immersion in the salt flood of passionate entanglement. This is the case with "Oread"; at the same time that the poem invokes purification by a sort of baptismal rite, it is on yet another level wryly and compellingly sexual. In the first two lines of "Oread," the sea, traditionally a feminine metaphor, takes on masculine attributes as the image fuses sea and tree: "Whirl up, sea—/ whirl your pointed pines." The sea-crests, hardened by their fanciful merging with thrusting pines, are urged to "whirl up," to "splash," to "hurl" themselves against a rocky coast, to "cover us," as male animals cover the female, perhaps to inseminate (insinuated by the oblique reference to fertility in the word "green"). The natural rhythm of the poem, abetted, as previously noted, by various prosodic and grammatical devices, suggests arousal, climax, and commingled torpor. On an elementary level, "Oread" is about events in the natural world; on another level, the landscape pictured evokes the austere classical world to which consciousness may retreat; and, on still another level, the natural landscape becomes a metaphor for the landscape of the body.

The superimposition of sexual metaphor occurs again and again throughout H. D.'s poetry. For example, the pubescence implied by "pools of fir" is an echo of the earlier poem, "Hermes of the Ways," where Hermes is invoked in his original form as a god of fertility: "Hermes, Hermes,/ the great sea foamed,/ gnashed its teeth about me;/ but you have waited,/ where seagrass tangles with shore-grass." "Priapus" (later retitled "Orchard"), a poem addressed to the Greek fertility god usually represented with an exaggerated phallus, celebrates the bounty of nature in lines transparent with reference to female genitalia: "grapes, red-purple,/ their berries/ dripping with wine,/ pomegranates already broken,/ and shrunken figs/ and quinces untouched,/ I bring you as offering." Feminine anatomy is also likened to coastal recesses or rocky chambers, as in the aforementioned "The Shrine," or in "Circe," a poem about the legendary enchantress who would "give up/ rock-fringes of coral/ and the inmost chamber/ of my island palace" for a glance from Odysseus. In H. D.'s metaphors for the sexual landscape, love and lovers meet where sea meets shore, on salt beaches, as in the refrain that haunts *Helen in Egypt*, on "the ledge of a desolate salt beach." This unusual coupling of rocky clefts with female sexuality and genitalia—perhaps suggested by the analogous promontory of the *mons veneris*—is typical of H. D.'s use of contrarieties and oxymora. Fire in ice, sweet in salt, soft and hard, male and female—these contrasts are used to create images of great vitality.

As H. D.'s art evolved, she developed a central feminine consciousness through a variety of images and personae and events, each of which lent associational meaning to the others. This feminine spirit is both delicate and durable, beautiful but tough, capable of surviving great buffeting, much as the "weighted leaf" in the poem "Storm," broken off by the vaguely masculine storm, "is hurled out,/ whirls up and sinks,/ a green stone." This spirit or consciousness may appear as an oread, as Helen of Troy or other figures from classical myth, or as a green stone, a sea-shell, a worm on a leaf, a hardy sea flower, a chrysalis—or as meldings of several of these. An image from *The Walls Do Not Fall* presents the poet as an "industrious worm" that survives calamity to tell its story, to "spin my own shroud"; in *Helen in Egypt*, Theseus (the character modeled on Freud) calls Helen "Psyche with/ half-dried wings." The portrayal of Psyche—in Greek myth, the personification of the soul, beloved by Eros—as a newly formed butterfly is a complex image into which are telescoped links to the figure of the oread and to other chrysalislike manifestations of H. D.'s poetic consciousness.

This consciousness grew out of the events and situations and characters of H. D.'s life, and each of her poems is a symbolic re-creation of some part of her life, thus giving a further, hidden meaning to the poetry. For example, the knowledge that the nickname bestowed upon H. D. by the green-eyed Ezra Pound was "Dryad" adds another dimension to "Oread." A dryad is a wood-nymph, and the nickname was perhaps a token of their early love among the apple trees of Pennsylvania, where H. D. was a virgin and Pound something of a satyr. Early poems such as "Oread" and "Priapus," with their bold sexual undercurrents, can thus also be read as amusing, half-mocking secret messages to the principal men in her life. Although not confessional poetry, H. D.'s work was intimately bound to her personal experiences, especially those of the period from 1911 to 1920, and though her poems may be grasped without knowing these circumstances, even a slight familiarity with them enhances the reader's pleasure and understanding. H. D. had no hesitation in acknowledging this autobiographical dimension: as she said of her thinly disguised autobiographical novel, *Bid Me to Live*, "It is a *roman à clef*, and the keys are all easy enough to find."

By poeticizing the story of her life, H. D. was consciously attempting, as she indicated in *Tribute to Freud* (1956), to create her own legend, to universalize her own experiences and emotional states, not for idiosyncratic self-glorification, but rather to capture a timeless expression of an age-old quest—a quest through the labyrinth of memory for enlightenment and love, for the truth of the soul, for mystical union, for her womanhood, for the purpose of her art. The goal was to "justify all the spiral-like meanderings of my mind and body," as she said of her analysis with Freud. She was concerned with preserving the intricate setting of her memories: "We wander in a labyrinth," she observed in *By Avon River;* "If we cut straight through, we destroy the shell-like curves and involutions." This quest motif furnishes a final, ontological, or even religious layer of meaning to "Oread" and other poems. The oread's venturing from her forested retreat to the sea-ledges can be interpreted as seeking the love of lover, mother, and father—and perhaps the godhead, since the image of merged sea and trees is suggestive of the Moravian doctrine of mystical union with Christ's body that influenced H. D. as a child and later as a poet.

H. D.'s poetry was original and manifested a new development in Western literature. Reversing the usual form of allegory, she drew images from the natural world and characters and situations from classical sources to transmute the story of her own life into poems expressing universal human experience. Exemplified by "Oread," her poems are like ideographic pictures or signs with many meanings coiled in single images—images that, in their distilled essence, contain the world seen by a gifted poet.

Other literary forms · Although H. D. is known chiefly for her poetry, she did produce works in other genres, including novels, a verse drama, a screenplay, and a children's novel. The nonfiction trilogy *Tribute to Freud, Writing on the Wall, Advent* (1974) presents an account of her psychoanalysis with Sigmund Freud in the 1930's. *End to Torment* (1979) is a memoir of Ezra Pound.

Other posthumous publications have included *HERmione* (1981), an autobiographical novel that was written in 1927, and *The Gift* (1982), a memoir about her childhood that was written in London during the Blitz of World War II. *HERmione* contains fictionalized depictions of young Ezra

Pound and others, and it lyrically describes young H. D.'s acceptance of herself as a woman and an artist. *The Gift*, as it shifts between recollections of childhood and descriptions of the destruction and fear in London wrought by the bombing during World War II, presents revealing looks at H. D.'s view of life.

Select works other than poetry

LONG FICTION: *Palimpsest*, 1926; *Hedylus*, 1928; *Kora and Ka*, 1934 (includes *Mira-Mare*); *The Usual Star*, 1934 (includes *Two Americans*); *Nights*, 1935; *Bid Me to Live*, 1960; *HERmione*, 1981.

SHORT FICTION: *The Hedgehog*, 1936.

NONFICTION: *Tribute to Freud*, 1956; *Tribute to Freud, Writing on the Wall, Advent*, 1974; *End to Torment*, 1979; *The Gift*, 1982.

DRAMA TRANSLATIONS: *Choruses from Iphigeneia in Aulis and the Hippolytus of Euripides*, 1919; *Euripides' Ion*, 1937; *Hippolytus Temporizes*, 1927 (adaptation of classical text).

John Clendenin Townsend

Bibliography · Barbara Guest, *Herself Defined: The Poet and Her World*, 1984, is the best starting place, a carefully and beautifully written book by a poet who is akin to her subject in sensibility and style. Janice S. Robinson, *H. D.: The Life and Work of an American Poet*, 1982, also combines biography with critical interpretation. An indispensable source is the late Robert Duncan's *The H. D. Book*, published over many years as a work-in-progress in diverse small magazines; for references to the scattered chapters of this critical magnum opus, see Robert J. Bertholf, *Robert Duncan: A Descriptive Bibliography*, 1986. Another useful source is Michael Boughn, *H. D.: A Bibliography, 1905-1990*, 1993. See also Gary Dean Burnett, *H. D. Between Image and Epic: The Mysteries of Her Poetics*, 1990; Angela DiPace Fritz, *Thought and Vision: A Critical Reading of H. D.'s Poetry*, 1988; and Susan Edmunds, *Out of Line: History, Psychoanalysis, and Montage in H. D.'s Long Poems*, 1994. Albert Gelpi, *A Coherent Splendor: The American Poetic Renaissance, 1910-1950*, 1987, includes a brilliant, monograph-length chapter on H. D. Rachel Blau DuPlessis, *H. D.: The Career of That Struggle*, 1986, a volume in a series of women writers, provides an introductory overview. DuPlessis also edited a special H. D. issue of *Sagetrieb* 6 (Fall, 1987). Other issues of *Sagetrieb* have offered articles on H. D., including Cyrena N. Pondrom, "H. D. and the Origins of Imagism," *Sagetrieb* 4 (Spring, 1985). *The H. D. Newsletter* features articles on H. D. and her circle. For other book-length studies of H. D. and Imagism, see John T. Gage, *In the Arresting*

Eye: The Rhetoric of Imagism, 1981; Glenn Hughes, *Imagism and the Imagists*, 1972; Vincent Quinn, *H. D.*, 1967, a volume in the Twayne series; William Pratt, *The Imagist Poem*, 1963; and Thomas Swann, *The Classical World of H. D.*, 1962. The period of H. D.'s life and the milieu in which she lived was a particularly fertile one for memoirists and writers of *romans à clef*. She figures in many of the accounts of this period, as well as having written her own. Among the many are Margaret Anderson, *My Thirty Years' War*, 1969; Robert McAlmon, *Being Geniuses Together*, 1968; Robert McAlmon, *A Hasty Bunch*, 1977; Winifred Bryher, *The Heart to Artemis: A Writer's Memoirs*, 1962; and John Cournos, *Miranda Masters*, 1926, which provides a resentfully distorted view of H. D. Many other contemporaries and friends of H. D. also wrote memoirs.

SEAMUS HEANEY

Born: Mossbawn, County Derry, Northern Ireland; April 13, 1939

Poetry · *Death of a Naturalist*, 1966 · *Door into the Dark*, 1969 · *Wintering Out*, 1972 · *North*, 1975 · *Field Work*, 1979 · *Poems, 1965-1975*, 1980 · *Sweeney Astray: A Version from the Irish*, 1984 (rev. as *Sweeney's Flight*, 1992) · *Station Island*, 1984 · *The Haw Lantern*, 1987 · *The Cure at Troy: A Version of Sophocles' "Philoctetes,"* 1990 · *New Selected Poems, 1966-1987*, 1990 · *Seeing Things*, 1991 · *The Midnight Verdict*, 1993 · *The Spirit Level*, 1996

Achievements · Almost from the beginning of his poetic career, Seamus Heaney gained public recognition for poems rooted deep in the soil of Northern Ireland and flowering in subtle rhythms and nuanced verbal melodies. In many respects he has pursued a return of twentieth century poetry to its foundations in Romantic meditations on nature and explorations of the triple relationship among words, emotions, and the imagination. Many awards accompanied Heaney's recognition. *Death of a Naturalist* garnered no fewer than four; thereafter, practically every volume earned at least one honor, with *North* gaining three. In 1982 Heaney was awarded D.H.L. degrees by Fordham University and Queen's University of Belfast; the two universities noted particularly that his reflection of the troubles of Northern Ireland in his poetry had universal application.

Biography · Seamus Heaney was born into a Roman Catholic farming family in rural Country Derry, Northern Ireland (Ulster), the predominantly Protestant and industrial province of the United Kingdom in the island of Ireland. Much of his boyhood was spent on a farm, one border of which was formed by a stream that also divided Ulster from Eire, the predominantly Catholic Republic of Ireland. As a schoolboy he won scholarships first at the age of eleven to St. Colomb's College, a Catholic preparatory school, and then to Queen's University, Belfast, from which he graduated in 1961 with a First Class Honors degree in English. There he joined a group of young poets working under the direction of creative writers on the faculty.

He began his professional career as a secondary school English teacher, after which he went into teacher education, eventually joining the English faculty of Queen's in 1966. When civil dissension broke out in Ulster in 1969, eventually leading to martial law, Heaney, as a Catholic-reared poet, became increasingly uncomfortable. In 1972 he relocated to a manor in the Eire countryside to write full-time, although he also became a faculty member of a college in Dublin. Beginning in 1979, he adopted the practice of accepting academic appointments at various American universities and spending the rest of the year in Dublin. In 1986 he was appointed Boylston Professor of Rhetoric and Oratory at Harvard University, and in 1989 he became professor of poetry at the University of Oxford.

Analysis · Seamus Heaney's distinctive quality as a poet is that he is at once parochial and universal, grounded in particular localities and microcultures yet branching out to touch every reader. Strangely, this unusual "here and everywhere" note remains with him even when he changes the basic subject matter of his poetry, as he has done frequently. His command of what William Blake called "minute particularity" allows him to conjure up a sense of the universal even when focusing on a distinct individuality—seeing "a world in a grain of sand." He makes the unique seem familiar. Because his success at this was recognized early, he was quickly branded with the label "greatest Irish poet since Yeats"—an appellation that, however laudatory, creates intolerable pressure and unrealizable expectations. Neoromantic he certainly is, but not in William Butler Yeats's vein; Heaney is less mythic, less apocalyptic, less mystical, and much more material and elemental.

In many respects Heaney's art is conservative, especially in technique. Unlike the forms of the iconoclastic leading poets of the first half of the twentieth century—T. S. Eliot, E. E. Cummings, Wallace Stevens, Ezra Pound, William Carlos Williams, and Dylan Thomas—Heaney's meters, figures, diction, and textures are all relatively straightforward. Also in contrast, his poetry is not "difficult" as theirs was; his sentences generally employ standard syntax. Nevertheless, he is a master technician with an ear for fine and subtle verbal melodies. Instead of breaking with the past, his poems much more often depend on forging links; his music often harks back to that of William Wordsworth, John Milton, or Edmund Spenser. Yet his diction is common and Irish as well as formal and English. Colloquial speech patterns of the brogue often counterpoint stately cadences of British rhetoric. The combination produces a varied music, blending the different strains in his personal history and in the history of his people and his region. His best poems ring in the memory with echoes of modulated phrase and evocative sound patterns.

Heaney's first book, *Death of a Naturalist*, laid the groundwork for his achievement. Centered firmly in the country scenes of his youth, these poems declare both his personal heritage from generations of Irish farm laborers and his emancipation from it, acquired by the mastery of a foreign tradition, the literature of the English. His art is Irish in origins and inspiration and English by training. The result is a surprisingly uniform and rich amalgam that incorporates much of Ulster's complex mix of cultures. The poems become what Heaney at the time hoped was possible for his region: the preservation of both Irish and English traditions by a fusion that transcends either of them separately.

"Digging," a celebrated poem from this volume, illustrates this idea. It memorializes the typical work he associated with his father's and grandfather's generations (and, by implication, those of their ancestors): cutting turf, digging. He deliberately contrasts their tool of choice, the spade, with his, the pen: "I've no spade to follow men like them." By his instrument he can raise their labor into art, in the process ennobling them.

"Follower" similarly contrasts his labor with his father's. It captures in paced phrases and exact images his father's skill at and identification with plowing. This was the ancestral craft of the Heaneys; it makes his father what he is. As a result, it serves as the model of what young Seamus believed he should grow up to become. Sent instead to school, however, he was not reared to the plow and could never do more than hobble in his father's wake. The poem ends in a complex and disturbing image:

> But today
> It is my father who keeps stumbling
> Behind me, and will not go away.

The meaning is clear and manifold. His father stumbles intellectually—because the son has climbed beyond him—and culturally, for he will never be able to reach this point or even appreciate it. His father also stumbles merely physically, as the older generation does, and he must be cared for by his son when he cannot care for himself. Finally, his father is a clog at Heaney's heels, hindering him by his heritage: The poet will never be able to evade his father's influence.

Three years later, *Door into the Dark* found Heaney continuing to explore this material from his upbringing, but it also showed him expanding his range and developing new moral insights. Increasingly he began sensing that the various pasts in his heritage—of family, race, and religion—were reincarnating themselves in the present, that the history of the people was recapitulating itself. This insight bound present and past indissolubly together. What unfolded in the here and now, then, became part of a gradually evolving theme and variations, revealing itself in event and place.

Some of the poems in this volume accordingly focus on events and occupations illustrating continuity in the Irish experience. "Thatcher," for example, celebrates an ancient Irish craft: thatching roofs out of by-products and discards. The fabric of the poem beautifully reflects and incorporates its subject, for its rhythms and rhymes form parallel patterns that imitate one another and interlock, although the dovetailing is not exact. Left unstated in the poem is an implied undertheme: The craft of the poet is equally ancient and equally intricate. A similar interweaving of past and present occurs in "The Wife's Tale," in which the persona—a farmwoman—re-creates simply the routine of laying out a field lunch for laborers during threshing. The narrative is matter-of-fact and prosaic, detached and unemotional, and unspecific in time: it could be almost anytime, a reiterative action. Her action thus binds the generations together, suggesting the sameness of human life regardless of time. The poem also subtly depicts the interdependence of husband and wife—he fights and plants, she nourishes and supports—and their failure to merge completely: "And that was it. I'd come and he had shown me,/ So I belonged no further to the work."

A number of the poems in this volume are simply musings on travels in Ireland and on the Continent. At first it is easy to pass over these pieces, because the simple, undramatic language and quiet tone do not attract much attention. In fact, however, these meditations are extremely important in the evolution of Heaney's poetic orientation, for they document his growing awareness of place as a determinant of sensibility. For Heaney, a person's surroundings, particularly the environment of his or her growing-up years, become the context to which he or she instinctively refers new experiences for evaluation. They become the norms of consciousness, the images from which the individual forms values. In "The Peninsula," for example, the persona spends a day touring the scenes of his youth. He discovers upon return that he still has "nothing to say," but he realizes that henceforth he will "uncode all landscapes/ By this." In "Night Drive" the speaker, driving through France and thinking of his love in Italy, finds his "ordinariness" renewed by simple things such as signposts and realizes that the same thing is happening to her. Environment forms and frames consciousness.

More important, it also frames historical consciousness, the intersection of the past with the present in the individual. In the poems that first document this idea, Heaney announces what is to be a major theme: the inescapable presence of the past. This emerges in "Requiem for the Croppies," a long-after-the-fact elegy for the insurrectionist Catholic peasants—designated "croppies" because in the 1790's they cropped their hair to indicate their support of the French revolutionaries—who were slaughtered by the thousands at Vinegar Hill at the end of the Uprising of 1798.

The poem, a simple sonnet, quietly recalls the mood of that campaign, in which unarmed, uneducated plowboys terrorized the great estates of the absent English overlords until they were hemmed in and mowed down by cavalry and cannon. At first, for the rabble the rebellion was a romp; finally, it became a nightmare and a shame. The poem documents this in one encircling image: The ultimate harvest of the battle is the spilled barley, carried for food, which sprouts from the mass graves the following summer. A better symbol of futility and helplessness could hardly be found. Written in 1969, the year of the recurrance of the "trouble" (ethnic conflicts in Ulster between Protestant unionists and Catholic secessionists), the poem both marks Heaney's allegiances—he was reared Catholic—and records his dismay over the renewal of pointless violence. Significantly, Heaney moved from Belfast that year, although his major motive was to devote his full time to writing.

In the same year, Heaney encountered the book *The Bog People* (1969) by the ethnologist and anthropologist P. V. Glob. This account of a race of Iron Age peoples who inhabited the boglands of northern Europe in the dark past, before the Indo-European migrations of the first millennium B.C., was based largely on excavated remains of bodies that had been preserved by immersion in bogs. The photographs of these bodies particularly fired Heaney's imagination, especially because many of them had been ritualistically sacrificed. Since the newspapers and magazines had recently been saturated with atrocity punishments and murders, often involving equally primitive rituals, Heaney postulated a connection between the two, forged by the history of terrorism between clans and religions in northern Ireland. Modern Ulster, despite centuries of alterations in its facade and supposed progress in its politics and civilization, was populated by a race different only in accidentals from its Iron Age progenitors. The same elemental passions and atavistic fears seethed beneath a deceptively civilized surface. Furthermore, those ancient dark mysteries that precipitated the superstitious sacrifices had not been superseded by civilization; they had merely receded into the background. Unsuspected, they continued to be inherited in the blood. Although he nowhere uses the Jungian terminology, Heaney seems to subscribe to the idea of the collective unconscious, the reservoir of instinctive, intuitive behavior acquired genetically.

These ideas bear first fruit in "Bogland," in which he invents a powerful metaphor for another of his central themes. He visualizes his kind, his culture, as centered on a bog: "Our unfenced country/ Is bog that keeps crusting/ Between the sights of the sun." The bog simultaneously buries and preserves, destroys and reconstitutes. Through it the past becomes continuous with the present, re-presented in it. The bog records all generations of humanity that have grown up alongside it, disclosing continuous occupation: "Every layer they strip/ Seems camped on before."

The bog is also an analogue of the human mind, which similarly buries and preserves, and which inherits the entire weight of the past. Furthermore, both have fathomless depths, brooding pools, and nameless terrors bubbling up from unplumbed regions. The bog becomes the perfect image of the inexplicable in the self and in society as a whole. Further, it provides Heaney with a device for illustrating the force behind the violence and a means of distancing himself from it. The bog becomes a link with humankind's preconscious, reptilian past: "The bogholes might be Atlantic seepage./ The wet centre is bottomless."

Heaney's third book, *Wintering Out*, secured his early reputation. Like his first two books, it is rooted in his homeland, but it also includes poems of departure. Places precisely realized play a large part in it; in particular, these places declare themselves through their ancient names. Heaney spins music out of them:

> *Anahorish*, soft gradient
> of consonant, vowel meadow,
>
> after-image of lamps
> swung through the yards
> on winter evenings.

Brough, Derrygarve, Ballyshannon voice related melodies, weaving together past and present, counterpointing also with English names: Castledawson, Upperlands. The two languages together stitch the present out of the past.

The volume opens with "Bog Oak," which Heaney makes into a symbol for his bog world: It is a relic from the past, wood preserved in a bog where no oaks now stand, excavated to make rafters for new buildings. Furthermore, It is saturated with the bog, so that images of past centuries may be imprinted in it, as on film, to be released as the wood is used and thus to redirect the present. In one more way, then, the past is reincarnated. Dreaming that the oak images will bring him contact with the spirits of past poets, Heaney reminds his readers that the history of poetry is also a means of realizing the past in the present.

Other species of the Irish environment also participate in this process of continuity. "Gifts of Rain," for example, memorializes the omnipresent threat of rain in the Irish weather. Yet the poem also makes the rain into a stream flowing through everything, a liquid voice from the past: "Soft voices of the dead/ Are whispering by the shore." It becomes a solvent of the Irish experience.

This awareness of and openness to all aspects of life, especially the dark and the violent, leads Heaney to treat some topics in this volume that are quite different from his past choices. Among them is one of the more inexplicable incidents of human cruelty: infanticide by mothers, or maternal rejection of infants. "Limbo" considers an infant drowned shortly after birth and netted by salmon fishermen. Heaney dispassionately records the ironies, beginning with the simple suggestion that this child's baptism was in fact murder, the most extreme sacrilege, although he fully sympathizes with the mother's agony. Still, the child died without baptism; hence, it is ineligible for Heaven and must be relegated to Limbo, a place of painless exile, according to orthodox Catholic doctrine. Such a conclusion, however, is so unjust that it seems incompatible with any God who claims to incarnate love: "Even Christ's palms, unhealed,/ Smart and cannot fish here."

Similarly, "Bye-Child" re-creates the perspective of a child shut up by his mother in a henhouse, without vital human contact. The inscription states that he could not speak. Heaney seems astounded that anyone could deny a human the possibility of communication: To be human is to communicate. This child, as a result, becomes in turn a curiosity, a rodent, an alien, a "moon man"–nothing human. Still, his response to his rescuers reveals an attempt to communicate, to reach "beyond love."

The experience that apparently enabled Heaney to contemplate such events took place through Glob's *The Bog People*. He was so struck by the images of some of the recovered bodies–particularly those sacrificed in earth mother rites and those punished for crimes–that he wrote poems about them. The first, the three-part "The Tolland Man," first published in *Wintering Out,* has become one of his most widely reprinted poems. Heaney first describes the body, now displayed at the State Museum at Århus, Denmark, and briefly alludes to his fate: Given a last meal, he was hauled in a tumbril to the bogside, strangled, and deposited as a consort to the bog goddess, who needed a male to guarantee another season of fertility. In the second section Heaney suggests that the ritual makes as much sense as the retaliatory, ritualistic executions of the troubles; the current practice is as likely to improve germination. The third section establishes a link between survivors and victims, past and present. It implies that all humans are equally involved, equally responsible, if only by complicity or failure to act. Heaney suggests that senseless violence and complacent acceptance of it are both parts of human nature.

Heaney's next book, *Stations,* marked both an advance and a setback.

The advance was compound, both formal and topical. Formally, the book consists of a series of prose poems; topically, they all deal with the experience of growing up rural and Catholic in an industrialized, Protestant-dominated culture. The title *Stations* alludes to this: The events detailed here constitute the contemporary equivalent of the Stations of the Cross, the sufferings Christ endured in his passion and death; moreover, they are the way stations of modern education, the stopping points of the soul. The poems show Heaney returning to his childhood to identify and document his indoctrination into the complicity he finds unacceptable in *Wintering Out*. In all these ways the book celebrates gains.

Yet the individual poems of *Stations* are less successful and less uniform than his earlier work. They disclose an artificiality, a staginess, a contrived quality formerly absent. They also depend on a good bit of private information for comprehension. In some respects this is curious, because Heaney managed to avoid any hint of these weaknesses elsewhere, either in his poetry or in the retrospective prose that also dates from around this time. To an extent this uneasiness must be associated with his private uncertainty during this period, when he was trying to justify his leaving Ulster rather than staying to take a stand.

Whatever the reason, it left the poetry of the same time intact. His second book of 1975, *North*, capitalized on his previous successes; significantly, the title indicates that all these poems still focus on the poet's Ulster experiences. The book includes more meditations on place and place-names, such as "Mossbawn"; there are also a few more nature pieces and reminiscences. Far and away the majority of the collection, however, deals with the cultural conflict of the North, the pagan heritage of Ireland, and the continuity of past and present through the mediation of the bog people. A series based on bone fragments from the past supplements the bog material. Practically all of Heaney's best-known poems are found in this volume.

Furthermore, this is the first of Heaney's books which is more than a mere collection. The order and arrangement are designed to create an integrated reading experience; groupings reflect, refract, and diffuse patterns and themes. The basic structure of the book is twofold, with each part using distinctive verse forms. Part 1 focuses on the "North" of northern Europe from the time of its first population to the present. The basic verse is the taut, unrhymed or off-rhymed quatrain developed for *Wintering Out;* much of the diction is formal or archaic, and the atmosphere is solemn and austere. Part 2 takes "North" as contemporary Ulster. The root verse is the standard pentametric rhymed quatrain; the diction and tone are informal and playful. The polarity seems to reflect the two kinds of poetry Heaney describes repeatedly in *Preoccupations:* poetry that is "made" and poetry that is "given."

Some of the poems in part 1 actually fall partly outside this overly neat division. "Funeral Rites," an often-praised poem, joins the urgency of funerals during the troubles with the legacy of pagan burials. The theme of the poem is that the frequent occurrence of funerals today has cheapened them: They lack the impact of ancient funerals, when death still meant something, still could be beautiful, and still could give promise of resurrection. The title poem also crosses the established border of the book. It centers in the imagination of the poet in the present, where he must work with what he finds—which falls far short of the epic standards of the past. Voices out of the water advise him to search the past of the race and express it through the roots of his language.

But the center of part 1 is the past. Here the bog poems take precedence. There are six of them, all powerful. "The Grauballe Man" depicts another victim of the bog mother cult, this one written as if the persona were in the presence of the body. Heaney arranges a series of metaphors drawn from biology to create the image of the body, then inserts the line "The head lifts"—and the body seems to come alive before the mind's eye. The persona explicitly denies that this can be called a "corpse." Previously, seen only in photographs, the man seemed dead, "bruised like a forceps baby." Now he is "hung in the scales/ with beauty and atrocity"—he has taken on the life of enduring art, yet also testifies to humanity's eternal and ongoing depravity. Violence creates beauty, and vice versa.

A second poem, "Punishment," portrays another category of victim among these people. According to the Roman historian Tacitus, the ancestral Germans punished adulteresses by shaving off their hair and immersing them naked in the bog, weighed down with stones and logs, until they drowned. The barely postadolescent girl of Heaney's poem illustrates the practice: undernourished, shaved, and blindfolded, she has no visible wounds. The persona sees her as a "scapegoat," a figure of terror: "her shaved head/ like a stubble of black corn." Yet she was also "beautiful," one who could arouse love. Nevertheless, he recognizes that had he been present, he "would have cast . . . / the stones of silence," in an allusion to the New Testament story of the woman taken in adultery. Heaney asserts that all human beings comply with the practices of their tribe, and then he finds the perfect modern parallel. In the early 1970's young Catholic women who consorted with British soldiers were punished similarly by the Irish Republican Army: They were shaved, tarred, feathered, and chained to public railings. Again all spectators comply, and the past, the primitive past, is present.

In "Strange Fruit" Heaney borrows the metaphor in the title from a black American civil rights protest song, in which "strange fruit" refers to the bodies of lynched blacks hanging from gallows. The fruit in the poem is ancient: an accidentally preserved severed head of a young woman. Here there is no justification in ritual; the woman is simply the victim of random violence or tribal conflict. Heaney, as before, suggests that exhuming the head from its bog grave is equivalent to restoring it to life and beauty. This time, however, he finds the consolation of art itself disturbing. He adds a new note, alluding to another Roman historian: "Diodorus Siculus confessed/ His gradual ease among the likes of this." Multiple atrocities generate complacency as well as complicity. Thus this girl stops short of beauty; far from attractive, she has "eyeholes blank as pools in the old workings." This is an image of the forlorn, the abandoned. These black eyeholes—lacking eyes—still outstare "what had begun to feel like reverence." Tolerating atrocities may not be the state human beings finally want to reach.

Heaney's next book, *Field Work*, poses a series of questions, mostly dealing with the relationship between art and social conscience. They thus cast doubts on both the attitude he had adopted toward contemporary violence and the resolution to which he had come about his life. Still, the answers he finds basically confirm his decisions. He chooses here the path of civilization, of art, the "field work" of the practicing artist. At the balancing point of this book rest the Glanmore sonnets, a series of ten sonnets reflecting his life at the country estate of Glanmore, County Wicklow, his retreat after Belfast. In terms of subject matter, he returns overtly to the natural settings and homely ways of his first two books. In this work, however, he is much more concerned with the poetic temperament, its influences, and its relation to society.

Accordingly, several of the sounds trace the parallels between Heaney and other figures who used rural solitude to comment on society: the Roman poets Horace and Vergil, the mythical Irish hero Sweeney, and the English poet William Wordsworth. The sonnets themselves are the densest, most intricate poems he had written to this point, rich and finely fashioned, delicate and subtle. Typical is sonnet 5, which commemorates the elderberry bush that served as refuge for the poet as a boy; he shapes it and his reminiscences about it into a symbol of his searches into the roots of language and memory.

Another major section of the book is devoted to elegies—three for victims of civil violence, three for fellow poets, and one for a relative killed in World War I. These are more conventional poems of mourning than his earlier meditations, which lamented but also accepted. They reflect a sense of absolute and final loss, the senseless wasting away that the pace of modern life leads people to take for granted, anger that so much good should be squandered so casually. Still, death is relentless and undiscriminating, taking the small with the great: "You were not keyed or pitched like these true-blue ones/ Though all of you consort now underground."

After *Field Work* Heaney moved for a while in a different direction. *Sweeney Astray: A Version from the Irish* is an adaptation of the medieval Gaelic epic *Buile Suibhne*. Heaney had long been fascinated by the character of Sweeney, at once king and poet, and had used him as one of the persona's alter egos in *Field Work*. In the poem Sweeney fails in a quest and suffers the curse of Saint Ronan, the peacemaker, after repeatedly violating truces and killing one of the saint's clerics. Already nicknamed "Mad" because of his battle rages, Sweeney is now transformed into a bird and driven into the wilderness, doomed to be hunted by human and beast alike and to suffer delusions. The poem is more an anthology of rhapsodic songs and laments made by Sweeney in his exile than the standard heroic quest-poem. It is easy to detect the sources of Heaney's fascination, which include the easily overlooked rhyme of Sweeney's name with his own–the kind of thing he would spot immediately. Like Heaney, Sweeney is driven out of a violent society, though given to violence himself; he feels a natural kinship with animals, birds, trees, plants, and the things of the wild; he identifies with the places of his exile; and he senses the elemental divine pulse beating in and unifying everything. Furthermore, he represents the wounded imagination, in love with and repelled by the ways of humans in the world.

Although widely praised and honored, *Sweeney Astray* seems to have fallen short of Heaney's expectations. It did receive some hostile reviews, from Irish critics who did not really believe that English is a suitable medium for anything Gaelic, and English critics who viewed Irish writers as plotting a hostile takeover of things British. The extent of Heaney's disappointment appears in the layout of *Selected Poems 1966-1987*, in which this book is the most scantily represented of his major works, having only sixteen pages in contrast to the sixty-six for *Station Island* and forty-four for *North*. Clearly, it is more difficult to cull from a continuous sequence than from a collection; yet it is also true that ever since the publication of *North* Heaney had paid considerable attention to the organization of his books, so that, theoretically at least, excerpting should be difficult from any of them.

Station Island is Heaney's amplest, most diversified, and most highly integrated book of poems. It consists essentially of three parts: a collection of separate lyrics, many family-centered and some combined into mini-sequences; the title sequence, centered on Station Island, also called

St. Patrick's Purgatory, in the west Ireland, a favorite Irish pilgrimage site; and a series named "Sweeney Redivivus," in which he creates new poems through the persona of the poet-hero brought back to life in himself and committed to reveal what remains of the past in the here and now. The lyrics show Heaney experimenting with new line lengths, new forms, and new approaches. They include W. H. Auden-like meditations, such as "Chekhov on Sakhalin," and a series on found objects called "Shelf Life"; both provide him with occasions for discovering unexpected epiphanies. Similarly, the Sweeney poems disclose Heaney deepening his vision. The identification with his mythic predecessor required by the translation brings him to a new vantage point: he realizes that perceptive and imaginative as Sweeney was, deeply as he penetrated to the soul of things, he still remained alien from the bulk of the people, and he had not changed much. Heaney writes out of a new humility, and also now out of relief. He concludes that he need not blame himself for having abandoned his people in the troubles. They were not really his people, in retrospect; his values were not theirs. He could not accomplish much for them that would last. Better to pursue his poetry.

The title series also teaches him that lesson, though in a different way. It is Heaney's major triumph, consolidating and drawing on strengths he had been establishing since early in his career. It is the quintessential place-poem, for Station Island has many places and provides multiple occasions for poetry. Situated on Lough Derg in County Tipperary, Eire, the island was originally a primitive settlement; in the eighth or ninth century it became a locus of pilgrimage, renowned as a place of penitence. A number of foundation rings remain, the relics of either monastic cells or primitive dwellings. Devotees complete the act of repentance by making a circuit of these, kneeling and praying at each in turn, and by this act gaining remission of punishment for past sins.

Heaney bases his cycle on the persona's return to the island in middle age. Although by this point in his life an unbeliever, he finds the island well populated with souls eager to establish common ground with the living. For the devout, as St. Patrick's Purgatory, this is a place of personal repentance, expiation, and rectification. For the literary, as a purgatorial site it has a forerunner in Dante's *Purgatorio* (c. 1320). Heaney uses the experience as a poetic examination of conscience, a Catholic devotional exercise: He reviews his career as a poet, attempting to determine once again the proper relationship between poetry and society. In this process he gains assistance and insight from the attendant ghosts, who include a number of figures from his private and literary past, notably including James Joyce. Heaney records their conversations, often weaving their voices together in terza rima, the verse form used by Dante. In the twelfth and last poem, Joyce advises Heaney to follow his lead in concentrating on art and ignoring the politics of the moment.

The Haw Lantern continues in the direction mapped out in *Station Island*. In volume it is among the slightest of Heaney's collections: thirty-one poems in fifty-two pages. His topics, too, are rather commonplace in comparison: hailstones, alphabets, fishing lures, a peacock's feather, and (in the title poem) the fruit of the hawthorn. Heaney transforms this brilliant red winter fruit metaphorically into a lantern, an instrument for seeing and for measuring human values. Commonly used for hedging in the British Isles, this thorny shrub becomes a means of testing human integrity in the daily situations that finally count. The book also contains another of Heaney's trademark sequences. "Clearances," a set of eight sonnets written to commemorate the death of Heaney's mother, moves him to another stage in the definition of his poetic character. Symbolically, this constitutes Heaney's prayer at his mother's deathbed, bonding him to the past and committing him to the future. It also sets him apart from Joyce, his spiritual mentor, who made his refusal to pray at his mother's bedside a pivotal scene in *A Portrait of the Artist as a Young Man* (1916) and *Ulysses* (1922).

Whatever direction Heaney follows in the future, his status as a major poet is assured. He has probed the Irish conscience and discovered a way to express it in the English language, to render the Irish soul afresh.

Other literary forms · *Preoccupations* (1980) is a collection of memoirs, lectures, reviews, and essays in which Seamus Heaney accounts for his development as a poet. *The Government of the Tongue* (1988) similarly gathers later reviews and lectures, developing his subsequent views on the relationship between society and poetry.

Select works other than poetry

NONFICTION: *Preoccupations: Selected Prose, 1968-1978*, 1980; *The Government of the Tongue: The T. S. Eliot Memorial Lectures and Other Critical Writings*, 1988 (pb. in U.S. with the subtitle "Selected Prose, 1978-1987," 1989); *The Redress of Poetry*, 1995; *Homage to Robert Frost*, 1996 (with Joseph Brodsky and Derek Walcott).

James Livingston

Bibliography · Two early book-length studies of Heaney's work broke ground for the many that have followed. Robert Buttel's *Seamus Heaney*,

1975, is limited by its date to the poet's first three volumes but has a focus on individual poems and a prescience about Heaney's poetic direction that make it a useful starting point. Blake Morrison, *Seamus Heaney*, 1982, is less willing to accept the poet on his own terms, questioning in particular what he sees as a romanticizing tendency in Heaney's evocations of rural Ireland. Michael Parker, *Seamus Heaney: The Making of the Poet*, 1993, provides valuable background for Heaney's poetry, if sometimes taking certain poems too literally as autobiographical statements. Useful collections of essays on Heaney's work are Tony Curtis, ed., *The Art of Seamus Heaney*, 1985, and Harold Bloom, ed., *Seamus Heaney*, 1986, part of the Modern Critical Views series. See also Neil Corcoran, *Seamus Heaney*, 1986, and Elmer Andrews, *The Poetry of Seamus Heaney: All the Realms of Whisper*, 1989. More narrowly focused discussion on specific aspects of Heaney's work can be found in *Eire-Ireland: A Journal of Irish Studies* (beginning in 1965), which generally prints several articles per year on Heaney, and *The Irish Literary Supplement* (beginning in 1982), which has published at least fourteen reviews and essays on Heaney since 1984.

HEINRICH HEINE

Born: Düsseldorf, Germany; December 13, 1797
Died: Paris, France; February 17, 1856

Poetry · *Gedichte*, 1822 (*Poems*, 1937) · *Tragödien, nebst einem lyrischen Intermezzo*, 1823 (*Tragedies, Together with Lyric Intermezzo*, 1905) · *Buch der Lieder*, 1827 (*Book of Songs*, 1856) · *Neue Gedichte*, 1844 (8 volumes; *New Poems*, 1858) · *Deutschland: Ein Wintermärchen*, 1844 (*Germany: A Winter's Tale*, 1892) · *Atta Troll*, 1847 (English translation, 1876) · *Ein Sommernachtstraum*, 1847 (*A Midsummer Night's Dream*, 1876) · *Romanzero*, 1851 (English translation, 1859) · *Gedichte*, 1851-1857 (4 volumes; *Poems*, 1937) · *Letzte Gedichte und Gedanken*, 1869 (*Last Poems and Thoughts*, 1937) · *Atta Troll and Other Poems*, 1876 (includes *Atta Troll* and *A Midsummer Night's Dream*) · *Heinrich Heine: The Poems*, 1937 · *The Complete Poems of Heinrich Heine*, 1982

Achievements · Second only to Johann Wolfgang von Goethe in impact on the history of German lyric poetry in the nineteenth century, Heine was unquestionably the most controversial poet of his time. He was a major representative of the post-Romantic literary crisis and became the most renowned love poet in Europe after Petrarch, yet for decades he was more celebrated abroad than in Germany. Anti-Semitism and negative reactions to his biting satire, to his radical inclinations, and to his seemingly unpatriotic love of France combined to prevent any consistent approbation in Heine's homeland. Nevertheless, he became the first Jewish author to break into the mainstream of German literature in modern times.

Heine's poetic reputation is based primarily on *Book of Songs*, which went through twelve editions during his lifetime. The collection achieved immediate popularity with the public and was well received by critics; since 1827, it has been translated into more than fifty languages. Lyrics that became part of the *Book of Songs* were set to music as early as 1822, and within a year after the book appeared, Franz Schubert used six poems from the "Heimkehr" ("Homecoming") section in his famous cycle *Schwanengesang* ("Swan Song"). Robert Schumann's *Dichterliebe* (love poems) features musical settings for sixteen poems from the "Lyric Intermezzo" cycle. By 1840, Heine's works had become prime texts for German lieder. In all, more than three thousand pieces of music have been written for the creations of Heine's early period.

In 1835, four years after he went into self-imposed exile in France,

Heine's works were banned in Germany, along with the writings of the Junges Deutschland (young Germany). The critics rejected him as a bad influence on Germany's youth. His immediate popularity waned as conflicts with government censors increased. In the late nineteenth century, attempts to reclaim his works for German literature touched off riots, yet by then his enchanting lyrics had become so ingrained in German culture that it was impossible to expel them. The measure of Heine's undying significance for German poetry is perhaps the fact that even the Nazis, who formally prohibited his works once again, could not exclude his poems completely from their anthologies of songs.

Biography · The son of a Jewish merchant, Chaim Harry Heine spent his early years working toward goals set for him by his family. His secondary education ended in 1814 when he left the Düsseldorf Lyceum without being graduated. After failing in two apprenticeships in Frankfurt, he was sent to Hamburg to prepare for a career in commerce under the direction of a wealthy uncle. While there, he fell in love with his cousin Amalie. This unfulfilled relationship was a stimulus for verse that the young poet published in a local periodical. In 1818, his uncle set him up in a retailing enterprise, but within a year Harry Heine and Co. was bankrupt. Acknowledging that his nephew was unsuited for business, Uncle Salomon at last agreed to underwrite his further education.

Between 1819 and 1825, Heine studied in Bonn, Berlin, and Göttingen. His university years were very important for his development as a poet. While in Bonn, he attended lectures given by August Wilhelm von Schlegel, whose interest in his work stimulated Heine's creativity. In the fall of 1820, he moved to Göttingen. Besides law, he studied German history and philology until January, 1821, when he challenged another student to a duel and was expelled from the university. He continued his studies in Berlin and was rapidly accepted into prominent literary circles. Included among the writers with whom he associated were Adelbert von Chamisso, Friedrich Schleiermacher, and Christian Dietrich Grabbe. Rahel von Varnhagen helped in the publication of Heine's first collection of poems in 1822, and he quickly became known as a promising talent. During a visit to Hamburg in 1823, he met Julius Campe, who afterward published all of Heine's works except a few commissioned essays that he wrote in Paris. Literary success persuaded him away from the study of law, but at his uncle's request Heine returned to Göttingen to complete work toward his degree. In the summer of 1825, he passed his examinations, though not with distinction. In order to facilitate a public career, he was baptized a Protestant, at which time he changed his name to Heinrich.

Travel was a significantly formative experience for Heine. Vacations in Cuxhaven and Norderney provided initial powerful impressions of the sea that informed the two North Sea cycles of the *Book of Songs*. Journeys through the Harz Mountains in 1824, to England in 1827, and to Italy the following year provided material for the *Pictures of Travel* series that elevated him to the literary mainstream of his time. Exposure to foreign points of view also aroused his interest in current political questions and led to a brief involvement as coeditor of Johann Friedrich von Cotta's *Politische Annalen* in Munich in 1827 and 1828.

When continued efforts to obtain permission to practice law in Hamburg failed, Heine moved to Paris in 1831, where he began to write articles for French and German newspapers and journals. Heine loved Paris, and during the next few years friendships with Honoré de Balzac, Victor Hugo, George Sand, Giacomo Meyerbeer, and other writers, artists, and composers contributed to his sense of well-being. When the German Federal Diet banned his writings, making it impossible for him to continue contributing to German periodicals, the French government granted him a modest pension.

The 1840's were a stormy period in Heine's life. In 1841, he married Cresence Eugénie Mirat (whom he called "Mathilde"), his mistress of seven years. Her lack of education and understanding of his writings placed a strain on their relationship and later contributed to the poet's increasing isolation from his friends. After returning from Hamburg in 1843, Heine met Karl Marx. Their association sharpened Heine's political attitudes and increased his aggressive activism. Salomon Heine's death in 1844 unleashed between the writer and his cousins a struggle for the inheritance. Eventually they reached an accommodation that guaranteed an annuity in exchange for Heine's promise not to criticize family members in his writings.

After a collapse in 1848, Heine spent his remaining years in unceasing pain. An apparent venereal disease attacked his nervous system, leaving him paralyzed. Physical infirmities, however, did not stifle his creative spirit, and from the torment and loneliness of his "mattress grave," he wrote some of the best poetry of his career.

Analysis · Unlike many poets, Heinrich Heine never stated a formal theory of poetry that could serve as a basis for interpreting his works and measuring his creative development. For that reason, confusion and critical controversy have clouded the picture of his oeuvre, resulting in misunderstandings of his literary orientation and intentions. The general concept that he was a poet of experience is, at the very least, an oversimplification.

To be sure, immediate personal observations of life were a consistent stimulus for Heine's writing, yet his product is not simply a stylized reproduction of individual encounters with reality. Each poem reveals a reflective processing of unique perceptions of people, milieus, and events that transforms seemingly specific descriptions into generally valid representations of humankind's confrontation with the times. The poet's ability to convey, with penetrating exactitude, feelings, existential problems, and elements of the human condition that correspond to the concerns and apperceptions of a broad readership enabled him to generate lyrics that belong more to the poetry of ideas than to the poetry of experience.

A characteristic of Heine's thought and verse is a purposeful poetic tension between the individual and the world. The dissonance between the artistic sensibility and reality is presented in unified constructs that represent qualities that were missing from the poet's era: unity, form, constancy, and continuity. By emphasizing condition rather than event, Heine was able to offer meaningful illustrations in the juxtaposition of antithetical concepts: sunny milieu and melancholy mood, pain and witticism, affirmation and negation, enchantment of feeling and practical wisdom of experience, enthusiasm and pessimism, love and hate, spirit and reality, tradition and anticipation of the future. The magic and power of his verse arise from his ability to clothe these dynamic conflicts in deceptively simple, compact forms, pure melodic sounds and rhythms, and playfully witty treatments of theme, substance, motif, and detail.

More than anything else, Heine was a poet of mood. His greatest strengths were his sensitivity and his capacity to analyze, create, and manipulate feeling. A colorful interchange of disillusionment, scorn, cynicism, rebellion, blasphemy, playful mockery, longing, and melancholy is the essence of his appeal to the reader's spirit. The goal, however, is not the arousal of emotion but rather the intensification of awareness, achieved by drawing the audience into a desired frame of feeling, then shattering the illusion in a breach of mood that typifies Heine's poetry.

Although he was not a true representative of any single German literary movement, Heine wrote poems that reflect clear relationships to definite intellectual and artistic traditions. Both the German Enlightenment and German Romanticism provided him with important models. In matters of form, attitude, and style, he was a child of the Enlightenment. Especially visible are his epigrammatic technique and the tendency toward didactic exemplification and pointed representation. Gotthold Ephraim Lessing was his favorite among Enlightenment authors. Heine combined the technical aspects of Enlightenment literary approach with a pronounced Romantic subjectivity in the handling of substance, theme, and motif, particularly in the examination of self, pain, experience, and condition. The absolute status of the self is a prominent characteristic of his works. In the emancipation of self, however, he carried the thoughtful exploration of personal individuality a step beyond that of the early Romantics and in so doing separated himself from them. Other Romantic traits in his lyrics include a dreamy fantasy of feeling and a pronounced element of irony. Where Friedrich Schlegel employed irony to transcend the restrictive material world and unite humankind with a spiritual cosmos, Heine used it to expand the self to encompass the cosmos. The feature of Romanticism with which Heine most consciously identified was the inclination of Joseph von Eichendorff and others toward simple musical poems modeled on the German folk song. Heine specifically acknowledged the influence of Wilhelm Müller, whose cultivation of pure sound and clear simplicity most closely approximated his own poetic ideal.

In many respects, the polish of language and form that marked Heine's *Book of Songs* was never surpassed in later collections. At most a strengthening of intonation, an increase in wit, a maturing of the intellect subtly and gradually enhanced his writings with the passing years. Nevertheless, his literary career can be divided into four distinct phases with regard to material focus and poetic concern.

Heine's initial creative period encompassed his university years and reached its peak in the mid-1820's. In *Poems*, the cycle of verse in *Tragedies, Together with Lyric Intermezzo*, and, finally, *Book of Songs*, the young poet opened a world of personal subjectivity at the center of which is a self that undergoes unceasing examination. Consciousness of the self, its suffering and loneliness, is the essence of melodic compositions that include poems of unrequited love, lyrical mood pictures, satires, romances, confessions, and parodies. Lines and stanzas deftly reflect Heine's ability to feel his way into nature, the magic of legend, and the spiritual substance of humanity, while the poetic world remains a fragmentary manifestation of the subjective truthfulness of the moment.

A major change in orientation coincided with Heine's move to Paris. The political upheaval in France and the death of Goethe signaled the end of an artistic era, and Heine looked forward to the possibility of a different literature that would replace the subjectivity of Romanticism with a new stress on life, time, and reality. He was especially attracted to the Saint-Simonian religion, which inspired within him a hope for a modern doctrine that would offer a new balance between Judeo-Christian ideals and those of classical antiquity. The lyrics in *New Poems*, the major document of this period, reveal a shift in emphasis from the self per se to the self as a mirror of the times. Heine's poetry of the 1830's is shallower than his earlier creations, yet it effectively presents the inner turmoil, confusion, and splintering of the era as Heine experienced it. Accompanying a slightly faded reprise of earlier themes is a new view of the poet as a heathen cosmopolitan who affirms material reality and champions the moment as having eternal value.

The third stage in Heine's career is best described as a period of political radicalization. It most visibly affected his poetry during the mid-1840's, the time of his friendship with Marx. In the aggressively satirical epics *Atta Troll* and *Germany: A Winter's Tale*, he paired sharp criticism of contemporary conditions with revelations of his love for Germany, specifically attacking his own critics, radical literature, militant nationalism, student organizations, the German hatred of the French, the fragmented condition of the German nation, and almost everything else that was valued by the establishment.

Profound isolation and intense physical pain provided the catalyst for a final poetic reorientation after Heine's physical collapse in 1848. Some of the poems that he wrote in his "mattress grave" are among his greatest masterpieces; they reflect a new religiosity in spiritual penetration of the self. In *Romanzero* and other late poems, the poet becomes a kind of martyr, experiencing the world's illness in his own heart. The act of suffering generates a poetry of bleak glosses of the human condition, heartrending laments, and songs about death unequaled in German literature.

Although Heine styled himself the last of the Romantics, a significant difference in approach to substance distinguishes his early poems from those of the Romantic movement. Where Clemens Maria Brentano and Eichendorff celebrated existence as it opened itself to them, Heine sang of a life that had closed its doors, shutting him out. The dominant themes of his *Book of Songs* are longing and suffering as aspects of the experience of disappointed love. Combining the sentimental pessimism of Lord Byron with the objective portrayal of tangible reality, he succeeded in exploring love's frustrations and pain more effectively, more impressively, and more imaginatively than any of his forerunners and contemporaries had done. In dream images, songs, romances, and sonnets that employ Romantic materials yet remain suspicious of the feelings that they symbolize, the poet transformed the barrier that he felt existed between himself and the world into deceptively simple, profoundly valid treatments of universal problems.

The poems of *Book of Songs* are extraordinarily flexible, self-contained productions that derive their charm from the combination of supple form and seemingly directly experienced and personally felt content. Colorful sketches of lime trees, an ancient bastion, a city pond, a whistling boy, gardens, people, fields, forests, a mill wheel, and an old tower contribute to a world of great fascination and sensual seduction. The verse is often bittersweet, however, focusing not on the sunny summer landscape but on the sadness of the poet who does not participate in a beauty that mocks him. The forceful presentation of the individual's isolation and conflict with the times represented a fresh direction in poetry that contributed greatly to Heine's early popularity. At the same time, the carefully constructed tension between the poet and his surroundings established a pattern that became characteristic of all of his works.

An extremely important feature of these early lyrics is the break in mood that typically occurs at several levels, including tone, setting, and the lyricist's subjective interpretation of his situation. The tone frequently shifts from emotional to conversational, from delicate to blunt, while the settings of the imagination are shattered by the banal reality of modern society. As the poet analyzes his position vis-à-vis his milieu, his positive feeling is broken by frustration and defeat, his hope collapses beneath the awareness of his delusion, and his attraction to his beloved is marred by her unthinking cruelty. There is never any resolution of these conflicts, and the poem itself provides the only mediation between the writer and a hostile world.

Among the most exquisite compositions in *Book of Songs* are the rustically simple lyric paintings from "Die Harzreise" ("The Journey to the Harz") and the rhythmically powerful, almost mystical studies from the two cycles of "Die Nordsee" ("The North Sea"). Filled with the fairy-tale atmosphere of the Rhine and the Harz Mountains, "The Journey to the Harz" poems exemplify Heine's ability to capture the compelling musicality and inner tone of the folk song and to combine these elements with an overwhelming power of feeling in the formation of an intense poetry of mood. In "The North Sea," he cultivated a new kind of language, anticipating twentieth century verse in free rhythms that sounded the depths of elemental human experience. Constant motion, changing patterns of light, play of wind, and movement of ships and fish combine as parts of a unified basic form. Heine pinpointed the individuality of the ocean in a given moment, reproducing atmosphere with precision and intensifying impact through mythological or human ornamentation. The rolling flow of impression is a consistent product of Heine's poetic art in its finest form.

Two years after moving to Paris, Heine published *Letters Auxiliary to the History of Modern Polite Literature in Germany*, his most significant theoretical treatise on literature and a work that marked his formal break with Romanticism. The major poetic document of this transition to a more realistic brand of expression is *New Poems*, a less integrated collection than

Book of Songs, containing both echoes of early themes and the first fruits of his increased political commitment of the 1840's. *New Poems* attests strongly a shift in approach and creative concern from poetry as an absolute to the demand for contemporary relevance.

The first cycle of *New Poems*, "Neuer Frühling" ("New Spring"), returns to the motifs that dominate the "Lyric Intermezzo" and "Homecoming" segments of *Book of Songs* yet presents them with greater polish and distance. New variations portray love as a distraction, a nuisance that causes emotional turmoil in the inherent knowledge of its transitoriness. The tone and direction of the entire volume are established in the prologue to "New Spring," in which the poet contrasts his own subjection to the hindering influence of love with the strivings of others in "the great struggle of the times."

Among the other sections of the book, "Verschiedene" ("Variae"), with its short cycles of rather acidic poems about the girls of Paris, its legendary ballad "Der Tannhäuser" ("Tannhäuser"), and its "Schöpfungslieder" ("Songs of Creation"), is the least coherent, most disturbing group of poems that Heine ever wrote. Campe, his publisher, decried the lyricist's creation of what he called "whore and chamber-pot stories" and was extremely reluctant to publish them. Nothing that Heine wrote, however, is without artistic value, and there are nuggets of brilliance even here. Despite its artificiality and seeming inconsistency with Heine's true poetic nature, "Tannhäuser," for example, must be regarded as one of his greatest masterpieces. The deeply psychological rejuvenation of the old folk epic, which served as the stimulus for Richard Wagner's opera, reflects the poet's all-encompassing and penetrating knowledge of the human heart.

"Zeitgedichte" ("Poems of the Times"), the concluding cycle in *New Poems*, sets the pattern for Heine's harsh political satire of the 1840's. Some of the lyrics were written expressly for Karl Marx's newspaper *Vorwärts*. Most of them are informed by homesickness, longing, and the bitter disappointment that Heine felt as the expected dawn of spiritual freedom in Germany failed to materialize in the evolution of a more cosmopolitan relationship with the rest of Europe. Powerful poems directed against cultural, social, and political dilettantes anticipate the incisively masterful tones of his most successful epics of the period, *Atta Troll* and *Germany: A Winter's Tale*; irreverent assaults on cherished institutions, superficial political activism, and his own critics accent his peculiar love-hate relationship with his homeland.

Regarded by many critics as Heine's finest collection of poems, *Romanzero* presents his final attempts to come to grips with his own mortality. Rich in their sophistication, more coherent in tone than the lyrics of *New*

Poems or even the *Book of Songs*, the romances, laments, and melodies of *Romanzero* reveal the wit, irony, and epigrammatic style for which Heine is famous in the service of a new, peculiarly transparent penetration of the self. Dominant in the poems is the theme of death, which confronts the individual in many forms. A new religiosity is present in the acknowledgment of a personal God with whom the poet quarrels about a divine justice that is out of phase with humankind's needs. Individual creations pass through the spectrum of human and religious history and into the future in the expectation of a new social order. Bitter pessimism unmasks the dreams of life, pointing to the defeat of that which is noble and beautiful and the triumph of the worse man over the better as the derisive law of the world. Voicing the mourning and bitter resistance of the tormented soul, Heine transforms personal confrontation with suffering and death into a timeless statement of universal experience.

Romanzero is divided into three main parts, each of which projects a substantial array of feeling: seriousness, despair, goodness, compassion, a longing for faith, bitterness, and mature composure. The first section, "Historien" ("Stories"), is composed of discursive, sometimes rambling narrative ballads and romances dealing with the tragedies of kings, heroes, and poets. Some of them process through a temporal distance such typical Heine themes as the yearning for love, clothing them in historical trappings. Others, such as the cruel poem "Vitzliputzli" that ends the cycle, are profound discourses on man's inhumanity to man. The poems of "Lamentationen" ("Lamentations"), the second major section, are directly confessional in form: deeply moving cries of anguish, sublime expressions of horror, statements of longing for home. The "Lazarus" poems that conclude this portion of *Romanzero* are especially vivid documents of the poet's individual suffering in a world where God seems to be indifferent. In "Hebräische Melodien" ("Hebrew Melodies"), the last segment of the collection, Heine presented the essence of his reidentification with Judaism. Three long poems explore the broad dimensions of Jewish culture, history, and tradition, ending with an almost sinister medieval disputation between Christian and Jew that evolves into a tragicomic anticlerical satire. Thumbing his nose at irrational action, intolerance, and superstition, the poet offers a dying plea for humanism.

No other volume presents Heine so thoroughly in all of his heights and depths, perfection and error, wit and seriousness. Captivating for the directness of despairing and contrite confession, repelling for its boastful, sometimes vicious cynicism, *Romanzero*, as perhaps no other work in the history of German lyric poetry, reveals the hubris of the problematic individual and penetrates the façade of the bright fool's drama that is life.

Other literary forms · Although Heinrich Heine is best remembered for his verse, he also made significant contributions to the development of the feuilleton and the political essay in Germany. Experiments with prose accelerated his rise to fame as a writer. Among the most important of his nonfiction works are *Reisebilder* (1826-1831; *Pictures of Travel*, 1855), a series of witty essays that are spiced with poetic imagination and penetrating social comment; *Zur Geschichte der neueren schönen Literatur in Deutschland* (1833; *Letters Auxiliary to the History of Modern Polite Literature in Germany*, 1836), which was later republished as *Die romantische Schule* (1836; *The Romantic School*, 1882) and constitutes Heine's personal settlement with German Romanticism; *Französische Zustände* (1833; *French Affairs*, 1889), a collection of sensitive newspaper articles about the contemporary political situation in France; and *Vermischte Schriften* (1854), a group of primarily political essays.

Heine's attempts to create in other genres were unsuccessful. During his student years in Berlin, he began a novel, *Der Rabbi von Bacherach* (1887; *The Rabbi of Bacherach*, 1891), but it remained a fragment. Two dramas, *Almansor* and *William Ratliff*, published in *Tragedies, Together with Lyric Intermezzo*, failed on the stage, although *William Ratliff* was later employed by Pietro Mascagni as the basis of an opera.

Select works other than poetry

LONG FICTION: *Der Rabbi von Bacherach*, 1887 (*The Rabbi of Bacherach*, 1891).

SHORT FICTION: *Aus den Memoiren des Herrn von Schnabelewopski*, 1933 (*The Memoirs of Herr von Schnabelewopski*, 1876).

NONFICTION: *Briefe aus Berlin*, 1822; *Reisebilder*, 1826-1831 (4 volumes; *Pictures of Travel*, 1855); *Die Bäder von Lucca*, 1829 (*The Baths of Lucca*, 1855); *Zur Geschichte der neueren schönen Literatur in Deutschland*, 1833 (*Letters Auxiliary to the History of Modern Polite Literature in Germany*, 1836); *Französische Zustände*, 1833 (*French Affairs*, 1889); *Der Salon*, 1834-1840 (4 volumes; *The Salon*, 1893); *Zur Geschichte der Religion und Philosophie in Deutschland*, 1835 (*On the History of Religion and Philosophy in Germany*, 1876); *Die romantische Schule*, 1836 (*The Romantic School*, 1876); *Über die französische Bühne*, 1837 (*Concerning the French Stage*, 1891-1905); *Shakespeares Mädchen und Frauen*, 1838 (*Shakespeare's Maidens and Ladies*, 1891); *Ludwig Börne: Eine Denkschrift von H. Heine*, 1840 (*Ludwig Börne: Recollections of a Revolutionist*, 1881); *Lutetia: Berichte über Politik, Kunst, und Volksleben*, 1854 (*Lutetia: Reports on Politics, Art, and Popular Life*, 1891-1905); *Vermischte Schriften*, 1854 (3 volumes); *De l'Allemagne*, 1855 (2 volumes).

MISCELLANEOUS: *The Works of Heinrich Heine*, 1891-1905 (12 volumes).

Lowell A. Bangerter

Bibliography · Introductions to Heine and his works include the Twayne's World Author Series volume by Hanna Spencer, *Heinrich Heine*, 1982, and the earlier eminently readable *Heinrich Heine: A Biography*, 1956, by E. M. Butler. By far the best researched study is Jeffrey L. Sammons, *Heinrich Heine: A Modern Biography*, 1979. Especially useful among the many English-language critical studies are Sammons, *Heinrich Heine: The Elusive Poet*, 1969, and Nigel Reeves, *Heinrich Heine: Poetry and Politics*, 1974. Older sources include William Rose's *Heinrich Heine: Two Studies of His Thought and Feeling*, 1956, and *The Early Love Poetry of Heinrich Heine: An Inquiry into Poetic Inspiration*, 1962; Siegbert Prawer's *Heine: "Buch der Lieder,"* 1960, and *Heine the Tragic Satirist: A Study of the Later Poetry 1827-1856*, 1961; Barker Fairley's *Heinrich Heine: An Interpretation*, 1954, 1977; and Laura Hofrichter, *Heinrich Heine*, trans. Barker Fairley, 1963. Commentary on a quarter-century of Heine scholarship is offered by Sammons in *Heinrich Heine: A Selected Critical Bibliography, 1956-1980*, 1982.

GEORGE HERBERT

Born: Montgomery, Wales; April 3, 1593
Died: Bemerton, England; March 1, 1633

Poetry · *Musae Responsoriae*, 1620, 1662 (printed) · *Passio Discerpta*, 1623 · *Lucus*, 1623 · *Memoriae Matris Sacrum*, 1627 · *The Temple*, 1633 · *Poems*, 1958, 1961

Achievements · George Herbert has always been and perhaps will continue to be read somewhat in the shadow of John Donne, arguably the greatest and most influential of the seventeenth century Metaphysical poets. At the same time, however, Herbert has rarely lacked an audience well aware of his remarkable poetic abilities and unique voice. During his lifetime, Herbert's English poems were most likely circulated in manuscript, no doubt within a rather restricted circle of friends, and were evidently highly regarded. Upon publication in 1633, the year of his death, *The Temple* began to reach an ever-widening group of readers, the number and variety of whom say something about Herbert's appeal. It is not enough to note that Herbert was extremely popular, though he certainly was that: At least eleven editions of *The Temple* came out in the seventeenth century. Perhaps more interesting is the fact that unlikely bedfellows shared an interest in Herbert and claimed him as their own. Members of the so-called "High Church" party found Herbert's deep attachment to Anglican ceremonial beauty particularly congenial, and they read *The Temple* as a record of how spiritual conflicts might evaporate in the face of simple faith, humility, and conformity. Several important poets, including Henry Vaughan and Richard Crashaw, along with a host of minor poets, including Christopher Harvey, Ralph Knevet, and Henry Colman, looked to Herbert as a guide in their devotions and a model for their poems. Other aspects of Herbert, however, appealed to many readers who could be called, for lack of a better term, Puritans. Though the Puritans are often criticized for a disinterest in, if not hostility to, art as an enemy of truth, Herbert's characteristic plainness, simplicity, and sincerity, coupled with his constant stress on the Bible as the center of the holy life, made him attractive to readers who were otherwise not greatly devoted to poetry. Richard Baxter and, later, John Wesley were extremely fond of Herbert, and it is no surprise that many poems from *The Temple* were subsequently adapted as hymns.

That Herbert could be appropriated so easily by such divergent readers indicates the richness of *The Temple*. Modern writers as varied as Gerard Manley Hopkins, T. S. Eliot, Dylan Thomas, Elizabeth Bishop, and Simone Weil have each in his or her own way learned from Herbert: as a poet who has a distinctive voice that nevertheless does not exclude other voices, particularly from the Bible and the Book of Common Prayer; as a man of purity and simplicity who is yet rarely naïve and often painfully sensitive to the intricacies of sin and self-deception; as a Christian, indeed a priest, wedded to humility but well aware that the resources of art can serve as resources of devotion.

Biography · George Herbert was born on April 3, 1593, into one of the most distinguished families of Montgomeryshire, active both in local politics and court service. The fifth son in a family of seven sons and three daughters, he was reared principally by his mother (his father died in 1596), by all reports a remarkable woman who left a deep impression on her children. Magdalene Herbert not only shrewdly managed an extremely large household—unlike the modern-day nuclear family, the upper-class household of the seventeenth century might contain upwards of a score of children, relatives, servants, and visitors—but also supervised the education of her children. Perhaps more important, as Donne relates in his commemorative sermon on her, she was a model of piety and took a great interest in the spiritual development of her family. Herbert's early childhood thus well-prepared him for a life of distinction and devotion, two clusters of values that he later spent much time trying to reconcile.

Herbert's formal education began at Westminster School, and upon entering Trinity College, Cambridge, he soon established himself as a young man of great promise. Moving quickly through B.A. and M.A. degrees and positions as a Minor, then a Major Fellow, Herbert became the University Orator in 1620. Such an appointment indicates not only the great verbal and oral skills that Herbert must have demonstrated, skills that he would later use to great advantage as both a poet and a preacher, but also testifies to the high regard in which he was held. The Orator was in some respects the public spokesperson for the university, constantly communicating with government officials and dignitaries, and it was only a small step to graduate from this office to a more prestigious position at court or in state service.

This was not, however, to be Herbert's path. Perhaps his attendance at two particularly troubling terms of Parliament (in 1624 and 1625) discouraged him from a life of secular employment. Perhaps the death of King James and the accession of Charles I left him without a strong group of supporters to back any possible ambitions. Perhaps as he grew older, passed through several serious illnesses, and deepened his devotions, he came to see that a secular career did not, in the long run, have nearly as much to offer as a life of holy service. For whatever reason, or, more likely, combination of reasons, Herbert chose to be ordained as a deacon by 1626, and four years later he became a priest. With his wife, whom he married in 1629, Herbert lived the remaining years of his life at Bemerton, a small parish near Salisbury. He died on March 1, 1633.

Herbert's poetry is often deeply personal, so that many readers insist on looking at *The Temple* as a kind of veiled autobiography. Surely the major themes of his life are indeed the major themes in his poetry: On one level, *The Temple* dramatizes Herbert's conflicting drives toward secular achievement and religious retreat, his search for a satisfying vocation, and his apparently constant self-doubts and worries about his unworthiness to be a lowly servant of God, let alone a priest. *The Temple* is ultimately, however, far more than autobiographical, and the reader should not assume that every statement made by Herbert the poet is literally true of Herbert the man. The persona who narrates and undergoes a variety of experiences in *The Temple* is very much like Herbert, but also very much like the readers of *The Temple*. Herbert's purpose in writing his poems was not so much to express his personal concerns as it was to clarify and perhaps resolve certain important problems that all Christians—some would broaden this to include all thoughtful readers—share. The details of Herbert's life thus figure largely in his poems, but as part of a design that is much more inclusive.

Analysis · *The Temple* is unquestionably one of the most inventive and varied collections of poems published in the seventeenth century, and a reader can go a long way toward appreciating George Herbert by studying this inventiveness and variety. At the same time, though, the full range of Herbert's intentions and impact may be missed if his technical virtuosity is seen as an end in itself. Everything known about Herbert suggests that he would not want to be described as a master craftsman or skilled technician of poetry unless it was also stressed that every effort of his artistry served a central purpose: helping him to know, love, and praise God, and to understand better his place in a world filled with sin but governed and redeemed by Christ. Such poems as "Jordan" (I) and (II) and "The Posie" are in fact critical of certain styles of poetry and show that Herbert is more than occasionally impatient with the subterfuge, indirection, and even pride that seem inevitable in producing a well-written work. Ultimately, however, poetic creativity and devotion are welded together in *The Temple*.

As the title suggests, Herbert imagines himself to be a builder, and nearly all the details, both large and small, of the structure he raises show it to be a place of intricate beauty as well as sacred worship.

Understanding the design of *The Temple* as a whole is no easy matter, in part because Herbert's natural inclination seems to be to "play" with structure, rather than to adopt a fixed schema as the pattern for the entire work. *The Temple* is divided into three parts, as though the reader is going to be led step-by-step through a physical temple. "The Church-porch," by far Herbert's longest single poem, offers a great deal of advice on moral matters to prepare a youth who is otherwise not yet ready for more serious devotions. After such an initiation, the reader is ready to enter the section called "The Church," a collection of lyrics that continues to describe various places or objects in the church (the altar, stained glass windows, and so on) but that in doing so dramatizes the spiritual conflicts of a believer trying to secure his faith. The final section, "The Church Militant," turns from the life of the individual believer to the corporate body of the church, which, like each individual, must endure a series of successes and failure throughout its history. While the tripartite structure of *The Temple* thus has a certain obvious coherence, there are limits to the usefulness of such a scheme. Though Herbert never completely drops his theme of tracing out the contours of the physical temple, he quickly shows that his main interest is in exploring the temple within the heart and mind of the worshiper.

Herbert's flexible and open-ended play with structure, his ability to make patterns that are stable enough to support a great weight of meaning but loose enough to avoid dull predictability, is seen to a great advantage in the way he arranges the poems of "The Church." Far from being a random miscellany, "The Church" is a carefully ordered collection in which the individual poems are placed in sequences and other kinds of groups, sometimes with poems that stand nearby in the volume, at other times with ones located many pages away. Although even a superficial reading of the poems soon advises readers that they must watch closely how the poems relate to one another, Herbert provides a good description of his method and a clue to where he learned it in his poem "The H. Scriptures" (II). Despite its many parts, the Bible, he suggests, has a basic unity, and in order to understand any particular story the reader needs to trace how "This verse marks that, and both do make a motion/ Unto a third, that ten leaves off doth lie." Like the Bible, "The Church" has a basic unity, and the reader understands the poems fully only when he or she Stakes into account how they comment on and echo one another.

Sometimes the patterns and sequences of the poems are rather straightforward. "The Church" opens with a series that moves through the events celebrated during Easter Week, and the cumulative effect of such poems as "The Sacrifice," "The Agonie," "Good Friday," "Easter," and "Easter-wings" is to reinforce a sense of the importance of this part of the Christian calendar. In another group, the typical progress of a Christian life is reflected in the succession of titles: "Affliction," "Repentance," "Faith," "Prayer," and "The H. Communion." Even when Herbert does not fully develop a sequence, there are many examples of paired poems, where one answers, corrects, or otherwise responds to another. "Church-monuments," one of Herbert's most impressive poems even though its theme is the body's inevitable decay, is immediately followed by "Church-musick," which focuses on the high-flying freedom of the soul once it is released from the body. The desperate pleas that fill "Longing" are short-lived; by the first line of the next poem, "The Bag"–"Away despair! My gracious Lord doth heare"–the pleas have been answered.

Toward the end of "The Church," the speaker in the poem "The Invitation" calls out to God, inviting him to a feast; the following poem, "The Banquet," not only shows that the invitation has been accepted but also that the feast is far more glorious than the speaker had imagined. The more the reader follows the many links drawing the poems closer and closer together, the more apparent it becomes that one aspect of Herbert's design in "The Church" is to use the entire collection to trace a believer's gradual attainment not only of wisdom but also, more important, of peace. Read as one long, continuous sequence, the poems of "The Church" do seem to have a general plot, as the tribulations so much in evidence early in the work gradually give way to a more subdued questioning and heightened moments of bliss. Many commentators have noted that Herbert marks out this general plot very clearly for his reader: At the beginning of "The Church" the reader is invited to "approach, and taste/ The churches mysticall repast," and the final poem in the section, "Love" (III), concludes quite simply–"So I did sit and eat"–showing that this task has been completed.

Without disregarding the broad movement in "The Church" from immaturity to maturity, pain to comfort, it is equally important to note that Herbert by no means presents a simple tale of easily achieved spiritual progress. The plot traced out by the lyrics in "The Church," while ultimately a hopeful one, is at the same time densely textured, complicated, filled with moments of weakness, backsliding, and lessons improperly learned. Numerous short sequences suggest that humanity's needs are answered by Christ, who is always nearby; for example, the momentary sense that Christ has vanished, and that even when He is near He is unapproachable, expressed in "The Search," "Grief," and "The Crosse," gives way to the blooming of joy in "The Flower"—joy that is both surprising and expected: "How fresh, O Lord, how sweet and clean/ Are thy returns! ev'n as the flowers in spring."

If comfort is predictable, though, so is despair, and many short sequences show how quickly humanity moves back again from wonder to worry; the exhilaration of "The Temper" (I), for example, is extremely precarious, over and done with, even by the time the next poem, "The Temper" (II), begins: "It cannot be. Where is that mightie joy,/ Which just now took up all my heart?" As confusing and frustrating as these constant oscillations may be, Herbert's purpose is not to undermine the reader's security. By linking his poems in a variety of ways, often teasing and challenging his reader, Herbert expands the limits of the lyric form, setting the entire collection up to do what no one lyric possibly could: to dramatize and analyze the various moods and rhythms of a faithful believer.

Herbert's structural skill is evident not only in the overall plan and order of *The Temple* but also, of course, in the individual poems. His playful sense of poetic structure, though, has often been misunderstood and held against him. Such obviously patterned poems as "The Altar" and "Easter-wings," both of which are typographically shaped to resemble the objects named in the title, often strike some readers as quaint at best. Eighteenth century critics, for example, viewed these poems rather condescendingly as typical of Herbert, and did not hesitate to consider him as a "false wit," incapable of more noble and creative effects. Looked at more sympathetically, though, "The Altar" and "Easter-wings" are typical of Herbert only in suggesting how important poetic form is for him. Besides being a statement and a dramatization, a poem by Herbert is also an artifact, whose structure, sometimes simply, at other times subtly, reinforces a particular theme. At one end of the scale, there are directly imitative poems such as "Paradise," a poem about pruning in which the rhyme words are, in fact, pruned; "Heaven," in which the last word of the speaker's questions echoes in a following line as an answer; and "Trinitie Sunday," composed of a trinity of three-line stanzas. Other poems show more subdued but nevertheless effective pictorial designs: The shape of the stanzas in "The Agonie" suggests the image of the winepress mentioned in the poem, which calls to mind the association between Christ's sacrificial blood and sacramental wine; and each stanza in "The Bag" seems to contain an open space, literally like the bag mentioned in the poem used to take messages from humankind straight to God.

Such directly imitative devices help to prepare the reader for Herbert's far more challenging uses of poetic form in other places in *The Temple*. The structure of "Church-monuments," for example, is meant not so much to imitate a gravestone, as the title seems to suggest, as to help the reader imagine the decay described in the poem that will sooner or later overcome gravestones, bodies, and the entire physical world. Because the lines are only occasionally end-stopped, the rhythm becomes somewhat unsettling, even ominous, and since the word "dust" is repeated again and again, the entire poem momentarily becomes like the hourglass mentioned in the last few lines, "which holds the dust/ That measures all our time; which also shall/ Be crumbled into dust."

Similarly, the theme and mood of the speaker in "The Collar" are powerfully and immediately conveyed by its structure: The poem is apparently unshaped, with irregularly alternating lines of different length to suggest the disordered mind of a man who has lost all control. By the concluding lines, though, the structure of the poem communicates the achievement of order. As the speaker exhausts himself to a moment of calmness, "normal" poetic form also surfaces in the relatively stable abab rhyme scheme of the last four lines: "But as I rav'd and grew more fierce and wilde/ At every word,/ Me thoughts I heard one calling, *Child!*/ And I reply'd, *My Lord.*" Because he so often shapes his poems to have a visual impact, Herbert is compared with the emblem writers of his time, whose verses were either appended to illustrative plates or were at least meant to call to mind and interpret such illustrations. Such poems as "Church-monuments" and "The Collar," however, show that one of Herbert's particular skills is an ability to use the structure of his poems to imitate not only objects and static scenes but also dramatic processes.

Herbert's attention to structure is matched by his loving care for the language of his poems. Especially when compared to other works of his period, *The Temple* seems remarkably simple and direct, with little of the straining against meaning that characterizes so many of William Shakespeare's sonnets, and with hardly any of Donne's self-conscious roughness and almost inconsiderate obscurity. As many critics have noted, though, Herbert's simplicity marks the triumph, not the abandonment, of art. The language of *The Temple* is that of the Bible (especially in the King James or Authorized Version, published in 1611) and the Book of Common Prayer: austere but resonant and multileveled. Herbert's delight in language reflects not only the deep influence of God's words, the Holy Scriptures, but also his awareness that human words, returned to God in prayer, praise, song, and poetry, are at least an acceptable celebration of God's Word made flesh in Christ. Throughout "The Church," Herbert struggles with the dilemma that humankind in poetry, as in all things, can give to God only what God has already given it; but though this undermines any pretense of human self-sufficiency, it is an arrangement in which Herbert ultimately finds a great deal of comfort. The heartfelt simplicity of the three poems entitled "Praise" and the two entitled "Antiphon," among many others in "The Church," signifies not only a poetic choice but also an acceptance of humankind's subservient place in God's world.

At the same time, however, Herbert's humility allows him to exploit the richness of the English language. Modern readers who consider puns to be at best a low form of wit need to be reminded that Herbert, like most other seventeenth century poets, used puns and wordplay not only for comic effects but also for much more serious purposes: to indicate deep correspondences between various things in the world, between language and reality, and between different levels of experience. In "The Sonne" Herbert confesses "I like our language well," in part because it lends itself so easily to one especially significant pun: The reader is led quickly through the multiple meanings of the title word, from "son" to "sun," and finally to Christ, who combines these meanings as Son of Man, Son of God, and the guiding and warming light of Christians: their sun. There may well be even another concealed pun here; "The Sonne" is written in the form of a *sonnet*. The title "The Holdfast" is also a pun that takes the reader into the central conflict of the poem: A "holdfast" is something one can cling securely to, in this case God; in addition, "holdfast" is a term for a stingy, self-reliant man, such as the speaker of the poem, who must first relax his hold on himself before he can truly understand "That all things were more ours by being his," that is, Christ's. Though it is sometimes difficult to determine where Herbert's wordplay leaves off and the reader's invention begins, the title "The Collar" sets off a series of associations that are relevant to the lines that follow: The collar is perhaps first and foremost the Christian's yoke of discipline and obedience from which the speaker flees; this word also suggests "choler," the anger and distress of the speaker as he raves on and on; finally, by a slight adjustment it also sounds like the "caller," alluding not only to the situation of the speaker calling out in anguish but also to the infinitely patient God who calls even his unruly servant "Child."

Herbert occasionally uses puns and wordplay to construct a puzzle, the explanation of which points the reader toward a comforting observation. In "Jesu," for example, the title word is "deeply carved" in the speaker's heart. When his heart is broken by "A great affliction," the letters become scattered, but even so they spell out an important message: the fragments *J* (often printed as *I* in the seventeenth century), *ES*, and *U* form the statement "I ease you," a welcome affirmation of the power of Christ. Not all of Herbert's poems are puzzles, but his constant reliance on puns keeps his otherwise short and compact lyrics from one-dimensional simplicity.

Even the smallest details in a poem are liable to expand into several important meanings. In "Christmas," for example, when he describes the "glorious, yet contracted light" of the Christchild, he not only marvels at how the greatness of God has taken the diminutive form of a baby, but also celebrates the fact that humankind is bound, by legal contract or covenant, to God.

When Herbert questions, in the ominously entitled poem "Discipline," "Who can scape his bow?," the various interpretations of the last word provide comforting associations. Besides being a weapon of war and traditional instrument of justice and wrath, the "bow" also calls to mind Cupid's bow and arrow, which are instruments of love; the rainbow, the sign after the Flood that God will change his ways of wrath; the bowlike cross, a common comparison found in many biblical commentators; and Christ's "bowing," taking human form in order to save humankind. Throughout *The Temple*, Herbert carefully avoids the two most common dangers of the pun—he is rarely ostentatious or ridiculous—and as a result his wordplay almost always adds allusiveness and depth to his poems.

What makes Herbert an enduring poet is not simply his structural and stylistic expertise, but also the application of these technical skills to themes of great importance. The general subject of *The Temple* is, in Herbert's own words as reported by Izaak Walton, his seventeenth century biographer, "the many spiritual Conflicts that have passed betwixt God and my Soul." Knowing this, it should be no surprise to see that the poems in "The Church" are constantly dramatic, most often revolving around a dual focus: human's inevitable sins and misunderstandings, and the processes through which they are comforted, instructed, and corrected.

Before telling humankind's tale, however, Herbert places human life within the frame of one larger event, the Crucifixion. Christ's drama must be told first, and, accordingly, the poem on "The Sacrifice" is placed near the beginning of "The Church." Although this poem is in many respects unusual for Herbert—it is very long, and uses Christ not only as the subject but also as the speaker—its pattern recurs in many other places: Unlike such poets as Donne and Richard Crashaw, who often try to sustain a high dramatic pitch for an entire poem, Herbert, here and elsewhere, normally works with quick, unexpected, striking dramatic moments. "The Sacrifice" has a startling immediacy as Christ narrates the humiliating events of his crucifixion, and yet the reader also senses a curiously triumphant detachment. Even though Christ's repeated refrain is "Was ever grief like mine?," his voice is calm and ironic as he lists in obsessive detail the incongruities of his situation, the Son of God tortured by the people he offers to serve and save. After more than two hundred lines showing Christ's rather impassive power, Herbert breaks his carefully established format: Christ suddenly cries out in anguish "*My God, my God*–," a broken, unfinished line that the reader presumably completes by adding, "why has thou forsaken me?" The refrain then changes in this stanza to the simple statement, "Never was grief like mine." Because of this sudden breakdown, the reader is drawn more surely into a fuller understanding of the sacrifice: Christ is not only serene and all-powerful but also, at least for one moment, vulnerable, human. Once "The Sacrifice" establishes to what extent Christ, despite his torment, is humanity's benefactor, the reader can realize more fully that the "spiritual Conflicts" in Herbert's poems are not truly between the individual and God but between the individual and self.

Throughout "The Church," the focus is on the many ways that humans find to resist God. Like Donne, Herbert is convinced of humankind's basic and inescapable sinfulness, and some of his poems, like Donne's Holy Sonnets, explore arrogant intellectual pride ("Vanitie" [I] and [II]), disobedience ("Affliction" [I], "The Collar"), and the general blackness of the human soul ("Sinne" [I] and [II]). Beyond these themes, however, and in a manner that distinguishes him from Donne, Herbert is primarily interested in dramatizing far more intricate modes of self-deception and far less obvious subtleties of pride. The speaker in "The Thanksgiving," for example, seems genuinely moved by his meditation on Christ, and his exuberant plan to dedicate his life to charitable works probably strikes every reader as praiseworthy. In a turn that is characteristic of Herbert, however, the last two lines suddenly undermine all that has come before. At the height of his confident offering to Christ, the speaker stumbles: "Then for thy passion– I will do for that–/ Alas, my God, I know not what." Herbert is by no means ridiculing the speaker or banishing exuberance and charity from the devotional life, but he dramatizes very effectively how evasive one can be even when trying to dedicate oneself to following Christ's example.

A similar reversal occurs in "Miserie." Here the speaker clearly abhors sin and spends most of his time criticizing humanity's foolishness in choosing a filthy life of "strange pollutions" over the moral purity that might have been within reach. The accusations are extreme but compelling, and it takes little arguing to convince the reader that man is "A lump of flesh, without a foot or wing/ To raise him to a glimpse of blisse:/ A sick toss'd vessel, dashing on each thing." The last line, however, changes the focus of the poem entirely: After seventy-seven lines describing the "strange wayes" around him, the speaker suddenly realizes that "My God, I mean my self." In this way Herbert shows that abhorrence of sin, while perhaps admirable, may be a mode of pride unless one includes oneself in the indictment.

"The Thanksgiving" and "Miserie" are also good examples of how Herbert typically includes the reader in his dramatic revelations and reversals. Although it might be overstating the case to say that Herbert traps his readers, many assent to and often identify with his speakers from the start of a poem. Because they accept their premises—the statements in both "The Thanksgiving" and "Miserie" seem plausible, if not praiseworthy, until the very end—they also share in their fall. The self-deception and pride of the speakers in many of Herbert's lyrics are thus, in a certain sense, duplicated in the reader, and as the speakers are dramatized, explored, and corrected, so is the reader.

Throughout *The Temple*, Herbert's subject is not merely the correction of humankind's numerous flaws: Equally dramatic are the lyrics of recovery and comfort where the speaker overcomes not pride but feelings of unworthiness, uselessness, and weakness. For all his moments of self-scrutiny and criticism, Herbert is a remarkably gentle poet, and he knows when to remind his readers how securely he feels that they are ground in God's mercy. Without God, he explains, human beings are nothing—a premise that many modern readers find extremely discouraging—but he goes on to add that human beings need not be without God. For Herbert, humankind is constantly cheered and renewed by God's presence: In "Aaron," feelings of worry about being a priest give way to calm confidence as soon as one sees that Christ "is not dead,/ But lives in me while I do rest"; in "The Flower," sadness about the fragility of life and poetry turns into a heightened sense of joy and beauty, truly "thy wonders"; and in "The Elixir," all human effort, as long as it is done "for thy sake," becomes "drudgerie divine," pleasant and ennobling.

God's voice and presence appear throughout the volume, but nowhere so movingly as in the last poem of "The Church," "Love" (III). Here God and man meet face to face, and though a lesser poet might not have been able to withstand the temptation to overembellish the scene, Herbert's dramatic lyric is as understated as it is powerful. God is Love, "quick-ey'd Love," whose every word and movement is meant to comfort an extremely shy human guest who is humbly aware that he is "Guiltie of dust and sinne." Humankind's unworthiness, however, is finally beside the point: Stated in its simplest possible terms, God knows, forgives, accepts, and redeems humanity. Simple words of paraphrase, however, can never tell the whole story. "Love" (III) is not a statement but an enactment, not a bit of theological argument or explanation but a dramatization of a devotional gesture. From the beginning of "The Church," as he notes at the conclusion of "The Reprisall," one of Herbert's main tasks is to show how "In thee [Christ] I will overcome/ The man, who once against thee fought." The particular action and quiet tone of the last lines of "Love" (III)—"You must sit down, sayes Love, and taste my meat:/ So I did sit and eat"—confirm that the battle, against God and against himself, is over, celebrated by a meal that is simultaneously a lover's banquet, a communion service, and his first true taste of heavenly joy.

Modern readers are justifiably impatient with and even suspicious of poets of belief. Generations of unskilled, moralizing, prescriptive, sanctimonious versifiers have spoiled the name of religious poetry, which despite its noble intentions, often seems to falsify and oversimplify life. Readers need not, however, be impatient with or suspicious of Herbert for these reasons. His faith encompasses and overcomes but does not exclude restlessness, doubt, and worry. *The Temple* records a wide range of spiritual experiences and moods, and Herbert flees from neither simplicity nor complexity, qualities which neither life nor art can long do without. Herbert's poems continue to strike readers as honest, perceptive, and compelling statements about his day-to-day affairs of the spirit, and perhaps about their own as well.

Other literary forms · George Herbert's most important work besides *The Temple* is his prose treatise *A Priest to the Temple: Or, The Country Parson His Character and Rule of Holy Life*, written when he was in fact a country parson at Bemerton during the last years of his life, though not published until 1652. However idealized it may be, *A Priest to the Temple* gives a good picture of the life of humble service that Herbert offered to his God and his parishioners. The volume of *Outlandish Proverbs Selected by Mr. G. H.*, published in 1640, testifies to Herbert's lifelong interest in the proverb, a form of literary and moral expression that is prominent throughout the poems in *The Temple*. Other minor works include a translation of *A Treatise of Temperance and Sobrietie of Luigi Cornaro*, (1634), and a series of "Briefe Notes" appended to, but indicating various disagreements with, *The Hundred and Ten Considerations of Signior Iohn Valdesso* (1638).

Select works other than poetry

NONFICTION: *A Treatise of Temperance and Sobrietie of Luigi Cornaro*, 1634 (translation); *Outlandish Proverbs Selected by Mr. G. H.*, 1640 (as *Jacula Prudentum*, 1651); *A Priest to the Temple: Or, The Country Parson His Character and Rule of Holy Life*, 1652.

MISCELLANEOUS: *The Works of George Herbert*, 1941, 1945 (F. E. Hutchinson, editor).

Sidney Gottlieb

Bibliography · Significant critical studies of George Herbert include James Boyd White, *"This Book of Starres": Learning to Read George Herbert*, 1994; Chana Bloch, *Spelling the Word: George Herbert and the Bible*, 1985; Diana Benet, *Secretary of Praise: The Poetic Vocation of George Herbert*, 1985; and Michael Schoenfeldt, *Prayer and Power: George Herbert and the Renaissance*, 1991. Two classic studies are Joseph Summer, *George Herbert*, 1954, and Rosemond Tuve, *A Reading of George Herbert*, 1952. See also Lewis Martz, *The Poetry of Meditation*, 1955.